EDUCATIONAL RESEARCH

EDUCATIONAL RESEARCH

SECOND EDITION

Edward L. Vockell
Purdue University—Calumet

J. William Asher
Purdue University—West Lafayette

Merrill,
an imprint of Prentice Hall

Upper Saddle River, NJ 07458

Library of Congress Cataloging-in-Publication Data

Vockell, Edward L.
    Educational research / Edward L. Vockell, J. William Asher. - 2nd ed.
    p.   cm.
    Includes bibliographical references and index.
    ISBN 0-02-423105-3
    1. Education-Research.   I. Asher, J. William.   II. Title.
LB1028.V88   1995
370'.78--dc20   94-5962
                                                        CIP

Cover Art: Steve Karp
Editor: Kevin Davis
Production Editor: Mary Irvin
Text Designer: Jill Bonar
Cover Designer: Thomas Mack
Production Buyer: Patricia Tonneman
Electronic Text Management: Marilyn Wilson Phelps, Matthew Williams, Jane Lopez,
    Karen L. Bretz

This book was set in Garamond by Prentice Hall
Merrill is an imprint of Prentice Hall

©1998 by Prentice-Hall, Inc.
A Pearson Education Company
Upper Saddle River, NJ 07458

Printed in the United States of America

10 9 8 7 6 5 4 3

ISBN   0-02-423105-3

Prentice-Hall International (UK) Limited, London
Prentice-Hall of Australia Pty. Limited, Sydney
Prentice-Hall Canada Inc., Toronto
Prentice-Hall Hispanoamericana, S.A., Mexico
Prentice-Hall of India Private Limited, New Delhi
Prentice-Hall of Japan, Inc., Tokyo
Pearson Education Asia Pte. Ltd., Singapore
Editoria Prentice-Hall do Brasil, Ltda., Rio De Janeiro

Dedications

To my father, Ray Vockell, who first taught me to think scientifically; and to my son, Marc Vockell, who first convinced me that I could pass scientific thinking along to someone else.

—Ed Vockell

To my teachers in my educational research methods courses over 35 years who have taught me a great deal about education and how to do research there.

—William Asher

PREFACE

Purpose and Scope of the Book

An educator is a person who is in some way responsible for helping people to learn. Most educators are professional teachers; but counselors, administrators, media specialists, instructional designers, and a host of others are also charged with the responsibility of helping people to learn. This book is written for all educators. Is purpose is to enable educators to apply research skills to their professional responsibilities and therefore be able to do a better job of promoting learning.

Research deals with the application of the scientific method to problem solving. In the past, research has been perceived as a highly mathematical activity that is pursued by research specialists. It has not always been obvious to teachers and other educators that scientific methodology can play an important role in the art of education. Very likely, this neglect of scientific methodology has occurred because research has been perceived as irrelevant to most educators. Teachers and other educators have too many practical problems for the to have time left over to worry about ivory tower research—or so the belief goes.

Although it covers most of the same topics, this book approaches research from a perspective different from that taken in many other educational research textbooks. The goal is to show educators that by understanding and applying principles of educational research they can become more effective in their job of promoting learning. The basic point is that you do not have to stop teaching to do research; research is something you can do while teaching. And if you do good research, you will do better teaching.

The book covers most of the topics treated in traditional educational research book, but in a different order and with a different emphasis. We have tried to avoid highly theoretical research issues and to focus on the practical application of research principles to teaching and learning. Our goal is to help readers not only to understand research reports in the published literature, but also to apply research principles in their own professional lives—when they are conducting formal research activities as well as when they are pursuing the usual activities of their professional lives.

Educators are decision makers whose decisions have important consequences for learners. The basic tenet of this book is that educators who understand how to apply the principles of scientific methodology to their professional activities will make better decisions about teaching and learning.

Changes in the Second Edition

The most obvious change in the second edition is that it is now the joint work of two authors. Ed Vockell wrote the first edition. Since its publication he has been pleased with the positive reaction of inservice educators to the book. Students who claim to have been "afraid of statistics" often say they "wish they had known this stuff earlier in their teaching careers." However, the book lacked a contemporary presentation of some of the most current issues and strategies in educational research. Bill Asher has long been active as a knowledgeable theorist in the field of educational research. He has held leadership roles in the Educational Psychology Division of the American Psychological Association and in the American Educational Research Association and has fostered the development of numerous educational researchers (including Ed Vockell). By combining out talents, we have tried to raise the level of scholarly insight while maintaining the informality and pedagogical soundness of the first edition.

The order of the chapters has changed radically in the second edition. The old order made sense, but it was difficult for students to undertake many course-related activities until they had read the first fourteen chapters. The new arrangement makes it easier for students to begin research activities earlier in the course and to develop them as they continue through the book.

A second major change is an emphasis on qualitative research. We believe that qualitative research should play a significant role in all formal and informal research activities. Therefore, we have not only added a chapter summarizing the key principles and strategies of qualitative research; we have also integrated qualitative insights into other chapters where this integration was appropriate.

A third major addition is the chapter on meta-analysis. This powerful tool was just coming into prominence when the first edition was published. All educators should now be familiar with the contributions and limitations of meta-analysis.

Finally, in addition to numerous other changes throughout the book, we have updated the treatment of the role of the computer in educational research. Since technology changes so rapidly, we have tried to deal with this by combining clear examples with a presentation of basic principles that will hold true even when a new generation of computers replaces the current one.

The Student Workbook, which was well received with the first edition, has also been upgraded. Like its first edition, the workbook contains instructional objectives for each chapter and references to where readers can find information relevant to each objective; multiple choice and short-answer review questions; semiprogrammed units to supplement and review the textbook materials; and supplementary exercises and activities that students can perform to apply and deepen their understanding of the concepts and principles discussed in each chapter. A new feature of the current workbook is a series of descriptions of possible problems that students are likely to encounter and guidelines for overcoming these problems.

Acknowledgments

The first edition of this book was born in the frustrations the first author faced in trying to make educational research relevant to the inservice teachers he taught in northwestern Indiana. Subsequent cohorts (see Chapter 12) reacted positively to the first edition and offered suggestions for further improvement. We acknowledge and appreciate the help of these students.

While we wrote this second edition, several more people were also extremely helpful. Jim Gaffney of Xavier University used the first edition, offered frequent comments, and made suggestions for the second edition. Eileen Schwartz of Purdue University Calumet likewise read both manuscripts and made suggestions for both editions. We would also like to thank the reviewers of the manuscript for this edition: David Bloome, The University of Massachusetts; Carolyn M. Cartledge, Columbus College; Jane Chauvin, Loyola University; Naim C. Gupta, Ball State University; Mary Huba, Iowa State University; Mark Isham, Eastern New Mexico University; Louise Jernigan, Eastern Michigan University; Patricia A. Kearney, John Carroll University; Bruce Rogers, The University of Northern Iowa; William M. Stallings, Georgia State University; Robert Wall, Towson State University; and William Webster, California State University, Stanislaus.

Finally, we want to thank Alice Vockell and Kay Asher for their help and patience as we became increasingly irritable with the many tasks involved in compiling this book.

CONTENTS

CHAPTER 7

REPORTING AND INTERPRETING THE RESULTS OF DATA COLLECTION PROCESSES   155

CHAPTER 8

SAMPLING STRATEGIES   169

CHAPTER 9

QUALITATIVE AND NATURALISTIC RESEARCH   191

CHAPTER 10

INTERNAL VALIDITY   217

CHAPTER 11

EXPERIMENTAL DESIGN:
CONTROLLING THE THREATS
TO INTERNAL VALIDITY   251

CHAPTER 12

EXPERIMENTAL DESIGN: WHAT TO
DO WHEN TRUE EXPERIMENTS
ARE IMPOSSIBLE   269

CHAPTER 13

CRITERION GROUP AND
CORRELATIONAL RESEARCH:
NONEXPERIMENTAL
METHODS FOR EXAMINING
RELATIONSHIPS   291

CHAPTER 14
TESTS OF STATISTICAL SIGNIFICANCE   315

CHAPTER 15
EXTERNAL VALIDITY: GENERALIZING RESULTS OF RESEARCH STUDIES   337

CHAPTER 16
META-ANALYSIS: COMBINING THE RESULTS OF SEVERAL STUDIES   353

CHAPTER 17
EXAMINING INTERACTIONS AND INTERPRETING THEORETICAL RESEARCH   375

CHAPTER 18
COMPUTERIZED DATA COLLECTION AND ANALYSIS   397

THE ROLE OF RESEARCH IN EDUCATION

■ THE PURPOSE OF THIS CHAPTER

This chapter will introduce the topic of research methods as a set of tools that enable educators to think better, develop and understand educational principles, and make increasingly broad and accurate generalizations.

■ WHAT COMES NEXT

In the next chapter we'll describe the process of identifying research variables and clarifying the research problem. Subsequent chapters will focus on ways to discover, operationally define, and measure research variables. The book will then focus on methods for designing and carrying out studies that collect data and test research hypotheses, for analyzing the results of these studies, and for evaluating the quality of research results.

■ CHAPTER PREVIEW

Simply stated, educational research is the application of the scientific method and other forms of disciplined inquiry to educational practice. Educational researchers look for relationships among variables in education. They suggest ways for teachers, instructional designers, and other educational decision makers to choose more productive methods of educational practice. Effective research helps increase the quality of educational decisions.

There are two overlapping perspectives from which educators should approach research: as consumers of research and as researchers themselves. This book will help you perform both of these roles better. After reading this chapter, you should be able to

1. Define and give examples of educational research.
2. Describe the scientific method and identify ways in which it applies to educational practice.

3. Describe the four levels of educational research and identify examples of research activities at each of these four levels.

4. Describe the role of validity in educational research.

■

THE SCIENCE OF EDUCATIONAL RESEARCH

Dictionaries tell us that *science* is a branch of study concerned with deriving verifiable general principles about the natural world through the process of induction, deduction, and hypothesis testing. *Scientific research* is a diligent and systematic inquiry or investigation of a subject to discover or revise facts, theories, or applications.

Scientific research is not a quest for certainty. It is a process of employing guidelines that enable us to make increasingly broad and accurate generalizations about the phenomena with which we are concerned. For educators, such phenomena include not only students but also factors related to the attitudes and performance of learners, teachers, instructional materials, administrators, and schools. The following examples are generalizations that educators may make regarding students:

1. Students learn effectively to the extent that they devote effective academic learning time to the tasks under consideration.

2. The reason American students lag behind Japanese students in math is that Japanese students spend more time actively engaged in the study of mathematics.

3. My students would spend more time actively involved in math and therefore learn more if they used computer games like *Math Blaster* to supplement their curriculum.

4. The only reason the students with the computer programs did better was that they spent more time studying math. If they had spent an equal amount of time on worksheets (which are cheaper), they would have done equally well.

5. The reason Nikki failed the anthropology quiz is that she studied for three hours in a single session instead of spreading her study time over a dozen 15-minute sessions.

Some of the preceding generalizations are broader or more global than others. Some may be topic sentences that summarize doctoral dissertations or major journal articles, while others may be the exasperated conclusions of a tired teacher. However, each generalization is likely to be perceived as important by the person making the statement. Each speaker would like to have evidence that the assertion is accurate. That is the role of educational research: it enables us to arrive at more solid conclusions and make more valid generalizations. And since we base our planning and decision making on our conclusions and generalizations, educational research can help us make better plans and decisions. This textbook will offer guidelines for testing the validity of statements like those in the preceding list.

Scientific research is a process of employing guidelines that enable us to make increasingly broad and accurate generalizations about the phenomena with which we are concerned.

You may feel that several terms used throughout this chapter require further clarification and specific definition (for example, what is a *valid generalization?*). If you feel this way, you are right. These terms represent key concepts that are discussed throughout this book. At this point in the text, it is sufficient that you understand these terms at an intuitive level (for example, a *valid generalization* is an accurate conclusion). Later we will clearly define these terms and put them in proper perspective.

THE SCIENTIFIC METHOD

One of the most popular and comprehensive descriptions of how scientists successfully derive verifiable principles, laws, and generalizations has been provided by John Dewey, who identified the following steps in the scientific process:

1. *Identification of a problem.* At this first step, the problem is often vague and loosely defined. For example, the scientist might wonder, "Why do some children remember things longer than others?"

2. *Formation of a hypothesis.* A hypothesis is nothing more than a conjectural statement that provides a tentative expression of what the scientist or thinker believes will be a resolution of the problem. It is based on the scientist's careful observations and insights into the problem. These insights are based on such processes as personally experiencing situations, reading the literature, and thinking. For example, the cognitive scientist might speculate: "Children will remember things longer if they organize the information themselves through discovery learning than if they receive the information in pre-organized form from the teacher."

3. *Reasoning and deduction.* The scientist analyzes the hypothesis and determines what observable events will follow as consequences if the hypothesis is correct. Usually, there are many observable phenomena that can be deduced from a single hypothesis. For example, the scientist's reasoning might lead to the following deduction: "When high school students use computer simulations to learn about the principles of biology, they can either be informed about a principle ahead of time and use the simulation as an example clarifying the principle, or they can perform the simulation without any prior explanation and discover the principle for themselves. If my hypothesis about discovery learning is correct, students who follow the second approach should do better six months later on test questions related to the principle than those who followed the first approach."

4. *Verification, modification, or rejection of the hypothesis.* The scientist observes the results of empirically collected data to see whether the predicted consequences actually do follow. For example, the scientist might assemble an experimental group and a control group of students, give one group the discovery-oriented approach described earlier and the other group the teacher-centered approach, and then see whether the results support the prediction that the discovery-oriented group will do better on a test and other criteria six months later.

Steps 3 and 4 are performed repeatedly. If a prediction based on the hypothesis formulated at Step 2 is supported, this is taken as an indication that the hypothesis is a valid answer to the problem identified at Step 1. If a prediction based on the hypothesis is not confirmed by the results of the experiment, this is taken as an indication that either the prediction was based on an unsound deduction, the hypothesis needs to be modified, or the hypothesis needs to be rejected completely. Each time the scientist completes Step 4, it is necessary to return to one of the earlier steps. The exact reaction will depend on what the outcome was at Step 4. If the results supported the hypothesis by confirming the prediction, then the researcher will probably go to Step 3 and generate another prediction. If the results were contrary to the prediction, then the researcher might return to Step 2 and modify the hypothesis before returning to Steps 3 and 4. If the results were so contradictory as to refute the entire hypothesis, then the scientist might return to Step 1, try to clarify the problem further, and eventually state a new hypothesis. By appropriately repeating the various steps in this process, the scientist is able to develop a useful theory that will serve as a solution to the problem.

Dewey's method is not the only one used for advancing scientific knowledge. However, it is similar to others in that the emphasis is on disciplined inquiry and the use of objective, factual, real-world, observable data in a hypothetical-deductive fashion to make inferences. (Readers interested in additional aspects of scientific theory development and its relationship to educational research should consult the references in the Annotated Bibliography at the end of this chapter.)

TEACHERS AS RESEARCHERS

No sensible educator should deliberately make decisions without basing them as much as possible on the findings of educational research. The important qualifier here is the phrase "as much as possible." A teacher or instructional designer who believes in and employs one method for teaching remedial reading should not necessarily abandon that method when an article in a professional journal proclaims that another method is superior. But a familiarity with the findings and methods of educational research will enable that educator to evaluate the relevance of the information in the journal article. Likewise, an elementary school teacher who is able to send her students to a computer lab to study science may not have the time to conduct a full-scale experiment to determine the validity of her belief that the laboratory experience enhances her students' knowledge of specific information as well as their general problem-solving skills. However, knowledge of the related findings and the methodology of educational research can help her decide whether it would be best to continue with the laboratory experience or instead try a different approach.

Decisions based on accurate conclusions and generalizations are likely to be better than those based on faulty generalizations.

Educational research is not just an abstract science. It is a useful tool for practical problem solving. It enables educators to identify outcomes, make predictions, and establish cause-and-effect relationships. Factors such as the intuition of sensitive teachers and instructional designers, philosophical insights, and legal restrictions all play legitimate roles in decision making. However, simply put, decisions based on accurate conclusions and generalizations are likely to be better than those based on faulty generalizations.

Teachers should do research every day. This would make their lives much easier. Yet many teachers do not seem to believe this is true. They believe that in order to do research they must temporarily or partially stop teaching; and most teachers either do not want to or cannot take time to do this. Without vitiating the concept of research, we suggest that important components of research are activities teachers can do *while* teaching. By employing appropriate strategies of educational research, teachers, instructional designers, and other educators can become more reflective and are likely to benefit from their personal experience. By behaving at all

times in our work at least partially as systematic observers and researchers, we can do our jobs more effectively.

FOUR LEVELS OF RESEARCH

Research can be conceived as occurring at four levels, summarized in Table 1.1. These levels are hierarchical in the sense that each higher level presupposes a knowledge of lower levels and employs the lower-level techniques. Most research textbooks speak of research as if everyone who does research is working at only the higher levels. This is not only a wasteful approach; it is destructive, because it discourages educators from taking advantage of the countless occasions that arise for them to do important, lower-level research.

Level I, data collection, is an authentic mode of research.[1] It is something that teachers should do every day. Let's take an example of a teacher who failed to accurately collect data. When in high school, one of the authors of this book took an English course in which the class studied the poetry

---

[1]A strong argument can be made that Level I research is not research at all. It can legitimately be considered *preresearch*. If research is defined as "the process of establishing scientific relationships," then only Levels II, III, and IV fit this definition. However, the concepts and principles discussed in this text under the label of Level I research (chapters 4 through 9) provide the foundation upon which cause-and-effect conclusions can be built. If a reader wishes to adhere to a strict definition of research, therefore, it would be appropriate to regard these chapters as describing data collection strategies or the tools of research, rather than as dealing with research itself. However, the application of the concepts and principles discussed in these chapters involves the use of disciplined inquiry and other scientific methodology. This methodology enables educators to step beyond haphazard measurement of educational outcomes and makes it more likely that desired results will occur.

Even if a teacher declines to advance to higher levels of research, the application of principles described at this first level will enhance teaching. Therefore, we have chosen to dignify this set of concepts and principles by labeling it as Level I research. The distinction described in this footnote is not essential to understanding the textbook. It is intended for readers who are jarred by an apparently nontraditional use of the term *research*. (If you think that this footnote has dealt with a nonproblem, feel free to ignore it. Read on!)

Table 1.1 The Four Levels of Research

Level I
Data collection

What is happening? (What is the problem? Is this what I want to happen? Is this what should happen?)

Examples: Can Johnny read?
Does Roberta enjoy Shakespeare?
Is Wanda more anxious now than she was in September?
Are only a relatively few students participating in class discussion?

Level II
Internal validity

What is causing this to happen? (Am I causing it? Can I change it?)

Examples: Johnny does read better this year. Is this because of my program? Or is it because he grew a year older? Or because his dad said he'd pound the heck out of him if he flunked?
Wanda is no longer anxious. Is this because of my self-concept program or because of something else?
Is the fact that my questions are directed at only a small minority of pupils causing others to "turn me off"?

Level III
External validity

Will the same thing happen under different circumstances? (How far can the results be generalized?)

Examples: Will the same program that taught Johnny how to read help him with math?
Will the self-concept program that helped Wanda also help Jeanette?
If I change to a different set of questions, will I still get intensive participation in class discussion? If so, how widely can such new sets of questions differ from those previously used?

Level IV
Theoretical research

Is there some underlying principle at work?

Examples: Did Johnny improve because I supplied him with an appropriate interaction of optimal discrepancy and reinforcement schedule?
Do children learn better if they organize the material themselves than if they receive the information in a highly structured format?
Does intrinsic reinforcement result in more effective learning than does extrinsic reinforcement?

of Emily Dickinson for about a week. The teacher was an intelligent, friendly person who wanted the class to develop an appreciation of Emily Dickinson's poetry. He wanted the class to develop a feeling for what the great poet was saying, to become excited about Emily Dickinson's ideas, to develop an affinity for her wisdom and insights.

Our student received a 95 on the unit quiz, but he did not appreciate Emily Dickinson at all. Probably nobody in the entire class of 30 students developed an appreciation of Dickinson's poetry. At class

reunions, they still joke about "Emily Dickinson—Mystique or Mistake?" The teacher had no idea that this was the case. He appreciated Emily Dickinson, and the students sat attentively and took notes and got reasonably good scores on his test; so he assumed that they all shared his appreciation. But he was wrong in his assumption. He was not doing his research. Had he found a way to assess the class's appreciation of the poet, it is likely that he would have modified his teaching strategy—and today Dickinson would have more admirers.

All subsequent levels of research depend on a sound foundation at Level I.

Level I research, then, consists of finding good ways to assess and describe what is happening. All subsequent levels of research depend on a solid foundation at Level I. There are, therefore, two good reasons for discussing Level I research at the beginning of this textbook. First, it is valuable for finding out what is happening in an educational setting, even when we have no intention of doing any higher-level research. Second, it gives us a firm basis for performing or interpreting the more sophisticated levels of cause-and-effect research.

Educators doing Level I research while teaching will often discover that something is not happening the way it should be, and they will try to make improvements. After they initiate changes, they will check again to see what is happening after their intervention. In many cases, such educators have not gone beyond Level I research; they have merely performed Level I research on repeated occasions, which is in itself useful and something all educators should do. But in other cases, educators should go

one step further and determine *why* a change has occurred. They should find out whether their intervention has *caused* the differences they have observed. They need Level II research, internal validation.

To pursue the example we started earlier, let us assume that our literature teacher has found a way to assess appreciation of Emily Dickinson and has discovered that none of his students appreciates the reclusive poet. After thinking it over, he develops and pursues what seems to be a better way to help his students. At the end of the unit of instruction, he measures the students again, and he finds that the appreciation of Dickinson's poetry has increased. In terms of Level I research, our teacher has discovered what he wanted to find out: he knows that he has not been wasting his time and that of his students. But has he shown that his new methods have *caused* the improvement? This is the question of Level II research. For reasons that will be discussed in later chapters, we would need to know more before we could say that this teacher has demonstrated a causal relationship. Other factors could have accounted for the change. For example, another teacher (say, in history or drama class) might have demonstrated the

---

BOX 1.1 | Classroom Assessment Techniques

In *Classroom Assessment Techniques: A Handbook for College Teachers,* Thomas A. Angelo and K. Patricia Cross argue that teachers themselves are the closest observers of learning as it takes place in their classroom; therefore they have the opportunity to become the most effective assessors and improvers of their own teaching. However, to make improvements they must first be able to discover when they are off course, how far they are off course, and how to get back on the right track.

Classroom Assessment Techniques provides detailed, practical guidelines for teachers who want to determine the degree to which their students are on track during the early and intermediate stages of learning. It includes strategies for assessing students' ability to recall and understand prior knowledge, their skill in problem solving and higher-order thinking skills, learner values and self-awareness, and other important outcomes. Most of the assessment techniques take little time and are unlikely to disrupt the normal flow of classroom activity—in fact, they are likely to stimulate as well as assess learning. The specific assessment techniques are presented along with step-by-step guidelines and case study examples that make it easy for teachers to learn how to use the techniques to collect valuable data.

value of Dickinson's insights, and this could have accounted for the improvement.

Has the teacher done a bad job of research? That depends on what he thought he was accomplishing with his little project. If he thought he was proving that the new method worked, then he may have done a bad job. On the other hand, if his main interest was to make sure that he was not turning loose on the world a group of Emily Dickinson haters, then his research was quite successful. He knew that a degree of appreciation existed among his students at the end of the unit. He did not especially care *why* the students had this attitude; the important thing was that the attitude existed.

What *should* his intention be? Again, that depends. Certainly he should have done at least Level I research. He seriously weakened the unit of instruction by failing to do so. But was Level II also necessary? If he spent a great deal of time or effort on his new method and it would be expensive or time-consuming to continue it, then knowledge of causality would be important. If his new method was inexpensive, however, then establishing a cause-and-effect relationship between his teaching and appreciation of Emily Dickinson's poetry would be less critical. If a cause-and-effect relationship can be established with little or no effort, then why not establish one? On the other hand, there might be better things on which the teacher should spend his time. Stopping at Level I is not necessarily weak or watered-down research, it is often the wisest use of one's resources.

If you think about it for a moment, you will realize that *all* decision making in education is based on cause-and-effect assumptions. A teacher makes Decision A instead of Decision B *because* there is reason to believe that Decision A will lead to more productive student learning. In many cases these decisions are based on custom, authority, or some factor other than the systematic examination of data that constitutes Level II research. What this book suggests is that Level II research provides an additional tool that will make decision making more constructive.

Once a possible causal relationship has been established at Level II, there is still room for increased sophistication. If we have demonstrated that something may have produced an effect in one isolated situation, we still don't know whether it would work somewhere else. At Level III, external validation, we examine the *generalizability* of research findings. It should be obvious that Level II is a prerequisite for Level III research, because if we have demonstrated no effect, then we have nothing to generalize.

In the case of the literature teacher, assume that he has established that his new method probably caused the improved attitudes toward Emily Dickinson's poetry. He then goes to the annual meeting in Canton, Ohio, of the International Association for the Advancement of the Appreciation of Emily Dickinson. There he finds a speaker bemoaning to a sleeping audience that high school students just don't appreciate Dickinson anymore. Our teacher jumps to his feet and excitedly proclaims that he can solve this problem. As the audience awakens, he announces that if they simply apply his method in their classrooms, their students will appreciate Emily Dickinson's poetry. He has scientific evidence!

What is the possibility that our teacher's method will work in other classrooms? If he has performed only Level II research, then we don't know. Numerous factors that might have operated in his own classroom perhaps are not present in the other classrooms. Level III research controls these numerous other factors and helps the researcher declare that it is the treatment *independent of the experimental situation* that caused the observed results.

Level III research is not performed by classroom teachers and instructional designers as often as Level I or II research. Such educators are most frequently concerned about solving pressing, unique problems in their own classrooms rather than generalizing about what might happen in someone else's classroom. Level III research becomes important when we want to share our results with someone else or adapt someone else's results to our own situation. If we are going to publish the results of our research, for example, and someone else plans to make use of these results, then we need to do Level III research.

A working knowledge of Level III research enables educators to make wiser decisions and avoid wasting time on educational fads.

Although educators do not often do Level III research, it is still important for them to understand it. A good way to obtain and evaluate new ideas is to read professional journals and talk to other educators about what they have been doing. When a project has worked somewhere else, teachers make decisions about whether it will work in their own situations. This becomes especially important if the innovation is expensive in terms of effort or money. A working knowledge of Level III research enables educators to make wiser decisions and avoid wasting time on educational fads. In other words, Level III research enables us to profit more effectively from the experience of others.

Finally, there is Level IV, theoretical research. This is the kind of research that social scientists do when they discover, for example, that a new behavior is learned most rapidly if it is reinforced continuously but that a behavior is maintained longer in the face of extinction if it has been reinforced on an intermittent schedule of reinforcement. Likewise, when Jean Piaget differentiated between concrete operational and formal operational thought, he was doing Level IV research. At this level, the researcher not only demonstrates that there are findings that can be generalized to new settings but gives theoretical reasons and explanations about why this happens. In turn, this theoretical explanation suggests other situations in which similar results would be likely to occur.

Let us return once more to our literature teacher. He has now done Level III research. He knows that he has caused an improvement in attitudes and that this is not unique to his isolated situation. Now he might wonder *why* the dramatic improvement occurred. Let us assume that his method was to give students lifelike vignettes and then to have them role-play, with the students taking turns adopting Emily Dickinson's viewpoint. At Level IV, he might draw a conclusion that "examining realistic situations from a poet's viewpoint in a lifelike situation enhances the high school junior's appreciation of that poet." He would have to work hard to demonstrate this theory, probably replicating the study in more situations with a wide variety of poets; but if he could successfully perform this research, he would have a principle with extremely wide generalizability. This principle could be applied through role-play, movies, interviews, and so forth. It could be extended to areas outside poetry, such as nonfiction literature, history, and psychology.

As you may have noticed, Level IV is really an extension of Level III research, with the results generalized *at a conceptual level* and much further beyond the original situation. Your first impression of Level IV may be that it is unnecessary, and you may think that you will never do Level IV research. Of course, we would reply that you need to understand Level IV so that you can read the results of scientists who do this kind of research. But there's an even better reason for knowing how to do Level IV research. At Level IV we apply what John Dewey called the *scientific method*. Many writers of research books have started with a chapter on the scientific method, treating it as if Dewey were primarily describing a good way to do scientific research. Actually, this is not what Dewey was doing. Rather, he was writing about how people in general develop complicated thoughts and advance their understanding of concepts. Hence, he called his book not *How to Do a Scientific Study* but *How We Think* (1910). The point we are making is that if this is how we think, then a careful analysis of the principles of Level IV research (which includes the earlier levels as prerequisites) will make us not only better researchers and readers of research but also better thinkers—whether we are thinking about how to get Johnny to read or how to achieve world peace. Furthermore—although this may sound grandiose—since Levels I, II, and III are hierarchical prerequisites of Level IV research, it seems clear that learning to do these things will not only help us solve specific problems but may eventually make us better thinkers overall.

The essential ingredient that distinguishes educational research from an educator's other professional activities is that it uses the scientific method or disciplined inquiry based on the collection of empirical data to solve problems. This means that at all four levels educational research is *systematic, logical, data referenced,* and *replicable.* These characteristics of educational research will be discussed throughout this book.

It is important to note that educational research is not the only endeavor in which the professional educator must engage. There are many problems that must be resolved through recourse to strategies other than research. For example, a decision about whether to include sex education in a school's curriculum must be based largely on philosophical or social considerations rather than purely on research information. School boards, principals, teachers, and parents who discuss this issue and must make decisions are likely to be concerned about such issues as the right to privacy, personal ethical convictions, the dangers of overpopulation and sexually transmitted diseases, political philosophies, and the nature of the social contract between the individual and the state as it applies to the educational setting. None of these issues focuses primarily on empirical data, and therefore the contribution of research will not be dominant. Although decision makers would be foolish to ignore the impact of research data when it is relevant, they sometimes base their decisions on values and goals that are not the direct subject of educational research.

Likewise, the results of educational research would probably not be the primary impetus to making decisions about how much emphasis to give to team sports in the local school, whether prayers should be allowed in public schools, and whether busing should be employed to achieve racial integration. Each of these may be an important question, but in each case the issue is going to be decided primarily on the basis of philosophical, legal, and social considerations rather than on the basis of information and principles obtained through the scientific method. However, placing the main emphasis on nonresearch considerations does not mean that research is completely irrelevant to such issues. For example, even though the matter of busing to achieve racial integration may focus primarily on legal issues, empirical data gained through research

enters the discussion at various points. For example, someone might argue that the time spent on buses significantly detracts from learning and that this loss outweighs any gains that might occur as a result of busing; and this assertion can be empirically tested through the scientific method. The empirical data arising from such an investigation could be used to influence the outcome of a discussion of this topic.

SOME SPECIFIC TYPES OF RESEARCH

Disciplined inquiry can serve many purposes in education. As you read the educational literature, you will see references to some specific types of research. Two of these are *evaluation research* and *action research.*

Evaluation Research

Evaluation research refers to the application of the scientific method or other forms of disciplined inquiry to the process of making decisions about the quality of educational processes, products, or outcomes. Educational evaluations usually focus on needs analyses, cost-benefit analyses, and the formative or summative evaluation (defined below) of educational products and programs. An educational evaluation consists of more than just the collection of research data. It uses the information obtained from the research process as one of several tools to *evaluate* a product or activity. Other components of the evaluation process include analyzing the goals of a program or the needs of a system, assessing the resources available for the program and the contexts of the program, determining the criteria or standards according to which decisions will be made, and interpreting the results after data have been collected.

There is a great deal of overlap between the literature on educational evaluation and the contents of the present textbook. This can be seen from the large number of books that contain the words *research* and *evaluation* in their titles (e.g., Buchanan & Feldhusen, 1991; Hagerty & Evans, 1985; Smith, 1987; Zapka, 1982). In addition, of the 53,108 articles indexed between 1983 and 1992 under *evalua-*

tion in ERIC's computerized data base, 15,913 were also indexed under *research*. The difference is that educational evaluation focuses heavily on value judgments that will lead to effective decisions; it uses research methods to collect data that can help lead to valid judgments. Whereas educational research in general focuses on testing hypotheses and building theories, educational evaluation usually has a noticeably practical and more limited purpose: to make decisions about a particular educational product or activity.

As you read the education literature, you will see references to two types of evaluation. *Formative evaluation* occurs during the planning and operation of a product or program. Its purpose is to provide information that may result in the improvement of the product or program. For example, by observing students during a cooperative learning activity, a teacher may obtain information that would suggest modifying the instructions given to the students. *Summative evaluation* occurs after a product has been developed or a program has been completed. Its purpose is to provide evidence regarding the quality of a product or program. For example, a teacher may examine test scores at the end of a cooperative learning unit and determine that the unit is worth repeating next year. In either case, the role of research is to provide valid data and effective comparisons to enable the teacher to make wise decisions.

Action Research

Action research refers to the practical application of the scientific method or other forms of disciplined inquiry to the process of dealing with everyday problems. It is particularly focused on teachers and other educators doing action research in order to make their particular educational activities more productive. It is more concerned with specific classes and programs and less concerned with generalized conclusions about other classes and programs. This book considers action research to be a valid enterprise and fully endorses the concept of teachers and students becoming involved in such research.

We will not devote further specific attention to distinctions among these topics. It is our belief that a sound understanding of the principles and strategies discussed herein will help educators perform evaluation and action research, as well as other forms of research.

VALIDITY

In this chapter we have already used the word *validity* several times without defining it. The word has an ordinary, commonsense meaning: a statement, argument, or judgment is valid to the extent that it is sound, accurate, or authoritative—free of illogical or imprecise contamination. Applied to the scientific method and other forms of empirical inquiry, the concepts of *validity* and *invalidity* refer to the best available approximation to the truth or falsity of propositions, including propositions about causality (Cook & Campbell, 1979). The major purpose of educational research at all levels is to produce valid data and valid results, which lead to valid generalizations. Validity, therefore, will be an important topic throughout this book. Researchers must validly identify and define the variables they intend to study. They must use valid processes to collect data that assess educational outcomes and other variables. They must examine the validity of cause-and-effect relationships and of generalizing results beyond the original setting.

The major purpose of educational research at all levels is to produce valid data and valid results, which lead to valid generalizations.

Because of human nature and the methods that must be applied in research, it is not possible to establish perfect validity in educational settings, only to approximate it. By employing the methods described throughout the rest of this book, however, you will be able to minimize threats to the validity of your generalizations and improve the quality of your educational decisions.

ORGANIZATION OF THIS BOOK

The present chapter has introduced the topic of research as a tool that enables educators to think more precisely and logically and make increasingly broad and accurate generalizations. Chapter 2 will describe how to begin the research process by identifying research variables and clarifying the research problem. Chapter 3 will discuss how to use the library and other reference materials as effective tools to gather information about research variables, to answer questions about relationships in education, and to lay the basis for educational research. Chapter 4 will describe strategies for operationally defining and measuring variables of interest to educators. By completing these four chapters, readers should be able to focus on research variables either to read research more effectively or to conduct research projects of their own.

Chapter 5 begins the discussion of data collection processes, focusing on how to collect consistent, accurate data by using methods that are reliable and valid. Chapter 6 describes specific data collection strategies, and chapter 7 describes ways to present and interpret the scores derived from these measurement processes. Chapter 8 discusses sampling strategies, which enable researchers and readers to draw conclusions about large groups by examining the characteristics of smaller numbers of group members. Chapter 9 describes strategies for conducting qualitative research, in which the researcher gives a comprehensive description of educational contexts, often by acting as a participant observer. By completing these chapters, readers should have a better understanding of how to assess educational outcomes and interpret the results of educational measurement processes.

Chapters 10 through 14 describe how to examine and establish relationships and to make predictions in education. To perform such research it is necessary to apply the methods and principles discussed not only in these five chapters but also in chapters 2 through 9.

Chapter 15 discusses the principles that must guide us in applying the generalizations we gain from a research setting to the other settings in which we intend to apply our findings. The validity of these generalizations depends on the correct implementation principles previously discussed in earlier chapters, as well as those discussed in chapter 15. Chapter 16 discusses meta-analysis, a strategy for combining the results from several studies to improve the quality of the conclusions of both Level II and Level III research and to move toward sound conclusions at Level IV research.

Chapter 17 integrates information discussed in previous chapters. It discusses interactions and theoretical research. Chapter 18 deals with the use of the computer as a tool for solving research problems. This tool can be employed at almost any stage of the research process. Finally, chapter 19 describes the appropriate strategies for carrying out and reporting upon a formal research project. In doing so, it integrates information discussed in chapters 2 through 18. The various aspects of educational research are highly interactive. While information in this book necessarily had to be presented in some order, there is not a linear path that can be followed from the early chapters to the end of the book. Chapter 19 shows how all the parts fit together into a productive research project. It also includes a discussion of both practical and ethical guidelines.

The authors of this book assume that most of its readers will be inservice educators—teachers, counselors, instructional designers, administrators, and others who are actively responsible for helping learners acquire new skills in a variety of settings, including schools, hospitals, industry, and training centers of various kinds. It has been arranged in the present format to make it as useful as possible for this audience. One of our main intentions has been to enable inservice teachers to use research strategies to solve practical problems; without losing sight of this focus, we have also tried to present guidelines for conducting and interpreting formal research projects.

PUTTING IT ALL TOGETHER

A section like this will appear near the end of each chapter, pursuing common problems throughout the book and pointing out the relevance of each chapter to the common problem. This will help the reader to integrate and apply the information as it accumulates throughout the text.

These sections will focus on the activities of the mythical Eugene Anderson, a specialist in humane education. Mr. Anderson works for an organization interested in promoting healthy attitudes toward animal life, and his job is to help schools and other organizations develop strategies for implementing humane education programs throughout the country. When these programs come into schools, they should have the effect of changing children's attitudes toward animal life.

Mr. Anderson read this textbook before he took his job, and he was shocked to discover that most humane educators worked with little research evidence to bolster their efforts. He realized that humane education would probably be more effective if it were pursued in a more scientific spirit, and so he entered upon the activities described in these "Putting It All Together" sections of this book.[2]

Of particular relevance to the present chapter is the overall plan of action that Mr. Anderson developed. He realized that if he was going to accomplish anything constructive, he would have a better chance if he followed the steps outlined here. First, he would find a way to determine what outcomes were actually occurring among the children he dealt with (Level I research). He needed to explore in some depth with the children their current thoughts and feelings about animals and their treatment of their pets. He needed to find a way to define and assess humane attitudes. When he went into a school classroom, he always *hoped* that something good was happening; but in reality he had only a vague idea of what the children's attitudes were. He needed a way to find out what was going on.

Second, he wanted to find out whether his educational efforts were causing anything to happen. This was Level II research. He wanted to find this out

right away, but he realized that he could not logically do this until he had first done his Level I groundwork. Once he found a way to assess what was going on in his classrooms, it was important to find out what cause-and-effect relationships existed between those outcomes and his own work. After all, his job was costing his organization thousands of dollars a year, and it would be desirable to spend this time and money as effectively as possible.

Third, if he did establish cause-and-effect relationships, he wanted to know whether the same outcomes would occur elsewhere. If something worked in one school, would the same strategy work in another school as well? In addition, Mr. Anderson went to several state and national conventions to share his results and conclusions with others and to learn from his colleagues. Level III research was important to Mr. Anderson.

Finally, Eugene Anderson was concerned with the concepts and principles that might be at work. In his highly speculative mind, he mulled over such questions as *What is a humane attitude anyway? How do such attitudes develop and how do they change? Is it possible that there's no such thing as a humane attitude, but only humane behavior?* Such problems filled his conversations at conventions and frequently kept him awake at night. Now he realized, after he did his Level I, II, and III research, that he would be able to dip into Level IV research and perhaps make original contributions to the theory of the development of humane attitudes.

(The adventures of Eugene Anderson will continue in this same section at the end of the next chapter.)

SUMMARY

This book examines educational research as the application of the scientific method to educational practice. Educational research tries to make it more easily possible for teachers, instructional designers, and other decision makers to make productive choices regarding educational practice. Effective research helps increase the *validity* of educational decisions.

---

[2]Mr. Anderson and his exploits are fictional. However, the examples are based on the humane education research of the first author. Interested readers can find further information in Vockell and Hodal (1978, 1980). See ERIC microfiche ED 196 799 and ED 199 118.

This chapter has introduced the topic of research as a tool that enables educators to think better, develop and understand educational principles, and make increasingly broad and accurate generalizations. Educational research can be regarded as a practical activity occurring at four levels. The first level consists of collecting data to find out what outcomes are occurring in an educational setting. At the second level, we attempt to establish cause-and-effect relationships. The third level concerns itself with determining how far the conclusions of a research study can be generalized. Finally, at the fourth level we examine the theoretical principles that explain the results we have observed in a research study or series of studies. Teachers and other educators should almost always be doing or applying some form of research in their educational practice. This book will help to determine the kind of research that is needed and will demonstrate how to perform it as efficiently and productively as possible.

FOR FURTHER THOUGHT

1. Is it reasonable to expect teachers and other educators to be researchers as well as do a good job educating students?

2. How does educational research differ from research that you might have conducted in high school or college science, social studies, or English classes?

3. The authors say that no sensible educator should deliberately make decisions without basing them as much as possible on the findings of educational research. Why don't more teachers and other educators seem to believe that this statement is true?

REFERENCES

Buchanan, N. K., & Feldhusen, J. F. (1991). *Conducting research and evaluation in gifted education: A handbook of methods and applications.* New York: Teachers College Press.

Hagerty, S., & Evans, P. (1985). *Research and evaluation methods in special education: Quantitative and qualitative techniques in case study work.* Philadelphia: NFER-Nelson.

Smith, M. L. (1987). *Research and evaluation in education and the social sciences.* Englewood Cliffs, NJ: Prentice-Hall.

Zapka, J. G. (1982). *Research and evaluation in health education.* Oakland, CA: Third Party Publishing Company.

ANNOTATED BIBLIOGRAPHY

Agnew, N. M., & Pyke, S. W. (1987). *The science game: An introduction to research in the behavioral sciences* (4th ed.). Englewood Cliffs, NJ: Prentice-Hall. The first two chapters of this book do a good job of presenting science and the scientific method in a human and social context.

Angelo, T. A., & Cross, K. P. (1993). *Classroom assessment techniques: A handbook for college teachers* (2nd ed.). San Francisco, CA: Jossey-Bass. This book suggests a large number of effective strategies for assessing student performance during the early and intermediate stages of learning, so that the students and instructor can make adjustments for more effective learning.

Cook, T. D., & Campbell, D. T. (1979). *Quasi-Experimentation: Design and analysis issues for field settings.* Chicago: Rand McNally. The first chapter discusses the basic logic of making causal inferences in the social sciences, including education.

Dewey, J. (1910, 1933, 1969). *How we think.* Boston: D.C. Heath. This book contains the original statement of Dewey's insights into the scientific method.

Eisner, E. W. (1991). *The enlightened eye.* New York: Macmillan. This book approaches the research process from a qualitative perspective, which will be discussed in chapter 9 of the present book.

Herman, J. L., Morris, L. L., & Fitz-Gibbon, C. T. (1987). *Evaluator's handbook* (2nd ed.). Newbury Park, CA: Sage. This is the lead book in a series called the Program Evaluation Kit. The series of nine books presents practical, step-by-step guidelines to assist practitioners in carrying out evaluations. The other books include *How to focus an evaluation, How to design a program evaluation, How to use qualitative methods in evaluation, How to assess program implementation, How to measure attitudes, How to measure performance and use tests, How to analyze data,* and *How to communicate evaluation findings.*

House, E. R. (1990). Trends in evaluation. *Educational Researcher, 19*(3), 24–28. This article covers the ways educational evaluation has evolved over the past 20 years.

Krathwohl, D. R. (1993). *Methods of educational and social science research: An integrated approach.* New York: Longman. The author presents an integrated view of educational research, focusing on how research findings make their way into knowledge and decision making. Chapters 1 through 5 deal with the nature of research, and chapters 12 through 14 deal with the nature of causal inference.

Mohr, M. M., & Maclean, M. S. (1987). *Working together: A guide for teacher-researchers.* Urbana, IL: National Council of Teachers of English. This book gives practical advice for conducting action research. It includes five examples as case studies of action research.

Stecher, B. M., & Davis, W. A. (1987). *How to focus an evaluation* (2nd ed.). Newbury Park, CA: Sage. This is part of the Program Evaluation Kit (see Herman, Morris, & Fitz-Gibbon). It provides guidelines for planning and effective evaluation.

Walford, G. (Ed.). (1991). *Doing educational research.* New York: Routledge. This book summarizes the experiences of 13 action researchers who conducted significant research activities in England and the United Kingdom.

Wittrock, M. (1985). *Handbook of research on teaching* (3rd ed.). New York: Macmillan. This book includes discussions of the theory behind research on teaching; several chapters review and synthesize the research on specific topics related to the field of teaching.

Worthen, B. R., & Sanders, J. R. (1987). *Educational evaluation: Alternative approaches and practical guidelines.* White Plains, NY: Longman. The authors present a comprehensive treatment of all types of educational evaluation. They focus on qualitative as well as quantitative methods.

CHAPTER 1

Research Report Analysis

At the end of each chapter, there will be a section like this, containing information and questions to analyze the research report found in Appendix C. This analysis of the research report will give you an opportunity to apply to a practical situation the principles discussed in each chapter.

The research report in Appendix C is an example of Level IV research. It provides evidence to support the theory that guided use of computer simulations gives students opportunities to practice thinking skills and receive reinforcement for successful use of these skills. This reinforced practice leads to improved problem-solving skills.

It is probably best not to try to answer these questions immediately after your first reading of each chapter. Wait until you review several chapters, then do all of the research analyses in the reviewed chapters as an integrated review of the topics covered in those chapters.

Now, on to the present chapter. . . .

According to chapter 1, Level IV research builds upon a foundation of lower-level skills. In what ways does this study demonstrate each of the other levels of research? Try answering the following questions:

1. How does the report in Appendix C demonstrate Level I research? (That is, what do the researchers do to find out what is happening?)

2. How does the report demonstrate Level II research? (That is, what do the researchers do to find out if the simulations are causing an outcome?)

3. How does the report demonstrate Level III research? (That is, what do the researchers do to examine the extent to which the same results would occur in other situations?)

ANSWERS:

1. The data collection processes described at the beginning of the report are examples of Level I research. The unit tests and the Watson-Glaser

tests collect evidence regarding what is happening in the classrooms.

2. The research design described in the report's introduction is an example of Level II research. The results of the data collected through that design are presented in the table in Appendix C, and these provide support for the belief that the simulations caused the students' improved performance on the tests.

3. The report deals with Level III by describing the types of students to whom the results can be generalized. This approach to Level III research is discussed in chapter 15. It would be a good idea to replicate this study to enhance its quality as Level III research. Improving the quality of Level III research would also enhance the quality of this report at Level IV research.

CLARIFYING THE RESEARCH PROBLEM

■ **WHERE WE'VE BEEN**

We have introduced the topic of research methods as a set of tools that enable educators to think better, develop and understand educational principles, and make increasingly broad and accurate generalizations.

■ **WHERE WE'RE GOING NOW**

In this chapter we'll describe the process of identifying research variables and clarifying the research problem. We will discuss several types of variables that can become part of a research study and ways to integrate these into the statement of a research question or hypothesis in order to lay the foundation for a well-conducted, well-interpreted, and well-reported research study.

■ **CHAPTER PREVIEW**

This chapter will introduce the concept of research variables[1]. No educational research—whether practical or theoretical—can be conducted without identifying, conceptually developing, and operationally defining or describing in detail the research variables. Much educational research consists of the conceptualization, description, or careful operational definition of educational variables. These descriptions enable educators to develop realistic depictions of persons, programs, and contexts related to education and to analyze and understand more accurately what is happening in various educational settings. While they are useful in their own right, these descriptions also lay a foundation for research that looks at more complex relationships among variables.

---

[1]We are going to use the term *variable* several times in this chapter before we eventually define it. If this does not bother you (that is, if the meaning is sufficiently obvious from the context), skip the rest of this footnote.

A variable is a *conceptual entity*, an invention based on reality that exists in the minds of people. Variables are so called because they *vary* (that is, they may take on any of several values—they are not constants).

The present chapter introduces variables studied in several types of educational research. The concepts introduced here will provide a useful foundation for understanding the ideas discussed in subsequent chapters. In addition, since many readers will be conducting research or writing research proposals while reading this book, it is important to enable them to begin identifying and examining research variables and investigating reference materials related to these variables as early as possible in their study of research methodology. All of the concepts introduced in this chapter will be discussed in greater detail and integrated with specific research methodologies in subsequent chapters.

To conduct research yourself at any level or to interpret the research of others, it is important to understand the nature of the variables in research studies. After reading this chapter, you should be able to

1. Identify examples of educational problems and specify the variables that constitute the statement of these problems.
2. Define and give examples of research questions and hypotheses.
3. Define and give examples of (a) quantitative descriptive, (b) qualitative, (c) experimental, (d) correlational, and (e) meta-analytic research studies.
4. Define and give examples of (a) dependent (or outcome or criterion), (b) independent (or treatment or predictor), (c) moderator, (d) control, (e) intervening, and (f) extraneous variables.
5. Combine a set of given variables into a correctly stated hypothesis.

■

EDUCATIONAL RESEARCH: A USEFUL TOOL

As we stated in chapter 1, educational research is a useful tool for both practical and theoretical problem solving. It helps us to identify concepts, contexts, treatments, and outcomes; to make predictions; and to determine the nature of relationships among variables in education. It helps us make generalizations about various aspects of education and to determine the degree of confidence we can have regarding these generalizations.

The educational research process begins with the realization that a problem exists. The following are examples of problems related to education:

1. Some of the members of a school board want to eliminate corporal punishment from the school system, but they are concerned that its removal may result in rampant anarchy. Members of a child advocacy group argue that the elimination of corporal punishment will actually improve self-discipline among the students.
2. The parents in a school system are aware that AIDS is a serious health risk for their children. They want their children to avoid this disease, but they are also concerned that introducing children to the issues could lead to sexual promiscuity.
3. A teacher needs to know whether his method of discipline, which definitely seems to enhance academic learning, might also be having the unpleasant side effect of promoting negative self-concepts among his students.

Educational research does not in itself solve these problems. It provides a tool that gives hard-working, conscientious educators some of the ammunition they need to successfully attack them.

Only after we start to know what the problem is can we take steps to solve it.

The first step in the educational research process involves identifying and clarifying the problem. Only after we start to know what the problem is can we take steps to solve it. We can identify and clarify research problems by specifying the variables involved in those problems, stating these variables in research questions or hypotheses, and operationally defining these variables or describing them in detail. Often the variables are not easy to identify, and

---

BOX 2.1   The Order of Chapters in This Book

Much of the subject matter of educational research is interactive rather than linear. That is, we cannot expect each new topic always to build consecutively upon previous topics. Earlier topics often do offer insight into later topics, but later topics may also offer insight into earlier topics. For this reason, you will sometimes discover that when you review a chapter after reading farther into the book, you will arrive at a more thorough understanding of the earlier chapter. To help you understand the concepts in chapter 2 as thoroughly as possible, we shall examine some of them again in chapter 17.

---

often they resist easy definition. However, only after we have identified and operationally defined the variables or described them in detail can we sensibly collect data, relate them to one another, and attempt to make generalizations that will help us solve our educational problems.

STATING RESEARCH QUESTIONS AND RESEARCH HYPOTHESES

Research questions ask about the nature of a variable or concept or about the relationship among two or more variables. *Research hypotheses* state the expected answers to these research questions. Research questions and hypotheses give focus, structure, and organization to the collection, analysis, and interpretation of the data collected by the person conducting the research.

A good researcher (or for that matter, a good thinker) would say that, stated in their present format, all three of the problems cited earlier (page 18) are too vaguely expressed to generate clear solutions. For example, what is the real problem in the first description?

1. Is the problem that somebody wants to know whether the removal of corporal punishment could objectively cause an increase in "rampant anarchy" (whatever that means)?

2. Is the problem that somebody doubts that the removal of corporal punishment could objectively cause an increase in "self-discipline" (whatever that means)?

3. Is the problem that somebody wants to know what it will take to placate the child advocacy group? If board members retain corporal punishment, can they withstand the hostile publicity that will be evoked from this group?

4. Or is the problem that the board members simply don't have enough information to make a sensible decision? Maybe they need answers to specific questions, like the following:

   a. How often is corporal punishment actually administered in the school system? How does the frequency of corporal punishment in this school system compare with that in the rest of the country?

   b. How does the frequency of corporal punishment compare with other forms of punishment?

   c. Do students really experience negative effects from corporal punishment? Assuming that there are negative effects, is corporal punishment more likely to cause negative effects than other strategies, such as detention or school suspension?

   d. What do teachers do when they give up corporal punishment? Do they become permissive and let students get by with anything? Do they resort to other strategies, which may be more harmful in the long run? Or do they begin to reason together with the students to arrive at solutions to disciplinary problems?

The preceding questions are more specific than the original problem. An educational researcher can now begin to offer information that will help solve the problem, because it is now more clear what the problem is. The difference between the original question and these refined questions is that the latter focus more on specific variables and the relationships among them.

RESEARCH VARIABLES

A variable is a concept that can assume any one of a range of values. *Factor* and *feature* are common English synonyms for *variable* in the following sentences (*outcome* is another word that often means *variable,* but note that not all variables are outcomes):

1. The parents in the school system are aware that AIDS is a factor (variable) that is a serious health risk for their children.
2. The teacher needs to know what features (variables) of his method of discipline might promote negative self-concepts among his students.
3. The teacher needs to know whether his method of discipline might promote negative outcomes (variables) among his students.

A variable *varies* in the sense that it can take on different values or conditions. It is a characteristic that can be the focus of a research study.

The definition of the term *variable* makes the concept seem more difficult than it really is. This is because it is a definition of an abstraction; and definitions of abstractions sometimes become very abstract (for example, it's easy to exist, but it's difficult to define *existence*). Therefore, it may be useful to look at some examples.

In the set of examples we started examining on page 18, *corporal punishment* is a variable. More specifically, *whether corporal punishment is permitted* is a variable. It can vary by either being permitted or not being permitted.

The *frequency of corporal punishment* could also be a variable. It can vary from, say, not happening

at all to happening once a day to happening several times a day.

If a researcher wondered whether corporal punishment might cause more anxiety than suspension from school, then *corporal punishment, anxiety,* and *suspension from school* could all become variables for this researcher to study.

If the researcher focused attention on any other factor, such as child abuse, self-discipline, religious beliefs, gender of the students or teachers, or ethnic background, these could become variables in a research study, or even merely in a thought process.

Variables are developed theoretically and abstractly in the mind of the researcher. The researcher draws on previous experience and theoretical knowledge to identify and specify variables, which serve as unifying factors to help organize the research process. All human thinking employs concepts, which are called variables when we focus attention on them, measure them, or deal with them in some other way as part of the research process. (The ways researchers define and measure variables will be the subject of later chapters.)

The next section of this chapter discusses the basic categories of studies that examine variables of interest to educators.

TYPES OF RESEARCH STUDIES

The following sections describe several basic categories of research studies that serve useful purposes in education. These descriptions should enable you to see what kinds of studies are possible and begin to identify research variables. These categories are not mutually exclusive. For example, the first category is called descriptive research, but actually *all* research is descriptive. At this point in the book, we are not going to worry about the degree of overlap among these categories. As Table 2.1 shows, strategies for conducting each type of research are covered in later chapters. We will wait until the distinctions among the types of research have practical significance before making those distinctions.

Table 2.1 Types of Educational Research Studies

Type of Study	Description	Chapter in Text
Quantitative descriptive research—status study	The researcher uses quantitative strategies (such as questionnaires or observational techniques) to collect information about the characteristics of a person, group, program, or other educational entity.	4 through 8
Qualitative research	The researcher uses qualitative strategies (such as ethnographies or detailed case studies) to collect detailed information about the characteristics of a person, group, program, or other educational entity.	9
Experimental/quasi-experimental research	The researcher assigns participants to treatments or otherwise structures conditions to determine whether a treatment has an effect on a specified outcome variable.	11–12
Correlational research	The researcher uses statistical techniques such as correlation coefficients to examine the relationships among two or more variables, without making generalizations about the causal nature of these relationships.	13
Criterion group research	The researcher examines the characteristics of existing groups (that is, groups not experimentally assigned to particular treatments) to determine the degree to which these groups differ with regard to specified characteristics.	13
Meta-analysis	The researcher combines and analyzes the results of several studies to examine the degree to which these combined results lead to generalizations regarding the variables in the studies.	16

Descriptive Studies—Status Research

In almost every educational research study, the researcher is interested in measuring an outcome. (The researcher may also be interested in other variables, but these will be discussed later in this chapter.) *Outcome variables* are concepts or characteristics of end results or products that can occur in educational settings. They are the results—the characteristics or events that teachers and other educators may wish to encourage or discourage in educational settings. In the first revised hypothesis of the corporal punishment problem, *anarchy* is the outcome upon which the question focuses. In the second example, the outcome variable is *self-discipline*. In the third example, the outcome is *the degree to*

which the board can withstand the hostility of the advocacy group. Try it yourself: What are the outcome variables in statements (a) through (d) of the fourth example on page 19?

Answers:

a. frequency of corporal punishment

b. frequency of corporal punishment and also frequency of other forms of punishment

c. negative side effects

d. types of punishment employed by teachers; permissiveness exhibited by teachers; other strategies employed by teachers; reasoning to arrive at solutions

In actual practice, the school board members would usually be interested in more than just one of these outcome variables. By refining the questions through identification of the outcome variables, they would be able to focus more accurately on a solution to their problems.

Outcome variables are the results—the character-istics or events that teachers and other educators may wish to encourage or discourage in educational settings.

Let's assume that one of the questions the school board actually wants answered is how often corporal punishment really occurs in the school system. How would a researcher collect data? Table 2.2 shows the steps that would be involved in answering this question (the next few chapters describe in detail how to conduct a research study of this kind). The second question asks about the frequency of corporal punishment in this school system compared with that in the rest of the country. The school board members could simply look that answer up in a professional publication; Table 2.3 shows the steps that would be undertaken by a researcher commissioned to find the answer to this second question.

Table 2.2 The Steps Used to Answer the Question "How Often Is Corporal Punishment Actually Administered in the School System?" (right-hand column indicates where each step is covered in this book)

Research Step	Chapter
1. Identify the outcome variable and clarify the research question	2
2. Check published literature to see what is known about measuring this outcome	3
3. Operationally define corporal punishment	4
4. Devise a set of strategies to measure corporal punishment	5–6
5. Administer the data collection process	5–6
6. Tabulate, summarize, and interpret the results	7

Table 2.3 The Steps Used to Answer the Question "How Often Is Corporal Punishment Administered in the Entire State?" (right-hand column indicates where each step is covered in this book)

Research Step	Chapter
1. Identify the outcome variable and clarify the research question	2
2. Check published literature to see what is known about measuring this outcome	3
3. Operationally define corporal punishment.	4
4. Devise a set of strategies to measure corporal punishment	5–6
5. Select an appropriate sample to whom data can be collected	8
6. Administer the data collection process to the selected sample	5–6
7. Tabulate, summarize, draw conclusions, and interpret the results	7–8
8. Write a report that will convey the results to a general readership	19

Descriptive research studies often focus exclusively on the measurement and description of outcome variables (in chapter 1 we referred to this as Level I research). The strategies for conducting descriptive studies are the focus of chapters 4 through 8. When these studies collect numerical data—for example, by counting how often corporal punishment occurs, by using a questionnaire to measure people's attitudes toward corporal punishment; by relating these variables to other variables, or by making predictions—these studies are referred to as *quantitative* descriptive studies. *Qualitative* studies (chapter 9), on the other hand, often study variables and outcomes in a more global sense; for example, a researcher may observe a classroom over a prolonged period of time and record anecdotal information regarding what happens when disruptions occur. Both of these are valid and important ways to describe educational contexts and outcomes.

Experimental Research

Experimental studies do more than describe contexts and outcomes—they examine cause-and-effect relationships. For example, if our school board members want to know whether the removal of corporal punishment may cause an increase in anarchy, they are asking about the causal nature of the relationship between *the removal of corporal punishment* and *anarchy*. To answer this question, they need more than descriptive research—they need to examine the results of experimental research.

An experimental study focuses on a treatment and an outcome. (The study may also include additional variables, such as the context in which the experiment is conducted.) The outcome that is expected to result from the treatment is referred to as the *dependent variable,* or *criterion variable.* Such outcome variables are *dependent* in the sense that they *depend* on the treatment. They offer a *criterion* that can become the basis for making a judgment about the results of the experiment. If the treatment has one effect, a person's score on the dependent variable may be low; whereas if the treatment had a different impact, that person's score on the dependent variable would be high.

An experimental study focuses on a treatment and an outcome.

The treatment, context, or condition that is expected to produce an outcome is referred to as the *independent* variable (the terms *independent variable* and *treatment* or *condition* are used synonymously in this text). The independent variable is *independent* in the sense that it *does not depend* on the outcome variable. Another way to say this is that in experimental research the independent variable is the cause and the dependent variable is the effect. The independent variable is the treatment; the dependent variable is the outcome.

REVIEW QUIZ 2.1

Examine each of the following hypotheses or questions and identify the dependent and independent variables (all answers to Review Quizzes in this text are at the end of each chapter):

1. Studying Shakespeare leads to a greater appreciation of Western culture.

2. Behavior modification leads to noncreative behavior among elementary school children.

3. Does programming in the Logo language cause improvement in higher-order thinking skills?

4. Delaying reading instruction until the sixth grade will have no adverse impact on reading ability by the time the child reaches adolescence.

5. Do classrooms that emphasize a language-rich environment have students who are more eager to share their opinions with their peers?

In each of the cases in the preceding quiz, the independent variable produces an outcome, and this outcome is referred to as the dependent variable.

You may have noticed that some of the variables (such as noncreative behavior, studying Shakespeare, and appreciation of Western culture) are vaguely defined. Operational definitions (discussed in chapter 4) will help remove this ambiguity.

Let's assume that one of the questions the school board actually wants answered is whether the removal of corporal punishment would increase disruptive behavior in the school system. How would a researcher collect data? Table 2.4 shows the steps that would be involved in answering this question (chapters 10 through 14 describe in detail how to conduct a research study of this kind). Note that while Table 2.4 recommends an experimental strategy to answer this question, it would also be possible to deal with this question through a qualitative research strategy (chapter 9) or a correlational strategy (chapter 13) or by conducting a meta-analysis (chapter 16).

Table 2.4 The Steps Used to Answer the Question "Will the Removal of Corporal Punishment Cause an Increase in Anarchy?" (right-hand column indicates the chapter in which each step is covered in this book)

Research Step	Chapter
1. Identify the dependent and independent variables and clarify the research question	2
2. Check published literature to see what is known about the effects of corporal punishment, especially with regard to disruptive behavior, which is probably what the school board means by "anarchy"	3
3. Operationally define corporal punishment and anarchy	4
4. Devise a set of strategies to measure anarchy	5–6
5. Devise an appropriate experimental strategy to test the impact of the independent variable on the dependent variable	11–12
6. Carry out the experimental strategy	11–12
7. Tabulate and interpret the results of the study	14
8. Write a report that will convey the results to a general readership	19

Correlational Studies

Correlational studies are descriptive studies in which the researcher not only describes variables but also examines the nature of the quantitative relationships among them. For example, a researcher might suspect that children who often receive corporal punishment are more likely to hit other children during recess. This researcher is interested not only in two variables (receiving corporal punishment and hitting other children during recess) but also in the relationship between these two variables (and perhaps others). The researcher could investigate this possibility by giving a questionnaire to a group of children to find out how often each child has received corporal punishment and by observing the same group of children on the playground to see how often (if ever) each child hit another child. If there was a tendency

for those who hit other children more often to be the same children who received corporal punishment more often, this evidence would support the belief that there is a relationship. This kind of study would enable the researcher to determine whether there is a *relationship* between corporal punishment and hitting other children in this group of children.

The existence of a relationship does not necessarily mean that one of the variables is the cause of the other.

Each of the following three hypotheses could be investigated by correlational methods:

The students who do well in algebra will also do well in gym.

People who arrive early for their therapy sessions usually arrive early for athletic events.

There is a strong positive relationship between GRE scores and success in this course.

The steps in a correlational research study are the same as those described in Table 2.4, except that the experimental design is replaced by a correlational method, which is discussed in chapter 13.

Note that the existence of a relationship does not necessarily mean that one of the variables is the cause of the other. For example, if there is a relationship between the incidence of corporal punishment and hitting other students, this could be because corporal punishment caused hitting, because hitting caused corporal punishment, or because some other prior factor (such as a negative self-concept) led to both increased corporal punishment and increased hitting.

MODERATOR VARIABLES

Moderator variables are characteristics that influence (moderate) the impact of the independent or treatment variable upon the dependent or criterion variable. Moderator variables appear only in studies that include independent and dependent variables—usually experimental studies. In the following hypothesis, for example, the sex of the child is a moderator variable:

The use of popular music will increase the appreciation of poetry among elementary school children. This impact will be greater among girls than among boys.

In this example, the use of popular music is the independent variable and appreciation of poetry is the dependent variable. The sex of the child is a moderator variable because the statement indicates that this factor influences *the degree to which* the independent variable will influence the dependent variable: if the child is a girl, popular music will tend to have one impact with regard to the appreciation of poetry; whereas if the child is a boy, the same independent variable will tend to have a different impact.

Moderator variables help us discover not only whether the treatment has had an impact but also under what circumstances or contexts this impact is likely to vary.

In the preceding example, the sex of the child was merely one of many variables that could have been chosen as moderator variables. The following are two other variations of the same hypothesis, with a different moderator variable inserted in each case:

The use of popular music will increase the appreciation of poetry among elementary school children. This impact will be greater among older children than among younger children.

The use of popular music will increase the appreciation of poetry among elementary school children. This impact will be greater when the teacher is of the same sex as the child than when the teacher is of the opposite sex.

You can easily see the advantage of using such moderator variables. The researcher (or reader) can discover not only *whether* the treatment has had the desired impact but also *under what circumstances or contexts this impact is likely to vary*. This is extremely useful information for helping us generalize the results to other situations, as well as for helping us selectively apply results to specific types of learners within a given educational setting.

The following are restatements of the first two hypotheses in Review Quiz 2.1. Moderator variables have been added to each hypothesis. To avoid stereotyped language and to show a fuller range of how moderator variables can be introduced into research studies, the wording has been varied in each hypothesis.

1. Studying Shakespeare leads to an increased appreciation of Western culture among college-bound students but not among non-college-bound students.

2. Behavior modification will reduce creative behavior among elementary school children in middle-class schools but will increase creative behavior in lower-middle-class schools.

Now you try to identify the moderator variables in the following hypotheses, again adapted from Review Quiz 2.1:

3. Programming in Logo will cause substantial improvements in higher-order thinking skills among slow readers who are not classified as having learning disabilities. However, no such improvements will occur among slow readers who are classified as having learning disabilities.

4. Delaying reading instruction until the sixth grade will have no adverse impact on reading ability by the time the child reaches adolescence. This absence of impact will be equally true among low-IQ, medium-IQ, and high-IQ students.

5. Elementary school classrooms that emphasize a language-rich environment will have students who are more eager to share their opinions with their peers. However, in middle school classrooms, language-rich environments will have no such impact.

The moderator variables in the preceding hypotheses are as follows:

3. being classified as having learning disabilities versus not being classified as having learning disabilities
4. IQ of students
5. grade level of classroom (elementary versus middle school)

In each of these examples the original hypothesis has been enriched by the addition of the moderator variable. In each case the moderator variable is a factor that could influence the impact of the independent variable upon the dependent variable. For each example, other factors could have been selected as moderator variables; the actual moderator variables selected in any study depend on what the researcher is interested in learning about the relationship between the independent and dependent variables.

CONTROL VARIABLES

Control variables are characteristics that are controlled by the experimenter to reduce any impact they might otherwise have on other variables or on the interpretation of the results of a study. They *control* extraneous variables (which are discussed later in this chapter). This control can be attained through any of the following methods:

1. *Isolation and elimination.* For example, a researcher can control the extraneous effect of intelligence by including only students of average intelligence in the study—excluding low-performing or gifted students. This is an effective strategy described further in the present chapter.
2. *Precise description of the context, treatment, or subjects.* A detailed, accurate, and unambiguous description enables persons applying the research findings to make a valid judgment regarding the degree to which the results of a particular study can be generalized to other settings. This is an effective strategy covered in chapters 9 and 15.

3. *Equating across groups.* This method is often used in experimental studies. For example, a researcher can control the extraneous effect of intelligence by randomly assigning subjects to the experimental and control groups, thereby making them similar with regard to intelligence (and many other variables). This.is an effective strategy described in chapter 11.

In any research study, the researcher can select and describe control variables to help define the limitations on how far the results of the study can be generalized. Furthermore, in experimental studies, the researcher may select control variables because these factors may otherwise influence the impact of the independent variable on the dependent variable. Such extraneous influences would make it difficult to determine the precise nature of the relationship between the independent and dependent variables. Therefore, the researcher controls these extraneous factors to balance or reduce their influence in a particular study.

Control variables enable the researcher to control extraneous factors to balance or reduce their influence in a particular study.

Let us examine two of the sample hypotheses that we have been following throughout this chapter, and this time we shall add control variables:

1. Among high school seniors, studying Shakespeare leads to a greater appreciation of Western culture.
2. Behavior modification leads to noncreative behavior among elementary school children in the public schools of Gotham City.

In the first hypothesis, "high school seniors" has been added as a control variable. It is possible that the effect of studying Shakespeare would be different for students of different ages; therefore, the grade level of the students might influence how they would respond to Shakespeare. Thus the researcher has decided to include *only* high school seniors in the research study. This constraint rules out the extraneous factor, but of course it also restricts the generalizations to those made about high school seniors only. The logic goes like this:

Students in the experimental group (who studied Shakespeare) were measured as displaying greater appreciation of Western culture than the students in the control group (who did not study Shakespeare).

Since there were only high school seniors in both groups, differences in appreciation of Shakespeare could not possibly have arisen from basic differences between juniors and seniors.

Therefore, the influence of grade level (seniors versus juniors) has been controlled; but generalizations from the experiment have also been restricted to those made about high school seniors only.

In the second hypothesis, there are three control variables: grade level of children (elementary rather than secondary or middle school), type of school (public rather than private), and location (Gotham City).

In the preceding examples we added control variables to the original hypotheses before they were enriched by the addition of moderator variables. It is possible (and often desirable) to have both control variables and moderator variables within the same research study. Each of the following examples contains independent, dependent, moderator, and control variables. The moderator variables are indicated by italics, the control variables by boldface.

3. **Among children between the ages of 9 and 11,** programming in Logo will cause substantial improvements in higher-order thinking skills among **slow readers** *who are not classified as having learning disabilities.* However, no such improvements will occur among 9- to 11-year-old **slow readers** *who are classified as having learning disabilities.*

4. **Among children who have no external pressure from their parents to learn to read,** delaying reading instruction until the sixth grade will have no adverse impact on reading ability by the time the children reach adolescence. *This will be equally true among low-IQ, medium-IQ, and high-IQ students.*

5. **In middle-class schools,** *elementary school classrooms* that emphasize a language-rich environment will have students who are more eager to share their opinions with their peers. However, *in middle school classrooms* **in similar schools,** language-rich environments will have no such impact.

In the third hypothesis, there are two control variables: age of child (9 to 11 years old) and level of reading ability (slow readers are included, but average and fast readers are excluded). There are no 8-year-olds or above-average readers in the study that tests this research hypothesis. The factors of age and level of ability are ruled out as contaminating factors, but the researcher can no longer generalize to students who fall beyond the restrictions set by these control variables.

Any variable that can be used as a moderator variable in an experimental study can also be used as a control variable, and vice versa.

You have probably noticed that there is considerable similarity between moderator and control variables. This similarity is a result of both types taking into account factors that may influence the impact of the independent variable upon the dependent variable. The distinction is that moderator variables control this extraneous influence and examine it in such a way as to describe its precise impact. Control variables, on the other hand, merely reduce or describe this extraneous influence without providing any information about its relationship to the independent and dependent variables. Thus, while moderator variables have the potential to restrict, refine, and elaborate generalizations, the role of the control variable is usually confined to merely restricting generalizations.

Because of the similarity stated in the preceding paragraph, any variable that can be used as a moderator variable in an experimental study can also be used as a control variable, and vice versa. A sensible strategy is to identify as many extraneous variables as possible that might influence the impact of the treatment on the dependent variable; then, some of these can be made into moderator variables and some into control variables, and some can be left uncontrolled. At first thought, it might appear that since the moderator variable does everything the control variable does and more, then we should use the moderator variable as often as possible. This would be good advice, except for an important practical consideration. It is often difficult to obtain the number or variety of subjects that is needed for analyzing a factor as a moderator variable. In addition, having a large number of moderator variables can make a study cumbersome. Similarly, it might at first seem that *no* extraneous factor should be left uncontrolled. Again, however, there is a problem of feasibility. There are so many factors that could influence the impact of the treatment on the outcome that it is not possible to isolate and control all of them.

This discussion of control variables has focused on their use in experimental studies. This focus has been useful to point out their relationship to moderator variables. However, control variables are also important in descriptive research. For example, notice the impact of the control variables italicized in the following research questions and hypotheses:

1. *Fifth graders* in the *public schools* of Oregon do better in reading than in mathematics.
2. A survey of *American businessmen* showed that they would support higher taxes if they could be assured that the quality of education would actually improve.
3. The *principals who responded to the survey* indicated strong opposition to corporal punishment.
4. The *students in the experimental school that used a whole-language approach* showed a strong tendency to want to share their opinions with their peers.

Each of the italicized control variables shows the limitations imposed by the context of the study that will restrict the degree to which the results of each of these descriptive studies can be generalized. If you noticed that many of these control variables were too vague to be of much use, you're right. The usefulness of these control variables would improve with operational definitions (the topic of chapter 4) or qualitative description (the topic of chapter 9).

INTERVENING VARIABLES

Intervening variables are hypothetical concepts assumed to be created by the treatment and to have an impact on the observable outcome. Treatments produce intervening variables (which are invisible—perhaps inside the brain of the learner), and intervening variables then produce observable outcomes. This variable *intervenes* in the sense that the treatment does not produce the observable outcome directly but rather through the mediation (intervention) of this invisible, conceptual, hypothetical, internalized process. The intervening variable is the basic subject matter of theoretical research (discussed in chapter 17).

To take a brief example, a researcher might find that computer simulations cause students to do well on science tests. In fact, the computer simulations themselves probably do not cause the improved performance on the tests. The simulations probably induce some internal change within the students (such as improved motivation, greater attention to the task, perceived relevance, or something else), and this internal change is what eventually leads to the difference in performance. Determining and examining intervening variables helps us understand educational principles better. In addition, such variables can be useful for practical reasons: we may be able to find less expensive ways to bring about these intervening variables than, for example, relatively expensive computer simulations.

The intervening variable is usually not stated as part of the hypothesis.

In the following examples the hypothesis is stated (without the moderator variables or control variables), and then a possible intervening variable is stated in parentheses:

1. Studying Shakespeare leads to a greater appreciation of Western culture. (perception of important similarities within Elizabethan and contemporary Western culture)
2. Behavior modification leads to noncreative behavior among elementary school children. (an urge to conform in order to be reinforced as efficiently as possible)

Now you try it. Identify possible intervening variables for the following hypotheses:

3. Because Logo offers opportunities for improved planning ability arising out of the involvement in microworlds, programming in Logo will cause improvements in higher-order thinking.
4. Delaying reading instruction until the sixth grade will have no adverse impact on reading ability by the time the child reaches adolescence.
5. Language-rich environments will make children more eager to share their opinions with their peers.

Here are possible intervening variables for the preceding hypotheses:

3. Improved planning ability arising out of the involvement in microworlds offered by the programming language
4. Self-motivation, which replaces external requirements
5. In this case, none is *stated*. A reader or researcher could construct one through such processes as reasoning about the evidence arising from the study and reflecting on theoretical information from the research literature. Through such reasoning, stimulation of language and social processes might emerge as the intervening variable.

In these examples, the intervening variable has been appended to the barest possible statement of the hypothesis. This has been done for the sake of simplicity. In actual practice, the moderator variable should take into account *all* the variables in the research hypothesis.

Unlike the other variables, the intervening variable is usually not stated as part of the hypothesis. Rather, it is stated at the culmination of the review of the literature (prior to the hypothesis) as the specific rationale behind why the hypothesis is going to be stated in the form it will take.

EXTRANEOUS VARIABLES

An extraneous variable is a factor that produces an uncontrolled, unpredictable impact upon the dependent variable. Extraneous variables weaken research studies because they introduce ambiguity into the research process. To the extent that they are uncontrolled, they render uncertain the conclusions we can draw from a study. The threats to internal and external validity, discussed in chapters 10 and 15, are extraneous variables, and the whole purpose of the strategies discussed in those chapters is to minimize the impact of such extraneous variables. To the extent that extraneous variables can be brought under control, the results of a study are strengthened. One good reason for replicating research (discussed later in this chapter) is to reduce the possibility that conclusions will be weakened by extraneous factors.

THE RESEARCH VARIABLES COMBINED

Table 2.5 summarizes the major characteristics of each of the research variables. Our discussion of research variables has focused largely on experimental research. This is because only in experimental studies are we likely to find *all* the research variables in a single hypothesis. We may have given the false impression that most educational research is experimental. Actually, only about 10% of published educational research is experimental; the rest is either descriptive, qualitative, or correlational. Table 2.1

briefly described these various types of research and indicated where each is discussed in this book. Also, the categories in that table are not mutually exclusive; for example, a quantitative or experimental study may also employ some qualitative methods, and a meta-analysis often combines the results of several experimental studies.

Most studies do not contain every type of variable. Whatever variables emerge from the analysis of a problem setting should be clearly identified and appropriately stated in a succinct research question or hypothesis. Subsequent chapters will describe how to operationally define these variables and incorporate them into effective research studies.

REVIEW QUIZ 2.2

1. Examine the following research hypothesis and identify each of the research variables requested below:

Formal operational high school biology students will use problem-solving heuristics to solve genetics problems, but concrete operational high school biology students will use a rote-memory strategy to solve the same kind of problems.

Identify the following variables:

Dependent

Control

Table 2.5 Summary of Research Variables

Variable	Definition	Mnemonic	Other Terms
Dependent	The outcome that is expected to result from a treatment	Such variables are dependent in the sense that they *depend* on the treatment	Outcome variable Effect Result Criterion variable (in prediction studies)
Independent	The treatment or condition that is expected to produce an outcome	The independent variable is independent in the sense that it *does not depend* on the outcome variable	Treatment Experimental procedure Case Predictor variable (in correlational studies)
Moderator	Characteristic that influences the impact of the independent variable upon the dependent variable	The word *moderate* can mean to *modify*, as one weather pattern may moderate the impact of another (If that doesn't help, *modify* and *moderate* both begin with *mod*)	Interaction Interactive factor
Control	Characteristic that is controlled by the experimenter in order to reduce any impact this factor might otherwise have on the interpretation of the results of a study	The whole purpose of this variable is to *control* extraneous influences	Context variable Limitation Restriction
Intervening	The hypothetical factor that is created by the independent variable and has an impact on the dependent variable	This variable *intervenes* in the sense that it occurs during the time that *intervenes* between the cause and the effect	Underlying cause Psychological construct
Extraneous	Factors that produce uncontrolled, unpredictable impacts upon the dependent variable	This variable is an *extra* factor, something that is *extraneous* to the current study and therefore may cause confusion, unless it is controlled	Contaminating factor Threat to internal or external validity

2. Examine the following research question and identify each of the research variables requested below:

How do K-3 students who use the whole-language method to study reading differ in their comprehension strategies from those who use a phonetic approach?

Identify the following variables:

    Independent

    Dependent

    Moderator

    Control

3. Examine the following research hypothesis and identify each of the research variables requested below:

High school students who study Latin for two years will develop better English vocabulary skills than those who do not study Latin. This difference will occur both among those who are in advanced-placement English classes and among those who are in regular English classes. This difference will occur because of an increased ability to break a word down into its component parts.

Identify the following variables:

    Independent

    Dependent

    Moderator

    Control

    Intervening

SELECTING RESEARCH PROBLEMS FOR YOUR OWN STUDIES

Many readers of this book will develop research proposals and conduct research projects of their own. An important consideration for these readers is the selection and exploration of their research problem. The following guidelines will be helpful:

1. It is not necessary to *invent* problems in education. Education is overwhelmed with problems. Pick one that is within your interests, abilities, and resources. To select a research problem, focus proper attention on questions and problems that already exist and that can feasibly be solved. Follow the guidelines in this chapter to state and clarify a problem that is meaningful, interesting, feasible, and important to you.

2. State the research question or hypothesis early, but be ready to modify, adapt, or expand it as your reading of the literature and early observations give you more information pertinent to the topic. This early focus will enable you to direct your attention to the problems of the research more effectively.

3. Use the library and reference sources discussed in chapter 3 to find out what has already been done with regard to your problem. Using reference materials will enable you to discover other variables, as well as how others have operationally defined and measured their variables, how they have carried out their research studies, and how they fit their ideas and methods into a theoretical framework.

4. It's often worthwhile to replicate previous research. As later chapters will show, replications not only check the accuracy of their original counterparts but also lead to refinement and expansion of generalizations. A replication can be almost a direct duplication, or you can make modifications, as the next guideline suggests.

5. Consider modifying previous research by using new control variables, moderator variables, or operational definitions of any of the variables.

6. If possible, conduct a pilot study before undertaking the full research project. Pilot studies often enable researchers to refine, clarify, and try out their variables, measurement processes, and other research strategies.

Strategies for getting research ideas from existing studies are summarized in Table 2.6. By following these guidelines and employing the strategies discussed throughout this book, you can plan and carry out an effective research project. The preceding list offers guidelines to stimulate your thinking, not steps to be followed in a linear sequence. The basic

Table 2.6 How to Get Research Ideas from Other Studies

Strategy	Comments	Chapter
Replicate the study		
1. Directly replicate the study	Use simple duplication to see whether it really works	
2. Replicate an old study in a new time	Increase external validity by controlling history	15
3. Replicate a study in a new place	Increase external validity by controlling setting	15
4. Replicate a study with new subjects	Increase external validity by controlling subjects	15
Alter a study		
5. Eliminate glitches in the procedures	Control threats to internal validity	10
6. Add control variables	Control threats to internal validity	2, 17
7. Intensify or reduce the treatment	Treatment may have been ineffective because it was too weak; or it may be useful to know whether less would still work	17
8. Use a more sensitive data collection process	Weak data collection may have missed real effects	5–9
9. Use new operational definitions of one or more research variables	Multiple operational definitions increases external validity	4
10. Add one or more new moderator variables	Control external validity by identifying interactions; also enhance internal validity	2, 15, 17
11. Use a different research design	For example, change from experimental to quasi-experimental or qualitative	9, 11, 12
12. Use more subjects	Rule out chance variation	13
13. Change the timing of data collection	For example, use delayed posttest	11, 12
14. Add levels to the treatment or other variables	For example, instead of treatment versus no treatment, add intermediate level of slight treatment or other treatment	17
15. Alter what the control group does	For example, instead of doing nothing, do an alternative activity	11, 12, 17
16. Perform a meta-analysis	Combine results of several studies to generalize results carefully	14
Where to get research ideas		
17. Follow author's suggestions for "further research"	These usually come at the end of the article (sometimes they are implied rather than stated)	18
18. Combine information from several studies	For example, by combining ideas from two different studies, you can have an original study	
19. Use analogical reasoning	Look for analogies between the study and other knowledge of your own	
20. Relate the study to your own experience	For example, perform an applied variation of a theoretical study	16
21. Contact the authors of interesting studies	For example, write directly or use computer bulletin boards	

strategy is to formulate an effective plan, to be willing to modify and adapt it, and to carry it out successfully.

PUTTING IT ALL TOGETHER

As we saw in the first chapter, Mr. Anderson, our humane educator, was interested in improving attitudes toward animal life. He did many forms of research, including descriptive, qualitative, and correlational studies, which will be described in subsequent chapters. The present chapter will focus on an experimental study he eventually conducted, because that research includes examples of a wide range of variables and is perhaps simpler to interpret.

The attitudes of children toward animal life were the outcome variable with which Mr. Anderson was concerned, and they became the dependent (or criterion) variable in his experimental research study. At the beginning of his work, he had no clear idea of how he could accomplish his goal. Nevertheless, he stated a rough hypothesis:

A program that I'll design will lead to improved attitudes toward animal life.

In this rough statement, Mr. Anderson's independent (or treatment) variable was *a program that he would develop*. He spent time searching library references, talking to colleagues, and using his imagination to find a program that he could present to children to help them improve their attitudes toward animal life. At the same time, he tried to find effective ways to measure attitudes toward animal life. After doing some preliminary descriptive and qualitative research, he eventually developed an Animal Life Program (ALP), which was based on theoretical principles of *induced dissonance* to produce attitude change. Once he had decided to test the ALP, it became his independent variable.

Since he planned to use his program with fourth, fifth, and sixth graders, the grade level of the children became Mr. Anderson's control variable. He also realized that children who owned pets may react differently to the ALP than other children, so he decided to examine this possibility during his research. Therefore, pet ownership became a moderator variable. His intervening variable was induced dissonance—the underlying principle that was supposed to make the ALP work. At this point Mr. Anderson's hypothesis could be stated like this:

Among fourth through sixth graders, the Animal Life Program (ALP) will lead to improved attitudes toward animal life. The program will lead to greater improvements among persons who do not own pets than among those who do own pets. (This impact will result from induced dissonance produced by the ALP, which will lead the children to change their attitudes.)

Subsequent chapters will describe how Mr. Anderson carried out his experimental study.

By stating his research variables and hypothesis in rough form at an early point in the project, Mr. Anderson could use them as a guide in his selection of measurement devices and in his choice of a research design. The earliest formulation would probably be changed and refined several times as he encountered new ideas and problems. The final product would be a guide for him in conducting the experiment, analyzing the results, and drawing conclusions.

SUMMARY

The first step in the educational research process involves identifying and clarifying the problem. We can begin to do this by specifying the variables involved in that problem and stating these variables in unambiguous research questions or hypotheses. *Research questions* ask about the nature of a variable or concept or about the relationship among two or more variables. *Research hypotheses* state the expected answers to these research questions. Research questions and hypotheses give focus, structure, and organization to the collection, analysis, and interpretation of the data collected by the person conducting the research and also help develop theory with regard to the variables in the study.

In many educational research studies, the researcher is interested in measuring or describing an outcome. Descriptive studies focus on the measurement, description, and interpretation of context and outcome variables. In experimental studies, the researcher is interested not only in the outcome (dependent) variable but also in the causal nature of relationships among variables. In experimental studies the outcomes are referred to as the *dependent* or criterion variables and the treatment as the *independent* variable.

Correlational studies also enable the researcher to examine relationships among variables. However, in this case the researcher merely describes the nature of the relationships, without making statements about whether one variable may have caused another.

Moderator variables are factors that influence the impact of the independent variable on the dependent variable. *Control* variables describe extraneous factors and provide a means to help reduce the impact of extraneous factors on a study. In all studies, control variables help determine the degree to which results can be generalized, and in many studies they enable the researcher or reader to understand better the nature of the relationship between the other variables in the study. *Intervening* variables are hypothetical concepts that mediate between the independent and the dependent variables.

By clearly understanding and identifying these variables, researchers can strengthen the quality of their work. In addition, a thorough understanding of these variables and their interactions will enable consumers of research to make more effective use of research that is performed by others and then communicated to us in some fashion.

What Comes Next

The next few chapters will focus on ways to discover, operationally define, and measure research variables. The book will then focus on how to design and carry out studies that collect data and test research hypotheses, how to analyze the results of these studies, and how to evaluate the quality of research results.

DOING YOUR OWN RESEARCH

In the first edition of this book, this chapter came near the end of the book. A major reason for moving it to the front of the book is to help readers begin to conduct a research study of their own. If you need to select a research topic and begin planning a research project, here are some strategies you can employ right now:

1. You can choose a problem that interests you, find a study that has already been done, and directly replicate that study. As later chapters will show, replication is an important part of the educational research process. Strategies for carrying out the replication will be discussed later in the book.

2. You can find a study that has already been done and replicate it using new operational definitions of at least some of the variables in the study. Strategies for operationally defining variables will be discussed in chapter 4.

3. You can find a study that has already been done and replicate it using additional moderator or control variables. As chapter 15 will show, replication with different moderator and control variables plays an important role in determining how far the results of educational research can be generalized.

4. You can find an existing study and develop a different way to test the same hypothesis.

5. You can choose a problem, analyze it as discussed in this chapter, and invent a completely new study of your own.

6. You can employ a combination of the preceding five strategies.

To actually carry out a study, you will need certain information that is presented later in this book. Right now, you can select a topic, determine what the variables are, and begin to think about what problems you are likely to encounter in conducting your own study. Be aware, however, that as you read subsequent chapters in this book or begin to read the literature related to your topic, you may change your mind. That's OK. What is important is that you eventually develop a good plan and carry it out.

Chapter 17 integrates the methods and principles discussed throughout this book; chapter 19 describes appropriate strategies for carrying out and reporting a formal research project. If you read this book in one course and later write a research paper in a subsequent course, then you should use those chapters—rather than the preceding list—as your primary source of guidelines for carrying out that project.

A few words of caution: Some studies may sound interesting, but they may involve the use of advanced methods, which will not be covered in this book. Therefore, there is a possibility that you will find an interesting hypothesis and discover (weeks later) that you are not going to be able to test that hypothesis with strategies covered in this book. The best way to deal with such a problem is to confer with your instructor and modify your hypothesis as you move on to appropriate chapters in this book.

FOR FURTHER THOUGHT

1. Complete this sentence by answering the designated questions: "The independent variable . . .(does what?) (To what or whom?) (When?) (Where?) (How?) (Why?)"

2. Complete this sentence by answering the designated questions: "The dependent variable . . .(does what?) (To what or whom?) (When?) (Where?) (How?) (Why?)"

3. Complete this sentence by answering the designated questions: "The moderator variable . . .(does what?) (To what or whom?) (When?) (Where?) (How?) (Why?)"

4. Complete this sentence by answering the designated questions: "The control variable . . .(does what?) (To what or whom?) (When?) (Where?) (How?) (Why?)"

5. Complete this sentence by answering the designated questions: "The intervening variable . . .(does what?) (To what or whom?) (When?) (Where?) (How?) (Why?)"

6. Complete this sentence by answering the designated questions: "The research hypothesis . . .(does what?) (To what or whom?) (When?) (Where?) (How?) (Why?)"

7. Complete this sentence by answering the designated questions: "The research prediction . . .(does what?) (To what or whom?) (When?) (Where?) (How?) (Why?)"

ANNOTATED BIBLIOGRAPHY

Martin, D. W. (1991). *Doing psychology experiments* (3rd ed.). Monterey, CA: Brooks/Cole. Chapter 4 provides good guidelines on how to select and define variables for formal research projects.

Smith, M. L., & Glass, G. V. (1987). *Research and evaluation in education and the social sciences.* Englewood Cliffs, NJ: Prentice-Hall. This up-to-date book gives good illustrations and different points of view regarding the research process.

Tuckman, B. W. (1988). *Conducting educational research* (3rd ed.). New York: Harcourt Brace Jovanovich. Chapter 4 discusses the formulation of hypotheses, and chapter 5 focuses on identifying and labeling variables.

ANSWERS TO QUIZZES

Review Quiz 2.1

1. Dependent variable: appreciation of Western culture

   Independent variable: studying Shakespeare

2. Dependent variable: noncreative behavior

   Independent variable: behavior modification

3. Dependent variable: higher-order thinking skills

   Independent variable: programming in Logo

4. Dependent variable: reading ability during adolescence

   Independent variable: delaying reading instruction until the sixth grade

5. Dependent variable: eagerness to share opinions with peers

   Independent variable: language-rich environment

Review Quiz 2.2

1. Dependent: strategies (heuristic versus rote)
   Control: High school biology students
2. Independent: reading method
   Dependent: comprehension strategies
   Moderator: (none stated)
   Control: K-3 students
   Intervening: (none stated)
3. Independent: studying Latin (versus not studying it)
   Dependent: vocabulary skills
   Moderator: English class placement (advanced placement versus regular)
   Control: high school students
   Intervening: increased ability to break a word into its component parts

CHAPTER 2
Research Report Analysis

The sample research report in Appendix C deals with computer simulations that are used to stimulate scientific problem solving. It provides evidence to support the theory that guided use of computer simulations gives students opportunities to practice thinking skills and to receive reinforcement for successful use of these skills. This reinforced practice leads to improved problem-solving skills. Try answering the following questions:

1. What is the hypothesis of this study?
2. What is the independent variable?
3. What is the dependent variable?
4. What is the moderator variable?
5. What is the control variable?
6. What is the intervening variable?

ANSWERS:

1. Guided use of computer simulations will cause students to develop problem-solving skills to a greater degree than either unguided use of computer simulations or the use of noncomputerized approaches to attain the same objectives. (This hypothesis is briefly stated on page 458 and is clarified on page 459.)

2. The independent variable is the way students study the instructional material (guided use of simulations versus unguided use of simulations versus noncomputerized approaches to the same objectives). (This variable is described on page 460 of the report.)

3. The dependent variable is problem-solving ability. (This variable is described on page 462 of the report.)

4. The moderator variable is gender of students. (This variable is described on page 463 of the report.)

5. The control variable is the type of students in the study. The subject matter content could also be considered a control variable. (This variable is described on page 459 of the report.)

6. The intervening variable is reinforced practice for the effective use of thinking skills. (This variable is described on page 464 of the report.)

RESEARCH TOOLS: LIBRARY AND REFERENCE MATERIALS

■ WHERE WE'VE BEEN

We have discussed the underlying logic of educational research and examined the variables typically included in a research study. We have seen that it is necessary to clarify the problem, identify the variables, and develop a plan for conducting the research study.

■ WHERE WE'RE GOING NOW

In this chapter we'll discuss effective ways to use the library, reference books, and other sources as tools to find information that will be helpful in clarifying the relationships among research variables and in conducting research at all levels.

■ CHAPTER PREVIEW

It is not necessary (nor advisable) to rely solely on our own knowledge and insights when we seek solutions to a research problem. Whatever problem is of concern to us, someone else has probably dealt with a similar one. We should bring such information to bear on our own problems so that we can benefit from the experience of others. A large amount of the information in library sources, reference books, data banks, and other places can be helpful to us, if only we know how to use these resources.

This chapter introduces many of the tools for researchers that can be found in libraries. Various types of services are becoming increasingly available in libraries and from computerized information agencies. By using these services effectively we can locate comprehensive sources of information that will enable us to deal effectively with our research problems. After reading this chapter, you should be able to

1. Identify the types of information that can be obtained from each of the following indexing and abstracting services:

   ERIC's *Current Index to Journals in Education (CIJE)* and *Resources in Education (RIE)*

   Psychological Abstracts

   Education Index

   Reader's Guide to Periodical Literature

   Social Science Citation Index (SSCI)

2. Use these sources to locate a specific piece or type of information.

3. Identify the types of information that can be obtained from journals, reviews, and books.

4. Describe effective strategies for conducting a review of the literature on a specific problem.

▪

USING THE LIBRARY TO SOLVE RESEARCH PROBLEMS

Every reader of this book has used the library, but most of us have not used it as effectively as we could. The library is a valuable tool for solving educational problems. Such value is obvious when the library is used for working on term papers and for formal research projects (where else would we find enough citations to fill the required four to six pages?), but this view reflects a narrow perception of the role of the library in educational research. It is more appropriate to consider the library an important resource that is available to help us keep abreast of what is going on in our field and solve specific educational problems when they arise.

The resources of the library can be helpful even when we are doing something informal, such as trying to devise a way to measure attitudes toward music or looking for a better way to teach Johnny to divide by two-digit numbers. The library can be equally helpful when we are doing something formal, such as writing a dissertation or preparing an article for a professional journal. In either case, our goal should be to use the library to help us clarify and solve our problem.

The following sections of this chapter will describe specific resources available in many libraries. Readers' familiarity with these different resources will vary considerably. In some cases you may already be aware of a resource and use it frequently and successfully; in other cases you may not be familiar with a resource. Your goal should be to become aware of what is available and to know how to use each of these resources to help you solve your educational problems.

When educators have information they want to share with their colleagues, they submit articles to professional journals or make presentations at professional meetings. Likewise, educators include such information in the reports they write for administrators and funding agencies. Because it is often useful to have ready access to such information, this chapter describes the major indexing and retrieval services that enable us to find it, whether it is distributed through a formal or an informal channel.

ERIC

The Educational Resources Information Center (ERIC) is a U.S. federal information system comprising 16 clearinghouses throughout the country. Each clearinghouse focuses on a specific area of educational interest, such as counseling or special education. The ERIC clearinghouses collect documents that contain information relevant to their areas of specialization. The specific clearinghouses vary widely in the unique services they offer; the easiest way to find out what is available in your area of interest is to contact the clearinghouses that you think may provide information useful to your professional interests. A listing of the clearinghouses and their mailing addresses can be found in many ERIC publications, including the two discussed in the following paragraphs.

The best way to find information through ERIC is to do a computer search. When accessing information via computer, it may not even be obvious which specific clearinghouse or ERIC resource you are using. We shall describe a computerized information search later (see Box 3.1 on p. 43). The following paragraphs will first describe two of the major ERIC information resources.

The *Current Index to Journals in Education* (*CIJE*) is an ERIC publication that attempts to keep abreast of what is published in the many journals directly or indirectly related to education. *CIJE* is published monthly, and a cumulative index is made available at the end of each year. It gives complete citations and brief abstracts for many of the thousands of articles on educational topics published each year. By examining the abstract, we can find out what the article is about; if we are interested enough to want to know more, the citation tells us the exact page numbers in a specific journal where we can read the entire article.

To use the hard-copy version of *CIJE*, we would start by referring to the index section. This might be the index of a monthly issue or the annual cumulative index. If we were starting our search with a specific topic in mind, we would go to the subject index. To take a specific example, assume we are looking for information on how to teach moral values to emotionally disturbed children. We might begin by looking at the most recent cumulative index under the subject headings of either "Emotionally Disturbed Children" or "Moral Values." In the January–June 1991 *CIJE* cumulative index under the subject "Emotionally Disturbed Children," we would find 17 articles listed on page 672. One of these is listed as follows:

Television's Impact on Emotionally Disturbed Children's Value Systems. *Child Study Journal.* v8 n3 p187-202 1978

EJ 192 901

The reference to EJ 192 901 tells us to look in the main entry section where that number appears in sequence. There we would find the entry shown in Figure 3.1.

The first part of this entry tells us where to find the article if we would want to pursue it further— the *Child Study Journal*. The information in paren-

---

> EJ 192 901   PS 507 193
>
> **Television's Impact on Emotionally Disturbed Children's Value Systems**. Donohue, Thomas R. *Child Study Journal:* v8 n3 p 187–202 1978 (Reprint: UMI)
>
> *Descriptors:* Elementary School Students; *Emotionally Disturbed Children; Identification (Psychological); *Modeling (Psychological); *Moral Values; Socialization; *Television Viewing
>
> This investigation studied the influences of television's behavioral models on institutionalized, emotionally disturbed children between the ages of 6 and 11. Investigated were children's perceptions and judgments of right and wrong, appropriate and inappropriate behaviors. (SE)

Figure 3.1   An Entry from the *Current Index to Journals in Education*

theses tells us that this article is also available as a reprint from University Microfilms. Next is a list of descriptors. A descriptor is a heading under which articles are listed in the subject index. This information, which at first might seem superfluous, is often helpful. By knowing what descriptors apply to the article we are currently examining, we can find out where similar articles are likely to be found. For example, in this case, we know that "Modeling (Psychological)" is a descriptor that applies to this article, and so we might want to look under that descriptor in the subject index to see whether there are any other articles that might be of interest to us. All the descriptors listed after the citation are pertinent to the article in question, but the article was actually indexed only under the descriptors marked by an asterisk. Therefore, we would have found this article indexed under "Emotionally Disturbed Children," "Modeling (Psychological)," "Moral Values," and "Television Viewing."

Finally, the abstract describes the contents of the article. By reading this abstract we can decide whether we want to pursue the article any further.

The initials in parentheses at the end of the abstract indicate who wrote the abstract. If it had been written by the author, it would say so at this point. (In this case, the abstract was written by one of ERIC's professional reviewers.)

Rather than merely plunging into *CIJE* to begin our search, we could be more systematic by referring first to the *Thesaurus of ERIC Descriptors* (Figure 3.2). By looking in this book we can find out what descriptors are actually used in *CIJE*. Moreover, we can find related terms, broader terms, and more specific terms, which would enable us to be more efficient and thorough in our search. (In addition, the *Thesaurus* lists the number of entries that have been indexed under any descriptor in *RIE* and *CIJE*, information that is helpful in determining how many citations we would be likely to get by looking under that descriptor.)

In the age of computers, the role of the *Thesaurus* has changed. If your library allows you to request that a specialist perform a search for you (the library may even *require* that you do so), then the role of the *Thesaurus* takes on new importance. Only if you give the library specialist an appropriate set of terms will that person be able to give you useful output from his or her search. (In addition, it is essential to give the specialist a correct set of logical operators, which are discussed later in the chapter. The form supplied by the specialist often makes choosing these operators a straightforward task.) On the other hand, if you conduct the search yourself, you may no longer need the *Thesaurus* at all. The computerized ERIC systems offer on-line help that is every bit as good as that offered by the *Thesaurus*—and sometimes better.

Figure 3.2 An entry from the *Thesaurus of ERIC Descriptors*

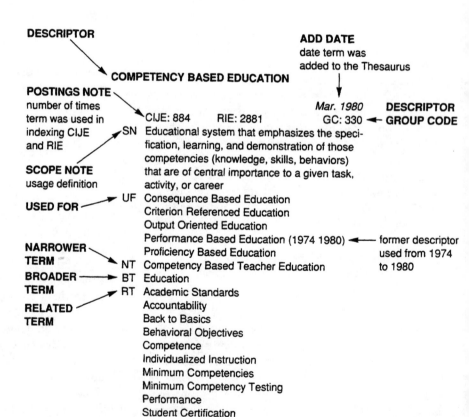

ERIC offers another important service through *Resources in Education* (*RIE*). This publication performs a service similar to *CIJE*, but it focuses on nonjournal sources of information. For example, doctoral dissertations, reports on government-funded projects, and papers given at conventions are often found in *RIE*. Such a report of a dissertation or a convention presentation may, of course, later be converted into a journal article and subsequently be indexed in *CIJE*, but in such cases the information is available much sooner through *RIE*. A sample entry from *RIE* is shown in Figure 3.3.

Most of the information contained in an *RIE* entry either is parallel to that provided by a *CIJE* entry or is self-explanatory. A unique feature of the *RIE* entry is that it indicates how much it would cost to buy the document if you wished to do so. In this example, the document can be purchased in microfiche for 83 cents or in hard copy for $1.67 plus postage. Instructions on how to order such documents can be found in the ERIC volume in which you found the entry. Many libraries that subscribe to *RIE* also purchase all the accompanying microfiche, and in such cases you can find the document by locating the microfiche and reading it on a microfiche card reader.

In many cases, researchers using *CIJE* or *RIE* will use the subject index to locate an article or research report. However, it is also possible to locate information by using the author index. In fact, since there are likely to be fewer entries listed under the author's name than under any given subject heading, it is easier to use the author index whenever the name of the author of the report is known. The author index is used in the same way as the subject index. Since many authors tend to have an area of interest and continue working in that area, it is often a good idea to look in the author index to find additional articles or reports by the same person who wrote a report that you found to be helpful.

RIE can also be searched by computer (see Box 3.1). Let us return to our *CIJE* example for a moment. In the January–June 1991 cumulative index there were 17 entries under "Emotionally Disturbed Children" and 18 entries under "Moral Values." Would it not be convenient to have immediate infor-

---

ED 133 695   CS 003 136

Burks, Ann T.

The Problem of Teenagers Reading on Elementary Levels: An Analysis of Approaches or How to Teach CVC to a Dude.

Pub Date 76

Note—13p.; Paper presented at the Annual Meeting of the International Reading Association Southeastern Regional Conference (4th, Jacksonville, Florida, February 18–21, 1976)

EDRS Price MF-$0.83 HC-$1.67 Plus Postage.

Descriptors—Diagnostic Teaching, Grouping (Instructional Purposes), *Individualized Reading, Learning Laboratories, *Reading Failure, *Reading Instruction, *Remedial Reading Programs, Resource Teachers, Secondary Education, Tutoring

To help an elementary-level reader in a secondary school learn to read, the program must not threaten the student's ego or undermine peer approval, and it must be individualized, in the diagnostic-prescriptive mold. Any organizational plan that meets these criteria should be workable. The characteristics of several possible approaches are described, including reading labs, tutorial situations, resource teachers, homogeneous groups in one-teacher classrooms, and heterogeneous groups in one-teacher classrooms. (AA)

Figure 3.3   An Entry from *Resources in Education*

---

mation about the articles that were indexed under *both* of these descriptors? This is exactly what the computer can do for us. Even better, the computer can make a search of a period of several years, and it can search both *CIJE* and *RIE* simultaneously. In addition, we could add more descriptors to narrow our search even further. By doing a computer search of ERIC, therefore, we can obtain a set of abstracts that zero in precisely on what interests us. After reading the abstracts, we may wish to choose for closer perusal the 5 or 10 that are of paramount interest to us.

Computer searches are often performed from terminals located in the library or via modem from one's home, office, or elsewhere. The computer obtains access to a CD-ROM storage disk on which the citations and abstracts are stored. Instead of searching through several separate volumes of *RIE* and *CIJE,* you can rapidly search through all the citations ever compiled by ERIC, or through some subset of these. For example, it would be easy for a researcher to find all the journal articles indexed by ERIC published since 1983 on the topic of computer-assisted instruction (CAI). It would be almost as easy to narrow this search to only those CAI articles published since 1983 that also deal with science education or thinking skills. Searches that used to take several hours now can be conducted via computer in 10–15 minutes.

While it is possible for individual researchers to do their searches by themselves, this may not be the procedure in all libraries. In some cases, a specialist who works for the library will do the actual search for you. Your role is to supply this specialist with the information needed to make an efficient and thorough search. Such preparation would probably include going to the *Thesaurus of ERIC Descriptors* to make sure that you have chosen terms that are actually employed by ERIC in its indexing system and to find out if there are additional terms that might help focus the search more appropriately. By providing your reference librarian with a good list of descriptors (or by using a good set yourself), you will lay the foundation for a useful search. Besides using descriptors to include and exclude citations, limits can be set in other ways. For example, you could request only those citations indexed since 1985 or only the 25 most recent citations. In many cases, search services are available free to users of libraries, but in other cases the library may charge the user a fee based on computer time and the number of abstracts obtained. In addition to providing searches in response to specific requests, many libraries and indexing services are willing to provide continuous updating with regard to research in an area of interest. In such a case, you would set up an initial search pattern, and then you would receive in the mail abstracts of whatever articles have recently appeared that meet your search requirements.

Persons writing formal research papers or articles for publication are not the only ones who benefit from these computerized ERIC searches. A teacher or researcher working on the problem of teaching moral values to emotionally disturbed children might want to know everything that has been published related to this area. On the other hand, teachers in public school classrooms planning to implement a new program might enter a much narrower search to find out if anyone else has done anything similar to their program, so that the ideas of others could be incorporated.

An additional resource provided by *CIJE* is a listing within each monthly issue of the tables of contents of the journals abstracted in that issue. By looking through these tables of contents, you can find out what is being published in journals related to your field. Although not all libraries subscribe to this resource, it is an especially useful one to which you have access through interlibrary loans.

When using indexing or abstracting services like ERIC, be aware of their shortcomings as well as their strengths. Articles are sometimes incompletely or even inaccurately indexed; for example, a computerized search for all research articles that deal with both science education and computers is not likely to derive a list consisting of all the research articles and *only* research articles on that combination of topics. Also be aware that there is a lack of quality control in the unpublished documents indexed in ERIC's *RIE*—while many of the RIE documents are useful, there may be a reason why some of these documents are not published in more formal channels.

PSYCHOLOGICAL ABSTRACTS

The services offered by *Psychological Abstracts* are similar to those provided by ERIC. In general, this source indexes and abstracts the more formal pieces of information in the field of psychology, including journal articles, books, doctoral dissertations, and convention proceedings. It does not include less for-

BOX 3.1

A Computerized Search of the ERIC Data Base

One of the authors of this book conducted a computerized ERIC search in his library. Here is what happened:

1. The author wanted to find recent journal articles on the subject of *cooperative learning in science education*. He took the steps necessary to get his system's ERIC main menu on the screen. His system splits the ERIC data base into two parts: entries indexed up to 1982 and entries indexed in 1983 or later. He chose the more recent part.
2. Our author then chose the *Easy Menu Search* option. (There are other, more efficient, ways to search the data base, but they are more difficult to learn. We won't discuss them in this example.)
3. From the next menu, he chose *Begin a New Search*.
4. From the next menu, he chose *Word/Phrase Index*. This would select for him all the entries indexed under words or phrases he would designate. (He could have instead chosen to have the computer begin by using other selection criteria—for example, all entries from a designated journal, all books, all entries published in 1992, etc.)
5. The author then typed the word *cooperative,* and that term appeared highlighted on the screen. The computer indicated that there were 8,845 entries indexed under *cooperative* in the data base. He decided that this term was too broad (it would probably include cooperative behavior and many other forms of cooperation), so he typed a space and the letter *l,* and the computer immediately highlighted *cooperative learning*. The screen indicated that there were 1,279 entries under this term. Our author pressed the enter key to select this phrase.
6. At this point he could have expanded the search—the computer screen indicated that there were 26 other terms related to cooperative learning. The author pressed the F2 key on his computer to see these related terms; after viewing them, he decided that he wasn't really interested in any of these additional terms, so he ignored this list.
7. He pressed the F10 key, and the computer indicated that it had selected all 1,279 entries identified in Step 5.
8. The computer asked whether he wanted to see the entries that had been selected, modify the search, begin a new search, save the strategy for later use, or quit. Since 1,279 articles were too many to manage, he selected *Modify the Search* from the menu.
9. From the next menu, he chose *Limit the Search with Additional Concepts or Terms*.
10. From the next menu, our author again chose *Word/Phrase Index,* and decided to search the list for *science*. As he typed the word *science,* the computer indicated that there were 32,301 entries on that word. He figured that this term was too broad—it would probably flag articles indexed under social science and other irrelevant entries. He decided to try *science education* instead, and so he typed a space and added *ed,* and the computer immediately highlighted *science education* and indicated that there were 13,508 entries under this phrase. He selected this phrase and pressed F2 to see related terms; among these he found *science teachers,* with 1,051 entries. When he pressed the enter key, the computer indicated that it had now selected two phrases (*science education* and *science teachers*), with a combined total of 13,838 entries so far during this step. (You might have noticed that 13,508 + 1,051 = 14,559, and are wondering why the running count was only 13,838. The count was lower because a large number of the *science teachers* entries had already been selected at the *science education* step.) He next selected *elementary school science,* with 3,284 entries (for a running total of 14,415 entries); *sci-*

ence instruction, with 6,595 entries (running total = 16,287); and *secondary school science,* with 6,158 entries (running total = 16,740 entries). He decided that he had found all the terms he wanted, and so he pressed the F10 key.

11. The computer indicated that there were 114 entries that met the criteria specified in Steps 5 and 10.

12. Since he wanted only journal articles, he chose *Modify the Search* from the main menu, *Limit the Search* from the next menu, and *Document Type* from the menu after that; then he typed the word *journal.* The computer indicated that there were 171,798 entries from journal articles in the data base. He pressed the F10 key.

13. The computer now indicated that there were 66 records on the combined topics of *cooperative learning* (Step 5) and *science education* (Step 10) that had been published in journals (Step 12). The author could have narrowed the search further, but he decided instead to look at the documents he had selected. He chose *Display the Selected Documents* from the main menu and *Complete Record* from the next menu. The computer displayed a screen with information much like that shown in Figure 3.1. As he continued to press the enter key, additional records appeared on the screen.

mal pieces of information—such as unpublished reports and curriculum guidelines—as would ERIC's *RIE. Psychological Abstracts* is published monthly, with semiannual cumulative indexes. An example of an abstract is shown in Figure 3.4.

As you can see, the information provided by *Psychological Abstracts* is much like that found in *CIJE* and *RIE.* One difference is that *Psychological Abstracts* indicates the institutional affiliation of the first author of the publication. Just as with ERIC sources, information is found in *Psychological Abstracts* by first referring to a subject or author index and then looking up the abstract.

Like other services, *Psychological Abstracts* can be accessed by computer for more rapid recovery of information. The output from the computer is slightly different from the hard-copy information. Figure 3.5 shows a computerized version of the entry shown in Figure 3.4. An important addition is that the computerized version contains a list of descriptors (e.g., in Figure 3.5, next to "MJ" in lines 12–14). With this information, we would know that we could find related articles under such descriptors as "Reading Skills," "Remedial Reading," and so forth.

Although *Psychological Abstracts* focuses on psychology rather than on education, most researchers find that there is a large amount of overlap between

14827. Lorenz, Linda & Vockell, Edward. (U Illinois Medical Ctr Disabled Children's Program, Chicago)
Using the Neurological Impress Method with learning disabled readers. *Journal of Learning Disabilities.*
1979(Jan-Jul). Vol 12(6), 420–422.—Evaluated the ability of the Neurological Impress Method (NIM) of remediation (teacher and child read together in unison) to increase comprehension and word recognition skills among mildly learning disabled students. 44 2nd-5th graders with below-grade-level reading skills were tested on the Reading Comprehension subtest of the Peabody Individual Achievement Test and the Word Recognition subtest of the Wide Range Achievement Test before and after receiving remedial reading instruction using the NIM (experimental group) or traditional techniques (control group). An ANOVA showed no significant differences between pretest, posttest, and gain scores for the 2 groups. Students with auditory and nonauditory disabilities were equally unlikely to benefit. Despite subjective positive impressions of the method, it is concluded that further replications of NIM effectiveness are needed before its use becomes widespread. (6 ref)—S. Sieracki.

Figure 3.4 An Entry from *Psychological Abstracts*

```
AN  14827 62-6.
AU  LORENZ-LINDA.     VOCKELL-EDWARD.
IN  U ILLINOIS MEDICAL CTR DISABLED CHILDREN'S PROGRAM, CHICAGO.
TI  USING THE NEUROLOGICAL IMPRESS METHOD WITH LEARNING DISABLED READERS.
SO  JOURNAL OF LEARNING DISABILITIES. 1979 JUN-JUL VOL 12(6) 420-422.
CD  JLDIAD.
IS  022-2194.
LG  EN.
YR  79.
CC  3570.
PT  10
MJ  READING-SKILLS. REMEDIAL-READING. LEARNING-DISABILITIES.
    READING-DISABILITIES. READING-COMPREHENSION.
    ELEMENTARY-SCHOOL-STUDENTS. RECOGNITION-LEARNING. TEACHING-METHODS.
AB  EVALUATED THE ABILITY OF THE NEUROLOGICAL IMPRESS METHOD (NIM) OF REMEDIATION
    (TEACHER AND CHILD READ TOGETHER IN UNISON) TO INCREASE COMPREHENSION AND WORD
    RECOGNITION SKILLS AMONG MILDLY LEARNING DISABLED STUDENTS. 44 2ND-5TH GRADERS
    WITH BELOW-GRADE-LEVEL READING SKILLS WERE TESTED ON THE READING COMPREHENSION
    SUBTEST OF THE PEABODY INDIVIDUAL ACHIEVEMENT TEST AND THE WORD RECOGNITION
    SUBTEST OF THE WIDE RANGE ACHIEVEMENT TEST BEFORE AND AFTER RECEIVING REMEDIAL
    READING INSTRUCTION USING THE NIM (EXPERIMENTAL GROUP) OR TRADITIONAL TECH-
    NIQUES (CONTROL GROUP). AN ANOVA SHOWED NO SIGNIFICANT DIFFERENCES BETWEEN
    PRETEST, POSTTEST, AND GAIN SCORES FOR THE 2 GROUPS. STUDENTS WITH AUDITORY AND
    NONAUDITORY DISABILITIES WERE EQUALLY UNLIKELY TO BENEFIT. DESPITE SUBJECTIVE
    POSITIVE IMPRESSIONS OF THE METHOD, IT IS CONCLUDED THAT FURTHER REPLICATIONS
    OF NIM EFFECTIVENESS ARE NEEDED BEFORE ITS USE BECOMES WIDESPREAD. (6 REF).
ID  NEUROLOGICAL IMPRESS METHOD, COMPREHENSION & WORD RECOGNITION SKILLS, MILDLY
    LEARNING DISABLED 2ND-5TH GRADERS WITH BELOW-GRADE-LEVEL READING SKILLS.
```

Figure 3.5 An Entry from the Computerized Version of *Psychological Abstracts* (this is the same abstract as that shown in Figure 3.4, but the computerized version contains some additional information)

these two fields. Researchers working at a theoretical level will find *Psychological Abstracts* an especially valuable source of information. Also, the American Psychological Association (APA) provides many additional information dissemination services, identified in each issue of *Psychological Abstracts*.

EDUCATION INDEX

The *Education Index* covers many of the same sources as does *CIJE*. However, although it provides an index of titles and citations arranged according to topic headings and author headings, it does not contain abstracts. The *Education Index* is published monthly, with an annual cumulative index. It can also be accessed by computer. Because it contains less information than *CIJE,* this index may offer a faster route to finding a citation of an article. Part of a page from the *Education Index* is shown in Figure 3.6.

READER'S GUIDE TO PERIODICAL LITERATURE

Like the *Education Index,* the *Reader's Guide to Periodical Literature* contains titles and citations, but no abstracts. It does not cover the field of education in the great depth that *CIJE* or *Education Index*

MASCOLINI, Marcia
    Vive la companie. Coll Comp & Comm
        29:301–2 O '78
MASCULINITY
    Father role and its relation to masculinity, femi-
        ninity, and androgyny. G. Russell, bibl Child
        Devel 49:1174–81 D '78
    Men in day care: you've come a long way,
        Buddy! R. E. Robinson and C. Hobson. bibl
        Child Care Q 7:156–63 Summ '78
            See also
    Androgyny (psychology)
    Femininity
MASDEN, H. Daniel
    Rural field-based education in Alaska: or, How
        we do it in the bush. Com Coll Front
        7:25–30 Wint '79
MASEK, Bruce J. See Epstein, L. H. jt. auth.
MASEMANN, Vandra L.
    Multicultural programs in Toronto schools. bibl
        Interchange 9 no 1:29–44 '78–79
MASIKUNAS, G. and Ryder, M.
    Caring is . . . running an induction course.
        Times Higher Educ Supp 360:13 O 6 '78
MASIN, Herman L.
    Writing for publication (one more time) Schol
        Coach 48:54 + Ja '79
MASKING (sound)
    Effect of contralateral noise on the middle com-
        ponents of the averaged electroencephalic
        response. H. N. Gutnick and R. Goldstein.
        bibl J Speech * Hearing Res 21:613–24 D '78
    Effects of noise and rhythmic simulation on the
        speech of stutterers. E. R. Brayton and E. G.
        Conture. bibl J Speech & Hearing Res
        21:285–94 Je '78

Figure 3.6   Part of a Page from the *Education Index*

does, but it covers a wider variety of related topics than either of the other two. It is published monthly, with an annual cumulative index. It is also accessible for computerized searches. A page from the *Reader's Guide* would look much like the page shown in Figure 3.6 from *Education Index*.

The *Reader's Guide* focuses on magazines that appeal to a general readership. If an article on education appears in *Time* or *Newsweek*, for example, it will be indexed in the *Reader's Guide* but not in such professional indexes as *CIJE* or *Psychological Abstracts*. Depending on the nature of research, these general and popular magazines may be what you want. In most cases, however, you will need to refer to the more professional sources described elsewhere in this chapter to obtain information that will help you solve your educational problems.

SUMMARY OF INDEXES

The comparative advantages and disadvantages of abstracting services that have been described in this chapter are summarized in Table 3.1. This table indicates that there is much similarity and overlap among the various services, but each of them has unique characteristics that may help you solve specific problems.

OTHER ABSTRACTING SERVICES

There are several other abstracting services that meet specific needs, but they are not discussed in detail here (see Table 3.2 on p. 48). For example, *Dissertation Abstracts International* indexes and summarizes dissertation research from major universities in all subject areas. *PsycBooks* is an indexing service offered by the American Psychological Association that indexes and summarizes books and individually authored chapters in books related to the field of psychology. In addition, major information services (such as Dialog and Compuserve) and independent electronic bulletin boards often index and summarize information on specific topics. Finally, teachers in specific subject areas will often find useful information in noneducation indexes (such as *Arts Index* or *Humanities Index*), which cannot be covered in this book. You should check with your professional organizations to see what specific services are available in your area of expertise.

Table 3.1   Comparison of Major Indexing and Abstracting Services in Educational Research

	ERIC	Psych Abstracts	Ed Index	SSCI	Reader's Guide	Social Sciences Index
Subject matter	Education	Psychology	Education	Social Sciences	General	Social Sciences
Abstracts	Yes	Yes	No	No	No	No
Available via computer	Yes	Yes	Yes	Yes	Yes	Yes
Author index	Monthly and Annual	Monthly and Semi-annual	With main entries	Three times per year	With main entries	With main entries
Starting year	CIJE – 1969 RIE – 1966	1927	1929	1973	1890	1973
Refereed journals	CIJE	Yes	Yes	Yes	Some—but mostly no	Yes
Unpublished documents	RIE	Some informal but high quality documents	No	No	No	No
Major advantage	Comprehensive source in education with abstracts	Comprehensive source in psychology with abstracts	Includes some journals not included in CIJE	Forward search to see where an article is cited	Good supplement for popular sources not in CIJE or Ed Index	Easy to use source that often overlaps with education
Major disadvantage	Some really weak materials in RIE	Mostly unrelated to education	No abstracts	Confusing for novices to use	Few scholarly education journals are included	Mostly unrelated to education

SOCIAL SCIENCE CITATION INDEX

A slightly different type of indexing and citation service is provided by the *Social Science Citation Index* (*SSCI*). One of the *SSCI* services is the forward search. To use this service, we need to know of at least one article that has useful information on the topic we are interested in. By entering the pertinent information about this first article into a computer search, we can quickly find out what other journals have cited this same article. It stands to reason that if a second article cites this first article (which we already know to be relevant), then the second article may also be of interest to us. Pursuing this line of reasoning a bit further, we might want to know what additional books and articles were cited by this sec-ond article. We can obtain this information from *SSCI*. Figure 3.7 (p. 49) shows an example of the sort of printout we can obtain from *SSCI*. By using *SSCI* in conjunction with ERIC, *Psychological Abstracts,* and the other indexing services, we can compile a comprehensive bibliography that will enable us to zero in on the information needed to attack a research problem.

COMPUTERIZED INFORMATION SERVICES

When the first edition of this book was published, in 1983, it was reasonable to assume that it was necessary (or at least appropriate) to go to a library to

Table 3.2   Indexes Related to Educational Research

Index	Topic or Field	Starting Year	Abstracts	Computer
British Education Index	English-language periodicals published in the British Isles	1954	No	Yes
Business Education Index	Business education	1940	No	Yes
Dissertation Abstracts International	Dissertations published at accredited institutions	1861	Yes	Yes
Educational Administration Abstracts	Educational Administration	1966	Yes	Yes
MEDLINE	Education of health professionals and information on communication disorders.	1966	Yes	Yes
New York Times Index	General topics of national or worldwide interest	1913	No	Yes
Sociological Abstracts	Sociology and related fields	1963	Yes	Yes

conduct a search of the literature. This is no longer true. Many universities and libraries allow users to access information services and their library catalogs via computer modem from their homes, offices, or schools. In addition, information services such as Compuserve and Dialog permit users to access on-line data bases that are as good as those found in high-quality libraries. These services are often free to students and faculty at participating institutions; for others, there may be a membership fee plus an additional cost for each minute the user accesses the data base.

Computerized access to information has become extremely user friendly, and the information is organized for efficient retrieval. The small amount of time it takes to learn to use these systems is usually rewarded by a vast return in terms of more efficient access to information. Table 3.3 (p. 50) shows an example of detailed, specific steps for accessing ERIC from a terminal on a local area network (LAN)—that is, from a computer terminal outside the library on a university campus.

Some of the more primitive computerized library catalogs and indexing services don't do much. They simply allow you to obtain on a computer screen the same information you would get by using a hard-copy catalog. For example, if you enter *science education*, the computer will give you a list of all titles that begin with those exact words or are indexed under that exact heading. If there are no matches, the catalog will give you no hints. With other systems, if you have no exact matches, the computer will show you a list of terms that come close. Others will allow you easy access to a set of related terms that will enable you to broaden or narrow your search, as the ERIC example in Box 3.1 showed.

Most research libraries, however, are moving toward using electronic catalogs that permit cross-referenced searches. If you want books on a combination of topics, you can enter your keywords and get a list of books related to that particular combination of topics. In the old days, you would have had to go through 100 books related to the first topic and 100 related to the second topic and screen each entry individually to find the 10 books that deal with *both* of the topics. A good electronic catalog, on the other hand, will immediately find the 10 books where the two topics overlap.

To take full advantage of the capability of electronic catalogs, you have to

1. Know what's in the catalog or data base.
2. Know how to move through the menus.
3. Know how to apply the basics of Boolean logic.

```
AN   78–11–08757.
AU   SCHWAB-M-R.    LUNDGREN-D-C.
IN   UNIV CINCINNATI, CINCINNATI, OH, 45221.
TI   BIRTH-ORDER, PERCEIVED APPRAISALS BY SIGNIFICANT OTHERS, AND SELF-ESTEEM.
SO   PSYCHOLOGICAL REPORTS 1978 VO043 #N2 P0443–0454.
RF   0036.
ON   FX825.
LG   EN.
YR   78.
CC   VI.
CR   ADAMS-B-N; 1972; VO035; P0411; SOCIOMETRY.
     ADLER-A; 1956; INDIVIDUAL-PSYCHOLOG.
     BERGER-E-M; 1952; VO047; P0778; J-ABNORMAL-SOCIAL-PS.
     BURKE-H-L; 1961; VO014; P0165; HUMAN-RELATIONS.
     COOLEY-C-H; 1922; HUMAN-NATURE-SOCIAL.
     COOPERSMITH-S; 1967; ANTECEDENTS-SELF-EST.
     CRONBACH-L-J; 1951; VO016; P0297; PSYCHOMETRIKA.
     EISENMAN-R; 1970; VO075; P0147; J-PSYCHOLOGY.
     FIEDLER-F-E; 1967; THEORY-LEADERSHIP-EF.
     FLAMMER-D-P; 1972; VO036; P0447; J-PERSONALITY-ASSESS.
     FORSLUND-M-A; 1972; VO009; P0413; PSYCHOLOGY-SCH.
     GREENBERG-H; 1963; VO060; P0221; J-SOCIAL-PSYCHOLOGY.
     HARTLEY-R-E; 1959; VO005; P0457; PSYCHOLOGICAL-REPORT.
     LUNDGREN-D-C; 1974; VO001; P0316; PERSONALITY-SOCIAL-P.
     MEAD-G-H; 1934; MIND-SELF-SOC.
     MILEY-C-H; 1969; VO025; P0064; J-INDIVIDUAL-PSYCHOL.
     MILLER-D-R; 1963; VO005; P0639; PSYCHOLOGY-STUDY-SCI.
     MILLER-N; 1976; VO033; P0123; J-PERSONAL-SOC-PSYCH.
     MIYAMOTO-S-F; 1956; VO061; P0399; AM-J-SOCIOLOGY.
     NASH-J-C; 1970; THESIS-OHIO-STATE-U.
     NORMAN-W-T; 1963; VO066; P0574; J-ABNORMAL-SOCIAL-PS.
     NYSTUL-M-S; 1974-VO030; P0211; J-INDIVIDUAL-PSYCHOL.
     PURPURA-P-A; 1970; THESIS-FORDHAM-U. RICE-W-C; 1971; THESIS-B-YOUNG-U.
     RING-K; 1965; VO079; PSYCHOLOGICAL-MONOGR.
     ROSENBERG-B-G; 1972; SEX-IDENTITY.
     ROSENBERG-M; 1965; SOC-ADOLESCENT-SELF.
     SAMPSON-E-E; 1972; F0086; PERSONALITY-SOCIALIZ.
     SCHACHTER-S; 1959; PSYCHOLOGY-AFFILIATI.
     SCHOOLER-C; 1972; VO078; P0161; PSYCHOL-B.
     SEARS-R-R; 1970; VO041; P0267; CHILD-DEVELOPMENT.
     SHERWOOD-J-J; 1965; VO028; P0066; SOCIOMETRY.
     STOTLAND-E; 1962; VO064; P0183; J-ABNORMAL-SOCIAL-PS.
     STOTLAND-E; 1962; VO076; PSYCHOLOGICAL-MONOGR.
     VOCKELL-E-L; 1973; VO029; P0039; J-INDIV-PSY.
     ZIMBARDO-P; 1963; VO031; P0141; J-PERSONALITY.
```

Figure 3.7   A Sample Printout from a Computer Search of the *Social Science Citation Index.* (The seach was conducted to find articles citing Vockell.)

Table 3.3 Steps in using a remote terminal to access the ERIC database through Purdue Calumet's LAN

What you do	Monitor responds
1. Turn on computer (Location of switch varies. Be sure any extension switches to which the computer may be connected are also turned on. It may be necessary to turn on the monitor separately.)	Screen lights up. Menu appears, permitting you to select stand-alone or network use of the computer.
2. Type N (for network) and press <enter>.	Screen shows several obscure messages and then prompts **Enter your login name:**
3. Type your login name. (I type Elvockel). Then press <enter>.	Screen shows prompt **Enter your password:**
4. Type your password. This will not appear on the screen, because a spy with binoculars may be trying to steal your password. When you have typed your invisible password, press <enter>.	Screen shows several obscure messages and then prompts **C:\>**
5. Type PULSE. Then press <enter>.	Screen shows several obscure messages and then shows the library main menu of the Purdue University Library Search (PULSE) system. From this point on, the screen will supply you with specific directions and help screens, if you request them.
6. Type INDEX and press <enter>.	The screen will show a menu listing several indexes.
7. Type ERIC and press <enter>.	The screen will give you a brief message about the ERIC database and will ask you for your Purdue ID number.
8. Type your Purdue ID Number. (For me this is my Social Security Number without the dashes.)	The screen will display prompts and instructions for using the ERIC database. Follow these guidelines to conduct a search.

* If you use the PULSE terminals in the library, start with Step 6.

Simple Boolean operations are easy to learn. For example, with a little thought it's easy to understand the difference between (a) books on science education *and* cooperative learning (which might include 10 books) and (b) books on science education *or* cooperative learning (which might include 200 books). Box 3.3 (pp. 52–53) shows a more complex example. It's worth the effort to learn how to use these logical operations effectively in order to profit from the effective use of electronic library catalogs.

JOURNALS

In addition to knowing how to find information through indexes and abstracts, it is a good idea to become familiar with the research currently being reported in your field of professional expertise. One way to keep abreast of developments is to attend conventions or read the summaries and proceedings of such conventions. Another way is to become a regular reader of the major journals in your field. Table 3.4 (p. 54) lists the 15 most frequently cited journals in education, according to a recent survey. Those cited most often in specific areas within this general field would vary from area to area. It is a good idea to identify the major journals in your field and read these frequently. Even if your library does not have access to certain journals, it is possible to monitor the contents through *CIJE* and to write to the authors or to a dissemination service (such as University Microfilms) for copies of important articles or to borrow the journals via interlibrary loan.

BOX 3.2	What Are Booleans and How Do They Operate?

Computerized data base searches use simple Boolean operators. Basically, that means the words *and* and *or* are used to combine descriptors to expand or narrow searches.

Here are the number of articles generated from a recent data base search using the descriptors listed below:

Cooperative learning = 1,279 documents

Computer-assisted instruction = 9,199 documents

Cooperative learning *and* computer-assisted instruction = 125 documents

Cooperative learning *or* computer-assisted instruction = 10,353 documents

(1) Cooperative learning *and* (2) computer-assisted instruction *and* (3) thinking skills = 4 documents

(1) Cooperative learning *and* (2) computer-assisted instruction *and* (3) thinking skills *or* thinking = 11 documents

(In the last two examples, we added the numbers to avoid confusion; otherwise, the *and*s would have become mixed up with the *or*s.)

In summary, *or* expands the number of citations that will be generated, and *and* narrows the number of citations. (However, an *or* within an *and*, as in the final example, narrows the number of citations.) All of this makes perfect sense, if you think about it. (Incidentally, if you are not familiar with the term *Boolean*, you're not alone. Our software's spelling checker thought we were trying to spell the word *bologna!*)

REVIEWS

It is helpful when someone gathers together and synthesizes the current information on some topic of importance. This is a service performed by reviewers. Several encyclopedias, handbooks, and other books publish reviews on a regular basis. A few of the most popular related to the field of education are shown in Table 3.5 (pp. 55–56). Some of these reviews are issued annually; others, at longer intervals. In each issue, important topics are identified, and the current information available on those topics is summarized in an integrated, scholarly fashion.

Many journals also carry review articles. The *Review of Educational Research*, sponsored by the American Educational Research Association, specializes in integrative reviews. Likewise, *Psychological Bulletin* publishes a number of reviews on important topics in psychology. *Educational Leadership*, published by the Association for Supervision and Curriculum Development, includes a synthesis of research on a topic of current interest in nearly every issue. *Phi Delta Kappan* likewise publishes summaries of research on topics of interest to educational leaders, and its sponsoring organization also publishes a *Fastback* series and occasional monographs that update information on pertinent topics. Many of the clearinghouses of ERIC intermittently issue reviews of the literature in areas for which they are responsible.

A good way to find a summary or synthesis of current research on a topic is to do a computer search of either ERIC or *Psychological Abstracts*, using your topic of interest plus either *meta-analysis* or *literature reviews* as descriptors. (Guidelines for interpreting meta-analyses are included in chapter 16.)

| BOX 3.3 | Variations of Keyword Searches |

Most electronic catalogs and searches permit powerful keyword searches. (A keyword is a word that occurs anywhere within an entry that is part of the database being searched.) The exact selection of keywords and the operators that combine them influence the results of the search. For example, Table A shows the results of nine different keyword searches of three separate library catalogs. This search was conducted from the first author's office after he entered his library's electronic cataloging system through his school's local area network by following the steps described in Table 3.3.

With the first strategy the user entered the word *computer*, hoping to find books dealing with computers. This strategy would find catalog entries with that exact word anywhere in the entry. Unfortunately, if an entry that would be of interest used the word *computers* or *computing*, this keyword strategy would not flag that entry. This problem could be solved by using the OR operator (computer or computers or computing); but the user used a wildcard (the question mark) instead. The Comput? keyword looks for any word beginning with comput; and so it will flag entries containing the words computer, computers, computing, computation, and so on. Notice that in each library the more inclusive comput? keyword flagged substantially more entries. A closer examination showed that most of these additional entries were true hits that were missed by the first strategy because the entry used the plural *computers* in the description.

The third strategy would select any catalog entry containing the word science. Since the user wanted books related to K-12 science education, this keyword was too broad. For example, it would flag entries dealing with computer science and social science.

With the fourth strategy the user wanted to find articles on cooperative learning. However, since this strategy did not specify the order in which the words had to occur, it flagged far too many entries. For example, this strategy selected a book that described a cooperative venture among several school districts to stimulate learning of basic skills. What the user actually wanted was accomplished by the fifth strategy. The ADJ operator tells the computer to flag words only if the first word comes immediately before the second—in other words, if the first word functions pretty much like an adjective. This strategy resulted in the selection of entries only if they contained the combination *cooperative learning*.

With the sixth and seventh strategies the user wanted to find books dealing with the use of computers in conjunction with cooperative learning. While both strategies yielded exactly the same results in all three libraries, the seventh is the preferred strategy. The user simply got lucky with the sixth strategy—*cooperative* appeared in these entries only when it came before the word *learning* rather than in some other sequence, and the exact word *computer* rather than a variation appeared in each of these entries. The eighth and ninth strategies are similar to the sixth and seventh, but in this case the difference in operators did make a difference.

Of course, in addition to showing how many entries were selected, each keyword search would make it possible to list all of these entries and to examine each entry. An examination of each entry would make it possible to determine such information as its catalog number and whether the book had already been checked out.

After the user had searched his own Purdue Calumet library catalog, he was able to search the other catalogs without retyping the entries. For example, he simply instructed his computer to "Choose IUCAT," and after a few seconds the screen indicated that he was ready to search the Indiana University catalog. He typed S9 (for Step 9, since this was the ninth strategy he had used in his original search) and discovered that there were nineteen books on science and cooperative learning in that library, compared to only one in his own library and two in the Purdue main campus library. (He was glad that Purdue formally competed with IU in football and basketball rather than library holdings.) If he wanted one of these books from the IU search, he could obtain it through interlibrary loan.

Table A Results of nine keyword searches of the Purdue University Calumet (PCAL), Purdue West Lafayette (WLAF), and Indiana University (IU) electronic library catalogs

Keyword Search Command	Notes	PCAL Hits	WLAF Hits	IU Hits
1. Computer	This will select an entry only if the exact word *computer* (not *computers* or *computing*) appears in it.	3,390	12,760	39,062
2. Comput?	This will select any entry that includes a word beginning with *comput*—including *computer, computers, computing,* and *computation.*	4,122	16,483	47,109
3. Science	This will select entries dealing with social science and computer science, as well as entries normally associated with science education.	6,366	36,068	over 99,999
4. Cooperative and Learning	This will select an entry if it contains the word *cooperative* and *learning* anywhere in it—even if the words are not adjacent.	35	46	310
5. Cooperative adj Learning	The ADJ (for adjective) causes an entry to be selected only if *learning* immediately follows *cooperative.*	25	25	183
6. Computer and Cooperative and Learning	This will select an entry if it has the exact words *computer, cooperative,* and *learning* anywhere in it.	0	4	5
7. Comput? and Cooperative and Learning	This will select an entry if it has any word beginning with *comput* that also contains the words *cooperative* and *learning* anywhere in it.	0	4	5
8. Science and Cooperative and Learning	This will select an entry if it contains the words *science, cooperative,* and *learning* anywhere in it.	3	4	28
9. Science and Cooperative adj Learning	This will select an entry if it contains the word *science* and the combination *cooperative learning.*	1	2	19

Table 3.4 The fifteen most frequently cited journals in the sixth edition of *Encyclopedia of Educational Research* (Based on Vockell, Asher, DiNuzzo, and Bartok, 1994)

Rank	Journal	Pre–64	64–67	68–71	72–75	76–79	80–83	84–87	88–91	Total
1	Review of Educational Research	0	0	1	2	2	3	7	6	21
2	American Psychologist	2	0	0	0	2	2	4	6	17
3	Educational Researcher	0	0	0	0	0	0	6	9	15
3	Phi Delta Kappan	0	1	0	0	1	2	5	6	15
5	Journal of Educational Psychology	2	0	0	0	2	3	3	4	14
6	American Educational Research Journal	0	0	0	0	1	1	6	3	12
7	Elementary School Journal	0	0	0	0	2	3	3	3	11
8	Educational Administration Quarterly	0	0	1	0	0	5	3	0	9
8	Harvard Educational Review	1	0	2	0	3	1	2	0	9
10	Curriculum Inquiry	0	0	0	0	2	3	1	2	8
10	Educational Evaluation and Policy Analysis	0	0	0	0	0	2	4	2	8
10	Educational Leadership	0	0	0	0	1	0	2	5	8
10	Psychological Bulletin	1	0	0	1	3	2	0	1	8
10	Sociology of Education	0	2	1	1	2	0	1	1	8
15	American Journal of Sociology	2	1	2	0	0	1	1	0	7

BOOKS

When research information is disseminated, it usually first goes through informal channels, then to conventions, then to journals, and finally to books. The information contained in books published by reputable companies is likely to be of high quality, but the advantage of this high quality is sometimes offset by the delay in getting it published. Nevertheless, books are an obviously important source of information to the researcher. Many books are indexed and abstracted by ERIC and the other abstracting services. *PsycBooks* even indexes individually authored chapters in books related to psychology. Researchers should become aware that these individually authored chapters in edited books have become a major source of disseminated information in the field of psychology.

Professional journals often provide reviews of current books in the various areas of education. *Contemporary Psychology* provides detailed monthly reviews on books dealing with psychology, and several books in each issue usually pertain to education. *Educational Researcher* offers detailed reviews on a small number of books on education in each issue; *Harvard Educational Review* usually includes one detailed review and several shorter reviews; and each issue of *Educational Leadership* typically contains several short reviews. Many other educational journals review books related to specific areas of education.

An activity that many researchers fail to do is carefully examine the entries in the library card catalog or electronic data base. An example of a card from a catalog is shown in Figure 3.8 (p. 57); electronic catalogs provide similar information, but in a more rapidly accessible format. Most users are aware that

Table 3.5 Encyclopedias and Handbooks on Topics Related to Educational Research

Title	Editor and Publisher	Sponsoring Organization	Contents
Educational Measurement (3rd Ed.)	Linn, R.L. (Macmillan, 1989)	National Council on Measurement in Education and American Council on Education	Integration of theory and research on (1) theory and principles of measurement, (2) construction, administration, and scoring of data collection processes, and (3) applications of measurement theory
Encyclopedia of Educational Research (6th Ed.)	Alkin, M.C. (Macmillan, 1992)	American Educational Research Association	Summarizes research on topics for a wide range of audiences, including novice college students, expert researchers, and educational practitioners
Handbook of Reading Research (Volume II)	Barr, R., Kamil, M.L., Mosenthal, P., & Pearson, P.D. (Longman, 1991)		Summary of research on (1) society and literacy, (2) task and format variables in reading research, (3) constructs of reader processes, and (4) literacy and schooling
Handbook of Research on Curriculum	Jackson, P.W. (Macmillan, 1992)	American Educational Research Association	Summary of research on (1) conceptual and methodological perspectives, (2) how the curriculum is shaped, (3) the curriculum as a shaping force, and (4) topics and issues within curricular categories
Handbook of Research on Educational Administration	Boyan, N.J. (Macmillan, 1988)	American Educational Research Association	Summary of research on (1) the administrator, (2) organizations, (3) economics and finance, (4) politics and policy, and (5) special topics related to educational administration
Handbook of Research on Mathematics Teaching and Learning	Grouws, D.A. (Macmillan, 1992)	National Council of Teachers of Mathematics.	Summary of research on all major aspects of mathematics education, including teaching, learning, and critical issues
Handbook of Research on Music Teaching and Learning	Colwell, R. (Schirmer, 1992)	Music Educators National Conference	Summary of research on (1) the conceptual framework of music education, (2) research modes and techniques, (3) evaluation methodology, (4) perception and cognition, (5) teaching and learning strategies, (6) instructional settings, (7) the curriculum, and (7) social and institutional contexts

Table 3.5 *continued*

Title	Editor and Publisher	Sponsoring Organization	Contents
Handbook of Research on Social Studies Teaching and Learning	Shaver, J.P. (Macmillan, 1991)	National Council for the Social Studies	Summary of research on (1) epistemology and methodology, (2) students, (3) teachers, (4) contexts, (5) outcomes, (6) components of instruction, (7) relationships to other curriculum areas, and (8) international perspectives in social studies education
Handbook of Research on Teacher Education	Houston, W.R., Haberman, M., & Sikula, J.	Association of Teacher Educators	Summary of research on (1) teacher education as a field of inquiry, (2) governance, (3) contexts and models, (4) participants, (5) curriculum, (6) processes, (7) evaluation and dissemination, (8) curricular areas, and (9) current issues in teacher education
Handbook of Research on Teaching (3rd Ed.)	Wittrock, M.C. (Macmillan, 1986)	American Educational Research Association	Detailed articles summarizing and synthesizing research related to numerous specific aspects of teaching
Handbook of Research on the Teaching of English	Flood, J. , Jensen, J.M., Lapp, D., & Squire, J.R. (Macmillan, 1991)	International Reading Association & National Council of Teachers of English	Summary of research on (1) theoretical bases for English language arts teaching, (2) teaching, (3) learners, (4) environments for teaching, and (5) specific aspects of the curriculum
Handbook of Research on the Education of Young Children	Spodek, B. (Macmillan, 1993)		Summary of research on (1) child development and early education, (2) early childhood educational curriculum, (3) early childhood education policy, and (4) research strategies for early childhood education

each entry can be accessed by searching by title, author, or subject heading. However, many users are unaware of the other information that is available on each entry. The card shown in Figure 3.8, for example, tells when the book was published, indicates how many pages are in it, and states that it contains a bibliography on pages 167–168 (this last piece of information would be helpful to you if you wanted to find more information on the topic covered by this book). Near the bottom of the card there are listed the three headings under which this book is indexed in the subject file of the catalog. By looking under these headings, you can find more books on the same topic. Both the Library of Congress number and the Dewey decimal number are listed at the bottom of the card. Since books are arranged according to similarity of topics, it might be a good idea for you to go to that part of the library where the book you want is shelved to see what other, related, books are located in this area. You may come across something that would otherwise have not even entered your mind.

In a growing number of libraries, the catalog of holdings can be accessed by computer; and in many cases the electronic data base will show whether the book is currently on the shelf. Some libraries now encourage users to access the catalog by computer from remote terminals and to order books or other documents; these books can be waiting at the library desk for the user to pick them up, with no need for the user to search the stacks or shelves.

INTERLIBRARY LOANS

Computerization has made it increasingly easy to borrow books from distant libraries. At a rapidly expanding number of libraries it is possible for a librarian to enter information into a computer terminal and be informed within seconds what libraries within a designated region of the country have a specified book or journal. By entering some additional information, the library is quickly and easily able to arrange to borrow the material on interlibrary loan. This means that even if your library does not have a book or journal, you can still have access to such publications. This can usually be accomplished at no cost to you or at only a minimal fee.

Figure 3.8 A Sample Entry from a Card Catalog

Punishment.

HQ	Vockell, Edward L.
770.4	Whatever happened to punishment / Edward L. Vockell. —
V62	Muncie, IN: Accelerated Development, 1977

xv, 175 p.: ill.; 23 cm.

Bibliography: p. 167–168.
Includes index.
ISBN 0–915202–11–5 : $7.95

1. Discipline of children. 2. Punishment. 3. Behavior modification. I. Title.

HQ770.4 V62   649*.6   77–80556
                                                          MARC

In practice, the catalog in your own library may not be the best place for you to look for information on a topic you are interested in. By using telecommunication services such as Compuserve and the Internet, data bases and the catalogs of libraries in distant cities can be searched. In many cases, limiting yourself to the holdings of a relatively small library will cause you to miss information to which you should have access. It is often better to look for sources of information in the indexing and abstracting services mentioned earlier in this chapter, in bibliographies of related publications, and in broader catalogs, and then to look for this specific information in your library. If it is not there, you can probably get it through an interlibrary loan. Check with your own library to see what services are available.

CONDUCTING A REVIEW OF THE LITERATURE

The sources of information mentioned in this chapter will enable you to carry out a successful search of the literature, provided you know what you are looking for. It is important that you define your problem as early as possible and continue to refine this definition so that you can focus more and more closely on solutions to it. By drawing upon published sources, you can avoid reinventing the wheel. You can take advantage of what is already known and build upon the knowledge of others.

In addition to the structured procedures covered in this chapter for finding published sources of information, there is a further strategy that is less formal. Once you find an article (or a book or report) that is directly related to the topic you are interested in, scrutinize the bibliography or list of references accompanying this piece of information. Then look up some of these articles in *CIJE* or *Psychological Abstracts* to see where they are indexed. In *CIJE*, examine the list of descriptors. This will enable you to get a good start; then it often becomes easier to find more sources.

Another strategy is to look through the list of references accompanying an article you have found and then look up the names of the authors in the author indexes of a more recent issue of an appropriate indexing or abstracting service. Since authors who publish important ideas on one topic will often do so again, this can lead you to additional sources of information that you might not otherwise have found.

A PRACTICAL EXAMPLE

One of the authors of this book wanted to find research information on the use of simulations in secondary science courses. He employed the following strategies:

1. Via his office modem, the author accessed his library's CD-ROM ERIC data base through the local area network (LAN). He used the topics *computer-assisted instruction* and *science education*. He realized that these categories were broad, but he wanted to err on the side of too much information—at least initially. He knew he could always limit the search with more specific descriptors later. This search generated a list of 592 titles. He instructed the computer to start printing the abstracts of these reports on the screen. They appeared in chronological order, starting with the most recent.

2. After looking at 20 of the 592 citations, our author realized that he was getting a large number of unpublished manuscripts and articles in which the computer was used for some purpose other than instruction. He was also getting too many articles related to elementary education. Therefore, he restarted his search, this time using these descriptors in combination: (1) *computer-assisted instruction*, (2) *science education*, and (3) *secondary education* or *middle schools*; he also instructed the computer to (4) select only journal articles and dissertations. The result of this search was a list of 136 articles. He instructed the computer to send this list with the abstracts to a printer, so that he could take these home to analyze them.

3. Before he left the computer, he decided to run one more search. He entered these descriptors:

(1) *computer-assisted instruction,* (2) *science education,* and (3) either *meta-analysis, synthesis,* or *literature reviews* that were (4) published in journals. He obtained 11 citations. Two of these were largely related to elementary education; our author felt that, although he did not want to read a large number of articles dealing with younger children, the *synthesis* of research in that area might yield some useful ideas.

4. Several of the articles were in his university library; he obtained these immediately. As he examined the articles, he noted that three authors seemed to be cited by most of the other researchers. He searched ERIC again for articles written by any of these authors. He discovered that while most of the articles were not directly related to simulations in science education, two of them were close enough to warrant further inspection. He also found several good articles by examining the lists of references at the end of each of the articles on his original list.

5. The author found one particularly useful article that was published jointly by two authors 10 years earlier. He entered these authors' names into the *Social Science Citation Index.* While he had performed the ERIC searches himself, he had to have a specialist in the library do the SSCI search for him because that data base was not available to general users in his library. This SSCI search yielded a list of 37 documents that had cited the original article, and several of these were not on his original list. These additional documents were on other topics (such as language arts and social studies), but some of them included a tangential discussion of computer simulations in science education.

6. He entered the set of descriptors from Step 2 into a computerized search of *Psychological Abstracts.* This led to a set of 33 citations; 25 of these differed from the entries on the ERIC list.

7. He went to the hard-copy volumes of *CIJE* and *Psychological Abstracts* and examined the issues that were more recent than the computerized data base. He had to search four issues of *CIJE* and three issues of *Psychological Abstracts* manually. When doing this, he was not able to do combination searches (e.g., selecting only articles that were about both computer-assisted instruction and science education)—he had to look through the citations for each descriptor individually; but since he had only a few issues to search, he felt this was worth the effort.

8. Our author searched his computerized library catalog under these descriptors: (1) *computers* or *technology* and (2) *science education.* He made the first descriptor more general than in the article search because he felt there would be fewer books, and a book on technology and science education might have a chapter on computer simulations in science education. He made a separate search with these descriptors: (1) *simulations* and (2) *science education.* From this second search of the library catalog he obtained 11 books, but although he got several new books (mostly on noncomputerized simulations in science), none of the new citations were of any interest to him.

9. He looked in the *Handbook of Research on Teaching* (Wittrock, 1986). He quickly discovered that this included no new information, since one of his synthesis articles was much more comprehensive than what he found there. However, he realized that had he started with this source, he might have found it more helpful. He resolved to look there earlier next time. He also looked in the *Encyclopedia of Educational Research,* but again found no new information. Although he found no new information in either of these sources, he had at least verified that in his earlier searches he had been looking in the right places.

10. The author found several citations to journals that were not available in his own library, but this did not mean that he had no access to them. His library, like many libraries, can obtain almost any journal article through the system of interlibrary loan. He filled out a form, and photocopies of the articles were sent to him within

a week or two. Several of these articles were obtained through University Microfilms, which maintains access to a large number of journals with permission to copy articles for a fee. He obtained these articles at no cost to himself. (His library feels that it is less expensive to absorb this cost than to subscribe to a vast number of journals that are rarely accessed.)

11. Likewise, a few books were not available, and our author obtained them through interlibrary loans. One book came from a library in his own state, and the other from a university library two thousand miles away. (Most libraries can obtain for you almost any book you need. Many libraries belong to a computerized network that permits them to find out which nearby libraries have a book that you may request. This more widespread access to books beyond the walls of your own library means that your own library's catalog may not be the best place to look for books on your research topic. It may be better to have your librarian help you search a catalog that extends beyond the scope of just one library.)

12. When he found a journal that contained several articles of interest, he went to the shelves and simply examined the most recent issues of that journal in their entirety. He found an article that was too recent to appear in the indexing services. In addition, he found an article on a closely related topic that had not appeared with his current set of descriptors. Finally, he found some information in an editorial that had not appeared during his computerized search.

13. When he found a relevant article, our author glanced at the descriptors under which it had been indexed. Knowing where that article was indexed gave him ideas for using descriptors more effectively as he continued to search for more citations.

This search of the literature enabled the author to arrive at a comprehensive grasp of the current status of literature on his topic.

NOTE TAKING

Most readers of this book already know how to take notes on their library research. In this section, we'll try to offer some creative ideas:

1. Make bibliographic entries for each source of information. Figure 3.9 shows a primitive but effective way to do this. Consider the following guidelines:

   a. Use a computerized strategy instead of index cards or other hard-copy formats. If you use a computer, you can usually avoid writing the same information more than once.

   b. If you do use index cards or paper, don't try to put too much information into a restricted space. (Don't make saving paper or cards a major priority.)

   c. Copy the information in the same format that you will want it in later. For example, if you will submit a report in the APA format (see chapter 19), make your bibliographic entries in that same format.

   d. Put *all* the information into your original entry. Going back to find and recopy information for a bibliography is a frustrating waste of time.

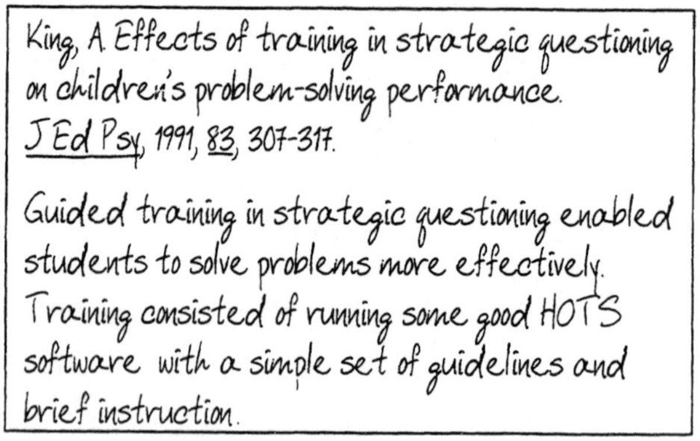

King, A Effects of training in strategic questioning on children's problem-solving performance. J Ed Psy, 1991, 83, 307-317.

Guided training in strategic questioning enabled students to solve problems more effectively. Training consisted of running some good HOTS software with a simple set of guidelines and brief instruction.

Figure 3.9 Bibliographic Index Card Entry

e. When you copy the entry, copy it carefully. Mistakes will haunt you later. Remember that even if you never return to an article yourself, someone who reads your report may wish to do so.

2. Summarize key points in a format that will enable you to find and use the information. Consider the following guidelines:

a. Use a computerized strategy instead of index cards or other hard-copy formats. If you use a computer, you can usually avoid writing the same information more than once.

b. Differentiate between direct quotations and your own ideas. You're going to have to make this distinction to avoid plagiarism when you write your report; it is easier to make the distinction at the time you are making the notes.

c. When you use direct quotations, check them for accuracy and be sure to get the exact page numbers for the citation. When you're summarizing or combining with your own ideas, it will be more difficult to cite exact pages, but a reasonable approximation may be helpful later.

d. Cross-reference your notes to your bibliographic citations. The best way to do this is usually to use the APA style (like in this book: e.g., Vockell & Asher, 1995). For short notes, you can write on the back of the card—or, even better, in your computer data base.

e. Find a way to code your notes for easy sorting. For example, you can put abbreviations in the corner of your index cards—or, even better, in a field of your data base.

As you may have noticed, we advocate using the computer as an appropriate tool for collecting data and developing a data base for reference purposes. The following guidelines will help you use the computer as an effective tool in your library research. (The discussion assumes that your computer will not be present with you in the library. If you have a laptop computer that you can take to the library, you have the ideal situation, and your job is much easier.)

1. Use an electronic data base—not a word processor—to store information that you may want to sort or rearrange later, which is often what you'll want to do. Figure 3.10 shows an example of a data base entry made by one of the authors of this book. The data base has the following advantages over the hard-copy approach:

a. The information can easily be sorted and reorganized. For example, entries can be arranged by topic for one purpose, then by author for another, then by date of publication for another.

b. It is easy to retrieve from a large file only the information you need.

c. If the information needs to be altered by additions or deletions, this can be done readily.

d. If the information needs to be copied, this can be done with much less effort than would be necessary in a hard-copy format. For example, bibliographic information can be easily transmitted to a list of references. Likewise, textual notes can be fed into the word processor for the body of a report.

2. For longer passages, use the word processor. Data bases are limited in two ways:

a. They accept only relatively short passages of text. For example, you may be able to enter only about 20 lines into the data base. (You can get around this problem by using the data base for short summaries on the card with the citation and the word processor for longer summaries or integrations of the information.)

b. The data base doesn't have the same typing capabilities as the word processor. For example, because of the limitation to 80 characters per line, it is much more difficult to make insertions at a later time. Also, most

Figure 3.10
Electronic Data
Base Entry

```
File: EdPsy File          01/18/94 11:29 am          Escape: Main Menu

Selection: All records


Record 461 of 788  (788 selected)
================================================================
Author: King, A.
Title: Effects of Training in Strategic Questioning on Children's
    T2: Problem-Solving Performance
Journal: Journal of Educational Psychology
Date: Sep 91
Page: 307
Topic: Thinking-skills Strategic-thinking Problem-solving CAI
Topic 2: File-Strategy
Date Read: Sep 30 91
Rating: 93
Summary: Guided training in strategic questioning enabled students to solve
    S2: problems more effectively. Training consists of running some good
    S3: HOTS software with a simple set of guidelines and brief instruction.
    S4: Use for Edpsy Book and Edres Book.

-------------------------------------------------------------------------------
Type entry or use @ commands                              @-? for Help
```

programs do not permit the use of the spelling checker in the data base.

The solution is to move data back and forth between the data base and the word processor. Do the work in the data base that requires sorting and retrieval, and then move information to the word processor for the final development of your ideas.

3. Consider the possibility of supplementary electronic tools. For example, ProCite enables users to store information in a data base that will automatically generate lists of references in the APA format.

4. Prepare for your trip to the library by entering information ahead of time into your computer. For example, if you have a list of articles to get from the library, enter the titles, authors, and other essential information into your data base before you go to the library. This enables you to sort your information and make lists of what you need. When you find further information, you can add it to the data base.

5. It's usually worth the effort to bring the sources of information to your computer, so that you can enter them directly into your word processor or data base. Copying information to cards in the library and then again to the computer consumes time. It is better to borrow materials from the library or to photocopy the information and bring it to your computer.

6. Very few libraries make computers available for people taking research notes. The irony is often that you'll be doing your library search on a computer, but you may not be permitted or able to use it for note taking. One way to get around this is to access the computer for your library search via modem from another location, where you have a second computer for note taking. As

time goes on, more computers will be available with windows-type programs, which will enable you to examine an information source on one part of the screen while you use your own data base or word processor on the other part. Another solution is to bring a laptop computer into the library.

7. Try to get the information transferred into your computer electronically, so that you don't have to do the initial typing at all. If you cannot transfer information directly from one computer to another, it may be possible to use a scanner. This mechanism works much like a photocopy machine; it scans printed information and transfers it to a computer, where it can be converted into a format that your word processor can use. At the present time, scanners read text imperfectly, but their accuracy is improving rapidly; the imperfections arise from the nature of the software. Once you get the data into your own computer, you can edit the information and delete what you don't want.

You will discover that it is worth the effort to become familiar with what the computer can do for you not only in retrieving information but in storing it and organizing it for your own purposes. Chapter 18 will describe some further uses of the computer for analyzing data and reporting your results.

SUMMARY

The resources discussed in this chapter will help you find information that will enable you to attack your educational problems more successfully. These library resources can be helpful at any level of research. Reading about them is not the best way to learn how to use them; the best strategy is to go into the library and actually try your hand at using each of the resources and services described. Even those who think they know a great deal about using the library (including the authors of this book) will discover that there is much to learn about how to get information from the modern library.

Several different indexing and abstracting services have been described here. Each service provides different advantages. Many are computerized. Such services enable us to go directly to the information we need rather than through a vast amount of irrelevant information before we find what is pertinent. In addition, a familiarity with the various journals, reviews, and books that present current research and ideas in our areas of specific educational interest will help identify, clarify, and solve our educational problems. An important point made in this chapter is that we should not confine ourselves to the physical limits of any one library when we search for information. The computerization of information resources and systems of interlibrary loans are becoming increasingly efficient, and such systems enable us to obtain quickly almost any information that we need.

What Comes Next

The rest of this book will describe strategies for operationally defining research variables, measuring them, designing and carrying out studies that generate and test research hypotheses, analyzing the results of these studies, and evaluating the authenticity and generalizability of these results.

DOING YOUR OWN RESEARCH

It is not appropriate to consider the review of the literature for your research project to be a mere formality. Rather, the library and reference materials should be valuable tools to stimulate and supplement your own thought processes. Unless you are already a highly skilled information user and unless you have taken advantage of your library's services within the last few years, this chapter probably contains information that will help you use the library and reference materials more effectively.

Keep in mind that using the library and reference materials should be a recursive process. That is, you should return to these tools at various points during your research project and feed the information you acquire into the particular research activity that is important at a given time. In addition, remember that by keeping accurate records of your use of reference materials you can have the material available to write an important segment of your research report.

FOR FURTHER THOUGHT

1. Wouldn't it be better for researchers to do their own thinking rather than to rely on what others have written for them in journals and reference books?

2. Identify a subject area that interests you. What sources of information in your school's library would be most helpful in keeping you abreast of information on that topic? Exactly what steps should you follow to stay current?

3. Experience shows that, as good as it is, ERIC sometimes makes mistakes in finding references on a given combination of topics. Do you think false positives or false negatives occur most often? (A false positive occurs when ERIC finds a document that is not really on the designated topics; a false negative occurs when there is a document that ERIC fails to find.) What causes false positives? What causes false negatives?

REFERENCE

Wittrock, M. C. (1986). *Handbook of research on teaching.* New York: Macmillan.

Vockell, E. L., Asher, W., DiNuzzo, N., & Bartok, M. (1994). Information sources in educational research literature. *Journal of experimental education.*

ANNOTATED BIBLIOGRAPHY

Cooper, H. M. (1987). *Integrating research: A guide for literature reviews* (2nd ed.). Newbury Park, CA: Sage. This short book describes strategies for both finding information and integrating and summarizing research findings in the social sciences.

Freed, M. N., Hess, R. K., & Ryan, J. M. (1989). *The educator's desk reference: A sourcebook of educational information and research.* New York: Macmillan. This book describes an array of information sources, research organizations, research methodologies, and other items of interest to educators who are looking for or evaluating research information.

Klein, B. T. (Ed.). (1980). *Guide to American educational directories* (5th ed.). Rye, NY: Todd Publications. This is a good guide to what you can find in other directories.

Yarborough, J. (1975). *How to prepare a computer search of ERIC: A non-technical approach.* Stanford, CA: ERIC Clearinghouse on Information Resources. This booklet briefly describes what is available through ERIC and offers step-by-step guidelines for performing a computerized search of ERIC.

CHAPTER 3

Research Report Analysis

The review of the literature contains information from several sources that are cited in the References at the end of the report. The outline in the commentary (located in the margins of Appendix C) briefly summarizes the logic of this review of the literature. The researchers already possessed a great deal of this information before they even began their study, but they also used library reference materials to acquire additional information. Try answering the following questions about how the researchers probably acquired this information.

1. What two sources of information would the authors probably have used to find this information?

2. Under what descriptors or keywords would the researchers look to find current information related to their topic in the computerized ERIC data base?

ANSWERS:

1. The two best sources would probably be the

computerized ERIC and *Psychological Abstracts* data bases.

2. The best approach would probably be to use this set of terms:

 a. *problem solving* or *thinking skills* (*thinking skills* is a broader term, and it would get some false positives; however, there will likely be several documents that deal with solving problems that happen not to be categorized under *problem solving*)

 b. *simulations* or *simulation* (and possibly other related terms that would appear during the search)

 c. *computers* or *computer-assisted instruction*

 d. *science education* or *biology* (since this is the subject matter)

They could stop the search at each level to check current citations before narrowing the search further. This would enable them to find, for example, the article by Beyer cited in the References, which would not appear if *science education* or *computers* were used to restrict the search. The complete set of four levels of terms would result in a manageable number of citations on the specific topic·of interest to the researchers.

OPERATIONALLY DEFINING AND MEASURING RESEARCH VARIABLES

■ **WHERE WE'VE BEEN**

We have introduced the topic of research as a tool that enables educators to make increasingly broad and accurate generalizations, and we have discussed examples of the various research variables. We have also examined reference sources that will help us clarify the relationships among variables and find out what research has already been conducted with regard to the problem under consideration.

■ **WHERE WE'RE GOING NOW**

In this chapter we'll describe the process of operationally defining and measuring research variables.

■ **CHAPTER PREVIEW**

Operational definitions are the evidence that teachers, researchers, and readers of research accept to indicate the degree to which a concept or context exists or that an outcome is occurring. These definitions enable teachers and researchers to clarify what they are talking about so that they can do their work more effectively and other observers can understand more precisely what the researchers have done or are doing. In addition to discussing strategies for developing operational definitions, this chapter also suggests strategies for making this evidence as solid or compelling as possible. After reading this chapter, you should be able to

1. Identify examples of well-written operational definitions of educational research variables.
2. Write operational definitions of given research variables.
3. Identify strategies for making the evidence acquired through operational definitions as solid or compelling as possible.
4. Write a correctly stated research prediction.

■

OPERATIONAL DEFINITIONS: KNOWING WHAT YOU'RE TALKING ABOUT

A major focus of educational research is the discussion and analysis of educational outcomes. These outcomes can be discussed effectively only if the discussants agree on operational definitions of these outcomes. Operational definitions are the *evidence* that a teacher or researcher is willing to accept to indicate that something of conceptual interest (such as an educational context or an instructional outcome) exists or is occurring. In some cases this evidence is direct, but in many more cases it is indirect.

Educational outcomes can be discussed effectively only if the discussants agree on operational definitions of these outcomes.

Although other types of research variables must also be operationally defined, we need an initial focus for the present discussion. We shall therefore focus on dependent variables—educational outcomes. The same logic applies to the operational definition of other research variables—including research contexts, treatments, and subjects; these applications will be discussed later. The following are examples of educational outcomes:

Reading ability

Spelling errors

Student anxiety

Teacher anxiety

Tardiness

Parental satisfaction

Moral behavior

Number of suspensions

Number of arrests

Attitude toward English

Extent of voluntary pupil participation in class discussion

Many of the problems that teachers and researchers encounter in education occur because they neglect to measure outcome variables. For example, the English teacher's failure to inculcate in his students an appreciation of Emily Dickinson (discussed in chapter 1) was a direct result of his failure to measure attitudes. Had he known what was happening, he could have attempted to change the state of affairs. Many teachers have discipline problems in their classrooms because they fail to assess the anxiety level among their pupils. Other teachers accidentally restrict the creativity of their students, because their tests measure conformity rather than insight. Many social studies teachers release into the world graduates who receive A's but will never vote in an election; these teachers could have avoided this outcome if they had taken steps to overcome this apathy—if only they had measured their students' attitudes toward participating in the democratic process. Principals often preside over a school filled with apathetic teachers, convinced that all is going well, since nobody complains. Counselors often waste weeks or months with unsuccessful guidance procedures, while they overlook indications that a different style of counseling would be in order. In each of these cases a problem exists because an outcome variable has gone unmeasured. The simple act of measurement would help educators become aware of such difficulties and focus their energies toward solving the problems.

The first step in measuring an outcome variable is to devise *operational definitions* of it. The operational definitions state as precisely as possible what set of observable events we should record in order to say that we have collected data regarding the variable under consideration.

In a few cases the behaviors we wish to observe or change are completely external and easily observable. In such cases, stating operational definitions is merely a matter of becoming precise—focusing directly on what we really want to observe and ignoring irrelevancies. Examples include in-seat behavior, frequency of tantrums, and tardiness. These are clearly observable and definable events, and all we need to do to measure them is to be in the proper place at the appropriate time and look for the specified behavior.

Most of what we try to accomplish in schools, however, involves an *internal change*, often referred to as learning. Learning cannot be observed directly. All we can do is collect evidence of internal activity by observing external behaviors performed by the person we think may have undergone the internal change.

In a few cases, the inference is very direct, and there is no reason whatsoever to doubt the validity of the inference. This is because the observable behavior is almost synonymous with the internal learning. This is the case when we want a person to learn how to perform a physical behavior. If we want to teach students to saw a board in half, we can ascertain that learning has occurred by giving the learners a saw and a board and asking them to saw the board in half. If the physical evidence shows that the board is in fact sawed in half, we can pretty well assume that learning has occurred. The slight remaining uncertainty can be eliminated by having them repeat the task several times, thus eliminating the likelihood of chance success. (Note: Even here we have not demonstrated that we *taught* them anything, but only that they have learned. They may have learned the behavior previously.) Likewise, we can directly observe that a child has stopped being tardy or that a child is throwing a tantrum. Little inference is necessary.

In other cases, the evidence is not so clearly related to the learning, and hence the inference that learning has occurred is more remote and needs to be buttressed by further reasoning and additional evidence. If we want to teach a child to understand a passage in a book, for example, can we ascertain from her correct answers that she has mastered the passage? Not really; for there is a good possibility that she is merely guessing well, incorporating information from other sources, or reading subtle cues from the question. By carefully structuring the testing situation, we *can* still make an accurate assessment of what the child has learned; but the point is that the evidence is much less direct, and we have to rely much more heavily on logical inferences and supporting evidence than in the case of the more external behavior.

Even more remotely connected with observable behaviors are the *affective* goals of education. Affective goals are important. Unless students appreciate or understand the value of subject matter, they are unlikely to take it with them beyond the classroom. But because of the more remote connection between the internal, affective change and any observable evidence, the inferential leap becomes considerable. Does this mean that we should not bother to teach these attitudes or collect evidence about them? Of course not; evidence is even more important here than in the other cases. The solution is to use *multiple operational definitions*—to collect *more evidence* and *more types* of evidence and to collect it more carefully. The methods for collecting such information will be discussed later. Here we shall simply point out that the problems of collecting data on extremely internal outcomes are often best surmounted by using unobtrusive forms of measurement and collecting more than a single form of evidence.

STATING OPERATIONAL DEFINITIONS OF COGNITIVE OUTCOME VARIABLES

As you read this section, if you already know how to write behavioral objectives, you may think that they are the same as operational definitions. This is technically not quite accurate. Actually, a behavioral objective is a *specific type* of operational definition, but there is little point in making an issue of the distinction here. If you can write good behavioral objectives, you can write good operational definitions of outcome variables. If you are interested in writing better operational definitions, the behavioral objectives literature provides worthwhile assistance. (See the Annotated Bibliography at the end of this chapter.)

If you can write good behavioral objectives, you can write good operational definitions of outcome variables.

To write an operational definition, state *observable behaviors* that you are willing to accept as evidence that the outcome is occurring. An observable behavior is one about which two or more observers would almost certainly agree with regard to its occurrence or nonoccurrence.

Let's have a little spot quiz. According to the definition of *observable behaviors,* that we just stated, which is the most readily observable behavior—understanding a reading passage, or paraphrasing a reading passage? The answer is paraphrasing. Since *understanding* involves no readily observable activity, it would be difficult to tell from purely objective, observable data whether a person understands something. It happens inside the person's head. An outsider would have to make an inference about it. However, it *is* possible to tell whether a person has paraphrased a passage merely by listening to that person.

Little inference is necessary to say, "That child is paraphrasing the passage I just told her to read!" Note, however, that it *does* take considerable inference to conclude that the paraphraser has *understood* the passage she is paraphrasing. Accurate paraphrasing is the objective, observable data that we are willing to accept as evidence to *support* our inference that understanding has occurred. Hence, "paraphrasing a reading passage" is just one of many operational definitions of understanding a reading passage. (Inadequacies of this specific operational definition will be discussed later.)

Note that we are not saying that paraphrasing is more important than understanding. Nor are we suggesting that the teacher should stop teaching students to understand passages and teach them to paraphrase instead. (This is what teachers sometimes do when they "teach for a test," and this is usually a bad idea.) In a few rare cases it might be important to teach students to paraphrase, but in most cases paraphrasing is a relatively trivial activity. What we really want is understanding. But even though it is trivial, paraphrasing is at least observable; and as Sherlock Holmes was wont to tell Dr. Watson, apparently trivial evidence can support important inferences.

Try another spot quiz. Which of the following are readily observable activities?

a. understanding Boyle's law
b. identifying correct applications of Boyle's law
c. distinguishing between correct and incorrect applications of Boyle's law
d. solving problems that require the application of Boyle's law

In this case, the answers are b, c, and d. By simply observing students we cannot tell what they understand. Understanding Boyle's law occurs inside the brain. We can, however, tell by simple, direct observation whether a person can identify correct applications or distinguish between correct and incorrect applications (assuming that "identify" and "distinguish" mean "point to," "select," or "circle on a test"). We can also tell whether a person can solve problems, simply by checking whether the answers are correct. However, from this observable data, we can only *infer* that the student *understands* Boyle's law.

If you got both of these spot quiz questions wrong, you probably do not understand what opera-

tional definitions are, do not know how to write them, and therefore need remedial help. On the other hand, if you got them both right, you probably understand this section of the chapter completely. Right? Not necessarily. Your understanding of this chapter occurs inside your own head, and we can only *infer* what you have learned. "Getting both of these questions wrong" is our operational definition of "failure to understand." But all we've really done is give you some examples of well-written and poorly written operational definitions and asked you to select the good ones. Failing to select the correct answers is *evidence* that you have not caught on, but there could be some other explanation (perhaps you read too much into our questions). Likewise, getting the answers right is only *evidence* that you understand what we are saying; there could be some other explanation for your correct answers (you might just be "test wise," or perhaps you answered the questions correctly by guessing, without possessing any real knowledge of the topic).

MAKING THE EVIDENCE MORE SOLID

As we indicated in the preceding section, before we can make solid inferences from operational definitions, we must rule out many other likely explanations for the occurrence or nonoccurrence of the designated activity. Let's look at the paraphrasing example. Assume that a reading student has paraphrased a passage correctly. For what reasons, other than that she actually understands the passage, might she have paraphrased correctly? The list of alternative explanations could be endless, but here are a few:

She could have guessed wildly but correctly.

She could have guessed accurately from context clues (such as pictures).

Another student could have whispered the paraphrase to her.

She could have memorized the paraphrase the night before.

She could have noticed that the teacher looked surprised when she began inaccurately and then

---

BOX 4.1

Dear Researcher: Young Love

Dear Researcher: I am a 12-year-old girl with a great personality. I'm pretty good-looking too. My problem is Dwayne, a great-looking guy in my class. I'm madly in love with him, but he doesn't care about me. I asked him to kiss me yesterday, but all he did was let out the grossest belch I've ever heard. I asked him to carry my books home, but he stuck them up in a tree, and I had to get an ugly 14-year-old to get them down. All Dwayne ever does is throw snowballs at me and my friends. Why won't Dwayne return my love? Why does he hate me? (signed) Young Love in Peoria

Dear Young: Your problem here is one of operational definition. You're interested in receiving Dwayne's affection, and you operationally define this as kissing, holding hands, and carrying books. Guys like Dwayne often operationalize affection by throwing snowballs at girls they like and sticking their books up in trees. It's also likely that Dwayne's misreading *you.* You're trying to show your affection by kissing, book-carrying, etc., but it's likely that Dwayne might view these activities as an operational definition of "weirdness." If I were you, I'd tie his coat in knots or hit him in the face with a pie. (On second thought, don't. I just noticed your letter was postmarked 14 years ago.) (signed) The Lonely Researcher

---

smiled when she changed to a more accurate paraphrase.

She might have deliberately and ingeniously worded the paraphrase in such vague verbiage that it would be considered correct even though she didn't know what she was talking about.

You can probably think of many more possibilities. In collecting evidence, the job of the teacher/researcher is to think carefully about the situation and the evidence and to rule out as many as possible of these alternative explanations. (The preceding sentence encompasses the basic logic of all scientific thinking; when teachers collect evidence about outcome variables, they are applying scientific thinking to their profession.) In our example it is not very hard to rule out the alternative explanations that we have suggested. Here are some ways to rule out each of the suggested alternatives:

Give the student three or four passages instead of just one. Wild guessing is no more likely to hold up over time than is extended luck at the roulette wheel.

Eliminate the context clues (such as pictures), or ask questions about things not mentioned in these clues.

Have the student sit where she cannot hear whispers, or stand between her and the person who is likely to whisper to her.

Give her a new passage at the moment of testing, so that she will not have time to seek help or memorize a paraphrase ahead of time.

Exclude "test wiseness" clues from your testing format.

If she gives you a vague paraphrase, ask more specific questions about the passage—don't let her be vague.

As the evidence collector, your responsibility is to rule out alternative explanations.

By doing these activities, we increase the accuracy of the inference that students who paraphrase a passage correctly actually understand it. But what if they paraphrase incorrectly? Would this mean that they did not understand the passage? No, there are many reasons for faulty paraphrasing, including the following:

The student might have good receptive skills but poor expressive abilities.

She might be shy or not like to talk to the teacher.

She might become anxious in testing situations.

She might feel that the original passage expressed the thought well enough and might see no reason to say the same thing in different words.

You can probably think of more reasons for failure to paraphrase. As the evidence collector, your responsibility is to rule out these alternative explanations. Here are some possible ways to do so:

If the student lacks expressive skills, teach these to her before you ask her to paraphrase.

If she doesn't like to talk to you, either make an effort to befriend her or have someone else with whom she enjoys conversation ask her to paraphrase the passage.

If she is shy or anxious, make the situation as nonthreatening as possible.

Make a deliberate effort, if necessary, to convince her that paraphrasing is a useful skill, if for no other reason than that this skill will enable her to communicate to you whether she has understood the passage.

By performing all these activities, we begin to maximize our confidence in the inference that a non-paraphraser is a nonunderstander. In many cases, validating evidence that learning has *not* occurred is much more difficult than validating evidence that it *has* occurred.

It is also an effective strategy to have multiple operational definitions and multiple methods for measuring outcome variables.

In addition to eliminating alternative explanations for the presence of evidence, there is a second route that the researcher should pursue to make the inference more solid—namely, *collect additional types of evidence.* Specifically, it is an effective strategy to have *multiple operational definitions* and *multiple methods* for measuring outcome variables. The logic of this strategy is that the weaknesses of a single operational definition can be mitigated by employing additional operational definitions, and a second or third method for collecting data can help overcome the biases and deficiencies inherent in any single measurement method. This strategy of attacking the measurement problem "from several different angles" is often referred to as *triangulation.* For example, we could have our reading student attempt *each* of the following:

1. Paraphrase the passage.
2. Answer questions about the passage.
3. Follow directions contained in the passage.
4. Tell us whether she thinks she understands the passage.

If the student cannot do 1 but can do 2, 3, and 4, we would probably conclude that she did understand the passage, especially if there was a plausible explanation for her inability to paraphrase. When there is a conflict in the evidence, we simply evaluate the evidence we have. Then we either make an inference based on our reconciliation of these conflicts or we seek further data. This kind of evidence collection may become quite detailed and can lead to useful diagnostic data that will help us work with the learner in the future.

In actual practice, while it is often helpful to use more than one approach for evidence collection when you are first working with a student, you will eventually find out which approaches are valid and which are invalid and be able to use one valid method of collecting data at a time. For example, experienced high school teachers can find out whether their students understand their lectures by asking questions that previous experience has shown will provide good evidence. Most college professors simply ask students whether they have understood a portion of the lecture. When the students nod yes, the professors take this as evidence that the students have understood. But the professors would do well to remember that the nods are *only evidence*—limited, partial evidence. The students may nod because they are reluctant to reveal their ignorance. Or they may know that the professor will talk longer if they do not nod.

In summary, there are two good ways to make the evidence supplied by operational definitions more solid:

Eliminate as many as possible of the plausible alternative explanations.

Collect more than one type of evidence, focusing on multiple operational definitions with minimal overlap in the methodology of data collection.

Neither of these methods can actually succeed in making the evidence foolproof, of course; but their combined use increases the probability that we are making sound inferences and decreases the probability of false conclusions.

CONCEPTUAL DEFINITIONS

This chapter's emphasis on the importance of operational definitions should not be taken to deny the value of *conceptual definitions* of the variables in a research study. The concepts behind the operational definitions are what really interests both the researcher and the reader of the research. Teachers are interested in promoting educational goals, not the operational definitions of these goals. We need operational definitions simply because it is impossible to observe internal concepts directly; therefore we must by necessity employ operational definitions to establish ground rules for collecting, interpreting, and discussing empirical data to support our conceptual thinking and decisions.

The concepts behind the operational definitions are what really interests both the researcher and the reader of the research.

When educational researchers work at the conceptual level, they follow the same rules of logic, critical thinking, and discourse as other persons engaging in cognitive activities. Researchers typically start at a conceptual level, then operationally define their variables, collect data, analyze and interpret them, and then return to the conceptual level. This return to the theoretical level and the integration of research into the scientific thought process will be discussed further in chapter 17.

DO YOU MEET THE OBJECTIVES OF THIS CHAPTER?

Let's stop to see whether we are accomplishing what we had hoped in this chapter. That is, do you understand what operational definitions are, and do you know how to write good ones? An operational definition of the goal of this chapter is as follows:

Given an undefined outcome variable and a set of several operational definitions of this variable, the student should be able to distinguish between those that are good operational definitions and those that are not.

To determine whether you have met this objective, take Part 1 of Review Quiz 4.1 (located on pp. 76–77). But before doing so, think: if you get 90–100% correct on this test, does that really mean that you understand what this chapter is all about? No, without knowing anything else about you, we cannot say that for certain. (In fact, we can seldom say anything "for certain," given the nature of goals and evidence in education and the social sciences.) For one thing, it would be easy to guess on Part 1, since there are only two alternatives to each question. However, if we have designed a good test, we can say that for most people, success on this test is a good indicator that they have met the objectives of this chapter. But there are many persons for whom this statement will not hold true, and we have no idea whether you are one of them. Two reasons why you might do well on Part 1 without having met the objectives are as follows: (1) you might be able to recognize good work in others without being able to write operational definitions yourself, or (2) you may have recognized subtle clues inadvertently included in the test items that tipped you off. In the second case, success on the test would actually be a good operational definition of test-taking ability, not understanding operational definitions or knowing how to write them.

Moreover, what should you conclude if you missed three or four of the items in Part 2 of Review Quiz 4.1? We are assuming that persons who miss items are displaying faulty performance with regard to the chapter objectives. Is this assumption correct for you? Again, we cannot tell without knowing anything about you. If we have written good items, then the vast majority of people who miss questions will do so because they lack an understanding of operational definitions. But there are other reasons for our errors of inference. For example, perhaps you got an item wrong because you read into it something that we did not intend to say (and perhaps *most* people would read the item exactly the way we intended it to be read). In such a case, your failure would not be an operational definition of failure to meet the goals of this chapter but rather of failure to perceive things from our perspective.

To get around the uncertainty surrounding the first operational definition, here is a second:

Given an undefined outcome variable, the student should be able to write a clearly expressed operational definition of it.

Review Quiz 4.2 was designed to determine whether you have met the goals of this chapter according to this second operational definition. Before you take this second test, pause for a moment. What will success or failure mean? If you succeed at matching our answer closely, that might be pretty good evidence that you have met the goal. But what if your answer does not match ours very closely? Then you might have to decide on your own whether you are right; and if you have not met the goal, how can you possibly make this decision? In this case, "success" might be a good operational definition of a lax conscience or low standards rather than of an understanding of how to write operational definitions.

To further circumvent uncertainties, we can state a third operational definition of understanding operational definitions:

The student should be able to restate in his/her own words the definition of the term *operational definition*.

Your status regarding this operational definition can be determined by your answer to Review Quiz 4.3. This quiz obviously has problems similar to the first two. But it is a third piece of evidence; and used in conjunction with the other two, it can strengthen our *inference* about your level of understanding.

If we were dealing with you on a one-to-one basis, we might find additional ways to collect evidence. For example, here is one more operational definition:

The student shall state that he/she understands what this is all about.

This final operational definition is measured by your answer to Review Quiz 4.4, simply by asking whether you are satisfied with your understanding. Note that this is often not a good operational definition of understanding of a classroom lecture. When a teacher finishes a part of a lecture and asks the whole class, "Do you understand what I am saying?" this question rarely elicits an accurate measure of understanding. Many students assume the question is rhetorical; others would prefer to leave the room and figure things out on their own; others are so unclear that they cannot even formulate a clear question; others feel that a question will embarrass the teacher by suggesting that there was an inadequacy in the lecture; and others will remain silent for other reasons. However, as a reader of this book, you are relatively free from the pressures expressed in the previous sentence and you probably really do want to understand the contents of this chapter, and so you can use this as a valid operational definition for yourself—especially in conjunction with one or two of the other operational definitions.

The preceding paragraphs have offered four acceptable operational definitions of "understanding operational definitions and knowing how to write them," with four accompanying tests to measure the degree of attainment of this goal. (It would be possible to write even more operational definitions and accompanying tests.) If you do well on all the tests, it is probably safe to infer that you have met the goal of this chapter. If you do poorly on all of them, you probably have not met the goal. If you do well on some and poorly on others, then the evidence is ambiguous, and it becomes necessary to evaluate the conflicting evidence (as described elsewhere in this chapter)—to decide which evidence is contaminated and which is a valid measure of the intended outcome. If your evaluation of the evidence indicates that you have met the goal, then it is time for you to go on to the next chapter. If the evidence indicates that you have not met the objectives, either reread the information, refer to the more detailed sources listed in the bibliography at the end of the chapter, study the parallel chapter in the workbook, or use some other means to help yourself master this information.

This detailed description of how to take these tests is intended as a model for collecting evidence in an instructional program. Teachers and other educators acting as researchers should follow this model, which includes these steps:

1. Focus on the specific outcome variable with which you are concerned.
2. Devise enough operational definitions of that outcome variable to enable you to collect adequate evidence to determine whether that outcome has been attained.
3. Devise tests based on these operational definitions and administer these tests (before, after, and/or during your instructional program) to collect evidence.
4. Evaluate your evidence.

Use these steps in your own instructional programs and in any other research you conduct.

REVIEW QUIZ 4.1

Part 1

Choose the best operational definition of the underlined terms in each general goal stated below.

1. General goal: to teach children to <u>appreciate</u> poetry
   a. The students will value poetry as much as their favorite hobbies.
   b. Given a list of topics and asked to choose which ones they value, the students will choose poetry.

2. General goal: to teach children to <u>understand</u> how smoking causes cancer
   a. The students will identify on a chart the parts of the body that are most likely to be adversely influenced by smoking-related carcinogens.
   b. The students will thoroughly know what does and what does not cause cancer in smokers.

3. General goal: to enhance children's <u>self-concept</u>
   a. The students will come to a better understanding of themselves as human beings.
   b. The students will verbalize accurate self-assessments of themselves in their school-work.

Part 2

Put an X next to all of the following operational definitions of "rapport with other students" that actually state an observable behavior.

a _____ Identifying each of the other students by name

b _____ Having a good sense of humor

c _____ Having respect for the opinions of others

d _____ Making no remarks to other students that are perceived by the observer as derogatory

e _____ Valuing the other students as persons

f ____ Naming one hobby that each of the other students is interested in

g ____ Being chosen frequently by other students on a "Who's your best friend?" questionnaire

h ____ Having other students smile when they talk to you

i ____ Initiating contacts with other students

REVIEW QUIZ 4.2

Below are several undefined outcome variables. Write a clearly expressed operational definition for each.

Goal 1: to teach children *how to do long division*

Goal 2: to teach student drivers *how to parallel park*

Goal 3: to eliminate *disruptive outbursts by children*

Goal 4: to have the students *develop moral standards*

REVIEW QUIZ 4.3

In your own words, explain what an operational definition is.

REVIEW QUIZ 4.4

Are you satisfied that you understand the term *operational definition* and know how to write operational definitions of outcomes you wish to measure?

THE RESEARCH PREDICTION

An important step in the formal research process is inserting the operational definitions into the research hypothesis. When the conceptual statements of the research variables are replaced by their operational definitions, the resulting statement is referred to as the *research prediction*. A research prediction is the same as a research hypothesis, except that it includes operational (rather than conceptual) definitions of the variables. In an experimental study, the research prediction is a statement of the expected relationship between the independent (or treatment) variable and the dependent (or criterion) variable, in which the conceptual terms employed in the research hypothesis have been replaced by their operational definitions. (In experimental studies, the research prediction leads directly to a research design, discussed in chapters 11 and 12.) The following five statements have taken the research hypotheses from Review Quiz 2.1 (chapter 2) and converted them to research predictions by replacing the dependent and independent variables with their respective operational definitions:

1. Reading *Julius Caesar* in accordance with our school's curriculum guidelines will cause sophomore students to make more references to a wider variety of aspects of Western civilization in an essay on Western culture written at the end of the semester than students who do not read *Julius Caesar*.

2. Students who receive token reinforcement in which it is contingently given according to prescribed guidelines will score lower on the Torrance Tests of Creative Thinking than students who receive no such token reinforcement program.

3. Students who write programs in Logo during a three-month, twice-a-week program consisting of hour-long sessions with two students at each computer using the software entitled *Logo Projects for Independent Thinkers* will have higher scores on the Watson-Glaser Test of Critical Thinking than similar students who do not take part in this program.

4. Children who are not required to learn to read until the sixth grade but are rather encouraged to read whenever they wish (according to guidelines discussed in the report) will score about the same on reading tests administered during the tenth grade as children who were required to start formal reading instruction in the first grade.

5. Students in a fifth-grade classroom in which the teacher emphasized the whole-language approach and stimulated expressive language by using the methods described in *The Language Rich Classroom* were found by a participant observer to be substantially more eager to share their opinions with their peers than were children in more traditional classrooms.

Each of these research predictions is stated in terms of operational definitions. In each case, the operational definitions could be written more specifically, and such clarified operational definitions should be contained within the full text of a research report. The brief statements contained in these predictions are satisfactory, provided they are backed up with more detailed descriptions in the text. In a good, published research report, major portions of the "methods" section provide operational definitions of the variables included in the study. As you examined some of these predictions, you may have been surprised, thinking that the prediction stated something different than what you expected from the original question or hypothesis. This is not unusual, since only the person doing the research can establish his or her own operational definition of the variables in a study. If *you* were performing a study to examine each of these hypotheses, the operational definitions (and hence the research predictions) might be different from those stated here.

The preceding research predictions contained only dependent and independent variables. Control and moderator variables should also be operationally defined in a complete and comprehensive research prediction. For instance, the third example can be further refined by the insertion of an operationally defined moderator variable:

3. Among children who fall outside the classification of "learning disabled" (according to state guidelines), those who write programs in Logo during a three-month, twice-a-week program consisting of hour-long sessions with two students at each computer using the software *Logo Projects for Independent Thinkers* will have higher scores on the Watson-Glaser Test of Critical Thinking than similar students who do not take part in this program.

This research prediction now includes "learning disabled" students as a moderator variable, and these students are operationally defined as those who fall within the classification system provided by the state guidelines.

Like all other variables, control variables benefit from operational definitions. While some control variables are easy to define operationally, others require considerable effort. For example, in the fourth hypothesis it would be important (although probably difficult) to operationally define external pressure from parents. Such an operational definition would be of crucial importance in determining the limits to generalizations arising from a study based on this hypothesis. Once such operational definitions have been stated, they can and should be inserted into the research prediction. For example:

Among children who receive a rating of 14 or less on the Parental Pressure Scale (PPS), those who are not required to learn to read until they reach the sixth grade but rather are encouraged to read whenever they wish to do so (according to the guidelines described in this report) will score about the same on standardized reading tests administered during the tenth grade as similar children who were required to start formal reading instruction in the first grade.

Readers of this prediction may not initially know what the PPS is, but they can find out by looking in the report, where the researcher should describe it in appropriate detail and make reference to citations that explain it further. These readers can judge for themselves how closely the operational definition of the children included in the study corresponds to the type of children they have in their own schools. They can use this information in deciding whether to examine the report more closely and in determining whether the results are applicable to their own schools. (This research prediction contains several terms that may seem insufficiently clear to be considered acceptable in an operational definition. For example, the typical reader would not know what a PPS is or what is meant by "whenever they wish." However, these terms are acceptable so long as they are backed up by clear descriptions in the text of the report. The relatively vague terms are merely shorthand indicators that stand for lengthier descriptions that would be too bulky to include in a simple research prediction.)

The intervening variable is the only one of the five types of research variables that is not operationally defined. This is because the research variable is by definition conceptual—that is, it is the assumed factor that can explain the observed results of a study. Although the intervening variable itself is not operationally defined, the validity of conclusions about this variable depends on the quality of the operational definitions of the other variables in the study. To the extent that these other variables are validly defined and measured and to the extent that the study has been validly conducted, it is likely that conclusions about the intervening variable will be valid.

The independent, dependent, moderator, and control variables should all be operationally defined. If possible, the operational definitions of these variables should be included in the statement of the research prediction. If the operational definitions of any of these variables are too complex to be stated succinctly in the research prediction, they should be operationally defined in greater detail in the methods section of the research report. Readers who are uncertain regarding a researcher's operational definitions should be able to find the operational definitions of all variables in the methods section of the research report.

The value of the research prediction is this: *Once such a prediction has been stated, then all the researcher has to do is find a way to determine whether the prediction is substantiated or not.* Such predictions can be tested by employing methods described later in this book—for example, by finding an appropriate research design, conducting an experiment, and performing statistical tests on the results. If this endeavor shows the results that were anticipated by the prediction, then we have supported our research hypothesis. The strength of this support depends on the strength of our operational defini-

tions and on the quality of the research design and procedures we used to test the prediction. On the other hand, if our experiment obtains results different from those anticipated by the research prediction, then we have evidence that our hypothesis was incorrect. Again, the strength of this evidence depends on the strength of our operational definitions and on the quality of the research design and procedures we used to test the prediction.

As you can see, there is a twofold advantage to having a clear statement of a research prediction. First, it enables *you as a researcher* to specify for yourself exactly what it is that you need to do to determine whether your hypothesis is correct. Once you have reached this point, you know exactly what it is that you have to find out; and you can identify strategies that will or will not test this prediction. You may still have trouble actually carrying out a given design, and in some cases you may find that it is unfeasible or impossible to test a given prediction, but with a well-stated prediction you have reached a point where you know exactly what is required to test the research hypothesis.

The second advantage to having a clear statement of a research prediction is that it enables you *as a consumer of research* to make a judgment about the relevance of the research for your own needs. By reading another person's research prediction, you can make a tentative judgment about the external validity of that person's report and make a decision regarding whether you want to pursue the matter any further. If the research prediction deals with something you are interested in, then you know that *if* the researcher has carried out the research design and other procedures appropriately, then there may be something of value to you in the research. On the other hand, if the research prediction deals with something you do not care about, then you know that no matter how high the technical quality of the research is, there is little likelihood that it is going to tell you anything that you can generalize upon for your own needs. By knowing how to locate and make intelligent use of research predictions, consumers of research can greatly increase the efficiency with which they derive useful ideas from the professional literature.

REVIEW QUIZ 4.5

1. Examine the following research prediction and identify each of the research variables requested below:

   Clients who enroll for counseling at Roberts Psychiatric Clinic and are initially diagnosed as passive-aggressive will later show more assertiveness by resisting a mock telephone solicitor with cogent reasons after treatment employing Transductive Role Modeling (TRM) than similar clients receiving the traditional treatment. However, clients at the same clinic diagnosed as passive-withdrawn will show more assertiveness after receiving the traditional method of treatment than clients receiving the TRM treatment.

   Identify the following variables:

   > Independent
   >
   > Dependent
   >
   > Moderator
   >
   > Control
   >
   > Intervening

2. Identify the operational definition of each of the research variables in Question 1.

PUTTING IT ALL TOGETHER

Eugene Anderson, our mythical humane educator, presents programs in school classrooms with the goal of helping children develop more favorable attitudes toward animal life. He recognizes that this is an affective outcome, which needs to be operationally defined—in several different ways, if possible. He therefore asks himself what evidence he would be willing to accept to indicate that this internal, affective change has taken place in the minds and hearts of the children he visits.

He draws up the following tentative list of behaviors he believes would indicate that a child has a favorable attitude toward animal life:

1. The child will talk enthusiastically about animals.
2. The child protects animals from harm.
3. The child appropriately reports stray or injured animals.
4. When others are talking about activities that are harmful to animals, the child will present arguments to help persuade these others to be kind to animals.
5. When presented with a list of statements, the child will agree with those that experts say show a respect for animal life.
6. If the child has a pet, he/she will care for it properly.
7. The child will show great interest during Mr. Anderson's presentation.
8. The child will ask Mr. Anderson to come back and talk about animals again.

Moreover, Mr. Anderson compiles a brief list of the following behaviors that would indicate an *un*favorable attitude toward animal life:

9. The child will inflict pain on animals.
10. The child will verbalize support for positions that are harmful to animal life.
11. If a child has a pet, he/she will neglect it.

Mr. Anderson reasons that children could be operationally defined as having a favorable attitude to the extent that they displayed the first set of behaviors and refrained from behaviors in the second set.

As he looks over his list, Mr. Anderson realizes that it has inadequacies. Taken alone, some items would not be very good operational definitions; but combined, they should at least provide him with better evidence than he has been receiving regarding what happens in his classrooms. In fact, he realizes that the operational definition he has implicitly been using up to this time has consisted of a combination of definitions 7 and 8. It has now occurred to him that these might be better operational definitions of "desire to escape ordinary schoolwork" than of "a favorable attitude toward animal life."

Eventually, Mr. Anderson will shorten his list and select only a few of these operational definitions as a basis for collecting data. His choice will be based largely on the empirical usefulness, or validity, of each operational definition (which will be discussed in chapter 5) and on his ability to collect the evidence suggested by each definition.

Once Mr. Anderson had his operational definitions, he was able to state his research prediction. One hypothesis that he wanted to test was this:

The Animal Life Program (ALP) will lead to improved attitudes toward animal life.

Let's examine his hypothesis with relation to each of the research variables and their operational definitions:

Independent variable: The ALP. We know almost nothing about the Animal Life Program. If Mr. Anderson were writing a report on the ALP, it would be important for him to include a detailed description of the program so that his readers could formulate an idea of how closely it resembled programs that they might have in mind; the description would also help readers replicate his study if they wished to do so.

Dependent variable: Attitudes toward animal life. This is operationally defined as the number of animals a child chooses on one or the other of the Fireman Tests (described in subsequent chapters). A second dependent variable is the number of good deeds and bad deeds that are reported to the school, the police, or the humane society. These would be operationally defined in terms of whatever criteria these agencies use. It would be helpful to clarify the operational definition of this second variable.

Control variables: These are not expressed in the hypothesis stated at the beginning of this section, but Mr. Anderson knew the study was confined to fourth, fifth, and sixth graders. It was also confined to a specific school; it would be useful in a complete report to describe this school in terms of its size, curriculum, teaching philosophies, and administrative orientation. Likewise, Mr. Anderson should specify demographic characteristics of the students (sex, race, ethnic background, etc.) and any other relevant characteristics that might influence generalizations (how many of them owned pets, etc.). Finally, he should specify the nature of the community in which the school is located.

Moderator variable: Mr. Anderson has specified no moderator variables. He could have included such variables in his design by selecting one or more of the control variables and using these as moderator variables. It would still be possible for him to do this with regard to any variable for which he has data (such as race, sex, or pet ownership), provided he has a sufficient number of subjects to subdivide them into levels for factorial analysis.

Intervening variable: Induced dissonance. Mr. Anderson felt that the ALP worked because it caused the children to feel dissatisfied with the way their present actions related to an image they had of themselves as generally good persons. The ALP treatment caused this dissonance; the dissonance caused changes in attitudes and behaviors; and one of the changes was the tendency shown on the Fireman Tests to save more animals. As we stated earlier in this chapter, intervening variables are not operationally defined.

These are the operational definitions of Mr. Anderson's research variables. He could state these in a research prediction as follows:

Among the fourth- through sixth-grade students in X school, the ALP humane education program described in this report will cause children to choose significantly more animals on the Fireman posttest than a group of similar children to whom the ALP has not been administered.

Mr. Anderson's operational definitions and research prediction are not perfect. He would continue to revise them as he conducted his research. By stating them in rough form at an early point in the project, he could use them as a guide in his selection of measurement devices and in his choice of a research design. The earliest formulation would probably be changed and refined several times as he encountered new ideas and new problems. The final product would be a guide for him in conducting the experiment, analyzing the results, and drawing conclusions. These operational definitions would also be an immense help to others in evaluating the relevance of this research to their own problems.

SUMMARY

Outcome variables are events of interest to teachers and other researchers. Many of the events we are concerned about in education involve learning and feelings, which are internal behaviors, impervious to direct observation by outsiders. Therefore, operational definitions become necessary if outside observers are going to ascertain whether learning or changes in feelings have occurred. The process of developing and using operational definitions is described in Figure 4.1.

Operational definitions are the evidence we are willing to accept as an indication that outcome variables are occurring. In some cases, the evidence is almost synonymous with the learning or the feeling under consideration; in such cases, the operational definition is very easy to devise. In other cases (especially with regard to higher-order and affective outcomes), the evidence is by no means nearly synonymous with the learning; therefore, much effort has to be made to ensure that the evidence is as solid as possible. The evidence can be made more solid by (1) ruling out contaminating factors and alternative explanations, (2) using more than one operational definition, and (3) using more than one method to measure outcome variables under consideration.

Once variables have been operationally defined, the operational definitions can be inserted into the research hypothesis. The resulting statement is referred to as the research prediction. Once the research prediction has been stated, the researcher has a specific description of what needs to be done to support or reject the hypothesis.

What Comes Next

The rest of this book will focus on ways to identify and measure research variables, design and carry out studies that test research hypotheses, analyze the results of these studies, and evaluate the authenticity and generalizability of these results.

DOING YOUR OWN RESEARCH

There are two practical implications of this chapter for doing your own research:

1. If you have identified a research problem of your own as a result of guidelines described in chapter 2, the process of operationally defining your research variables is essential. Do this as early as possible in your research study.

Figure 4.1 The process of operationally defining a variable and collecting data about it

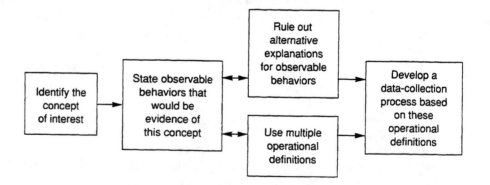

2. If you are looking for a research project to do, it is often a good idea to replicate an existing study with a new operational definition of one or more of the research variables.

When considering either of the preceding implications, it is important to remember that *multiple* operational definitions often improve the quality of a study. Thus, even if you already have a good operational definition of a research variable or if the study you are examining has good operational definitions, it may still be useful to improve the process of operationally defining the research variables more clearly.

FOR FURTHER THOUGHT

1. Educators often claim that an important goal of education is to promote higher-order thinking skills. How could a combination of conceptual and operational definitions clarify whether a given program helps students attain this goal?
2. Why does this chapter place such strong emphasis on the importance of multiple operational definitions?
3. Identify some instances from your own experience where faulty operational definitions have led to serious problems in the education process or in other social activities.

ANNOTATED BIBLIOGRAPHY

Mager, R. F. (1984). *Preparing instructional objectives* (2nd ed.). Belmont, CA: David S. Lake. This book provides a branching, programmed instruction approach to the topic of operationally defining the goals of instruction.

Martin, D. W. (1991). *Doing psychology experiments* (3rd ed.). Monterey, CA: Brooks/Cole. Chapter 4 provides good guidelines on how to select and define variables for formal research projects.

ANSWERS TO QUIZZES

Review Quiz 4.1

Part 1
1. b
2. a
3. b

Part 2
a, d, f, g, h, i

Review Quiz 4.2

(Note that these are only *sample* answers. Other answers that state definite, clearly observable behaviors are also acceptable. It is almost always scientifically worthwhile to develop multiple operational definitions and multiple measurement methodologies for defining outcome variables.)

Goal 1: Given a series of problems set up in long-division format, the children will obtain the exact answers.

Goal 2: The student driver will parallel park the practice car within a 25-foot boundary without bumping the barriers or the curb. He/she will do this within one minute. When the car is parked, it will be no more than one foot from the curb.

Goal 3: The child will refrain from engaging in the following behaviors: shouting, hitting, throwing things. (Note: If you envisioned a different sort of child, your answer could be substantially different from the one given.)

Goal 4: The students will verbalize reasons for their behavior that reflect increasingly higher levels of moral reasoning according to Kohlberg's scale of moral development. The students will stop engaging in behavior that the teacher and other objective observers label as selfish. Given hypothetical situations in which moral decisions are possible, the students will increasingly explain their decisions on the basis of a social benefit standard rather than a personal goal standard.

(This goal is highly internalized. Many operational definitions are possible. Again, in actual practice, one should use more than one operational definition and more than one method for measuring it.)

Review Quiz 4.3

Your answer should paraphrase the following sentence:

An operational definition is the observable evidence you are willing to accept to indicate that an (internal) outcome is occurring.

Review Quiz 4.4

Your answer should be yes.

Review Quiz 4.5

1. The research variables are as follows:

   Independent: type of treatment (TRM versus traditional)

   Dependent: assertiveness

   Moderator: initial diagnosis

   Control: clients

   Intervening: None is stated. A research prediction contains operationally defined variables; an intervening variable is defined in conceptual (not operational) terms, and therefore it has no place in a research prediction.

2. The operational definitions are as follows:

   Independent: Transductive Role Modeling (as opposed to the regular treatment)

   Dependent: number of cogent reasons given in resistance to the mock telephone solicitor

   Moderator: passive-aggressive versus passive-withdrawn (criteria should be further defined)

   Control: persons who enroll for counseling at the Roberts Psychiatric Clinic

   Intervening: None. An intervening variable is defined in conceptual (not operational) terms, and therefore it has no place in a research prediction.

CHAPTER 4

Research Report Analysis

The research report in Appendix C tests the hypothesis that guided use of computer simulations will cause students to develop problem-solving skills to a greater degree than either unguided use of computer simulations or the use of noncomputerized approaches to attain the same objectives. According to the present chapter, the variables in this hypothesis should be operationally defined. Try answering the following questions about the operational definitions in this study.

1. What is the operational definition of the independent variable?

2. What is the operational definition of the dependent variable?

3. What is the operational definition of the control variable?

4. What is the operational definition of the moderator variable?

5. What is the operational definition of the intervening variable?

6. What is the research prediction in this study?

ANSWERS:

1. The independent variable is the way in which students study the instructional material (guided use of simulations versus unguided use of simulations versus noncomputerized approaches to the same objectives). The simulations are operationally defined in the section of the report entitled "Treatment." The guided use of these simulations is operationally defined by the specific example and is pointed out in the commentary in

the margins. As the report indicates, the unguided use of simulations is operationally defined as the use of the same programs without the guidance.

2. The dependent variable is problem-solving ability. This is operationally defined in two ways (see the commentary in the margins). One operational definition is improved performance on successive pretests. The logic of this operational definition is pointed out where the authors argue that if students improve their problem-solving abilities they are likely to have an edge over other students on subsequent pretests. The logic of this operational definition is relatively weak; used alone, it would not be convincing. However, it becomes more convincing in light of the second operational definition of problem-solving ability, which is performance on the Watson-Glaser test.

3. The control variable is the type of students in the study. This variable is operationally defined in the section entitled "Methodology," where the authors describe the type of students involved in the study.

4. The moderator variable is gender of students. This variable is described at the end of the section entitled "Results." The authors give no operational definition. They simply assume that readers know the difference between males and females.

5. The intervening variable is reinforced practice for the effective use of thinking skills. This variable is not operationally defined. (Intervening variables are abstractions—they are never operationally defined.)

6. Among students like those in this study, both boys and girls who use the computerized materials with the guidance described in the treatment section will score higher on the Watson-Glaser test and on subsequent pretests than students who do not use these materials without the guidance. (This research prediction is not specifically stated in the research report, but it was present in the minds of the researchers to guide their efforts.)

RELIABILITY AND VALIDITY OF DATA COLLECTION PROCESSES

■ WHERE WE'VE BEEN

We've described how to identify research variables, use reference sources to obtain information about these variables, and devise operational definitions of them.

■ WHERE WE'RE GOING NOW

We're going to discuss how to make data collection processes reliable and valid—that is, how to make sure that our measurement processes do not generate evidence that is self-contradictory because of internal inconsistency or instability and make it more likely that they actually zero in on the outcome we want them to measure rather than on extraneous outcomes or no outcome at all.

■ CHAPTER PREVIEW

Once you have decided on the operational definitions of an outcome variable, you can collect data regarding the occurrence of that outcome. This chapter describes reliability and validity—two essential characteristics of all good data collection techniques.

The present chapter defines *reliability* in terms of how consistently a data collection process measures whatever it measures. This consistency concerns the level of agreement among independent tests, testing occasions, observers, or items that purport to be measuring the same outcome. The confidence we can place in judgments based on data collection processes will be greater to the extent that they are reliable. This chapter discusses ways to increase the prospect that you can make consistent decisions based on your tests and observations. We also introduce here the concept of *validity* of data collection processes—the extent to which a data collection process really measures what it is designed to measure. We will discuss the factors that influence validity of data collection processes and methods of establishing validity.

After reading this chapter, you should be able to

1. Define *reliability* and *validity*.

2. Identify examples of data collection processes with strong reliability and validity and examples with weaker reliability and validity.

3. Identify factors that contribute to the unreliability and invalidity of a data collection process.

4. Identify effective ways to increase the reliability and validity of a data collection process.

5. Identify appropriate statistical procedures for estimating the reliability of a data collection process and identify proper situations in which each of these procedures would be appropriately employed.

6. Identify the weaknesses and limitations for each of these statistical procedures for estimating the reliability of data collection processes.

7. Describe how to use the concept of reliability in selecting and improving techniques for measuring outcome variables.

8. Describe the use of the standard error of measurement in interpreting test scores.

9. Describe the process for establishing the validity of data collection processes.

10. Describe the role of evidence from content validity, criterion-related validity, and construct validity in establishing the validity of data collection processes.

■

RELIABILITY

Reliability addresses the question of whether the results of measuring processes are consistent on occasions when they should be consistent. *Consistent* means what the dictionary says it means: "not self-contradictory." If a person possesses a certain degree of knowledge about a topic, for example, the estimate of knowledge that appears as a test score should not be contradicted by other administrations of the same or similar tests. The estimate should be approximately the same whether the test is taken today or tomorrow. If different tests are given to students in the first and third period, we should be able to assume that our judgments about the person's knowledge would have been about the same on either test; and we should be free from the impression that the score would have been substantially different if someone else had graded the test. A data collection process is *less reliable* if the results are influenced by irrelevant factors that cause our judgments to fluctuate when they should not fluctuate. Measurement is *reliable* to the extent that the results are similar every time they *should* be similar.

If a mother wants to measure the body temperature of a sick child, she will expect her assessment to be reliable. If she measures his temperature once, and the temperature is 102.4, then tries again two minutes later and gets a reading of 99.9, she has an unreliable thermometer. (Of course, if she gives him medication and then takes his temperature two hours later and discovers a large drop, this would have nothing to do with unreliability. The temperature would not be expected to be similar on the second occasion, since the medicine is likely to have had an effect.)

Reliability can be applied in the same way to an instructional or research situation. If you ask a child a question and conclude on the basis of her response that she has achieved an educational outcome, you would hope that if you questioned her a few minutes later you would still come to the same conclusion. To the extent that the result is similar on repeated occasions, you are dealing with a reliable method of data collection. However, if you concluded the second time that she had *not* achieved the outcome, then you would be dealing with an *unreliable* data collection process. (If a week goes by and it is plausible that the child might have forgotten something in the intervening week, then a different result on the second occasion would have nothing to do with unreliability, any more than a reduction in temperature after a child has been cured would indicate unreliability of the thermometer.)

An important point to keep in mind is that it is the reliability of the data collection *process*—not of the data collection *instrument*—that must be demonstrated. What we are really looking for is consistency in the *decisions* we make based on the data collection process; we don't want to draw conclusions that would be likely to change if we took another estimate of the outcome variable. It is technically incorrect to refer to the reliability *of a test*. A test, a checklist, an interview schedule, or any other measurement device that is reliable in one setting or for one purpose may be unreliable in another setting or for a different purpose. Therefore, this chapter always refers to the reliability of data collection *processes*. It is important to remember this distinction.

REVIEW QUIZ 5.1

Examine each of the following descriptions and indicate whether it is reliable, is unreliable, or provides no information about reliability.

1. Ralph got a B when Mrs. Washington scored his essay test. However, he got a D when Mr. Lincoln scored the same test.

2. Both witnesses independently told the police that the suspect had been carrying a violin case when he got on the train.

3. Thelma got a C in third-grade spelling, but she got a B in fourth-grade spelling.

4. The students filled out a rating sheet on Mr. Rivers on Monday, and they rated him as an overall good instructor. On Wednesday, they filled out the same rating sheet and rated him a mediocre instructor.

5. On Tuesday, the counselor concluded that the client had a severe neurosis. On Friday, she concluded that he was probably as well adjusted as anyone else. On the next Tuesday, she concluded again that he had a severe neurosis.

6. Steve did not know much about reliability, and so when he took this review quiz he guessed wildly. The first time he got six right. He tried again, without any further studying, and this time he got three right.

7. Mr. Monroe's class had to study a list of 1,000 spelling words. The exam consisted of two 50-word tests. The average score on both tests was about 85% correct.

8. Mr. Roth's new novel was rated the number one best-seller in the *Chicago Tribune* poll, but it did not even make the list in the *Time* magazine best-seller poll.

9. Miss Mears wanted to rate the degree to which students in her classroom accepted cultural attitudes of students from other cultures. She collected data that indicated that they were more accepting than most classes. She asked the principal to make a similar rating of her classroom, and he came to the same conclusion.

If you got most of the questions in Review Quiz 5.1 correct, or if you easily saw the logic of the explanations, then you probably have a good basic grasp of the concept of reliability. If not, reread the chapter to this point, check the chapter in the workbook, refer to the recommended readings, or ask your instructor or a peer for help. Be sure that you understand the summary in the following paragraph so that you will profit from the rest of this chapter.

In summary, reliability refers to whether a data collection process is consistent. Unreliability occurs when the data collection process contradicts itself: when observations, observers, items, or alternate forms of the same test give contradictory evidence. Reliability is not an all-or-nothing characteristic; data collection processes range from strong reliability to weak reliability. Because of the highly internalized nature of educational outcomes, measurement processes in education can never be perfectly reliable. If the scores on a data collection process vary when they should not, then the test is less reliable. If a data collection process produces consistent, noncontradictory results over a span of time or in varying settings, then it is said to be reliable.

As you read the rest of this chapter, remember that *reliability is not synonymous with reliability coefficients*. The technical reliability coefficients are often irrelevant, unnecessary, or at least more trouble than they are worth in practical situations. However, a major goal of professionals in education is to achieve respect and effectiveness by engaging in scholarly activity that is authentic, public, and replicable. Decisions or statements at any level are more worthy of respect and more likely to be fruitful if they are based on sound reasoning rooted in the scientific method. A major part of the scientific method is to be public in one's methods and results and to show that they are replicable—that others can independently arrive at much the same conclusion. Establishing that our data collection processes are reliable is an important step in this process of public, scientific thinking.

SOURCES OF UNRELIABILITY

The best way to increase the reliability of our measuring instruments is to determine what causes unreliability and then to make sure that these causes of inconsistency are not present in the data collection strategies we employ. The following paragraphs summarize the major sources of unreliability.

1. *Faulty items and observations.* Questions on a test, items on a checklist, or statements on a questionnaire or interview schedule can be ambiguous, tricky, or presented in a confusing format. When people are presented with such faulty items, it is hard for them to respond consistently. If the respondents do not know what they are expected to do, it will be hard for them to respond reliably.

2. *Excessively difficult elements of the data collection process.* This factor is a problem primarily with tests designed to measure students' knowledge or learning. If a test is too difficult, the test taker is likely to guess at the answers, and the result will be problems similar to those described in the previous paragraph. Some types of test items promote guessing on difficult items more readily than other types. For example, if a true–false item is too difficult, the student still has a 50–50 chance of getting it right; whereas on a short-answer test the probability of guessing correctly is considerably smaller.

3. *Excessively easy elements of the data collection process.* This is another factor that presents problems on tests designed to measure students' knowledge or learning. If we ask you a question that is extraordinarily simple for you to answer, we may learn nothing about what you really know. This is especially true if the correct answer is obtained from extraneous clues that are unrelated to the learning task. Asking an excessively easy question is like asking no question at all. This becomes a problem of reliability if we are asking a student several questions on a test and plan to combine the responses to get a total score. If we ask you 10 questions, and 9 of them are absurdly easy, then we are really basing our decision about you on the single good question that was not excessively easy. We might *think* we have a 10-item test, but it is really a 1-item test camouflaged by 9 non-items. The problem of length is discussed in the next paragraph. The point here is that excessively easy items contribute nothing to increasing the sample of consistent items included on our instrument. The same effect occurs with attitude questionnaires. If you ask everyone in your class to fill out a 10-item agree–disagree questionnaire, and if 9 of them are written in such a way that practically everyone is guaranteed to answer "strongly agree," then you really have a 1-item questionnaire.

4. *Inadequate number of observations or items.* A general rule about reliability is that the shorter the measuring instrument or the smaller the number of observations, the greater the opportunity for chance factors to operate, and the more likely that unreliability will be present.

5. *Accidentally focusing on multiple outcomes.* If all the items on a test or all the aspects of a data collection process focus on pretty much the same characteristic, then the reliability of the data collection process will likely be high; whereas if the items or observations focus on several different characteristics, the reliability will be lower. In fact, when the data collection process focuses on several different characteristics, you really have a large number of very short data collection processes (each of which are therefore likely to be inconsistent) rather than a single longer data collection process. The point is this: if you are going to combine scores or observations to obtain a measure of a single characteristic (such as English-speaking ability, test anxiety, or attitude toward cooperative learning), then you should

be certain that all the items are actually measuring much the same thing.

6. *Characteristics of the respondents.* Reliability is reduced by any temporary characteristic of the respondents that causes them to respond or act differently than they would have responded under normal conditions. Such characteristics include inability to concentrate at a given time because of surround-ing conditions, fluctuations in mood, and inconsis-tent recall of information.

7. *Faulty administration of the data collection process.* The way a data collection process is admin-istered can render the results inconsistent. If a test is given in a room that is extremely hot or full of dis-tractions, the results may be affected. If the teacher gives one set of instructions to one class and a differ-

ent set to another class, performance may be inconsistent and class comparisons will be based on less reliable test scores. In addition, the mannerisms, idiosyncrasies, and other characteristics of the person administering the instrument or conducting observations can influence reliability.

8. *Faulty scoring procedures.* After the students or respondents have done their share of responding, inconsistency can still creep in when the scorer tries to assign values to the respondents' performance. The scorer could simply record information inaccurately or count the number of right answers incorrectly. If the answer sheet was at all ambiguous, it might be hard to determine what the respondent actually meant. Extended-answer essay tests are particularly notorious for the inconsistency with which they are graded. Research has shown that it is possible for one grader to give an essay an A, while another might give the same paper an F. Furthermore, even after the instrument has been accurately scored, it is still possible to introduce inconsistency through faulty record keeping.

HOW TO INCREASE RELIABILITY

The reliability of educational measurement can never be perfect. However, it can be improved by designing and administering data collection processes carefully. The way to increase reliability is to minimize the sources of unreliability cited in the previous section. There are statistical procedures for determining coefficients of reliability, and one of the ambitions of professional test constructors is to get this coefficient to be high. The use of these coefficients will be discussed in the next section of this chapter. At this point, let us say that it is possible (and important) to take steps to improve reliability (and to verify that others have done so) even if you never intend to compute a reliability coefficient outside an assignment for a college course. The following are specific guidelines for improving the reliability of measuring instruments:

1. *Use technically correct, unambiguous items.* Make sure that the respondents are able to give the answers they really want to give. There are excellent

textbooks available on educational and psychological measurement that offer specific guidelines on how to write technically correct items in various formats and for various content areas and how to develop effective observational systems. Teachers frequently collect data with instruments they have not even proofread properly, and such laxity is likely to lead to unreliability. A simple procedure for improving the technical quality of a data collection process is to have someone else look it over or take the test before the target audience actually sees it.

2. *Standardize the administration procedures.* Collect the data in such a way as to promote consistency. Eliminate distractions. Don't make your personality a part of the data collection process. If more than one person will collect data, make sure they are using precisely the same set of instructions. The key point is to make it as likely as possible that each person administering the data collection procedure will make the same decisions when these decisions can influence the way an outcome will be recorded. This standardization is accomplished by writing the interview schedule or observation checklist as clearly as possible (covering as many as possible of the responses and behaviors that are likely to arise) and training the interviewers or observers carefully before they go into the field. (Strategies for standardizing interviews and observations are discussed in chapter 6.)

3. *Standardize the scoring procedures.* Develop systematic strategies for consistency during the scoring process. This is easy with objectively scored instruments like true–false and multiple-choice tests, simple checklists, and Likert questionnaires. It becomes more difficult with extended-length essays, open-ended interviews, and unstructured observations. The idea here is that you want to allow the respondent to make as much of the decision as possible regarding what response will be recorded. Otherwise, you will have two sources of inconsistency—yours and the respondent's. When you do have to make decisions about how to record a response, make your decisions according to as structured a format as possible. An excellent way to get evidence that your scoring format is sufficiently structured and reliable is to let someone else indepen-

dently examine the respondent's answers using the same scoring format and see if that person arrives at the same decisions about the outcome as you did.

4. *Be alert for respondent irregularities.* Do not give tests or make observations when respondents or classrooms are in atypical moods or conditions. If everyone in a class is giggling, if someone is extremely anxious, if half the group is sick—such temporary characteristics will get you an unrepresentative (and inconsistent) sample of the respondents' performance.

5. *Make the data collection process comprehensive enough to include a good sample of behaviors.* The difficulties presented by a short (e.g., one-item) test were discussed in the previous section. Overcome these difficulties by making sure you include enough items or observations so that you are confident that you are measuring a stable performance, not a chance result. Be sure to include a good sample of items or observations for every separate outcome you are trying to measure.

6. *Be certain that each item or aspect of the data collection process focuses on the same outcome or set of outcomes.* As we discussed in the previous section, if you have a 10-item test that measures 10 separate outcomes, then you really have 10 separate 1-item tests. Consequently, any decision you make based on any one of these "subtests" is likely to be unreliable; and a decision based on the whole test is both unreliable and meaningless. If you have several distinct outcomes to test, develop appropriate data collection procedures of sufficient length and reliability for each. For each measurement procedure your goal should be to make each item measure the same outcome.

7. *Construct items of an appropriate level of difficulty.* When measuring knowledge or learning, be sure you are measuring what the respondents actually know and not their luck at guessing answers or figuring out what your question really means. Also remember that excessively easy items often add nothing meaningful to the length of the test. When measuring feelings or attitudes, make sure that difficult reading level does not make it more difficult for the participants to respond.

REVIEW QUIZ 5.2

Write R next to each sentence that describes a factor contributing to the reliability of the measuring technique. Write U next to each sentence that describes a source of unreliability.

1 ____ Mrs. Stallings decides to base the spelling grades on a 100-item test rather than her previous 10-item testing pattern.

2 ____ Mr. Carol is proud of his 10-item English test, because it contains 5 "mind benders" that nobody got right.

3 ____ Miss Harmon gives a 50-item test every two weeks. Previously she has tried to base her tests on a common set of objectives, but now she has decided to save time by testing on five distinctly different sets of objectives on each 50-item test.

4 ____ Mrs. Rogers has decided to see if Curt is creative by giving him a highly imaginative problem and asking him to solve it.

5 ____ Mr. Peters considers each of the 10 subscales on a 100-item standardized test to be more useful than the entire test, and so he bases his decisions entirely on these subscales.

6 ____ Miss Adams planned to give a test on Friday, but she postponed it when she heard that the biggest pep rally of the year would occur during the period immediately after her class.

7 ____ Mrs. Wolf likes to promote informality with her students, because she believes that this makes them work to the best of their ability. Therefore, she sets aside the instructions accompanying the standardized test and instead gives the directions in her own words, which she thinks are more understandable to her students.

8 ____ There is a wide range of mastery of skills in Mrs. Johnson's Spanish class. On the test, most of the items are answered correctly by 40–70% of the students.

If you missed several of these items, refer back to the appropriate sections of this chapter for clarification.

It is important to understand this information before proceeding. If you are a true skeptic, you might by now realize that this quiz may itself be unreliable. If that worries you, try the appropriate exercises in the workbook. A longer test will enable you to make a more reliable (consistent) judgment regarding your knowledge of this material.

STATISTICAL PROCEDURES FOR ESTIMATING RELIABILITY

Reliability coefficients are statistical procedures for estimating how consistent a data collection process is. These are important tools. Even if you do not feel a particular urge to compute these statistics, you should still be concerned about the reliability of your data collection techniques. These procedures are described here because they are relatively easy to understand and can be helpful to you. In addition, you will often want to administer professionally prepared data collection procedures, interpret the results of such procedures, or read about them in the published literature. Understanding the meaning of these statistical procedures can be extremely helpful for these purposes.

The following are the basic types of statistical reliability coefficients:

1. *Test-retest reliability (stability)*. The purpose of test-retest reliability is to estimate the likelihood that the results of the data collection process would have been the same if it had been administered on a different occasion. In other words, it helps us determine whether the measurement of the characteristic is likely to be *stable*. To compute this reliability coefficient, you would administer your data collection procedure, let some time pass, and then administer the same procedure a second time to the same people. Then you would compute a correlation coefficient between the two sets of scores.[1] A high correlation coefficient (near 1.00) indicates that respondents performed comparably on both tests,

whereas a low coefficient (near .00) indicates that their performance was inconsistent.

A frequent misapplication of this concept of reliability is to give a pretest, then offer instruction to the students, then give them a posttest after the instruction, and finally compute a correlation coefficient. Actually, this coefficient has little to do with reliability—the two sets of scores would be subject to change because of the intervening instruction. If instruction has been successful, there is no reason why a person's score on the posttest should be at the same level as the pretest score.

2. *Equivalent-forms reliability (consistency among data collection procedures)*. The purpose of equivalent-forms reliability is to provide evidence that the results of a data collection process would have been similar if the results were obtained with a variant form of the data collection procedure. This form of reliability is useful when it is necessary to make comparisons or common judgments about people even though they could not be measured by exactly the same procedure. For example, if there are six forms of the SAT, it is important to know that a score of 1,100 by a student taking form A has the same meaning as a score of 1,100 by a student taking form B. To compute this form of statistical reliability, you would administer one form of the test to a group and then administer a different form of the same test to the same group. A high correlation between the two sets of scores would indicate that the respondents performed comparably on both tests; and this would mean that the two forms are essentially equivalent—that they consistently measure the same outcome.

This form of reliability is especially useful when you need to determine the effectiveness of instruction by using one form of a test as a pretest and the other as a posttest. If you have a reliable test (that is, if the pretest and posttest data collection strategies are essentially equivalent), you can more logically attribute any improvements in performance to the intervening situation; whereas if the test is unreliable, then the improvements (or absence of improvements) could be the result of chance fluctuations resulting from the inconsistency of the test.

---

[1]Correlation coefficients are discussed in chapter 13.

3. *Test-retest with equivalent-forms reliability.* The purpose of this form of reliability is to provide evidence that the results of a data collection process would have been similar if they were obtained both on a different occasion and with a variant form of the data collection procedure. To compute this coefficient, you would administer one form of the test, let some time pass, and then administer the other form of the test to the same group of people. A resulting high correlation coefficient would indicate that there is a stable characteristic of some sort that both forms of the test are measuring. (This coefficient is a combination of the first two types.)

4. *Internal consistency reliability.* The purpose of internal consistency reliability is to provide an estimate of the degree to which the items or elements that constitute a data collection process measure a single outcome rather than several diverse outcomes. The term *internal consistency* refers to the degree that all the elements or aspects composing the data collection process appear to be measuring the same thing. Internal consistency is expressed by coefficients arising from mathematical formulas that correlate scores on different items or separate parts of a data collection procedure with other items or parts of the same procedure. Unlike the other types of statistical reliability, internal consistency can be calculated from the administration of a single data collection process to a single group of people. The following are three common statistical estimates of internal consistency:

Coefficient alpha is the internal consistency reliability coefficient that can be used with the widest variety of data collection procedures.

The *Kuder-Richardson* reliability coefficient is used with measurement procedures (such as test items) that can be scored on a right–wrong or yes—no basis. (It is a special case of coefficient alpha.)

The *split-half* reliability coefficient can be computed for tests by splitting the test in half and comparing the students' performance on each half of the test. (It is now considered to be obsolete, having been superseded by coefficient alpha.)

The main value of the split-half procedure is that it can easily be computed by hand; but it is not as precise as the others, and computers have rendered it obsolete. The Kuder-Richardson coefficient is a better estimate of internal consistency than the split-half procedure, and it is frequently reported with computerized scoring packages for objectively scored tests. Since it is applicable to every situation in which the other two can be used and to other situations as well, coefficient alpha is clearly the most important indicator of internal consistency.

Internal consistency reliability sets the upper limit for the other statistics that measure relationships among variables (including the other reliability coefficients). The statistical logic to support this statement will not be presented in this book. In practical terms, this means that it is a good strategy to use internal consistency as a *starting point* for developing reliable data collection procedures. If you develop solid, internally consistent procedures and then do other things right, you will be able to conduct reliable measurements of outcome variables. If you fail to develop internally consistent procedures, then it is unlikely that your attempts to measure outcome variables will be reliable.

5. *Interscorer reliability.* The purpose of this procedure is to rule out the possibility that unreliability has been introduced by the person recording the results of a data collection process. In other words, it provides evidence that the scores would have been similar, regardless of who calculated the results of the data collection process. In using this procedure, you would have two different persons score the same set of tests (or make the same set of observations or conduct the same set of interviews), and then you would compare the two sets of results. A high correlation coefficient between the two sets of scores would indicate that both persons were interpreting the data collection process similarly. A low coefficient would indicate that differences among the scores of the persons being measured might be the result of the way the data collection procedure was scored rather than the result of real differences

among the respondents. (Some Olympics events are scored by ratings of observing judges. When spectators and critics charge that these events are inconsistently judged, this is actually a statement about poor interscorer reliability among the observers.)

With many educational tests, interscorer reliability is irrelevant. This is particularly true of "objective tests," which would be described more specifically as "objectively scored tests." There is little chance that two scorings by a machine will differ significantly in giving the results of a multiple-choice test. With more subjective data collection processes, such as essay tests and ratings of personality characteristics or classroom social climate, an evaluation of the consistency of the scoring process is much more important.

Like internal consistency, interscorer reliability sets an upper limit on the other types of reliability and on correlations with other variables. That is, if there is unreliability in the scoring process, these other types of reliability will be lower than if the scoring process were perfectly reliable. This is because the scoring process provides chances for error and disagreement *in addition to* whatever inconsistencies are inherent in the respondent's actual performance during the data collection process. This means, for example, that if the test-retest reliability of a data collection procedure is low and if its interscorer reliability is also low, the test-retest reliability can be increased by improving the interscorer reliability. This would occur because a major source of error would be removed on both testing occasions.

6. Interobserver agreement. The purpose of this procedure is to verify that different observers can agree that an event has or has not occurred. This estimate of reliability differs from the others in that it is stated as a percentage rather than as a correlation coefficient. It is used when a rater is trying to observe a person or a group; it is also used to determine whether a behavior or a set of social conditions is occurring. The interobserver reliability is determined by having a second person simultaneously make the same set of observations. After this has been done on a certain number of occasions, a percentage is calculated to determine how often the two raters agreed. For example, a teacher might be concerned about the disruptive behavior of a kindergarten child. *Disruptive behavior* might be operationally defined as "being out of one's seat when children are supposed to be in their seats." It should be relatively easy to ascertain whether a child is or is not seated; but in actual practice it may be difficult to discern when children "should" be in their seats or when a child has actually left his seat at the wrong time. To establish reliability, the teacher could have two observers independently but simultaneously observe the child and record how often he is out of his seat. They might each watch the child for 10-second intervals and mark him as being in-seat or out-of-seat during each interval. Afterwards, they would compute their percentage of agreement. If they watched the child for 50 intervals and agreed on 40 of these, then their interobserver reliability would be 80%. Upon examining their data more closely, the raters might discover that 8 out of their 10 disagreements occurred when the student was out of his seat but still in the vicinity of his desk, as when reaching down below for something. By agreeing on whether this was in-seat or out-of-seat behavior and writing this into the guidelines for administering the observation instrument, the interobserver agreement could become much higher on subsequent administrations.

Interobserver agreement is used only when a yes/no decision is made regarding the occurrence or nonoccurrence of an event. When the observer makes a rating, interscorer agreement (which was discussed earlier in this section) is the appropriate estimate of reliability. Interobserver reliability is very important in situations (such as behavior modification programs) where the test consists of observing a child to determine whether he is performing some predefined behavior.

In a very real sense, you may not *need* any reliability coefficient. What you need is the *concept* of reliability, because you want your measurements, observations, and interviews to be consistent. A coefficient is merely a tool to help estimate consistency. The question, therefore, is what kind of statistical reliability is going to be helpful to you in determining whether your measuring instruments are consis-

Table 5.1 Statistical Methods of Estimating Reliability

	Purpose	Procedure	Statistic
Test-retest reliability	To ensure stability; to rule out the possibility that results fluctuate widely on different administrations of same instrument to same people	Administer the same test twice to the same group with a time interval in between; then compute the correlation	Correlation coefficient
Equivalent-forms reliability	To ensure that two forms of a test are actually equivalent	Administer two forms of the same test to the same group in close succession; then compute correlation	Correlation coefficient
Test-retest with equivalent forms	To ensure both stability and equivalence (combines first two methods)	Administer one form; let time pass; administer second form; compute correlation	Correlation coefficient
Internal consistency reliability	To determine the extent to which the items on a test are measuring a common characteristic (to ensure internal consistency)	Administer test only once; apply formula to results	Coefficient alpha
Interscorer reliability	To determine the extent to which the results are objective; i.e., will be the same no matter who scores the test	Administer the test once; have two different persons score the test; compute correlation between the two sets of scores	Correlation coefficient
Interobserver agreement	To determine the extent to which different observers can agree whether an outcome is occurring	Have two observers watch for the occurrence of an event during a designated number of intervals; compute the percentage of intervals during which they agree	Percentage of agreement

tent. The preceding descriptions (summarized in Table 5.1) should help you make decisions regarding whether a statistical procedure may be helpful to you and to interpret these statistics when other researchers report them.

REVIEW QUIZ 5.3

Identify the type of statistical reliability that would be helpful in determining whether the stated data collection technique is consistent.

1. Mr. Perkins had decided to help Jamahl control his aggressive behavior. He has defined *aggressive behavior* as any attempt to inflict physical harm on another person. He plans to count how often such attempts occur during an hour-long period each day for two weeks.

2. Ms. Wilkes is going to give her music students a test of tonal discrimination. She doesn't want to waste her time with a test that will give one result today and a different result next week.

3. Mrs. Johns is a vocational education supervisor. She has developed a rating scale to determine how ready each student is to take a full-time job in an out-of-school situation. She plans to have each of the teachers use this instrument to rate their students, and she expects that the scores will reflect the students' capabilities, not the eccentricities of the teachers.

4. Mr. Byrd teaches Freshman composition. He has developed an end-of-the-year test that he claims gives a good indication of an overall skill he labels "proficiency in the basics." Students are required to get a score of at least 80 on this test before they can take more advanced courses.

5. Miss Gordon wants to find out whether her new method of teaching speed reading works. She wants to give one test of speed and comprehension at the beginning of her course and another at the end. She hopes to be able to determine that speed will increase while comprehension stays about the same.

STANDARD ERROR OF MEASUREMENT

While correlation coefficients give good estimates of the reliability of data collection processes, they are not directly useful for communicating information about the degree to which a specific score is likely to be accurate. The standard error of measurement is a statistic that is based on reliability coefficients and gives information about the relative accuracy of individual scores. The standard error of measurement indicates the range within which the "true" score of the individual is likely to fall—taking into consideration the unreliability of the test. For example, if a student received a score of 85 on a test with a standard error of measurement of 4.0, then her true score would probably range somewhere between 81.0 and 89.0. If the standard error of the test were 7.0, then this student's true score would probably lie in the range of 78.0 to 92.0. (The word *probably* in the previous two sentences means that the statistical formula gives about a 68% probability that the true score falls in the designated range.) Since the standard error of measurement is based on the reliability of the data collection process, higher test reliability leads to a smaller standard error of measurement—that is, to a more narrow range of scores within which the true score would be likely to fall.

The standard error of measurement has considerable practical importance. Within the context of the preceding paragraph, it is reasonable to think of the standard error of measurement as an estimate of the "likely error" of a data collection process. For example, if a person scores 115 one year on an IQ test that has a standard error of measurement of 5 and then scores 112 on a parallel form of the test the next year, we would assume that this probably represents a normal fluctuation of scores rather than an actual deterioration in performance. The standard error of measurement is closely related to the concept of standard deviations (discussed in chapter 7) and to the concept of confidence intervals (discussed in chapter 8). A major advantage of standardized tests (discussed in chapter 6) is that their test manuals almost always include information on the standard error of measurement.

HOW RELIABLE DOES A DATA COLLECTION PROCESS HAVE TO BE?

It is an axiom that no data collection process in education can ever be perfectly reliable. Whether you use statistical procedures or not, it is obvious that some data collection processes are more reliable than others. The reliability of almost any given data collection process could be improved, if you worked a little harder or added more items or observations. How reliable is reliable enough? The answer is that the necessary degree of reliability depends on what you plan to do with the results of your data collection.

If you are giving a weekly arithmetic test, and you happen to make an inaccurate decision based on it, this is probably not a serious problem. If you give a child credit for mastering a topic and you discover a day later that she has not mastered it after all, then you can simply change your decision and offer her some additional instruction. Although you would not want to make frivolous decisions even in such cases, it is obvious that you could settle for a more unreliable instrument than you would require if you were deciding whether that same student should embark upon a college preparatory curriculum in mathematics. Therefore, the first answer to your question is that the data collection process needs to be more reliable to the extent that the decisions based on it are likely to be permanent or irreversible.

A second, closely related factor is whether the results of the data collection process will be the only source of information in making a decision or whether they will be supplemented by other sources of data. In chapter 4 we recommended multiple operational definitions of outcome variables and multiple methods to measure these outcomes. To the extent that a data collection process is effectively supplemented by other sources of information, lower reliability is tolerable. The inconsistencies and imprecision in one set of data will be counterbalanced by information from other sources.

The point is this: The more confidence you want to be able to place in the score an individual attains, the greater the reliability you should require from your instrument.

The situation is somewhat different when you are examining *group* accomplishments rather than diagnosing the performance of an individual. The factors that lead to unreliability (inconsistency) on a data collection process are often essentially random, and they tend to average out over the long run. In other words, if one student improves his score by guessing accurately on a test, it is probable that someone else's score has been hurt to a similar proportion by poor guessing on the same test. Therefore, a chance factor like guessing is likely to contribute less to inconsistency when group evaluations rather than individual evaluations are being considered. For this reason, substantially lower reliabilities are acceptable for comparing group scores than for comparing individual scores. In addition, note that when statistical comparisons are made among groups (see chapter 14), the statistical estimates of reliability will be accounted for in the computation of the statistical comparison.

Although it would often be absurd to evaluate an individual's performance in a history course based on her answer to a small set of questions, it would nevertheless make sense to evaluate the performance of a group based on the group's answer to that same set of questions. (Of course, it is still relevant to ascertain that the questions properly sample the topics covered in the history course; see the discussion of content validity later in this chapter.) In fact, this is exactly what the highly reputable National Assessment of Educational Progress (NAEP) is attempting. The NAEP is asking several questions to carefully selected groups of students in schools throughout the United States. On the basis of NAEP results, it would be possible to conclude something like, "In 1980, only 70% of fifth graders knew who Christopher Columbus was, whereas in 1990, 95% of fifth graders knew who he was." On the other hand, it would not be appropriate to use one child's

answer to that same question to draw reliable conclusions about his knowledge of history.

Finally, one must consider how high reliabilities should be for commercially prepared tests. If we're paying the pros to come up with good tests, shouldn't we expect the tests to be highly reliable? Here again, it depends on what kind of test you're looking for. Commercially available intelligence tests often report reliabilities of .90 or higher. On the other hand, some personality tests used for group research report reliabilities of only .60. The general strategy is to determine what you want to use the test for, and then to look for information regarding the specific type of reliability needed to achieve that goal. (For example, look for equivalent-forms reliability, not just internal consistency, if you are interested in using one form for a pretest and another for a posttest.) It's a good idea to look in a source like *The Eleventh Mental Measurements Yearbook* (Kramer & Conoley, 1992) to find out what levels of reliability are available for tests of the sort you're looking for. If there are five tests of the same sort, and four of them report reliabilities of .85 or better, then the fifth one with a coefficient of .60 is substantially less reliable.

VALIDITY OF DATA COLLECTION PROCESSES

Validity of data collection addresses the question of *whether a data collection process is really measuring what it purports to be measuring.* A data collection process is valid to the extent that the results are actually a measurement of the characteristic the process was designed to measure, free from the influence of extraneous factors. *Validity is the most important characteristic of a data collection process.*

A data collection process is *invalid* to the extent that the results have been influenced by irrelevant characteristics rather than by the factors the process was intended to measure. For example, if a teacher gives a reading test and the test does not really measure reading performance, the test is useless. There is no logical way that the invalid test can help the teacher measure the outcome in which she is interested. If she gives a self-concept test that is so difficult to read that the third graders taking it are unable to interpret it correctly, the test cannot validly measure self-concept among those students. It is invalid for that purpose, because it is so heavily influenced by reading skills that self-concept is not likely to come to the surface. This test cannot help the teachers make decisions about the outcome variable "self-concept." For example, if they ran a self-concept program for their students and their students' "self-concept" scores improved, how could they know whether it was really self-concept and not just reading ability that improved? In designing and carrying out any sort of data collection process, therefore, validity is of paramount importance.

As we said with regard to reliability, it is important to keep in mind that it is the validity of the data collection *process*—not of the data collection *instrument*—that must be demonstrated. What we really want to do is strengthen the validity of the *conclusions* we draw based on the data collection process; we don't want to draw conclusions based on the measurement of the wrong outcomes. It is technically incorrect to refer to the validity *of a test*. A test, a checklist, an interview schedule, or any other data collection device that is valid in one setting or for one purpose may be invalid in another or for another purpose. Therefore, this chapter always refers to the validity of data collection *processes*. It is important to remember this distinction.

A CONTINUOUSLY INVALID TEST

A TEST THAT MAY BE INVALID IN A MORE SUBTLE WAY

SOURCES OF INVALIDITY

What makes a data collection process valid or invalid? A data collection process is valid to the extent that it meets the triple criteria of (1) employing a logically appropriate operational definition, (2) matching the items to the operational definition, and (3) possessing a reasonable degree of reliability. Invalidity enters the picture when the data collection strategy fails seriously with regard to one of these criteria or fails to lesser degrees in a combination of these criteria.

It may be instructive to look at some examples of invalid data collection processes. Assume that a researcher wants to develop an intelligence test. He operationally defines *intelligence* as follows: "A person is intelligent to the extent that he/she agrees with me." He then makes up a list of 100 of his opinions and has people indicate whether they agree or disagree with each item on this list. A person agreeing with 95 of the items would be defined as being more intelligent than one who agreed with 90, and so on. This is an invalid measure of intelligence, because the operational definition has nothing to do with intelligence as any reputable theorist has ever defined it.

Not all invalid data collection processes are so blatantly invalid. For example, one of the most heated arguments in psychology today is over the question of what intelligence tests actually measure. This whole question is one of validity. The advocates of many IQ tests argue that intelligence can be defined as general problem-solving ability. They operationally define *intelligence* as something like, "People are intelligent to the extent that they can solve new problems presented to them." They test for intelligence by giving a child a series of problems and counting how many she can solve. A child who can solve a large number of problems is more intelligent than one who can solve only a few. The opponents of such tests argue that the tests are invalid. They say that general problem-solving ability is not the only quality—or even the most important one—required to do well on such tests. The tests, they argue, really measure how well a person has adapted to a specific middle-class culture. Success on such tests, therefore, is really an operational definition of "ability to adapt to middle-class culture." Since the

test is *designed* to measure intelligence but really measures a different ability, it is invalid. The argument over the validity of IQ tests is far from settled. Important theorists continue to line up on both sides, and others continue to suggest compromises— such as recommending new tests or redefining the concept of intelligence.

Consider another hypothetical intelligence test. Assume that we ask the child *one* question directly related to a valid operational definition. This is an excessively short test, and thus it is likely to provide an unreliable estimate of intelligence. Our result is also likely to be invalid, because our conclusion that a child is a genius for answering 100% of the questions correctly is about as likely to be a result of chance factors (unreliability) as it is to be a result of real ability related to the concept of intelligence[2].

The factors that determine the validity of a data collection process are diagrammed in Figure 5.1. The first test cited in this section was invalid because the operational definition was inappropriate. In the second case, the operational definition was logically appropriate, but it was not clear whether the tasks the child performed were really related to this operational definition. The final IQ test was considerably limited in its validity because the test was unreliable.

ESTABLISHING VALIDITY

From the preceding discussion, it can be seen that there are three steps to establishing the validity of a data collection process designed to measure an outcome variable:

1. *Demonstrate that the operational definition upon which the data collection process is based is actually a logically appropriate operational definition of the outcome variable under consideration. The*

---

[2]Since reliability can be defined mathematically, its relationship to validity can be defined by a formula:

$$v_{11} = \sqrt{r_{11}\, r_{22}}$$

This means that the correlations between two data collection processes—one definition of validity—can never be higher than the square root of the product of the reliabilities of the two data collection processes.

Figure 5.1 Factors
Leading to Test Validity
or Invalidity

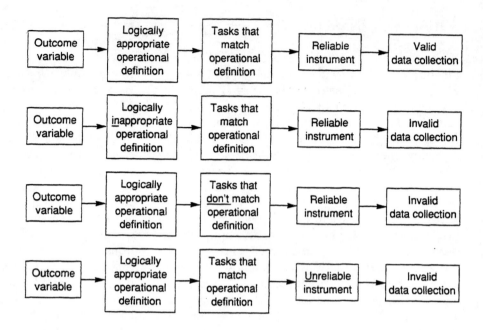

strategy for demonstrating logical appropriateness was discussed in detail in chapter 4, where we pointed out that operational definitions are not actually synonymous with the outcome variable but rather represent the *evidence* that we are willing to accept to indicate that an internal behavior is occurring. Table 5.2 lists some cases where the operational definitions are to varying degrees logically inappropriate. For example, if the instructors in English 101 administer an anonymous questionnaire at the end of the semester to evaluate their performance in the course, they might *think* that the students are responding to questions about how they performed during the course. However, it's possible that the students who are completing the questionnaire are thinking, "If we tell them what we really think, they'll be upset and come down hard on us when they grade the exam. I think we should play it safe and give them good ratings for the course." If this is what students are thinking, then the favorable comments on the questionnaire are actually an operational definition of "anxiety over alienating instructor" rather than of "quality teaching."

In many cases, the logical connection is easy to establish, and hence the logical fallacies found in Table 5.2 are often easy to avoid. For example, the connection between the operational definitions and the outcome variables in Table 5.3 are much more obvious than the connections in Table 5.2. It's still possible for a person to perform behaviors described in the operational definitions without having achieved the outcome variable, but it is much less likely than was the case in the situations in Table 5.2.

Logical inappropriateness is most likely to occur when the outcome variable under consideration is a highly internalized one. Affective outcomes present particularly difficult problems, because the evidence is much less directly connected to the internal outcome than is the case with behavioral, psychomotor, and cognitive outcomes. The guidelines presented in chapter 4 are applicable here—namely, rule out as many alternative explanations as possible, and use more than one operational definition.

2. *Demonstrate that the tasks the respondent has to perform to generate a score during the data collec-*

Table 5.2   Some Examples of Logically Inappropriate Operational Definitions of Outcome Variables

Assumed Outcome Variable	Operational Definition	Conceivable Real Outcome Variable
Ability to understand reading passages	The pupil paraphrases a passage he/she has read silently	Ability to guess from context clues
Love of Shakespearean drama	The student will carry a copy of Shakespeare's plays with him to class	Eagerness to impress professor
Appreciation of English 101	The student will indicate on a questionnaire that she liked the course	Anxiety over alienating instructor
Knowledge of driving laws	The candidate will get at least 17 out of 20 true-false questions right on license test	Ability to take true–false tests with subtle clues present in them
Friendliness toward peers	The pupil will stand near other children on the playground	Anxiety over being beaten up if he or she stands alone
Appreciation of American heritage	Child will voluntarily attend the Fourth of July picnic given by the American Legion	Appreciation of watching fireworks explode

Table 5.3   Some Examples of Operational Definitions That Are Almost Certain to Be Appropriate for the Designated Outcome Variables

Ability to add single-digit integers	The student will add single-digit integers presented to him ten at a time on a test sheet
Ability to tie one's own shoes	The student will tie her own shoes after they have been presented to her untied
Ability to bench press 150 pounds	The student will bench press 150 pounds
Ability to spell correctly from memory	The student will write down from memory the correct spelling of each word from dictation
Ability to spell correctly on essays with use of dictionary	The student will make no more than two spelling errors in a 200-word essay written during class with the aid of a dictionary
Ability to type 60 words per minute	The student will type a 300-word passage in five minutes or less
Ability to raise hand before talking in class	The student will raise his hand before talking in class.
Ability to recall the quadratic equation	The student will write from memory the quadratic equation
Ability to apply the quadratic equation	Given the quadratic equation and ten problems that can be solved using the equation, the student will solve at least nine

tion process match the task suggested by the operational definition. The benefits of stating operational definitions can be completely nullified if the tasks that generate a score during the data collection process do not match the tasks stated in the operational definitions.

Table 5.4 provides examples of such mismatches. The first three are not intended to be facetious. Mismatches this obvious actually do occur on teacher-designed tests. They *say* they are going to measure one thing, and then they measure something else. The other examples in Table 5.4 are more subtle. In these cases, the teacher has one behavior in mind; and in fact, many of the persons responding to the data collection process will perform the behavior anticipated by the teacher. But the mismatch occurs whenever a respondent performs the different or additional tasks indicated in the second column of the table.

When questions arise concerning various sorts of bias in the data collection process, it is often the mismatch between task and operational definition that is being challenged. For example, with regard to bias in IQ tests, one of the most common arguments is essentially that middle-class youngsters who take the test are actually performing behaviors related to the operational definition, whereas equally intelligent lower-class youngsters are taking a test where there is a discrepancy between what they are doing and the operational definition of *intelligence.*

It is important to be aware of the various kinds of bias and other contaminating factors that could cause discrepancies, and to carefully rule these out. Such sources of mismatching include cultural bias, test-wiseness, reading ability, writing ability, ability to put oneself in a hypothetical framework, tendency to guess, and social responsibility bias. The preceding list is not to be considered exhaustive. There are

Table 5.4 Some Examples of a Mismatch Between the Operational Definition and the Task the Respondent Has to Perform on the Instrument

Operational Definition	Task on Instrument
The student will add single-digit integers presented to him ten at a time on a test sheet	"If I have three apples and you give me two more apples, how many do I have?"
The student will solve problems using the quadratic equation	"Explain the derivation of the quadratic equation."
The student will use prepositions correctly in her essays	"Write the definition of a preposition."
The student will apply the principles of operant conditioning to hypothetical situations	The student first has to unscramble a complex multiple-choice thought pattern and then apply the principles
Given a (culturally familiar) novel problem to solve, the test taker will be able to solve the problem	The student is presented with a problem entirely foreign to his cultural background
The student will describe the relationship between nuclear energy and atmospheric pollution	The student will write, in correct grammatical structures, a description of the relationship between nuclear energy and atmospheric pollution
The student will circle each of the prepositions in the paragraph provided	The student will first decipher the teacher's unintelligible directions and then circle each of the prepositions
The respondent will place herself in the simulated job situation provided to her and will indicate how she would perform in that situation	The respondent has to first ignore that the situation is absurdly artificial and highly different from the real world and then still respond as she would perform in the hypothetical situation

other factors unique to specific individuals that produce a similar effect. A good way to assure a match is to have several different qualified persons examine the data collection process and state whether the task matches the operational definition.

A special type of mismatch between operational definition and task is worth mentioning. Some data collection strategies are so obtrusive that the respondent is more likely to be responding to the data collection process itself than to be performing the tasks indicated in the operational definition. For example, if a child *knows* that a questionnaire is measuring prejudice and that it is not nice to be prejudiced, the child may answer what he thinks he *should* answer instead of revealing his true attitude. (This is referred to as a social-desirability bias.) Likewise, if a researcher comes into the classroom and sits in a prominent position with a behavioral checklist, children may be acutely aware that something unusual is happening; and so the behavior recorded on the checklist is more a reaction to the data collection strategy than an indication of actual behavioral tendencies. (Specific strategies for overcoming obtrusiveness are discussed in chapter 6.)

3. *Demonstrate that the data collection process is reliable.* Reliability was discussed extensively earlier in this chapter. The contribution of reliability to validity was mentioned in Figure 5.1 and in the accompanying discussion. The relationship between reliability and validity is diagrammed more specifically in Figure 5.2. As this diagram suggests, a certain amount of reliability is necessary before a data collection process can possess validity. In other words, a data collection process cannot measure what it's supposed to measure if it measures nothing consistently. In demonstrating that data collection processes are valid, professional test constructors first demonstrate that their data collection processes are reliable—that they measure *something* consistently; then they demonstrate that this something is the characteristic that the data collection processes are supposed to measure. In other words, they first demonstrate reliability in several ways, and then they demonstrate validity.

An important caution is necessary in discussing the relationship between reliability and validity. It is crucial to realize that it is possible (but undesirable and inappropriate) to increase reliability *while simul-*

Figure 5.2 How Reliability Influences Validity

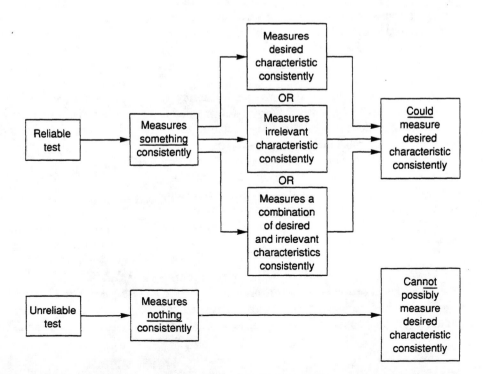

taneously reducing the validity of a data collection process*. This can be done by either (1) narrowing or changing the operational definition so that it is no longer logically appropriate or (2) changing the tasks based on the operational definition to less directly related tasks and then (3) devising a more reliable data collection process based on the more measurable but less appropriate operational definition or tasks. This is obviously a bad idea, because the result is that the data collection now measures a less valid or wrong outcome "more reliably."

Such an increase in reliability accompanied by a reduction in validity occurs, for example, if a teacher introduces unnecessarily complex language into a data collection process. A data collection process that had previously measured "ability to apply scientific concepts" might now instead measure "ability to decipher complex language and then apply scientific concepts." The resulting reliability might be higher; but if the teacher is still making decisions about the original outcome, the data collection process has become less valid.

Overemphasis on reliability is one of the arguments against culturally biased norm-referenced tests. Their detractors argue that many standardized tests become more reliable when cultural bias is added, because such bias is a relatively stable (consistent) factor, which is likely to work the same way on all questions and on all administrations of the test. However, the cultural bias detracts from the validity of the test.

It is important to be alert to the tendency to accept spuriously high statistical estimates of reliability as solid evidence of validity. The fact that a certain amount of reliability is a necessary prerequisite for validity does not mean that the most reliable data collection process is also the most valid. Statistical reliability is only one factor in establishing the validity of a data collection process. Another way to state this is to say that reliability is a necessary but not sufficient condition for validity.

As you can see, establishing validity is predominantly a logical process.

Finally, before leaving this introduction to the validity of data collection processes, it is important to note that a data collection process that provides valid data for group decisions will not always provide valid data for decisions about individuals. On the other hand, a data collection process that provides valid data for decisions about individuals will always provide valid data for group decisions. This is not as complicated as it sounds. To take an example, we might operationally define *appreciation of Shakespeare* as "borrowing Shakespearean books from the library without being required to do so." Even if Janet Jones borrows books on Shakespeare without being required to do so, it is not possible to diagnose her specifically as either appreciating or not appreciating the bard using this operational definition. There are too many competing explanations for her behavior, and these would invalidate this data collection process as an estimate of her appreciation. (For example, she might hate the subject but need to pass the exam; and so she has to borrow a vast number of books to do burdensome, additional studying. Or she might like Shakespeare so much that she owns annotated copies of all the plays and never has to borrow from any library except her own.) Nevertheless, it would still be valid to evaluate the *group* based on this operational definition. If you teach the Shakespeare plays a certain way one year and only 2% of the students ever borrow related books from the library, and the next year you teach the same subject differently and 50% of the students spontaneously borrow books, it is probably valid to infer from their available documented records that appreciation of Shakespeare has increased. The group decision, at any rate, is more likely to be valid than is the individual diagnosis.

REVIEW QUIZ 5.4

Part 1

Identify the item from each pair that is most likely to be an *invalid* measure of the outcome variable given in parentheses.

1. a. The child will correspond intelligibly with an assigned Spanish-speaking pen pal. (understands Spanish)

BOX 5.1

An Argument-Based Approach to Validity

Kane (1992) presents the practical yet sophisticated idea that validity should be discussed in terms of the practical effectiveness of the argument to support the interpretation of the results of a data collection process for a particular purpose. The researcher or user of the research chooses an interpretation of the data, specifies the interpretive argument associated with that interpretation, identifies competing interpretations, and develops evidence to support the intended interpretation and refute the competing interpretations. The amount and type of evidence needed in a particular case depend on the inferences and assumptions associated with a particular application.

The key points in this approach are that the interpretive argument and the associated assumptions be stated as clearly as possible and that the assumptions be carefully tested by whatever strategies will best rule out bias and other sources of faulty conclusions. As the most questionable inferences and assumptions are checked and either supported by the evidence or adjusted so that they become more plausible, the plausibility (validity) of the interpretive argument increases.

This interpretation of validity is compatible with the discussion presented in this chapter. In addition, it has the advantage of presenting validity as a special instance of the overall application of formal and informal reasoning to solving problems. From this viewpoint, when educators do research, they are under the same obligation as any other person making public statements to demonstrate that those statements really do mean what the speaker or writer says they mean. Statistical procedures and other specific techniques are merely pieces of evidence to check the quality of inferences and the authenticity of the assumptions underlying a particular interpretation.

(Source: Kane, M. T. [1992]. An argument-based approach to validity. Psychological Bulletin, 112, 527–535.)

b. The child will correspond intelligibly with an assigned Spanish-speaking pen pal. (appreciates Spanish culture)

2. a. The student will identify examples of the principles of physics in the kitchen at home. (understands principles of physics)

   b. The student will choose to take optional courses in the physical sciences. (appreciates physical sciences)

Part 2

Write *Invalid* next to statements that indicate an invalid data collection process; write *Valid* next to those that indicate a valid data collection process; write *N* if no relevant information regarding validity is contained in the statement.

1 ____ The questions were so hard that I was reduced to flipping a coin to guess the answers.

2 ____ The test measures mere trivia, not the important outcomes of the course.

3 ____ To rule out the influence of memorized information regarding a problem, only topics that were entirely novel to all the students were included on the problem-solving test.

4 ____ The only way he got an A was by having his girlfriend write the term paper for him.

5 ____ The length of the true–false English test was increased from 30 to 50 items to minimize the chances of getting a high score by guessing.

6 ____ The teacher ruled out the likelihood of cheating by giving each of the students seated at the same table a different form of the test.

7 ____ Since the personality test had such a difficult vocabulary level, it probably was influenced more by intelligence than by personality factors.

8 ____ The observer rated the classroom as displaying a hostile environment toward handicapped people, but the teacher argued that the observer's judgment was clouded because she observed from a position where she was next to students who were not at all typical of the entire class.

9 ____ The observer rated the atmosphere of the school board meeting as being supportive of innovative teaching, but the newspaper critic pointed out that this was because the board members were local residents with business interests and were therefore very likely to be supportive of innovation.

If you got most of the questions in Review Quiz 5.4 correct, or if you easily saw the logic of the explanations, then you probably have a good basic grasp of the concept of validity. If you do not understand the concept, reread the chapter to this point, check the chapter in the workbook, refer to the recommended readings, or ask your instructor or a peer for help. Be sure that you understand the summary in the following paragraph so that you will profit from the rest of this chapter.

In summary, validity refers to whether a data collection process really measures what it is designed to measure. Invalidity occurs to the extent that the data collection process measures an incorrect variable or no consistent variable at all. The main sources of invalidity are logically inappropriate operational definitions, mismatches between operational definitions and the tasks employed to measure them, and unreliability of data collection processes. Validity is not an all-or-nothing characteristic; data collection processes range from strong validity to weak validity. Because of the highly internalized nature of educational outcomes, data collection processes in education can never be perfectly valid. By carefully stating appropriate operational definitions, ascertaining that tasks employed in data collection processes are directly related to the operational definitions, and designing reliable data collection processes, we can increase the validity of our data collection processes and the probability that we will draw valid conclusions from them.

SPECIFIC, TECHNICAL EVIDENCE OF MEASUREMENT VALIDITY

If you read a test manual or look up the citation of a test in *The Eleventh Mental Measurements Yearbook* (Kramer & Conoley, 1992), you will find references to three basic types of evidence to support measurement validity. These have been defined by several major organizations interested in mental measurement (American Educational Research Association et al., 1985). The technical types of evidence for validity are rooted in the theory discussed earlier in this chapter, and it is not difficult to achieve a fundamental understanding of these concepts. A brief discussion of these types of evidence for validity can help teachers and researchers develop more valid data collection processes for their own use. In addition, an understanding of these concepts will be especially useful when selecting or using standardized tests, reading the professional literature, and attempting to measure psychological or theoretical characteristics beyond those that are typically covered by classroom tests. These three types of evidence for validity are (1) content validity, (2) criterion-related validity, and (3) construct validity.

Content Validity

Content validity refers to the extent to which a data collection process measures a representative sample of the subject matter or behavior that should be encompassed by the operational definition. A high school English teacher's midterm exam, for example, lacks content validity when it focuses exclusively on what was covered in the last two weeks of the term and inadvertently ignores the first six weeks of the grading period. Likewise, a self-concept test would lack content validity if all the items focused on academic situations, ignoring the impact of home, church, and other factors outside the school. Content validity is assured by logically analyzing the domain of subject matter or behavior that would be appropriate for inclusion on a data collection process and examining the items to make sure that a representative sample of the possible domain is included. In classroom tests, a frequent violation of content validity occurs when test items are written that focus on knowledge and comprehension levels (because such items are easy to write) while ignoring the important higher levels, such as synthesis and application of principles (because such items are difficult to write).

Criterion-Related Validity

Criterion-related validity refers to how closely performance on a data collection process is related to some other measure of performance. There are two types of criterion-related validity: predictive and concurrent.

Predictive validity refers to how well a data collection process predicts some future performance. If a university uses the Graduate Record Exam (GRE) as a criterion for admission to graduate school, for example, the predictive validity of the GRE must be known. This predictive validity would have been established by administering the GRE to a group of students entering a school and determining how closely performance on the GRE corresponded with performance in that school. It would be expressed as a correlation coefficient. A high positive coefficient would indicate that persons who did well on the exam tended to do well in graduate school, whereas those who scored low on the GRE tended to perform poorly in school. A low correlation would indicate that there was little relationship between GRE performance and success in graduate school.

Concurrent validity refers to how well a data collection process correlates with some current crite-

rion—usually another test. It "predicts" the present. At first glance it sounds like an exercise in futility to predict what is already known, but more careful consideration will suggest two important uses for concurrent validity. First, it is a useful predecessor for predictive validity. If the GRE, for example, does not even correlate with success among those who are going to school right now, then there is little value in doing the more expensive, time-consuming, predictive validity study. Second, concurrent validity enables us to use one measuring strategy instead of another. If a university wants to require that students either take freshman composition or take a test to "test out" of the course, concurrent validity would enable the English department to demonstrate that a high score on the alternative test has a similar meaning to a high grade in the course. Like predictive validity, concurrent validity is expressed by a correlation coefficient.

Construct Validity

Construct validity refers to the extent to which the results of a data collection process can be interpreted in terms of underlying psychological constructs. A construct is a label or hypothetical interpretation of an internal behavior or psychological quality—such as self-confidence, motivation, or intelligence—that we assume exists to explain some observed behavior. Construct validity often necessitates an extremely complicated process of validation. To state it briefly, the researcher develops a theory about how people should perform during the data collection process if it really measures the alleged construct and then collects data to see whether this is what really happens. The process is complicated because the researcher is doing two separate things: (1) proving that the data collection process possesses construct validity and (2) refining the theory about the construct. Note that this process of validation can never be completed; the goal of researchers engaging in construct validation is to *refine* concepts and data collection processes, not to arrive at ultimate conclusions. Construct validity often deals with the intervening variable (discussed in chapter 2), and it is of greatest relevance to theoretical research (discussed in chapter 17).

Remember: The three technical types of evidence for validity are merely tools for demonstrating that a data collection process measures what the test designer or researcher *says* it measures. The fundamental logic behind them is relatively straightforward. The difficulty lies in carrying out the procedures to collect these types of evidence for validity. The information presented here (summarized in Table 5.5) should be enough to enable you to deal with applying and interpreting these concepts in most situations. If you find that you need further information (for example, if your job requires that you select people accurately for various programs), consult the more technical references in the Annotated Bibliography at the end of this chapter.

Table 5.5 Summary of the Three Major Types of Psychological Validity

Type of Validity	Definition	Mnemonic	Examples of How to Achieve and Demonstrate It
Content	The extent to which a data collection process measures a representative sample of the topic encompassed by the operational definition.	The *content* c: the data collection process is a good sample of the *content* that it should cover.	1. Use a plan (such as an item matrix) to plan a test so that all areas are properly represented. 2. Logically show that nothing has been omitted or overrepresented in the data collection process.
Predictive	How well a data collection process predicts some future performance.	The data collection process *predicts* something that has not yet occurred.	1. Select students for an advanced algebra class based on a standardized math test. Then see if those who did well on the math test actually do better in the course. 2. Give students the SAT before they enter college. Then compute a correlation coefficient with college GPA to see if the SAT accurately predicts college performance.
Concurrent	How well a data collection process correlates with a current criterion.	Both data collection processes occur at the same time (*concurrently*). We want to demonstrate that one can be considered a substitute for the other.	1. Determine that success in English composition classes has already demonstrated writing skill, making it unnecessary for the student to take the English exit exam (which measures the same thing). 2. Compute a correlation coefficient between the performance of students on the computerized and noncomputerized versions of the GRE (so that we can consider performance on one to be equivalent to performance on the other).
Construct	The extent to which the results of a data collection process can be interpreted in terms of underlying psychological constructs.	A psychological *construct* (accent on first syllable) is something that exists inside a person's head. We *construct* it (accent on second syllable) by reasoning about observable information (such as test results).	1. A person's test results show whites are smarter than blacks. We challenge this person by demonstrating that the test measures cultural familiarity rather than intelligence. 2. A person shows that her moral development test really does measure something that can be called moral reasoning—rather than reading ability, conformity, intelligence, or some other unrelated characteristic.

REVIEW QUIZ 5.5

Indicate the type of technical evidence for validity called for in each of the following situations. Choose from this list:

a. content validity

b. predictive validity

c. concurrent validity

d. construct validity

1. A test designer has developed an Anxiety Measurement Scale and wants to verify that it really measures a characteristic that can be labeled "anxiety."
2. A counselor wants to select students into his school's college preparatory program based on the likelihood that they will succeed in college, and he wants to know whether a certain data collection process can help him accomplish this selection process.
3. A test designer has developed a new, 10-minute IQ test and wants to demonstrate that it measures about the same thing as the more expensive Stanford-Binet IQ test.
4. The dean wants to make sure that all the exams in the English composition course cover all the objectives they are supposed to cover.
5. A teacher wants to find out whether the students who fail her final comprehensive exam really are the ones who will have trouble with related materials the next year.

PUTTING IT ALL TOGETHER

As you will recall, Eugene Anderson, the humane educator, had written several operational definitions of "attitude toward animal life." Several of these will be discussed in the next few chapters, but here we shall focus on just one of them. Based on his second operational definition ("The child protects animals from harm"), he devised the paper-and-pencil test shown in Figure 5.3. He reasoned that a person with

a favorable attitude would want the fireman to save animals before he or she saved objects from a burning building. (The validity of this belief will be discussed next.)

Mr. Anderson planned to give each respondent a score between 0 and 3, depending on how many animals the child selected on this test. Of course, he wanted to be reasonably certain that the score a child received on any testing occasion would actually represent that child's feelings toward animals, not some irrelevant or transient factor. In addition, he wanted to have two forms of the test; and so he devised a second test ("Billy and the Fireman"—not shown here), which contained a different set of animals and objects. Mr. Anderson needed to ascertain that both tests really were equivalent forms of the same test. If they were really equivalent forms, then he could give one as a pretest and the other as a posttest, to determine whether attitudes really changed as a result of his visits.

Mr. Anderson tried to follow all the nonstatistical guidelines listed in this chapter to make the test as reliable as possible. As he completed his task, the only guideline that caused him any real concern was the one about making the test long enough. Was a range of 0 to 3 a big enough span of scores? On the one hand, he thought it might be a good idea to increase the number of choices; but on the other hand, he felt that the larger number of choices might needlessly confuse his respondents, since many of them would be in only the third or fourth grade.

Because of his doubts about the length of the test, he decided to use statistical techniques to check its reliability. If the test was too short, he would obtain a low reliability coefficient; if he obtained high coefficients, he would know that the brevity of the test was not a serious problem. In addition, the statistical procedures would be helpful in establishing the equivalence of the two tests. He had tried to obtain equivalence by pairing items and assigning them from a larger pool, but he would feel more secure if he had statistical evidence to demonstrate that they were parallel. Finally, the statistical evidence would be helpful to Mr. Anderson when he presented his results to his colleagues at meetings. With the statistical reliability data, he would not have to persuade them of his personal capability as an item writer. He

---

Johnny and the Fireman

Johnny is a boy about your age. One night his house catches fire. He and all the members of his family escape, but they have time to bring nothing with them. A fireman comes up to Johnny and says, "The house is going to be a total loss. Is there anything you would like us to try to get out of the house before it burns down?"

Here is a list of some of the things in the house. Choose the three things that Johnny should tell the firemen to try to save if there is time. Then explain the reasons for your choice.

Color portable TV (brand new: cost $450).
Father's wallet ($75 and credit cards).
Johnny's dog (1 year old: cost $30).
Johnny's stamp collection (worth $75).
His sister's cat (she got it free a year ago).
Dad's car keys (car is safely parked on the street).
Mother's expensive coat (worth $300).
CB radio (worth $210).
Little brother's pet gerbil.
Dad's checkbook.

What is the first thing to save? _____

What is the second thing to save? _____

What is the third thing to save? _____

Figure 5.3 Mr. Anderson's Humane Attitudes Test

could simply show them the numbers to prove that the tests were consistent.

He found several schools in which he was allowed to field test his instrument. In some cases, he had the same students take the same form of the test with an interval of a week or two in between (test-retest reliability). In other cases, he had them take the alternate forms after an interval of only a day or so (equivalent-forms reliability). In two cases, he gave the alternate forms with two weeks between the two testing occasions (test-retest with equivalent-forms reliability). The results are summarized in Table 5.6. As Mr. Anderson looked at his results, he was quite satisfied. The reliability coefficients showed that he had devised a reasonably consistent instrument. In addition, the alternate forms of the test really did appear to be equivalent. When one of his colleagues pointed out that his correlation coefficients were not

as high as the correlations of .90 often reported for good standardized tests, Mr. Anderson replied that he was not concerned about that. The standardized tests were intended for diagnosing *individual* abilities, and a higher degree of reliability was necessary for that purpose. All that Mr. Anderson wanted to do was examine *group* attitudes, and his statistical reliabilities were more than sufficient for his needs. Mr. Anderson had indeed developed a consistent test. His next problem was to demonstrate that the trait he was consistently measuring could legitimately be called "attitude toward animal life."

An even more important concern for Mr. Anderson was that his tests should be valid. He was concerned about the validity of *all* his measuring instruments, but in this section we'll focus exclusively on how he established the validity of his Fireman Test.

Table 5.6 Reliability Data on the Fireman Tests

Test	Test-Retest Reliability		
	Grade Level	Time Interval	Correlation
Johnny	5th (n=20)	1 week	.63
Johnny	4th (n=24)	1 week	.75
Johnny	6th (n=25)	2 weeks	.70
Billy	5th (n=20)	1 week	.69
Billy	4th (n=23)	1 week	.70
	Equivalent-Forms Reliability		
	Grade Level	Time Interval	Correlation
	4th (n=47)	1 week	.70
	4th (n=26)	2 days	.64
	3rd (n=35)	1 day	.73
	4th (n=24)	4 days	.55
	5th (n=65)	1 day	.71
	5th (n=65)	1 day	.73

In determining the validity of this data collection process, Mr. Anderson followed the guidelines suggested in this chapter. First he looked at the operational definition to ascertain that it was really logically valid. This operational definition had been revised to state, "Given a hypothetical situation in which animals might undergo pain and suffering, the respondent will choose to save the animals from that pain and suffering." He talked this over with several of his colleagues, and they agreed that saving the animals was the behavior they would expect from a person with humane values.

Next, he ascertained that the children involved in the data collection process would actually be doing what the operational definition said they should be doing. At this point, he had to rule out such irrelevant tasks as reading ability and the tendency to give false but socially desirable answers. He ruled out the reading variable by consulting some reading specialists. They agreed that for most third through seventh graders, the vocabulary would not be excessively difficult. They suggested that in case of uncertainty, Mr. Anderson should simply read the test to the respondents. Next he ruled out the social-desirability factor by reasoning that all the objects in the house were socially desirable. In addition, since it would be

introduced as part of a discussion of fire prevention, the test would be presented in such a way that the children would not even know that it had anything to do with attitudes toward animals. Finally, he noted that he had already established the reliability of the data collection process.

Mr. Anderson decided to use some statistical procedures to further authenticate validity. The procedures he used were a combination of criterion-related (concurrent) validity and construct validity. (It is not very important for you to distinguish precisely between the various techniques he used.) He asked himself, "If my data collection process is valid, what can I expect the results to be?" He answered this question with three predictions:

If the test is valid, it will correlate strongly with other tests of humane attitudes.

If the test is valid, people who are known to have good attitudes will score higher on the test than those who are known to have negative attitudes.

If the test is valid, it will *not* correlate very strongly with irrelevant factors, such as reading ability, IQ, and general grades in school.

He set out to check each of these predictions.

Mr. Anderson found it hard to check his first prediction. This was because he could not find any other good tests of humane attitudes. What he did, therefore, was compare the results of the Fireman Tests with the results of some other measuring techniques he ad derived from his own set of operational definitions. (Some of these other tests are described in chapter 6.) He found a definite pattern. Those who did well on the Fireman Test also did well on the other instruments. This information seemed to verify his first prediction.

His second prediction was much easier to check. He knew from his professional reading that one specific geographic region of the country was noted for its humane attitudes. The largest humane organizations were in that part of the country, and the incidence of pet and animal abuse was very low there. He also knew of another area that was generally considered by experts to be populated by much less humane people. He arranged to have his test given at the same grade levels in comparable schools in each of these communities. The results overwhelmingly supported his prediction. The students from the part of the country where the attitudes were known to be favorable scored higher on the test than the other students. This provided very strong support for the validity of his data collection process.

Then Mr. Anderson checked his third prediction. He correlated the test scores with scores on reading tests, math tests, and intelligence tests. The Fireman Test did not correlate substantially with any of these other scores. This is what he had hoped for. If the Fireman Test *had* correlated strongly with reading ability, for example, this might have indicated that the test was really a measure of reading ability rather than humane attitudes.

Mr. Anderson was happy with his validity data. He had demonstrated both logically and with empirical data that his data collection process really id seem to measure attitude toward animal life. ie still intended to supplement the Fireman Test with other measuring techniques (described in the next chapter), but at least he knew he was off to a good start.

SUMMARY

Reliability refers to the degree to which measuring techniques are *consistent* rather than self-contradictory. Reliability is important because you will want to make decisions about your programs and students based on internally consistent and stable data rather than fleeting information that would change if you simply took the time to collect the information a second time. This chapter has discussed factors that introduce inconsistency into data collection procedures as well as strategies for controlling these factors. In addition to presenting these guidelines, this chapter has described statistical procedures that can be useful tools to help assure reliability.

Validity refers to the extent to which a data collection process really measures what it is designed to measure. The validity of a data collection process is established by demonstrating that (1) the operational definitions upon which the data collection process is based are actually logically appropriate operational definitions of the outcome variable under consideration, (2) the tasks the respondent performs during the data collection process match the task suggested by the operational definitions, and (3) the data collection process is reliable.

What Comes Next

In the next few chapters we'll discuss how to collect, report, and interpret reliable and valid data. Later we'll integrate this information into strategies for effectively conducting and interpreting research in education.

DOING YOUR OWN RESEARCH

When conducting quantitative research, it is essential that your data collection processes be valid. (The issue of validity of qualitative research is discussed in chapter 9.) The following guidelines emerge from the principles discussed in this chapter:

1. Develop good operational definitions of your outcome variables. Use the guidelines discussed in chapter 4.

2. Keep your operational definitions in mind when developing or selecting data collection processes. Be aware of sources of invalidity, and design or select only data collection processes that are directly related to your operational definitions.

3. Develop or select reliable data collection processes, but remember that reliability is only a tool for establishing validity—it is not an end in itself.

4. Increase validity by triangulating—that is, by using more than one operational definition and more than one data collection process for each outcome variable.

5. Check the reliability and validity of your data collection processes during the early stages of your research.

6. Collect information about reliability and validity from published sources like those described in chapter 6 and from information in the methods section of published articles.

In addition, even if your research plan emphasizes quantitative methods, consider enhancing validity by supplementing quantitative methods with the qualitative strategies described in chapter 9.

FOR FURTHER THOUGHT

1. Why is it that the same steps that increase reliability often interfere with the validity of a data collection process?

2. Complete this sentence by answering the designated questions: "The concept of reliability . . .(does what?) (To what or whom?) (When?) (Where?) (How?) (Why?)"

3. Complete this sentence by answering the designated questions: "The concept of validity . . .(does what?) (To what or whom?) (When?) (Where?) (How?) (Why?)"

ANNOTATED BIBLIOGRAPHY

The following sources provide more detailed information on the general topics of reliability and validity:

American Educational Research Association, American Psychological Association, & National Council for Measurement in Education. (1985). *Standards for educational and psychological testing.* Washington, DC: American Psychological Association. This booklet includes the guidelines for reliability and validity recommended by the three corporate authors. A familiarity with these guidelines will help you make better use of published information regarding data collection processes.

Ebel, R. L., & Frisbie, D. A. (1979). *Essentials of educational measurement* (5th ed.). Englewood Cliffs, NJ: Prentice-Hall. Chapter 5, "The Reliability of Test Scores," presents a clear statement of the theoretical rationale behind the traditional methods of assessing reliability, with a special emphasis on how to apply these methods to educational practice. Chapter 6, "Validity: Interpretation and Use," offers guidelines to help teachers enhance the validity of their tests by making sure they are appropriate for the purposes for which they are intended. Chapter 13, "Evaluating Test and Item Characteristics," describes important techniques for promoting internal consistency and generally revising early versions of data collection procedures.

Gronlund, N. E., & Linn, R. L. (1990). *Measurement and evaluation in teaching* (6th ed.). New York: Macmillan. Chapter 3, "Validity," provides some very useful guidelines for teachers to increase the validity of their classroom tests. Part of Chapter 11, "Appraising Classroom Tests," describes item analysis, an important technique for promoting internal consistency. Chapter 4, "Reliability and Other Desired Characteristics," discusses the traditional methods of establishing reliability and gives concrete advice on how to apply these to improving classroom tests.

Kramer, J. J., & Conoley, J. C. (Eds.). (1992). *The Eleventh Mental Measurements Yearbook.* Lincoln, NE: Buros Institute of Mental Measurements. This book and earlier volumes in the series provide critical, scholarly information about the reliability, validity, and other characteristics of published, standardized data collection materials.

Mager, R. (1984). *Measuring instructional results* (2nd ed.). Belmont, CA: David S. Lake. This book addresses the very important problem of matching test items to behavioral objectives (operational definitions of outcome variables). Although Mager does not use the specific term *validity,* this little programmed text offers an excellent guide to one of the most important validity-related problems the classroom teacher faces.

Worthen, B. R., Borg, W. R., & White, K. R. (1993). *Measurement and evaluation in the schools.* New York: Longman. Chapters 6 and 7 offer practical and useful answers to the questions "Why worry about reliability?" and "Why worry about validity?" Chapter 8 focuses on "Cutting Down Test Score Pollution" by discussing ways to increase the reliability and validity of data collection processes.

The following source is useful for readers who are interested in more theoretical information on reliability:

Feldt, L. S., & Brennen, R. L. (1989). Reliability. In R. L. Linn (Ed.), *Educational measurement* (3rd ed.). New York: American Council on Education. This is a brief but comprehensive treatment of the major issues relating to reliability. It's heavy on statistical formulas.

The following sources are useful for readers who are interested in more detailed information on validity:

Cole, N. S. (1989). Bias in test use. In R. L. Linn (Ed.), *Educational measurement* (3rd ed.). New York: American Council on Education. This is a detailed treatment of one of the major sources of invalidity in the interpretation of data collection processes.

Messick, S. (1989). Validity. In R. L. Linn (Ed.), *Educational measurement* (3rd ed.). New York: American Council on Education. This is probably the most authoritative discussion available regarding the status of current thought on validity. Anyone doing serious work on validity of data collection processes should consult this chapter.

The following source provides more detailed information on the specific topic of reliability of criterion-referenced tests:

Popham, W. J. (1978). *Criterion referenced measurement.* Englewood Cliffs, NJ: Prentice-Hall. Chapter 2, "Traditional Measurement Practices," discusses tradi-tional approaches to reliability and points out some of the problems that are likely to occur when we try to apply these same approaches to the kinds of tests that teachers should be using to evaluate student performance. Chapter 7, "Reliability, Validity, and Performance Standards," is probably the most comprehensive treatment available on the reliability and validity of criterion-referenced tests.

ANSWERS TO QUIZZES

Review Quiz 5.1

1. Unreliable. If they were measuring Ralph's ability consistently, they should be able to agree on his score. Ralph's score depends on who scores the test, not on what he wrote down. This is like having two parents read the thermometer and one conclude that the child is sick, while the other concludes that he is healthy.

2. Reliable. Of course, you may need more than two witnesses to convince a jury. Their testimony could be *invalid* (discussed elsewhere in the chapter) if they had conspired to lie about seeing the violin case. However, in the sense that we are using the word here, their testimony is reliable.

3. No information is provided about reliability. It is quite possible that her performance could have changed during the intervening year. The difference *could* be the result of unreliability, but we have no way to know. There is no solid reason to expect the two grades to be identical.

4. Unreliable. If the same students are rating his overall ability as a teacher, there does not seem to be any good reason why this should change between Monday and Wednesday. If factors such as mood swings on the part of the students or teacher are causing the ratings to vary, these are sources of unreliability. (Note that if the students were rating him on how well he taught a specific lesson, then it might be plausible to say that he did well on one lesson and less well on another. In this case, the different scores would be a reflection of his actual performance, and the variation would not be evidence of unre-liability.)

5. Unreliable. Neuroses are supposed to be relatively permanent personality characteristics. They do not come one day and go the next. *Neurosis* is a vague term, and the counselor is probably having trouble operationally defining what she means.

6. Unreliable. The test should prove him equally ignorant both times. Wild guessing is one of the most frequent sources of unreliability on "objectively" scored tests.

7. Reliable. Mr. Monroe has essentially measured them twice and has come up with the same result. That's consistency. (This measurement of the class is apparently reliable; it still may be an unreliable way to diagnose individual students. The distinction is treated elsewhere in the chapter.)

8. Unreliable. If both pollsters are trying to measure popularity of novels, then their results should be much alike. However, if one is measuring nationwide popularity and the other is measuring popularity in Chicago, then discrepancies are plausible, provided there is an actual reason (other than inaccuracy of the measuring process) for the differences.

9. Reliable. The two persons have made independent ratings of the same students and have come to similar conclusions.

REVIEW QUIZ 5.2

1. R. She is increasing the length of the test and getting a better sample of student behavior.

2. U. He is using excessively difficult items.

3. U. She is making the items more *dis*similar. Items that are added into a *single* score should be on a common topic.

4. U. This is an excessively short (one-item) test.

5. U. Each of these subtests is very short. Mr. Peters would be on solid ground if he knew that each of the subscales had adequate reliability.

6. R. Miss Adams is avoiding the chance that temporary characteristics of the students anticipating the pep rally will lead to inconsistency.

7. U. Mrs. Wolf is adding an additional source of inconsistency (the chance that she will make a mistake in instructions) to the sources that the students themselves bring to the test.

8. R. Mrs. Johnson is using items of medium difficulty in a situation in which it is plausible to expect less than perfect mastery.

REVIEW QUIZ 5.3

1. interobserver agreement
2. test-retest reliability
3. interscorer reliability
4. internal consistency reliability
5. equivalent-forms reliability

REVIEW QUIZ 5.4

Part 1

Pair 1: b
Pair 2: b

In both cases, the second item requires a greater inferential leap to conclude that it is evidence for the occurrence of the outcome variable. The first item in each pair offers more direct evidence.

Part 2

1. Invalid. The test is unreliable and therefore invalid.

2. Invalid. The tasks do not match the designated outcome variable.

3. Valid. The selection of topics is designed to rule out a major source of bias.

4. Invalid. Having someone else do your assignment is a different task than writing the assignment on one's own.

5. Valid. This would increase reliability and hence validity—provided the true–false items are all appropriate for the outcome variable.

6. Valid. Ruling out cheating increases the probability that the students will, in fact, respond to the correct tasks.

7. Invalid. Intelligence and personality are different outcomes.

8. Invalid. The observer's task was to observe the whole class. The teacher's criticism is that the observer has instead performed the different task of observing atypical students.

9. Valid. The observer's job was to observe the atmosphere of the meeting, not to determine the causes for this atmosphere. The observer apparently assessed this information correctly.

REVIEW QUIZ 5.5

1. d. She is interested in finding evidence that the characteristic (construct) being measured is really anxiety.

2. b. This one should have been easy. The counselor is interested in finding evidence about the accuracy of predictions.

3. c. The test designer wants evidence that the two tests really measure the same outcome.

4. a. The dean is interested in finding evidence that the test samples the subject matter appropriately.

5. b. The teacher is trying to predict who will have trouble with related materials the next year, and she wants evidence regarding whether predictions based on the comprehensive exam are likely to be accurate.

CHAPTER 5

Research Report Analysis

The research report in Appendix C uses two strategies to measure the ability of students to solve problems. Evaluate the reliability of each strategy separately.

1. How reliable were the unit pretests as a measure of problem-solving ability?

2. How valid were the unit pretests as a measure of problem-solving ability?

3. How reliable was the Watson-Glaser test as a measure of problem-solving ability?

4. How valid was the Watson-Glaser test as a measure of problem-solving ability?

5. How satisfactory was the overall data collection process with regard to reliability and validity?

ANSWERS:

1. Information about the reliability of the unit pretests is not clearly stated. The fact that the pretest and posttest items were based on the same set of objectives would tend to make it likely that changes in performance from pretest to posttest reflected real gains rather than a change in the test, but this report does not focus on the pretest–posttest comparisons. The fact that the tests were administered under standardized conditions would also tend to make them more reliable. However, it would have been useful to have evidence from a reliability coefficient.

2. The fact that the tests were taken from the manual suggests good content validity for the objectives of the unit, but we don't know how strongly the objectives of the unit are related to the concept of problem solving. In fact, it seems likely that the improved performance of students on subsequent tests could be a result of generalization of learning rather than problem solving. Actually, since the first author of this textbook was the second author of this study, he knows that the tests actually did measure problem-solving ability, but this information is not clearly expressed in the report.

3. The report itself contains no specific information regarding the reliability of the Watson-Glaser test, except to say that it was administered in accordance with the instructions in the manual. However, since this is a commercial test, interested readers could find information regarding reliability in several sources: the reference to Watson and Glaser cited in the text, the *Mental Measurements Yearbook* or a similar source, or the test manual.

4. The report itself contains no specific information regarding the validity of the Watson-Glaser test. However, since this is a commercial test, interested readers could find information regarding validity in several sources: the reference to Watson and Glaser cited in the text, the *Mental Measurements Yearbook* or a similar source, or the test manual.

5. If these tests were going to be used to diagnose the problem-solving ability of individual students, they would not be considered valid. However, since they were used to assess the performance of groups, they provide good evidence. (This distinction between individual diagnosis and group research is discussed on page 99 of this textbook.) By using two forms of data collection in tandem, the researchers enhanced validity. It would have been useful to use other methods as well. (In the original report, the researchers also reported using the Test of Integrated Process Skills and the Biological Sciences Curriculum Study Test.)

DATA COLLECTION INSTRUMENTS AND PROCESSES

■ WHERE WE'VE BEEN

We've described the fundamentals of the educational research process and discussed how to operationally define and measure outcome variables in such a way that our data collection processes are as reliable and valid as possible.

■ WHERE WE'RE GOING NOW

We're going to apply the principles from the previous chapters to designing or selecting specific types of instruments to collect reliable and valid data regarding operationally defined outcome variables.

■ CHAPTER PREVIEW

Chapters 4 and 5 dealt with the technical characteristics of good data collection processes. These characteristics are general; they can be applied to any specific data collection technique. The present chapter deals with the many different formats through which data can be collected. These formats range from very open-ended to very structured approaches.

Different formats have different purposes, and each solves one set of problems while opening the door for others. Your goal in designing or selecting a data collection process is to devise a combination of various techniques that will enable you to collect reliable and valid information about the operationally defined outcome variables with which you are concerned.

After reading this chapter, you should be able to

1. Identify examples of well-designed data collection processes of each of the following types:

   Classroom achievement tests

   Questionnaires

Interviews

Observational techniques

Unobtrusive techniques

Standardized tests

2. Identify the purposes of each of these data collection techniques.

3. Identify the strengths and weaknesses of each of these techniques when they are used for a particular purpose.

4. Devise strategies for integrating several of the formats into a useful data collection process.

■

This chapter and chapter 9 come close to overlapping with regard to several topics. Both chapters discuss strategies for making observations and conducting interviews. The major distinction lies in the purpose behind the use of the strategies, and consequently there is a difference in the way the strategies are implemented. The present chapter focuses on *quantitative* data collection. Researchers use the strategies described in this chapter when they have already identified target behaviors and are trying to count these behaviors or in some other way assign numeric values to them. Chapter 9 deals with *qualitative* data collection. Researchers using qualitative strategies often do not approach the situation with pretargeted behaviors to observe; instead, they collect information in a natural setting in order to develop a richer or more complete interpretation of what is happening or to conduct effective quantitative research on a subsequent occasion.

This distinction will be clarified when interview and observation techniques are discussed in this chapter and in chapter 9. For now, let's begin our discussion of data collection processes that help us to *quantify* behaviors, thoughts, and feelings that occur in educational settings.

TEACHER-DESIGNED ACHIEVEMENT TESTS

Attainment of knowledge and mastery of skills or concepts are certainly among the most important desired outcomes in most educational settings. Educators spend a great deal of time promoting cognitive outcomes. They therefore spend much time developing and administering classroom tests to assess these cognitive outcomes. The results of these tests can serve as useful sources of data.

This chapter will briefly discuss strategies for designing, administering, and interpreting achievement tests. Most teacher education programs have at least one specific course devoted to the construction and interpretation of such tests, and so the present text will not attempt to duplicate that important effort. This section will not tell you everything you always wanted to know about classroom test construction. Only a few important, general guidelines will be presented here. If you are interested in more detailed information, Osterlind (1989) and several of the other references in this chapter's Annotated Bibliography will prove helpful.

The logic behind designing a classroom test is exactly the same as that behind any other data collection process.

The logic behind designing a classroom test is exactly the same as that behind designing any other data collection process. Your goal is to determine whether your students have mastered an educational outcome. There are three simple steps in designing a good classroom test.

The first step is to *determine exactly what it is that you are trying to measure.* If your course objectives are stated in specific, observable terms, this will be easy to do. Chapter 4 has provided useful guidelines for operational definitions, and these guidelines are applicable to writing objectives for units of instruction. Teachers who have clearly stated, valid objectives of worthwhile outcomes find it relatively easy to design valid classroom tests. One caution: avoid the tendency to test only low-level learning, such as knowledge and comprehension, while ignoring such higher levels as application and synthesis. Teachers often tend to do this because it is easier to write operational definitions and to design items for lower-level objectives.

The second step is to *match the testing technique to the operational definition*. The goal of one of our colleagues who teaches introductory psychology is to help students understand the important principles of psychology. When we asked him what he meant by this general goal, he agreed that "being able to identify concrete instances of important concepts and principles" would be an operational definition of about 95% of what he is trying to teach. And yet he always uses *essay tests*. When asked for a reason, he replied, "Multiple-choice tests are multiple-guess tests. They measure mere trivia." But the truth of the matter is that using well-written multiple-choice tests is probably one of the best ways to measure what this professor is trying to teach—how to identify concrete instances of important principles. With a valid multiple-choice format, the student is able to focus on clear anecdotes applying psychological principles and identify these principles.

The multiple-choice format has two advantages for a course like the one described: (1) such tests are designed to measure recall, understanding, and application of specific concepts or principles, and, (2) because a student can answer a large number of questions in a short time, a large sample of items covering a wide range of topics can be incorporated into the test. The essay test, on the other hand, would be an inadequate way for this instructor to evaluate his students with regard to his stated objectives. The essay test would be weak in this case because (1) well-written essay tests are more appropriate for measuring higher-order processes, such as the ability to organize and integrate information, whereas the instructor is measuring mastery of concepts, and (2), since a relatively long time would be required to answer each question, only a few topics could be covered.

We are not trying to argue for wider use of multiple-choice tests but rather to point out the illegitimacy of deciding *ahead of time* what kind of test is best in all situations. The correct strategy is first to determine the appropriate operational definition of the educational outcome and then to match the testing technique to that definition.

The third step is to *write good items using the chosen testing format*. Our colleague's dissatisfaction with multiple-choice tests probably arose either because he himself wrote terrible multiple-choice items or because as a student he was subjected to bad multiple-choice items by his own teachers. Several books in this chapter's Annotated Bibliography provide useful guidelines to writing good items of a designated type.

In designing your tests, avoid falling into a rut. Be creative. Look for new ideas for writing or selecting good items. Bloom, Hastings, and Madaus (1971), for example, present innovative ways to write good items in several different subject areas. If you administer a good standardized test (discussed at the end of this chapter), look through it and imitate good ideas. For example, many good standardized tests currently use "interpretive exercises" rather than isolated multiple-choice items. These interpretive exercises often use the multiple-choice format to test higher-order abilities more efficiently than would be possible with an ordinary essay test. Many of the exercises in the workbook that accompanies this textbook are interpretive.

Computer technology can make important contributions to classroom achievement testing. Most school systems make available to teachers the capability to score tests and analyze results by computer. Many teachers use these programs without even knowing the name of the program or the type of computer being employed; they just write good test items, have the students put the answers on "scan sheets," submit the items to someone who runs the computer, and eventually interpret the results. By using these services sensibly, it is possible not only to save time but also to improve the quality of the tests. For example, most test-scoring systems provide information on internal consistency reliability as well as an item analysis, which helps identify items that detract from validity. Teachers who prefer to exercise more direct control over the scoring process often use a program like Excelsior's *Quiz2*. By following simple guidelines, teachers with a basic knowledge of the principles of measurement can easily administer, score, interpret, and improve the quality of their classroom tests.

There are also many computer programs that enable teachers to store test items and generate tests from a bank of such items. Some programs, such as *Create-a-Test* by Cross Educational Software, supply a large number of prewritten items for a subject area (such as American history, biology, or genetics) and permit teachers to both select from this item bank and add their own questions. Some of these programs simply permit teachers to store and retrieve items for printed tests; others store the items and randomly generate printed tests; and others actually permit students to take tests interactively, while the computer not only stores the students' scores but also identifies areas where the students need further review and instruction. Table 6.1 lists a number of important characteristics that teachers might expect from a test-generating program, and Table 6.2 indicates the degree to which a number of popular computer programs provide each of these services.

One of the disheartening aspects of these programs is that most of them do not take advantage of the computer's full range of word processing capabilities. The editing systems are weak, and during the revision process they usually require teachers to reenter entire items (or at least major portions of the items) rather than simply make insertions and deletions. For example, the word processor on which we are writing this book would accommodate our decision to add a two-line sentence between the first and second sentences. Most test-generating programs, on the other hand, would require us to retype every line after the point of insertion. Teachers who have become accustomed to the efficiency of word processors find this lack of function to be demoralizing, and they often choose to use a word processor instead of a test-generating program to design their achievement tests.

A technical note is in order here. Teacher-designed achievement tests are often examples of criterion-referenced measurement, which is discussed in chapter 7. (Note: Do not confuse the notion of criterion-referenced measurement with criterion-related validity, which was discussed in chapter 5.) As we indicated in chapter 5, when the range of scores from tests is restricted, the internal consistency reliability of the test is lowered. With criterion-referenced tests, grades are often tightly clustered. Therefore, although criterion-referenced measures may be the better way to measure achievement and assign grades to student performance, they may present some problems when they are used in statistical computations that build upon internal consistency reliability.

When you need a test to measure classroom achievement, find the most valid way to measure the outcome you're interested in observing. Then devise good items within that format. .

QUESTIONNAIRES

As its name implies, a questionnaire is a device that enables respondents to answer questions. In this section, the term will refer to any data collecting instrument other than an achievement or ability test, where respondents directly supply their own answers to a set of questions. This definition is not intended to be technical; it is merely stated for convenience. Other sections in this chapter discuss achievement tests, interviews, and observation techniques.

The answers that respondents will give on a questionnaire are determined by the nature of the questions and the respondents' reactions to these questions. This reaction will be based on factors such as students' knowledge, attitudes, and willingness to respond completely and accurately. The questionnaire designer's job is to plan the instrument in such a way as to facilitate rather than impede the respondents' ability to provide the desired information. In the case of specific demographic or factual information, writing a good questionnaire item is largely a matter of using language clearly and concisely. However, if the questionnaire focuses on attitudes, personality traits, or other internalized characteristics, then the job of item construction becomes more difficult. In this case, it is necessary to write the item in such a way as to help the respondents reveal what the questionnaire is looking for, rather than some alternate characteristic, such as how eagerly they want to please the person administering the questionnaire or how they think society would like them to answer the questions.

Figure 6.1 on p. 126 presents six ways to ask essentially the same question in order to ascertain respondents' attitudes toward participation in various sports. Note that the way each question is stated

Table 6.1   Characteristics Desired in Electronic Test Generating Programs

1.   Allow the teacher to store and retrieve from the computer the same sort of items that the teacher would otherwise store in a test-item bank.
2.   Generate tests at random from these electronic item banks, using the same (or better) selection strategies that the teacher would normally use.
3.   Permit entry of questions from a normal word processing program (such as Microsoft Works).
4.   Permit the use of spelling and grammar checking programs.
5.   Select items for tests according to prescribed criteria (such as item format, level of difficulty, or instructional objectives).
6.   Generate equivalent alternate forms of the same test.
7.   Permit the students to take tests interactively at the computer terminal, as well as in the normal printed format.
8.   Provide statistical analyses (including item difficulty and item discrimination) that would enable the teacher to improve the quality of the test.

Table 6.2   Data Entry Features of Eleven Major Test Generating Programs

Program (Publisher)	Word Processing	Menus	Other Comments
Classified Test Bank (Classified Software)	Fair	Main & Submenus—good	Stores items manually after each question
Create a Test (Cross)	Cumbersome—often requires control key and letter	Nice layout and easy access	Accompanied by sets of predesigned items
Excelsior Quiz2 (Excelsior)	Excellent—compatible with major word processors	Clear—easy to follow	Tutorial helps understand the numerous options
Final Exam (Earthware)	Cumbersome—but acceptable	Generally clear	Minor confusion with menus
Grand Inquisitor (Cross)	Cumbersome—cluttered screen	Good menus—but few defaults	Very complex because of screen clutter and options
Question Bank (Teaching Technologies)	Excellent—compatible with word processor	Good menus—Easy to use	Can generate 100 versions of same test
Teacher Management Tools (Bertamax)	Cumbersome—but acceptable	Good—but limited options	Not obvious how it is better than a word processor
Test Generator (Gamco)	Fair—Many control keys—Useful reference card	Easy to use and to access	Awkward security system
Test It Deluxe (EduSoft)	Very good basic word processing	Good menus and submenus	Allows selection of level of difficulty
Testmaster (Midwest Software)	Good basic editing system	Easy to use	Allows on-screen previewing and selection of difficulty level
Testworks (Milliken)	Cumbersome but acceptable	Large number of good menus and options	Saves after 10 items (User may change interval)

imposes a somewhat different task upon the respondents, and therefore the answer obtained by each item is likely to give slightly different information.

Question 1 asks the respondents to make up their own list of sports. This open-ended approach has the advantage of imposing no artificial constraints upon the respondents; if, alternatively, we supplied them with even an extremely long list, we could still possibly omit their favorite sports. A major disadvantage of the open-ended approach is that we give the respondents little information about the framework within which we want them to respond.

For example, they have to make up their own definition of what a sport is. It's possible (and even likely) that different persons answering this same question will define the term differently. Is jogging a sport? Perhaps someone would consider jogging to be a sport if done with another jogger, but merely an exercise if done alone. And what about exercise? Are people engaging in a sport if they do 50 sit-ups every morning as soon as they get out of bed? How about chess—is that a sport? A closely related problem is that some people would focus only on sports in which they have participated during the last month

1. List the five sports you enjoy participating in the most.

a.

b.

c.

d.

e.

2. Rank the following sports in order of preference. Give a ranking of "1" to the sport you would like to participate in the most, "2" to the one you'd next like to participate in, etc.

_____ tennis
_____ bowling
_____ baseball
_____ basketball
_____ volleyball
_____ swimming
_____ jogging

3. In each of the following pairs of sports, circle the one that you would prefer to participate in. You should circle 24 sports altogether—one from each pair.

tennis-bowling	volleyball-basketball	swimming-basketball
basketball-jogging	swimming-baseball	tennis-basketball
jogging-tennis	bowling-basketball	volleyball-baseball
swimming-jogging	baseball-basketball	bowling-jogging
jogging-baseball	volleyball-swimming	tennis-swimming
bowling-volleyball	swimming-baseball	swimming-jogging
volleyball-jogging	tennis-baseball	tennis-baseball
baseball-bowling	volleyball-tennis	jogging-basketball

Figure 6.1 Six Ways to Determine Sports Preference

or so, and they might ignore favorite sports that occur during a different season. Indeed, it is possible that some people might enjoy skiing immensely but may not have had a chance to participate in it in the five years since they moved to Hawaii. What are they likely to give as their answer? Many of these problems could be solved by rephrasing the question more carefully: "List the five sports in which you would most like to participate, if given a chance. In making this list, consider a sport to be any athletic activity in which a person participates for enjoyable competition. Be sure to consider all possible sports

from all seasons of the year." This would solve some problems, but others would still emerge.

The major difficulty with open-ended questions is that different respondents are likely to supply different contexts for answering the same questions. If our intention is to compare these different respondents with one another or to combine the responses, then we need a common context.

Questions 2 through 6 solve this context problem by presenting lists of sports. Since language is not sufficiently precise, it is still possible that various respondents will understand the nature of their tasks

---

4. Check all of the following sports that you enjoy participating in:

   _____ tennis
   _____ bowling
   _____ baseball
   _____ basketball
   _____ volleyball
   _____ swimming
   _____ jogging

5. Rate each of the sports below on the following scale:

   1—I enjoy participating in this sport very much.
   2—I enjoy participating in this sport.
   3—I'm rather indifferent about this sport.
   4—I dislike participating in this sport.
   5—I hate participating in this sport.

   _____ tennis
   _____ bowling
   _____ baseball
   _____ basketball
   _____ volleyball
   _____ swimming
   _____ jogging

6. Assume that you have to spend all of your recreation time for the next year participating in some combination of the following sports. Indicate the percentage of time you would spend in each sport. (The total should add up to 100%).

   _____ % tennis
   _____ % bowling
   _____ % baseball
   _____ % basketball
   _____ % volleyball
   _____ % swimming
   _____ % jogging

differently; but the likelihood of unique reactions to Questions 2 through 6 is considerably less than even to the revised version of Question 1. The major difficulty with these questions, however, is that the respondents' favorite sports may not even be on the list. This problem can be partially solved by lengthening the list, but this leads to other difficulties. A longer list makes the task of responding more time-consuming, and this strategy adds to the complexity of answering the questions. Just imagine Question 3 with 50 sports matched up in a two-by-two pairing! Even if the list is lengthened, there is still the possibility that a favorite sport will be omitted. Adding an additional space marked "other (specify)_____" is not a perfect solution, because this involves the same sort of problems inherent in Question 1.

Question 2 differs from Questions 4 and 6 in that it requires a *ranking* of the sports. A person who likes both tennis and volleyball, for instance, has to choose one over the other. There's a certain validity in requiring this forced choice, because in fact most people would probably prefer one over the other. On the other hand, what if this person doesn't care at all about bowling or jogging? Is it valid to force the person to decide which she is least unconcerned about? Another problem with the ranking method is that it is difficult to rank large numbers of items. Young children cannot handle more than 3 to 5 items to rank; even sophisticated adults dislike being asked to rank more than 9 or 10 items. Finally, rankings tend to distort the true differences among people's choices.

Question 3 is similar in principle to Question 2. In a sense, the task of putting sports in order is simplified, because the respondent never has to consider more than two sports at a time. If a person is logically consistent, the rank ordering resulting from Number 3 would be the same as the ordering derived from Number 2. A disadvantage of this approach is that respondents often find it irritating to have to make so many comparisons. Since it is necessary to match each of the sports with every other sport, the number of comparisons becomes quite large as the number of sports increases. For example, if 25 sports were included on the list, it would be necessary to have 300 comparisons. For 50 sports, 1,225 comparisons would be necessary!

Question 4 has the advantage of not requiring the artificial, forced choices found in Questions 2 and 3. In addition, it is usually not considered fatiguing or frustrating to go through even a long list of this kind and mark choices. The respondents simply check what they like and pass by those they do not like. Of course, a severe disadvantage of this approach is that from the results it is impossible to tell which sports are liked more than the others. All the "likes" look alike.

Question 5 is similar to Question 4, except that it allows the respondent to state a degree of preference. (Actually, Question 4 *is* Question 5, except there are only two choices: 1 = like and 2 = dislike.) It takes only slightly more effort to fill out this sort of ranking, with a lot of tied ranks. However, allowing tied ranks (for example, by allowing the respondent to rate all three of his favorite sports "like very much") often gives a false impression, because there is probably some difference in the rater's actual preference.

Question 6 tries to get the best of all worlds. It enables the respondents to rank the sports (by giving greater amounts of time to more preferred sports), while deliberately allowing ties if the respondents wish (by giving an equal amount of time to each of two sports) and allowing them to give different weights to different rankings. A serious shortcoming, however, is that this sort of ranking is a complex activity, requiring patience and intelligence. Young children and even unmotivated adults will not use it to its full potential. A further problem with this example is that a person might spend eight hours a week jogging (which he does not particularly like) in order to train for his Saturday tennis match (which he dearly loves).

In summary, each of the formats in Figure 6.1 has both advantages and disadvantages. The disadvantages can often be minimized. For example, if it is necessary to have a respondent rate 15 items (as in the Question 2 format), it is possible to give helpful directions to the respondent (e.g., the instructions might say, "It is often a good idea to find your two or three top choices and mark these. Then find your two or three bottom choices and mark these. Continue until you have ranked all the items."). An even more helpful idea for younger children is to have each of the items written on a card, and let the children physically sort the responses; it is easier to stack cards in order of preference than it is to rank intangible ideas. A similar idea with regard to the Question 6 format is to give the respondents a certain amount of play money and have them put amounts in envelopes, corresponding to the amount they would spend on each activity.

It is essential that the teacher or researcher, as well as any other users of the results, know what the answers to questionnaire items actually mean.

It is essential that the teacher or researcher, as well as any other users of the results, know what the answers to questionnaire items actually mean. Assume that a physical education teacher is using questions from Figure 6.1 to assess attitudes toward jogging among her students.

The results from Question 1 would enable her to conclude that "35% of the students spontaneously listed jogging as a favorite sport on the pretest, and this placed it fourth. On the posttest, 65% mentioned jogging, which placed it first."

Question 2 would enable her to conclude that "jogging received an average ranking of 3.5 among the seven sports listed on the pretest. This ranked third out of seven. On the posttest, jogging ranked second out of seven, with an average ranking of 2.5."

Question 3 would enable her to say, "Jogging received an average of 2.5 choices out of a possible 7 on the pretest, putting it third out of the seven listed sports. On the posttest, jogging received an average of 3.5 choices, putting it in second place."

Using Question 4, she could say that "80% chose jogging as a sport they would enjoy participating in, which ranked it in second place among the seven listed. On the posttest, jogging was selected by 85% of the respondents and still ranked in second place."

With Question 5, she could find that "jogging received an average score of 2.7 on a scale of 1 to 5 on the posttest. There were two sports higher. On the posttest, jogging was rated 1.9, with only one sport rated higher."

Using Question 6, she could discover that "according to the pretest, the respondents were willing to spend an average of 30% of their time jogging. This was the highest of any sport on the list. On the posttest, the average increased to 40%, which was still the highest of all the sports listed."

It is apparent that there are subtle differences among these statements. These slight distinctions may not make any real difference to the data collection process, and in such cases the decision about which format to use would be based on which one could be used most efficiently. In other cases, the researcher might want to focus on the nuances uncovered more effectively by one format more than others, and the decision would be to use that format. As will be pointed out later in this chapter, many of the shortcomings of questionnaire strategies can be overcome by supplementing them with data from nonquestionnaire techniques, or vice versa. You should not limit yourself ahead of time to any single method of data collection.

Open-Ended versus Structured Formats

When we were examining Figure 6.1, it was obvious that Question 1 differed more from the other five than these others differed among themselves. This was because Question 1 is an open-ended question, whereas all the others employed a structured format. The major advantage of the open-ended format over the structured format is that with the open-ended format it is the respondents themselves who take the initiative in deciding what answer to supply; whereas with the structured format the respondents merely select from a set of answers supplied by the writer of the questionnaire. On the other hand, the structured format has the advantage of requiring all the respondents to answer within the same framework; with the open-ended format it is possible for two respondents to adopt such divergent frameworks that it is hardly accurate to view their responses as replies to the same question.

> *The major advantage of the open-ended format over the structured format is that with the open-ended format it is the respondents themselves who take the initiative in deciding what answer to supply.*

Let us pursue the difference a little further. For our example, we shall use one of the most frequent situations in which teachers use questionnaires: course evaluation. An open-ended format might consist of asking the students to write a statement about how they felt about the course; with a structured format, the teacher might pass out a form with 25 statements and ask the students to rate each on an agree–disagree scale. The type of information the teacher gets could vary considerably, depending on which method was used. For example, what would the teacher conclude if 3 students out of 25 in her class indicated in an open-ended format that "the teacher has an annoying habit of talking about her own family too much"? On an open-ended questionnaire, respondents can only put down what comes into their minds. How can this teacher tell how the other 22 students felt about this issue? Did they disagree with the statement, or did they like the fact that the teacher talked about her own family, or what? How likely is it that another student in the same class would spontaneously write down, "It doesn't move me one way or another when the teacher talks about her own family so much"? It's not very likely. Chances are, the topic would not even enter the minds of most respondents. The students in this example are all responding to their own separate questionnaires, and it is difficult to discern what the consensus is on most issues.

> *The structured format has the advantage of requiring all the respondents to answer within the same framework.*

An alternative would be to use a structured format. The teacher would present her list of 25 questions, and the students would respond to each. Then she would know how each student felt about each issue on the questionnaire. The trouble with this approach is that there may be things on the students' minds that were not even included on the questionnaire. The teacher might feel good about her performance because she did well at the things *she* was concerned about; whereas the students might be extremely dissatisfied because she did poorly at things *they* were concerned about but which did not appear on the teacher-designed questionnaire.

One way to solve the dilemma this teacher faces would be to give the structured questionnaire and ask the students to add additional comments at the end. This is only a partial solution, because the open-ended part of the questionnaire entails the problems discussed earlier. A better solution to the dilemma is represented in Figures 6.2 and 6.3. The teacher follows a two-step process. First she asks the students to write down the three things they liked best, the three things they liked least, and the three changes they'd most like to see in the course. From the students' responses to these open-ended questions, the teacher generates the questionnaire shown in Figure 6.2 and asks all the students to respond to this structured questionnaire. She therefore has a questionnaire generated from ideas submitted by all the students (gaining the major advantage of the open-ended format) and completed by all the students (gaining the major advantage of the structured format).

Similar strategies are useful in developing questionnaires and general data collection strategies for purposes other than classroom evaluation. Such strategies would increase the probability that a research study could identify important outcomes occurring in the course being evaluated. (Note that the naturalistic research strategies described in chapter 9 could also be used to evaluate classroom instruction; such strategies may be especially useful in situations where some of the desired outcomes have not been clearly defined.)

The issues discussed in this section are pertinent for designing not only questionnaires and interviews but all forms of data collection. The field of cognitive psychology offers insights about formats to use to obtain data regarding cognitive outcomes. For example, Bennett and Ward (1993) discuss the potential advantages and pitfalls of multiple-choice and constructed-response formats, performance test-

```
3 Best
    The pretests are very useful
    The instructor is well prepared for class
    The instructor shows enthusiasm for the
        subject matter.

3 Worst
    Too much time is spent on class discussions.
    Major questions are left unanswered.
    The instructor calls on students who
        are not volunteering.

3 Changes
    Get a new textbook.
    Don't call on us unless we raise our hands
    Try fewer films.
```

Figure 6.2 The Open-Ended Part of a Two-Step Procedure to Obtain a Valid Course Evaluation from Students

ing, and portfolio assessment; the main point emerging from the discussion in this book is that students are engaged in different cognitive tasks when responding to these various formats and the selection of the format will strongly influence what we learn about the respondents.

Computer-Generated Questionnaires

One of the advantages of structured questionnaires is that they are easily adapted to computerized scoring. (Specific advantages of computerization will be explored in chapter 18.) Figures 6.4 through 6.6 demonstrate a technique for using the computer to simplify the process of questionnaire usage. (This "cafeteria" format was developed by the Center for Instructional Services at Purdue University.) Figure 6.4 (pp. 134–135) shows part of a form instructors use to select the items they want on their unique

course evaluation questionnaires (the sheet on which they would enter these coded selections is not shown). This procedure enables the instructors to select up to 40 items that they feel are uniquely useful for their courses. Figure 6.5 (p. 136) shows the questionnaire that is generated by the computer from the instructor's request. Figure 6.6 (pp. 138–139) presents the results of one evaluation. The results give the number of persons who gave each response, the average (median) response based on a 1-to-5 scale, and a percentile indicating how the instructor compares with other instructors at the university. Further programming of the computer would enable the instructors to do cross-tabulations. For example, they could find out what percentage of the students who thought they had clearly stated objectives also felt the course was intellectually fulfilling.

LIKERT QUESTIONNAIRES

The format shown in Figure 6.6—often referred to as a five-point scale—is technically known as a Likert scale. The essential component is not the five points on the scale but rather the continuum ranging from "strongly agree" to "strongly disagree." The following guidelines are suggested by Anderson (1981) for developing Likert scales:

1. Write or select statements that are clearly either favorable or unfavorable with regard to the feeling or characteristic under consideration.
2. Ask several judges to react to the statements. These judges should examine each statement and classify it as either positive, negative, or neutral with regard to the feeling or characteristic under consideration.
3. Eliminate or clarify statements that are not unanimously classified as positive or negative.
4. Decide on the number of alternatives to be listed on the continuum of choices for responding to each statement.
5. Prepare the actual instrument. Include instructions that indicate that the respondents should rate each item according to the designated scale.

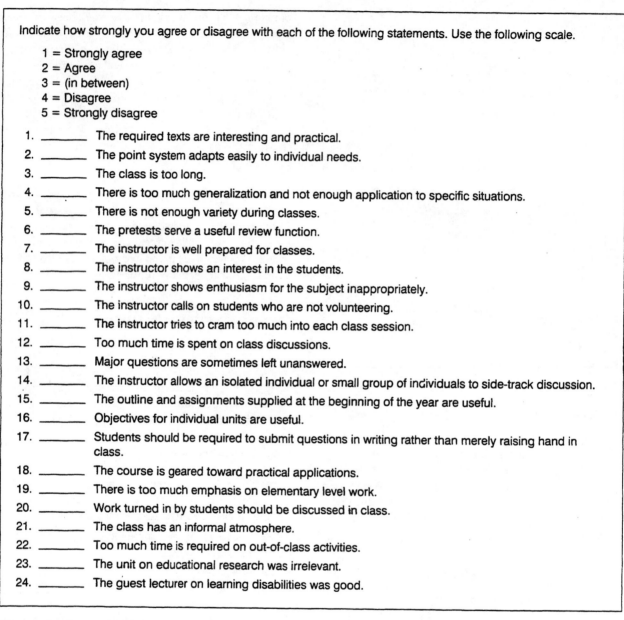

Indicate how strongly you agree or disagree with each of the following statements. Use the following scale.

    1 = Strongly agree
    2 = Agree
    3 = (in between)
    4 = Disagree
    5 = Strongly disagree

1. _____ The required texts are interesting and practical.
2. _____ The point system adapts easily to individual needs.
3. _____ The class is too long.
4. _____ There is too much generalization and not enough application to specific situations.
5. _____ There is not enough variety during classes.
6. _____ The pretests serve a useful review function.
7. _____ The instructor is well prepared for classes.
8. _____ The instructor shows an interest in the students.
9. _____ The instructor shows enthusiasm for the subject inappropriately.
10. _____ The instructor calls on students who are not volunteering.
11. _____ The instructor tries to cram too much into each class session.
12. _____ Too much time is spent on class discussions.
13. _____ Major questions are sometimes left unanswered.
14. _____ The instructor allows an isolated individual or small group of individuals to side-track discussion.
15. _____ The outline and assignments supplied at the beginning of the year are useful.
16. _____ Objectives for individual units are useful.
17. _____ Students should be required to submit questions in writing rather than merely raising hand in class.
18. _____ The course is geared toward practical applications.
19. _____ There is too much emphasis on elementary level work.
20. _____ Work turned in by students should be discussed in class.
21. _____ The class has an informal atmosphere.
22. _____ Too much time is required on out-of-class activities.
23. _____ The unit on educational research was irrelevant.
24. _____ The guest lecturer on learning disabilities was good.

Figure 6.3   Part of the Structured Half of a Two-Step Procedure to Obtain a Valid Course Evaluation from Students

6. Administer the scale to a sample of the audience for whom the instrument is intended.

7. Use item analysis (discussed in measurement textbooks, such as Ebel & Frisbie, 1986; Gronlund & Linn, 1990; and Osterlind, 1989) to evaluate the quality of each item.

8. Eliminate or revise items that the item analysis indicates are weak. (If revision was necessary, repeat appropriate steps to evaluate the revised questionnaire.)

As the preceding guidelines suggest, this type of scale for measuring attitudes and other affective characteristics has the advantage of being both easy to design and easy for the respondent to complete.

Summary Regarding Questionnaires

There are several other specific strategies for generating, administering, and scoring questionnaires. For example, sociometric techniques, the semantic differential, and the Q-sort are all examples of specific techniques for obtaining input from respondents. These more specialized techniques are not discussed in this book. If you need more detailed information, consult other sources listed in this chapter's Annotated Bibliography, especially Borg (1989), Kerlinger (1986), and Krathwohl (1993). The important thing to remember in designing a questionnaire is to determine what it is that you want the respondents to tell you, and then devise an instrument that will make it as likely as possible that you will actually obtain that information. The general strategies and specific examples presented on the preceding pages should help you accomplish this goal.

INTERVIEWS

Like a questionnaire, an interview is designed to enable respondents to supply information to the researcher. The interview, however, differs from the ordinary questionnaire because of the personal presence of the interviewer while the respondents supply their answers. This personal presence of the interviewer has both advantages and disadvantages. One of the disadvantages is that this one-to-one approach takes much longer than an ordinary questionnaire. Another disadvantage is that the personal presence of the interviewer may reduce the respondents' spontaneity. Anonymity is gone, and so the willingness to be completely frank and honest might be reduced.

The interview differs from the ordinary questionnaire because of the personal presence of the interviewer while the respondents supply their answers.

The major advantage of the interview over the ordinary questionnaire lies in its flexibility and wide range of data that can be collected. For example, it is possible to combine both open-ended and structured formats in a single interview. This could be done, for instance, by asking the respondent several open-ended questions and then following up with one of several different sets of structured questions. In addition, ambiguity is reduced, since it is possible for either the interviewer or the respondent to ask for clarifications during the interview.

Interviews can vary in their degree of structure. Naturalistic interviews, which are often conducted by participant observers, sometimes without the interviewee even knowing that an interview is being conducted, are discussed in chapter 9. The present chapter discusses exploratory and structured interviews that are designed to collect quantitative data to answer specific questions.

An *exploratory* interview is much like an open-ended questionnaire. One of its most important functions is to elicit ideas, thoughts, and feelings to lay the foundation for subsequent, more structured data collection. The exploratory interview is informal and relatively unstructured. The researcher probes with general questions, records the answers, and decides on the basis of one question what to ask next. Such exploratory interviews are usually of little direct use for evaluation and decision-making purposes. In fact, it is difficult even to make a comparison between two persons' responses to such interviews, because in many cases the two don't even answer the same set of questions. For the

Instructor and Course Appraisal: Cafeteria System
Measurement and Research Center
Copyright © 1974 Purdue Research Foundation

CAFETERIA is a computer-assisted course and instructor appraisal system developed and administered by the Measurement and Research Center, Purdue University. CAFETERIA is intended to serve faculty and all information pertaining to individual instructors, courses, and departments is treated confidentially.

Directions

To initiate CAFETERIA service, an instructor should obtain an *item selection form* for each class to be evaluated. From the following 200-item catalog, the instructor may select *up to 40 items*. Selections are recorded on the item selection form by darkening the numbered space which corresponds to the number of the desired catalog item. In addition to the selected catalog items, each rating form will contain demographic questions and 5 University core items which are added automatically when the rating forms are printed. The University core is not considered part of the 40 items an instructor is permitted to choose.

If your department has requested that you select certain specific items as part of the 40 items you may choose, commonly referred to as departmental core, please mark those items on your item selection form.

Item Catalog

Clarity and Effectiveness of Presentations
001   I understand easily what my instructor is saying.
002   My instructor displays a clear understanding of course topics.
003   My instructor is able to simplify difficult materials.
004   My instructor explains experiments and/or assignments clearly.
005   Difficult topics are structured in easily understood ways.
006   My instructor has an effective style of presentation.
007   My instructor seems well prepared for class.
008   My instructor talks at a pace suitable for maximum comprehension.
009   My instructor speaks audibly and clearly.
010   My instructor draws and explains diagrams effectively.

Figure 6.4   Page 1 of Cafeteria Item Catalog for Course Evaluation

exploratory interview to provide useful data, it usually must be followed by a more structured technique. This follow-up could be a structured interview, but it could also be a questionnaire or an observation strategy. Exploratory interviews are in many respects similar to the naturalistic interviews discussed in chapter 9.

A section from a *structured* interview is shown in Figure 6.7 (p. 140). (The printed format for a structured interview is referred to as a schedule.) This example is part of a 19-page schedule, which was developed after a series of exploratory interviews. The schedule was devised in such a way as to permit 15 different interviewers to be in the field at the same time, and yet the researcher had reasonable assurance that all of them were gathering information that could legitimately be combined and compared. This assurance was based on the fact that the schedule had been carefully devised to take into consideration almost any possible answer that could be given. At junctures where unusual responses could be given, the interviewers were instructed to make notes about the unusual events and to continue or stop as appropriate.

Notice that with the schedule in Figure 6.7, the interviewer has to do little writing during the interview. As much as possible, the interviewer merely asks questions, listens to what the respondent says,

---

011 My instructor writes legibly on the blackboard.
012 My instructor has no distracting peculiarities.

Student Interest/Involvement in Learning
013 My instructor makes learning easy and interesting.
014 My instructor holds the attention of the class.
015 My instructor senses when students are bored.
016 My instructor stimulates interest in the course.
017 My instructor displays enthusiasm when teaching.
018 This course supplies me with an effective range of challenges.
019 In this course, many methods are used to involve me in learning.
020 My instructor makes me feel involved with this course.
021 In this course, I always felt challenged and motivated to learn.
022 My instructor motivates me to do further independent study.
023 This course motivates me to take additional related courses.
024 This course has been intellectually fulfilling for me.

Broadening Student Outlook
025 My instructor has stimulated my thinking.
026 My instructor has provided many challenging new viewpoints.
027 My instructor teaches one to value the viewpoint of others.
028 This course caused me to reconsider many of my former attitudes.
029 In this course, I have learned to value new viewpoints.
030 This course fosters respect for new points of view.
031 This course stretched and broadened my views greatly.
032 This course has effectively challenged me to think.
033 The class meetings helped me to see other points of view.
034 This course develops the creative ability of students.
035 My instructor encourages student creativity.

---

and circles appropriate items. This simplified recording is an important characteristic of a good structured interview schedule. Respondents usually do not like long pauses during an interview, while the interviewer writes a verbatim summary of the responses. Also notice that the interviewer is instructed to hand the respondent a card to accompany Question 2. There is a twofold purpose in using this card: (1) the respondent does not have to rely on memory while the interviewer reads the list, and (2) the strategy avoids any uncomfortable feeling that would arise if the respondent were allowed to look at the questionnaire itself while the interviewer recorded the responses.

This 19-page interview schedule was easily completed in 20 to 40 minutes by pet owners and in less than 5 minutes by non–pet owners (the longer period of time it took to interview pet owners occurred primarily because of differences in how much the respondents elaborated upon details during the interviews). The interviewers asked each question, noted the responses, and then did whatever the schedule instructed them to do next. These structured interviews provided useful information upon which to base intelligent comparisons and decisions. A great deal of information was collected from a large number of respondents without much disruption to their lives.

Class	School	Sex	Expected Grade	Course Required
_____	_____	_____	_____	_____

Please read each statement carefully, then select one of these five alternatives: Strongly Agree (SA), Agree (A), Undecided (U), Disagree (D), Strongly Disagree (SD).

My instructor has an effective style of presentation.	SA	A	U	D	SD
This course supplies me with an effective range of challenges.	SA	A	U	D	SD
My instructor motivates me to do further independent study.	SA	A	U	D	SD
My instructor has provided many challenging new viewpoints.	SA	A	U	D	SD
In this course I have learned to value new viewpoints.	SA	A	U	D	SD
My instructor emphasizes relationships between and among topics.	SA	A	U	D	SD
My instructor emphasizes conceptual understanding of material.	SA	A	U	D	SD
This course builds understanding of concepts and principles.	SA	A	U	D	SD
My instructor is actively helpful when students have problems.	SA	A	U	D	SD
My instructor suggests specific ways I can improve.	SA	A	U	D	SD
My instructor returns papers quickly enough to benefit me.	SA	A	U	D	SD
My instructor adjusts to fit individual abilities and interests.	SA	A	U	D	SD
I am free to express and explain my own views in class.	SA	A	U	D	SD
I feel free to challenge my instructor's ideas in class.	SA	A	U	D	SD
My instructor relates to me as an individual.	SA	A	U	D	SD
My instructor readily maintains rapport with this class.	SA	A	U	D	SD
The objectives of this course were clearly explained to me.	SA	A	U	D	SD
I was able to set and achieve some of my own goals.	SA	A	U	D	SD
This course contributes significantly to my professional growth.	SA	A	U	D	SD
There is sufficient time in class for questions and discussions.	SA	A	U	D	SD
This course provides an opportunity to learn from other students.	SA	A	U	D	SD
My final grade will accurately reflect my overall performance.	SA	A	U	D	SD

Figure 6.5 Sample Cafeteria Format Evaluation

A major disadvantage of the interview compared with the simple questionnaire is that while the interview covers a greater range and offers greater depth of information, it is much more time-consuming. If you are going to have 50 persons answer a set of questions, you can usually have the entire group fill out the questionnaire in the time it takes to conduct a personal interview with just a single person from the same group. Advantages gained by spending the additional time interviewing respondents need to be balanced against the major added costs. Interviews are more appropriate if a wide range of in-depth thoughts and feelings is sought or if a limited range of possible responses is of interest; if the question cannot be easily asked and answered in an impersonal, printed format but must be accompanied by a personal explanation; if the nature of a follow-up question can be determined only after the respondent has answered a prior question; or if it is unlikely that the respondents will return the questionnaire if left on their own. In most other situations, the simple questionnaire format is preferable.

A second major disadvantage of the interview format is that the interviewer becomes a part of the data collection process, in the sense that the respondent reacts not only to the questions but to the person asking them as well. Anonymity is lost, and this loss can result in a reduction in spontaneity, frankness, and honesty. In addition, such irrelevant factors as the physical appearance and personality of the interviewer can interfere with the validity of the responses. For example, the typical person on the street might respond differently to an interview regarding racial prejudice if the questions are asked by a six-foot-four, middle-aged black man than if the same questions were asked by a five-foot-four, fragile-looking, white, female college student.

OBSERVATIONAL TECHNIQUES

The techniques discussed so far ask the respondents to write down or verbally describe the outcome variables occurring within themselves. With observational techniques, however, an observer watches behaviors in a natural setting and records that behavior in some way. Therefore, observation differs from the strategies discussed previously in that the person recording the scores takes more responsibility than the respondents for what is actually recorded. Observation will also be an important topic of chapter 9, where we will focus on fairly unstructured strategies for gathering information and insights when the purpose is to undertake initial explorations, to probe further but nonspecifically, or to find interpretations for data that have already been collected. The present chapter will focus on more structured techniques that quantify observed behaviors by counting them or assigning ratings to those behaviors.

Another way to state the difference is that the purpose of observations discussed in this chapter is to measure outcomes that have already been targeted, whereas the purpose of observations discussed in chapter 9 is to gather comprehensive, detailed, rich, in-depth information without previously identifying which behaviors to observe. Both types of observations can provide useful information to educators.

Observations of specific behaviors are likely to be reliable and valid to the extent that the behaviors are clearly and operationally defined, based on good conceptual definitions.

There are two manners in which structured observations can be conducted and recorded. First, the observer can look for the occurrence or nonoccurrence of a designated behavior. Second, the observer can observe the performance of a target behavior and record a rating of the quality of that behavior. These two strategies will be discussed separately.

Observing the Occurrence or Nonoccurrence of a Behavior

This observational strategy has become especially important in the implementation of behavior modification strategies and in the evaluation of special-education programs, which often focus on changes in specific, observable behaviors performed by individual subjects. It is important to note, however, that behavioral observations can be of considerable use to *all* teachers and researchers.

With this strategy, the observer defines a specific, observable behavior and watches over a period of time to ascertain whether that behavior occurs. In making such observations, it is often useful to distinguish between *discrete* and *continuous* behaviors.

Discrete Behavior A *discrete* behavior is one that can be counted as a separate event. Examples include children raising their hands in class, players swinging at a bad pitch in a baseball game, and teachers making supportive comments. The number of times such events occur can be counted over a period of time, and then the rate per unit of time can be computed. For example, it would be possible to say that Marilyn raised her hand an average of 3.1 times per hour, that Chris swung at bad pitches about 3 times out of 10, and that Miss Jordan made an average of 49.6 supportive comments per hour. Discrete behaviors are often easy to observe; it is merely necessary to operationally define the behaviors clearly and then count how often they occur.

Continuous Behavior A *continuous* behavior is one that cannot meaningfully be recorded by merely counting it. Attending behavior, on-task activity, and out-of-seat behavior are all examples of continuous behaviors. It is not meaningful to count how often these behaviors occur. For example, if a child sat

STUDENT DEMOGRAPHICS —   A604 ED VOCKELL ED 530-51   1/25/78

CLASS		SCHOOL		SEX		EXPECTED GRADE		COURSE REQUIRED	
FRESHMAN	1	AGR	0	FEMALE	26	A/PASS	26	YES	26
SOPHOMORE	0	BAS	0	MALE	4	B	3	NO	3
JUNIOR	0	HOME EC	1			C	0		
SENIOR	4	HESS	2			D	0		
GRADUATE	28	COMM CLGE	0			F/FAIL	0		
OTHER	0	GRAD	26						

CATALOG NUMBER		SA (5)	A (4)	U (3)	D (2)	SD (1)	MEDIAN	PERCENTILE
3	MY INSTRUCTOR IS ABLE TO SIMPLIFY DIFFICULT MATERIALS.	23	10	1	0	0	4.8	96
6	MY INSTRUCTOR HAS AN EFFECTIVE STYLE OF PRESENTATION.	20	11	3	0	0	4.7	90
7	MY INSTRUCTOR SEEMS WELL-PREPARED FOR CLASS.	24	9	1	0	0	4.8	84
8	MY INSTRUCTOR TALKS AT A PACE SUITABLE FOR MAXIMUM COMPREHENSION.	8	12	6	7	1	3.8	21
10	MY INSTRUCTOR DRAWS AND EXPLAINS DIAGRAMS EFFECTIVELY.	15	16	2	1	0	4.4	79
12	MY INSTRUCTOR HAS NO DISTRACTING PECULIARITIES.	7	15	5	7	0	3.8	21
13	MY INSTRUCTOR MAKES LEARNING EASY AND INTERESTING.	22	8	2	2	0	4.7	89
14	MY INSTRUCTOR HOLDS THE ATTENTION OF THE CLASS.	22	9	3	0	0	4.7	91
15	MY INSTRUCTOR SENSES WHEN STUDENTS ARE BORED.	20	8	6	0	0	4.7	98
17	MY INSTRUCTOR DISPLAYS ENTHUSIASM WHEN TEACHING.	28	6	0	0	0	4.9	94
21	IN THIS COURSE, I ALWAYS FELT CHALLENGED AND MOTIVATED TO LEARN.	9	17	6	2	0	4.0	74
24	THIS COURSE HAS BEEN INTELLECTUALLY FULFILLING FOR ME.	13	12	5	4	0	4.2	67
25	MY INSTRUCTOR HAS STIMULATED MY THINKING.	12	17	3	2	0	4.2	68
30	THIS COURSE FOSTERS RESPECT FOR NEW POINTS OF VIEW.	16	14	3	1	0	4.4	79
35	MY INSTRUCTOR ENCOURAGES STUDENT CREATIVITY.	20	10	2	2	0	4.7	78
44	MY INSTRUCTOR IS ACTIVELY HELPFUL WHEN STUDENTS HAVE PROBLEMS.	20	10	2	2	0	4.7	77

Figure 6.6 Sample Printout from Cafeteria Evaluation

138

	Item	5	4	3	2	1	Mean	%ile
45	17. MY INSTRUCTOR RECOGNIZES WHEN SOME STUDENTS FAIL TO COMPREHEND.	13	16	3	1	0	4.3	89
51	18. MY INSTRUCTOR IS READILY AVAILABLE FOR CONSULTATION.	18	11	3	1	1	4.6	82
56	19. EXAMS ARE USED TO HELP ME FIND MY STRENGTHS AND WEAKNESSES.	21	10	2	1	0	4.7	99
58	20. THIS COURSE SHOWS A SENSITIVITY TO INDIVIDUAL INTERESTS/ABILITIES.	14	13	5	1	0	4.3	69
61	21. MY INSTRUCTOR TAILORS THIS COURSE TO HELP MANY KINDS OF STUDENTS.	17	11	4	2	0	4.5	90
68	22. I AM FREE TO EXPRESS AND EXPLAIN MY OWN VIEWS IN CLASS.	22	7	3	1	0	4.8	86
79	23. THIS INSTRUCTOR ENCOURAGES DIVERGENT THINKING.	20	10	2	2	0	4.7	86
81	24. THIS COURSE HAS CLEARLY STATED OBJECTIVES.	29	4	1	0	0	4.9	98
84	25. I UNDERSTAND WHAT IS EXPECTED OF ME IN THIS COURSE.	29	5	0	0	0	4.9	99
90	26. THIS COURSE MATERIAL IS PERTINENT IN MY PROFESSIONAL TRAINING.	21	11	2	0	0	4.7	80
105	27. MY INSTRUCTOR DEVELOPS CLASSROOM DISCUSSION SKILLFULLY.	15	16	3	0	0	4.4	84
114	28. EXAMS ARE FAIR.	30	3	1	0	0	4.9	99
131	29. LENGTH AND DIFFICULTY OF ASSIGNED READINGS ARE REASONABLE.	19	13	1	0	0	4.6	94
151	30. MEDIA (FILMS, TV, ETC.) USED IN THIS COURSE ARE WELL CHOSEN.	20	11	3	0	0	4.7	96
CORE 1	31. MY INSTRUCTOR MOTIVATES ME TO DO MY BEST WORK.	14	13	6	1	0	4.3	85
CORE 2	32. MY INSTRUCTOR EXPLAINS DIFFICULT MATERIAL CLEARLY.	16	15	3	0	0	4.4	85
CORE 3	33. COURSE ASSIGNMENTS ARE INTERESTING AND STIMULATING.	15	12	6	1	0	4.3	90
CORE 4	34. OVERALL, THIS COURSE IS AMONG THE BEST I HAVE EVER TAKEN.	15	13	3	3	0	4.3	87
CORE 5	35. OVERALL, THIS INSTRUCTOR IS AMONG THE BEST TEACHERS I HAVE KNOWN.	18	10	5	1	0	4.6	84

REPORT BASED ON 34 STUDENTS.   01/25/78   COPYRIGHT 1975 PRF.

Figure 6.6 continued

139

Figure 6.7 Example of a Structured Interview Format

Section Two: In this section I have a series of questions about pets.

1. Do you own any pets such as dogs, cats, rabbits, gerbils, birds or fish?

Yes........1 (Ask A & C)   NO.......2 (Ask B)

A. What animals do you own? What others do you own?	B. During the last 3 years have you owned any pets?
Code all animals mentioned: then for each type, ask:	Yes _____ No _____(Go to next sec.) **
How many ___1___ do you own?	If Yes, ask: WHY do you no longer have these pets?
Type of animal (code) No. of animals	RECORD RESPONSE verbatim:

Dog	1	①2 3 4 5 6 7 8									
Cat	2	1 2 3 4 5 6 7 8									
Rabbit	3	1 2 3 4 5 6 7 8									
Gerbil	4	1 2 3 4 5 6 7 8									
Bird	5	1 2 3 4 5 6 7 8									
Snake	6	1 2 3 4 5 6 7 8									
Fish	7	1 2 3 4 5 6 7 8									
Other											
(Specify)	8	1 2 3 4 5 6 7 8									

Then code all that apply:

Too costly to keep	1
Pet needed more care than expected	2
Pet was noisy, destroyed property	3
Pet attacked people (bit, dangerous to children)	4
Pet was very sick	5
Pet was very old	6
Not enough space to keep	7
Pet died	8
Other (Specify) _____	9

C. During the last three years have you owned any pets which you no longer have?

YES _____   (NO ___X___)

IF YES, GO TO **

2. This card lists some reasons people give for owning pets and small animals. Of the things listed on this card, which come closest to your reasons for owning a pet/pets? PROBE AS DIRECTED.

IN COLUMN A, CODE "1" FOR ALL REASONS MENTIONED: CODE "2" for reasons not mentioned. Then, if more than one reason is mentioned, ask which of the given reasons is the most/more important and code response in column B. (If more than one reason is given in A, ASK: "WHICH ONE OF THESE REASONS WOULD YOU SAY IS THE MOST IMPORTANT TO YOU?" and code.)

		A		B
		YES	NO	Most important
HAND	a. companionship _____	①	2	1
CARD	b. recreation (sport, hunting?) _____	1	②	1
1	c. protection _____	1	②	1
	d. educational for children _____	①	2	1
	e. enjoy animals_____	①	2	①
	f. no special reason _____	1	②	1
	g. other (Specify) _____	1	②	1

GO ON TO NEXT PAGE

down at 8:30 and paid attention continuously until 12:00, this child would get credit for attending once, if we merely counted the behavior. On the other hand, a child who was continuously distracted might get a score of 95 attending behaviors, if we recorded each time he started paying attention. Rather than counting the occurrence of such behaviors, it is necessary to determine a number of equally sized time intervals, observe the child during these time intervals, and determine the percentage of the intervals during which the behavior occurs. For example, children could be defined as attending if they were on-task during the whole interval, if they were on-task at all during the interval, or if they paid attention

according to some other criteria. It is up to the observer or researcher to operationally define the standards. Based on such observations, it might be possible to say that Jennifer was paying attention during 35% of the intervals on the pretest and during 60% of the intervals on the posttest. An example of a continuous-behavior recording sheet is shown in Figure 6.8.

Observations of specific behaviors are likely to be reliable and valid to the extent that the behaviors are clearly and operationally defined, based on good conceptual definitions. It is always a good policy to check the interobserver agreement, using the guidelines described in chapter 5.

Figure 6.8 An Example of a Recording Sheet for Observing Continuous Behavior

Name of child ___Jane Doe___   Date __March 14, 1980__
                                     Time Started __9:10 a.m.__
                                     Time Finished __9:19 a.m.__

Directions: 1. Watch the child for ten seconds.
               2. During the next five seconds, record whether or not he was out-of-seat at all during that period. (Consider the child out-of-seat if his/her posterior is not in contact with the chair.)
               3. Repeat this process until you have done this for ten minutes.

X = in seat   O = Out of seat

MINUTE				
1	X	X	X	O
2	O	O	O	O
3	O	O	X	X
4	X	X	O	O
5	X	O	X	O
6	X	X	X	X
7	X	X	O	O
8	O	O	O	O
9	X	X	X	X
10	X	X	O	O

Total number of intervals ___40___
Number of intervals in seat ___21___
Number of intervals out of seat ___19___   Percentage in seat ___53%___
                                                Percentage out of seat ___47%___

Rating the Quality of Observed Behavior

Instead of merely counting the occurrence or nonoccurrence of a behavior, an observer can use a rating scale to assign a value to observed behaviors. Some examples of rating scales are shown in Figure 6.9. Question 1 is an example of one of the simplest sorts of rating scales. The rater observes the behavior and writes a number in the space provided before each statement. Question 2 is also quite simple. The rater merely circles one of the numbers from the set accompanying each statement. Question 3 and 4 present the same questions in a more graphic format. Questions 1 and 2 are easier to devise, whereas Questions 3 and 4 are often easier for a trained rater to employ.

The reliability of the rating scale can be estimated using the interscorer method described in chapter 5. Rating scales will be reliable to the extent that they refer to observable behaviors with clearly defined criteria for the various quality levels. Since the rating scales involve a certain amount of subjectivity, however, the reliability of such scales will usually be lower than the reliability of observational strategies that count continuous or discrete behaviors. Furthermore, the question of *validity* must also be taken into consideration. For example, is it valid to use an observational strategy to classify a person as either (a) paying attention or (b) not paying attention? Since there are varying degrees of attention, a statement that a pupil received an average rating of 3.1 on a 1-to-5 scale during the past week might be more useful than stating that the pupil attended during 45% of the one-minute timed intervals. As with all data collection strategies, it is important to determine what it is that you want to know, then operationally define it, and finally find a way to collect data using the selected operational definitions.

The reliability of rating scales can be increased if teachers and researchers become familiar with certain rating errors. One set of such errors is referred to as *personal bias errors:*

Some people rate everyone high. They display a *generosity error.*

Others rate everyone low. This is referred to as a *severity error.*

Still others have a tendency to rate everyone about average, and this is referred to as a *central tendency error.*

Another type of rating error is known as the *halo effect.* When this error is operating, it leads a rater to rate designated traits of an individual on the basis of an overall impression of that person. For example, a teacher might rate a student as extremely intelligent because the student is a very friendly person rather than because the student has shown a high degree of intelligence.

By knowing about these errors and training raters to avoid them, researchers can greatly reduce their impact on the reliability of rating scales.

Concluding Remarks Regarding Observational Techniques

The discussion in this section has focused on observing *people.* It is also possible to observe *products* and *contexts.* Most current measurement textbooks discuss such data collection procedures as portfolio assessment and work sample analysis. For example, it would be possible to examine a sample of a student's written essays to determine overall quality, evaluate specific aspects of writing (such as spelling, penmanship, and analytic style), and observe and describe the atmosphere or context in which writing instruction takes place. In effect, the same guidelines that apply to observing people can also be applied to observing products and contexts.

UNOBTRUSIVE MEASUREMENT

A potential problem with most of the common data collection techniques arises when the persons about whom data are being collected know that this data collection is taking place. In some cases this awareness makes no difference. In other instances, however, the person whose behavior is being measured *reacts* to the process. The data collector, therefore, is often uncertain whether the data collection strategy is collecting information on the real outcome variables or on versions of the outcome variables that have been altered because of reactions to the data

Figure 6.9 Four Ways to
Phrase an Item in a Rating
Scale

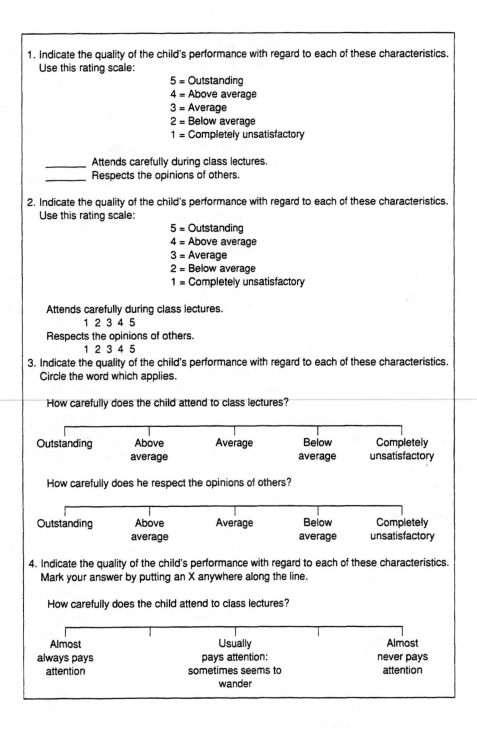

1. Indicate the quality of the child's performance with regard to each of these characteristics. Use this rating scale:

   5 = Outstanding
   4 = Above average
   3 = Average
   2 = Below average
   1 = Completely unsatisfactory

   _____ Attends carefully during class lectures.
   _____ Respects the opinions of others.

2. Indicate the quality of the child's performance with regard to each of these characteristics. Use this rating scale:

   5 = Outstanding
   4 = Above average
   3 = Average
   2 = Below average
   1 = Completely unsatisfactory

   Attends carefully during class lectures.
        1 2 3 4 5
   Respects the opinions of others.
        1 2 3 4 5

3. Indicate the quality of the child's performance with regard to each of these characteristics. Circle the word which applies.

   How carefully does the child attend to class lectures?

   | Outstanding | Above average | Average | Below average | Completely unsatisfactory |

   How carefully does he respect the opinions of others?

   | Outstanding | Above average | Average | Below average | Completely unsatisfactory |

4. Indicate the quality of the child's performance with regard to each of these characteristics. Mark your answer by putting an X anywhere along the line.

   How carefully does the child attend to class lectures?

   | Almost always pays attention | Usually pays attention: sometimes seems to wander | Almost never pays attention |

143

collection strategy. The alterations in the observed outcome variables that result from such reactions are often a significant source of invalidity. To the extent that a data collection strategy promotes such reactions, the strategy can be referred to as a *reactive measurement strategy*. A major effort has been made in recent years to use nonreactive, or *unobtrusive*, data collection techniques to reduce the threats to validity that arise from reactive measurement.

A data collection technique is unobtrusive to the extent that it reduces the likelihood of the respondent's reacting to it, thus reducing the validity of the data collection process.

A data collection technique is unobtrusive to the extent that it reduces the likelihood of the respondent's reacting to it, thus reducing the validity of the data collection process. One way to minimize reactiveness is to establish rapport with the people being interviewed or observed; by blending in with the situation, researchers can minimize reactiveness. In addition, researchers can minimize artificial reactions by guaranteeing anonymity, assuring confidentially, and promising that the data will be used in an ethical manner. As we showed earlier, there are many sources of invalidity in data collection processes, and the tendency to "fudge" data is one more source of invalidity. For this reason, it is often desirable to take a real-life sample of the behavior of interest. For example, it may be better to watch an adolescent boy interact with adolescent girls at a dance than to ask him to fill out a questionnaire regarding how well he gets along with girls.

In some cases, collecting unobtrusive data requires considerable ingenuity. For example, if a researcher asks someone how much alcohol he consumes per week, the respondent might react to the question and give an answer that he thinks might meet more socially acceptable standards. On the other hand, if the researcher secretly goes through the respondent's garbage can each week and counts the empty beer cans and wine and liquor bottles, the person will not know that his behavior is being observed and therefore cannot react to the data collection process. The

book *Nonreactive Measures in the Social Sciences* (Webb et al., 1981) cites numerous examples of effective ways to collect data unobtrusively. Table 6.3 lists several suggestions that may help you generate some ideas for your own use.

An ethical caution is in order here. Unobtrusive measurement, like all forms of research and measurement, should not be undertaken in a frivolous or an unethical manner. It would be possible to measure attitudes toward school, for example, by placing hidden microphones in a classroom and monitoring the teachers' and students' conversations there; but this would be an invasion of privacy. In fact, the garbage-can example cited in the previous paragraph was mentioned facetiously, not as a recommended invasion of your neighbor's privacy. Common sense and appropriate ethical codes should regulate all forms of data collection. It should be obvious that there are many circumstances in which unobtrusive strategies like those listed in Table 6.3 can be employed without violating the privacy of the persons whose actions are being assessed.

It should be apparent from an examination of Table 6.3 that while unobtrusive techniques often reduce one source of invalidity (arising from reactions to the data collection process), they may introduce other sources of invalidity. For example, when the nosy garbage collector examines a garbage can and discovers 10 liquor bottles and no soft drink containers, his conclusion that the owner of the garbage can had thrown a particularly wild party and served only hard liquor and no soft drinks might be invalid. One source of invalidity in this conclusion may be that liquor often comes in throwaway bottles, whereas soft drinks often come in recyclable cans. Unobtrusive data collection techniques, by their nature, are indirect; and indirect strategies often require inferential leaps to support their validity. All of the unobtrusive techniques noted in Table 6.3 are susceptible to possible invalidity. For this reason, unobtrusive measurement is often recommended as a strategy to *supplement* other data collection strategies. As we mentioned earlier, the process of triangulation—employing multiple operational definitions and multiple data collection strategies—will lead to the most valid conclusions about

Table 6.3   Some Examples of Unobtrusive Measurement Techniques

Outcome to be Measured	Measurement Technique
Number of cigarettes smoked per hour	Let respondents have a discussion in lounge for an hour and then count the cigarette butts in the ashtray after they leave.
Preference for a political candidate	Leave some postcards around with a message relevant to one or the other candidate on one side and a standard address on the other. People are more likely to pick up and mail the ones for the candidate they prefer and throw away the ones for the candidate they dislike.
Feelings toward a film shown in class	Watch to see how often the students turn around to see how close the film is to being over.
Extent to which physical education students actually clean themselves while taking shower after gym class	Weigh the soap before and after the shower session (or obtain its volume by immersing it in a measurement device).
Appreciation of Shakespeare	Count number of books about Shakespeare borrowed from library.
Child's favorite color	Measure size of crayons. Favorite colors will be shorter.
Favorite radio station	Turn car radio on and see what station it's tuned to. Also see where the buttons are set.
Children's bedtime	Ask them what TV shows they watched last night. Then check to see what time the shows were on.
Racial prejudice	Watch whether the students sit in racially isolated or mixed groups at various activities.

outcome variables. In most cases, it is desirable to collect more than one sort of data. If both an obtrusive and an unobtrusive strategy give the same result, then the researcher can have greater confidence in that result; but if the obtrusive strategy gives one result and the unobtrusive strategy gives a different result, then the researcher should look for possible sources of invalidity that might be contaminating the data collection process. For example, a teacher could give a questionnaire about prejudice and also watch to see where people sit in the lunchroom. The strategies are quite divergent and control different sources of invalidity. It is often useful to supplement more formal data collection strategies with several unobtrusive techniques.

It is not correct to classify data collection processes as either purely obtrusive or purely unobtrusive. Data collection techniques exist along a con-

tinuum ranging from extremely reactive to not at all reactive. By being aware of this factor and selecting less obtrusive techniques whenever possible, you can reduce a significant source of invalidity in your data collection efforts.

STANDARDIZED DATA COLLECTION INSTRUMENTS

You should not always have to develop your own data collection processes. Sometimes you will want to use data collection strategies that have already been developed and are accompanied by known reliability and validity information. In addition, you will sometimes want to be able to compare the performance of the people you measure with the performance of other persons who have responded to the same data collection process. The term *standardized instrument* refers to professionally designed measurement devices that are accompanied by information regarding their reliability and validity and by normative data. The *normative data* permits users to compare the performance of their current respondents with the typical performance of norm groups—representative samples of respondents who responded to the same data collection process as part of the standardization process. There are many issues involved in the selection and use of standardized instruments, and persons who often use these devices should consult books specifically devoted to this topic, such as Anastasi (1988) and *The Eleventh Mental Measurements Yearbook* (Kramer & Conoley, 1992).

The logic behind selecting a data collection process is the same as that behind designing one, which has been described in previous sections of this chapter. Decide what variables you want to measure, and then look for a data collection process that will do that. Also, remember that standardized data collection processes do not have to be the *only* data collection techniques you employ to measure the variables under consideration.

Information on professionally developed data collection procedures is available in reviews and research reports in many professional journals. Table 6.4 on p. 148 summarizes information about several sources. Two excellent sources of information are *Tests in Print* and the *Mental Measurements Yearbook* (Figure 6.10). By consulting these sources you can acquire basic information about the contents of the instrument, the type of respondents for whom the instrument is intended and on whom it was normed, and the reliability and validity of the instrument. These sources will also help you find reviews by specialists in the appropriate field. In addition, a good data collection device is accompanied by manuals containing the information necessary to evaluate and use the device correctly. Worthen et al. (1993) describe more detailed steps for selecting a data collection process.

It is often less costly and almost always less time-consuming to purchase an instrument than to develop your own.

BOX 6.1	Norms Are Not Standards!

Since norms accompany standardized tests, there is a tendency to think that norms are synonymous with standards. This is not true. In the English language, the word *standard* is used to refer to an "approved model." In the field of education, a standard refers to a level of performance that has been designated as a goal. A norm group consists of representative respondents who were involved in a measurement process as part of the standardization process. The norms describe the typical performance of this comparison group.

Sometimes we use norms to set standards, but this is not always a sensible procedure. For example, a school may run a remedial program to try to get 80% of its students above the 50th percentile according to the norms of a test of mathematical problem solving. This decision would be based on the judgment that this was a reasonable goal. On the other hand, if a study indicated that the "normal" age for a teenage boy in a community to drop out of school was between 16 and 17, it is not likely that educators would set this norm as a standard for other young men to achieve.

Norms describe the way things are. Standards describe the way someone wants things to be. The difference is important.

The ABC Inventory to Determine Kindergarten and School Readiness. Purpose: Measures kindergarten and school readiness and identifies children too immature for kindergarten or first grade before enrollment. Ages 3.5–6.5; 1965–85; individual; an individualized computer-generated narrative report, The Learning Temperament Profile (based on child's ABC Inventory scores), available from publisher; 1985 price data: $8 per 50 copies of Inventory and administration and scoring procedures ('85, 4 pages); $.48 per child per Learning Temperament Profile; (10) minutes; Normand Adair and George Blesch; Educational Studies & Development.*

See T3:7 (2 references); see also T2:1691 (2 references); for a review by David P. Weikart, see 7:739 (2 references).

Figure 6.10 An Entry from the *Mental Measurements Yearbook*

Standardized data collection processes have the advantage of being developed by persons who are experts in an appropriate field. It is often less costly and almost always less time-consuming to purchase an instrument than to develop your own. When you want to measure complex behavior, such expertise may lead to more reliable and valid results than would be obtained through your own efforts at measuring that outcome variable. Furthermore, the normative data from standardized data collection processes may be helpful in interpreting your results. However, the fact that standardized data collection processes are designed by an outside specialist is sometimes a disadvantage. There is often a less-than-perfect match between what the standardized instrument measures and what you want to measure. For example, since the designers of standardized achievement tests want to sell their instruments to as many schools as possible, they will cover content that is likely to be covered in a large number of schools. In addition, for reasons related to reliability described in chapter 5, designers of standardized achievement tests usually omit items that can be answered correctly by a large number of respondents. For these reasons, it is unlikely that the content covered by the standardized achievement test will perfectly match the unique content of your course or curriculum. Therefore, if your intention is to assess how well your students are achieving the outcomes intended by your course or curriculum, it is wise to use standardized achievement tests largely as a useful supplement to your own evaluation strategies.

CHOOSING AND USING DATA COLLECTION TECHNIQUES

Data collection strategies are effective tools for gathering information about the degree to which variables are occurring. The present chapter has reviewed several general data collection strategies. The principles discussed in chapters 4 and 5 have to be carefully integrated with those covered in this chapter to select and develop strategies useful for your own purposes.

Validity should be an important factor in choosing the format of the data collection process as well as in determining the content of any instrument you might use.

The most important quality of any data collection process is its validity. Therefore, validity should be an important factor in choosing the format of data collection processes as well as in determining the content of any instrument you might use. There are four steps in constructing a valid measurement instrument or data collection process:

1. Identify the variables you want to measure.
2. State valid, multiple operational definitions of those outcome variables.
3. Select data collection formats that match the requirements of your operational definitions.
4. Within the requirements of that format, design data collection processes that match your operational definitions as closely as possible.

Table 6.4 Sources of Information Regarding Professionally Developed Data Collection Instruments

Source	Publisher	Summary of Contents
Assessment by J. Salvia & J. E. Ysseldyke	Boston, MA: Houghton Mifflin (5th edition published in 1991).	Often used as a textbook for assessment courses in special education and as a reference by special educators, this book is organized by topic and has the advantage of offering comparisons of several tests that might be available to measure a designated outcome.
A *Consumer's Guide to Tests in Print* by D. D. Hammill, L. Brown, & B. R. Bryant	Austin, TX: Pro-Ed. (2nd edition published in 1992).	Brief tabular summaries of evaluative information about a large number of data collection processes, with a specific slant toward diagnosing the strengths and weaknesses of learners with special needs.
ETS Test Collection Bibliographies	Educational Testing Service (Various dates—frequently updated)	Extremely brief information on a large number of tests, arranged by category. Available in print from ETS. Also widely available on microfiche in university libraries.
Mental Measurements Yearbooks	Lincoln, NE: Buros Institute of Mental Measurement (11th edition published in 1992)	Detailed descriptions of tests include the title and descriptive information, intended examinees, reliability and validity information, normative information, administration details, cost, etc. Descriptions also include references to the use or evaluation of the test in the published literature. Comprehensive indexes make it easy to find needed data collection processes.
Test Critiques by D. J. Keyser and R. C. Sweetland	Kansas City, MO: Test Corporation of America (Seven volumes published between 1984 and 1988).	More detailed reviews of a smaller number of tests than appear in the *Mental Measurements Yearbooks*. Cumulative indexes with each current volume keep track of previous issues. The main advantage is the depth of coverage.
Tests in Print	Lincoln, NE: Buros Institute of Mental Measurement (3rd volume published in 1983)	Serves as a comprehensive index to the *Mental Measurements Yearbook*. Each edition of the *Yearbook* includes only data collection processes that were published or revised since the last edition. *Tests in Print* helps coordinate the various editions.

Chapter 2 has provided direction with regard to the first step; chapter 4 discussed the second step; and chapter 5 focused on the final step. The present chapter deals with the third step. The information from all four of these chapters has to be fused and integrated to develop useful strategies to help you determine what variables are occurring in your educational settings. This is the essence of Level I research.

Table 6.5 summarizes the strengths and weaknesses of each of the data collection formats discussed in this chapter. These principles can be readily understood from reading the table, and all have been discussed in appropriate sections of this chapter. The important point is that each of the formats serves a certain purpose and solves certain problems; but at the same time, any single technique entails certain basic weaknesses. For this reason, it is often a good idea to use more than one format and method for measuring any designated variable. The full process for developing or selecting appropriate data collection strategies is diagrammed in Figure 6.11. An important feature of this diagram is the feedback loop, which indicates that the second through fourth steps should be repeated as often as necessary to assure a valid data collection process. For example, it

Table 6.5 Purposes and Weaknesses of Various Measurement Formats

Format Technique	Purpose of Format	Weaknesses of Format
Classroom achievement tests	Estimate academic achievement	Really only an indirect measure of internal learning; ignores affective outcomes
Questionnaires	Enable respondent to provide answers without personal presence of data collector	Less flexible than interview; rely on respondent to state accurately what he/she feels or will do
Interviews	Enable respondent to provide answers with personal presence of data collector	Interviewer often increases reactivity to instrument
Observational techniques	Focus on actual performance rather than introspection or accuracy of respondent	Data is recorded by outsider (observer), who provides an additional source of error; only completely external behaviors can be recorded
Unobtrusive techniques	Minimize tendency for responses to be reactions to the instrument rather than true indications about the outcome variable	Often only indirectly connected to outcome variable
Standardized tests	Designed and field-tested by professionals with a great deal of experience with regard to a given outcome variable	Often the content of the standardized instrument matches up imperfectly with the data collector's goals

might be a good strategy to give a child an achievement test on scientific concepts and also unobtrusively observe the child to determine whether she really applies the concepts in appropriate situations. Likewise, it might be effective to give an adolescent boy a questionnaire regarding his attitude toward female classmates, observe him to see how he really interacts with girls in social and academic situations, and also interview him about his thoughts and feelings toward girls. By using the various formats in this complementary fashion, you can retain the strengths of each data collection technique while canceling out the weaknesses.

Before concluding this chapter, it is important to note that no attempt has been made to discuss *all* possible data collection techniques. For example, there has been no discussion of specific guidelines for constructing particular types of achievement tests, such as completion items, essay tests, and true–false tests. Likewise, we have not discussed such specific techniques as the semantic differential, focus groups, and checklists for evaluation purposes. Nor has there been a detailed discussion of the many nuances that could occur when any of the many data collection

strategies are employed, such as the differences between telephone interviews and other kinds of interviews. Rather, this chapter has attempted to point out the important guidelines to use in selecting and implementing data collection strategies. The principles discussed in this chapter can be applied to any of the additional techniques that have been omitted. Readers interested in more specific guidelines or technical details should consult current issues of measurement journals (such as the *Journal of Educational Measurement*) and the references in the Annotated Bibliography at the end of this chapter.

PUTTING IT ALL TOGETHER

Eugene Anderson, the humane educator, followed the steps suggested in Figure 6.11 when he was developing his data collection strategies. His use of these steps will be summarized in the following paragraphs.

Initially, he knew that the outcome variable he wanted to measure was "attitude toward animal life." He had previously drawn up a list of possible operational definitions (chapters 4 and 5). From this

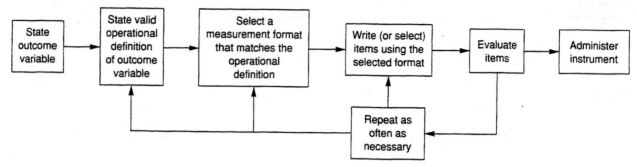

Figure 6.11   The Complete Process for Developing Valid Strategies for Measuring an Outcome Variable

list, he selected one that he thought was especially good: "Given a hypothetical situation in which animals might undergo pain and suffering, the respondent will choose to save the animals from that pain and suffering." He examined this operational definition, talked it over with a few colleagues, and decided that this was indeed a good operational definition of his outcome variable.

Next, he looked for a format with which he could assess the occurrence of this operational definition. He decided against observational techniques, because he felt that it would take too long to wait for such events to occur in a natural setting, and ethical considerations clearly militated against inflicting pain on animals just so that Mr. Anderson could obtain his data. Therefore, he decided to use the questionnaire format. Specifically, he decided to use the hypothetical situation of the burning house and to ask each respondent how he or she would respond in that situation. (See Figure 5.3 on page 112 for a copy of his instrument.) He incorporated some ideas from unobtrusive measurement into his data collection strategy, because he reasoned that students filling out the questionnaire would have no idea that the questionnaire had anything to do with animal life, and therefore they would be unlikely to react to the data collection process.

After he wrote the first version of the Fireman Test, he revised the items several times based on trial runs, reliability coefficients, validity information, and item analysis, as described in chapter 5. He eventually arrived at two valid forms of the Fireman Test, so that he could use one as a pretest and the other as a posttest.

At this point, Mr. Anderson started using the Fireman Tests to evaluate some of the presentations he gave. While doing so, he continued to go through the feedback loop described in Figure 6.11. He asked himself whether he needed any further data. Was his evidence already strong enough to require no further data collection, or should he look for more evidence? He decided he needed more evidence, and so he returned to the second step in the diagram and selected another operational definition from the list he had previously devised. He then went through Steps 3 and 4 and the feedback loop as often as he felt he still needed more evidence. He continued this process until he had the following set of data collection techniques:

Two versions of the Fireman Tests

A questionnaire that he administered to the students after he gave presentations, asking them to describe their feelings about animal life

An observation sheet that he left with the teachers, asking them to record specific behaviors that the children might display which would reveal different attitudes toward animal life

A values rating scale that listed a whole series of worthwhile values, one of which was attitude toward animal life; the children were asked to rank these in order of priority

A form that he submitted to veterinary clinics and animal control programs to ascertain whether certain animal-related behaviors increased or decreased in the area after his presentations

He could have developed even more data collection strategies, but he decided that it would be best to do a good job with what he had rather than run the risk of overwhelming himself with too much information. He felt that these strategies would get him some fairly good evidence, and he knew that he could always resort to additional operational definitions and more data collection strategies if he later discovered that he needed them.

Mr. Anderson did not always use all of the preceding data collection techniques in every school he visited. In some cases, circumstances prohibited him from collecting any data at all. However, whenever possible he collected what evidence he could. This information made it possible for him to change some of his methods of presentation and evaluate the effectiveness of some of his new ideas. He developed new confidence that his presentations were actually accomplishing useful goals.

SUMMARY

With well-designed measurement and data collection strategies, we can collect reliable and valid evidence concerning the outcomes of interest to us in educational settings. This chapter has discussed the major types of data collection strategies. Table 6.5 summarized the strengths and weaknesses of each of these major strategies. Many specific strategies for collecting data have not been discussed in this chapter, but the guidelines presented here will help you evaluate and implement these other strategies as the need arises.

To measure variables, it is necessary to follow these steps:

1. Identify and conceptually define the variable.
2. State valid operational definitions of that variable.
3. Select data collection formats compatible with that operational definition.
4. Design (or select) data collection procedures using the chosen formats.
5. Evaluate the procedures and make changes as necessary.
6. Administer the data collection process and tabulate the data appropriately.

What Comes Next

In chapter 7 we'll discuss ways to present and interpret the scores that result from our data collection processes. In chapter 8 we'll discuss how to use sampling strategies to collect reliable and valid data about a large group by sampling from a smaller group, and in chapter 9 we'll discuss how to use effective strategies to make observations and conduct interviews in naturalistic settings.

DOING YOUR OWN RESEARCH

When designing or selecting data collection processes, the most important criterion is that they be valid. The following guidelines emerge from the principles discussed in this and preceding chapters:

1. Develop good operational definitions of your outcome variables. Use the guidelines discussed in chapter 4.
2. Keep your operational definitions in mind when developing or selecting the format for data collection processes. Select a format not because you or someone else likes it but rather because it will contribute to the validity of the data collection process.
3. Be aware of the strengths and weaknesses of the various data collection formats. Select and use formats in such a way as to maximize the strengths and to avoid the pitfalls.

Whenever possible, use more than a single format. By using a variety of formats, you can gain the strengths of each and cancel out the weaknesses.

FOR FURTHER THOUGHT

1. Evaluate this statement: "True–False tests are totally useless for measuring academic performance. Students who know none of the answers can guess too easily."
2. Evaluate this statement: "Professionally designed tests and measurement devices are more likely to derive valid and useful information than those designed by nonprofessionals."

3. Evaluate this statement: "Open-ended question-naire items usually give more valid information than more structured items."

4. Evaluate this statement: "If time and money are available, it's usually better to conduct a personal interview than to have respondents complete a questionnaire."

ANNOTATED BIBLIOGRAPHY

These citations are subdivided by topics related to sections in this chapter. However, many of these sources contain information on other topics as well, and so it may be useful to examine the entire bibliography for information relevant to your interests.

The following sources offer useful information regarding classroom achievement tests:

Angelo, T. A., & Cross, K. P. (1993). *Classroom assessment techniques: A handbook for college teachers.* San Francisco: Jossey-Bass. This book suggests a large number of informal but effective strategies for assessing student performance during the early and intermediate stages of learning, so that the students and instructor can make adjustments to make instruction more effective.

Bennett, R. E., & Ward, W. C. (1993). *Construction versus choice in cognitive measurement.* Hillsdale, NJ: Lawrence Erlbaum. This book offers insights into the theoretical and technical considerations behind selecting a format for measuring cognitive outcomes. It focuses especially on issues in constructed-response formats, performance testing, and portfolio assessment.

Bloom, B. S., Hastings, J. T., and Madaus, G. F. (1971). *Handbook of formative and summative evaluation of student learning.* New York: McGraw-Hill. Although there have been important developments in the years since this book was published, this book has stood the test of time. Part I provides overall strategies for constructing achievement test items. Part II offers specific guidelines for constructing good items in specific subject matter areas.

Ebel, R. L., & Frisbie, D. A. (1986). *Essentials of educational measurement* (4th ed.). Englewood Cliffs, NJ: Prentice-Hall. Chapters 6 through 9 offer specific guidelines on how to write good items for various types of achievement tests.

Educational Testing Service. (1985). *Creative classroom testing: 10 designs for assessment and instruction.* Princeton, NJ: Educational Testing Service. This book describes a number of options other than essay, multiple-choice, and true–false items for assessing academic performance.

Gronlund, N. E. (1993). *How to make achievement tests and assessments* (5th ed.). Boston: Allyn and Bacon. This is a concise treatment of all the major information related to the construction of classroom achievement tests.

Gronlund, N. E., and Linn, R. L. (1990). *Measurement and evaluation in teaching* (6th ed.). New York: Macmillan. Part 2 of this book gives useful guidelines for constructing classroom tests. Chapter 8 presents especially good information on the interpretive exercise. Part 4 offers useful guidelines for observational techniques and rating scales.

Osterlind, S. J. (1989). *Constructing test items.* Boston: Kluwer Academic Press. This truly outstanding book presents concise, clear, and practical guidelines on how to write achievement test items. It should serve as a useful reference for both professional test designers and classroom teachers.

Popham, W. J. (1990). *Modern educational measurement* (2nd ed.). Englewood Cliffs, NJ: Prentice-Hall. This book is especially useful in its discussion of criterion-referenced measurement (especially in chapter 9).

Roid, G. H., & Haladyna, T. M. (1982). *A technology for test item writing.* New York: Academic Press. This book offers a practical and effective perspective on writing good test items.

The following sources offer useful information regarding the construction and use of questionnaires:

Anderson, L. W. (1981). *Assessing affective characteristics in the schools.* Boston: Allyn and Bacon. As its title suggests, this book includes recommendations for assessing affective outcomes. This excellent source of theoretical information on affective measurement is also probably the most frequently cited source for guidelines on the development of Likert scales.

Anderson, L. W. (1988). Attitudes and their measurement. In J. P. Keeves (Ed.), *Educational research, methodology, and measurement: An international handbook.* Oxford: Pergamon Press. This is a six-page summary of the key points discussed in the previous citation.

Angleitner, A., & Wiggins, J. S. (Eds.). (1986). *Personality assessment via questionnaire.* New York: Springer-Verlag. This book is more useful for interpreting personality assessments than for constructing them. The information is up to date.

Berdie, D. R., Anderson, J. F., & Niebuhr, M. A. (1986). *Questionnaires: Design and use* (2nd ed.). Metuchen, NJ: Scarecrow Press. In addition to offering excellent guidelines and examples, this book includes an annotated bibliography of 494 publications that have reported research on questionnaire usage.

Converse, J. M., & Presser, S. (1986). *Survey questions: Handcrafting the standardized questionnaire.* Newbury Park, CA: Sage. This book is especially useful for developing effective wording of survey questions.

Devaus, D. A. (1986). *Surveys in social research.* Boston, MA: Allen & Unwin. This book focuses in clear, nontechnical language on both designing and analyzing the results of survey instruments.

Fowler, F. J. (1988). *Survey research methods* (2nd ed.). Newbury Park, CA: Sage. This book covers all aspects of survey design and use.

Sedman, S., & Bradburn, M. M. (1982). *Asking questions: A practical guide to questionnaire design.* San Francisco, CA: Jossey-Bass. This is a practical guide to the nuances of writing effective structured questionnaires and interview guides.

The following sources offer useful information regarding the measurement of affective outcomes:

Gable, R. K. (1986). *Instrument development in the affective domain.* Boston: Kluwer-Nijhoff Publishing. This book summarizes the important data collection principles that relate to the measurement of affective characteristics.
(Several of the sources cited for questionnaires, especially Anderson [1981, 1988], are also pertinent to measuring affective characteristics.)

The following sources offer useful information regarding observational strategies:

Alberto, P., & Troutman, A. (1990). *Applied behavior analysis for teachers* (3rd ed.). Columbus, OH: Merrill. Chapter 4 of this book offers useful guidelines for collecting and graphing data. It includes discussion of such techniques as time sampling and latency recording. These guidelines are especially effective in evaluating behavior modification programs in special-education settings.

Bakeman, R., & Gottman, J. M. (1986). *Observing interaction: An introduction to sequential analysis.* New York: Cambridge University Press. This book focuses on collecting sequential data—that is, information about continuous processes or interactions in educational settings.

Evertson, C. M., & Green, J. L. (1986). Observation as inquiry and method. In M. C. Wittrock (Ed.), *Handbook of research on teaching* (3rd ed.). New York: Macmillan. The first author has been active in some of the best observational studies published with regard to instructional activities. This book clearly describes how to conduct good observational research.

Fryer, B. J. (1989). Twenty years of classroom climate work: Progress and prospect. *Journal of Curriculum Studies, 21*(4), 307–327. This article not only describes the instruments, it also summarizes the research on classroom climate.

Gronlund, N. E. (1959). *Sociometry in the classroom.* New York: Harper. This is an old citation, but it is probably still the best single source on the topic of measuring the social interactions in a classroom through sociograms and similar techniques.

The following sources offer useful information regarding interviewing techniques:

Gordon, R. (1992). *Basic interviewing skills.* Itasca, IL: Peacock. This book covers a wide range of interviewing skills, from designing relevant and motivating questions to recording and interpreting the data.

Krathwohl, D. R. (1993). *Methods of educational and social science research: An integrated approach.* New York: Longman. Chapter 16 includes a useful discussion of the critical characteristics of the individual interview, the group interview, the telephone interview, and the mailed questionnaire.

Lavrakas, P. J. (1987). *Telephone survey methods: Sampling, selection, and supervision.* Newbury Park, CA: Sage. This short book provides guidelines for effective data collection via telephone.

Tolar, A. (Ed.). (1985). *Effective interviewing.* Springfield, IL: Charles Thomas. This book discusses a large variety of interviewing techniques, including several that would be useful for educators collecting research data.

The following source offers useful information regarding unobtrusive data collection processes:

Webb, E. J., Campbell, D. T., Schwartz, R. D., Sechrest, L., & Grove, J. B. (1981). *Nonreactive measures in the social sciences* (2nd ed.). Boston: Houghton Mifflin. This is the second edition of an old but renowned book that presents in detail the theory behind unobtrusive measurement, as well as numerous specific strategies and examples of the successful use of such strategies.

The following sources offer useful information regarding standardized data collection processes:

American Educational Research Association, American Psychological Association, & National Council for Measurement in Education. (1985). *Standards for educational and psychological testing.* Washington, DC: American Psychological Association. These are the standards that the three corporate authors recommend test developers follow for developing, publishing, and interpreting data collection instruments. A familiarity with these standards will help you make better use of standardized materials.

Anastasi, A. (1988). *Psychological testing*. New York: Macmillan. This book approaches data collection from the perspective of standardized tests. It will be useful for persons who interpret such tests as well as for those who design them.

Kramer, J. J., & Conoley, J. C. (Eds.). (1992). *The Eleventh Mental Measurements Yearbook*. Lincoln, NE: Buros Institute of Mental Measurements. This book and earlier volumes in the series provide critical, scholarly evaluations of published standardized data collection materials.

Mehrens, W. A., & Lehmann, I. J. (1987). *Using standardized tests in education* (3rd ed.). New York: Longman. This book offers detailed descriptions of achievement, personality, and aptitude tests that may be useful to educational researchers.

Each of the following sources covers more than one of the preceding areas:

Borg, W. R. (1989). *Educational research: An introduction*. New York: Longman. Chapter 9 includes detailed information on standardized tests. Chapter 11 discusses interviews and questionnaires. Chapter 12 discusses observational strategies.

Kerlinger, F. N. (1986). *Foundations of behavioral research* (3rd ed.). New York: Holt, Rinehart and Winston. Chapters 28 through 34 present detailed and sometimes complex information on the use of specific methods of data collection.

McKillip, J. (1987). *Need analysis: Tools for the human services and education*. Newbury Park, CA: Sage. This book describes in moderate detail specific strategies for ascertaining needs through data collection and analysis.

Worthen, B. R., Borg, W. R., & White, K. R. (1993). *Measurement and evaluation in the schools*. New York: Longman. This book is an excellent source of suggestions for developing and using data collection processes of all kinds. Chapter 16 provides useful guidelines for selecting professionally developed instruments.

CHAPTER 6

Research Report Analysis

The research report in Appendix C uses two strategies to measure the ability of students to solve problems: the unit pretests and the Watson-Glaser Test of Critical Thinking.

1. How useful were the unit pretests as a measure of problem-solving ability?

2. How useful was the Watson-Glaser test as a measure of problem-solving ability?

ANSWERS:

1. Although they were commercially produced, the unit tests should be regarded as classroom achievement tests. They had the advantage of being directly related to the objectives of the units of instruction. The major disadvantages were that it was not clear that they were really valid measures of problem-solving ability, and there were no norms to compare the performance of the students in the experimental and control groups with that of other students.

2. The Watson-Glaser Test of Critical Thinking was an example of a standardized test. Its major advantages were that there was information regarding its reliability and validity as a measure of critical thinking, and there were norms to compare the performance of students on this test with that of other students in the standardization group. Its main weakness was that it was not clear that critical thinking as measured by this test was really the same thing as problem solving as most science teachers or other educators would define that concept.

To a certain extent, these two data collection strategies supplemented each other nicely. That is, the strengths of the Watson-Glaser test almost directly duplicated the weaknesses of the unit pretests.

REPORTING AND INTERPRETING THE RESULTS OF DATA COLLECTION PROCESSES

■ **WHERE WE'VE BEEN**

We've described the overall principles for operationally defining and measuring variables reliably and validly and have examined strategies for implementing specific types of measurement processes.

■ **WHERE WE'RE GOING NOW**

We're going to discuss ways to present and interpret the scores that result from our measurement processes.

■ **CHAPTER PREVIEW**

Once you have designed and administered a data collection process, the scores have to be tabulated, summarized, presented, and interpreted. This chapter deals with the basic principles of score use and interpretation, topics that are approached in a conceptual rather than a mathematical manner. After understanding the concepts, you should be able to make better use of your own results and interpret the data that others present to you.

In previous chapters we focused on the reliability and validity of data collection processes for assessing operationally defined outcome variables; this chapter focuses on presenting and interpreting the scores that result from such processes. After reading this chapter, you should be able to

1. Identify examples of nominal, ordinal, interval, and ratio scale data.
2. Define the mode, the median, and the mean and identify situations in which each is used.
3. Describe and interpret examples of ways to express individual differences in group scores, such as using the standard deviation.

4. Distinguish between norm-referenced and criterion-referenced measurement techniques.

5. Interpret examples of percentiles and derived scores.

■

Other topics related to reporting and interpreting the results of data collection processes are presented elsewhere in this book: correlation coefficients and scattergrams are discussed in chapter 13; inferential statistics are discussed in chapter 14; and strategies for graphing data, which are briefly mentioned in this chapter, are discussed more completely in chapter 19.

MEASUREMENT SCALES

Examine the questionnaire in Figure 7.1. The person who completed it has given the answer "2" to questions 1, 2, 4, 5, 7, 9A, and 9E. Does "2" have the same meaning in each of these responses? For example, does it always mean twice as much as 1 and half as much as 4? Actually, it has this meaning only in question 5. There is no logic behind the assumption that a female is twice a male, that single is twice married and half widowed, or that "disagree" is twice "strongly disagree" and half "agree"; the answer "2" is meaningful in these items, but the meaning is different from that in question 5, where a person who has two children does have twice as many offspring as a person with one child and half as many as a person with four children. These differences in meaning are related to the concept of scales of measurement.

There are four levels of meaning (scales) of measurement: the nominal, ordinal, interval, and ratio scales. With *nominal* scale data, the number merely attaches a label to a piece of information. The response "2" in question 1 is nominal scale data. The nominal scale does not indicate rank or order, nor do the sizes of the intervals between the numbers mean anything significant. It would be just as appropriate to classify males as "2" and females as "1," or even to classify males as "2" and females as "7." All that the numbers do here is attach a label to the respondent's answer.

| BOX 7.1 | Why Bother with Nominal Numbers? |

If nominal scale numbers convey so little information, why bother with them at all? The answer is that they are often convenient for tabulating data, especially in a computerized format.

Many computer programs that perform statistical analyses are designed to deal with numbers, not with words. Therefore, these programs can easily handle a comparison of 1s and 2s, but they would have more trouble comparing experimentals to controls.

In addition, it is sometimes a great deal more convenient to label a person or a group with a number than with a more descriptive name. In sports, for example, it is easier for a referee to call a foul on number 22 than on Patrick Hornschemeier—even though both the number and the name refer to exactly the same person.

The important point is that a nominal number cannot be treated the same way as other numbers. It makes no sense to say that Patrick Hornschemeier (number 22) is twice as good as Zeke Zimmerman (number 11) or even that he is better or worse than Michael Jordan (number 23). On the other hand, if Hornschemeier had 22 points and Zimmerman had 11, then it would be safe to say that Hornschemeier had scored twice as many points as Zimmerman. By knowing the scale of measurement, we can determine what restrictions we must put on our use and interpretation of the numbers.

Figure 7.1 Samples of the Three Scales of Measurement

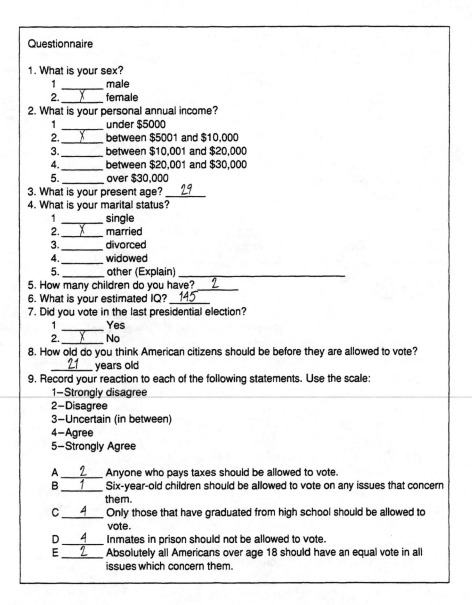

Questionnaire

1. What is your sex?
   1 _____ male
   2. __X__ female
2. What is your personal annual income?
   1 _____ under $5000
   2. __X__ between $5001 and $10,000
   3. _____ between $10,001 and $20,000
   4. _____ between $20,001 and $30,000
   5. _____ over $30,000
3. What is your present age? __29__
4. What is your marital status?
   1 _____ single
   2. __X__ married
   3. _____ divorced
   4. _____ widowed
   5. _____ other (Explain) _____
5. How many children do you have? __2__
6. What is your estimated IQ? __145__
7. Did you vote in the last presidential election?
   1 _____ Yes
   2. __X__ No
8. How old do you think American citizens should be before they are allowed to vote?
   __21__ years old
9. Record your reaction to each of the following statements. Use the scale:
   1–Strongly disagree
   2–Disagree
   3–Uncertain (in between)
   4–Agree
   5–Strongly Agree

   A __2__ Anyone who pays taxes should be allowed to vote.
   B __1__ Six-year-old children should be allowed to vote on any issues that concern them.
   C __4__ Only those that have graduated from high school should be allowed to vote.
   D __4__ Inmates in prison should not be allowed to vote.
   E __2__ Absolutely all Americans over age 18 should have an equal vote in all issues which concern them.

With *ordinal* scale data, the number not only attaches a label, it also indicates an ordering of data. For example, in question 2, the answer of "2" had a level of income between the levels indicated by "1" and "3." The ordinal scale "2" attaches a label and assigns an ordering, but this arrangement is *only* an ordering. The size of the interval between items in the ordering is not constant, nor is it meaningful to multiply and divide the ordered numbers. For example, it is not accurate to assume that a person answer-

ing "2" is as much more affluent than a person answering "1" as a person answering "5" is more affluent than a person answering "4." (If this last part confuses you, just remember that ordinal data indicate *only* an ordering of data. They are more precise than nominal data but less specific than interval data.)

Of the four scales, the interval and ratio scales provide the most specific information. With *interval* scale and *ratio* scale data, the number not only attaches a label and indicates an ordering, but the intervals between the numbers are also meaningful. Many standardized test scores (but not percentiles) employ interval scales. For example, verbal SAT scores range from 200 to 800. The difference between 450 and 500 is considered to be the same as that between 500 and 550. In an example of ratio scale data, a person with two children has one more child than a person with only one child; and likewise a person with five children has one more child than a person with four children.

Many students find it difficult to distinguish between examples at interval and ratio levels. Our feeling is that it is not worth the effort needed to overcome this difficulty. It is reasonable to simply view ratio data as a specific type of interval data. There are no instances in educational research where it is important for researchers or readers of research to make the distinction between interval and ratio scales of measurement. It is, however, important to distinguish among nominal, ordinal, and interval/ratio scales. We have listed all four levels for the sake of completeness. Although this book will use the words correctly, it will place no further emphasis on this distinction.

At this point, you may ask, "Who cares about scales of measurement?" In a moment we'll show you the difference this all makes, but first here's a little quiz.

REVIEW QUIZ 7.1

Indicate which scale of data is provided by the underlined number in each statement.

Betty had the <u>second</u> highest score with <u>14</u> correct.

Mary wore the number <u>2</u> during her varsity days.

<u>Fourteen</u> players wear the number <u>12</u> in the NFL.

1. <u>Second</u> is _____ scale.
2. <u>14</u> is _____ scale.
3. <u>2</u> is _____ scale.
4. <u>Fourteen</u> is _____ scale.
5. <u>12</u> is _____ scale.

There are two reasons why understanding scales of measurement is important. First, since the higher levels of measurement convey more information, you should choose measurement strategies that use the higher levels whenever appropriate. For example, if you construct a questionnaire with question 2 written the way it appears in Figure 7.1, then you would not be able to compute a precise average of incomes. However, if you asked the respondents to indicate their exact incomes, then you would have ratio data, and your analysis would be more precise. The second important reason for understanding measurement scales is that some statistical analyses can be employed only when the data fit the proper scale, so you can perform more appropriate analyses if you know what the scales mean.

Sometimes the scale of data is dictated by factors other than the preference of the data collector. For example, although a specific salary figure gives interval data and permits more precise analysis, persons being interviewed may consider a specific question about their income to be an invasion of their privacy; if this is the case, the data collector would be well advised to collect the less specific ordinal data shown in question 2 of Figure 7.1. (Imprecise information is better than none at all.) On the other hand, if the interviewer is copying information from a personnel file, it would probably be a mistake to convert the data to the question 2 format, since this would unnecessarily reduce the precision of the available data.

WAYS TO REPORT SCORES

When you have just one score on a single person, it is easy to report that score. However, when you have either a large number of scores on a single test for a whole group of people or scores on a large number of tests for an individual, a listing of all these scores at once may overwhelm the reader. It would be much more convenient to report a single score that summarizes all the other scores. One of the most common ways to summarize scores is to use a measure of *central tendency*—often referred to as an *average*. A

Table 7.1 The Relationship between Scales of Measurement and Measures of Central Tendency That Can Be Used with Each

	Scales of Measurement		
	Nominal	Ordinal	Interval
Allowable Measures of Central Tendency	Mode	Mode Median	Mode Median Mean

measure of central tendency gives a single score as typical or representative of all the other scores. There are three kinds of measures of central tendency: the mode, the median, and the mean.

A measure of central tendency gives a single score as typical or representative of all the other scores.

The *mode* is the most frequently occurring score in a set of scores. You *must* use the mode to indicate the average when all you have is nominal data; any other average would be meaningless. If you wanted to know what color eyes the average American has, the answer would be expressed in terms of the mode. A certain color of eyes would be the most frequent color. If we said that the average respondent to a questionnaire was a 23-year-old white female, *white* and *female* would be modes, indicating that more respondents were female than male and more were white than any other race. Age could also be expressed as a mode, but it would be more meaningful to use a median or mean to express age.

The *median* is the midpoint in a set of scores.[1] It can be the middle score or an imaginary dividing point that splits the distribution of scores in half. You *must* use the median instead of the mean (discussed next) when you have ordinal data, but with interval or ratio data you can take your choice of the mean or median, depending on which would give

the better picture. In the example from the previous paragraph, the age would probably be given as a median, since the person with the middle age would be a reasonable representation of what is typical.

The *mean* is the arithmetic average, obtained by adding all the scores together and dividing by the number of scores that went into computing that total. The mean is popular because it is easy to compute and gives equal weight to all the scores. In statistics, the mean is also popular because it can be used as the basis for a vast number of useful analyses. However, it can be meaningfully calculated only for interval or ratio data. Table 7.1 summarizes the three measures of central tendency and their relationship to nominal, ordinal, and interval data.

Table 7.2 presents some SAT scores and averages obtained by each of the methods of computing central tendency. Since SAT scores are interval data, it is possible to compute either a mode, a median, or a mean for such scores. The researcher can choose the measure of central tendency that presents the most accurate picture.

For these scores, the mode is not very meaningful (in our example, two students had scores of 870, but it is not reasonable to say that theirs is the typical score in this group). The mean would not be the best scale to use either (the mean is 1040.7, but this is strongly influenced by the single 1560 score, which is far higher than anyone else's score; without Chris's score, the mean would have been only 1002.9). In presenting these scores, the median seems to be the best scale to use (in our example, the median score is 980, and it seems reasonable that for this group of students, such a score is more typical than either the mode or the mean—half are above the median and half are below it).

---

[1]To calculate the median, it is necessary to first put the scores in order from highest to lowest and then select the middle score. It would be a mistake to arrange scores haphazardly and to consider the middle score to be the median.

Table 7.2 Combined Verbal and Nonverbal SAT Scores for a Group of Students (scores are arranged in descending order)%

Chris	1570	
Todd	1150	
Marian	1140	
Isiah	1120	
Tony	1100	
Marcia	1080	
Ylonda	1000	Mode = 870
Annette	980	Median = 980
Ralph	970	Mean = 1040.7
Marge	960	
Alphonse	950	
Wanda	940	
Lee Anne	910	
Wendy	870	
Pat	870	

Note that the group of students whose scores are presented in Table 7.2 is atypical. In most large groups, the mean, median, and mode of cognitive characteristics are approximately the same. When the data meet the mathematical specifications of the normal distribution (discussed later in this chapter), the mode, median, and mean are all represented by the same score; in such cases, the mean is most frequently reported. Even when the data deviate somewhat from the normal curve, the mean is still the most popular measure of central tendency. In general, when it is possible to do so (that is, when you have interval or ratio data), compute and report the mean unless there is a good reason to do otherwise, such as in the following two cases:

1. When the scores are badly skewed—that is, when they depart radically from the normal distribution (e.g., when there are many scores at the very top or bottom of the distribution). In this case, it would be better to use the median to represent the typical score.

2. When a distribution of scores is artificially truncated (e.g., if 5 of 17 runners do not complete a race and therefore have no numerical scores). In this case, the median is easy to compute—it would be the time of the 9th runner.

REVIEW QUIZ 7.2

What is the mode, median, and mean of each of the following sets of scores?

1. 45, 35, 48, 39, 41, 44, 45
2. 25, 18, 17, 18, 27, 18, 23, 17, 14

In addition to knowing the typical (average) score by examining a measure of central tendency, it is useful to know the degree of spread or individual differences among the scores. The spread can be expressed roughly by stating the *range,* which is simply the difference between the highest and lowest scores. If we told you that scores on a test averaged 45 with a range of 3 to 95, you would easily perceive that these scores would be more spread out than if we told you that the average was 45 with a range of 40 to 50. The range is actually a rough estimate of the spread in scores. A much better practice is to report the *standard deviation.* As its name implies, this is simply a description of the average magnitude of the differences among individual scores in a set of scores. The larger the standard deviation, the greater the spread among the scores. For example, if we told you that a test had a mean of 45 and a standard deviation of 12.3, you would know that the scores were spread further apart than if the mean was 45 with a standard deviation of 2.1.

The standard deviation is simply a description of the average magnitude of the differences among individual scores in a set of scores.

When scores approximately fit the normal distribution, then the standard deviation conveys even more useful information. In general, when scores in large samples are normally distributed, the highest score will be about three standard deviations above the mean, and the lowest score will be about three standard deviations below the mean. With this brief introduction, you should be able to conclude that a test with a mean of 65 and a standard deviation of 10 has both lower and higher scores than a test with a mean of 80 and a standard deviation of 2. (The mean and the standard deviation are important concepts and will appear again in our discussion of derived scores [Figure 7.3].)

This is not a statistics course, so the method for computing the standard deviation will not be presented here. (You can easily calculate these statistics by computer, if you have access to appropriate programs.)

REVIEW QUIZ 7.3

In each of the following two sets of descriptions, which scores are most spread out? Which scores are most closely clustered together? Which test is likely to have the highest score? Which is likely to have the lowest score?

1. a. a test with a mean of 60 and a standard deviation of 6.3

    b. a test with a mean of 60 and a standard deviation of 16.3

    c. a test with a mean of 60 and a standard deviation of 1.3

2. a. a test with a mean of 50 and a standard deviation of 5.4

    b. a test with a mean of 60 and a standard deviation of 9.5

    c. a test with a mean of 70 and a standard deviation of 17.5

It is useful to graph data so that a person reading the report has a visual representation of the scores. As chapter 18 will indicate, it is often useful to tabulate the results of research projects in electronic databases or spreadsheets, and the best of these often provide tools for drawing effective and readable graphs. Figure 7.2 shows examples of graphs that are often employed to present the findings of educational research. Although graphs will be used in the later chapters of this book, specific graphing strategies will not be discussed here. Useful specific strategies can be found in the measurement and statistics

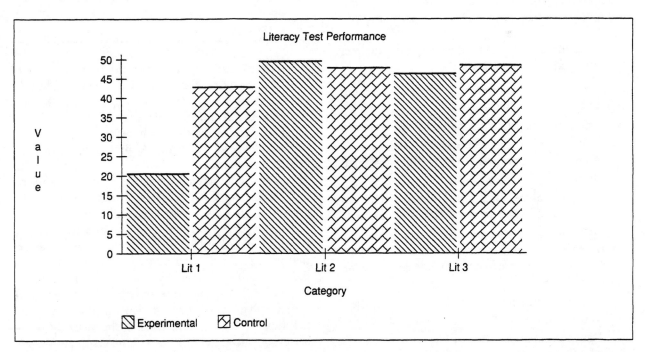

Figure 7.2 An Example of a Bar Graph Generated from the Microsoft Works Spreadsheet (Note: This graph is based on the data that is used as an example in Figures 18.7 and 18.8)

books referred to in the Annotated Bibliography at the end of this chapter.

In presenting your data, use whatever statistics and graphs give an accurate and meaningful picture. By using the wrong statistic or a badly drawn graph, you can seriously mislead yourself and your readers. This information is also useful to you as a reader of reports written by others. Watch for misleading presentations of data. In *How to Lie with Statistics,* Huff (1954) demonstrates some grotesque falsifications that can be achieved by simply using the wrong statistic or graph. Huff's book is highly recommended to help you understand what *not* to do when presenting your information.

DESCRIBING AND COMPARING TEST PERFORMANCE

There are three basic ways to compare a person's performance during a data collection process: with an absolute standard, with a criterion-referenced standard, or with a norm-referenced standard. Some examples from physical and educational measurement may make this clear:

Absolute scores simply state the observed outcome.

Physical measurement: He is 5'10" tall.

Educational measurement: He spelled 43 out of 50 words correctly.

Criterion-referenced scores compare the person's performance with a standard, or criterion.

Physical measurement: He is tall enough to dunk the ball in the basket.

Educational measurement: His score of 43 out of 50 put him past the cutoff point to go on to the next lesson.

Norm-referenced scores compare a person's performance with that of other people in the same context.

Physical measurement: He is the third smallest and second fastest player on the squad of 15.

Educational measurement: His score of 43 out of 50 was not very good; 75% of his classmates did better.

All three types of scores are useful, depending on the purpose for which you are conducting the measurement.

Percentiles

A *percentile* indicates the percentage of scores that a raw score exceeds. (Percentiles are ordinal data.) A percentile must necessarily be based on a reference to some specific group. Thus, if you score at the 75th percentile on the final exam in a course, this means that you finished above 75% of the students who took the same exam.

Percentiles are not the same as percentages of correct answers—finishing at the 75th percentile does not mean that you answered 75% of the questions correctly. If all the other students on the test did very well, it might take a percentage of 95% correct answers to be at the 75th percentile, whereas if everyone else did poorly, a score of 60% correct answers might put you at the 75th percentile.

Percentiles are not the same as percentages of correct answers.

Percentiles are often used in the interpretation of standardized tests. For example, a person might take the Graduate Record Exam (GRE) and find that she scored at the 80th percentile with regard to the overall norm group, at the 50th percentile compared with students at University A, and at the 95th percentile compared with University B students. This means that compared with all the students who typically take the GRE (that is, compared with the "norm group"), her score exceeded 80% of them. However, if the student is interested in going to graduate school at University A, she should be aware that her score exceeded only 50% of the students at that school. On the other hand, if she is interested in University B, she can relax and realize that her score is better than 95% of the students at that school. In practical terms, this means that she is likely to do better at University B than at University A—assuming that the skills measured by the GRE are important at both schools.

Normal Curve and Derived Scores

The normal distribution (normal curve) is a graph of a mathematical probability formula. Its derivation and theory will not be discussed here, except to say that many events in nature approximate the normal curve. It is a mathematically convenient formula. It is useful in education because many human characteristics (such as intelligence, spatial ability, and manual dexterity) are distributed nearly normally and are well represented by this theoretical distribution.

Because of the mathematical convenience and because many educational abilities do fit this curve, the normal curve has become popular as a means of interpreting educational and psychological tests. When test designers discovered that some of their tests did not fit the normal curve, they artificially redesigned the tests so that they would fit the curve. This may sound illogical, and sometimes it is. But to the extent that student ability and learning is influenced by many random factors, the normal distribution is logical. Whether we approve of the logic or not, the results of many standardized tests are pre-sented in terms based on the normal curve; and so an understanding of these terms will be helpful to you as an educator.

The normal curve is diagrammed in Figure 7.3. In this curve, 68% of the scores fall within plus or minus one standard deviation of the mean (34% above and 34% below the mean). Try reading the percentages yourself. What percentage of the scores falls below two standard deviations above the mean? The answer is 98%. What percentage of IQ scores falls between 85 and 130? The answer is 82%.

By applying some straightforward mathematical computations (which are not discussed in this text), it is possible to compute *derived scores*. These are scores based on the normal distribution that have arbitrarily assigned means and standard deviations. This may sound complicated, but the interpretation of such scores is actually simple. For example, a *standard score* is a derived score with a mean of 0 and a standard deviation of 1. Standard scores are not particularly important, except as a basis for computing nearly all other derived scores.

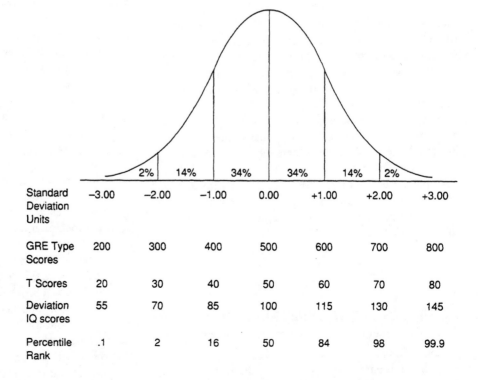

Figure 7.3 The Normal Curve and Several Derived Scores Based on It

	2%	14%	34%	34%	14%	2%
Standard Deviation Units	−3.00	−2.00	−1.00	0.00	+1.00	+2.00	+3.00
GRE Type Scores	200	300	400	500	600	700	800
T Scores	20	30	40	50	60	70	80
Deviation IQ scores	55	70	85	100	115	130	145
Percentile Rank	.1	2	16	50	84	98	99.9

REVIEW QUIZ 7.4

A popular derived score is the IQ score, which usually has a mean of 100 and a standard deviation of 15. With this information, answer the following questions.

1. What percentage of people have an IQ below 100?

2. What percentage of people have an IQ above 100?

3. What percentage of people have an IQ between 85 and 115?

4. What percentage of people have an IQ below 115?

5. What percentage of people have an IQ below 85?

Another common type of score is the T score, which has a mean of 50 and a standard deviation of 10. Two other derived scores, popular for reporting on standardized achievement tests, are the GRE-type and SAT-type scores, both of which have a mean of 500 and a standard deviation of 100. The quantitative interpretation of all these scores is exactly the same, and they serve as a good way to compare the performances of different people on the same test, or even to compare the performance of the same person on different tests.

It is always possible to convert a derived score to a percentile. This can be done by using the diagram in Figure 7.3 or using more detailed tables based on the formula from which that figure was derived. For example, a person with a GRE score of 500 is at the 50th percentile of graduate students on that test, and one with a score of 600 is at the 84th percentile of the same norm group.

REVIEW QUIZ 7.5

1. What percentage of T scores falls below 60?

2. What percentage of T scores falls between 30 and 40?

3. What percentage of GRE scores falls above 600?

4. What percentage of GRE scores falls between 400 and 600?

5. Is there the same number of persons between GRE scores of 400 and 500 as there is between 500 and 600?

6. Is there the same number of persons between GRE scores of 500 and 600 as there is between 600 and 700?

A technical note is in order here. Percentiles are ordinal data. For mathematical reasons, a slight change in raw scores near the middle of the distribution (near the 50th percentile) results in a greater shift in the percentiles than does a change of the same size near the extremes of the distribution. Because of this irregularity, it is *not* appropriate to compute means or to do many other statistical calculations with percentile scores. When all the scores are clustered around the mean or around some other common point in the distribution, little distortion results. However, attempts to treat ordinal data (percentiles) as interval scores often result in unanticipated distortions. This is important to remember. A frequent error that teachers make is to obtain the mean percentile scores of students on tests and to use average (mean) percentile scores as indicators of achievement or improvement. This procedure is *not* appropriate; it is likely to give misleading results. The correct procedure is to use the original, raw (nonderived) scores for the mathematical calculations.

Many readers will understand the discussion in the preceding paragraph quite easily if they reread that paragraph and look at Figure 7.3. Others will find this whole discussion mystifying. It is not worth losing sleep over. Just remember—do *not* average percentiles—when you compute means, use raw scores.

More specific information on the computation and use of various derived standard scores can be found in a good measurement textbook. When interpreting such scores, remember that they are always based on a norm group. A score that is high in one norm group might be low in another. If the norm group is appropriate, then the use of such scores provides a convenient framework for comparison. Only to the extent that the norm group resembles your own group do you really want to compare your scores with theirs.

PUTTING IT ALL TOGETHER

When Mr. Anderson had the teacher administer his Fireman Test a week before he presented his program at Warren Harding School, he found a mean of 1.2 (out of a possible 3.0) with a standard deviation of .37. Since the scores were pretty well spread out (much like a normal curve), he decided that stating the mean would be a good way to report the data. This average meant that in the class of 30 children, the typical child chose "about 1.2" animals to save from the fire. (One of Mr. Anderson's friends commented that she'd hate to be the "two-tenths of an animal" that was saved.) Mr. Anderson knew that his mean was a convenient way to summarize the data.

A week after the pretest, Mr. Anderson visited the school and gave what he considered to be a good program. The children seemed to respond happily and enthusiastically. A week later, the teacher gave the alternate form of the Fireman Test. This time the students chose an average of 1.3 animals with a standard deviation of .41. Mr. Anderson was slightly discouraged, because these results showed that the children's attitudes had not changed much as a result of his efforts. He resolved to try some new strategies the next time he visited a classroom.

When Mr. Anderson reported his results to the teacher, she was amazed. She remarked, "How can these children be so cruel? Where have I gone wrong?" Mr. Anderson agreed that it would be desirable to see higher scores among her pupils, but he also pointed out that their performance was actually typical of how most students throughout the country responded on the same test. During the validation process, the test had been administered all over the country. He had gotten averages as low as 0.6 and as high as 2.3. The performance of the present group was typical, according to these norms.

Although he was reassured by his awareness that these results were typical, Mr. Anderson was still concerned. After all, it was not exactly inspiring to know that the typical child would save only one out of three living things from certain death in a fire. Several children had chosen to save no animals—they chose to save credit cards and other material things instead. The fact that several schools stressing humane values toward animals had averaged so much

higher suggested to him that it was possible (and desirable) to develop attitudes that would persuade children to be more concerned about animal life. Mr. Anderson resolved to keep working on his project.

SUMMARY

When collecting or interpreting data, it is important to know that numbers can have different levels of meaning. For example, a number can be used merely to label or categorize a response. This sort of number (nominal scale) has a low level of meaning. A higher level of meaning comes with numbers that order responses (ordinal data). An even higher level of meaning (interval or ratio data) is present when numbers attempt to present exact scores, such as when we state that a person got 17 correct out of 20. Although even the lowest scale is useful, higher-level scales give more precise information and are more easily adapted to many statistical procedures.

Scores can be summarized by using either the mode (most frequent score), the median (midpoint of the scores), or the mean (arithmetic average) to indicate typical performance. When reporting data, you should choose the measure of central tendency that gives the most accurate picture of what is typical in a set of scores. In addition, it is possible to report the standard deviation to indicate the spread of the scores around the mean.

Scores from measurement processes can be either absolute, criterion referenced, or norm referenced. An absolute score simply states a measure of performance without comparing it with any standard. However, scores are not particularly useful unless they are compared with something. Criterion-referenced scores compare test performance with a specific standard; such a comparison enables the test interpreter to decide whether the scores are satisfactory according to established standards. Norm-referenced tests compare test performance with that of others who were measured by the same procedure. Teachers are usually more interested in knowing how children compare with a useful standard than how they compare with other children; but norm-referenced comparisons may also provide useful insights.

Criterion-referenced scores are easy to understand because they are usually straightforward raw scores or percentages. Norm-referenced scores are often converted to percentiles or other derived standard scores. A student's percentile score on a test indicates what percentage of other students who took the same test fell below that student's score. Derived scores are often based on the normal curve. They use an arbitrary mean to make comparisons showing how respondents compare with other persons who took the same test.

What Comes Next

In the next two chapters we'll discuss how to use sampling strategies to learn about a large group by sampling from a smaller group, and how to use effective observation and interview strategies in naturalistic settings. Then we'll move on to strategies for examining cause-and-effect relationships in education.

DOING YOUR OWN RESEARCH

With proper planning, you can use the statistical packages described in chapter 18 to facilitate the tabulation and presentation of data from your research studies.

FOR FURTHER THOUGHT

1. The British statesman Benjamin Disraeli has been quoted as saying, "There are lies, damned lies, and statistics." Why are people so suspicious of statistics?

2. A person scored 600 on the verbal portion of the SAT, which has a mean of 500 and a standard deviation of 100. His friend scored 115 on an IQ test, which has a mean of 100 and a standard deviation of 15. He hears an education professor say that the SAT is really nothing more than a verbal intelligence test. He therefore concludes that he and his friend have almost exactly the same level of intelligence, since they both scored one standard deviation above the mean. What's wrong with this reasoning?

REFERENCE

Huff, D. (1954). *How to lie with statistics.* New York: Norton.

ANNOTATED BIBLIOGRAPHY

Bertrand, A., & Cebula, J. P. (1980). *Tests, measurement, and evaluation: A developmental approach.* Reading, MA: Addison-Wesley. Chapter 7 provides an innovative presentation of most of the topics covered in the present chapter.

Ebel, R. L., & Frisbie, D. A. (1991). *Essentials of educational measurement* (5th ed.). Englewood Cliffs, NJ: Prentice-Hall. Chapters 7 through 12 are especially useful for helping teachers develop classroom achievement tests. Chapter 14 discusses observation and informal data collection techniques. Chapters 16 through 18 provide useful information on using standardized tests.

Hills, J. R. (1986). *All of Hills' handy hints.* Columbus, OH: Merrill. This is a collection of articles originally published in *Educational measurement: Issues and practice.* The articles offer practical and interesting insights into fallacies in the interpretation of test scores. (Incidentally, the original journal provides theoretically sound guidelines that are easy to understand.)

Kubiszyn, T., & Borich, G. (1987). *Educational tests and measurement: Classroom application and practice.* Glenview, IL: Scott, Foresman and Company. The chapter on data presentation provides useful and practical guidelines for communicating data effectively through graphs and diagrams.

Lyman, H. B. (1986). *Test scores and what they mean* (4th ed.). Englewood Cliffs, NJ: Prentice-Hall. This book provides a detailed discussion of the interpretation of test scores.

Tufte, E. R. (1983). *The visual display of quantitative information.* Cheshire, CT: Graphic Press. This book offers interesting examples of how to display information and discusses strategies for presenting data graphically.

Wainer, H. (1992). Understanding graphs and tables. *Educational Researcher, 21,* 14–23. This article presents strategies for employing and interpreting sophisticated yet understandable graphs to display quantitative data.

Worthen, B. R., Borg, W. R., & White, K. R. (1993). *Measurement and evaluation in the schools.* New York: Longman. Chapter 5 presents a practical discussion of the meaning of test scores.

ANSWERS TO QUIZZES

Review Quiz 7.1

1. ordinal
2. interval or ratio
3. nominal
4. interval or ratio
5. nominal

Review Quiz 7.2

1. mode: 45; median: 44; mean: 42.4
2. mode: 18; median: 18; mean: 19.7

Review Quiz 7.3

1. Most spread out: Test b
   Most closely clustered: Test c
   Highest score: Test b
   Lowest score: Test b
2. Most spread out: Test c

Most closely clustered: Test a
Highest score: Test c
Lowest score: Test c

Review Quiz 7.4

1. 50% (34% + 14% + 2%)
2. 50% (34% + 14% + 2%)
3. 68% (34% + 34%)
4. 84% (34% + 34% + 14% + 2%)
5. 16% (14% + 2%)

Review Quiz 7.5

1. 84% (34% + 34% + 14% + 2%)
2. 14%
3. 16% (14% + 2%)
4. 68% (34% + 34%)
5. Yes (34% each)
6. No (34% between 500 and 600; 14% between 600 and 700)

CHAPTER 7

Research Report Analysis

The research report in Appendix C uses several types of scores to present the results of the study.

1. The control group scored 47.26 on the pretest. Does this score represent nominal, ordinal, or interval scale data?
2. The control group's score of 47.26 on the pretest put it at the 26th percentile. Does this percentile score represent nominal, ordinal, or interval scale data?
3. The control group had a standard deviation of 7.78 on the pretest. Does this standard deviation represent nominal, ordinal, or interval scale data? What does it mean?

ANSWERS:

1. interval
2. ordinal
3. interval; it means that about 34% of the students in the control group scored about 7.78 above the mean and about the same number scored about that much below the mean

SAMPLING STRATEGIES

We've discussed how to operationally define outcome variables, how to develop and administer various data collection processes to measure variables so that reliable and valid results can be obtained, and how to report and interpret the results of measurement processes.

We're going to discuss how to use sampling strategies to collect reliable and valid data about a large group by sampling the characteristics of a smaller group. We'll discuss various types of sampling processes and determine how large a sample should be to lead to sensible inferences.

The preceding chapters have described strategies for operationally defining and developing measurement processes to assess variables. In most cases, when we assess variables we identify the group of people whose abilities, feelings, or attitudes are of interest to us and then measure the performance of each individual within that group. However, when the numbers of people become very large or measurement strategies become complex, it is more practical to use the performance of a subgroup to estimate the performance of the entire group. This estimate can be obtained using the sampling procedures discussed in this chapter.

After reading this chapter, you should be able to

1. Describe the purpose of sampling and identify situations where sampling would be useful.
2. Identify examples of each of the major sampling procedures.
3. Identify the major sources of bias in sampling.

4. Identify the major strengths and weaknesses of each of the major sampling procedures.

5. Given a sampling situation, specify how to use each of the major sampling techniques and evaluate the relative strengths and weaknesses of each.

6. Determine how large a sample would be needed to estimate population characteristics at a designated level of accuracy.

7. Describe strategies for dealing with nonrespondents in surveys.

■

THE IDEA BEHIND SAMPLING

As every baseball fan knows, the only really perfect way to find out how the 700 major league baseball players feel about the designated hitter rule is to ask all 700 of them for their opinions. Only then can we conclude with perfect accuracy, for example, that 84% (but only 63% of the nonpitchers) are opposed to that rule. Even here, however, our conclusions would be inaccurate if there were anything ambiguous about our questioning technique or about the responses of the players or if we tried to generalize about next year's players. But what if we wanted to know the answer to this question but could not (because of lack of time or money) afford to contact all 700 players? Obviously, if we asked *some* of the players, we would have a better idea about their opinions than if we asked none of them. If we asked 10 players, it seems obvious that we could be more confident in our conclusions than if we asked only 2. Likewise, 50 would probably be better than 10. In addition, if these 50 players were evenly split between the National and American leagues, would that not make our conclusions more convincing? And certainly it would be better to have players from several different positions, rather than all pitchers or all designated hitters. How big does the group of players have to be before we can make useful decisions? How can we be confident of getting a representative sample of all the major league players? What does *better* mean when we talk about finding players to whom we can direct our questions?

The problems mentioned in the preceding paragraph focus on sampling. The term *sampling* refers to strategies that enable us to pick a subgroup from a larger group and then use this subgroup as a basis for making *inferences* about the larger group—the researcher's goal is always to generalize about the population based on observations of the sample. Sampling strategies not only make it possible to collect data from a smaller number of respondents, but these strategies also make it possible to go into greater depth with this smaller number—by asking more and deeper questions or by following up the structured questions with more open-ended or qualitative questions (see chapter 9) than would be possible with a larger group of respondents. When using such a subgroup to make decisions about the larger group, the subgroup must be as closely representative of the larger group as possible.

In discussing sampling procedures, the term *sample* refers to the *subgroup,* and the term *population* refers to the entire group from which the sample was drawn. In the example at the beginning of this chapter, the 700 major league baseball players are the population (assuming that this is the entire group we are talking about); whereas the smaller group of 50 players to whom we might address our questions would be a sample. The terms *sample* and *population* will be used in this way throughout the chapter.

There are many situations in which sampling is not necessary at all. If we want to know how many of the 26 graduate students in our educational research class plan to enroll in the advanced class next semester, the best way to find out would be to ask all the students in the class this question. Likewise, if a third-grade teacher wanted to know how many of her students could add three-digit numbers, the best way to answer this question would be to administer to all the students a valid test involving three-digit addition.

Sampling techniques are useful when we want to know how a large group would be described with regard to several variables, but there would be major added costs, narrow restrictions on the number of questions that could be asked, or some other difficulty in administering the data collection procedure to every member of the target population. If we wanted to find out how many graduate students in our entire university were interested in taking a certain advanced course next semester, it would be difficult and expensive to ask every graduate student this question. Even if we had a list of all their names, it would be difficult to get them all to reply to a questionnaire. Finally, we would probably have time to ask only one question, and it would be unlikely that we would be able to uncover the qualitative reasons behind interest or lack of interest in the course. Similarly, if we wanted to know how many third-grade children throughout the entire United States can add two-digit numbers, we would find it a lot more convenient to administer our test to a sample of third graders than to every third grader in the nation.

The following are a few examples of questions related to education where sampling would be helpful in finding the answers:

In a school with 500 children, how many more parents would come to PTA meetings each month if baby-sitting and child-care services were provided?

What percentage of the 200 freshman in your high school would be considered formal operational according to Piaget's standards, as determined by an interview format that takes an hour to administer to each student?

What percentage of the English teachers in the state of Pennsylvania approves of a set of proposed changes in the English curriculum, and how is approval related to such factors as school size, grade level, and teaching experience?

How many of Smith's *5000 Books for High School Libraries* does our high school have in its library? What percentage of these books has been borrowed in the past year?

Would the alumni support our athletic program more enthusiastically if we built a new stadium? Would this additional support offset the cost of construction?

How would the 1,000 teachers of our school system view a new system of teacher incentives based on student performance?

What percentage of the 600 elementary school teachers is satisfied with the current policies regarding mainstreaming of children with learning disabilities in their classrooms? Do these attitudes vary at different grade levels? Do these attitudes depend on previous experience with such children? Do teachers who attended a two-hour workshop on mainstreaming have attitudes different from those of other teachers?

In many of the preceding cases, sampling would be helpful simply because there is a large number of persons in the target population. In other cases, there would be a small number of respondents, but the amount of time needed to collect the data from each person would make it desirable to deal with a smaller group. By dealing with a smaller number of freshman students, for example, a single teacher might be able to find the time necessary to discover how many children use Piaget's formal operational skills in the second example. Likewise, by dealing with a smaller number of teachers in the sixth example, the researcher could spend time with all the teachers in the sample to make sure that they have clearly understood the incentive system before expressing an opinion about it.

There are several different types of samples that could be drawn from a population. For instance, the PTA survey in the first example could be administered to any of the following samples:

The president could ask for a show of hands at a meeting to see how many people would come to more meetings if baby-sitting and child-care services were provided.

The president and three other officers could each call 10 parents and find out the opinions of the 40 people they would interview.

A note could be sent home with each of the 500 children asking the parents to give their input. (Then the responses of the four persons who responded could be carefully tabulated.)

Each of the preceding approaches has a fundamental weakness. As you read the rest of this chapter, you will see the flaws in these approaches. You will see that *the quality of a sampling strategy depends on how the sample is drawn (including the response rate) and how many persons are in the sample.* These factors will be discussed in the following sections. As you proceed with this chapter, keep in mind that the sampling strategy is not the only factor that contributes to the validity and usefulness of inferences drawn from a sample of a population. It is also essential that the data collection process (the questionnaire, the interviewing procedure, the observational strategy, etc.) be valid. A solid sampling strategy can be rendered useless by a measurement process that is invalid or lacking in depth.

A solid sampling strategy can be rendered useless by a measurement process that is invalid or lacking in depth.

THE BASIC SAMPLING STRATEGIES

The manner in which a sample is drawn is an important factor in determining how useful the sample will be for making inferences about the population from which it is drawn. It is quite possible to have a very large sample upon which no sound decision can be based. This occurs because the respondents in the sample are not really similar to the population about which we want to make generalizations. For example, it is not at all uncommon for magazines to report the results of surveys based on the responses of thousands of readers. A close examination of such surveys often reveals that the results are far less useful than if they were based on 25–50 representative respondents rather than the reported thousands. To be useful, *the sample must be representative of the population about which we wish to make generalizations.* To provide useful information, magazines should let their readers know what the population is to which the survey results can be generalized, but few popular magazines do this. (Their reluctance to do so is probably based on their awareness of how bad the surveys really are.)

To be useful, the sample must be representative of the population about which we wish to make generalizations.

Random Sampling

Random sampling is generally the best and simplest way to draw a sample from a population. With random sampling, every member of the population has an equal opportunity to be included in the sample, and pure chance is the only factor that determines who actually goes into the sample. Keeping this definition in mind, which of the following is an example of random sampling?

Going to a shopping mall and asking every fifth person for his or her opinion about presidential candidates.

Calling the third name from the top of each page of the telephone directory and asking the first adult who comes to the phone his or her opinion about presidential candidates.

Going to the local high school football game and asking equal numbers of Democrats and Republicans for their opinions about presidential candidates.

The answer is that *none of the above* is an example of random selection, because in each case some factor in addition to chance includes or excludes respondents who could be part of the sample. If the population about which we wish to generalize comprises all adult citizens who are eligible to vote in the city, then we cannot use any of the preceding examples to make valid generalizations about this population.

In the first example, it is possible that the people at the mall are not typical of adult citizens who are eligible to vote in the city (e.g., wealthy people may go shopping out of town; poor people may seldom go to the mall).

In the second example, not all of the adult citizens who are eligible to vote in the city are likely to have listed phone numbers in the directory.

In the third example, the people at the football game are not likely to represent all the adult citizens who are eligible to vote in the city (people who don't like football would be notably absent; in addition, the assumption that the group would be more representative if the interviewer solicited equal numbers of Republicans and Democrats would make no sense unless it were already established that the community was equally divided between these two parties).

The following are examples of random selection to obtain a sample of the adult citizens who are eligible to vote in the city:

Getting a list of all the adult citizens who are eligible to vote in the city, putting each name on a card, mixing the cards up thoroughly, and selecting the cards on the basis of pure chance, as by drawing blindly from a large box.

Obtaining a list of all the adult citizens who are eligible to vote in the city, assigning a number to each name on the list, and then using a table of random numbers to select names off this list. (The use of a table of random numbers is described in Box 8.1.)

In both of these cases, chance is the *only* factor that determines who will be selected for the sample.

To select a strictly random sample, it is essential to have a complete list of all the members of the population.

To select a strictly random sample, it is essential to have a complete list of all the members of the population. This is often difficult to accomplish. For instance, in the example under consideration, if the target population about which we wish to generalize includes registered voters as well as eligible voters who have not registered, a list of such voters would be hard to obtain—it may be difficult to get a list of people who have not registered to vote. On the other hand, if we decided to limit our generalizations to registered voters, then a list would be more

readily accessible, although we would have to be aware that our inferences would not necessarily apply to eligible voters who had not registered, voters who had become eligible since the last election, and voters who had recently moved into town. In addition, it would be possible that some voters who had been eligible in the last election had become *in*eligible since that time. As we said, it is sometimes very difficult to obtain a complete list of the entire population.

When we deal with smaller, more clearly defined populations, the process of devising a comprehensive list is much simpler. For example, for each of the hypothetical voter populations described earlier, a list would be readily available or could easily be compiled. To draw a random sample, it would be necessary merely to draw a sample of names from the list at random.

Random sampling has such a clear advantage over most other methods with regard to generalizations we can make that it should be used as often as possible. This means, for example, that if we have a choice of collecting responses from 50 persons selected at random or from 300 respondents selected through a nonrandom process, the small but random sample is preferred.

Biased Sampling

Biased sampling is the worst way to draw a sample. With this method, we put together our sample by using naturally occurring or artificially constructed groups of subjects without the benefit of random selection. For example, if a professor wants to determine how many students would enroll in an experimental course, she could ask the 30 students taking her Introductory Educational Research course this question. If she tried to generalize beyond these 30 students, she would have a biased sample. There is no good reason to believe that these 30 students are typical of the 970 other graduate education students in her university. Likewise, if a researcher stood in a shopping mall and questioned whoever walked past, she would be getting a biased sample. How would she know that the people who walked past were representative of anyone about whom she

BOX 8.1

Using the Table of Random Numbers

There are 525 students who have taken graduate courses at the university during the past year. Ms. Jefferson has all the names and addresses in an *AppleWorks* (electronic) data base. She has decided to select a random sample of 100 of these students to survey. The electronic data base automatically assigns numbers to each record (e.g., Janet Jones is record number 116 of 525). If the computer did not do this, Ms. Jefferson would simply have to assign numbers to each student herself.

The names and addresses happen to be stored in alphabetical order, but this is not essential. The main reason for listing the numbers in alphabetical order is that a systematic order makes it easier to keep records accurately (in this case, also to ensure that all the students are really listed).

Ms. Jefferson gets a printout of a table of random numbers like that in Appendix B of this book. However, there is a problem: the table has only two-digit numbers, and most of Ms. Jefferson's students have been assigned three-digit numbers. What can she do? Well, she could use pairs of numbers. For example, she could select a two-digit number and the two-digit number to the right of it. By putting them together, she would have a four-digit number. She could then read the "hundreds" values of these combined numbers (ignoring the left-most digit). This strategy is what Ms. Jefferson will employ, and the reason will become clear in the following paragraphs. Ms. Jefferson decides that she will place her finger in the table at random and then move downward. When she reaches the bottom of a column, her plan is to move to the top of the next column.

Ms. Jefferson follows this plan and enters the table in the 11th line from the top of the third column, where she finds the number 72. Immediately to the right is 58. Combining these two numbers, she gets 7258. She drops the 7 and gets 258, and so she selects student number 258 from her data base.

Going down the page, she comes to 73 and 57, and so she selects student 357 from the data base.

Next, she finds 65 and 27. Since there are only 525 students in her population, there is no number 527, and so she skips this number and goes down the column.

She next finds 23 and 09 and selects student 309. She continues doing this until she has the 100 subjects she needs for her sample.

This strategy would work. However, since we know that Ms. Jefferson has access to a computer, there are two much more efficient ways to draw her sample:

1. Computers are capable of generating lists of random numbers. If Ms. Jefferson knew how to program in a language like BASIC, she could give the computer a simple set of commands that would automatically generate a list of numbers ranging from 1 to 525.
2. If she has the names in an *AppleWorks* data base, she can easily transfer them to an *AppleWorks* spreadsheet. She could then program the spreadsheet to select the names at random for her.

Either of these strategies would be equivalent to the use of the table of random numbers.

The table of random numbers can also be used to draw a systematic sample. For example, Ms. Jefferson could use the table to select a number between 1 and 525. She could then take every fifth student on the list until she had 100 students. (When she reached the end of the list, she would simply "wrap around" and continue at the beginning.)

would wish to generalize? And furthermore, what makes her think that the person who is willing to talk to her is similar to the person who looks down and avoids eye contact in order to evade being interviewed?

The magazine surveys cited earlier are examples of biased sampling, and it is this bias that renders them useless. We know of a magazine that each month published the results of a "reader survey." The editors decided that they wanted a representative sample of readers each month, and so they decided to do something random. They reasoned that the expiration dates on magazines occurred in a near random manner, so with each renewal notice they sent a survey form. This way they were able to get what they presented as a representative sample of

views on interesting issues to publish each month. The respondents simply enclosed the survey in the postage-paid envelope when sending in payment for the next year's subscription! The problem, of course, is that neither subscribers who did not renew nor new subscribers would be included in the sample. This may be an interesting sales method, but it is not a good technique for obtaining a representative sample of opinions on the topics covered in the questionnaires.

In recent years, television news programs have begun conducting surveys by instructing viewers with one opinion to call one number and those with the opposite opinion to call another. There is usually a "small charge" for making the phone call. (Some day we expect to see a survey that instructs us to dial

---

BOX 8.2	Biases and Really Bad Biases

The textbook says that "if a professor wants to determine how many students would enroll in an experimental course, she could ask the 30 students taking her Introductory Educational Research course this question. If she tried to generalize beyond these 30 students, she would have a biased sample. There is no good reason to believe that these 30 students are typical of the 970 other graduate education students in her university."

Our students ask, "Why not? How do you *know* the sample is biased?"

Our reply is that *we don't know*. That's the whole point.

With random selection, *we do know* that mathematical probability is the only factor that can account for differences between the sample and the population from which it was drawn. And mathematicians have given us precise ways to estimate how likely it is that these differences exist.

Random selection does not *guarantee* an accurate sample. It rather lets us rule out all sources of bias other than random variability and offers us an estimate of this degree of variability. Short of our collecting data from the entire population, a suitably large random sample gives the best estimate of population characteristics.

Yet our students still ask, "But isn't it *possible* that this professor's class of 30 students could be more representative of the entire population than a random sample of 30 from the whole school?"

And our final answer is this: Yes. Anything is *possible*, but our concern is what is *probable*. Basing her decisions on this group of 30 would obviously be better than putting an ad in the newspaper asking for people interested in the experimental course and then conducting a survey with 30 of these respondents. But without random sampling, the professor simply does not have a clear idea how representative her sample is or how far inferences can be generalized. However, by using some of the other sampling strategies discussed in this chapter, such as quota sampling, she can improve the quality of her biased sample—and this would enable her to have greater confidence in her conclusions.

one number if we value such surveys and another if we think they are a waste of time. The results would undoubtedly show that people overwhelmingly think these are valuable!) If you do not by this time see the problem of bias in such surveys, you should reread the chapter to this point. The newscasters sometimes have the integrity to point out that these are "not scientific surveys," but the situation would be more accurately stated if the newscaster prefaced the results by saying, "This just in from an unreliable and biased source. . . ."

On the other hand, many reputable researchers and organizations are forced to rely on nonrandom sampling. This is because random sampling is sometimes difficult to accomplish. If we want to find out, for example, how American teenagers feel about sex or drugs, it would be difficult to obtain a random sample of all the teenagers in the country—and it would be very expensive even to come close. It would be possible to obtain a random sample of all the teenagers in a specific city, perhaps, but once we try to use the results of a few small-scale surveys to generalize about the whole country, we're really dealing with a biased sample. Nonrandom sampling is most justified in cases where it is actually impossible to derive a true random sample. In such cases, reputable researchers upgrade their nonrandom sample by making it a quota or stratified sample (discussed next in this section) and by carefully delineating the precise nature of the sample and the limitations in generalizing about specific populations. These limitations should be kept in mind when we interpret these surveys.

In most cases when educators need to use a sampling strategy, they can do better than using a badly biased technique. In spite of this, various forms of biased sampling seem to be the most prevalent sampling techniques in educational settings. Unfortunately, most of the persons who use biased techniques are not aware of what they are doing wrongly. For example, many actually believe that talking to every fifth person who walks through the door or talking to whoever happens to be in the lounge are ways to get representative opinions. Such methods are examples of biased sampling, and they often result in nonrepresentative results.

In most cases when educators need to use a sampling strategy, they can do better than using a badly biased technique.

It is important to cite one more example before moving beyond biased samples. What happens if you have a population of 1,000 people and select a genuine random sample of 200, then mail out a survey to which only 25% respond? Are these 50 respondents a random sample? The answer is no! This would represent a biased sampling strategy. The obvious bias is that only those who volunteered to respond are part of the actual sample available for analysis. People who volunteer to respond are by definition different from those who do not. A much better strategy would be to select a smaller sample and attempt to get 100% responses via direct contacts. In this case, responses from 50 out of 50 respondents selected in a sample would be vastly superior to 50 responses out of 200 from the entire population.

To summarize, random sampling is the best technique; biased sampling is the worst. The strategies discussed next help make a nonrandom sample come as close as possible to possessing the characteristics of a random sample.

Quota Sampling

Quota sampling provides a way to give respectability to a nonrandom sample. If done well, quota sampling can lead to strong inferences. When using this strategy, researchers identify important characteristics that they already know the target population possesses, and then they select the nonrandom sample in such a way as to make it correspond to the population with regard to these known characteristics. We might get a quota sample of American teenagers in a city by consulting census information and discovering what percentage of teenagers in that city is of each sex, what percentage belongs to each of the various races, and what percentage lives in each of several different neighborhoods. Based on this information, we would set quotas even before we set out to conduct our survey, determining that we would get a certain number of males, a certain number of females, a certain number of whites, of blacks, and so forth. When conducting the survey, we would use these quotas to set the limit on how many persons possessing each characteristic we would include in our survey.

Although it is desirable to set quotas *before* selecting the sample, it is also possible to use quota sampling strategies retrospectively. For example, a researcher who needs a sample but is forced to deal with an intact group might feel compelled to do no research at all. Instead, in addition to questions related to his outcome variables, this researcher might include on his questionnaire some questions about the characteristics of his respondents. These additional questions should focus on areas that are most likely to introduce biases. When analyzing the data, the researcher could compare the characteristics of the sample with those of the population to verify that there are no obvious biases.

For example, an organization with a small budget may be interested in knowing the attitudes of American college students regarding drug and alcohol use. Realizing that students are likely to react to questions by giving socially desirable answers, this organization might hire a researcher at a nearby university who is known for her ability to establish rapport and obtain frank answers from students. Because of time and travel restrictions, this researcher would have to collect her data from respondents at her own university. She might obtain detailed responses to a wide variety of questions from all 200 of the students in her classes, which all sophomores are required to take. Can the organization use these results to generalize about "American college students"? A further examination indicates that these students had SAT scores typical of American college students, and that there were percentages of whites, blacks, Hispanics, Orientals, males, females, old students, young students, rich students, poor students, liberal arts majors, engineering majors, etc. comparable with the percentages known to be typical of the rest of the country. The researcher also notes that two of her many questions overlapped almost exactly with those asked by a nationally prominent survey organization, and the

responses of her students were almost identical to those. At this point, the organization has good reason to believe that these results can be generalized. Their confidence cannot be as great as if they had conducted a random survey with an equally good interviewer, but they are more confident than if they had sent their interviewer over to the local bar to interview students or if they had conducted a random survey in a manner very likely to obtain reactive, false responses.

The flaw in this after-the-fact quota sampling is that the demographics of the sample may indeed reveal obvious biases with regard to the targeted characteristics. Then the researcher is left with nothing more than a limitation that can be stated but no longer corrected. For instance, in the preceding example, what would the organization do if the researcher reported that her group included an overrepresentation of Oriental students and education majors? This would be a difficult problem with after-the-fact quota sampling. Preplanned quota sampling is more likely to minimize differences. In the preceding example, the problems would be minimized by selecting fewer Oriental students or education majors for the sample. Retrospective strategy can increase our confidence in nonrandom samples when the subjects meet the quotas and caution us regarding the nature of biases when the subjects do not meet the quotas. (This retrospective strategy will be discussed again later in this chapter, when we discuss *essentially random* samples.)

Systematic Sampling

Systematic sampling is a strategy whereby only two factors determine membership in the sample—chance and "the system." The system is simply a way of facilitating the random selection process. For example, instead of using a table of random numbers to select a sample of 100 individuals from a list of 1,000 names, a researcher might randomly select a number between 1 and 10, start with the name that corresponds to that number, and then take every 10th name on the list thereafter. The resulting sample is essentially the same as a random sample, unless there is a systematic bias in the way the names appear on the list. However, if the system employed were related to any sort of system in the list, this could be a very bad technique. For example, if a classroom were arranged so that boys and girls sat in alternate seats throughout the room, when the researcher took every 2nd or 10th child she would get an atypical sample of either all boys or all girls. Likewise, if she had a list of 2,000 names and obtained a sample of 100 by starting with a random number between 1 and 10 and selecting every 10th name, this would exclude the whole second half of the list, which would likely be a serious bias. (This problem would be overcome by taking every 20th name instead of every 10th name.) It is usually relatively easy to identify and eliminate such sources of bias in the selection of subjects by examining the lists ahead of time and asking the compilers how they were assembled.

Stratified Sampling

Stratified sampling is a strategy whereby members of a sample are selected in such a way as to guarantee appropriate numbers of subjects for subsequent subdivisions and groupings during the analysis of data. For stratified sampling to be most effective, the respondents within each stratum should be selected at random. Such random stratified sampling is mistakenly thought by many novice researchers to be the ideal sampling technique. This is not quite the case. In general, simple random sampling is the easiest and most desirable procedure. Stratified sampling is useful only when you plan to subdivide the subjects for subsequent analysis to make various comparisons and decisions or when you have too large a population to be able to assign each subject a number in advance. Readers of this book are most likely to use stratified sampling for the first reason. National marketing and political polling organizations often use it for both reasons.

The use of stratified sampling can be clearly illustrated with an example from a political survey. Let's say we are going to conduct a survey during which we will ask respondents to indicate (1) their race, (2) the candidate for whom they intend to vote, and (3) their attitude toward environmental issues. A random sample of 200 people from a town of 50,000

would generally give us a good estimate of (1) how many persons of each race live in the town, (2) how many persons planned to vote for each candidate, and (3) the percentage of persons for and against each environmental issue. However, what if we wanted to know whether black Democrats were more similar to white Democrats than to black Republicans, or whether within the Democratic Party blacks and whites differed on environmental issues? If there were only 10% blacks in the town, this would give us a probability of 20 blacks in the sample. If blacks tended to be 80% Democrat in this town, this would give us 4 black Republicans and 16 black Democrats.

As we shall discover in the next section, the validity of inferences based on 4 or 16 subjects is not nearly as strong as the validity of inferences based on 200 subjects. If we want to make such subanalyses, we should "stack" the sample by including many more blacks, so that we would have more for the subanalysis. Such a move, of course, would bias the overall sample by giving disproportionate weight to black subjects. This overrepresentation would have to be countered by a weighting strategy to correct this false emphasis. Stratified sampling would be used in this case specifically to provide ample numbers of subjects for later subdivision, subanalysis, and reporting.

What is the difference between stratified sampling and quota sampling? They are similar in that both specify numbers of subjects to be included in the sample based on selected characteristics. However, they differ sharply in their purpose. The purpose of quota sampling is to make the sample as closely representative as possible of the larger population with regard to important characteristics. This is done by selecting proportional numbers of subjects with specific characteristics. To pursue the example from the preceding paragraph, if the original population had 10% blacks, then the quota sample should have 10% blacks. On the other hand, the purpose of stratified sampling is to ensure sufficient numbers for subanalysis. To do this, the researcher will often select subjects in such a way as to deliberately make the entire sample dissimilar to the larger population with regard to the specified characteristics. For example, the researcher might select 30% blacks so that there will be enough black respondents in the sample to permit meaningful subanalysis based on the race of respondents.

Stratified sampling and quota sampling are similar in that both specify numbers of subjects to be included in the sample based on selected characteristics. However, they differ sharply in their purpose.

Essentially Random Sampling

Essentially random is a term often applied to a sample that was not randomly selected but that the researcher thinks is unbiased anyway. For example, there might be 300 students in the freshman class at your high school, and you might want to find out what percentage of them can read with at least sixth-grade ability. Testing all 300 would be expensive and time-consuming, but you could easily test 30 of them. Pursuing the matter, assume you discover that the English classes are heterogeneously grouped. The only factor that appears to influence who goes into what English class is when they eat lunch. This, in turn, depends on a combination of alphabetical order and what electives the students are taking. At this point, you might argue that such classes are "essentially randomly selected." However, you could improve your logic further by using quota sampling strategies. You might select one of the classes at random and discover that it contains about the expected number of males and females, the expected number of persons from various racial and ethnic groups, the expected number of persons from various academic tracks, and so forth. This would further strengthen your case that the sample is free of bias. To top it off, you might examine their most recent standardized test scores and note that these are similar to the mean of the entire class. Having done all this, your conclusion that only 35% of the freshmen can read at the level of a sixth grader or better would have a great deal more weight than if you had no reason to believe that your sample was essentially random.

The comparative advantages and disadvantages of the four major sampling strategies are summarized in Table 8.1. The table summarizes the following points: (1) random sampling is the simplest and best strategy if there is a complete list of the population; (2) systematic sampling is almost as good as random sampling; (3) quota sampling gives respectability to nonrandom samples; and (4) stratified sampling is useful in situations where no list of the population is available or when subdivision of the sample is intended and adequate numbers are not likely to be present in the subunits through regular random sampling. (Additional sampling strategies, as well as combinations of the preceding strategies, are discussed in Asher [1976]. Purposive sampling, which is often employed in qualitative research studies, is described in chapter 9.)

Table 8.1 The Relative Advantages and Disadvantages of the Five Basic Sampling Techniques

Technique	Advantages	Disadvantages
Random sampling	Theoretically most accurate Influenced only by chance	Sometimes a list of the entire population is unavailable or practical considerations prevent random sampling
Systematic sampling	Similar to random sampling Often easier than random	The system can sometimes be biased
Quota sampling	Can be used when random sampling is impossible Quick to do	There may still be biases not controlled by the quota system
Stratified sampling	Ensures large enough sample to subdivide on important variables Needed when population is too large to list Can be combined with other techniques	Can be biased if strata are given false weights, unless weighting procedure is used for overall analysis

REVIEW QUIZ 8.1

Part 1

Categorize each of the following as either badly biased sampling, random sampling, systematic sampling, quota sampling, or stratified sampling:

1. Miss Gilligan is surveying attitudes of students at her college toward intercollegiate football. She goes to a home football game and gets her sample by interviewing all the students standing in line at one of the hot dog stands.

2. Mr. Quinn wants to find out how many people in his town watch certain evening television shows. He selects the numbers 2 and 10 at random, and he calls the 10th person in the second column of every page in the telephone directory. If this is a business phone, he goes to the next number in the same column.

3. Ms. Billings selects her sample of college students by obtaining an alphabetical computer printout of all the students, assigning them each a number, and selecting 200 of them by using a table of random numbers.

4. Mr. Vockell wanted to analyze the quality of ERIC's *Resources in Education (RIE)* microfiche service for his doctoral dissertation. He obtained a list of all the documents published during a designated year, chose the number 64 at random, and then selected every 50th document starting at number 64 for his sample of documents for that year.

5. Mrs. Jacobs wanted a sample of students from her Educational Psychology course. She put all the names of her students on cards, shuffled the cards, and dealt them into two stacks. The cards in her left-hand stack were included in her sample.

6. Mrs. Rahner wanted to analyze the attitudes of her city elementary school children toward busing to achieve integration. She had time to interview only about 600 students. She selected 3 schools out of the 75 in her city and interviewed all third, fifth, and seventh graders. This gave her 22 classes, with 601 students all together. She selected these schools because these children were known to be similar to those in the rest of the city in intellectual ability, in ratio of whites to nonwhites, and in the percentage of students who rode buses to school.

7. Reverend Wachel wanted to find out how people reacted to his sermons. He specifically wanted to know whether there were differences in reactions related to age level, so he obtained a sample of 300 people to interview by obtaining a list of all 2,000 adult members of the congregation and using a table of random numbers to select 100 young adults, 100 middle-aged adults, and 100 elderly adults from this list.

Part 2

Evaluate the quality of each of the sampling techniques from Part 1. How good would the sample be if the strategy were carried out?

HOW LARGE SHOULD THE SAMPLE BE?

In addition to depending on the procedure by which it is selected, the quality of a sample depends upon its size. *In general, if a sample is scientifically selected, we can place more confidence in the results of a larger sample than we can in the results of a smaller sample.* This is because the likelihood that the characteristics of a discrepant minority will improperly influence our perceptions of the whole population decreases as the sample grows larger. (Note, however, that adding 25 people to a sample of 5 will result in a much greater increase in accuracy than will adding 25 people to a sample of 100.) At a certain point, the benefits from increasing the size of the sample may be outweighed by the cost of sampling a larger number of respondents.

In general, if a sample is scientifically selected, we can place more confidence in the results of a larger sample than we can in the results of a smaller sample.

How large should a sample be? To answer this question, we need to undertake a brief exploration of *confidence intervals*. (These are closely related to the concept of the standard error of measurement, which was discussed in chapter 5.) A confidence interval states a range of numbers such as ±5% or ±10%. When we use a sample to estimate a population characteristic, we are aware that it is just that—an estimate. The confidence interval states how accurate we think this estimate is. (Newscasters often use the term *probable error* when they indicate the confidence intervals of survey results.) The confidence interval can be applied to the sample estimate to indicate the range within which the population characteristic almost certainly falls.

This can best be understood by considering an example. Imagine a PTA president who has found that 37% of a sample of parents responding to a survey indicated that they would come to a meeting on Thursday night if child-care services were provided. She would make an inference from this sample that about 37% of the entire population of parents would have been likely to give this same answer, if they would have been asked. She would be aware that her estimate of 37% is not an exact measurement, as could be obtained by asking all 1,000 parents for their answer to the survey question. If she had a confidence interval of ±15% for this estimate, this would mean that the true percentage of persons who would have said yes to this question is likely to fall somewhere in the range between 52% and 22%. This is a very wide range.[1] (The true percentage, of course, could be ascertained by directing the question to everyone in the population.) If the confidence interval were smaller, the range within which the true percentage would be likely to fall would have been smaller. For example, if her confidence interval were ±5%, then it would be expected that the actual number of persons willing to come to the meeting would

probably be somewhere between 42% and 32%. If the confidence interval were ±1%, then she would expect the actual number to fall somewhere within the range of 38% and 36%. (A confidence interval of ±3% is considered desirable in high-quality surveys, like those performed by major polling organizations to make projections regarding presidential elections. That's why these national surveys often report a sample size of about 1,300.)

As you can see, by keeping the confidence intervals narrow we increase the expectation that we are making an accurate estimate. These confidence intervals are based on sound mathematical theory, which will not be explored here. The critical factor in determining confidence intervals is the number of persons constituting a sample. As the size of the sample increases, the confidence intervals become more narrow, and our estimates are likely to be more accurate. By applying some simple mathematical procedures or consulting an appropriate table before we conduct a survey, we can estimate ahead of time how large a sample we will need in order to obtain confidence intervals that will give us a satisfactory amount of confidence in the accuracy of the results we expect to receive from the sample.

Table 8.2 presents estimates of confidence intervals based on sample size[2]. A sample of 100 gives confidence intervals of ±9.8%. A sample of 200 gives smaller confidence intervals, ±6.9%. By using this table, you can easily estimate the confidence intervals surrounding results obtained from surveys. In addition, you can use this table to decide how large a sample you need in order to have an acceptable degree of confidence in your results. For example, if you live in a city of 500,000 and want to estimate a characteristic with ±5% confidence intervals, a sample of 400 would accomplish this.

---

[1] Actually, a confidence interval of ±15% typically means that there's a 95% probability that the percentage falls between 52% and 22%. The tables in this book are based on 95% confidence intervals. Other possibilities (such as 99% confidence intervals) could be used as well. Technical language is avoided in this discussion.

[2] The confidence intervals in Table 8.2 are sometimes conservative estimates. A more complete treatment of sampling theory (e.g., Asher, 1976) would describe *correction factors*. A correction factor is used when the sample is a major part of the population. For instance, a sample of 50 from a population of 50,000 would yield confidence intervals of ±14%, as shown in Table 8.2. However, a sample of 50 from a population of 100 would yield more narrow confidence intervals—about ±9.9%, which could be ascertained by using a correction factor not discussed in this book.

Analyzing Subgroups from Surveys

Survey results can be put to valuable use to perform various subanalyses. For example, a principal might want to know whether the responses of parents who attended PTA meetings the previous year differed from those who had not previously attended meetings. She might also want to know whether parents with more than one child in the school gave different responses than parents with only one child in attendance. Likewise, she might be interested in knowing whether the answers from one-parent families were different from those from two-parent families. Such information can be useful in helping her make decisions.

It is important to remember that whenever we subdivide the original sample for such subanalyses, we reduce the size of our sample—and therefore increase the size of our confidence intervals. The result is a reduction in accuracy. For example, assume that a principal decided to sample 100 families to estimate their attitudes toward a proposed change. This would give her a confidence interval of ±9.8% for her whole sample. What if she wanted to compare the responses of persons who had attended meetings the previous year with those who had not done so? Let's assume that 25% had attended the previous year. This would mean that her sample of 100 would probably contain about 75 nonattenders

Table 8.2 Initial Estimates of Confidence Intervals Based on Sample Size

Sample Size	Plus and Minus Confidence Interval Limit
5	±44%
10	±31%
20	±22%
30	±18%
40	±16%
50	±14%
60	±13%
70	±12%
80	±11%
90	±10.3%
100	±9.8%
125	±8.8%
150	±8.0%
175	±7.4%
200	±6.9%
225	±6.5%
250	±6.2%
275	±5.9%
300	±5.6%
400	±4.9%
500	±4.4%
750	±3.6%
1000	±3.1%
2000	±2.2%
5000	±1.4%

Technical note: These are 95% confidence intervals, based on the formula

$$\frac{1.96\sqrt{2500}}{\sqrt{n}}$$

and 25 attenders. What kind of confidence intervals would she have for her analysis of the responses of attenders? Considering the interval levels given in Table 8.2, we would have an interval of about ±20% for 25 people. On the other hand, since their subsample is larger, the 75 nonattenders would have a confidence interval of about ±12%.

Faced with such difficulties, the principal would be left with two alternatives: (1) keep the same sample and merely acknowledge the weaknesses of the confidence intervals in the subanalyses, or (2) draw the sample in such a way as to ensure a sufficiently large subsample for the subanalyses. Accepting the first alternative would be a reasonable decision in many circumstances; it would merely be necessary to keep in mind that inferences based on the subanalysis would not be on as firm a footing as those derived from the overall sample. The second alternative requires stratified sampling, which was discussed earlier in this chapter.

To use stratified sampling, we would select our sample in such a way that each subsample (stratum) for subanalysis will have enough members to provide the desired confidence intervals. Thus, if our principal wanted to do the subanalysis comparing attenders and nonattenders, she would have to select 100 families *from each category* in order to provide 10% confidence intervals for each of these subgroups. This would be good for the subanalysis, but notice what has happened to the overall analysis. In the original population, there were 75% nonattenders and 25% attenders. In the sample, however, there are now 50% nonattenders and 50% attenders. Thus, the adjustment to improve the confidence intervals has resulted in a bias in the overall sample. A mathematical adjustment (see Asher, 1976) would be necessary to restore the proper proportions in the overall sample.

REVIEW QUIZ 8.2

1. Mr. Fenwick, the school librarian, wants to find out what proportion of the books listed in Smith's *5000 Books for School Libraries* is in his library. He wants to be within ±5% in his esti-

mate. He wants to take a random sample from Smith's book and check to see whether each selected book is in the library. How many entries would Mr. Fenwick have to sample to be within ±5%?

2. Mrs. Peters, a probation officer, wants to find out what proportion of the adolescents in her caseload would be willing to take a day off from school (with their parents' permission) to go on a field trip to a nearby penal institution. She has 250 young men and women in her caseload. How many would she have to sample to have a confidence interval of ±10%?

3. There are 500 teachers in the Nice City School System. Miss Good, the superintendent, wants to find out how many of them would be willing to accept a system of incentive pay based on student performance. She knows that this is a volatile issue, and she fears that if a questionnaire is mailed, people will react without thinking. She feels that it is necessary for an interviewer to explain to each respondent individually what is meant by the incentive plan before answering. Since this will take time and cost money, she wants to keep the sample as small as possible. She also wants to know whether secondary teachers react differently to the survey than elementary teachers. There are 300 elementary teachers and 200 secondary teachers in the system. How many does Miss Good have to include in the sample in order to be within ±10% for all her analyses?

WHAT TO DO ABOUT NONRESPONDENTS

In an ideal world, a researcher would identify a sample of 100 persons to interview, would interview all 100 of them, and would be able to interpret the results according to the confidence intervals derived from Table 8.2. In reality, however, things go wrong. Some people are impossible to find, and others simply refuse to answer our questions.

It is better to aim for complete responses from a smaller sample than incomplete responses from a larger sample.

The confidence intervals listed in Table 8.2 are based on the assumption of random selection of respondents. Collecting data from a badly biased sample of 5,000 people who call a "900" telephone number to register an opinion is no better than collecting data from 5 people who called the same number. But what happens when a researcher makes a legitimate attempt to collect data about a large population but is still able to collect data from only 200 of the 250 respondents selected for the sample? The following questions and answers focus on this problem of what to do when not everyone in a sample responds.

1.   If the researcher looks at the characteristics of the respondents and determines that they match appropriate quotas for the target population, is it at all legitimate to use Table 8.2 to suggest that the results have a ±6.9% confidence interval?

Strictly speaking, the ±6.9% confidence interval applies only to random samples. To the extent that the researcher departs from random sampling, it becomes necessary to rely on logic that does not include mathematical probability to estimate the degree to which a sample resembles the population from which it was derived.

2.   Isn't it at least obvious that collecting data from 200 out of 250 respondents is better than collecting similar data from 100 out of 150 respondents?

Yes, it is better. The trouble is that it is not possible to use mathematical principles of probability to estimate *how much* better.

The following guidelines should influence your choice of strategies for dealing with the problem that occurs when people selected to be part of a sample choose not to respond:

1.   It is better to aim for complete responses from a smaller sample than incomplete responses from a larger sample. In many cases a 100% response rate *is* possible, especially if smaller samples are used.

2.   Highest response rates are likely when respondents do not feel that you are intruding on their time. If you are using a questionnaire, you should make it brief and accompany it with a cover letter giving the potential respondents an incentive to participate. Sometimes it is better to use a strategy that puts the work and time demands on *you* instead of on the respondents. For example, if you use an observational checklist, it becomes your job (not the respondent's) to see to it that data get collected.

3.   Follow up on your initial contacts to try to obtain 100% participation. If you let potential participants respond anonymously, follow-ups may be difficult. Therefore, you should consider carefully whether you really want to encourage anonymous responses. Many persons are willing to sign their names to a questionnaire, as long as it is not of a personal nature. If disclosing their names will not contaminate their responses, then it may be best to obtain the names of persons returning questionnaires. If it is necessary to retain anonymity, it is still possible to send reminders to everyone or to have participants do two things: (1) complete the questionnaire and (2) return a separate form indicating that they have responded.

4.   It is often good practice to simply report the nonrespondents as part of the results (e.g., "64% agreed, 30% disagreed, and 6% declined to answer or could not be reached").

5.   It is good practice to use the retrospective quota sampling strategy described earlier in this chapter to help authenticate your sample (e.g., "The respondents closely resembled the overall population regarding these important characteristics. Therefore, we assume that the absence of data from the nonrespondents does not contaminate the conclusions drawn from the sample").

6.   To the extent that it is possible to do so, obtain an estimate of the characteristics of the nonrespondents and use these to help interpret the data. For example, Rosenthal and Rosnow (1975) have delineated the characteristics of vol-

unteers and nonvolunteers for typical research projects. By knowing that nonrespondents are also nonvolunteers, researchers can use this information to estimate how the absence of the nonrespondents influences the results. Likewise, if the respondents to a questionnaire are above the class average in academic ability, then the nonrespondents must be below average; this information can help interpret the results.

7. When reporting survey data, include a complete description of your sampling methods and data collection procedures. Give your readers enough data to determine the quality of the sample and the biases likely to be present.

8. Remember that even a perfect sampling method does not guarantee a perfect survey. The survey consists of both a sampling technique and a data collection process. If the data collection process is seriously flawed, a good sampling strategy will not correct this. Similarly, it is possible that the activities you conduct to ensure a high rate of participation will interfere with the validity of the measurement process.

The moral of the story is that it's best to use random sampling. However, when random strategies are impossible, the next best course of action may be to plan to use random sampling, even though you fail to carry out this plan, but to be aware of how you failed and to use this information to help interpret the data.

BOX 8.3	Interpreting the Results of Nonrandom Surveys

The discussion in this chapter tries to clarify sampling theory by describing how to obtain appropriate samples. If you understand how to draw a good sample, you should be able to interpret the results of surveys reported in professional journals or in the public media. However, a few guidelines may be helpful:

1. Be seriously skeptical of nonrandom samples with huge numbers of respondents. (When television newscasters say that a sample is "nonscientific," we might wonder why they bother to report it at all. As we mentioned earlier, perhaps they should preface the results with a comment like, "This just in from an extremely unreliable source. . . .")

2. When reading the results of surveys to which there were imperfect response rates, try to determine why the nonrespondents chose not to respond. Try to determine the likelihood that the actual sample (that is, the persons who actually did respond) is truly typical of the population about which the author of the report wishes to generalize.

   For example, if there is a huge percentage of nonrespondents, the results may be useless. A response rate of 100 out of a random sample of 125 from a population of 1,000 is likely to be more representative than a response rate of 100 out of the entire population.

   Try to determine the characteristics of the nonrespondents, and judge whether these characteristics are likely to be related to the conclusions of the report. For example, if a researcher sent out 200 questionnaires and received 100 responses, it would be useful to realize that students in the top half of the class responded more often than those in the bottom half. If the report focused on the income of the alumni or the rate at which they graduated from college, this would be an obvious bias. On the other hand, if the top and bottom halves of the class were about equally represented among the 100 respondents, then it would be much more likely that the results would be authentic.

3. When reading the results of surveys of intact groups, be critical of the ways the author tries to generalize these results to other groups. For example, if an author finds that 87% of the freshmen but only 26% of the seniors at a designated high school display a high degree of computer anxiety, you would obviously like to know how closely that school resembles your own, before making decisions based on this survey.

The basic method for interpreting nonrandom samples is to employ the retrospective quota strategies described earlier. The quality of the sample is likely to improve to the extent that the researcher followed the prescribed steps. The author of the report should supply enough information for you to determine how closely the sample of actual respondents resembles the population to which you would like to generalize the results.

LONGITUDINAL VERSUS CROSS-SECTIONAL SURVEYS

A frequent goal of researchers is to study the characteristics of persons as they go through a program or an institution. For example, a researcher may want to find out how the percentages of students in grades 9 through 12 differ regarding drug use or ability to think at a specified level of abstraction. The following are conclusions that may arise from surveys of learners:

> Fifty percent of the freshmen in School X reported using illegal drugs; 60% of the seniors in the same school reported illegal drug use.
>
> Twenty percent of 13-year-olds, 40% of 14-year-olds, and 80% of 15-year-olds were able to solve problems of a designated type.

Longitudinal Surveys

When researchers continue to survey the same persons as they move through a program or an institution, this is referred to as a *longitudinal survey*. The preceding conclusions could be based on longitudinal surveys. (If this were the case, the conclusions should be phrased more carefully to state that the same subjects were followed throughout the study.)

A serious problem that often occurs during longitudinal research is that persons surveyed during an initial stage of a study may be unavailable to be surveyed during later stages. This presents problems comparable to experimental mortality, which will be discussed in chapter 10. Changes in response patterns of the group may occur because the composi-

tion of the group changed rather than because of changes in the attitudes or behaviors that the researcher intends to measure. In addition, a serious difficulty in conducting longitudinal research is that it takes a long time to collect the data.

Cross-Sectional Research

Researchers may solve some of the problems of longitudinal studies by conducting *cross-sectional research*. With this method, researchers survey different groups of persons who are simultaneously moving through a program or an institution. Instead of following a single group of students through a program or institution, the researchers examine participants currently at different levels when the survey is conducted. With this approach, there is no problem with dropouts. However, it is possible that differences among the different levels may occur because of differences in the subjects arising from sampling or from factors unrelated to the institution or program being studied. Sometimes researchers combine both methods by following groups of students from several grade levels as they move through a program. This combined method would permit both cross-sectional and longitudinal comparisons.

When researchers conduct either longitudinal or cross-sectional research, they typically employ sampling strategies. It is important to know how the researchers obtained their samples and to evaluate the quality of these samples according to the criteria described in this chapter.

Researchers planning to conduct or interpret extensive surveys should realize that both longitudinal and cross-sectional methods may entail unexpected difficulties. More detailed books (e.g., Magnusson & Bergman, 1990) will provide guidelines to avoid pitfalls. It is also important to note that both longitudinal and cross-sectional studies are descriptive strategies. It is difficult to demonstrate cause-and-effect relationships with survey data. To establish causality, it is best to employ the experimental or quasi-experimental methods described in chapters 11 and 12 of this book. For example, in the drug usage example cited at the beginning of this section, the relative absence of change may occur because more drug users drop out of school, thus reducing the percentage of seniors reporting illegal drug use.

PUTTING IT ALL TOGETHER

To collect background data for his research, Eugene Anderson decided to find out how many people within his city owned pets, what percentage of the pet owners had their pets altered to prevent unwanted pregnancies, and how various groups of people felt about increasing licensing fees for pets. There were 750,000 people living in his city. He wanted to sample 500 respondents, but the task of locating 500 randomly selected people seemed overwhelming, even if he could handle most of the work by telephone. The people would be too spread out and too hard to reach. Therefore, Mr. Anderson contacted a friend at a local marketing research firm, and he discovered that there was a shopping center at which the marketing firm did most of its research. The marketing firm had discovered that samples drawn from this shopping center were usually very similar to the rest of the city with regard to most characteristics. Indeed, the conclusions of the research that the firm conducted at this one location were usually representative of what would have been concluded if the whole city were surveyed.

This was a valuable discovery. By drawing his participants from the shopping center, Mr. Anderson would have a high-quality quota sample. He followed the same procedure his friend at the marketing firm followed. He stood near the fountain in the mall and asked his question to the first person to approach him from the west at the end of each two-minute interval. In this way, he easily got his sample of 500 within two weeks. He found that 62% of the people he interviewed owned pets, 36% did not, and 2% refused to talk to him. (For purposes of his research, he restricted his definition of *pets* to dogs and cats.) Of those who owned pets, 20% had them spayed or neutered, whereas the other 80% had not done so. Of those who had their pets altered, 45% favored raising the licensing fee. Of those who had not had their pets altered, only 40% favored raising the fee.

Mr. Anderson started to conclude that pet owners who had their pets spayed or neutered were slightly more willing to favor an increase in fees. However, first he checked his confidence intervals. The interval for a sample of 500 was ±4.4%, and therefore he felt that his estimate that 62% owned pets and 36% did not was pretty accurate. Since there were about 300 persons who stated that they owned pets, this gave him a confidence interval of ±5.6% for his question about altering pets. He had 240 respondents who owned unaltered pets and 60 who owned altered pets. This meant that his estimate for the first group (alterers) was within a satisfactory ±6.2%, but his confidence interval for the second group (nonalterers) was a high ±13%. This estimate was too imprecise. Therefore, he decided that it would be rash to base any inferences on the relatively small discrepancy in opinions he had discovered.

SUMMARY

Sampling makes it possible to estimate the characteristics of a larger group by examining the characteristics of a smaller group drawn from the larger one. The larger, entire group is referred to as a *population*. The smaller group drawn from the population is called a *sample*. To provide an accurate estimate of the characteristics of a population, a sampling procedure should provide a sample that resembles the population as closely as possible. Random sampling is the best procedure for drawing a sample from a population, since it maximizes the probability that the sample will be like the population in all respects except chance variations. Biased sampling is the worst way to draw a sample; since it allows uncontrolled biases into the sample, we no longer know how closely the biased sample resembles the overall population. Quota sampling attempts to upgrade nonrandom sampling by removing some of the most obvious biases. Systematic sampling is very similar to random sampling; it starts at a random point in a population and then systematically selects members for the sample. Stratified sampling is useful when we have no list of the population or when we want to guarantee that we shall have enough members of subgroups within our sample to allow us to perform further subanalyses of the data.

Larger samples are more likely to furnish accurate estimates of their populations than are smaller samples. It is possible to estimate how accurately a sample of a given size from a designated population will represent the characteristics of that population. This information can be used to determine ahead of time how many individuals we should sample to be within a designated degree of accuracy in estimating the characteristics of a target population.

What Comes Next

In chapter 9 we'll study principles regarding the collection of reliable and valid data of an exploratory or interpretive nature in naturalistic settings. Starting in chapter 10, we'll begin to focus on conducting and interpreting research that deals with cause-and-effect relationships and on generalizing results in education. To apply these forms of research, we shall build upon the principles discussed in the first eight chapters.

DOING YOUR OWN RESEARCH

When conducting survey research, it is important to keep in mind that the goal of selecting a sample is to obtain a small group that is as representative as possible of the larger group about which you are going to make generalizations. The following guidelines from this chapter will be helpful:

1. Try to rely as much as possible on mathematical probability to obtain a random sample. For most situations, this means using random sampling.

2. It is important to come as close as possible to a 100% response rate in a random survey. Each nonrespondent makes the sample a little less random. To obtain a high response rate, it may be necessary to make such trade-offs as the following:

   a. Select a smaller sample and spend greater effort getting all the respondents to participate. This will usually be more useful than spending the same amount of effort getting a lower response rate from a larger sample.

   b. Don't use anonymous respondents unless anonymity serves a useful purpose. It's difficult to follow up on nonrespondents when the respondents are anonymous. Sometimes anonymity is necessary because it improves the quality of the responses, but you should think carefully before giving up the identity of your respondents. (You can still guarantee confidentiality even if you have the names of the respondents.)

3. When response rates are incomplete, you are essentially dealing with volunteer respondents. Try to estimate as accurately as possible how the respondents are likely to differ from the nonrespondents, and use this information as part of your analysis.

FOR FURTHER THOUGHT

1. Some of the most widely publicized surveys are those related to elections. Sometimes the projections made even a day before an election are grotesquely inaccurate, yet the exit polls on the day of election are almost always accurate. How do you explain this difference in the degree of accuracy?

2. Groups that do excellent national surveys often do not rely on purely random sampling. Why not?

3. On a television game show, one of the reviewers heard the question, "According to a recent survey, what percentage of Americans consider washing the dishes to be their most unpleasant chore?" The answer was 17%. How likely is it that this is a reasonably close estimate of the percentage of Americans who actually detest dish washing? What factors influence this degree of accuracy?

ANNOTATED BIBLIOGRAPHY

Asher, J. W. (1976). *Educational research and evaluation methods*. Boston: Little, Brown and Company. Chapter 7 provides a thorough discussion of the rationale behind the determination of sample size and sampling methodologies. Tables are given for correction factors (described in the present chapter's footnote 1).

Freedman, D., Pisani, R., & Purves, R. (1988). *Statistics* (2nd ed.). New York: W.W. Norton. Chapters 19 to 23 offer a clear and comprehensive treatment of sampling theory. The discussion is replete with useful examples. The presentation is advanced yet comprehensible to the serious reader who wants to learn more about sampling than is contained in the present textbook.

Jaeger, R. M. (1984). *Sampling in education and the social sciences*. New York: Longman. This book is both theoretically accurate and readable. Practically oriented readers can easily skim over the technical parts. Any educator planning to do serious sampling research should consult this or a similar book.

Krathwohl, D. R. (1993). *Methods of educational and social science research: An integrated approach*. New York: Longman. Chapter 8 discusses a wider range of sampling strategies than the present chapter has described. In addition, on pages 386–388 of chapter 16, Krathwohl provides a good discussion of dealing with nonrespondents and interpreting survey results with imperfect response rates.

Magnusson, D., & Bergman, L. R. (1990). *Data quality in longitudinal research*. New York: Cambridge University Press. This book gives a comprehensive treatment for the problems likely to arise in collecting longitudinal data.

Rosenthal, R., & Rosnow, R. L. (1975). *The volunteer subject*. New York: John Wiley. The authors describe the characteristics that tend to apply to persons who volunteer to take part in surveys or experiments. This kind of information can help us determine how far we can generalize the results of research that employs volunteers.

ANSWERS TO QUIZZES

Review Quiz 8.1

Part 1

1. badly biased sampling
2. biased sampling of whole population; systematic sampling of listed phone numbers
3. random sampling
4. systematic sampling of that year's documents
5. random sampling
6. quota sampling
7. stratified sampling

Part 2

1. This is similar to the person-on-the-street interviews discussed earlier in this chapter and is likely to be extremely biased. There is no reason to assume that the subjects are typical of the target population.

2. If the researcher tries to generalize the results to everyone living in the town, this would be a biased technique. (If everyone owned a single telephone and all had listed numbers, then this would be a systematic sample—provided that when the researcher chose the numbers 2 and 10 he was choosing from a range that covered the number of columns in the phone book and the number of entries in each column.)

3. This sampling is perfectly valid.

4. As long as the researcher limits his generalizations to that one year, this would be a valid sample.

5. This sampling is perfectly valid.

6. The researcher's sample is probably biased, because her very small sample of 3 out of 75 is not likely to be representative. However, the use of the quotas would improve the authenticity of the sample.

7. This sampling is perfectly valid for the subanalyses. The researcher should use a weighting procedure if he intends to make any generalizations about the overall attitudes of his congregation.

Review Quiz 8.2

1. He would have to sample 400 books. His actual confidence interval would be ±4.9% (see Table 8.2).

2. She would have to sample 100 persons. Table 8.2 gives an interval of ±9.8% for a sample size of 100.

3. She would have to include 200 teachers (100 elementary and 100 secondary). Note that correction factors (see footnote 1) would result in smaller samples.

QUALITATIVE AND NATURALISTIC RESEARCH

■ WHERE WE'VE BEEN

We've described how to operationally define and measure variables in such a way that our measurement processes are as reliable and valid as possible. We've also discussed ways to present and interpret the scores that result from our measurement processes and the strategies we use for designing instruments that assist us in the data collection process.

■ WHERE WE'RE GOING NOW

In this chapter we'll describe how to collect reliable and valid data in naturalistic settings—such as schools, classrooms, and communities. This kind of information is often informal, interpretive, and of direct value to educators. In addition, it often supplements the kind of data described in preceding chapters and provides input and a context for cause-and-effect research, which will be covered in later chapters.

■ CHAPTER PREVIEW

As we stated in chapter 1, the purpose of Level I research is to ascertain what outcomes are occurring in an educational setting. When teachers or researchers already know what variables to observe and can easily operationally define them, it is often a straightforward (though sometimes difficult) process to apply the strategies described in chapters 4–8 to assess the degree to which these variables are occurring.

In other cases, however, while it is obvious that there are problems to solve, it is necessary to conduct research to clarify what the problems really are and to identify variables that may need to be measured by more structured methods. In addition, sometimes the variables are unknown or genuinely difficult to operationally define, so it may be necessary to conduct interpretive research to explore and develop variables and to give deeper, fuller meaning to them. The labels *qualitative, interpretive,* and *naturalistic* have been applied to these kinds of broad-based research efforts to describe or interpret educational settings.

After reading this chapter, you should be able to

1. Define and give examples of qualitative research.

2. Describe the relationship between qualitative research in education and research methodologies in ethnography, human ecology, and sociology.

3. Describe the role of the participant observer in qualitative research.

4. Describe effective qualitative research strategies, including interviews, observations, and content analysis.

5. Describe how samples are selected for qualitative research.

6. Describe the four types of field data.

7. Describe the important issues in establishing the reliability and validity of qualitative research.

8. Describe four major phases of qualitative research and the activities typically conducted during each phase.

9. Describe the characteristics of a good qualitative research report.

10. Describe the major problems that occur in qualitative research and provide strategies for overcoming these problems.

■

Qualitative research admits that the analysis of human activities is by necessity largely subjective and attempts to make the subjective analysis of human behavior as unbiased as possible.

The strategies described in the preceding chapters are quantitative in the sense that researchers using them will count or rate behaviors or in some other way assign scores as a result of a data collection process. On the other hand, researchers using the strategies in the present chapter will collect data not to assign scores but rather to develop well-founded, deep, general interpretations of a situation. Quantitative research strives to be objective, but the human nature and the imprecision of measurement processes in education guarantee that research in education can never be as objective as that in physics and biology. Qualitative research, on the other hand, admits that the analysis of human activities is by necessity largely subjective and attempts to make the subjective analysis of human behavior as unbiased as possible. Specific strategies within this category of research often include the following:

The use of field studies

The use of participant observers

A major concern with the personal feelings and thoughts of an individual or the members of a group with respect to events in their lives

The use of broad descriptions of the context of social communities

An awareness of the invisibility of everyday social and personal events and structures

An awareness of personal, local, and different meanings of seemingly the same structures, events, and social rules

The questioning of assumptions and existing social systems

The holistic, broad, deep perception of existing social systems and the people in them

Qualitative research is not new. In some areas of the social sciences, such as anthropology, qualitative research has long been the primary strategy for developing and testing hypotheses. Qualitative research has likewise had a long history in education, dating back at least to Barker's (1964) *Large Schools, Small Schools,* which presented overwhelming evidence of the benefits of small schools for the personal and social growth of adolescents. The results of that study were all but ignored by educational administrators, who were on a campaign to consolidate schools, partially on the promise that larger schools would be more efficient to run—a promise that was little supported by research and was seldom fulfilled. Coleman (1961) studied the culture of adolescents in high schools in the Chicago area and concluded, among other things, that adolescents do form a society and that a psychology of learning based on students as isolated entities would be markedly incomplete. In such ways, qualitative research has played a prominent role by contributing to our understanding of the educational process and its context.

Quantitative and qualitative educational researchers have simply responded in different ways to the challenge posed by the fact that experimental control, in the tradition of physics and biology, is clearly impossible in education and the other social sciences.

In another sense, however, qualitative research in education is a new field. There has been a tendency to consider as "true research" only the quantitative and experimental research described in the other chapters of this book. Recent theorists have balked at this perception and have pointed out that since human behavior is complex and often highly subjective, interpretive research strategies are necessary to supplement traditional, quantitative educational research (Erickson, 1986). Quantitative and qualitative researchers have simply responded in different ways to the challenge posed by the fact that experimental control, in the tradition of physics and biology, is clearly impossible in education and the other social sciences. Quantitative researchers have responded by developing or applying numerical data collection processes, research designs, and statistical procedures that enable research and measurement in social sciences to parallel closely the work of natural science researchers. Qualitative researchers, on the other hand, have responded by using strategies focusing on the "objective analysis of subjective meaning" (Erickson, 1986). There is considerable validity in both of these approaches.

In this book, we take the position that there is an objectivity and subjectivity continuum and that it is improper to force all research studies into one category or another. In fact, the two types of research are perhaps of greatest value when combined. An appropriate strategy is to understand the basic principles of both qualitative and quantitative research, to know the strengths and limitations of each, and to be able to interpret the results of both methods.

The newness of some aspects of the emphasis on qualitative research presents certain problems in discussing it. The terms, labels, and methodologies are sometimes not well defined. One of our goals is to clarify some of these ambiguities in later sections of this chapter.

THE ORIGINS AND IMPACT OF QUALITATIVE RESEARCH

When they conduct qualitative studies, educational researchers often borrow from such scientific fields as social anthropology, ethnography, ecology, clinical psychology, sociology, social psychology, child development, and family studies. When you read qualitative research reports, you will sometimes see them referred to as *ethnographic* or *ecological* studies. What this means is that the researchers borrowed heavily from the field of ethnography in conducting their research or relied heavily on the methodologies employed in the field of human ecology.

Students and researchers specializing in the qualitative sciences like anthropology and ethnology take one course or more on the research methodology unique to that field. It is safe to assume, therefore, that we are not likely to convey to you within a few pages "how to become an excellent researcher" in any of these qualitative fields. Rather, the following pages will offer examples and guidelines from a few of these fields so that you can understand what the researchers do and can interpret their findings more fruitfully. In our brief examination of these fields, we shall focus immediately on how they can be applied to educational settings.

Ethnography

Ethnography is a part of cultural anthropology. Ethnographers view human actions in broad social contexts and look for multiple meanings about these

---

BOX 9.1	Good and Bad Reasons for Doing Qualitative Research

As university faculty members, we often encounter students and colleagues who tell us they "want to do qualitative research." What they mean is that they become nervous when they hear the words *measurement* and *statistics* and they think they have found a way around these distasteful topics. (Sometimes it's even worse: they are simply inept thinkers who want to avoid hard work, and they think qualitative research is easy.) They think they have found a way to do research without doing statistics and without the careful thought and time-consuming planning that must go into effective data collection processes or good research designs.

This line of reasoning is seriously wrong! Quantitative research is not really all that difficult to conduct. It is not necessarily highly mathematical. It requires logic and planning—but so does qualitative research.

Good qualitative research is no easier to conduct than good quantitative research. Teachers do not conduct qualitative research simply by visiting an innovative school, conversing with some students and teachers, and refraining from using structured measurement processes. They do not conduct qualitative research by simply taking a sabbatical, visiting the school for a whole year, reading many books related to the strategies employed in the school, theorizing carefully about the philosophy behind the school, and writing a 400-page book about their experiences. To conduct qualitative research, they would have to apply strategies like those described in this chapter.

The right reason to do qualitative research is because the situation calls for qualitative research.

---

actions. They study such topics as languages, loss of cultural elements, the influence of exceptional individuals, taboos, religion, child-rearing patterns, marriage, eating habits, housing patterns, gender roles, and games and recreation. By vividly bringing to our attention the extraordinary variability of cultural behavior, ethnography helps make us far more conscious of our own behavioral patterns. It is a science aimed at understanding the diversity of human cultures.

The ethnographer's task is to describe, interpret, and understand in considerable depth people and the cultural scenes in which they exist. Ethnographers do not make value judgments or evaluate people's actions; they would be concerned if researchers tried to "improve" the people or the cultural situations with which these participants are involved. The ethnographer's orientation is to discover how things are and how they got that way, rather than how they ought to be. The interest is long term—they examine cultural scenes for years or decades rather than for days or weeks. In educational settings, ethnographers

believe it is critical to focus on environments such as classrooms, school buildings, school systems, and central offices as cultural scenes.

Ethnographers do not make value judgments or evaluate people's actions; they would be concerned if researchers tried to "improve" the people or the cultural situations with which these participants are involved.

Ethnographies are analytic descriptions of intact cultural scenes. These descriptions present the shared beliefs, practices, artifacts, folk knowledge, and behaviors of peoples. Ethnographies are both empirical and naturalistic. They are first-hand, holistic descriptions of a total phenomenon in its context. From these in-depth descriptions, ethnographers generate the major variables and phenomena affecting the participants' beliefs and behavior. The findings that are generated often give rise to or support emerging theories.

Human Ecology

Human ecology is the study of the total system of influences surrounding people. As teachers well know, the classroom is a complex environment of cultures and overt and covert message exchanges expressed in a number of ways. Variables in an ecological study of a classroom could include the written and spoken language; the body language of movement, gestures, and posture; changes of tone, speed, tempo, pitch, and intensity of voice, including pauses and any intruding sounds; the social processes of negotiation and turn-taking; humor in communications; and patterns of thought, feelings, behavior, and inner responses. All of these variables influence what is communicated, how it is communicated, and from and to whom the communications are sent in the classroom.

In a classroom ecology, the communicators include the students and teachers, any announcements over the intercom, and any messengers, parents, visitors, administrators, or special teachers who come into the classroom. An examination of these communicators and their activities can help develop a rich, descriptive understanding of the social and cultural foundations of a classroom. Thus, they are important sources of information in educational research. Further, classroom teachers are continual, active participant observers of many classroom variables and thus can be full partners in ecological qualitative research. Classrooms (and school buildings and school systems) are culturally complex entities in which students, teachers, administrators, secretaries, janitors, parents, and the community play roles. All of these groups and individuals interact with one another. They all have their own contexts, cultures, patterns, and methods of relating. In addition, schools exhibit both formal and informal curricula. Finally, the classroom ecology includes various patterns of formal and informal social control.

Sociology

A part of education's task is to aid in the socialization and acculturation of children and adolescents. How this is done, whose culture is passed on, and how it is communicated in schools should be a major part of educational research. Sociology looks at the functioning of groups of people and the influences of social structure. It is concerned with such factors as social change, social status and stratification, social power, social problems (such as crime, poverty, ethnic tension, and overpopulation), bureaucracies, families, and social institutions. In addition, sociologists are concerned with interpersonal relationships, conflicts, and management styles. They also study evasion tactics such as ambiguity, ignorance, avoidance, and the use of intermediaries, rituals, secrecy, lying, and joking in social relationships. Sociologists study education and view it as a major cultural learning experience for everyone in our society.

BOX 9.2	Margaret Mead: Qualitative Researcher

Anthropologists have pioneered the social research methodology of the active participant observer. When anthropologist Margaret Mead lived with the Samoans in the South Pacific, she was not too much older than the adolescent Samoan girls; she was thus able to gain the girls' confidence and that of their parents and other members of the community. She described in detail the cultural aspects and events in all of their lives and the physical, biological, and social environments in which they lived. Her book *Coming of Age in Samoa* (Mead, 1928) not only described the lives of adolescent Samoan girls but gave Americans considerable new insight about their own culture and about how adolescent girls are treated in the United States. Young women have been reading the book ever since, to gain deeper insights and broader perspectives about their own lives, feelings, and behaviors.

One of the problems of educators is to deal effectively with all the social classes. Perhaps some educators "tolerate" lower-class habits and values and reinforce "good" middle-class values, while trying to convince the "elites" of society to financially support the schools. Family poverty is another problem for which schools make accommodations, by providing free lunches, special tutoring, and often public health services. An additional problem is that teachers are predominantly from the middle classes and tend to emphasize the middle-class values of attendance at school, punctuality, respect for property, and personal responsibility, while school boards may be drawn from business and professional groups or, in rural areas, from landowning farmers.

The preceding paragraphs have shown the degree of overlap between sociology and education. In fact, there is a well-developed field of the sociology of education, which itself conducts educational research. Educational sociologists point out that schools are a part of society and not apart from it; thus, schools cannot be understood without some understanding of society, which schools reflect. They tell us that schools seek out students and indoctrinate them with specific knowledge and social values. In fact, one of the major goals of teaching is to change the beliefs of the students. It is clear that the content and methodologies of sociology have much to offer education.

Summary: The Impact of Qualitative Sciences

We have summarized only a few of the qualitative sciences whose research methodologies are relevant to education. As you read these descriptions, it probably became obvious to you that there is considerable overlap among the activities that researchers in these various fields perform. For example, ethnographers and human ecologists often focus on the same variables as do sociologists, but from a slightly different perspective. The recommendation of qualitative theorists in education is that educators similarly borrow from these fields and apply these methodologies in proper perspective to education.

Most readers of this book will realize that they have at least briefly encountered the methodologies of qualitative research as part of their liberal arts training to become teachers.

To exhibit a broad understanding of students, teachers, administrators, and parents in educational research it is important to be knowledgeable of the theories and research methodologies of such fields as anthropology, ethnography, human ecology, and sociology, as well as their data collection, analysis, and interpretation methods. Most readers of this book will realize that they have at least briefly encountered the methodologies of these fields as part of their liberal arts training to become teachers. As qualitative research reports continue to be increasingly available in the professional literature, you will have opportunities to review these methodologies, understand their applicability to education, interpret their findings more appropriately, and perhaps begin to employ them yourself in further understanding educational problems.

QUALITATIVE DATA COLLECTION METHODS

Once we have realized the value of qualitative research, it is useful to examine specific methods for recording a continuing sequence of events and a wide range of variables. Effective qualitative methods enable the researcher to probe situations in considerable depth and breadth, learn the participants' personal feelings and views of activities, determine the social structure and context of the classroom or other educational setting, and put all the observations into a holistic, all-encompassing, phenomenological picture.

The Participant Observer

The key data collector in many forms of qualitative research is the participant observer. As the name indicates, this is a person who participates in the setting or process being studied and also makes careful observations of what is happening. Participant observers (who in classrooms can certainly be teachers) are not strangers to the situation; therefore they know the language, phrases, and particular vocabulary common in educational situations. This knowledge allows the participant observer an understanding of the events in the classroom and educational culture from the beginning phases of the data collection. The participant observer can ask sensible questions about educational events and can develop a strategy for data collection of all kinds: observations, interviews, questionnaires, visual and auditory recordings, content analysis, and formal and informal testing.

It takes practice to be a good participant observer. Explicit awareness must be built. A good way to develop this expertise is to work with a colleague—each of you should write detailed, explicit descriptions of rather ordinary educational processes which you observe, or conduct separate interviews of the same people. Then compare notes with your colleague to see how they agree and to see which variables were reported by one but not the other. Discuss the reports of your observations and interviews to determine what you may have misinterpreted, overinterpreted, or omitted. Then repeat these activities several times with different observers and interviewers with progressively more complex social events and interviews. Continue this process until you see and hear variables in much the same way.

The process described in the preceding paragraph will produce observers and interviewers who are in general agreement with one another (in psychometric terms, these researchers develop reliability). Through this process the observers and interviewers can demonstrate that there are real social and psychological (but subjective) variables in the educational world that can be observed by others. Being reliable data collectors doesn't necessarily indicate that the participant observers are valid reporters and interpreters of that reality, but without replicable data there is little hope of having valid data.

It takes practice to be a good participant observer. Explicit awareness must be built.

Bernard (1988, p. 159) suggests that even with prior training and practice and good rapport, "it takes at least three months to achieve reasonable intellectual competence in another culture and be accepted as a participant observer." He suggests that researchers pick sites that are easy to enter, have their research project well documented, use contacts with the participants who can help them gain access to the culture, and think through in advance their responses to questions about what they are doing, what they want to learn, what good their research is, and whom it will benefit.

Classroom teachers can be heavily involved and often full partners in qualitative research, certainly at Level I research. They can be collaborators and participant observers with others at Levels II, III, and IV. Teachers are deeply and personally involved in the classrooms and with their students. They are only too aware of discrepancies between learned theories of human behavior and actions and what they see everyday. Further, they see unusual students and social events for which there are few descriptions in the published literature. They know through personal experience that family, neighborhood, and community contexts are important. Every classroom has a distinctly local, unique, and compelling reality.

A teacher serving as a participant observer can markedly reduce the problem of reactivity of the members of the class or school being observed. Teachers understand educational systems and how they operate. They fit in well, and the class and school participants soon go on with the business of teaching and learning and let the participant observer conduct interviews, make observations, and generally collect data with a minimum of change in behavior. Teachers acting as participant observers can facilitate collecting field data on-site in the classroom or other educational setting in which they participate.

One of the problems of being a teacher participant observer is that teachers and other educators are not naive about the culture they are observing, and familiarity with the classroom can serve as a biasing factor that will interfere with objective data collection. Much of what teachers do every day is done so automatically that perhaps they are intellectually almost unaware of it, or they read their own motivations and thoughts into what others are doing as they go about their tasks. In either event, they can form an inaccurate interpretation of observed events or, perhaps worse, not recognize that an event or a response is taking place.

In spite of the problems, however, the participation of teachers in qualitative research, collaboratively or individually, holds the promise of contributing markedly to the profession of teaching, to education, and to one's personal growth and insight.

TYPES OF QUALITATIVE DATA

Generally, qualitative research data fall into four classifications: observations, interviews, documents, and research instruments of various kinds (such as questionnaires, surveys, and personality, attitude, and cognitive tests). Many of these qualitative data collection methods are available to teachers, counselors, and administrators, who should use them in understanding their educational milieu. However, in some cases, qualitative researchers remain deliberately uninformed about variables and relationships until after their data collection; this enables them to approach the situation without preconceptions that may bias their research. In other cases, the participant observers approach the research setting with a more specific plan and listed variables, behaviors, events, and settings of probable interest to them. This preplanning is based on prior experiences and reviews of the literature and gives them a tentative organization for their data collection in the field.

Seidman (1991) points out that effective qualitative interviewing and observation must take into consideration the power of the social and organizational context of people's experience. He urges researchers to become aware of their own experience with issues of race, class, gender, and age, as well as the way these factors may be influencing the participants.

The information obtained by these less formal means of data collection needs to be organized and interpreted (the characteristics of a good report are summarized later in this chapter). The results of qualitative studies often provide a useful basis for developing other data collection strategies, including further qualitative research, structured interviews, questionnaires, and surveys.

Many qualitative data collection methods are available to teachers, counselors, and administrators, who should use them in understanding their educational milieu.

Observations

Some observational methods can be (and in some instances should be) conducted under rigorously controlled conditions—highly trained researchers can observe specific, operationally defined units of behavior that are easily agreed upon and counted, as was discussed in chapter 6. However, in this chapter we shall consider *open-ended* observations, which are broadly defined as observations of behaviors under ongoing, natural conditions. These observations involve seeing and hearing events that people take part in, not asking after the fact what people have done or why. For example, researchers can observe types of teacher–pupil exchange in a naturalistic situation to look for patterns based on ethnic, social status, or gender differences or based on the type of program in which students are participating. In addition, it is possible to observe administrative as well as instructional activities. For example, continuous observations of the principal can help determine the kinds of problems encountered during a typical day and how these tend to be handled—essentially, a day, a week, a month, or a year in the life of a principal.

The obtrusiveness or unobtrusiveness of these observations, as discussed in chapter 6, must always be a consideration. Here, the emphasis of qualitative research leans heavily toward observations and measures that are as unobtrusive as possible. Reactivity of the participants being observed or interviewed is a major problem for qualitative researchers. They want to see behaviors essentially unmodified by their own presence. Mixing in (or "hanging out") with those observed, if this is possible, is more friendly, builds rapport, and is certainly less reactive than more systematic time sampling, behavior counting, or videotaping of social groups. However, the more informal approach requires much more reliance on the observer's memory and increases the possibility of bias. If such biases can be minimized, the quality of the natural data is likely to be better and more meaningful.

Interviews

Interviews are another major form of data collection in qualitative research. The richness of the responses in both breadth and depth can add markedly to the understanding of the classroom or school. In qualitative data collection the informal interview essentially has no structure. These interviews resemble ordinary conversations, except that the participant observer often makes a point of ensuring that the conversations take place and continue. Notes are afterwards made of the informal interview's contents based on the memory of the conversation. The informal interview is used to explore interesting phenomena in the cultural scene and to establish rapport. At a slightly higher level of structure, there can still be a minimum of control, but there is a clear plan in the interviewer's head about the areas and people of which information is wanted. The purpose of the informal interview is to allow a structure so that the persons being interviewed tell the interviewer their information in their own terms. Tape recordings of interviews are often helpful to preserve and cross-check information.

In qualitative research, the interviewer is often shopping for information but is not totally certain regarding what that information may be; he or she doesn't know the aspects and topics about the social group that the informant knows. It is wise to guarantee the informants' anonymity and to explain to them why they have been chosen (e.g., because they have observations and feelings about particular situa-

tions, events, or social relationships; or they were picked at random to obtain a sample that represents a group of people).

The informant must have the needed information and must be available to give the interviewer the time to talk. The interview tone should be cordial, supportive, and nonthreatening. The general principle of many interview formats is to tell the informant, in rather general terms, what it is the interviewer wants to know, and then let the informant talk.

The general approach of the qualitative interview is nondirective and Rogerian in style.

Counselors and teachers with counseling courses should be especially good interviewers. They will recognize the general approach of the qualitative interview as nondirective and Rogerian in style. Teachers and counselors typically have the genuine interest in people that is so necessary to be a good interviewer. They are often able to develop an open, reflective communication pattern with the informant and build a feeling of trust and rapport. Being supportive of responses with smiles, nods, and a nondirective "uh-huh" is important. Showing attentive silence and learning to wait are both valuable interviewing skills. Another effective skill is to be able to reflect the gist of the last statements in a questioning manner, indicating that you want either affirmation that your notes are right or further clarification of the responses.

The purpose of naturalistic interviewing strategies is to keep the informants talking and to express your interest in what they have to say. Interviewers should not indicate an approving or disapproving valuation by their words, tone of voice, or gestures. It is important to probe to obtain further, more detailed, and relevant information, but if it is necessary to interrupt, this should be done gracefully and not accidentally. The interviewers must reduce their reactions and interventions to a minimum. Reinterviewing the informant a second and third time after a lapse will sometimes allow even more information to be obtained.

Often, it is useful to take on-the-spot notes or use a tape recorder and have a list of topics available that should be covered. If there are sensitive issues to be discussed, it is better to ask the informant about them in the middle of the interview and begin and end with questions about less sensitive topics. As part of the interview, it is useful to take notes on the surroundings in which the interview was held and to record the date and time. It is also important to record the informant's attitude (e.g., was the informant open? evasive? cordial? nervous? afraid?).

Documents and Other Artifacts

Formal and standardized instruments (such as questionnaires, surveys, and tests, which are discussed in chapters 4–8) and documents can also be part of qualitative research data. Documents in this sense are often referred to as *artifacts*. They can include either current information (e.g., instructional materials and communications within the school building or school system) or archival information (e.g., newspapers, school board minutes, teachers' union records of contract negotiations, court records, architects' plans for school buildings, tapes of televised programs, diaries, tax roll data, transcripts, and textbooks). Archival documents are often valuable even though they may have errors and could well be incomplete. The data from both types of documents should be collected unobtrusively, although the records could have been made under obtrusive conditions (e.g., perhaps newspaper reporters asked pointed questions about school board meeting procedures).

One of the main ways to analyze documents and other qualitative data is through a process called *content analysis,* whereby the researchers look for themes or concepts in the natural language. For example, they could count or analyze the number of references to administrators, teachers, students, and parents to ascertain the relative importance of each of these groups in a school system's communications. In children's themes, the relative emphasis on the concepts of cooperation and competition could be assessed. The several concepts in teachers' evaluation statements about pupils could be coded and counted

to determine the curricular and social goals of the teachers. Newspaper articles reporting on the activities in schools could be counted, their length noted, and the topics analyzed; this would indicate the public's interest in education or the facets of the system that the administrators would like the public to know about. Variables can be both conceptually and operationally defined, as well as illustrated with examples from the documents themselves. Current documents can be generated by having students write themes on various topics for content analysis.

SELECTING SUBJECTS AND INTERPRETING QUALITATIVE DATA

The sampling of situations, sites, and informants for qualitative research is usually not done in the same way as for quantitative research. As chapter 8 showed, *quantitative* researchers often sample people and sites at random. Whatever findings are true in the random samples can be generalized, within limits, to the populations from which they are drawn. In *qualitative* research, informants and events are selected for their unique ability to explain, understand, and yield information about the meaning of expressive behavior or the way the social system works. This is called *theoretical sampling.* *Purposive* samples can also be chosen to yield maximum information related to specific issues.

The samples may be unique or unusual in order to promote insight about a behavior that is not usual. For example, a researcher may be interested in understanding the feelings of a child with a specific disability, the dynamics of a chaotic classroom, the effect of unusual school building architecture (such as an open classroom) on class instruction, or the educational progress of a newly immigrated Vietnamese community. All of these situations are unusual, and subjects to be observed or interviewed may be selected specifically to learn about social and personal variables operating in the educational situation or to gain insight about ways a class or school functions. Informants are chosen because of their key involvement in a social group and their competence to tell the participant observer what they observe, feel, and

Figure 9.1 Example of
Field Jottings

Tues, Jan 25 (Written at 9:30 am)

J & KV worked on interactive part of their hyperstack.
Had trouble with button for video portion.
Solved problem by copying Bill & Carl's use of Voyager materials
Teacher intervened - "Don't just do it for them - Show them so they'll know
   how to do it next time."

think; they are chosen also because they are believed to reflect the views of others in the social group.

At other times, convenience samples are selected simply because they are available. Precautions need to be taken to determine whether such samples are reasonably representative of a more general population. This can sometimes be done by checking the sample's demographic variables (e.g., sex, age, social class) against the population of interest. The logic of sampling (discussed in chapter 8) indicates that nonrandom samples are often biased; these biases present a problem that must be considered when interpreting qualitative research.

The logic of sampling indicates that nonrandom samples are often biased; these biases must be considered when interpreting qualitative research.

THE FOUR TYPES OF FIELD DATA

A major problem with qualitative data collection is remembering the data long enough to record it. Bernard (1988) recommends collecting four basic types of field data: field jottings, field notes, a field diary, and a field log. *Field jottings* (Figure 9.1) are taken whenever the researcher observes or hears something important. They are written on the spot to avoid the problems of forgetfulness and selective memories.

Field jottings serve as a source for *field notes* (Figure 9.2), which are summaries of field data col-

lected during the day or over another designated period of time. The notes are supplemented by all the other information collected, including recordings, documents, and notes about the overview and understanding of the social scene as the participant observer sees it at that time. These notes are compiled immediately, at least on a day-to-day basis, so that the data are fresh and other activities do not interfere with recollections. Bernard suggests spending an hour or two per day collating and integrating a day's field jottings and writing the field diary. The field notes are a precursor to the reports the participant observers will ultimately compile.

The *field diary* (Figure 9.3) is a personal chronicle of how the participant observer feels about the social situation that he or she is in; it should also chronicle the relationship of the observer to those being observed. Later this diary will help the participant observer to more fully interpret the field notes and be alert for personal biases. The *field log* (Figure 9.4), much like a ship's log, relates the chronicle of daily events: how the participant observer planned to spend time, how time was actually spent, who was seen, what their names are, what they talked about, and who else needed to be seen and what needed to be asked. The plan of the day and the actual activities of the participant observer may actually be quite different, but the log helps keep the data collection organized.

Eventually, the sheer bulk of field notes becomes unwieldy, so organizing and summarizing becomes important. An essential step is coding the information to help structure and report the field data. The coding process (Figure 9.5) consists of looking for

Figure 9.2 Example of
Field Notes

Tues, Jan 25 (Written around 3:00 pm)

All 8 groups worked on their stacks for full 60 minutes.
Examples of students imitating others:
    J & KV copied Bill & Carl's Voyager approach.
    Mona's group expanded on Maria's use of submenus by adding a second
        level.
    Arlene's group used the same pictures as Dan's, but added new
        questions of their own.

Examples of preparation for computer sessions:
    19 out of 20 students brought new materials from home today.
    Maria brought in her twelfth book with pictures of whales.

Figure 9.3 Example of
a Field Diary

Mon, Jan 24 (Written at 3:00 that day)

High level of participation, but some frustration when John & Ken had trouble
    with interactive portion of their stack. Others were too busy to help.

Tues, Jan 25 (Written at 3:00 that day)

High level of participation. Children are helping one another and teacher is
    playing a supportive role.

Wed, Jan 26 (Written at 3:00 that day)

Computer session canceled because of school assembly. Students were
    upset. Teacher promised extra time tomorrow if they would finish math
    assignments at home.

Figure 9.4 Example of a Field Log

Mon, Jan 24

Sit near back of room and scan class as evenly as possible

OK
Bill & Carl's video drew attention. Watch J & KV tomorrow.

Tues, Jan 25

Start at back of room but move to scenes of frustration or intense interaction.

OK
Everyone wanted to add video. Focused on J & KV, but observed others from there.

Look for evidence of preparation.

Counted students with materials from home.

Wed, Jan 26

Session canceled - No data except to note frustration of kids & teacher's plan of action

Sit at side of room to focus on Mona's group while monitoring everyone else.

(Left column was written _before_ observation session)

(Right column was written at the end of the day)

patterns and organizing information around these patterns. At a minimum, coding should note the informant's name, the names of those observed, the place of the observation, the date and time of the data recording, and the initial indications of the variables involved. It is during this coding process that concepts and insights arising from the data collection begin to emerge. This development of insights about categories, concepts, social structures, and meanings is one of the principal aims of qualitative research. The codings should also summarize the methodological techniques used and describe the events that occurred during the period of data collection.

A valuable aspect of qualitative research is that it allows you to develop variables and an understanding of patterns of behavior in social groups over a large number of naturally occurring events.

Analytic notes (Figure 9.6) are essentially the result of the qualitative researcher's conceptualizations of how he or she thinks the culture and social groupings are structured and organized. They result from a careful examination of the field notes, jottings, diaries, and logs. They are inductive. They look for broad, speculative explanations, organizing

Figure 9.5 Example of Coding of Field Data

Help Seeking by Students

1. Initially they sought help only from the teacher.
(Examples omitted)

Exception - Mona & Maria got help from one another from the start
(Example omitted)

2. Eventually they sought help from group members
(Examples omitted)

3. Later they started looking to other groups for ideas and help.
(Earlier examples omitted)

Jan 25 - When J & KV had trouble on their interactive button, they copied Bill & Carl's use of Voyager materials.

(Later examples omitted)

4. Teacher prompted students to seek & give help effectively.
(Examples omitted)

principles, and concepts that explain and give structure to the many observations and data that are contained in the field notes. Analytic notes will not be many, but they are the key to good results from qualitative research. They are inductive generalizations arising from specifics and operational definitions. They result from "eyeball" analyses and sometimes from discussions with objective, insightful colleagues who have expertise as qualitative researchers but have not been so close to the field setting. This inductive procedure leads to the generation or refinement of theory. This is often referred to as grounded theory because it is generated from the data rather than developed first and then tested through the collection of data.

Qualitative researchers must be open to negative evidence as well as positive evidence about a theory,

and they must deal with unusual cases in the proposed explanations of behavior. As they seem to understand and can explain the behaviors, qualitative researchers develop alternative explanations (hypotheses) and check them against the data as well. A valuable aspect of qualitative research is that it allows you to develop variables and an understanding of patterns of behavior in social groups over a large number of naturally occurring events. The field data descriptions are used to help operationally define the variables and describe in rich, natural language how these variables change in relationship to other variables and circumstances. Good field data depend on systematic fieldwork conducted over a long period of time.

The human mind is a fast and effective organizer and recognizes patterns in data, but it is not too

Students seemed to start by working in isolation. Even within the small groups, members did not interact with one another except by showing partners what they had done. By the second day, interaction was accelerating *within* groups. When the teacher suggested looking at the work of other groups, interaction increased greatly. Groups began sending delegates to other groups to find good ideas that they might use.

When groups first started sharing ideas, at first the group with the good idea simply did the work for the group that requested help. The teacher discouraged this. She showed them how to help by giving ideas without doing all the work for the group receiving the assistance. . . .

Figure 9.6 Example of Analytic Notes from Field Data

effective in storing large amounts of finite bits of data. Thus, qualitative researchers should make copious notes on a timely basis, add to these field notes daily in a reflective and structured mode, and record their feelings about the situation as well. On the basis of these voluminous amounts of data, researchers should then make interpretations of it, impose a meaningful structure, develop variables, and finally present their readers with their understanding of the social entity with which they have been involved. This process of repeatedly looking for patterns of data and variables in field notes and developing constructs that account for these patterns, comparing them with each other, and redefining and reconceptualizing them into more coherent variables and patterns has been called the "constant comparative method" (Goetz & LeCompte, 1984).

RELIABILITY AND VALIDITY OF QUALITATIVE DATA

The concepts of reliability and validity (discussed in chapter 5) must be reexamined and expanded for qualitative data. While some qualitative theorists (e.g., Wolcott) would maintain that such quantitative

terms do not apply at all in qualitative research, others would maintain that the essential definitions still apply in this chapter. *Reliability* means that the data collection process is not self-contradictory—that the data collection is both consistent and stable. *Validity* means that the observations, interviews, or content analysis really contain the information that the researcher thinks they contain. At their most general level of definition, these concepts are obviously important in any form of research; otherwise, why should anyone pay attention to such research? However, because of its more subjective nature, qualitative research introduces some nuances into the use of these terms.

> *Because of its subjective nature, qualitative research introduces some nuances into the use of the terms reliability and validity.*

The concept of reliability is sometimes ignored in qualitative research. If an event is rare, how can two independent observers describe it and then later check their level of agreement? Qualitative research is enormously labor intensive. Many groups and individuals are observed and interviewed over long periods of time, up to a year or more. Many sources of data are tapped, and extensive written records are made. Then more writing is done to further elaborate on the descriptions. To have more than one person do all of this is rare. Clearly, to attempt even to duplicate these observations would be enormously time-consuming and expensive. However, for educational research to maintain credibility as a science, the concern with reliability must be addressed.

Kirk and Miller (1986), two anthropologists, refer to the types of reliability relevant to qualitative research as synchronic and diachronic. *Synchronic reliability* is the similarity of observations made within the same time period (agreement among observers or measures). *Diachronic reliability* is the stability of an observation over time. The general rule is that diachronic reliability is distinctly limited by the reliability of observations of phenomena at a given point in time. (In addition, the validity of one's interpretations are limited by both types of reliability.)

Aside from the problems of interpretation arising from low reliability, biases of various types are a major threat to the *validity* of qualitative research. One type of bias concerns the time span or settings sampled, which may not be typical of those to which the results of the data collection process will be generalized. This problem is treated by collecting data over a lengthy time span and by selecting settings judiciously.

Another major bias concerns the subjectivity of observers. They tend to be biased about what they see, and since qualitative research often involves interpretation, further problems occur when they misinterpret what is really happening. Much of what teachers and educators do every day is done so automatically that they are almost unaware of it, or they read their own motivations and thoughts into what others are doing. In either event, they can form wrong interpretations of observed events or not recognize that an event or a response is taking place. In phenomenological terms, they are reporting their own reality rather than the reality they should be observing. The way to deal with this source of bias is to train researchers to be aware of and control their tendencies to be biased. An effective strategy to increase validity is to do a *member check*—that is, ask participants if they think your interpretation is valid (but do this in a way that avoids obtrusive interference with the natural setting).

Although there are problems with validity, compared with more traditional quantitative research, qualitative methods are more valid in that they really do get at the underlying concepts being observed rather than measure an artificial entity created by a data collection process. To the extent that interpretation is necessary and the interpreter has interpreted correctly, then the subjective qualitative measurement will be superior to a more objective, quantitative assessment of the same outcome or situation. The problem, of course, is that there is no good, objective way to assess the quality of subjective interpretations and insights. We can muster empirical evidence to demonstrate the validity of quantitative instruments, but this is much more difficult to accomplish for qualitative strategies. This does not mean that quanti-

tative strategies are superior. As we have stressed from the beginning of this book, multiple methods of data collection are always preferable to a single method. Teachers and researchers should derive the benefits from both approaches to research problems.

Maxwell (1992) has identified five general types of validity in qualitative research:

Descriptive validity refers to the overall accuracy of the descriptions making up a study.

Interpretive validity refers to the degree to which the researcher correctly interprets the activities and feelings of the people in the study (i.e., as the participants themselves would interpret them).

Theoretical validity refers to the degree to which the researcher's explanations represent a legitimate application of the concepts or theories that the researcher thinks they represent.

Generalizability refers to the degree to which an account can be extended to situations or populations not directly studied (both within the study and beyond the study).

Evaluative validity refers to the degree to which judgments based on the study are legitimate.

The validity of any type of research is established by logical methods. Some research studies rely heavily on the mathematical, statistical, or research design strategies described in chapters 5, 10, and 11 of this book to support their validity; this is why they are often referred to as quantitative studies. On the other hand, researchers who use the qualitative methods described in this chapter rely on experience, insight, and reasoning to demonstrate the validity of their studies. The preceding presentation of Maxwell's discussion of validity meshes very well with the phases of qualitative research described by Kirk and Miller (1986), which are described next.

THE PHASES OF QUALITATIVE RESEARCH

Kirk and Miller (1986) describe four phases of qualitative research methodology, which serve as a useful synthesis of what has been discussed in this chapter. These phases are as follows:

1. Invention or preparation
2. Discovery
3. Interpretation
4. Explanation

Invention or Preparation

The first phase is *invention* or *preparation*. This phase involves reviewing the literature about a problem; developing the aspects of the context and social group that might be of particular interest; gaining access to and becoming accepted by the social group and developing social networks and contacts within it; having your preconceptions challenged or changed; dealing with practical constraints to data collection as they emerge; and identifying your own biases. Developing questions about interesting aspects of the field situation, locating key informants, and developing research instruments are also part of the preparation for data collection.

Kirk and Miller state that taking notes during the first views of a cultural scene and its social context are crucial. They point out that first observations of social scenes and cultural settings in the field seem to evaporate as soon as the ethnographers get close to them. The same may be true of too much prior knowledge of a social scene from personal experience or a study of the literature. This knowledge can bias researchers and lead them to think that they understand (only too well) certain personal reactions of the individuals involved or to recognize only certain variables. Thus, some purists in qualitative research refuse to bias themselves by reviewing the prior literature and theory about classrooms or school systems. Nevertheless, it is important for researchers to document their first impressions about a social context and scene because such impressions will fade rapidly, and much will be lost.

A feature common to all qualitative research is the need to become acquainted with the participants and

to build rapport. At an early stage in the research process, it is useful to learn where the participants usually work and gather informally; to map the physical characteristics of the classroom, building, and neighborhood; to record the demographics of the participants by role; and, in general, to create a preliminary description of the social and physical scenes to be studied. The demographics should include the participant's age, gender, education, socioeconomic status, ethnic identity, and position in the various social organizations. In addition, use-of-time maps and a record of daily, weekly, and monthly episodes are useful. It is also helpful to determine the concerns of the students, teachers, community, and parents—perhaps by collecting anecdotes, stories, and even gossip about how the participants view one another. These data will suggest what is socially and personally important to the participants and how they evaluate their role in the group. At this point, too, the observer develops trust and rapport with the participants. He or she also takes care to note unusual features of the physical and social functioning of the group because all too soon these features will fade from consciousness, seem familiar, and no longer be questioned or perhaps even recorded.

At an early stage it is also important to note the location of documents—records, minutes, curriculum guides, memos, letters, public relations handouts, newspapers, policy statements, etc.—that will form the collection to further inform and substantiate the observer's description of the group. Observations, interviews, document collection and analysis, depiction of physical structures, content analysis, open-ended questions, focus groups, role playing, formal and informal tests, and product analysis can each form a part of the all-encompassing description of the group.

Discovery

The second phase, *discovery*, occurs when the researchers identify specific places and times to make their observations, conduct interviews, and collect other types of data. An initial plan for the research needs to be developed. In even simple social groups, an almost unlimited number of observations could be made. A research plan lists the most interesting situations, events, people, and data that can be used.

This phase is conducted initially to allocate the researcher's time to accumulate most efficiently data that will shed light on the questions, individuals, and social events of interest. Research in general is a continual, circular process of asking questions and collecting data so that you can ask better questions, collect more data, and so on. One of qualitative research's great strengths is in the broad observational abilities of the researchers to see far more than they expected to see and hear far more than they expected to hear.

The scholarly preparation, planning, and first phases of data collection are essential; but an alert, open mind eager to follow interesting clues, identify and record surprises in the first observations, develop more interesting questions, and follow the more intriguing social events is a great strength of qualitative research. It is practically a certainty that these initial research plans will be reworked, in some cases radically. (In one example, an initial qualitative study of school dropouts and underachievers showed that one aspect of the problem was the lure of major money to be made by adolescent boys becoming homosexual prostitutes [Reiss & Rhodes, 1959]. This was totally unanticipated and was a major diversion of the research effort as first planned.) All new questions, variables, and events must be incorporated into the total scope of the data collection plans on-site in the field. In addition, the data collection plans continue to change throughout the fieldwork as more new opportunities arise. Kirk and Miller (1986, pp. 66–67) state that "qualitative research is defined by the location of hypothesis-testing activity in the discovery, rather than the interpretation, phase." The discovery phase ends with all the field data in hand for the attainment of the research objectives, as modified during the fieldwork. The discovery phase fully ends when the researchers exit from the field site.

Interpretation

Interpretation is the third phase of qualitative research and constitutes an ongoing analysis of the field data and its overall meaning. (Some would argue that this should be done, in part, in the field also, where further inquiries are possible.) Interpretation occurs partly through a reconsideration of the reliability and validity of all the data, considering whether the conceptual interpretations of the variables are reasonably correct and the overall understanding of the social scene, its context, and those involved in it are also reasonably correct.

This phase involves a repeated, careful examination and consideration of all the field data combined with the researcher's insights gained from his or her personal involvement on the scene in the field. Data related to the same event from several sources are brought together, further hypotheses are developed, and old and new hypotheses are further tested against other data and alternative hypotheses until a theory evolves from the field data that appears to be a general explanation. The field data are converted into categories and relationships through a process of multiple readings and sorting multiple sources of records into piles relating to such aspects as themes, concepts, individuals, groups, and scenes. This can be done by making multiple copies of the raw data and cutting them up before sorting. File cards can be used, but computers are commonly used these days. Various software programs are available, and the computer's natural language storage capacity and ability to classify, subclassify, and organize data are nearly ideal for the functions that go into developing grounded theory. Assertions are made, tested, and then retested against many examples in the data. During interpretation, the researcher also looks for discrepant cases to see how they fit the theory or whether other theories and explanations are needed.

Data are pieced together to help determine patterns. The search is made for key links that pull together data related to the same event, person, or scene. The whole process of interpretation and explanation is one of pattern analysis, and the attempt is to bring together in a meaningful fashion as many items of data as possible into a meaningful whole. This can be done in part by maps, figures, diagrams, and tables. The aim is to persuade the readers of the research that sufficient evidence exists to support the assertions made and that the patterns of evidence do exist and the theory (i.e., the conceptual explanations) is indeed valid. It is not the thick, rich descriptions—quotations, vignettes, frequency counts, etc.—that demonstrate the descriptive validity of the report, but all of these combined with the interpretive perspective make the overall presentation valid.

Explanation

The final of Kirk and Miller's four phases of qualitative research is *explanation*. In this phase a message is produced to communicate the data, findings, and broad, deep understanding of the social and personal relationships of the field site. The report must present the organized data and the relationships among the variables that the data represent; this is the evidence that will support the ultimate assertions. The links between the concrete data and the abstract concepts must be made clear. Researchers should make explicit their own expertise, possible biases, and interpretive stance. Next, they should consider carefully the audiences who will read the report; these could include fellow researchers, administrators, policymakers, teachers, and members of the context community. For the research audience the adequacy of the research methods and data will be of importance, and the interpretations and particularly the hypotheses generated need to be taken into consideration in future research. For policymakers and administrators it is appropriate to present a wider range of alternative policy options that have been generated by the research and some data about the consequences of each. For this group it is particularly helpful to present the practical constraints, inhibitions, and frustrations of those in the classrooms and school buildings.

For the practitioners the concern is whether the field situation is similar to their own classroom or building and whether there are suggestions, prescriptions, or recipes in the report for what works. Also, researchers should question whether the theories and explanations generated help explain the actions, behaviors, and responses of others and themselves. In part, the value of these explanations lies in the specificity of the qualitative descriptions of the contextual situation and the classroom or building so that the teachers and principals can determine whether there is enough similarity between the research and their own situations to allow them to generalize about their own rooms and buildings.

The last audience includes members of the community, parents, other school staff, and students. These people may want to be more generally informed about their school—what is news and not news, what might be regarded as a positive, negative, or neutral evaluation. It is crucial that for this group (as well as to some extent the professional group) reputations and privacy be protected. Certain material may have to be excluded from the public reports. In any event, for all of the audiences the researchers must be judicious and consider that everything they write may ultimately become public information.

CHARACTERISTICS OF A GOOD QUALITATIVE RESEARCH REPORT

The amount of writing included in field notes, logs, diaries, and reflections—especially for the long periods of time involved—is considerable. By necessity, the reporting of the research is lengthy—a good qualitative thesis may run 500 pages or more, and many qualitative research projects are reported at book length. Further, the writing itself must almost be of novelistic quality to gain and keep the attention of the readers. Some of the greatest insights about human actions, thoughts, and feelings are presented in novels, and at least one psychologist has said that to be a good clinician requires taking a few psychology courses and reading Dostoyevsky. With this advice in mind, we have found that English and history teachers are among the best qualitative researchers. Erickson (1986) says that the narrator must convey to the readers the particulars and meaning of the everyday life contained in the social scene; ground the abstract analysis concept results in concrete particulars; provide evidence for the analytical results; and present vignettes and quotations in the rhetoric to convince the readers that what is presented is typical of the social unit and that the results can be generalized to other similar events and social units.

> *Teachers doing any informal observation can bene-*
> *fit from applying aspects of what we have described*
> *in this chapter.*

Having stated that qualitative research is often time-consuming and that qualitative reports are often extensive, we should hasten to indicate that it is possible—and often desirable—to conduct and report abbreviated forms of qualitative research. For example, teachers doing *any* informal observation can benefit from applying aspects of what we have described in this chapter. Following guidelines of qualitative research will help make these observations a better "objective analysis of subjective meaning" and will lead to more insightful interpretations of what has been observed. In addition, when we discuss external validity in chapter 15, it will become evident that the results of higher-level research can be generalized more accurately if researchers employ qualitative methods in collecting, reporting, and interpreting data. As later chapters will show, good educational research is often an integration of effective qualitative and quantitative strategies.

PROBLEMS AND LIMITATIONS OF QUALITATIVE RESEARCH

Erickson (1986, p. 140) lists four types of problems that can occur because of poor procedures in qualitative research:

1. *Inadequate amounts of evidence.* Assertions in research conclusions may be unwarranted by the data or may not include events and scenes that would have confirmed the statements.

2. *Inadequate varieties of kinds of evidence.* The researcher may have failed to employ triangulation of data by using several sources or field sites, or may have failed to employ the multimethod, multitrait, and alternative hypothesis approaches to data collection and analysis.

3. *Inadequate attention to disconfirming evidence.* Erickson strongly recommends deliberate searches for potential disconfirming data.

4. *Lack of attention to discrepant cases.* The researcher may fail to examine on a comparative basis individuals and instances that do not conform to the initial theories and explanations that seem to hold for most individuals and cases. Discrepant case analysis also needs to be done as data collection is in process to help change and sharpen theoretical presuppositions. Discrepant cases and individuals' data analyses help suggest alternative hypotheses that need examination. (Ethnography places in the foreground discrepant cases, which may contain more information than the normative cases.)

Sadler (1981) has indicated areas of pitfalls and cautions for those attempting to observe and make generalizations and inferences in qualitative research (as well as providing commonsense approaches to drawing conclusions from evidence). Sadler lists 10 such problem areas:

1. *Data overload.* It is well known that humans have severe limitations on the amount of data they can process. While the human brain is unexcelled in its capacity to extract patterns and relationships from noisy environments, it has distinct limits on receiving, recalling, and processing data. Naturalistic observations can severely tax these cognitive processing limits.

2. *First impression.* It is also well known that the order in which observations are made is important. First impressions tend to dominate observers' later inferences and assertions. Closely related is the problem of confidence in judgment. Researchers (and also administrators) tend to stick to a decision once it is made, even in light of considerable contrary evidence.

3. *Availability of information.* The ease with which an observer can obtain data influences conclusions. Personal relationships can ease or

hamper data collection. Data that are readily obtained will be relied on more than data that are difficult to obtain. When initial hypotheses are developed, instances of positive observations that confirm the hypotheses will tend to be unconsciously selected, noticed, depended upon, and later stated as fact. Even when there are later negative or conflicting observations, they tend not to be noticed.

4. *Positive and negative instances.* Even balances between negative and positive observations do not cancel out. Sadler notes that to be aware of ambiguity is not the same as to be ignorant.

5. *Redundancy versus novelty of information.* Novelties and extreme observations tend to be overweighted and given more importance than redundant or consistent data.

6. *Uneven reliability of information.* Lack of notice of uneven reliability of data causes all data to be given equal consideration.

7. *Missing information.* Missing data tend to be filled in by the observers later when making interpretations, often in unpredictable ways.

8. *Base-rate proportion.* Base-rate proportions against which later comparisons are made are often unstable as the result of observations on one or a few cases. Faulty or unstable base-rate proportions produce inaccurate comparisons and interpretations later.

9. *Sampling considerations.* From the study of sampling theory (see chapter 8) it is well known that small samples are unstable and that humans tend to be insensitive to sampling considerations. In qualitative research, where samples are often small (e.g., a class, a student, or a school building), the local sample results may not hold true for the larger population.

10. *Co-occurrences and correlations.* There is a problem with interpretation of co-occurrences and correlations. A documented correlation is not necessarily a cause-and-effect relationship; rather, it is merely a co-occurrence of events, perhaps caused by some prior condition. (See chapter 13.) Exacerbating the problem, many observers tend to rely on positive co-occurrence instances as evidence of a strong correlation.

WHAT IS THE ROLE OF QUALITATIVE RESEARCH IN EDUCATION?

At the beginning of this book we argued that teachers should do research every day. This is true of qualitative research as well as quantitative research. While a careful, full-fledged qualitative study consumes a large amount of time and energy, the basic strategies of qualitative research are applicable to the daily life of teachers. For example, teachers can benefit from becoming more skillful at observing their students in their natural environments, from being aware of the wide variety of factors that interact with one another to influence their students, from taking and using field notes, and from generally being more aware of the impact in their classrooms of variables they cannot yet quantify.

Scientific research methodologies have been developed over a span of 400 years to reduce the human errors of observation and logical inference. Research methods in the human sciences are much newer than that, but numerous problems of biased observation and inaccurate inferences and explanation have been noted, and methods have been designed to reduce these errors. These methods and concerns need to be heeded by all in the human sciences. Qualitative, sociological, cultural and social anthropological, and human ecological research methods are valuable in developing the basic understandings of students, teachers, administrators, parents, and the social contexts, scenes, and events in which these people live, study, and work.

Qualitative research reports are valuable as instructional tools. For example, they have the "you are there" quality, which allows education students to obtain the "feel" of classrooms, school buildings, and systems. Teaching itself requires an ethno-

---

BOX 9.3 | Examples of Qualitative Research Studies

Health, S. B. (1982). What no bedtime story means: Narrative skills at home and school. Language and Society, ii, 49–76. This study provides a good qualitative description of how students in homes with various socioeconomic backgrounds differ in the language skills that relate to educational success.

Jankowski, M. G. (1991). Islands in the Street: Gangs and American Urban Society. Berkeley: University of California Press. Without personally committing criminal behavior, the author became a participant observer of gangs in Los Angeles, New York, and Boston over a period of ten years. His report gives useful insights into why young people join gangs, what gangs do, and how people react to gangs.

McAuliffe, S. (1993). Toward understanding one another: Second graders' use of gendered language and story styles. Reading Teacher, 47, 302–309. The author uses qualitative strategies to determine that boys and girls have distinct styles of communicating during story time and to explore the nature of these different styles.

Wong, E. D. (1993). Self-generated analogies as a tool for constructing and evaluating explanation of research in science teaching. Journal of Research in Science Teaching, 30, 367–378. The author uses a systematic anecdotal approach to describe students coming to new insights because of their use of analogies to understand unfamiliar phenomena.

---

graphic perspective toward the students and a knowledge of the social learning environment and context. The reports of the human sciences of social and cultural anthropology are about as close and involved with the real life of education as one can get out of books. They serve as excellent entrees to the educational world prior to the students actually becoming a part of it. Reading books is not as good as the real thing, but it gives a much wider perspective than can be obtained in a few classrooms; and, of course, it is less disruptive and cheaper.

Good educational research is time-consuming and labor intensive. There are many important educational problems that need better solutions than now exist. Therefore, the best-quality, most informative research needs to be done, research that will give us the broadest, deepest understandings that can be obtained. Inevitably, qualitative and interpretive data and methodology will be part of all educational research that provides these roads to understanding.

The present chapter has focused on the contribution of qualitative research toward determining what is going on in educational settings and presenting causal explanations for what is happening. In addition, qualitative methods can be integrated with quantitative methods to contribute to higher levels of research as well. These contributions will be discussed in later chapters.

PUTTING IT ALL TOGETHER

Let us return now to the days when Mr. Anderson was first planning to do research on children's attitudes toward animals. At about that same time, a colleague, Helen Witherspoon, expressed a similar interest in doing research, but she took a different approach.

Mrs. Witherspoon was working on a graduate degree and needed a research project for her thesis. She identified two schools in her area. In one, the principal, who was a friend of hers, was concerned that the children seemed to display a flagrant disregard for animal life. The other school was recommended by the local humane society as a place where students had a reputation for being especially kind to animals.

Mrs. Witherspoon conferred with some teachers and the principals at both schools. She arranged to visit the classrooms on a regular basis and to make observations and conduct interviews with the students. She agreed to do this without disrupting the normal classroom routines. Two third-grade teachers were very receptive in each school, and these four teachers agreed to keep detailed notes. Mrs. Witherspoon prepared guidelines that listed general behaviors she wanted these teachers to look for.

For the entire school year, Mrs. Witherspoon spent two hours each week in each of the four classrooms. The teachers in each class considered it to be a useful language arts activity for the children to converse about interesting topics, and so Mrs. Witherspoon was able to hold individual and group interviews with the children. The teachers introduced her as a teacher who was taking a college course and needed to talk to children. The students seemed to like her, and they spoke freely. The conversations ranged among many topics—sometimes focusing directly on animals but also covering matters only indirectly related to animal life. During these sessions, Mrs. Witherspoon let the children talk freely. She tape recorded the conversations, so it was not necessary to take notes while she talked with the children. Shortly after each session she listened to the recordings and took notes based on these interviews and her other observations. In addition, the teachers had the students write occasional essays on topics of interest to Mrs. Witherspoon, and they shared these essays with her. The teachers were pleased that as time went on the children seemed to be developing both written and oral thoughts more effectively.

In addition, Mrs. Witherspoon spent a half hour each week interviewing the four teachers.

At the end of the year, Mrs. Witherspoon spent a week summarizing her data. She agreed that the students in the second school really were more humane in their attitudes than those in the other school. She drew many conclusions, which are too numerous to summarize here. One of the most interesting was that perhaps materialism was an important factor in attitudes toward animal life. In the past, she had thought that programs on humane values should focus on bringing cute animals into the classroom, but her insight about materialism suggested to her that it may be more important to find ways to reduce personal greed and materialism among the children. She needed to collect more data to confirm and expand her ideas.

When Mrs. Witherspoon shared her findings with Mr. Anderson, he found her ideas to be helpful. He arranged for Mrs. Witherspoon to administer his Fireman Tests in her classrooms. With Mrs. Witherspoon's detailed knowledge of the children, Mr. Anderson felt that she could provide valuable information to help validate these tests. In addition, he was particularly struck by her ideas on materialism. He found that her insights helped him to better understand the results he had found in his own research.

SUMMARY

Qualitative researchers examine naturalistic settings to look for factors that might give meaning to those situations. Qualitative research can be either exploratory or fully interpretive in nature. It is useful in its own right and frequently provides a basis for subsequent quantitative and experimental research. It offers insights into the reasons behind the events that occur in experimental research settings. Qualitative research is often conducted by participant observers, who have the advantage of being very close to the situation and can observe it in as natural a manner as possible. Participant observers have to take deliberate efforts to avoid biases and collect information as objectively as possible.

This chapter has described the basic methods of qualitative researchers and the types of data they collect. Good qualitative research depends upon systematic fieldwork over a lengthy period of time. This chapter has also discussed problems of reliability and validity in the collection of qualitative data and has examined factors that are likely to interfere with the qualitative research process. In addition, this chapter has described the characteristics of a good qualitative research report and has discussed the role that qualitative research can play in education.

What Comes Next

Starting in chapter 10, we'll begin to focus on conducting and interpreting other types of research—quantitative research that deals with cause-and-effect relationships and with generalizing results in education.

DOING YOUR OWN RESEARCH

When conducting qualitative research, your goal is to collect and report objective data that are free of the artificial constraints often imposed by quantitative methods. Consider the following guidelines, which are based on principles discussed in this chapter:

1. Use the naturalistic strategies described in this chapter to examine the whole picture. Avoid the accidental exclusion of important elements.

2. Avoid personal biases. The best way to do this is to be aware of the sources of bias described in this chapter and to take steps to prevent their occurrence.

3. Employ a reasonable strategy to compile data completely but unobtrusively. Bernard's (1988) suggestion to use field jottings, field notes, a field diary, and a field log is one good strategy.

4. Be aware of the problems that can occur in qualitative research, and avoid them. An awareness of the lists compiled by Erickson (1986) and Sadler (1981) can help you prevent costly mistakes in planning and implementation.

5. Remember that there's no law against integrating quantitative methods with your qualitative methods, if this can be done without disrupting the collection of data in a naturalistic setting.

In addition, even if your research plan emphasizes quantitative methods, consider supplementing them with the qualitative strategies described in this chapter.

FOR FURTHER THOUGHT

1. Is it reasonable to expect teachers and other educators to both do a good job educating students and to engage in qualitative research?

2. What types of problems in education are most amenable to qualitative research?

3. Complete this sentence by answering the designated questions: "Qualitative research . . .(does what?) (To what or whom?) (When?) (Where?) (How?) (Why?)"

REFERENCES

Barker, R. (1964). *Large schools, small schools: High school size and student behavior*. Stanford, CA: Stanford University Press.

Bernard, H. R. (1988). *Research methods in cultural anthropology*. Beverly Hills, CA: Sage.

Coleman, J. S. (1961). *The adolescent society: The social life of the teenager and its impact on education*. New York: Free Press of Glencoe.

Erickson, F. (1986). Qualitative methods in research on teaching. In M. C. Wittrock (Ed.), *Handbook of research on teaching* (3rd ed.). New York: Macmillan.

Goetz, J. P., & LeCompte, M. D. (1984). *Ethnography and qualitative design in educational research*. Orlando, FL: Academic Press.

Kirk, J., & Miller, M. L. (1986). *Reliability and validity in qualitative research*. Beverly Hills, CA: Sage.

Maxwell, J. A. (1992). Understanding and validity in qualitative research. *Harvard Educational Review, 62*, 279–300.

Mead, M. (1928). *Coming of age in Samoa*. New York: Morrow.

Reiss, A. J., & Rhodes, A. L. (1959). *A sociopsychological study of adolescent uniformity and deviation*. Oct. 31, 1959, CRP 507, ERIC ED 002 890.

Sadler, D. R. (1981). Intuitive data processing as a potential source of bias in naturalistic evaluations. *Educational Evaluation and Policy Analysis, 3*(4), 25–31.

Wolcott, H. F. (1990). On seeking—and rejecting—validity in qualitative research. In E. W. Eisner & A. Peshkin (Eds.), *Qualitative inquiry in education: The continuing debate* (pp. 121–152). New York: Teachers College Press.

ANNOTATED BIBLIOGRAPHY

Bernard, H. R. (1988). *Research methods in cultural anthropology*. Beverly Hills, CA: Sage. This is a good textbook from the field of cultural anthropology, a field that relies heavily on qualitative research and in which methodologists have developed and perfected numerous effective strategies.

Erickson, F. (1986). Qualitative methods in research on teaching. In M. C. Wittrock (Ed.), *Handbook of research on teaching* (3rd ed.). New York: Macmillan.

This chapter presents a good summary of the status and methods of qualitative research in education.

Finders, M. (1992). Looking at lives through ethnography. *Educational Leadership, 50*(1), 60–65. This article includes excerpts from several ethnographic studies. These can give teachers insight into how qualitative research can contribute to their daily practice.

Patton, M. Q. (1987). *How to use qualitative methods in evaluation*. Newbury Park, CA: Sage. This book covers issues to consider when deciding whether to use qualitative research methods as well as strategies for conducting qualitative studies.

Seidman, I. E. (1991). *Interviewing as qualitative research: A guide for researchers in education and the social sciences*. New York: Teachers College Press. This is a good introductory text for researchers with no background in qualitative research. It connects interviewing techniques with broader issues in qualitative research.

CHAPTER 9

Research Report Analysis

The research report in Appendix C is primarily an example of quantitative rather than qualitative research. However, the conclusions section incorporates an important qualitative component that makes the report more meaningful. Find that qualitative component on page 464 and answer the following questions:

1. In what way does this qualitative information enhance the research report?

2. In what other ways could qualitative research strategies be incorporated into this study and report?

3. What would a primarily qualitative study of the same topic look like? (Give a brief description of what the report of a qualitative study could say.)

Note that similar qualitative components could improve the quality of most quantitative research.

ANSWERS:

1. This qualitative information gives us an anecdotal example of what the numbers in the report tell us. The reader of the report can vividly picture the conversation described in this anecdote, and this puts the quantitative descriptions into perspective.

2. Additional anecdotal descriptions could further elucidate the thinking processes the students went through. For example, the report says that a major advantage of the computer simulations is that students can run programs repeatedly and learn from their mistakes. The report could describe how some students did this and how they acted differently on subsequent runs of the programs. Likewise, an anecdotal description of how the teachers implemented the programs and what the students did while running them would help support external validity, because teachers reading the report could more easily decide how closely the activities on which the report is based resemble what goes on in their own classrooms.

3. A fully qualitative study would devote attention exclusively to issues such as those described in the second paragraph of the "Discussion and Conclusions" section and in the answer to the preceding question. For example, a participant observer could watch students running the set of programs and report on the sorts of things that the students and teachers did when using them as a tool for studying the designated topics. The report could focus on the thinking and feelings expressed by the students and teacher and on specific behaviors the students engaged in that would seem to demonstrate known psychological principles such as cooperative learning, attribution theory, and strategic thinking. Additional descriptions could describe the social context (e.g., parental, administrative, and community pressures, forms of support, and interests).

INTERNAL VALIDITY

■ WHERE WE'VE BEEN

We have completed our treatment of Level I research. We have discussed how to operationally define outcome variables, how to develop and administer various data collection processes to measure outcome variables in such a way as to obtain reliable and valid results, and how to report and interpret the results of measurement processes. We have also examined strategies for collecting reliable and valid data in naturalistic settings and for making inferences about a population by administering a measurement process to a sample of that population.

■ WHERE WE'RE GOING NOW

This chapter begins the treatment of Level II research—examining the causes that generate outcome variables in education. In this chapter, we'll discuss the major threats to internal validity—factors that interfere with causal inferences regarding whether a treatment has produced an outcome. By controlling these threats, we increase the confidence we can place in the conclusions of our research.

■ CHAPTER PREVIEW

Internal validity deals with the authenticity of cause-and-effect relationships. It asks the question "Did the treatment really cause the observed outcome, or are there some other factors at work?" *The way to establish internal validity is by ruling out the threats to internal validity.* These threats are factors—variables or conditions other than the treatment—that could produce an impact on the outcome variable. It is true that teachers do not always have the time or money necessary to conduct good scientific experiments in their classroom. Nevertheless, it is also true that the ability to rule out threats to internal validity will help one draw correct conclusions about the cause-and-effect relationships observed in educational settings. In addition, the ability to identify these threats will help you avoid drawing false conclusions when you are confronted with faulty research in the professional literature and in other sources.

After reading this chapter, you should be able to

1. Define *internal validity*.
2. Define and give examples of each of the major threats to internal validity.
3. Describe how each of these threats operates to weaken the internal validity of a conclusion about a treatment and describe strategies for controlling these threats.

■

FINDING CAUSE-AND-EFFECT RELATIONSHIPS

Mrs. Johnson is a science teacher at a large metropolitan high school. She has taken a course at a nearby university and has learned how to design and use computer simulations in her classroom. She has discovered that by interacting with the computer, her students can experience many realistic situations that would otherwise be too expensive, physically difficult, or dangerous to undertake in her normal science lab. Mrs. Johnson believes that this interaction will provide her students with the motivations and insights necessary to understand science. She thinks that the computer simulations should be introduced in science courses throughout the school's science program.

It would cost $20,000 to purchase the necessary hardware and software to implement Mrs. Johnson's idea in all the science classes. These expenditures would occur only during the first year; thereafter, a budget of about $2,000 a year would easily keep the computers running with updated simulations.

Mrs. Johnson brings her idea to the principal, who says that the project is not worth spending $20,000 of the school's budget. Mrs. Johnson persists, however, and finally the principal agrees that if she can actually provide evidence that the computer simulations *cause* improvements in scientific skills and attitudes, they would be worth the expenditure. He is even able to help her with a small supply budget, which she combines with her own ingenuity and the assistance from the local university to run a pilot project in one of her classes.

Mrs. Johnson has carefully read this textbook up to this point, and she realizes that she needs a good way to find out what outcomes are occurring in her classes and how these outcomes relate to what she would like to see happening. She carefully selects a standardized science test that measures both knowledge of science facts and problem-solving abilities. She feels that this test validly measures what she wants to teach. She and the principal are satisfied that if the students score high on this test they will be demonstrating scientific proficiency.

Mrs. Johnson pretests her third-period students and finds that at the beginning of the year their average score is equivalent to about the 34th percentile of the norm group on the test. She then integrates the computer into the curriculum for her class. At the end of the year, she retests the students and finds that their average score is now at about the 57th percentile. Moreover, attitudes that were negative at the beginning of the year have become positive by the end of the year. She concludes that the computer simulations did in fact *cause* an improvement in science skills and in attitudes toward science.

Is Mrs. Johnson right? Did working with the computers cause the observed improvements? The answer is that she would need better evidence before any sensible person would give her $20,000.

Mrs. Johnson is assuming that the process diagrammed in Figure 10.1 has occurred among her students. Use of the computer simulations, she believes, has produced favorable motivation and new insights, leading to improved test performance. Mrs. Johnson has shown that high test scores have occurred, but has she shown that her simulations have *caused* these effects? To make this claim, Mrs. Johnson has to rule out the possibility that the process diagrammed in Figure 10.2 (rather than the simulations) could explain the improvements in the scores. This diagram suggests that a combination of a nice social studies teacher who was enthusiastic about science, a good TV show during the year that dealt with science, and the other information that presented science in the ordinary curriculum all led to the appropriate motivation and insights, which in turn led to improved test scores. To build a really convincing argument that the computer simulations themselves *caused* the change, Mrs. Johnson has to rule out these and many similar alternative explanations for the higher scores.

Mrs. Johnson needs to know more than *what* is happening. She needs to know *why* it is happening.

INTERNAL VALIDITY

Internal validity deals with the question of *whether the treatment actually caused the observed outcomes in an experiment*. In other words, it deals with the authenticity of a stated cause-and-effect relationship between the treatment and the outcome variables. The appropriate way to establish internal validity is to identify and rule out as many of the threats to internal validity as possible. These threats are other factors—variables and conditions other than the deliberately imposed treatment—that could have an

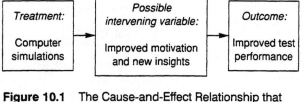

Figure 10.1 The Cause-and-Effect Relationship that Mrs. Johnson Assumes Has Produced the Observed Outcome

impact on the outcome variable. By showing that these other factors did not produce the effect observed in an experiment, you increase the strength of your argument that the treatment is indeed the factor that produced the observed outcome.

Let us return to the example discussed in the preceding section of this chapter. Mrs. Johnson and her principal should be concerned about the internal validity of the cause-and-effect relationship she claims to have established. Did the treatment (computer simulations) cause the observed improvements, or was some other factor (such as the nice social studies teacher from Figure 10.2) actually responsible for the improvement? Would the improvements have occurred even if there were no computer simulations? To the extent that it is likely that any of these other factors caused the improvement, Mrs. Johnson's theory has weak internal validity. On the other hand, to the extent that she can rule out these and other irrelevant explanations, Mrs. Johnson has strengthened her theory's internal validity.

Figure 10.2 An Alternative Explanation of the Outcome That Mrs. Johnson Observed. It is impossible to know for sure what actually caused the observed outcome.

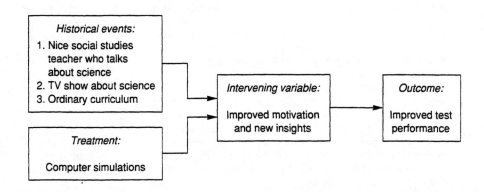

BOX 10.1	Colonel Mustard Did It

Establishing internal validity is very much like the work of a detective. You may have at some time played the board game called "Clue." In this game, a highly effective way to find out "who did it" is to rule out suspects who *didn't* commit the crime. For instance, if you know that everyone other than Colonel Mustard is innocent, then you can conclude that Colonel Mustard is guilty. The same logic can be applied to establishing internal validity. If we can rule out all the other possible explanations for an observed outcome (that is, if we can rule out all the threats to internal validity), then we can conclude that the treatment (and not any of the other irrelevant, extraneous factors) caused the observed impact.

Theorists in social science research have developed a comprehensive list of the threats to internal validity. This chapter will present a discussion of the major such threats, and chapters 11 and 12 will provide a discussion of the most popular, effective strategies for overcoming them.[1] Even as you read the present chapter, however, it should be obvious to you that these threats are not insurmountable. With proper planning and reasoning, a teacher can rule out most of the threats to internal validity and thereby increase the soundness of decisions based on the observation of apparent cause-and-effect relationships in the classroom.

---

[1] In order to make this chapter as straightforward and unconfusing as possible, we have written it as if internal validity referred simply to whether an observed effect is a real effect of an experimental treatment. This is just slightly inaccurate—or at least incomplete. Our approach is an oversimplification because it ignores the fact that internal validity would also be involved if a researcher wanted to know whether the absence of any effect was truly an absence of that effect. For example, if a researcher gave a reading program to a group of students, they might actually improve, but problems with internal validity might make it look as if there had been no improvement. The questions of whether a non-effect is really a non-effect, therefore is a valid concern of internal validity. It's actually not a very complicated concept, and the reader who understands this chapter will almost automatically apply the principles correctly to both effects and non-effects. The only problem is that if we try to include both concepts while we are writing this chapter, we wind up with hopelessly tangled, complex sentences. Our solution has been to allow this slight inaccuracy in this chapter and to rectify the situation by informing you in this footnote of our deliberate error.

REVIEW QUIZ 10.1

Place an X before each of the following statements where the issue is one of internal validity.

1 ____ Joey Schneider was extremely shy around girls when he was in the seventh grade. His father bought Joey a sex education book to read during the summer. During the eighth grade, Joey got along well with girls. Mr. Schneider wonders whether the book really caused the difference in Joey.

2 ____ The superintendent of police wonders about the location of the nearest center at which he can train new police officers.

3 ____ The teacher wants to know how her fifth graders compare with the national norms in reading and math.

4 ____ The school board abolished corporal punishment one year. The next year, there was much more vandalism than there had ever been before. The superintendent wanted to know whether the change in policy regarding corporal punishment caused this difference.

5 ____ The teacher wondered whether a film he wanted to show met the guidelines of the local PTA. He has done a careful study of all the available guidelines and has determined that the PTA's are the most pertinent to his situation.

6 ____ After Mr. Jacobson showed his fourth graders his slides about his trip to Russia, the pupils

seemed to be much more interested in world affairs. He wondered whether his slide show had helped cause this change in attitudes.

7 ____ Mr. Campbell is a probation officer. Thirty percent of his charges were rearrested for criminal offenses last year. He has tried a new method of working with them, but still 30% were rearrested. He looked at the statistics from other probation officers in the same area, and he discovered that most of their rates had jumped to about 50%. He wanted to know whether his new method had actually acted as a deterrent to prevent an increase of crime in his own group.

8 ____ Mrs. Smith tried a new reading program. The children did no better after the program than before it. However, she realized that there had been extreme unrest in her school that year because of racial problems. She wondered whether the program might have actually been effective and whether the unrelated problems might have lowered the scores.

Subsequent sections of this chapter describe in detail each of the major threats to internal validity. As you read these sections, examine the figures carefully. These figures are all specific variations of Figure 10.2, and they diagram in detail exactly how each threat works. The text of each section provides a theoretical explanation of each threat and several anecdotal applications of each threat to realistic situations. Finally, each section concludes with a Review Quiz, which provides interactive questions about additional anecdotes related to each threat. By care-

fully comparing positive examples of a concept with the negative instances in these anecdotes, you can verify that you understand each concept before moving on to the next. A careful study of all the components of each section will enable you to come to a comprehensive understanding of each threat. If you need extra help, the Student Workbook offers additional programmed instruction and further interactive anecdotes to help you achieve mastery of these concepts.

HISTORY

One of the major threats to internal validity is history. The term *history* refers to *any additional, concurrent, extraneous events occurring in the environment at the same time the experimental variable (the treatment) is being tested.* It is not past history with which we are concerned, but rather current history—the events that occur *while* the treatment is being tested. (See Figure 10.3.) For example, if a science teacher tried a new science curriculum for adolescents during the same year that a brilliant new show related to science appeared on television or at about the same time that a major development took place in space exploration, it is possible that improvements in science performance might be more a result of these related, concurrent, historical events than of the science curriculum. In this example, the new TV show and the development in space exploration are historical events that pose a threat to the internal validity of the conclusion that the new science curriculum actually caused improved performance in science.

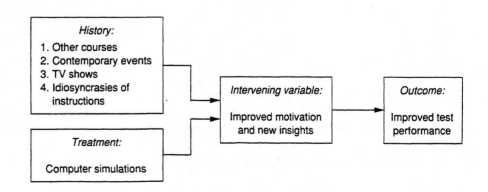

Figure 10.3 History as a Threat to Internal Validity. There has been an actual change in motivation and insights, but it is impossible to tell whether this change has occurred because of history, because of the treatment, or because of some combination of the two.

History:
1. Other courses
2. Contemporary events
3. TV shows
4. Idiosyncrasies of instructions

Treatment:
Computer simulations

Intervening variable:
Improved motivation and new insights

Outcome:
Improved test performance

History is a serious and obvious threat to internal validity whenever we compare two different periods of time and try to demonstrate that the different outcomes are the result of one major factor (such as an innovative teaching program) that has changed. For example, many schools that now ban corporal punishment have more disruptions than in the "good ole days" before the ban. Does this prove that banning corporal punishment *caused* the increase in disruptions and that reintroducing corporal punishment would reduce the disruptions? Without further evidence, we cannot draw this conclusion, for it is possible that some other extraneous factor (such as new patterns of child rearing or other problems in society) has caused the increased disruptions. In this example, many different events could pose a threat to internal validity. Additional examples of such historical threats include variations in teacher morale, changes in the social context of the school or community, shifts in curriculum content, concurrent television programming, and peer pressures. When we refer to these as threats to internal validity, we mean that before we can conclude that banning corporal punishment has led to an increase in disruptions, we have to rule out other plausible explanations for the same phenomenon.

Note that we are not saying in the first example that any of these other factors actually did cause the improved performance in science. Nor are we saying that variations in child rearing or any of the other proposed factors actually did cause the increased disruptions in the second example. All we are saying is that because the historical context was not properly taken into consideration, we cannot come to a sound conclusion. Numerous events are so confounded that we simply *do not know* why the differences occurred.

When we speak of history as a threat to internal validity, we are referring to any contextual events that occur at the same time as the treatment—not just to those that might show up in history books. For example, a researcher might find two groups of students that are exactly the same. (It is impossible to find two groups that are exactly the same, but for the sake of this example, we are going to imagine that it is possible.) He might give one of these groups a special reading treatment and withhold it from the other group and then use a standardized test to measure improvements in reading comprehension. If during the experiment several star athletes in one of the classes announced that they thought reading was "for nerds," this would be a historical event that would make the historical context different for the two groups of pupils.

As part of establishing the internal validity of a study, therefore, it is important to ascertain that there are no extraneous events occurring in the environment at the same time as the experimental variable that could plausibly explain the observed results. We are not able to stop history from occurring, but we can arrange events so that history does not interfere with our inferences. To the extent that we can reduce the plausibility of such extraneous explanations, we can increase the internal validity of our conclusions.

REVIEW QUIZ 10.2

Put an *X* before the description if it contains an example of history as a threat to internal validity.

1 _____ The students were not doing as well as the math teacher had hoped in long division. She purchased a series of videotapes in which a small rodent talked to a chirping insect of the gryllidae family about the merits of long division. Unbeknownst to the math teacher, after the third of the eight video sequences the gym teacher announced in his class that there would be a contest. The 10 students with the highest baseball batting averages would receive trophies. A large number of students started computing their own batting averages and comparing statistics every day. At the end of the year, several months after completing the entire series of videotapes, the teacher was impressed to see long division performance greatly improved. She was heard commenting to a colleague, "The kids sure seemed bored during those videotapes, but at least they learned from them. I think I'll use them every year."

2 ___ The students were not doing as well as their teacher had hoped in spelling, and so she decided to hold weekly spelling bees. Unbeknownst to the teacher, after the third of the eight spelling bees the gym teacher announced in his class that there would be a contest. The 10 students with the highest baseball batting averages would receive trophies. A large number of students started computing their own batting averages and comparing statistics every day. At the end of the year, the teacher was impressed to see spelling performance greatly improved. She was heard commenting to a colleague, "The kids didn't seem very excited about those spelling bees, but at least they learned from them. I think I'll use them every year."

SELECTION BIAS

A second threat to internal validity is selection bias, which refers to the fact that *a group's performance on an outcome variable may arise from the particular composition of the group itself (as compared with another group) rather than from the treatment that was intended to produce the outcome.* (See Figure 10.4.) In an experiment, this most often means that the experimental group may have possessed the desired outcome or the ability to acquire it even prior to the administration of the treatment. For example, if a certain baseball team adapts an innovative training procedure and then wins the championship, this could mean either that the technique was effective or that they were good players who would have won the championship regardless of how they had trained. Whenever someone claims that a treatment produced an outcome, a very useful question to ask is "What would the group have done if their performance had simply been measured without the treatment?" This question focuses on selection bias as a threat to internal validity.

Selection bias is most commonly a threat to internal validity when the teacher/researcher deals with intact groups or volunteers. An intact group is one that already exists or was formed independently of the decision to administer the treatment. For example, if a criminal court system decided to try a new probation method in a midwestern city and compare the results with the outcomes in a southern city, it is possible that the observed differences might have occurred because of the nature of the people in the two groups rather than because of the nature of the treatment. The same confusion would occur if a teacher tried one method with his first-period English class and another with his last-period class.

Figure 10.4 Selection Bias as a Threat to Internal Validity. There may have actually been no change at all in motivation and insights. It might merely *look* as if a change has come about, because previously existing abilities are revealed when the outcome variable is measured. It is impossible to tell whether the improved test performance has occurred because of the treatment, because of selection bias, or because of some combination of the two.

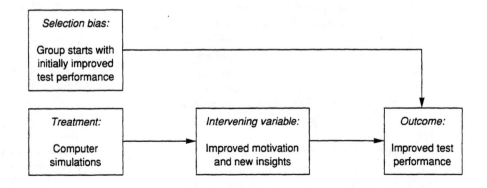

How would he know whether the observed differences on the essay test were because of the treatment or because the subjects were different to begin with? For example, there may be fewer varsity athletes in one of the classes because of scheduled team practices; or better students may have a tendency to sign up for an elective course that conflicts with one of the class periods.

When a researcher asks for volunteers for an experimental treatment, it is always possible (and sometimes likely) that the persons who volunteer will, in important respects, be different from the nonvolunteers. If the researcher then tries to compare the volunteers with the nonvolunteers after some kind of educational innovation, it is difficult to determine whether the differences arose because of the treatment or because of preexisting differences between the two groups. For example, if you asked for volunteers to go on a specific weight control diet, would you really be surprised to see the volunteers lose more weight than people who would decline to volunteer for such a program? Probably not. Persons who would volunteer for such a program are likely to be more interested than others in losing weight, and so they would be more likely to lose weight with any treatment—or with no treatment at all, for that matter. In addition, persons who volunteer are already making a commitment and might therefore have a vested interest in seeing that the experiment worked. Likewise, if there are two adjacent school systems and one of them volunteers for a federally funded project and the other declines to participate, could you really say that the project *caused* the improvements that occurred in the first system but not in the other?

The examples of selection bias as a threat to internal validity are not always as obvious as those presented in the preceding paragraphs. The important point to keep in mind is that you have to rule out the possibility that the observed outcomes might have arisen from the original composition and differences of the group to which the treatment is administered rather than from the treatment itself. This threat to internal validity is especially likely to be a problem when you are dealing with intact groups or volunteers. To the extent that you can rule out the likelihood that the composition of the group has had an impact on the outcome variable, you are increasing the internal validity of your conclusions.

REVIEW QUIZ 10.3

Place an X next to the description if it contains an example of selection bias as a threat to internal validity.

1 ____ The coach wanted to find out whether mental practice exercises would help her players shoot free throws more accurately. She had 16 players on her team. She asked for 8 volunteers. These volunteers spent only 10 minutes a day shooting free throws; they spent an additional 20 minutes each day sitting in a relaxed position in a quiet room while they meditated and imagined that they were shooting free throws. The other 8 players spent 30 minutes a day practicing free throws. After two weeks the coach tested the players. Those using mental practice exercises made an average of 8.9 out of 10 shots, whereas the other players made only 6.7 out of 10 shots. She concluded that the mental practice was more effective than traditional practice.

2 ____ Another coach felt that collective pressure exercises would help her players shoot free throws. She had 16 players. She randomly picked 8 of them. These 8 were sent to one end of the gym and practiced their free throws; they were not allowed to shower and go home until all 8 of them had ultimately made 5 shots in a row. The others could leave separately as soon as each individual made 10 in a row. After two weeks the coach tested all the players, and those using collective pressure exercises made an average of 8.9 out of 10 shots, whereas the others averaged only 6.7 out of 10 shots. The coach concluded that collective pressure exercises worked effectively.

3 ____ A third coach felt that progressive distance training was the best way to teach foul shooting. She took all 16 players and had them

start 5 feet from the basket. They would shoot at the basket until they made 5 shots in a row. Then they moved back 2 feet and repeated this process. They kept moving back until they reached a distance of 15 feet or had done this for an hour. After two weeks the coach tested her players. They made an average of 8.9 out of 10 shots, whereas her teams in the past had averaged only 6.7 out of 10 shots. She concluded that progressive distance training was an extremely effective technique.

4 ____ The last coach believed in theoretical knowledge. She, like the other coaches, had 16 players on her team. She asked for volunteers, and 8 came forward. She randomly selected 4 of these and had them read *The Golden Book of Basketball,* while everyone else on the team (including the other 4 volunteers) merely continued their regular program. Two weeks later the coach tested her players. The Golden Girls averaged 8.9 out of 10 shots, the other volunteers averaged 7.1 out of 10, and the rest of the players averaged 6.7 out of 10. She concluded that theoretical knowledge worked effectively as a technique to improve foul shooting.

MATURATION

As a threat to internal validity, maturation refers to the fact that *changes in an outcome variable may* *routinely occur as a result of the passage of time and natural changes that occur as part of human development rather than as a result of the treatment that occurred while time was passing.* (See Figure 10.5.) For example, a certain amount of biological maturity is necessary for a child to pay attention to a teacher for a prolonged period of time. If a psychiatrist treats a hyperactive child and demonstrates his success by pointing out that the child is much more attentive at the end of the second grade than he was at the beginning of the second grade, the threat of maturation would weaken the internal validity of his conclusion that his treatment had increased the child's attention span. In other words, the psychiatrist would have to rule out the likelihood that the biological maturation that occurred with the mere passage of time (which would have occurred without any psychiatric intervention) led to the same improvement.

Maturation is a serious problem only when some sort of change related to the treatment or outcome variable is likely to occur as time passes. Although maturation was a plausible problem in the example of the hyperactive child cited in the previous paragraph, it would hardly be a threat to the internal validity of the conclusion that a 50-year-old adult underwent a similar reduction in hyperactivity within the same period of time. If a person has been hyperactive for 50 years and suddenly calms down after psychiatric treatment, there is no compelling reason to attribute this change to maturation.

It is important to note that maturation does not refer exclusively to those biological and psychologi-

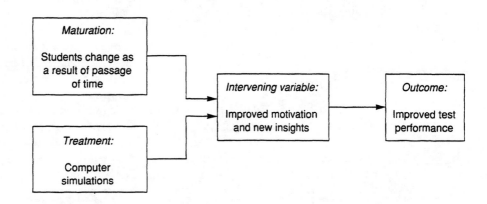

Figure 10.5 Maturation as a Threat to Internal Validity. There has actually been a change in motivation and insights, but it is impossible to tell whether this change has occurred because of maturation, because of history, or because of some combination of the two.

cal phenomena usually labeled as *maturation* in human development textbooks. The term encompasses any factors that produce change as time passes. Thus the term is used in research to include the possibility that a person might change because he gets tired or gets acclimated to someone or something as time passes. Imagine that a baby who has not been crying suddenly starts to cry when her father picks her up. This change could have occurred because of maturation (getting tired or hungry as time passed) rather than because of the treatment (being picked up by the father).

Maturation often creeps in as a problem in research where two groups being compared over a period of time are likely to mature at different rates. If you have a group of slow-learning fourth graders who read poorly, you might use experimental instructional materials with this group and compare their performance with that of a class of bright second graders who are initially at about the same reading level. You might discover that the second graders learn more quickly and conclude that the materials are ineffective. In fact, it might be possible that the fourth graders have benefitted from the materials but that their progress is masked because the second graders are maturing much more rapidly (because of their comparative growth in age), and this maturation makes it look as if more learning has taken place.

It is important, therefore, to keep in mind that change will occur as time passes. If you can rule out the possibility that it is these maturational changes rather than the treatment that has caused the observed outcome, you will take another step toward strengthening the internal validity of your conclusions.

REVIEW QUIZ 10.4

Place an X next to the description if it contains an example of maturation as a threat to internal validity.

1 ____ The fourth-grade students were reading at only the 3.1 grade level according to a standardized test. The scores went up to 5.1 after

six months of training with computerized materials. The teacher concluded that the computerized materials were effective.

2 ____ The slow-learning 12th-grade students were reading at only the 3.1 grade level according to a standardized test. The scores went up to 4.1 after six months of training with computerized materials. The teacher concluded that the computerized materials were effective.

INSTRUMENTATION

The only way we can measure the impact of a treatment upon an outcome variable is to use a measurement process of some kind. Instrumentation as a threat to internal validity refers to the fact that *observed differences in an outcome variable could be the result of changes in the measurement process rather than a result of the treatment itself.* (See Figure 10.6.) Changes in an instrument (e.g., the questionnaire or the way it is administered) include not only changes in the questions or items, but also changes in the way the measurement process is administered, differences in observers or interviewers, and any other variations in the data collection process that may influence the way performance on the outcome variable is recorded.

Although changes in the instrument itself are rare in the published literature, such changes are frequent in informal classroom research. For example, after giving a pretest, a teacher might discover that some of the students missed items largely because the items were ambiguous. Therefore, she might (quite logically) try to write better items for the posttest. If she does this, and if the scores of the students improve, how can she tell whether the improvements are the result of her treatment (good instruction) or the result of changes in the test (instrumentation)?

A more frequent difficulty with regard to instrumentation occurs when subtle, accidental changes are made in the way the instrument is administered. This often occurs in interviewing and observation. For example, changed performance of respondents between a pretreatment interview and a posttreat-

Figure 10.6 Instrumentation as a Threat to Internal Validity. There may actually have been no change at all in motivation and insights. The improved test performance might have occurred merely as a result of the change in the instrument. It is impossible to tell whether this change has occurred because of the treatment, because of the change in the instrument, or because of some combination of the two.

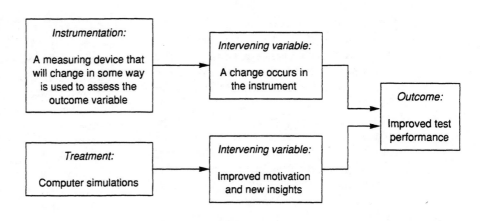

ment interview might occur not because the respondents have actually changed, but rather because the interviewers have gotten better at interviewing as they gained more practice. Similarly, if a white female administers a racial attitudes pretest and a black male administers the same questionnaire as a posttest, have the respondents really responded to the same set of behaviors?

A related problem occurs even if you are using seemingly impartial interviewers, observers, or raters. If these persons become aware of the purpose of the study as it progresses, it is well known that they may (even unconsciously) make adjustments to make the results come out "the way they're supposed to."

A similar problem occurs when the grade point average (GPA) is used as a measure of student performance. If students enter a new school (or a new program) and their GPAs increase, this increase could be the result of differences in grading policies rather than the result of accelerated achievement. Differences in competition or in the attitudes of school personnel toward grades or record keeping could make high grades easier to obtain at one school than at another. If the two GPAs are interpreted as having the same general meaning, this would be an example of instrumentation as a threat to internal validity.

It is important, therefore, to be sure that changes you observe are actually in the outcome variable itself, not merely in the measurement process you

are using to collect data about that outcome. The techniques discussed in earlier chapters of this book (Level I research) will help you devise and use data collection methods as effectively as possible. To the extent that you can say that your observed differences are really the result of the treatment and not the result of changes in measurement processes, you will increase the internal validity of your conclusions.

REVIEW QUIZ 10.5

Place an X next to the description if it contains an example of instrumentation as a threat to internal validity.

1 ____ Mr. Schultz designed two versions of his test on basic geography facts. He accomplished this by writing 100 items, matching them in pairs based on topics, and then randomly putting one item from each pair on the first version of the test and the other item on the second version. He gave the first version as a pretest. The students did poorly, averaging just 21.9 correct out of 50. He felt they should have averaged at least 45 out of 50. The students complained about what they considered to be unclear items on the test, but Mr. Schultz considered this to be a mere

rationalization to excuse poor performance. The next day Mr. Schultz sent a letter home to each of the parents, stressing that the students should know the basic facts before starting this important unit of instruction and urging the parents to see to it that their children reviewed properly. He also announced that there would be another test the next Friday. When that Friday came, he administered the second form of the test, and the students averaged 47.3 out of 50 correct. Mr. Schultz considered the letter to the parents and the retest to be quite successful.

2 ____ Mrs. Snyder designed two versions of her test on basic mathematics facts. She accomplished this by writing 100 items, matching them in pairs based on topics, and then randomly putting one item from each pair on the first version of the test and the other item on the second version. She gave the first version as a pretest. The students did poorly, averaging just 21.9 correct out of 50. She felt they should have averaged at least 45 out of 50. The students complained about what they considered to be unclear items on the test, and when Mrs. Snyder examined the items more carefully, she found a number of unclear items; therefore, she reworded many of the items on the parallel second version of the test. Mrs. Snyder also sent a letter home to each of the parents, stressing that the students should know the basic facts before starting this important unit of instruction and urging the parents to see to it that their children reviewed properly. She also instituted a program of cooperative review, which permitted the students to review together for the test, which she announced would occur the next Friday. When that Friday came, she administered the second form of the test, and the students averaged 47.3 out of 50 correct. Mrs. Snyder considered the cooperative review strategy and the retest to be quite successful.

STATISTICAL REGRESSION

Statistical regression occurs when a subgroup is selected from a larger group based on the extreme (high or low) scores of the subgroup. The term refers to the *tendency of the subgroup, when retested on the same or related variables, to have a mean score closer to the mean of the original group.* (See Figure 10.7.) When retested, therefore, subgroups selected because they originally displayed extremely high scores are likely to score lower, but still above the mean of the original group. On the other hand, subgroups selected because they originally scored extremely low will tend to score higher, but still below the mean of the original group. This regression toward the mean occurs because of statistical unreliability in the measuring instrument. If a test were perfectly reliable (and none is or can be), there would be no regression. If the test is extremely unreliable, then there is likely to be a large amount of regression. When regression occurs, the average of the lowest 10% of the scorers on the first test will move *up* on the second test, and the average of the top 10% on the first test will move *down* on the second test.

This concept sounds complicated and mysterious. Simply stated, however, the reason such regression occurs is because the chance factors that operate in data collection processes (discussed in chapter 5) are more likely to have a significant impact on extreme scores within a group. Such chance factors are unlikely to reoccur in the same manner on subsequent testing occasions. For example, the occurrence of headaches and unusually good or bad luck in guessing are most likely to influence the scores of people at the extreme bottom or top of a distribution of scores and to have less impact on scores around the middle of the distribution. It is unlikely that the same persons will have unbearable headaches or fantastic guessing streaks on each testing occasion.

Even if you find the mathematics behind this concept hard to understand, statistical regression is relatively easy to recognize and avoid. A situation where statistical regression often occurs is in programs for students who need remediation. Assume that a

Figure 10.7 Statistical Regression as a Threat to Internal Validity. There may actually have been no change at all in motivation and insights. It may merely look like a change has occurred because the scores have shifted toward the mean of the original group. It is impossible to tell whether this change has occurred because of the treatment, because of the statistical regression, or because of some combination of the two.

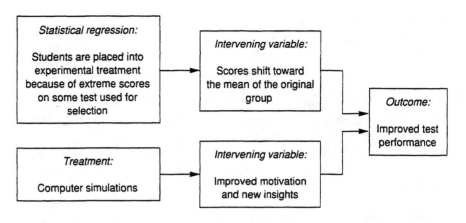

school has 100 third graders who take a reading screening test at the beginning of the year. The 10 who score lowest are designated as remedial readers and receive special attention from a reading specialist for half an hour each day for the rest of the school year. When they are retested, these remedial readers score considerably higher—their rate of improvement is better than that of the other students in the class. At least part of this improvement has to be attributed to regression toward the mean. Even if they had gained no more from this special instruction than they would have from traditional instruction, their mean scores would have moved up, in the direction of the mean of the whole class, on the second testing occasion, simply because of regression toward the mean.

The same phenomenon will occur with groups selected on the basis of extremely high scores. If you retest gifted and talented students a year after they have been selected, statistical regression is likely to pull their scores down in the direction of the mean of the original group. This means that if the school mentioned in the previous paragraph took its 10 best readers (based on the screening test) and gave them an accelerated program, the program's gains would be clouded by regression toward the mean. In other words, the accelerated program might result in substantial improvements, but those gains might show up as slight or nonexistent because statistical regression pulled the scores toward the mean of the original group.[2] What happened here is that some pupils got lucky on the screening test and looked smarter than they really were. When they retook the test, the luck balanced out. The average of the entire class would tend to be the same (or show a gain, if the intervening program were successful), but different people would move into and out of the top and bottom 10. When they retook the test, luck balanced out. It would be possible for members of this initially high group to improve in actual ability and still have their scores show little improvement or even a loss.

Note that regression toward the mean occurs only when the group being measured was *selected on the basis of extreme scores.* (Regression will be a problem either if the same measurement procedure is readministered or if another procedure is used on the second occasion. For example, students could be selected for a gifted education class on the basis of either high IQ scores, high musical ability, or high initial performance on the SAT. If they were tested a year later for SAT performance, the students selected on the basis of high SAT scores would regress toward the mean the least; those selected on the basis of music scores would regress the most; and those selected on the basis of IQ scores would regress an intermediate amount.

---

[2]This is a good example of the phenomenon cited in footnote 1.

Regression will be greater to the extent that the data collection process is unreliable or the two measures are unrelated.)

If the principal of Public School 101 discovers that the students in the third grade scored at the 2.1 grade level on their reading test, judged this to be inadequate, implemented a program to remediate this deficiency, and then saw the scores rise substantially, regression would not be a major problem. This is because the third graders were not selected from a larger group on the basis of their extreme scores. The mean of the entire group was 2.1, and if the group were immediately retested, the most likely guess for the group's score on the retest would again be near 2.1. However, if the superintendent gave the reading test to all the third graders in the city (with a mean of 3.2) and then assigned the 25 lowest-performing students (with a mean of 2.1) to the remedial program at Public School 101, then regression would be a factor. This is because they were selected on the basis of their extreme scores, and if these 25 were immediately retested, the most likely guess for their new mean would be somewhere between 2.1 and 3.2. With this grouping, there would tend to be a disproportionate number of people in the remedial group whose scores were reduced by chance factors on the first test, and chances are that their bad luck would not be equally present the next time they were tested.

In summary, statistical regression occurs when individuals or subgroups are selected from some larger group based on their extreme scores. The more extreme the group, the more likely it is that regression will occur. Likewise, the more unreliable the test and/or the longer it is between testing occasions, the greater the regression is likely to be. When retested, the extreme subgroup will regress in the direction of the mean. Extreme groups with high scores will move down on retests, and extreme groups with low scores will move up. If a group progresses in the direction predicted by statistical regression, you should view this progress with skepticism. If you can rule out the likelihood that your results are artificially influenced by statistical regression, you will strengthen the internal validity of your conclusions.

REVIEW QUIZ 10.6

Place an X next to the description if it contains an example of statistical regression as a threat to internal validity.

1 ____ The 300 freshmen at Gotham City High School averaged 65.7 on the English admissions test. The lowest-scoring 30 (who had an average of 39.6 on the test) were put in the remedial class. At the end of just one semester in this class, their scores went up to 52.8, and so the remedial class was considered to be a success.

2 ____ The 300 freshmen at Gotham City High School averaged 65.7 on the English admissions test. The highest-scoring 30 (who had an average of 90.4 on the test) were put in the gifted/talented English class. At the end of just one semester in this class, their scores actually went down slightly to 90.3. The gifted/talented English class was considered to be a waste of money.

3 ____ The 300 freshmen at Central High School averaged 50.3 on the English admissions test. This was lower than expected. A random group of 30 (who had an average of 50.5 on the test) were put in the remedial class. At the end of just one semester in this class, their scores went up to 65.6, and so the remedial class was considered to be a success.

4 ____ The 300 freshmen at Gotham City High School averaged 65.7 on the English admissions test. The lowest-scoring 30 (who had an average of 39.6 on the test) were randomly divided into two subgroups, and one of these groups of 15 was put in the remedial class. At the end of just one semester in this class, the scores of these 15 remedial students went up to 52.8, while the nonremedial students averaged only 41.3. The remedial class was thus considered to be a success.

5 ____ The 300 freshmen at Gotham City High School averaged 65.7 on the English admissions test. The highest-scoring 30 (who had

an average of 90.4 on the test) were randomly divided into two subgroups, and one of these groups of 15 was put in the gifted/talented English class. At the end of one semester in this class, these 15 students averaged 90.3 on the same test, while the other 15 averaged 81.4 on the retest. The gifted/talented English class was considered to be a success.

EXPERIMENTAL MORTALITY

From time to time, subjects drop out of an experimental or control group, and the absence of these dropouts influences the computed average performance of that group. Experimental mortality refers to the fact that *differences in performance on the outcome variable after a treatment might occur because of changes in group composition rather than as a result of the treatment that the group experienced.* (See Figure 10.8.) To put it another way, we can get the average score of 25 pupils to become higher simply by omitting the 5 lowest scores from the computation of the mean. After such a recalculation, the 20 remaining pupils would possess no greater ability or achievement than before, but the group's average would be higher, since the lower scores would no longer be used in computing the mean.

Imagine a high school situation in which students have previously been offered only academic courses.

BOX 10.2

Dear Researcher: I'm the principal of a junior high school. We have 300 students at each grade level, sixth through eighth. Mrs. Smith (not her real name) had always been a rather mediocre teacher until one summer when she took a course on educational research. That year when she came back to school, she made a deal with me. She would take the 25 slowest seventh graders (based on standardized tests) and teach them for one year. Mr. Jones (not his real name) would teach the 25 brightest seventh graders during the same time period. If Mrs. Smith's students improved more than Mr. Jones's, she'd get double pay. If hers did worse, she'd resign. This sounded like a good way to ease a weak but tenured teacher out of the system. I'm sure Mr. Jones is the better teacher, but Mrs. Smith has taken me to the cleaners eight years in a row now. What's wrong?
(signed) *Dismayed Principal*

Dear Dismayed: You've been the victim of the old regression-toward-the-mean scam. It's the oldest trick in the book. If you select a group based on the extreme scores from a larger group, the extreme scores will regress toward the mean on subsequent tests simply because of the unreliability of the tests. If you want to solve your problem, give Mrs. Smith a "break" and insist that she take the 25 brightest students next year and give Jones the 25 weakest. I'm sure the pattern will reverse itself. If it's any consolation to you, this scam goes on all over the world. In major league baseball, for example, when a team comes in last at the end of a season, the owners go through the ritual of firing the manager and hiring a new one. The new manager is inevitably some guy who has coached other losing teams before, and nobody seriously believes he's actually any better than the one who was fired. Almost always the team improves under the new leadership. Why? Regression toward the mean. There was also an obscure millionaire named Harold Ewes who got rich by applying regression toward the mean to the stock market. I'm not at liberty to disclose how Mr. Ewes did it, however. It was a condition of his will.
(signed) *The Lonely Researcher*

Figure 10.8 Experimental Mortality as a Threat to Internal Validity. There may have actually been no change at all in motivation or insights. It may merely *look* as if a change has occurred because the means have shifted in the absence of certain students on the posttest. It is impossible to tell whether the observed difference has occurred because of the treatment, because of this experimental mortality, or because of some combination of the two.

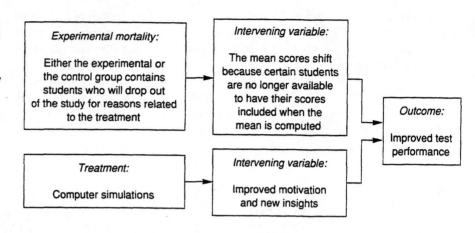

One year the principal announces that an experimental word processing program will be offered to juniors. Fifty students sign up for the new program, but the program has a capacity of 25 students. To be fair, the administrators select 25 of the 50 applicants at random for the new program. The principal decides to use the other 25 applicants as a control group for comparison purposes. (As you will see in the next chapter, so far this is an excellent procedure.) The students are pretested in some way, and the two groups are about even. At the end of the year, the students are retested, and their scores are still about even. Has the program been ineffective? The principal looks at the results more closely and notices that all 25 students are still in the experimental group, but only 20 are left in the control group—5 of the control students are no longer in the school. The comparison has become clouded because of experimental mortality. It is likely that the performance of the experimental students improved because of actual gains in knowledge or skills, whereas the improvement in the control group probably occurred because slower students were more likely than stronger students to leave the school.

To be a threat to internal validity, changes in group composition must be related to the outcome variable. The situation described in the preceding paragraph provides an example of a threat to internal validity because the students who dropped out did so in such a way as to have a specific impact on the outcome variable. If 5 students dropped out of each group and if it could be shown that these students dropped out because of routine relocations arising from the employment of their parents, then this mortality would not be a threat to internal validity.

Experimental mortality, then, is a problem when a group that finishes an experiment (completes a treatment or control condition) is not the same group that started it. When such mortality occurs, it is important to check to see whether it is related to the outcome variable in any way. If you can rule out experimental mortality as an explanation of the results of an experiment, you will strengthen the internal validity of your conclusions.

REVIEW QUIZ 10.7

Place an X next to the description if it contains an example of experimental mortality as a threat to internal validity.

1 ____ Gotham State University has a rugged chemistry program. Over half the students who take chemistry fail the courses, and as a result many of these students are forced to drop out of the university. The administrators point out, however, that students who persist until graduation receive quality educa-

tion. Gotham graduates average 87.4 (78th percentile) on the National Chemistry Exam. This can be compared with the average of students at Mickey Mouse University, where students are similar according to admissions tests but few flunk out because of chemistry. MMU graduates average only 63.8 (61st percentile) on the National Chemistry Exam. Gotham faculty and alumni are quite proud of their fine chemistry program.

2 ____ Students at Public School 101 and Public School 202 are from similar neighborhoods and possess similar abilities. At PS 101 the school board has asked the faculty to introduce the new mastery approach to teaching biology. At PS 202 the faculty continues to use the old approach. At PS 101, 84% of the mastery students finish the year and average 77.6 (80th percentile) on the Biology Knowledge Test. At PS 202, however, 90% finish the year and average 62.8 (47th percentile) on the same test. These dropout rates and percentiles are about the same as they have always been and appear to be related to family mobility rather than to anything relating to school. The school board concludes that the mastery approach is superior and recommends that it be implemented throughout the entire school system.

PRETESTING

With regard to internal validity, the threat of pretesting refers to the fact that *changes in an outcome variable might be a result of the measurement process before the treatment rather than the impact of the treatment itself.* (See Figure 10.9.) For example, at the beginning of an antismoking program the therapist running it might have the participants write down the number of cigarettes they smoke each day for a week. Then he might show them a film about the ill effects of smoking. Finally, the week after the film, he might again have them record the number of cigarettes they smoke. If the average number of cigarettes smoked is substantially lower after the film, the therapist might assume that the film helped cause this cutback. The threat to internal validity is that it is plausible that the measurement process could have focused attention on the need for the participants to change their behavior patterns and motivated them to stop smoking, and it could have been this reaction to the measurement process rather than the treatment itself that caused the reduction in the number of cigarettes smoked. Likewise, a history teacher might give a pretest before presenting an innovative approach to a unit on the Civil War. Even if the teacher did not give the students the answers, they might do better on the posttest not because the unit was effective but rather because the pretest alerted them to some important concepts about the Civil War.

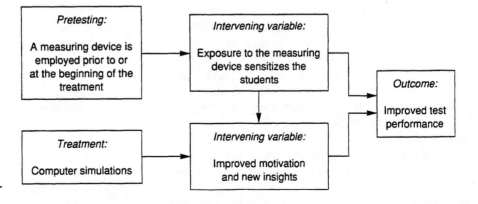

Figure 10.9 Pretesting as a Threat to Internal Validity.   There may actually have been no change at all in motivation or insights. It might merely *appear* that there has been a change, because exposure to the pretest has led the students to react differently to the posttest. Even if there has been a change in motivation and insights, it is possible that this change occurred as a reaction to the sensitization arising from the pretest rather than from the treatment.

Pretesting is a problem only when there is data collected before the treatment. (The terms *pretest* and *posttest* refer to the administration of any measurement process before or after the treatment—not merely to measurement strategies normally referred to as tests.) With regard to achievement tests, pretesting is a problem because an initial test may familiarize the students with the type or the actual content of the test questions they will have to deal with on the posttest and therefore artificially inflate their scores. In cases where the pretest and posttest are identical, such familiarity with the measurement process may even be more useful to uninformed students than the instructional lesson itself. For example, if a teacher gives students a set of 20 spelling words as a pretest, then teaches them a lesson on a list of 200 words for the next two weeks, and finally retests them with the identical set of 20 words, the teacher should not be surprised to see improvement on the posttest. It is obvious that increased scores could result from previous experience with the list of words on the pretest. The threat to internal validity would be greatly reduced by using one random set of words on the pretest and a different set on the posttest.

The problem is somewhat different with regard to attitude and personality testing, observations, and interviews. In these cases, the pretest may serve to *sensitize* the person whose performance is being measured, and this sensitization may act as an added treatment. If we give a person a questionnaire measuring attitudes toward a specified ethnic group, for example, and then follow this up with some kind of ethnic awareness program, it is possible that the test taker might do some thinking to sort out his feelings while answering the questions. It might be this self-analysis at the time of the pretesting and during the interval between the pretest and posttest (rather than the ethnic awareness program) that would lead to an improved attitude.

In many cases in education, pretesting probably does not have the distracting effect described in the preceding paragraph. Nevertheless, the possibility of a threat to internal validity exists, and the teacher/researcher must take precautions to reduce

the chances that pretesting will produce artificial results. By using unobtrusive data collection techniques (discussed in chapter 6) and multiple assessment techniques to cross-check one another, this threat can be reduced. If you can rule out pretesting as an explanation of the results of an experiment, you will strengthen the internal validity of your conclusions.

REVIEW QUIZ 10.8

Place an X next to the description if it contains an example of pretesting as a threat to internal validity.

1 _____ The students averaged 60 correct answers on the punctuation exam at the end of the first semester. The English teacher was concerned about the low scores and gave the students detailed programmed materials to help them learn to punctuate more effectively. The students used the materials, and then these same students averaged 84 correct when the same test was administered at the end of the second semester. The English teacher concluded that the programmed materials had been effective and recommended spending 40% of the English department's supplies budget for the year to purchase enough of these materials to accommodate all the students.

2 _____ The students averaged 60 correct answers on the punctuation exam at the end of the first semester. The English teacher was concerned about these low scores. He taught four sections of composition. To two of these sections he gave detailed programmed materials to help the students learn how to punctuate more effectively; to the other two sections he gave no new materials, but rather continued with the usual method of instruction. At the end of the second semester, he gave the same students the same punctuation test. The students with the new materials averaged 84 correct, but those with the old materials averaged only 63 correct. The English

Figure 10.10 Instability as a Threat to Internal Validity. There may actually have been no change at all in motivation or insights. It may merely *look* as if there has been a change because of the instability in the test scores. It is impossible to tell whether the improved test performance occurred because of the treatment, because of the instability, or because of some combination of the two.

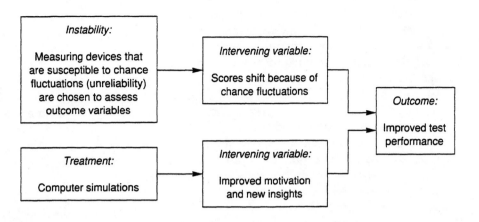

teacher concluded that the programmed materials had been effective and recommended spending 40% of the English department's supplies budget for the year to purchase enough of these materials to accommodate all the students.

3 _____ The students in the English class turned in essays that were to be graded on the basis of content rather than mechanics. As the teacher looked over the papers he was concerned about the poor quality of the punctuation. Without making any marks on the papers, he recorded a separate mechanics score for each student. He did not convey this mechanics score to the students, nor did he let it influence their grades. The students did not even know they were being scored for mechanics. He then gave the students detailed programmed materials to teach them to punctuate effectively. Three months later he examined a similar assignment and again checked it for mechanics. Whereas the students had made 11.4 errors per 500 words on the first testing occasion, on the posttest they made only 2.1 errors per 500 words. The English teacher concluded that the programmed materials had been effective and recommended spending 40% of the English department's supplies budget for the year to purchase enough of these materials to accommodate all the students.

INSTABILITY

Instability is a threat to the internal validity of an experiment to the extent that *chance fluctuations in the scores derived from the measurement process rather than the actual treatment can account for observed differences between groups.* (See Figure 10.10.) Such instability can be reduced by designing more reliable measurement devices and by using larger groups. In addition, the likelihood that a result will occur by chance can be estimated statistically, and such statistical information can be useful in helping you draw conclusions from an experiment. Note that of all the threats to internal validity, instability is the only one that is effectively controlled by statistical analysis. (These statistical procedures will be discussed in chapter 14. Also, since instability is more appropriately treated there, no Review Quiz on this topic is presented here.)

EXPECTANCY EFFECTS

If either the experimenter or the subjects expect a certain outcome in an experiment, it is possible that their behavior will be (perhaps unconsciously) influenced by these expectations. The fact that *it could be these expectations rather than the actual treatment that produce the observed outcomes* is referred to as an expectancy effect. (See Figure 10.11.) It has been shown that researchers are sometimes biased in unconscious, subtle ways to obtain the anticipated results. "Smart" rats genetically identical to "dumb" rats have been known to run mazes better simply because the people training them were convinced by the false labeling and unconsciously paid more attention to the "smart" rats. In addition, people who take part in experiments often try to figure out what the experiment is about and then act the way they think they are supposed to act. In addition, sometimes the opposite effect occurs: a participant tries to figure out what the result is supposed to be and does things to produce the opposite effect, in order to thwart the experimenter.

In all these cases, it could be the artificial expectations aroused by the experiment rather than the actual treatment that accounts for the outcome. If you can rule out the impact of such artificial expectations, you can increase the internal validity of your conclusions.

REVIEW QUIZ 10.9

Place an *X* next to the description if it contains an example of expectancy as a threat to internal validity.

1 _____ Mr. Sherman had developed a computer program that he believed would help students develop thinking skills in science. He had two sections of comparable biology students. He used his computer programs in one of these sections and continued to teach the other section without the programs. At the end of the semester, the students who used Mr. Sherman's computer programs scored much higher than the other students on a test of thinking skills. Mr. Sherman concluded that the computer program had been effective.

2 _____ Mrs. Wayne had developed a computer program that she felt would help students develop English composition skills. Her colleague, Mrs. Jefferson, had two sections of comparable English students. Mrs. Wayne gave Mrs. Jefferson her own computer program and another set of new materials. Mrs. Jefferson agreed to use both sets of innovative materials, but Mrs. Wayne did not tell her colleague which one she thought would work best. Mrs. Jefferson used the computer program in one of her sections and the other materials in the other section. At the end of the semester, the students who used the computer program scored much higher than the other students on a test of composition skills. Mrs. Wayne concluded that the computer program had been effective.

Figure 10.11 Expectancy as a Threat to Internal Validity. There may have been an actual change in motivation or insights, but it is impossible to tell whether this change occurred because of the treatment, because of an urge to make the experiment come out "right," or because of some combination of the two. It is also possible that motivation and insights did not change at all. It might merely *appear* that a change has occurred, because the participants' urge to make the results come out "right" led them to react differently to the posttest.

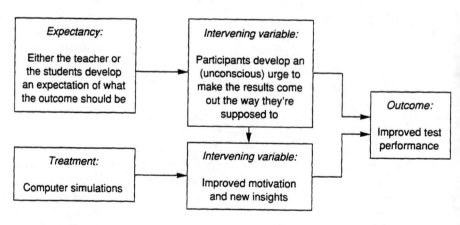

3 ____ Dr. Price had developed a computer program that she felt would help students develop mathematics skills. Mr. Jordan was a new teacher at the school who was scheduled to teach two sections of comparable math students. Dr. Price gave Mr. Jordan her computer program to use with one section and the previously used materials for the other section. Mr. Jordan did not know which materials were Dr. Price's, nor did Dr. Price tell her colleague which materials she thought would work best. At the end of the semester, the students who used the computer programs scored much higher than the other students on a test of mathematics skills. Dr. Price concluded that the computer program had been effective.

4 ____ Mrs. Feldman had developed a computer program that she felt would help students develop French conversation skills. Her colleague, Mrs. Benton, had two comparable sections of French students. Although Mrs. Benton was skeptical about the usefulness of Mrs. Feldman's program, she agreed to field test the computer program with one section and to use another set of materials with the other. At the end of the semester, the students who used the computer program scored much higher than the other students on a test of French conversation skills. Mrs. Feldman concluded that the computer program had been effective.

(Expectancy effects are also an important consideration with regard to external validity. Because these effects will be discussed more fully in chapter 15, no further discussion will be given to them at this time. Many students find it difficult to distinguish between expectancy as a threat to internal validity and as a threat to external validity. There is a clear distinction, but it is not particularly important at this time to isolate what aspects of expectancy influence internal validity and what aspects influence external validity. The important thing is to reduce such artificial influences so that you can draw valid conclusions from the experiment at hand.)

SOCIAL-PSYCHOLOGICAL THREATS

There are four additional threats that arise out of the psychological dynamics of the social situation surrounding the introduction of the treatment. These are referred to as social-psychological threats to internal validity. They are as follows:

1. Diffusion
2. Compensatory equalization of treatments
3. Compensatory rivalry
4. Compensatory demoralization

In each case, the dynamics of the social situation may generate a response that could influence the treatment or the outcome variable and thereby cloud the nature of any cause-and-effect relationships.

Diffusion

Diffusion occurs when participants in one group (usually the experimental group) communicate information to members of another group in such a way as to influence their behavior with regard to the outcome variables. For example, if one group of students has learned an exciting, innovative approach to studying mathematics, they may tend to share their excitement (and hence the treatment) with their friends. This threat often has the impact of making it look as if there was no impact even though the treatment was effective. In the preceding example, the children with the innovative math program and those without it might do equally well on a test of math skills—not because the program was ineffective but because it was so effective that the students had spontaneously disseminated the program. Diffusion can be reduced by deemphasizing the fact that there is an experiment in progress and by encouraging teachers to avoid accentuating the differences between the two groups. Another effective strategy is to isolate the students receiving the experimental treatment so that they are unlikely to spread it to other students.

Compensatory Equalization of Treatments

Compensatory equalization of treatments occurs when administrators or others perceive an unfairness in giving benefits solely to the experimental group and demand that these be extended to the control group as well. For example, if a school system wants to test the effectiveness of computers for teaching science by running a pilot study in one of the schools, the people in the other schools might perceive it to be unfair to give computers to one school while neglecting the others. If the school system responds by giving equivalent "perks" to these other schools, then the computers might be perceived to fail not because they were ineffective but because the other schools essentially were receiving other "treatments" of their own.

Compensatory Rivalry

Compensatory rivalry occurs when subjects in one group have emotional responses to the other group and try (perhaps subconsciously) to work harder to compete with that group. For example, in the preceding example teachers who worked without computers and liked it that way might work harder in their noncomputerized setting, because there would be a tendency for them to want to "beat" the computers. This problem is especially likely to occur when the students who do not receive the treatment (or their teachers) feel that they will be at a disadvantage if the experimental program is successful.

Compensatory Demoralization

Compensatory demoralization occurs when subjects in one group feel neglected, perceive that effort is futile, or for some other emotional reason put forth less effort than the members of the other group. To pursue the science computers example, the teachers and students who did not receive the computers might either deliberately reduce their efforts in retaliation or inadvertently lose heart and set lower goals. In either case the resulting improvements of the innovative group may occur not because that method was superior but because the other students reduced their efforts and performed more poorly.

In general, the best way to deal with these problems is to reduce the obtrusiveness and perceived threat of the treatment by presenting it as a natural part of the school routine. For example, if all the schools in the system are going to receive new equipment, then there may be no problem in evaluating the use of computers for science education in one of these schools but not in others. Likewise, if the principals of all the schools realize that it is important to run an experimental pilot study in a single school first, that their own schools will derive benefits if the experiment can be carried out successfully, and that their own schools will have the innovative opportunities on other occasions—and if they can convey these feelings to the teachers and students in their own schools—then these social-psychological threats are likely to be minimized. By seeing to it that the treatment is nonobtrusive and perceived as fair to all parties, the researcher can make it less likely that persons who do not receive the treatment will react artificially to its absence, and this will improve the internal validity of the conclusions that can be drawn from the study.

INTERACTION OF SEVERAL FACTORS

The examples given so far in this chapter have focused on one effect at a time. It should be obvious that several of these threats could simultaneously threaten the internal validity of the same study. What may not be so obvious is that these factors not only accumulate, *they also interact.* In other words, *the different threats sometimes mix together in such a way as to provide unique threats in their own rights.* (See Figure 10.12.)

To take an example, history and selection bias often interact in experiments when volunteers are used. This occurs because it is often true that persons who volunteer to be part of an experiment are also likely to be more attuned to what is going on around them. For this reason, volunteers may react to history differently than persons who do not volunteer. In a very real sense, therefore, history is different for the volunteer. Technically, the threat is not history itself (concurrent events would be the same for both groups). Likewise, selection bias itself is not a prob-

Figure 10.12 The Interaction of Several Factors as a Threat to Internal Validity.   It is possible that there has been a change in motivation and insights, but this change may have occurred because of differences in the way the separate groups reacted to the pretest. It is also possible that it merely *appears* that there has been a change, because one of the groups (but not the other) was sensitized by the pretest to do better on the posttest.

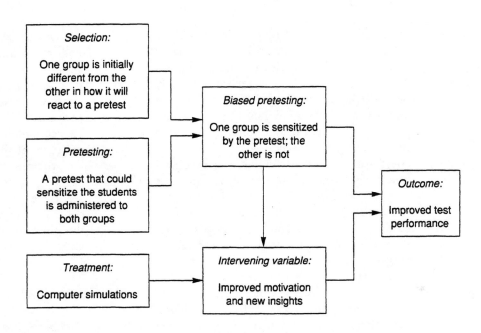

lem (the volunteers did not already possess the outcome variable). Rather, the problem is the unique interaction of both history and selection bias (the volunteers had a tendency to deal with concurrent events differently than the nonvolunteers, and this could affect their performance on the outcome variable). In a sense, a new variable (called biased history, perhaps) has been created. In this way, history and selection bias can interact to threaten the internal validity of a study.

When you are examining an experiment to rule out each of the threats to internal validity, therefore, it is important to look for them in interaction with one another, as well as operating separately. For example, although the volunteers receiving a treatment might be similar in all other respects to nonvolunteers, it is still possible that the subtle interaction of volunteering and history or pretesting or some other factor could contaminate the internal validity of the study. If you can rule out such interactions, you can strengthen the internal validity of your conclusions.

Many readers will find it hard to distinguish between the simple impact of the threats discussed earlier in this chapter and the interactive effects described in this section. There is a difference, and it

is important to control both simple threats and interactive threats. However, the distinction appears needlessly subtle to many readers. If you examine the exercises at the end of this section and see that there are problems with internal validity but have trouble explaining why these are interactive rather than simple threats, you should probably not be concerned. The important point is to recognize and control the threats when doing or reading experimental research, not to define and classify them.

REVIEW QUIZ 10.10

Place an X next to the description if it contains an example of two or more factors interacting to pose a threat to internal validity.

1 ____ Mr. Sander's first-grade pupils were doing poorly on their basic math. He had given them a test on which the average for first graders should have been about 50, but his students had averaged only 25.2. (The skills were related to abilities that, according to the theory of Jean Piaget, developed around the time a child was in the first grade.) Mr.

Sander knew of a technique that might help his students, but it would be time-consuming. Therefore, he decided to do an experiment, because unless the technique really worked, he did not want to bother with it again the next year. Since there were no other first graders in the building, he asked the second-grade teacher, Mrs. Adams, if he could use some of her children as a control group. He chose 10 of her slower students who also averaged 25.2 on the same test. He then used his new technique with his first graders, while the second graders continued with their normal instruction. He tested everyone at the end of the year with an alternative form of the test. His first graders scored 42, whereas the control group of second graders scored only 32. He concluded that although he would have liked to see even more improvement, the new technique did seem to have a beneficial effect. And so he decided to use the technique regularly in the future.

2 ____ Miss Dawson wanted to find out whether the use of computer simulations would help her science students learn the skills of scientific problem solving. She had 24 students in her class. She asked for 12 volunteers to use the simulations; the other 12 served as a control group. She gave them a pretest, on which both groups averaged about 35. Four months later, she gave them a posttest. This time the control group scored about 55, whereas the students who had used the computer simulations averaged nearly 65. Miss Dawson concluded that the computer simulations were more effective than the ordinary instruction in teaching scientific problem-solving skills.

3 ____ Mr. Bellow wanted to find out if a physical fitness program would promote an improved self-concept among adults. He posted a notice on a college bulletin board, stating that he needed volunteers for a project involving physical exercise. One hundred volunteers signed up. From these, Mr. Bellow randomly selected 25 to serve as an experimental group (who got the exercise program) and 25 to serve as a control group (who were tested but did not get the exercise program). He told the other 50 that he appreciated their interest, but he could not use them at this time. After three months in his program, the people receiving the physical fitness training had significantly better self-concepts than those who were in the control group. Mr. Bellow concluded that the physical fitness program had caused an improved self-concept among these people.

PUTTING IT ALL TOGETHER

Eugene Anderson, our humane educator, had developed an Animal Life Program (ALP), which he believed would help children develop favorable attitudes toward animals. He wanted to field test it to make sure it worked, and then he wanted to promote its use throughout the country.

He got out his Fireman Tests (chapters 2–7), which existed in two forms. He went to Mortimer Peterson Elementary School, where he gave one form of the test as a pretest to all fourth through sixth graders. Two weeks later he presented the ALP to the same classes. He returned in another two weeks to administer the other form of the test as a posttest. He found that on the pretest the children had chosen to save an average of only 1.34 animals apiece, but after the treatment they chose 2.21 animals each. He was impressed with his findings.

However, as fate would have it, that afternoon Mr. Anderson chanced upon this very textbook. He found it, tattered and well worn from avid reading, in the principal's office. He perused the chapter on internal validity. Was it possible that his study was weakened by threats to internal validity? Was it possible that something other than the ALP had caused the enhanced performance on the posttest?

After a sleepless night, Mr. Anderson spent the next day evaluating the threats to the internal validity of his study. He found good news and bad news. The good news was that he had no serious threats from selection bias, history, maturation, instrumentation, instability, statistical regression, experimental mortality, or the interactive effects of any of these.

He ruled out selection bias as a threat because if the children had already possessed favorable attitudes, this would have shown up on the pretest. He eliminated history because after interviewing the participants and making a careful examination of everything that happened at school, on TV, and around the neighborhood, he uncovered nothing that would logically have caused them to improve their attitudes. Maturation was no problem because there was no apparent reason why the passage of four weeks should suddenly lead to improved attitudes toward animals. He ruled out both instrumentation and instability because he had already established that his tests possessed both test-retest and alternate-form reliability. Statistical regression was no problem because there had been no selection from extreme groups. Finally, experimental mortality was no threat since all the children had been present for both the pretest and the posttest.

The bad news was that he had serious problems with regard to expectancy and pretesting. Mr. Anderson interviewed the principal at the end of the experiment and discovered that she had announced to the teachers and children that Mr. Anderson was an expert who was going to present an excellent program about animals and she hoped they would do well. That certainly could lead to expectancy problems. Even worse, Mr. Anderson discovered that after they took the pretest, several of the students had been heard talking about the test and commenting that they thought that "saving animals was the right answer." Mr. Anderson had to admit that he could not really tell whether it had been the ALP, the exhortation from the principal, or the reaction of the children to the pretest that had led to the improved test scores.

Mr. Anderson realized the error of his ways and eagerly read the next two chapters of this book to discover effective strategies for controlling these threats to internal validity.

SUMMARY

The threats to internal validity and ways to control them are summarized in Table 10.1. Each of the threats described in this chapter creates problems for one of two reasons. First, they may bring about a change in the desired outcome that may be mistakenly attributed to the impact of the treatment. Second, they may influence the measurement of the outcome variable in such a way as to make it appear that an outcome has occurred when, in fact, no such outcome has actually occurred. To the extent that we can rule out these threats, therefore, we can strengthen the logic of our conclusion that it is the treatment that is responsible for the observed effects.

As you read the following summaries for each of the threats to internal validity, follow the logic through Figure 10.13, and determine whether you understand the principles involved. If you do not, you should reexamine the relevant sections of this chapter before proceeding to chapter 11.

History refers to the threat that some simultaneous, extraneous event (or combination of events) during the time frame of the experiment other than the treatment is responsible for the observed outcome.

Selection bias is concerned with the problem that a group's performance during a measurement process after a treatment may arise from the selection or composition of the group itself rather than from the treatment.

Maturation refers to the fact that changes in an outcome variable may occur as a routine result of the passage of time rather than because of the treatment.

Instrumentation can be a problem because observed differences in an outcome variable could be the result of changes in the data collection process rather than the treatment itself.

Statistical regression is a threat because subgroups selected on the basis of extremely high or low scores tend to give a false impression of change by shifting their average toward the mean of the original group on subsequent administrations of the same or related measurement processes.

Table 10.1 Summary of Threats to Internal Validity and Ways to Control Them

Threat	Description	How to Control Threat
History	Extraneous events occurring at the same time as the treatment may influence performance with regard to the outcome variable	• Carefully ascertain that no extraneous events occur • Make sure that what happens to one group happens to other(s)
Selection bias	It may be the composition of the group rather than the treatment that accounts for performance with regard to the outcome variable	• Make groups initially equal—preferably by random assignment • Pretest to check initial performance of group(s)
Maturation	Improvements between one testing occasion and another may result from routine changes that occur as time passes	• Randomly assign groups to true experiment • Rule out maturation logically (e.g., developmentally implausible)
Instrumentation	Differences on various testing occasions may occur because the data collection process has somehow changed	• Carefully ascertain that no changes occur in the data collection process • If changes do occur, make them happen to both groups
Statistical regression	Groups selected on the basis of extreme scores tend to shift toward the mean of the original group when retested	• Don't select on the basis of extreme scores • If you do select extreme groups, use random assignment afterwards
Experimental mortality	Differences on subsequent testing occasions may occur because the composition of the group has changed	• Strive to prevent dropouts • Analyze characteristics of dropouts • Use a matching strategy with subsequent random assignment
Pretesting	The experience of taking the pretest may sensitize subjects to perform better on the posttest	• Do not use a pretest • Use an unobtrusive pretest • Use random assignment to true experiment
Instability	Chance fluctuations in scores arising from unreliability may cause changes in performance on various testing occasions	• Use reliable tests • Use tests of significance—after random assignment, if possible
Social-psychological threats	Dynamics of the experimental situation may set up alternative treatments that may account for differences	• Make the experiment as natural and unobtrusive as possible
Expectancy effects	Outcomes may occur because experimenter or subjects expected those outcomes	• Discourage expectancies • Foster opposite rather than supportive expectancies

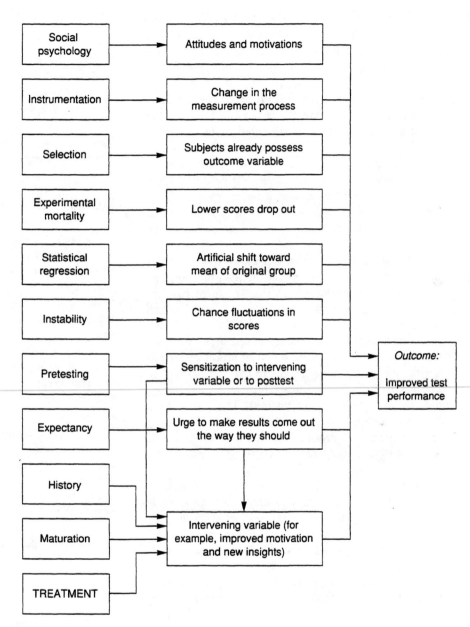

Figure 10.13 Summary of the Major Threats to Internal Validity. Interactions are not included in this diagram as a separate threat. The role of the teacher/researcher is to rule out each of these threats and therefore make it possible to conclude that the treatment (and not one of these irrelevant threats) actually caused the observed outcome. It is not always possible to control all these threats, but to the extent that they can be controlled, the validity of your conclusions will be strengthened.

Experimental mortality is a threat when the composition of a group changes because of dropouts, and this change gives the false impression that the performance of the members of the group has changed.

Pretesting refers to the fact that it might be the reaction to an initial administration of the measurement process rather than the treatment itself that has resulted in the differences observed in the outcome variable.

Instability consists of chance fluctuations in the scores obtained from a measurement process, which give a false impression that differences have been found where there are none. This is the only threat to internal validity that is controlled by statistical analysis.

Expectancy refers to the fact that artificial expectations arising from the experimental situation can give the false impression that the treatment has had an impact (or, conversely, that the treatment has had no impact).

Social-psychological threats arise out of the psychological dynamics of the social situation surrounding the introduction of the treatment. Participants in one group may communicate information to members of another group (*diffusion*). There may be a demand that the apparent benefits of the experimental treatment be extended to the control group as well (*compensatory equalization of treatments*). Subjects in one group may have emotional responses to the other group and work harder to compete with that group (*compensatory rivalry*) or reduce their efforts for emotional reasons (*compensatory demoralization*). These factors have the impact of setting up rival treatments, which compete with the experimental treatment.

The interaction of several factors refers to the possibility that several factors can act in combination as well as alone to constitute a threat to the internal validity of a study.

The job of the teacher/researcher/decision maker or reader of research is to rule out or account for each of the threats summarized in Figure 10.13. The next chapter will begin with a discussion of how to control these threats and thereby increase the internal validity of your cause-and-effect conclusions.

What Comes Next

Chapters 11 and 12 will describe strategies that help control the threats to internal validity. Chapters 13 and 14 will discuss statistical tools that help report relationships and estimate the likelihood that relationships are not merely the result of chance fluctuations in data. Chapter 15 will begin the treatment of Level III research, which builds upon well-conducted Level II research.

DOING YOUR OWN RESEARCH

It is practically impossible in a single study to control all the threats to internal validity. The best you can usually do is to control as many of the threats as possible and demonstrate an awareness of the rest. When conducting, interpreting, and reporting the results of research, it is important to acknowledge these threats and to specify the extent to which they are likely to influence the results of your study.

In addition, replication is an important way to control threats to internal validity. For that reason, you may find it useful to replicate someone else's study, while controlling threats to internal validity that were uncontrolled in that earlier study.

Finally, it is important to note that there are often tradeoffs between internal and external validity. Strategies that enhance the internal validity of a study may reduce your ability to generalize the results as widely as you would like. Therefore, what you want to strive for is the best possible balance between internal and external validity

FOR FURTHER THOUGHT

1. What's internal about internal validity?

2. Politicians often take responsibility for improvements that occur after they take office. What threats to internal validity typically threaten the conclusion that their policies (rather than some other factor) account for these improvements?

3. Complete this sentence by answering the designated questions: "The threat of history . . .(does

what?) (To what or whom?) (When?) (Where?) (How?) (Why?)"

4. Complete this sentence by answering the designated questions: "The threat of selection bias ...(does what?) (To what or whom?) (When?) (Where?) (How?) (Why?)"

5. Complete this sentence by answering the designated questions: "The threat of maturation ...(does what?) (To what or whom?) (When?) (Where?) (How?) (Why?)"

6. Complete this sentence by answering the designated questions: "The threat of instrumentation ...(does what?) (To what or whom?) (When?) (Where?) (How?) (Why?)"

7. Complete this sentence by answering the designated questions: "The threat of statistical regression ...(does what?) (To what or whom?) (When?) (Where?) (How?) (Why?)"

8. Complete this sentence by answering the designated questions: "The threat of experimental mortality ...(does what?) (To what or whom?) (When?) (Where?) (How?) (Why?)"

9. Complete this sentence by answering the designated questions: "The threat of pretesting ...(does what?) (To what or whom?) (When?) (Where?) (How?) (Why?)"

10. Complete this sentence by answering the designated questions: "The threat of instability ...(does what?) (To what or whom?) (When?) (Where?) (How?) (Why?)"

11. Complete this sentence by answering the designated questions: "The threat of expectancy ...(does what?) (To what or whom?) (When?) (Where?) (How?) (Why?)"

12. Complete this sentence by answering the designated questions: "The social-psychological threats ...(do what?) (To what or whom?) (When?) (Where?) (How?) (Why?)"

REFERENCE

Wittrock, M. C. (Ed.). (1986). *Handbook of research on teaching*. New York: Macmillan.

ANNOTATED BIBLIOGRAPHY

Campbell, D. T., & Stanley, J. C. (1966). *Experimental and quasi-experimental designs for research*. Chicago: Rand McNally. Until it is eventually supplanted by Cook and Campbell (1979), this will continue to be the most widely cited work on the threats to internal validity.

Cook, T. D., & Campbell, D. T. (1979). *Quasi-Experimentation: Design and analysis issues for field settings*. Chicago: Rand McNally. Chapter 2 contains the most complete treatment available on the concept of internal validity. Although a few chapters in this book are extremely technical and complex, chapter 2 is easily understandable and useful to teachers and other professionals interested in doing serious applied research.

ANSWERS TO QUIZZES

Review Quiz 10.1

1. The issue is one of internal validity. Mr. Schneider is vaguely aware that something else (perhaps growing a year older or something Joey's friends said) may have helped change Joey's behavior.

2. The issue is not one of internal validity. The superintendent is concerned about a piece of factual information, not about a cause-and-effect relationship.

3. The issue is not one of internal validity. The teacher is concerned about a comparison, not about a cause-and-effect relationship. If she thought that her teaching methods *caused* her students to be different than other students, then she might become concerned about the internal validity of that conclusion.

4. The issue is one of internal validity. It would be possible that something else (such as improved police patrols or other changes in the discipline policy) was responsible for the reduction in vandalism. The superintendent would want to rule out these possibilities.

5. The issue is not one of internal validity. The teacher simply wants to compare his film with

the PTA guidelines. He does not seem to believe that his film and the PTA are in any way causally related.

6. The issue is one of internal validity. Mr. Jacobson would have to rule out the possibility that something else (perhaps a series of news reports or simple maturation) had caused the increased interest in world affairs.

7. The issue is one of internal validity. Mr. Campbell should consider the possibility that perhaps his charges behaved better because of some factor other than his new method of working with them. (Perhaps his personal expectations of improved performance made the difference.)

8. The issue is one of internal validity. She is concerned that some extraneous factor—the unrest in the school—impeded the effectiveness of the reading program.

Review Quiz 10.2

1. There is a threat here. It is obvious that computing batting averages (the result of a historical event) could have caused improved ability in long division. Concluding that the videotapes caused the improvement is therefore untenable.

2. There is no obvious threat here. There is no apparent logic behind the possible belief that the historical event (computing batting averages) caused children to spell words more accurately. The historical event appears to be irrelevant and does not jeopardize the conclusion that the spelling bees paid off.

Review Quiz 10.3

1. There is a problem here. It is quite possible that the players with the inclination to volunteer would also have an incentive to work harder. They might have volunteered precisely because they wanted to become better. This is a serious threat to the conclusion that the mental practice exercises actually accomplished anything.

2. There is no apparent threat here. There is no obvious reason why one group would have a pre-existing advantage over the other. Random assignment to comparison groups is an excellent way to rule out selection bias. (This method will be discussed in chapter 11.)

3. There is a problem here. The coach is comparing this year's players with teams from other years, and it is not at all obvious that the groups are similar. Teams do vary markedly from year to year. Her conclusion would be strengthened if she had evidence to show that the group was, in fact, similar to previous groups. (Note that a sensible coach might still use the new method. She would merely be a bit wary. She has not proven anything, and she would look for further evidence to support her conclusion.)

4. There is no problem of selection bias here. The important comparison is between the 4 *Golden Book* volunteers and the 4 volunteers who did not get the book. All 8 of these were volunteers, and so if volunteers had unique characteristics, all 8 would share these attributes. Random assignment of these 8 to two subgroups (as in example 2) helped eliminate selection bias. (If you were concerned that there were only 4 players in each group, your concern was well founded. Random assignment works better with larger groups. However, this is technically not a problem of selection bias but of instability, which will be discussed later. If you are concerned that the results cannot be *generalized* to players who do not volunteer, you are right again—but that's a problem of *external* validity, which is discussed in chapter 15.)

Review Quiz 10.4

1. There is an obvious problem here. It is perfectly normal for fourth graders to mature as the year goes on, and at least part of their improvement would be the result of maturation rather than the computerized materials.

2. There is no apparent problem arising from maturation here. If 12th graders have progressed only

to the third-grade level in 12 years of schooling, it would be illogical to expect them to mature two full years in only six months. They have progressed further than would be expected by maturation alone.

Review Quiz 10.5

1. There is no apparent threat of instrumentation. The tests were apparently equivalent and administered in the same manner.

2. There is a problem here with regard to instrumentation. The test the students took after the cooperative review was actually slightly different from the one they took before the treatment. It is possible that the improved performance on the posttest occurred because it was a technically better test rather than because the students knew more.

Review Quiz 10.6

1. There is a problem of statistical regression here. The 30 students in the remedial class were selected for that class because they had extremely low scores on the admissions test. On the retest, therefore, their scores would be likely to move toward the mean of the original group of 300 students.

2. There is a problem of statistical regression here. The 30 students in the gifted/talented English class were selected for that class because they had extremely high scores on the admissions test. On the retest, therefore, their scores would be likely to move toward the mean of the original group of 300 students.

3. There is no problem of statistical regression here. The 30 students in the remedial class were not selected for that class because they had extremely low scores on the admissions test. Rather, their mean was about equal to the mean of the original group, and no regression would be expected.

4. There is no problem of statistical regression here. The 15 students who went into the remedial class and the 15 who were selected but not placed in that class were selected because they had extremely low scores on the admissions test. But since both groups were equally likely to regress toward the mean, this statistical regression cannot account for the difference in scores between the two groups on the retest. Therefore, although regression toward the mean occurred for both groups, it was not a threat to the internal validity of the study.

5. There is no problem of statistical regression here. The reasoning is the same as in number 4. Regression occurred, but it occurred about equally for both groups, and so it did not threaten the internal validity of the study.

Review Quiz 10.7

1. There is a problem of experimental mortality here. The average of GSU students is probably high on the National Chemistry Exam not so much because of a high rate of learning but rather because the students who would have lowered the GSU average were eliminated before they could take the exam. This would lead to an artificial inflation of the GSU average.

2. There is no apparent threat from experimental mortality here. The higher dropout rate at PS 101 is about the same as it had been before the experimental treatment. The dropout rate at PS 101 was higher than at PS 202, but this had also been the case in previous years. The mortality appears to be unrelated to the outcome variable. (That is, the PS 101 students probably did not have their scores inflated by having more weak students than usual excluded from the calculation of their mean.) Therefore, although the dropout rates were slightly different, this does not constitute a threat to internal validity.

Review Quiz 10.8

1. Since the same test was used on both the pretest and the posttest, there is a serious problem here.

For example, it is possible that students who thought they got items wrong asked their friends for the correct answers or were merely sensitized to attend more carefully to ordinary instruction, and assistance of this kind might have helped them do better when they saw the same questions again. Without further evidence, it would be rash to conclude that the programmed materials had caused a substantial improvement.

2. Pretesting is not a problem here. If pretesting were causing the improvement, this effect would occur for all four groups, not just the sections receiving the treatment. There may be other problems here (such as selection bias), but pretesting is not a threat to the internal validity of this study.

3. There is no apparent problem with pretesting here. The measurement process was unobtrusive. There was no information from the pretest that was likely to enhance student performance on the posttest. It seems unlikely that this pretest alone would produce the posttest results.

Review Quiz 10.9

1. There is a problem here. The science teacher had a personal interest in proving that the materials were effective. Whenever the inventor of a treatment is its evaluator, you should be skeptical of positive findings.

2. There is no apparent problem here. Mrs. Jefferson was an impartial observer who did not have expectations regarding the success of the experiment.

3. There is no apparent problem here. Mr. Jordan was an impartial observer who did not have expectations regarding the success of the experiment.

4. There is no apparent problem here. Mrs. Benton possessed expectations regarding the success of the experiment, but the results came out exactly the opposite of these expectations.

Review Quiz 10.10

1. There is a problem here, consisting of an interaction between selection bias and maturation. The subjects who were selected for one group (second graders) probably responded differently to maturation than did those selected for the other group (first graders). That is, the first graders were at a stage of development where developmental maturation was likely to help them, whereas the second graders were already beyond this point. (Note that if you identified statistical regression as a possible problem, you were wrong—but on the right track. The second graders were selected from the overall group of second graders based on their extremely low scores; therefore, their scores would be likely to shift upward on a retest. They regressed, but the experimental group improved even beyond this regression. With regression taken into account, therefore, the gains of the first graders are even more impressive. If the experiment would have shown that the first graders advanced to an average of 32, while the second graders also advanced to an average of 32, then the interaction of selection and statistical regression would have been a problem, because one group would have regressed while the other did not; this regression would have made a real difference look nonexistent.)

2. There is a problem here involving the interaction of selection bias and pretesting. The subjects in one group (volunteers) could possibly be more likely to react differently to pretesting than the subjects in the other group (nonvolunteers). It cannot be stated for certain that this interaction occurred, but the possibility has not been ruled out.

3. There are no apparent uncontrolled threats to internal validity in this study. With regard to internal validity, this is an excellent study. This kind of randomized assignment to experimental and control groups will be described in the next chapter as an excellent way to control many of the threats to internal validity.

CHAPTER 10
Research Report Analysis

The study described in the report in Appendix C is an example of quasi-experimental research. It attempts to show that the guided use of computer simulations caused the students to develop problem-solving abilities to a greater extent than would have been possible with the traditional approach to teaching the same topics or with the unguided use of the same programs.

1. How well does the program deal with each of the following threats to internal validity?

   a. history

   b. selection bias

   c. maturation

   d. instrumentation

   e. statistical regression

   f. experimental mortality

   g. pretesting

   h. instability

   i. expectancy effects

   j. social-psychological threats

2. What could have been done to enhance the internal validity of the research described in this report?

Answers:

1. The threats to internal validity are controlled in the following ways:

   a. There is no evidence that anything different happened to the guided or unguided groups than to the control group. If something happened to make history a threat, we would expect the authors to mention this. Therefore, we can assume that history is not a serious threat to internal validity.

   b. Selection bias is controlled by the Watson-Glaser pretest. Since the groups were not different on that test at the beginning of the experiment, we can assume that selection bias was not likely to be a critical factor.

   c. Young high school students would be likely to mature with regard to formal operational abilities, and this would lead to improvements in problem-solving ability. However, this would be equally likely to happen to the students in all three groups, not just to the guided group. Therefore, we can assume that maturation is not a serious threat to internal validity.

   d. Instrumentation is not a threat. The tests did change on different occasions. For example, each pretest was different from the previous one, and the students took a different form of the Watson-Glaser test as a posttest. But these changes occurred for all three groups, and so instrumentation cannot account for the superior performance of the guided group.

   e. Statistical regression is not a threat. The students were weak at the start of the study, but all three of the groups were weak. No group was selected because of its extremely high or low scores. If there were any regression toward the mean, it would be roughly equal for all three groups.

   f. Experimental mortality is probably not a problem. The researchers do not report the dropout rates. It would have been better to include a sentence describing how many students who took the pretests also took the posttests. If experimental mortality were a threat, the authors should have mentioned this.

g. Pretesting is not a problem. The pretests could have sensitized the students to do better on subsequent versions of the same or similar tests, but this would be equally likely for all three groups.

h. Instability is taken into consideration by the statistical tests of significance. Since there were plenty of subjects in each treatment group, there is unlikely to be much random variation in the averages of the groups, and therefore it is not likely that instability was a serious threat to the results of this study.

i. Expectancy is likely to be a problem. The teachers knew they were part of an experiment, and they may have felt an inclination to see the innovative materials become successful. However, the teachers did not know whether the guided or unguided materials were supposed to be more effective. Therefore, unless the teachers developed more subtle expectancies (and we don't know whether this happened), the threat of expectancy was probably minimal. (It may have been a good idea as part of the qualitative description to interview the teachers and thereby ascertain the degree to which expectancy was a problem.) In addition to expectancy among the teachers, it is also possible that the students themselves could develop expectancies that would interfere with the internal validity of the study.

j. Social-psychological threats could present a problem. For example, we do not know the extent to which the nonsimulation students or teachers decided to work harder to compensate for their lack of innovative materials. The researchers appear not to have examined this possibility. (They could have included it as a qualitative description of the research setting.) However, social-psychological problems would not be likely to account for the differences between the guided and unguided students, and these differences represented the major finding of the study.

2. The best way to enhance the overall internal validity of the study would be to have more qualitative information to supplement the quantitative data. For example, qualitative interviews with the students and teachers or observations of them would help us assess whether expectancy or social-psychological threats were likely to be problems.

EXPERIMENTAL DESIGN: CONTROLLING THE THREATS TO INTERNAL VALIDITY

■ **WHERE WE'VE BEEN**

We have begun our discussion of Level II research, which examines cause-and-effect relationships. In chapter 10, we discussed the major threats to internal validity—factors that interfere with causal inferences regarding whether a treatment produced an outcome.

■ **WHERE WE'RE GOING NOW**

This chapter continues our treatment of Level II research. Here we will discuss experimental research design, which is the most important strategy for controlling the major threats to internal validity. This chapter will examine the principles behind random assignment of subjects and will demonstrate how this strategy can increase our confidence that outcomes of experiments are produced by the treatment rather than by extraneous factors.

■ **CHAPTER PREVIEW**

Chapter 10 introduced the concept of internal validity and identified the major threats to it. The present chapter introduces the basic strategies for minimizing these threats through the careful scheduling of treatments and observations of the persons to whom the treatments are administered. These strategies are called *experimental design*.

This chapter introduces the ideal strategies for dealing with threats and identifies ways to put such strategies into practice. Chapter 12 will introduce ways to modify and adapt these strategies to provide as much control of the threats as possible in situations where it is impossible to attain the high degree of control described in the present chapter.

After reading this chapter, you should be able to

1. Define *experimental design* and identify its purpose.

2. Define and give examples of the important terms used in discussing experimental design.

3. Describe the basic strategy of experimental design and apply it to concrete situations.

4. Define and give examples of random assignment of subjects to experimental and control or comparison group treatments.

5. Describe how to apply random assignment of participants in a concrete experimental situation.

6. Describe the underlying theory regarding how random allocation or assignment overcomes some of the major threats to internal validity.

7. Describe the problems in the use of matching and its relationship to random assignment.

8. Describe strategies for controlling internal validity threats that are not controlled by random assignment of subjects to experimental and control groups.

9. Describe the strategy of two true experimental designs and apply these designs to concrete research settings.

■

EXPERIMENTAL DESIGN

Experimental design refers to the systematic scheduling of the times when treatments are administered to subjects and data are collected about the performance of the subjects. This careful scheduling of the treatments and observations can be helpful in reducing the threats to internal validity that were discussed in the previous chapter. *Experimental design is not a replacement for careful data collection, analysis, and reasoning.* It is rather an important component of the overall research process of establishing cause-and-effect relationships. By combining careful experimental design with appropriate data collection, analysis, and reasoning, we can strengthen the validity of the conclusions we draw from our research efforts.

To overcome the threats to internal validity, we can reason carefully about what happened in our treatment, use a well-planned experimental design, or do both. The two strategies are not mutually exclusive; a good experimental design makes reasoning easier. Many educators by necessity have no alternative but to accept whatever data they can obtain—and a good experimental design is not always available. Under such circumstances, carefully thinking about the threats to internal validity and weighing their impact upon the conclusions under consideration is a valid and important endeavor. Teachers and other professionals may have to do much of their thinking and decision making without the benefit of a good experimental design.

Nevertheless, in this and the next chapter, priority will be given to discussing effective experimental design. This is because correct experimental design is by far the best course of action and easiest to interpret, and you should always come as close as possible to using a good experimental design to support your conclusions; also, the alternative routes are often really "patched up" techniques to improvise a poor experimental design when a good one is not available. An understanding of the principles of experimental design will sharpen your ability to deal with the threats to internal validity in order to strengthen your conclusions.

THE BASIC STRATEGY OF EXPERIMENTAL DESIGN

In theory, the most straightforward strategy for ascertaining cause-and-effect relationships is extremely simple. This basic strategy of experimental design can be summarized as follows:

Compare the performance of the group receiving the treatment with the performance of another group that is *exactly* the same in all respects except that this second group has not received the treatment.

If the group that received the treatment subsequently performs differently with regard to a set of specified outcomes than the group that

| BOX 11.1 | Important Terms Used in Discussing Research Design |

When discussing research design, it is useful to understand some basic terms. The definitions of many of these terms are probably self-evident to many readers, but it seems appropriate to state these definitions at this time.

An *experiment* refers to an attempt to establish a cause-and-effect relationship by some strategy such as administering a treatment to one group and withholding it from another. In a very strict sense, the term is used only when there is *manipulation* of the subjects, as when one set of subjects receives a treatment and another set does not receive that treatment. In a looser but still adequate sense, the term refers to situations where there is an attempt to establish cause-and-effect relationships even when there is no manipulation of subjects, conditions, or treatments by the researcher. For example, it might be suggested that the condition of gender of the subjects in a study may cause certain attitudes, even if boys and girls cannot be assigned to the boy and girl designations.

A *subject* is a person who takes part in an experiment. Subjects can also be referred to as *participants*. The subject receives the treatment. (Subjects in the control group have the treatment withheld, or they receive a standard treatment or condition.) In educational research, subjects are usually students, teachers, or administrators, but in certain cases, something other than a person (a school system or textbook, for instance) can be the subject of an experiment.

A *treatment* is an event, a condition, or an activity that is expected to produce an outcome. The term *condition* is sometimes used as a synonym for this term. Reading programs, cooperative learning environments, and the practice of keeping children after school for detention are examples of treatments. (In chapter 2, treatments or conditions were referred to as *independent variables*.)

An *observation* is the act of collecting data about the performance of a subject. The term covers all types of data collection procedures, not just those accomplished through visual observation. Observations conducted prior to a treatment are called *pretests;* observations conducted after the treatment has been administered are called *posttests.*

The *experimental group* is the group of subjects that receives the treatment.

The *control group* is the group of subjects from whom the treatment is withheld or who receive the usual, standard treatment and conditions and whose performance is compared with that of the experimental group. A related term is *comparison group;* the two terms are often used interchangeably. The distinction, when there is one, is that the control group receives no treatment, whereas a comparison group receives an alternative treatment.

Let us summarize these terms with an example. If a teacher wants to determine whether a new reading program is effective, she can do this by setting up an *experiment*. She would *manipulate* the *subjects* by randomly assigning half to the *experimental group* and half to the *control group*. She would conduct *pretest* and *posttest observations* and make comparisons afterwards to see whether the *treatment* caused the improvements among those who received it.

Additional terms (such as *random assignment* and *quasi-experiment*) will be defined later in this chapter and in further chapters as the need for them arises.

received no treatment (or a standard treatment), then the best inference is that this effect must have been caused by the experimental treatment.

On the other hand, if the group that received the treatment still performs the same as the group that did not receive the treatment, then the treatment must have made no difference.

This basic strategy of experimental design is diagrammed in Figure 11.1. If this design could readily be implemented, it would be easy to conduct experimental research in education. The problem is that it is actually difficult (usually impossible) to put this "simple" theory into practice with absolute precision. This difficulty arises from the two great problems in educational experiments:

It is not possible to find two groups that are initially exactly identical in all respects except with regard to the experimental treatment.

Because educational data collection cannot be perfectly reliable or perfectly valid, it is often difficult to tell whether the two groups actually differ after a treatment.

In many of the "hard" sciences, such as chemistry and physics, the preceding problems do not seriously interfere with drawing cause-and-effect inferences. This is because in such sciences it is known that some materials are exceptionally stable over time (and thus no control group is needed), and it is actually possible to find perfectly standardized materials and make extremely precise measurements in comparison with

those in sociology, psychology, and education. Educational research, however, does have to deal with these problems. The problem of finding equal groups—or of accommodating to their absence—will be dealt with in this chapter and in chapter 12. The problem of dealing with unreliab data collection strategies has already been discussed in chapter 5 and will be discussed further in chapter 14.

HOW TO FIND EQUAL GROUPS

Assume that you want to know whether a new method for teaching reading to fifth graders is really better than your traditional method. According to the basic strategy of experimental design, you should use the new method with one group while you simultaneously use the traditional method with another group that is initially identical to the experimental group. How would you go about finding two groups that are exactly identical? The answer is that you cannot—it's impossible. So, how could you go about finding two groups that are as nearly identical as possible? Which of the following procedures would be the best to follow?

Examine all 45 fifth-grade classes in the school system and find two that are closest to each other with regard to average age and IQ. (You would choose age and IQ because these factors are likely to be related to reading ability.) Then give the new reading treatment to one of these classes and the traditional method to the other.

Figure 11.1
The Basic Strategy
of Experimental
Design

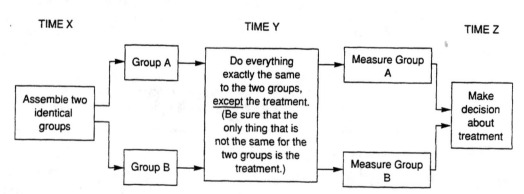

Find two fifth grades within one school with 30 students in each class. Compute the average IQ and age of each. Then eliminate 5 students from each class so that the two classes are as nearly equal as possible with regard to IQ and age. Then give the new reading treatment to one of these classes and the traditional method to the other.

Find a school with two fifth-grade classes within the same building. Simply give one of these classes the new program and the other the old program.

Find a school that is going to assign its fifth graders to two separate classes. Have the students assigned to these classes completely at random (without reference to age, IQ, or any other factor). Then choose one of these groups at random and have it use the new program. Have the other class use the traditional program.

Which of these would be the best strategy? The answer is the last one, because this strategy relies completely upon random assignment. Nothing other than chance influences the choice of persons for the treatment. In the other cases, some factor(s) other than chance went into the formation of the groups, and therefore the groups are likely to be biased in ways related to their ability to profit from the program.

One of the most important realizations in the history of social science research has been that random assignment is the most powerful way to make it likely that two or more groups are initially equivalent. Therefore, comparisons that are based on random assignment are the most powerful comparisons, and random assignment is by far the preferred and most powerful strategy for examining cause-and-effect relationships.

HOW RANDOM ASSIGNMENT WORKS

If we wanted to divide a class of 50 graduate students randomly into two groups, how could we accomplish this?

Should we get to the classroom before anyone arrived, and then count the first 25 who happen to come into the room, placing them in one group and the remaining 25 in the other group?

Should we wait until all 50 were in the room and then count 25 from the front of the room, putting these in one group and the other 25 in the other group?

Should we take the class list and put the first 25 in alphabetical order into one group and the remaining 25 in the other group?

The answer is that **none of the above** is an example of random assignment, and none is likely to produce equated groups. In the first case, it seems obvious that those who arrive early for a class probably possess certain characteristics that make them different from those who arrive later. Even if we waited until everyone was in the room (the second case), there is a reasonable chance that friends will sit together, that everyone who comes early goes to the back of the room, or that some other unknown factors will cause the groups to be different. In the case of using the alphabetical list, the biasing factors are perhaps more subtle, but is it not possible (for example) that persons close together in the alphabet might become friends and that friends might be more alike? Indeed, names that are adjacent in the alphabet are more likely to belong to husbands and wives or to mothers and daughters than are names separated in the alphabet.

In its logic, random assignment is similar to random sampling, which was discussed in chapter 8. In the nonrandomized examples cited in the previous paragraph, we don't *know* that biases exist. However, without random assignment, we cannot rule them out. With random assignment, we can state the *probability* that the groups are initially comparable. Random assignment is a strategy whereby chance alone determines whether subjects will be placed in an experimental or a control condition. It minimizes the chance that biases will occur in the selection of groups. The only factor that determines group placement is chance alone, and chance can be logically and mathematically defined. In the class of graduate students, random assignment could be accomplished in several ways:

Take the list of 50 students and assign each student a number between 1 and 50. Then go to a list of random numbers and select 25 of them at random between 1 and 50. Put the students whose names correspond to these numbers into one group and the rest into the second group. Then flip a coin to decide which is the experimental group.

Take the list of 50 students and put the names on index cards. Shuffle the cards thoroughly and then deal them into two stacks. Make the cards on the left the members of your control group and those on the right members of your experimental group.

Match the students into pairs, based on important characteristics such as age, GRE scores, or previous course grades. Obtain 25 pairs in this way. Then flip a coin for each pair and assign the person who gets heads to the control group and the one who gets tails to the experimental group.

All three of these strategies would provide randomly assigned groups. Each is more likely to give equivalent groups with regard to all variables than the non-random strategies cited at the beginning of this section. The third strategy is an example of random assignment with matching. This strategy will be discussed later in this chapter, but it should be pointed out here that either of the first two is almost always just as effective as the third, and quite a bit simpler.

Because there are strong similarities in strategies, many readers have trouble telling the difference between random assignment and random sampling, which was discussed in chapter 8. Table 11.1 summarizes the differences. The major difference lies in their purpose. Random assignment is designed to form two (or more) groups that are likely to be initially similar; random sampling, on the other hand, is designed to select a small group from a larger population and use data collected from this small group to make estimates about characteristics of the population from which the sample was drawn.

HOW TO USE A TABLE OF RANDOM NUMBERS

A table of random numbers (see Appendix B) is a list of numbers arranged in random order—in other

Table 11.1   The Differences between Random Assignment and Random Sampling

	Random Assignment	Random Sampling
Purpose	To create two groups that are initially as equal as possible, except as they happen to differ by chance	To create a small group that can be investigated, so that inferences can be drawn about a larger group
When it occurs	After subjects have been selected for an experiment, when some of them are assigned to an experimental group and some to a control group	Usually before a survey is conducted
Outcome	Two groups that are initially as equal as possible, except as they happen to differ by chance	A smaller group that is similar to a larger group (the population), except as it happens to differ by chance
Relative size of resulting groups	Usually (but not necessarily) two groups of equal size	The sample is much smaller than the population
Chapter in textbook	11	8
Relationship to validity	Internal validity (cause-and-effect relationships)	External validity (how far results can be generalized)

words, with no perceptible order or pattern. By using this list to select a sample for a survey (see chapter 8) or assign members to experimental and control groups, we can be sure we are doing so with no bias influencing our selection or assignment.

There are actually many ways we could use such a list. All we have to do is be sure we do not accidentally introduce some sort of bias into our selection of subjects. The following paragraph will describe one of the methods for using the table of random numbers found in Appendix B to assign subjects to experimental and control groups.

Assume that we have 60 people whom we wish to assign to two groups, an experimental and a control group. First we would list all 60 names and assign the numbers 1 through 60 to them. (At this point, it does not matter how systematically or unsystematically the names are arranged. It would probably be best to arrange them systematically—perhaps alphabetically—for purposes of proofreading, but this decision is unrelated to random assignment.) Next, we would turn to the table of random numbers and choose a number at a point determined by chance. (A blind pointing will do.) We would then read in a direction determined in advance—up, down, right, left, or diagonally. For example, such a chance entry into the table of random numbers might give us a starting point of the 31st number down in the third row. In our table in Appendix B, this number is 72. Since 72 is greater than 60, we ignore it (because no person in this group has a number greater than 60). Next we might go horizontally to the right across the page, selecting any number that falls between 1 and 60 (the decision to follow this pattern would be made in advance, before determining the starting number). The next number in the table is 85, which is still too high. Next comes 22, which falls within our range of 1 through 60, and so we select that person for Group A. We would continue across the page, putting persons 38, 56, 01, and 30 into Group A. When we reached the end of the line, we would continue down to the left on the next line in the table—unless we had made a decision to follow some other pattern. If we came to a number we had already selected, we would skip that number.

Eventually, we would select 30 subjects for Group A. We would then put the remaining 30 persons in Group B. Finally, we would flip a coin to decide which group would get the treatment and which would be the control group.

The preceding method would result in a random assignment of subjects to groups. Of course, if we wanted three groups instead of two, or if we had 150 subjects to put into two groups, we would have to vary the process somewhat to accommodate. The important thing is to let no biasing factor enter our random assignment process.

An example of biased use of the table would be to have students sign a list as they arrived, then assign numbers based on order of arrival, and finally select a random number from the table, putting the first 30 names after that number into the experimental treatment. This would be a biased method because subjects would be clustered together on the list in a nonrandom fashion. Likewise, if a teacher assigned subjects to groups at random and then decided to give the treatment to Group B after examining the lists of names because he felt this group would be more cooperative, this choice of Group B would be nonrandom and would jeopardize the authenticity of the experiment.

The availability of computers has made it even easier to select random samples and assign subjects to groups at random. For example, a BASIC program like the following would generate a list of 30 random numbers ranging from 1 to 500, which could be used to select 30 names at random from a list of 500 names:

```
100 FOR I = 1 TO 30
110 LET X = RND(500)
120 PRINT X
130 NEXT I
```

It is important to note, however, that different computers have varying eccentricities with regard to the random number selector; if you don't check your manual, you may accidentally inject patterns into your "random" process. For example, with the Apple II series of computers, it is necessary to initialize the random number generator before selecting random numbers. Without the first two lines below, the computer would select the same 30 random numbers every time you turned on the computer and immediately try to generate a list of random numbers:

```
 90 LET Y = PEEK(78) + 256 * PEEK(79):
        X = RND(-Y)
100 FOR I = 1 TO 30
110 LET X = INT(RND(1) * 500 + 1)
120 PRINT X
130 NEXT I
```

More sophisticated programs (or prewritten application software) will not only generate lists of random numbers but also print a list of names selected at random.

WHY RANDOM ASSIGNMENT WORKS

Random assignment is based on principles of probability. Simply summarized, these principles state that when subjects have been assigned to groups at random, *the groups are likely to differ with regard to any and all characteristics only to the extent that they would be expected to differ by chance, both now and in the future.* This is slightly different from saying that they are likely to be equal, but it's close. The groups will, in fact, be slightly different from one another, and if we assigned them again at random, we would get slightly different variations. However, when chance is the only factor operating, it is possible to state statistically the degree of confidence that these differences will fall within a certain range. Once we know this range of probability, then we can examine data after a treatment to determine whether our results fall inside or outside this range. By doing this, we can make a conclusion about how likely it is that our treatment caused the outcome. To the extent that some factor other than chance influenced the composition of the groups, this line of reasoning would be invalid. (Confidence intervals are the basis behind statistical tests of significance, which will be discussed in chapter 14.)

The preceding paragraph is a brief but accurate statement of the theory behind random assignment. Since it involves mathematical assumptions and implies statistical analysis, it may seem incomprehensible to many readers at this point. This is not because educators lack mathematical aptitude but rather because many of us have developed conditioned reflexes that cause us to turn off any ideas involving mathematics or statistics. With this in mind, we would recommend that you reexamine the preceding paragraph if either now or later you have a further desire to understand the underlying logic behind random assignment of subjects to groups. If you do not have such an urge, read on.

To take a concrete example, assume that we have two really bright students among our 50 graduate students about to be assigned to an experimental and a control group. If we use any one of the three methods described on page 254 to assign these students to experimental and control groups, there is a pretty good chance that they will both wind up in the same group. This is because of biases such as those mentioned earlier. On the other hand, if we assign them at random (through one of the strategies described on page 256), there is a 50–50 chance that each one will be in the experimental group and a 50–50 chance that each will be in the control group. There is still a reasonable chance (50–50) that both will wind up in the same group. A major difference between the random and the nonrandom procedure is that in the case of random assignment *we know what the probability is* that both will be in the same group (it's a 50% probability), whereas in the nonrandom case we don't know this probability.

The larger the group becomes, the more likely it is that random assignment will minimize chance biases with regard to any characteristic. For example, assume that we have 6 exceptionally able mathematics students in a class of 300. If we used any of the biased (nonrandom) strategies mentioned earlier to put them in experimental and control groups, there would still be a good chance that subtle biases would result in the majority being in the same group. On the other hand, the odds are much more remote that all 6 of them would be in the same group if we had used random assignment. Again, a statistician could state the precise odds against getting all 6 in one group to be 1 in 64.

Random assignment has the advantage of statistically equating *all* characteristics of people, even if we do not know what all these characteristics are. For example, it might not even occur to us that there are in our graduate class six students who are excessively shy and prone to avoid novel teaching techniques and who sit together near the back of the room. If we used one of the biased methods described earlier, we might inadvertently put most or all of these students in one group. We might then look at our groups and notice that they both were similar with regard to age and previous test scores, and this might convince us that the groups were equal. Unbeknownst to us, the groups would differ with regard to an important variable related to the outcome of our experiment. On the other hand, if we used random assignment, these six shy students would have a good chance of being evenly distributed—even though we would not be aware of this characteristic at the time of random assignment (or at any other time, for that matter).

The larger the groups become, the less likely it is that discrepant characteristics will arise in randomly assigned groups. The logic is precisely the same as in coin tossing. If a friend tosses a coin twice and gets heads both times, you are not going to accuse him of cheating. But if he tosses the coin 15 times and gets 15 heads, then you are going to be suspicious. This is because you would intuitively know that 15 in a row is improbable. In the same way, as randomly assigned groups become larger, we can make more precise statements about how likely it is that two groups will be about the same with regard to *all* variables, both known and unknown, both now and at any time in the future, unless something intervenes to make the groups differ. The larger the groups become, the less likely it is that randomly assigned groups will differ substantially with regard to any specified characteristic.

Random assignment sounds mysterious—even eerie—to some readers. But it works, and it is an enormously powerful and valuable research method. It is based on perfectly sound mathematical theory. An experimental study employing random assignment gives a much more solid basis for drawing conclusions than much larger studies employing biased assignment to treatments. Through careful planning, it is frequently possible to use random assignment in education. In fact, random assignment can often be

reasonably parallel to ordinary means of assigning students to classes, and by combining random assignment with educational treatment of students, it is possible to derive useful research information from ordinary educational activities. This often requires the foresight to seek cooperation from the person who assigns students to classes. Whenever possible, use random assignment in your experiments.

THE EFFECTIVENESS OF RANDOM ASSIGNMENT

The purpose of random assignment is to make groups initially as equal as possible with regard to all variables, and this equivalence will persist into the future until something causes it to change. As Figure 11.1 has indicated, if a treatment is administered to one randomly assigned group while a second randomly assigned group receives no treatment, then any differences in the two groups that appear on subsequent data collections are the result of either chance, one or more of the other threats to internal validity discussed in the preceding chapter, or the treatment. The probable impact of chance can be estimated through statistical procedures and can often be ruled out as a plausible explanation (ways to do this are discussed in chapter 14). Likewise, the threats to internal validity can be controlled by strategies discussed in this and the next chapters. When chance and the other threats to internal validity are ruled out, the treatment remains by far the most plausible explanation for the observed differences.

Essential to integrating the previous chapter with the present chapter is the idea that random assignment makes the groups initially as equal as possible with regard to each of the threats to internal validity. Selection bias is removed as a threat, because random assignment systematically controls this factor. In addition, subjects in one group are likely to be initially comparable with those in the other group with regard to their past histories, their tendencies to mature during the experiment, and their reactions to pretests and data collection instruments. Both groups are equally likely to regress to the mean, if regression is a consideration. The initial proclivities of the subjects in the two groups to drop out of the experiment, to display unstable test results, or to develop attitudes of expectancy are also likely to be similar.

Although random assignment thus minimizes most of the threats to internal validity, some threats still remain. Experimental mortality, social-psychological threats, and expectancy are problems that arise after the start of the treatment, and therefore they cannot be controlled simply by making the groups initially equivalent. Furthermore, even though random assignment makes it likely that the subjects in both groups will be comparable with regard to past, present, and future history *outside* the experiment, this does not rule out the possibility that the social context (history) could differ *within* the experiment. For example, if one group in an experiment meets before lunch and the other after lunch, this could produce aspects of history not controlled by random assignment.

By making the groups as equal as possible in their susceptibility to the threats to internal validity, therefore, random assignment emerges as a highly effective tool for strengthening the internal validity of our cause-and-effect inferences. It is also among the simplest tools to implement and interpret. Although random assignment is not perfect in its control of these extraneous factors, it is by far the best single strategy available for group research. Supplemented by additional careful procedures and qualitative descriptions of contexts and circumstances, random assignment lends major strength to our ability to draw cause-and-effect inferences from experimental research.

MATCHING AND RANDOM ASSIGNMENT

Sometimes you may have to deal with intact groups—groups over which you have no control regarding who gets or does not get the experimental treatment (i.e., they are already formed at the beginning of an experiment). Under such circumstances, some novice researchers resort to a process called *matching* in order to artificially acquire two groups to use in the experiment. As intuitively appealing as this procedure may be, this is an *absolutely wrong* way to proceed. This erroneous process is described here only to help you avoid it. See if you can understand the reasons

why this is an improper method for assembling experimental and control groups. (Hint: the mistake has to do with statistical regression.)

Assume that a high school basketball coach wants to try a new method to teach his players how to shoot free throws. He decides to use his varsity players for the experimental group and his junior varsity players as the control group. He checks out his statistics and discovers that his 12 varsity players have averaged 80% from the foul line this year, whereas the 12 junior varsity players have averaged only 60%. The groups clearly are not equal. So he decides to *create* two equal groups by taking 5 of the worst varsity players and matching them up with 5 of the best junior varsity players so that the two groups have seemingly identical free throw percentages. The coach therefore has an experimental group of 5 varsity players with a free throw average of 70% and a control group of 5 junior varsity players with a free throw average of 70% (see Figure 11.2). The groups seem exactly equal, but are they?

The problem that the coach has ignored is that of statistical regression. As you may recall from chapter 10, statistical regression refers to the tendency of the

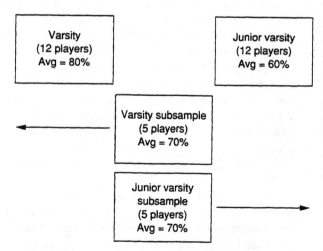

Figure 11.2 An Example of Regression Toward the Mean Resulting from Matching. Each of the subsamples will regress toward the mean of the group from which it was originally selected. The arrows indicate the direction of this statistical regression.

scores of extreme subgroups to regress on subsequent testing occasions toward the mean of the group from which they were taken. In the present example, the coach has two extreme subgroups, as shown in Figure 11.2. To get his 70% shooters from the varsity, he had to select 5 of the players with the lowest averages on that squad. When retested (that is, after they have shot some more free throws), these extreme low scorers are likely to score closer to the mean of their original group—closer to 80%. Likewise, to get his group of 70% shooters from the junior varsity, the coach had to select 5 of the best shooters on that squad. When retested, these extreme high scorers will score closer to the mean of their original group—in this case, closer to 60%. Even if the coach's treatment is worthless, it will look good because his experimental group will regress up and his control group will regress down. In his attempt to obtain two identical groups, the coach has in fact taken steps to guarantee that the groups are actually *unequal!*

Matching is a valid strategy only when it can be followed by random assignment to groups. For example, if the coach in the previous example took his 12 varsity players and matched them in pairs based on nearly equal scores, he could have *then* assigned one member of each pair to the experimental and the other to the control group. Such matching *followed by random assignment* is a perfectly valid strategy, since it involves no bias or problems of interpreting regression. It is not an especially useful strategy, however, since the resulting groups are seldom superior for research purposes to groups assembled with simple random sampling without matching. There are only a few instances when the matching plus random assignment procedure is preferred. For example, if you expect experimental mortality during an experiment, then matching plus random assignment can help you decide which subjects to delete from posttest analysis to possibly overcome the threat to internal validity. (This problem is discussed in the next section of the chapter.) In addition, if you have subjects with widely varying scores in a situation where it is obviously undesirable to have a disproportionate number of these discrepant scorers in a single group, then matching plus random assignment

would be preferable to simple random assignment. This would most often be the case when only a few subjects are available for a study and some of them have unusual scores.

The preceding discussion may be viewed as unnecessarily technical by some readers. If this is the case for you, then just remember the following simple rule. *Never match from intact groups. If you do match, always follow the matching with random assignment to groups.* Or, as the Bard says:

Don't tug on Superman's cape.
Don't spit into the wind.
And never match from intact groups without subsequent random assignment to treatment groups.

SOME THREATS NOT CONTROLLED BY RANDOM ASSIGNMENT

The previous section indicated that random assignment helps assemble two groups that are likely to be as equal as possible with regard to the following threats to internal validity: selection bias, maturation, some aspects of history, pretesting, statistical regression, most aspects of instrumentation, and the interaction of any of these variables. However, some threats are completely or partially beyond the control of random assignment. Random assignment does nothing to control factors that arise *after* the groups have been assembled. For example, experimental mortality, expectancy, and social-psychological effects are not at all controlled by random assignment. In addition, while random assignment is a basis for ultimate testing for instability, further steps help control that threat. Finally, there are "local" aspects of history and instrumentation that random assignment cannot control (the use of the term *local* will be explained later in the chapter).

None of the experimental designs discussed in this chapter or the next controls the threats to internal validity described at the end of the preceding paragraph. These threats have to be controlled through methods other than simple experimental design. The following paragraphs will briefly describe methods for controlling these threats. As you read about the experimental designs in this chapter and the next, remember that *experimental design alone cannot overcome all the threats to internal validity.* The additional steps described in this section, plus careful thought, are also necessary.

Experimental Mortality

Experimental mortality refers to the fact that measures of group performance might change because self-selected subjects drop out of the group rather than because the members of the group have actually altered their performance. The most certain way to rule out the threat of experimental mortality is to have no dropouts. Complete participation on pretest and posttest data collections is often possible, and researchers might strive for this goal. If there is likely to be a problem with dropouts, then it is a good idea to try for 100% posttest performance from a small group of subjects rather than a lower percentage of posttest participation from an initially larger group of subjects.

If subjects do drop out of your experiment (and sometimes this is inevitable), there are a few steps you can take. First, you can compare the pretest scores (if you have them) of the subjects who dropped out with the pretest scores of those who remained in the experiment. If the scores are approximately the same, then it is likely that the dropouts have not biased your study. (However, this is a statement of probability, not certainty. Since the dropping out is a nonrandom process, you will encounter subtle problems similar to the interaction of selection bias with other factors, discussed in chapters 10 and 15. This complex issue will not be discussed further in this book.)

Second, you can examine the *reasons why* subjects dropped out. Interview them, if possible. If they dropped out because of reasons completely unrelated to the treatment or the outcome variable, then your problems are minimal. On the other hand, if there appears to be a connection between the decision to drop out and either the treatment or the outcome variable, then this is a threat to your internal validity. Finally, if you assigned subjects to groups by random assignment after matching them into pairs, then

you can exclude from the posttest analysis the subject who was matched with the person who dropped out. This is an imperfect, partial solution, but, when available, it is better than the other methods.

The strategies described in the preceding paragraphs *help* control the threat of experimental mortality. The only perfect way to control this threat, however, is to have no dropouts.

Expectancy Effects

Expectancy effects arise when subtle expectations of the experimenter or of the subjects influence the outcome of an experiment. Such effects occur most often when the experiment is an obviously artificial situation or when someone (such as the experimenter) has a vested interest in the success or failure of the experimental treatment. Expectancy effects influence external as well as internal validity; a detailed discussion of how to deal with them will be delayed until chapter 15. At this time, only the following important point will be made: In most cases, a true experimental design is preferable to a quasi-experimental design for controlling the threats to internal validity. The threat of invalidity arising from expectancy is often an exception to this rule. If the process of random assignment results in an artificial situation that is likely to arouse expectancy effects, then the true experiment is actually more likely to lead to this source of invalidity than a less obtrusive quasi-experimental design. In such cases the quasi-experimental design (which does not use random assignment) may be preferable. Such artificiality, however, is not an integral component of random assignment; it is possible in many cases to use true experimental designs that do not produce expectancy threats to internal validity.

Instability

Instability refers to the tendency of a result to appear on one experimental occasion but not on another. It occurs because of the innate lack of complete reliability of data collection strategies and the use of small groups. It is controlled by using reliable data collection techniques and large groups and by stating the probability of instability in statistical terms. The use and interpretation of these statistical procedures will be discussed in chapter 14.

Local Threats

The term *local threat* can be applied to events that happen to one group but not the other after experimental and control groups have been formed. For example, *local history* would be a threat if the experimental class watches a television show and the control group does not. A similar problem would occur with instrumentation if the teacher gives faulty test instructions to one class but correct instructions to the other. The ways to control these threats are to standardize events so that they are as similar as possible for both groups and to observe, interview, and check during and after the study to determine possible contextual, treatment, and perceptual effects on the participants in one or the other group.

THE TRUE EXPERIMENTS

A true experiment is one in which a clear-cut comparison is possible between an experimental group and a control group, both of which were initially considered to be equal with regard to all variables because of random assignment to experimental conditions. The term *true experiment* is used to distinguish such strategies from *quasi-experiments,* which

do not have randomly assigned groups but compensate for this weakness through various strategies, to be discussed in the next chapter.

The *posttest-only control group design* is a true experimental design. (Remember that the term *test* is really shorthand for any data collection method—usually a set consisting of more than one method—rather than a test in a narrow, academic sense.) This design can be diagrammed as follows:

$$R \quad X \quad O_1$$
$$R \qquad \quad O_2$$

In this design, the members from one original pool of subjects are assigned at random to an experimental and a control group. This random assignment is accomplished according to the guidelines discussed earlier in this chapter. The strengths and weaknesses of random assignment discussed in the section entitled "The Effectiveness of Random Assignment" accompany this design.

Similar to the previous design is the *pretest-posttest control group design,* which is diagrammed as follows:

$$R \quad O_1 \quad X \quad O_2$$
$$R \quad O_3 \qquad \quad O_4$$

BOX 11.2	The Symbols Used in Diagrams of Experimental Designs

R at the beginning of a line indicates that the subjects described on that line were randomly assigned to the indicated treatment.

X stands for the administration of the treatment.

O stands for an observation or measurement of the subjects in the designated treatment.

Subscripts, such as O_1 and O_2, simply differentiate among various observations. For example, O_1 might refer to the pretest and O_2 to the posttest.

Additional symbols will be described in the next chapter.

The only difference between this and the previous design is that this one includes a pretest for both groups. The presence of the pretest makes this design differ from the preceding design in the following ways: (1) pretesting consumes additional time and effort on the part of the experimenter; (2) it might make the experimental situation more obtrusive and arouse expectancy effects; (3) it can provide a check to verify whether the groups were really equal regarding the outcome variable—a check that is usually unnecessary except in the case of small numbers of subjects; (4) it creates the possibility that the observed differences in scores might actually be the result of a combination (interaction) of the treatment and the pretest—in other words, the treatment might work only after a pretest; (5) it enables the researcher to measure *gains* rather than merely differences among posttest scores; and (6) if subjects drop out of the experiment, it enables the researcher to ascertain whether the dropouts were initially similar to those who remained in the experiment.

None of these factors is strong enough to warrant a blanket recommendation that one strategy be preferred to the other. Many novice researchers have a tendency to use pretests unnecessarily in randomized designs, simply because they do not *believe* that random assignment really works. This is not a good reason to use the pretests. On the other hand, the major weaknesses of the second design occur because pretests take time and are obtrusive. If data collection can be efficiently and unobtrusively done (see chapter 6), then these disadvantages vanish. Of course, if pretest data already exist (as in the case of yearly schoolwide testing), they can be incorporated into the experimental design.

A major advantage of true experimental designs is that the results are extremely easy to interpret. In Figure 11.3, diagrams A and B present the results for an experimental and a control group who have received a treatment and then had their performance measured in some way afterwards (posttest-only control group design). The results presented in diagram A indicate that the treatment did, in fact, make a difference, since the experimental group has scored

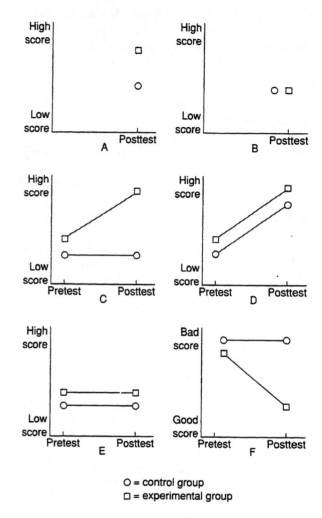

Figure 11.3 Sample Outcomes for the Posttest-Only Control Design and the Pretest-Posttest Control Group Design

higher than the control group.[1] On the other hand, the results in diagram B indicate that the treatment did not cause an observable difference, since the scores are approximately equal.

---

[1]The problem of whether such differences are big enough to be significant will be discussed in chapter 14.

Likewise, the results for the pretest-posttest control group design (diagrams C through E) are easy to interpret. Diagram C indicates that the treatment probably caused a difference, since the two groups started out the same and became different. Diagrams D and E, on the other hand, indicate no causal effect, since the two groups were approximately the same both before and after the experimental treatment. Because of the random assignment to treatments, these results are straightforward and easy to interpret. In the next chapter, you will discover that some of the other designs present considerably more ambiguous results for interpretation.

Diagram F is included in Figure 11.3 to clarify a point that often confuses readers who are looking at this sort of diagram for the first time. Many novice researchers think that diagram F indicates that the treatment has failed, since the experimental group has scored lower than the control group. This is not the case; in this diagram a low score is considered good, and therefore a low score is a sign of success. For example, if a treatment were undertaken to reduce rude behavior among high school freshmen, the results in diagram F would indicate that the treatment had been successful, since instances of rude behavior decreased after the treatment. It is important, therefore, to understand what such diagrams mean before attempting to interpret them.

True experiments present powerful designs. Carefully applied in conjunction with other appropriate procedures, they can control many of the major threats to internal validity. Whenever they are plausible and logistically possible, they are simple to initiate and easy to interpret. They should be used whenever appropriate and possible. They should be supplemented by qualitative data of many types and by quasi-experimental designs to further reduce threats to internal validity, to verify and expand the findings, and to generate hypotheses for further research.

WHEN NOT TO USE TRUE EXPERIMENTS

Even though random assignment is highly desirable, there are five good reasons why random assignment to groups might be undesirable:

The resulting groups may be absurdly small (e.g., one or two persons to a group) or impossibly small (e.g., one-half person to a group).

The logistics of the situation may prohibit altering the group structure in a way that would permit random assignment.

Your goal may be to examine individual, not group, performance.

It is impossible to assign people at random to some conditions (e.g., people cannot be randomly assigned to gender, people cannot have IQs randomly assigned to them, etc.).

Random assignment may produce a highly artificial situation, which would produce expectancy effects or lessen the degree to which the research can be generalized. (This refers to external validity, which is discussed in chapter 15.)

In such cases, your goal is to accomplish the same thing that random assignment accomplishes by using other strategies. Since these other strategies are almost always less effective than random assignment, this usually means that you will have to do the best you can, be aware of your weaknesses, and interpret your results in terms of these weaknesses, if possible.

REVIEW QUESTIONS

Throughout most of the chapters in this book, there have been review questions after short segments of presentation. The idea has been to let you read a segment and then test yourself to make sure you have understood that portion before proceeding to the next section. Such questions have been omitted from the present chapter (and several others), not because such self-review is unnecessary but rather because the type of questions needed to review the material requires a considerable amount of stage setting. Thus, they would become long questions, resulting in a highly disjointed presentation.

Review questions regarding the information in this chapter are available in the workbook accompanying the text; it would be to your advantage to examine these questions before proceeding to the next chapter.

PUTTING IT ALL TOGETHER

Mr. Anderson had been seriously disheartened to discover that his first attempt at researching the effectiveness of the Animal Life Program (ALP) had been seriously weakened by major threats to internal validity (see chapter 10). He resolved to try again and to do his research right this time.

As luck would have it, he came across another copy of this textbook. He was at a professional basketball game, and he noticed that an elderly lady sitting next to him was reading the book during lulls in the action. He asked to borrow the book, and during the first and second overtimes he eagerly devoured the chapter "Experimental Design: Controlling the Threats to Internal Validity."

Armed with the information from this chapter, he set forth to apply the basic strategy of experimental design. His determination withered into discouragement, however, as colleague after colleague informed him that the classes in their schools were not established through pure random assignment. A well-meaning principal said that there were two fifth grades at her school, and it would probably meet with the board's approval for Mr. Anderson to select a matched group from each class and use one for the experimental and one for the control group. Mr. Anderson explained to this principal the problems of statistical regression that were likely to accompany such matching without subsequent random assignment to groups. The principal replied that she had known that all along and was merely testing him. Mr. Anderson was not sure he believed her.

On several occasions, teachers and principals offered to take intact classes and split the students into two groups at random. Then Mr. Anderson could take half of the students to a different room for the ALP and use the others for a control group. It would even be possible to give the control group some sort of placebo treatment. Mr. Anderson thought these offers over carefully, but in the end he decided not to accept them, because the resulting experimental situations would be too artificial. The ALP was designed to work in a regular classroom as a normal part of the classroom routine. To demonstrate that it caused improved attitudes in a highly artificial setting would be of no great benefit.

Although Mr. Anderson was saddened at his repeated failure to find a setting in which he could run a true experiment, at the same time he felt glad that he at least knew his limitations and had refrained from jumping to false conclusions. Indeed, he knew there were ways around his obstacles. At that fateful basketball game, just before the elderly lady smiled and snatched her book out of his hands as the winning basket swished through the hoop at the final buzzer, he had glanced at the title of the next chapter, "Experimental Design: What to Do When True Experiments Are Impossible." He knew that some day, somewhere, fate would lead him again to that priceless volume. How he envied those readers who could turn immediately to the next chapter and find out how to control the threats to internal validity when true experiments were impossible!

SUMMARY

The basic strategy of experimental design suggests that if we could find two groups that are exactly the same, then we could give one of them an experimental treatment while we withheld this treatment from the other. If the groups were then treated exactly the same in all respects except for the treatment, any differences on a posttest would have to be attributed to the experimental treatment. Therefore, if the experimental group differed from the control after the treatment, this would be strong evidence the treatment had caused the impact.

The problem is that it is impossible to find groups that are identical. The closest approximation to this ideal situation is brought about by random assignment, whereby the groups are expected to be equal with regard to all characteristics except as they happen to differ by chance. The larger the groups become, the less likely it is that chance will result in major differences with regard to any characteristics.

In addition, there are statistical methods for estimating the likelihood that chance is a major factor in an experiment based on random assignment. Therefore, experiments based on random assignment of subjects to treatment and control groups are most effective for controlling the major threats to internal validity. When such true experiments are carried out with additional proper concern for experimental mortality, expectancy effects, social-psychological effects, instability, and local threats, all the major threats to internal validity can be controlled.

Matching subjects to obtain equivalent experimental and control groups is an acceptable strategy only if the matching is followed by subsequent random assignment to treatment conditions. Otherwise, matching will inevitably lead to problems of statistical regression, which will pose a serious threat to internal validity.

True experiments should be used whenever they are feasible, possible, and appropriate, but in situations where they are inappropriate, other designs are possible. These other designs are the subject of the next chapter.

What Comes Next

Chapter 12 will describe strategies that help control the threats to internal validity when the true experimental designs described in the present chapter are impossible to implement. Chapters 13 and 14 will discuss statistical tools that help report relationships and estimate the likelihood that the results of experiments are not merely the result of chance fluctuations in data.

DOING YOUR OWN RESEARCH

Beginning researchers often believe that true experiments must be more difficult to perform than the quasi-experiments described in the next chapter. This is not necessarily true. There are many occasions when random assignment to treatment is easy to carry out, and in such cases it is likely to be the preferred experimental design for examining cause-and-effect relationships.

To conduct a true experiment, find a large group of subjects and follow the guidelines from this chapter to randomly assign them to experimental and control groups. Note that the pretest is not really necessary with the experimental group; it *will* be necessary with the untreated control group design described in the next chapter. After you have collected your data, use the statistical procedures described in chapter 14 to estimate the level of significance of your results.

FOR FURTHER THOUGHT

1. Some critics refer to experimental research as "horse race research." They suggest that researchers be concerned with more important things than holding contests between two groups and using statistics to establish the validity of their findings. How much validity is there in this criticism?

2. This chapter states that the pretest contributes very little when subjects have been randomly assigned to experimental and control conditions. Yet our experience shows that most people who conduct true experimental research include a pretest in their design. Why do they do this?

3. Complete this sentence by answering the designated questions: "Random assignment . . .(does what?) (To what or whom?) (When?) (Where?) (How?) (Why?)"

ANNOTATED BIBLIOGRAPHY

Agnew, N. M., & Pyke, S. W. (1987). *The science game: An introduction to research in the behavioral sciences* (4th ed.). Englewood Cliffs, NJ: Prentice-Hall. Chapter 8 presents an excellent discussion of experimental control from a novel perspective.

Anderson, B. F. (1971). *The psychology experiment* (2nd ed.). Belmont, CA: Brooks/Cole. Chapters 3 and 4 give a simple and straightforward description of how to conduct a psychological experiment.

Asher, J. W. (1976). *Educational research and evaluation methods*. Boston: Little, Brown and Company. Chapter 2 provides a good discussion of the underlying rationale behind experimental research in education.

Cook, T. D., & Campbell, D. T. (1979). *Quasi-Experimentation: Design and analysis issues for field settings*. Chicago: Rand McNally. The final chapter in this book provides a thorough discussion of the rationale behind true experimental research as well as useful strategies for actually carrying out randomized experiments in real-life settings.

Mitchell, M., & Jolley, J. (1992). *Research design explained* (2nd ed.). San Diego, CA: Harcourt Brace. This book is written for the psychology student rather than teachers, but its detailed treatment of many of the topics of research design will be interesting to many readers of the present text.

CHAPTER 11

Research Report Analysis

The study described in the report in Appendix C attempts to show that the guided use of computer simulations caused the students to develop problem-solving abilities to a greater extent than would have been possible with the traditional approach to teaching the same topics or with the unguided use of the same programs.

1. How does this study incorporate the basic logic of experimental research?

2. Which research design described in the current chapter does this study employ?

ANSWERS:

1. The basic logic of a true experiment states that the researcher should start with initially equal groups, handle them exactly the same except for the treatment, and then see whether they are still the same. In this case, the groups were not initially equal. The experimenters chose intact groups and then checked to see how close they were to being equal. This imperfect strategy flaws but does not destroy the basic logic of the quasi-experimental research in this study.

2. This study does not use any research design described in the current chapter. It uses a quasi-experimental design, which is described in chapter 12.

EXPERIMENTAL DESIGN: WHAT TO DO WHEN TRUE EXPERIMENTS ARE IMPOSSIBLE

■ **WHERE WE'VE BEEN**

We have examined the major threats to internal validity and have seen how experimental research design serves as the most important strategy for controlling these threats.

■ **WHERE WE'RE GOING NOW**

In this chapter we'll discuss strategies that help control the threats to internal validity when the true experimental designs described in chapter 11 are impossible to implement. The strategies described in this chapter do not use random assignment, but they employ careful scheduling of observations and treatments to rule out as many as possible of the threats to internal validity.

■ **CHAPTER PREVIEW**

The preceding chapter described useful procedures for controlling the major threats to internal validity as effectively as possible through a combination of random assignment and the appropriate scheduling of treatments and observations. Sometimes, however, such careful control of these threats is not possible. The present chapter deals with quasi-experimental procedures—research designs that do not use random assignment. Quasi-experimental procedures attempt to compensate for the weakness of not using random assignment through additional attention to careful scheduling of observations and treatments in such a way as to rule out many of the threats to internal validity.

After reading this chapter, you should be able to

1. Identify the major weaknesses of so-called nondesigns.
2. Define and give examples of quasi-experiments.

3. Describe the logic behind each of the following quasi-experimental designs:

> Untreated control group design with pretest and posttest
>
> Nonequivalent dependent variables design
>
> Repeated treatment design
>
> Interrupted time series design
>
> Cohort designs

4. Identify the major strengths and weaknesses of each of the preceding quasi-experimental designs.

5. Apply the preceding quasi-experimental designs to real-life settings.

6. Describe the differences among true experimental designs, quasi-experimental designs, and nondesigns with regard to their ability to control the threats to internal validity.

7. Describe strategies for combining several quasi-experimental designs to evaluate a single treatment.

■

THE NONDESIGNS

The true experiments described in the previous chapter represent the strongest contribution that experimental design can make to the process of ascertaining cause-and-effect relationships. The designs discussed in this section represent the weakest designs. They are so weak, in fact, that they are often ignominiously referred to as *nondesigns,* suggesting that they contribute little to the process of improving internal validity. True experiments require careful planning and occur relatively rarely in classroom research. Nondesigns, on the other hand, require little planning. Almost anyone can carry out a nondesign.

There are two reasons for discussing nondesigns at this point in the text. First, even though they have severe weaknesses, the nondesigns are not totally without merit. It is possible (but difficult) to draw valid inferences from some experiments employing nondesigns. Second, they provide a good basis for approaching the quasi-experimental designs discussed in the next section. In a true sense, quasi-experiments modify and improve the nondesigns in such a way as to make them come as close as possible to providing the impact of true experiments. Therefore, by understanding the logic of true experiments and the weaknesses of the nondesigns, it is possible to derive a good understanding of how to proceed when it is desirable to do cause-and-effect research but impossible to perform a true experiment.

One-Group Pretest-Posttest Design

The *one-group pretest-posttest design* is one of the most frequently used designs in education. It can be diagrammed as follows:

$$O_1 \qquad X \qquad O_2 \text{ (Just one group)}$$

A pretest is given to a group of subjects. Then the experimental treatment is administered to that group, and finally a posttest is administered. Although this design is far from useless, it is obviously the weakest design discussed so far. The reason for its weakness is that this design controls almost none of the major threats to internal validity. Since the pretest comparison makes it possible to see whether the initial composition of the group accounts for outcomes observed after the treatment, simple selection bias *can* be ruled out. However, none of the other threats is controlled by this design. If there is a change between O_1 and O_2, this change can plausibly be attributed to an extraneous historical event, to maturation, to the pretest, to changes in instrumentation, to statistical regression, or to some combination of these. The design makes no provision to control any of these major threats to internal validity.

Why do we say, then, that this design is far from useless? The design does have some redeeming value, because at least it controls selection bias and provides data (acquired before and after the measurement process) on the performance of the subjects. *It is simply necessary to rule out the uncontrolled threats through some process other than experimental design.* However, the word *simply* in the preceding sentence is an understatement; ruling out these threats through processes other than experimental design is often a formidable task.

The task is much easier for the physical or biological scientist than for the educational researcher. If a certain chemical in a carefully controlled environment has always reacted to another chemical in a certain way but reacts differently when a third chemical is simultaneously introduced, the chemist can safely conclude that this third chemical caused the difference. There is no reason to worry about history, maturation, statistical regression, or the other threats that assail the educational researcher.

In the absence of controlled experimental designs, however, the educational researcher has to look for other information to rule out each of these threats to internal validity. For example, if she is dealing with 18-year-old nonreaders, it is unlikely that maturation would cause the improvements in reading ability after an experimental reading program; therefore, she can rule out this threat, even though it is not controlled by her experimental design. Likewise, if it can carefully be demonstrated that the students were not selected for treatment based on extreme scores, then it is safe to conclude that statistical regression did not cause the change. In the same way, if the teacher can demonstrate that the pretest was so unobtrusive as to be almost certain not to stimulate altered performance and that the instrument did not change between pretest and posttest, then she can safely rule out pretesting and instrumentation as threats to internal validity.

History is one of the most difficult threats to control without help from the experimental design. It is often difficult to demonstrate that there were no extraneous, related historical events occurring at the same time as the treatment that could explain the observed outcomes. Any events going on in the world at large (political events, social activities, sports activities, music videos, etc.) or incidental activities in the school (other subjects, wisecracks by classmates, teacher illness, etc.) that could have an impact on the outcome variable constitute a threat to internal validity. The researcher may not even know

of the existence of some of these threats. However, if our researcher can succeed in demonstrating that the time during which this event occurred was typical in all respects, then she can rule out history as a threat to internal validity.

Replication of the study under different circumstances is an excellent idea when a researcher is forced to use a weak design. Indeed, replication is probably the *best* way to control the problem of history cited in the preceding paragraph. If the results consistently are the same under different historical circumstances, then it is unlikely that an extraneous historical event is responsible for these results. In addition, replicating a study a second or third time helps control the other threats to internal validity that are not controlled by a single administration of a weak design. (As will be seen in chapter 15, replication is also helpful with regard to external validity.)

One-Group Posttest-Only Design

The *one-group posttest-only design* is the weakest of all the designs discussed in this book. It is diagrammed as follows:

$$X \quad O \quad \text{(Just one group)}$$

A treatment is given, and then a measurement is taken. That's all there is! This design controls none of the threats to internal validity. If you use this design, then you have to find other ways to rule out each of the threats to internal validity. The design provides you with no help whatsoever in this regard.

As weak as it is, however, this design still has some merit. It does include observations after the treatment, and such observations are an improvement over merely giving the treatment and just hoping that something happened. To take an extreme example, if a distraught student comes into a counselor's fifth-floor office, steps onto the window sill, and prepares to commit suicide, the counselor might engage in some sort of crisis intervention. If she talks him off the window sill and has him imbued with a love of life before he leaves, the counselor might believe that her treatment helped, and rightly so. Her efforts seemed to cause the improvement, and she would want to try them again if a similar occasion were to arise. She could give the student a posttest to establish his posttreatment sanity, but the fact that the fellow was not courteous enough to come in for a pretest relegates the counselor to a very weak, one-group posttest-only design. If she examines all the circumstances carefully and rules out all the threats to internal validity, then the counselor can say that her treatment caused the change. If you are a careful, critical reader, you are perhaps at this point muttering, "Fat chance!" And you would be right. This is such a weak design that it is difficult to rule out the various threats to internal validity.

Remember how easy it was to interpret the results of the true experimental designs in Figure 11.1? The situation is drastically different with the nondesigns. Diagram A in Figure 12.1 presents the results of a one-group posttest-only design. A treatment was administered to a group of subjects, a posttest was administered, and the group's performance is indicated in the diagram. For use in making causal inferences, the result is nearly devoid of meaning. Similarly, in diagram B, although we at least know that the group scored higher after the treatment, it is still quite possible that the group would have followed this pattern even in the absence of a treatment. Likewise, diagram C seems to indicate that the treatment had no impact, but how do we know what the performance of this group would have been in the absence of the treatment? For all we know, the group might have scored even lower on the posttest if it were not exposed to the treatment, and arresting such a downward trend is surely a sign of a successful treatment.

The basic problem with the results presented in Figure 12.1 is that we have no good basis for comparison, and therefore interpreting the results *on the basis of the design alone* is nearly impossible. Recall, however, that it is possible (but difficult) to use strategies other than experimental design to interpret these results. Also note that even though we have said that these nondesigns provide little direct basis for causal inference, this does not render the researcher's efforts completely worthless for experimental purposes. For one thing, the results of such designs can provide useful hypotheses to be tested by

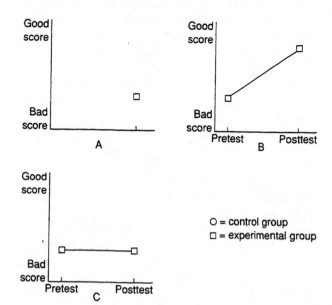

Figure 12.1 Sample Results from the Nondesigns

better designs. In addition, the data already collected can sometimes be patched up and incorporated into a more useful quasi-experimental design, to be discussed in the following sections of this chapter.

In spite of the weaknesses of these two nondesigns, they are probably the most widely used designs in education. By this we do not mean that they are widely used in reputable research journals, but rather that when teachers in classrooms draw cause-and-effect conclusions, they often base their conclusions on designs like these. We hope that you will realize that these experimental designs are prevalent and that you will profit in several ways from reading this chapter. First, you should realize that these designs are better than nothing. They at least include data, and some conclusions can be based on such data. Second, you should understand the weaknesses of these designs and develop the habit of looking for other than research design strategies for ruling out the threats to internal validity left uncontrolled by these designs. And finally you should realize that it is often possible (and worthwhile) to move from one of these weak designs to a much stronger design. The difference between the weak designs and the stronger designs often lies in the planning of the experimental research strategy. For a moderate amount of time invested at the planning stage, the returns may be great in terms of the strength of the inferences that can be drawn after the experiment.

As you can see from reading this section, it is an exceedingly difficult task to eliminate the threats to internal validity without the help of a good experimental design. Under such circumstances, the researcher must isolate each of the threats separately and demonstrate why they are not plausible. In many cases, this is an impossible task; evidence for such reasoning simply does not exist, and the conclusion must remain ambiguous. It is much more effective to use, if possible, a better experimental design. By scheduling the timing of the treatments and observations more appropriately (that is, by using an experimental design), a researcher can control many extraneous factors that otherwise can be dealt with only through extensive data collection and laborious efforts at reasoning, if they can be controlled at all. In many cases, by planning more carefully it is easy for a researcher to move from one of these nondesigns to a quasi-experimental or even a true experimental design. In terms of the control obtained over threats to internal validity and the ease of interpretation of the results, this extra planning is always worth the effort.

QUASI-EXPERIMENTAL DESIGNS

Quasi-experimental designs are not based on random assignment of subjects to experimental and control groups. However, *they attempt to compensate for this shortcoming through the careful scheduling of observations and treatments in such a way as to eliminate many of the threats to internal validity.* Quasi-experimental designs do not employ random assignment—they are almost always weaker than the true experimental designs—but since they do employ careful scheduling of treatments and observations, they provide a solid basis for reasoning about the threats to internal validity and are therefore generally stronger than the nondesigns. In addition, it is possible to combine several quasi-experimental designs in a single experiment. By doing so, it is pos-

sible to take advantage of the strengths of several different designs in such a way as to control the threats to internal validity almost as effectively as if a true experimental design had been employed.

There are many more quasi-experimental designs than can be discussed in this brief chapter. A sensible procedure to follow in reading this text is to gain an understanding of the basic principles of quasi-experimenting and then invent or adapt your own designs. If you do this carefully, many of the designs you invent will be those discussed in this chapter and in the books cited in the Annotated Bibliography. Only a few of the most common and representative designs will be discussed in the following pages. In examining these designs, your task is not to memorize the labels or diagrams but rather to understand how each design eliminates certain threats to internal validity while leaving others uncontrolled. Your goal should be to eventually learn to use these designs in your daily work and your professional reading in such a way as to strengthen the validity of your cause-and-effect inferences and thereby improve your ability to promote useful educational outcomes.

THE UNTREATED CONTROL GROUP DESIGN WITH PRETEST AND POSTTEST

The untreated control group design with pretest and posttest is the most common quasi-experimental design. It is diagrammed as follows:

$$O_1 \quad X \quad O_2 \qquad \text{Experimental}$$
$$\text{---------------}$$
$$O_3 \qquad O_4 \qquad \text{Control}$$

As you can see, this diagram is the same as that for one of the true experimental designs (page 263), except that the R for random assignment has been removed and a line of dashes has been inserted between the two groups. (The dotted line means that existing, nonrandomly assigned groups have been used for the experimental and control groups.) Thus, this design can be viewed as a weakened variation of a true experiment. Another way to look at this diagram is to regard it as similar to one of the nonde-signs (page 270), with a second line added to the diagram. This second line adds a control group for comparison, and therefore this quasi-experimental design can be viewed as a strengthened variation of this nondesign.

To use this design, you would find two intact groups of subjects—perhaps two classrooms of sixth graders. (An intact group is one that is already formed or assembled on some basis other than random assignment before the treatment is administered. For example, you might use your seventh-period students as the experimental group and your third-period students as the control group, or the students in the chemistry class at School A as the experimentals and the chemistry students at School B as the controls.) You would pretest both groups, then administer the treatment to one group while withholding it from the other, and finally administer the posttest to both groups.

Note that with the true experimental design, the pretest was optional. When subjects are not randomly assigned to groups, however, the pretest is much more crucial. It is only by comparing the pretest scores of the two groups that we can rule out initial selection differences as a threat to internal validity. If the two groups perform comparably before the treatment but differently afterwards, we can rule out selection as a threat to internal validity. If we had no pretest, we would not have this evidence for ruling out the possibility that the observed differences on the posttest were merely indications of differences that would have existed even if there were no treatment.

In addition to selection bias, what other threats to internal validity are controlled by this design? If maturation were likely to occur, it would be equally likely to affect both groups, and therefore a simple comparison of the experimental and control groups rules out maturation as a threat. The same reasoning holds true for pretesting. If it were exposure to the pretest (rather than the treatment) that led to improved performance, then such spurious improvements would have appeared in both groups. The same reasoning holds true for statistical regression (as long as neither group was selected on the basis of

extreme scores while the other was not), instrumentation, and history. These factors are controlled in this setting by the same logic that prevails in a true experimental setting.

Interaction of Selection Bias and Maturation

However, some threats are not controlled by this design. Note that all of these uncontrolled threats arise out of an interaction of selection and one of the other threats to internal validity. An example of one of these interactive threats is that of the *interaction of selection bias and maturation*. In the preceding paragraph we stated that maturation was not a problem because the subjects in each group would have equal opportunity to mature. Therefore, if maturation did occur, it would happen to both groups and even on the posttest. This statement assumes that both groups are equal in their *susceptibility* to maturation. But what happens if one of the groups is more susceptible to maturation than the other? In such a case, maturation would no longer be controlled. This is what is meant by the interaction of selection bias and maturation. The subjects may have been selected into the two groups in such a way that one group is more likely than the other to change because of maturation.

A specific example of the interaction of selection bias and maturation will be helpful. Assume that a preschool teacher has a group of 10 children who are labeled nonverbal; that is, they are five-year-olds who do not yet speak in coherent sentence structures. She has purchased a computer program designed to help such children develop verbal skills. To find out whether the program really works, she decides to use her children as an experimental group and another group of 10 children as the controls. The only comparably nonverbal children she can find are in a group of three-year-olds. She pretests and finds the groups roughly equal. After using the program with her children for six months, she posttests and discovers that her children have gained no more than the control children. This comparison is clouded by the possible interaction of selection bias and maturation. The groups were selected in such a way that the three-year-olds were much more likely to improve in verbal abilities as time passed—the time between ages three and four is when this kind of change generally occurs. In other words, the two groups were assembled in such a way that the control subjects were much more likely to benefit from maturation than were the experimental subjects. Of course, it would be possible to do the opposite. If the teacher selected a group of 12-year-olds as controls, then her five-year-olds would have had the edge with regard to maturation; in such a case, the interaction of maturation and selection would have operated in favor of the control group.

Note that all the interactions discussed in this section work in exactly the same fashion. Subjects are put into groups in such a way that one group is more susceptible to one of the major threats to internal validity than the other. These threats are controlled in true experimental designs, because random assignment equalizes on *all* variables—even those on which we do not focus specific attention. In the present quasi-experimental design, the groups are not equalized by random assignment, but we check for comparability with pretests. However, it is difficult to use a pretest to check for *susceptibility* to threats, which is why these interactive threats are uncontrolled in this otherwise effective design.

Interaction of Selection Bias and History

Let us next examine the *interaction of selection bias and history*. Such an interaction would occur, for example, if the experimental group met before lunch and the control group immediately after lunch. This would provide a sort of local history for each group. Unique historical events could have an impact on either group without influencing the other. A more common problem is that one group might simply be more attentive to history than the other. For example, if volunteers are put in an experimental group and nonvolunteers in the control group, the experimental subjects might simply tend to pay more attention to life in general and therefore notice events around them that the nonvolunteers ignore. In this case, both groups would experience the same history, but the experimental subjects would be more likely to be influenced by extraneous events.

Interaction of Selection Bias and Instrumentation

Another frequent problem is the *interaction of selection bias and instrumentation*. It is possible to select subjects in such a way that an instrument undergoes subtle changes for one group but not for the other. For example, assume that one group averages at the 50th percentile on a pretest and the other at the 90th percentile on the same pretest. Both groups take an alternate form of the same instrument as a posttest. At the time of the posttest, the second group will be taking a test on which it scored very near the ceiling on the pretest; it is going to be difficult for them to show improvements on the posttest. In such a case, these subjects might improve with regard to an outcome variable, but the test may simply be incapable of reflecting these gains. On the other hand, the group that scored at the 50th percentile would have plenty of room for improvement. If these subjects gained as much as the others did in reality, these gains would show up as improved scores, because the test would be sensitive enough to reflect these improvements. In a real sense, the two groups are no longer taking the same test; that is, the high-scoring group took a test on which it was hard to improve, while the lower-scoring group took a test on which it was relatively easy to display improvement. This type of situation can confuse the comparisons that a researcher might try to make between the two groups.

Regression toward the Mean

It would also be possible to select subjects in such a way that one group would be more susceptible than the other to *regression toward the mean*. This would occur, for instance, if a group of children from a special-education program was used for an experimental group and a group of children with similar scores from an ordinary classroom was used for the control group. The special-education children might score low on the pretest. When retested on the posttest, they would be likely to score about the same. They would not be likely to shift toward the mean because of regression. However, to get children from the ordinary classroom with scores comparable with those of the special-education children, it would be necessary to select children with the lowest scores from that group. The control group would have an average score far below the average of the group from which it was selected, and the average of this group would be likely to regress upward on the posttest. Thus, the interaction refers to the fact that the scores of one group will artificially increase between pretest and posttest, while the other group will receive no similar artificial boost from regression. This artificial increase in one group but not the other will cloud any comparisons made at the time of the posttest.

In summary, the untreated control group design with pretest and posttest is a quasi-experimental design that controls the same threats to internal validity that would be controlled by a true experiment, except those that arise out of interactions. The reason that these interactions are controlled in true experiments is that the subjects are assigned to groups at random, and random assignment makes it probable that the two groups will be equal on all characteristics, including their susceptibility to react to threats to internal validity. In the absence of random assignment, this quasi-experimental design is not able to control the impact of such interactions. Therefore, the threats to internal validity from these interactions have to be controlled by either reasoning carefully about the probability of such interactions occurring or adding something to the quasi-experimental design to rule out the impact of these interactions.

The results of this quasi-experimental design are relatively easy to interpret *if* the groups score about the same on the pretest and *if* there is no obvious occurrence of the interactive threats to internal validity discussed in this section. Examine Figure 12.2 and decide whether the treatment had an impact in each diagram. Diagram A indicates that the treatment was successful (caused an improvement), whereas diagrams B and C indicate no causal impact. In diagram B, neither group improved, and so it is apparent that the treatment did not have an effect. In diagram C, the experimental group improved, but so did the control group; it seems likely that in this case some extraneous factor (such as history, pretesting, or maturation) caused comparable improvements in both groups.

When the groups are not comparable on the pretest or when we cannot rule out interactive threats, the interpretation of the results of this design becomes difficult. Some of these more ambiguous possibilities are presented in Figure 12.3. In diagram D, the experimental group improves slightly, but the control group improves even more. Is this an indication that the treatment failed to produce an impact? That could be the explanation, but it is also possible that the control group regressed more toward its mean or that the experimental group was more susceptible to a ceiling (instrumentation) effect. Likewise, the same sort of interactive effects of selection with one of the other factors could account for the results shown in diagram E. In this case, perhaps the control group was hampered by a ceiling effect that would not have impeded the progress of the experimental group. Diagram F, on the other hand, seems to present results that have a stronger indication of a causal effect. In this diagram, the experimental group has started out below the control group and finished above it; it is hard to imagine an interaction of selection bias and one of the major threats that would account for this result.

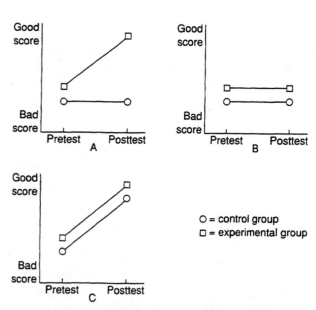

Figure 12.2 Sample Results from Untreated Control Group Design with Pretest and Posttest

From the preceding discussion, you can see that the results of the first quasi-experimental design are more difficult to interpret than the results of true experiments, but they are also far more useful for causal inferences than the results of the nondesigns. What can we do to improve the quality of inferences drawn from this design? There are two answers: First, we can reason carefully about each of the factors that could interact with selection to contaminate our results and try through such logic to rule out these interactive threats. Sometimes we will be able to rule out these threats, but in many cases we will have to admit that we cannot eliminate certain ones, and in such cases we are left with a weakened inference. Second, we can improve the design by combining it with other quasi-experimental designs. For example, we can rule out the threat of statistical regression or maturation by using a second or third pretest (the interrupted time series design) in conjunction with the design just discussed. Additional quasi-experimental design strategies and ideas for implementing them will be discussed later in this chapter.

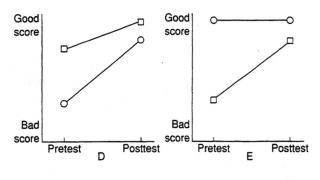

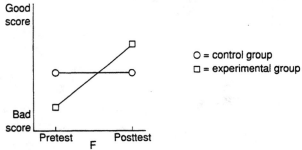

Figure 12.3   Some Ambiguous Results from the Untreated Control Group Design with Pretest and Posttest

A COMPARISON OF THREE DESIGNS

Before we go on, it will be useful to make a systematic comparison of three of the basic designs we have discussed so far. Table 12.1 lists three of the distinctly different designs that we have discussed. They are similar to the extent that they all have a pretest–treatment–posttest format. They differ with regard to the variables that are controlled by the design and with regard to the inferences we can draw. The second column of the table indicates what events are controlled (i.e., likely to be identical) for both the experimental and the control group. (Of course, with the nondesign there is no control group.) The third column indicates what events are uncontrolled (i.e., allowed to be different).

Recall that the basic logic of experimental design can be stated as follows:

If two groups start out the same at time A, but are different at time B, then the cause of the differ-

ence has to be something that was different between time A and time B.

Using this logic, the fourth column in Table 12.1 lists the possible causes of observed differences (if there were any) after an experimental treatment using each of these three designs. The fifth column reverses this logic and lists the possible causes of the absence of a difference using each of these designs. As this table indicates, when we use a true experimental design, there is only one major plausible explanation if the results show a difference and only one major plausible explanation if the results show no difference. This is why it is easy to draw inferences from true experiments.

On the other hand, with the nondesign the treatment is only one of several possible explanations of the outcome if the experiment shows a difference; and likewise the inference that the treatment failed to make an impact is only one of a host of valid conclusions if the experiment shows no difference between the pretest and posttest.

Table 12.1 Comparison of Three Research Designs with Regard to Possible Explanations of Observed Differences

Design and diagram	Events that are controlled (likely to be the same for both the experimental and control groups)	Events that are allowed to be different for the experimental and control groups	What could possibly explain the difference between groups (if there is a difference)?	What could possibly explain the absence of a difference between groups (if there is no difference)?
Pretest-posttest control group design (true experiment) $R\ O_1\ X\ O_2$ $R\ O_3\ \ \ \ O_4$	Selection bias Maturation History Pretesting Statistical regression Instrumentation Interactions of the above factors	Treatment	Treatment	Treatment did not make a difference.
One-group pretest-posttest design (nondesign) $O_1\ X\ O_2$	(Selection bias)	Treatment Maturation History Pretesting Statistical regression Instrumentation Interactions of the above factors	Treatment Maturation History Pretesting Statistical regression Instrumentation Interaction of the above factors	Treatment did not make a difference or treatment made a difference but its impact was suppressed by the other factors.
Untreated control group design with pretest and posttest (quasi-experimental design) $O_1\ X\ O_2$ $O_3\ \ \ \ O_4$	(Selection bias) Maturation History Pretesting Statistical regression Instrumentation	Treatment Interaction of the major threats with selection bias treatment	Treatment Interaction of the major threats with selection bias treatment	Treatment did not make a difference or treatment made a difference but its impact was suppressed by the interaction of selection and one or more of the threats.

For simplicity and clarity, this table assumes that expectancy, social-psychological effects, experimental mortality, instability, and local threats have been controlled through strategies other than research design.

Finally, with the quasi-experimental design, if differences are observed after a treatment, the inference has to be that either the treatment or an interaction of selection and one of the other threats has caused the outcome. The list of possible causes is considerably shorter than the list for the nondesign, but not as restricted as that for the true experimental design. If the results of the quasi-experimental design indicate no difference after the treatment, this means either that the treatment produced no effect or that there was an impact that was suppressed by the interaction of selection and one of the other threats. Again, this finding of no difference from this design is much more subject to clear interpretation than the nondesign, but not as clearly interpretable as the true experimental design. In fact, from meta-analysis, which integrates the results from a number of experiments (discussed in chapter 16), we know that the results of true and quasi-experimental designs tend to be the same—perhaps 80–90% of the time.

NONEQUIVALENT DEPENDENT VARIABLES DESIGN

The nonequivalent dependent variable design is a good design to use when you have access to only one group for your experiment. It uses this one group—which could be even a single subject—as a sort of control for itself. This design can be diagrammed as follows:

O_{A1} X O_{A2} First (critical) variable
O_{B1} O_{B2} Second (non-critical) variable

In this diagram, subscript A stands for the outcome variable that is expected to change as a result of the treatment, whereas subscript B stands for an outcome variable that is *not* expected to change as a result of the treatment. In using this design, you would measure a single group with regard to both outcome variables, then you would administer the treatment, and then you would measure the group again with regard to both outcome variables after the treatment. If the treatment worked, then the group's performance would improve on outcome variable A but not on outcome variable B. (If the group improved on both variables, it would be assumed that some other factor—such as history or maturation—caused the improvement.)

In using this design, a researcher has to be careful in selecting the second outcome variable. Variable A is easy to choose; it is the outcome the researcher expects the treatment to achieve. However, variable B is much more difficult to select. This second variable should show a gain if an extraneous factor (such as history, maturation, or pretesting) had caused the improvement but should *not* increase if the treatment were not responsible for the improvement.

An example will help make this clear. Suppose a speech therapist is working with a child who is having problems articulating several sounds. The therapist attends a convention where he hears of a new speech enhancement technique that is expected to accomplish exactly what he is trying to do with this child. He decides to apply this new technique to teaching one sound—and only to teaching that one sound. He continues to use his traditional technique with all other sounds. He identifies the percentage of correct pronunciations for this target sound, which becomes variable A as in the diagram. He selects another sound (for which he is still using the traditional method), and records the percentage of correct pronunciations for this sound as variable B. After two weeks, he discovers that the child has made substantial improvements in pronouncing the first sound (variable A) but has remained approximately the same with regard to the second sound (variable B). Such data would provide a solid basis for the inference that the speech enhancement technique caused the improvement in the pronunciation of the first sound. If history, maturation, or pretesting had been responsible for improved pronunciation of the first sound, then it is likely that this same, extraneous factor would have had a similar impact on the second sound. This use of logic is not as solid as in a true experimental design. For example, if the child developed a new tooth, which would influence the pronunciation of one sound but not the other, maturation *could* be responsible for the difference.

In the preceding example, if the therapist had used performance on a speech test as variable A and performance on a math test as variable B, this would have provided little (if any) support for the inference that the new treatment worked. This is because it could easily be argued that a threat to internal validity could plausibly have had an impact on the child's speech without influencing the child's math performance. For instance, someone might argue that children of that age are more likely to routinely develop improved speech as they grow older (maturation) than they are to spontaneously acquire improved math skills. Likewise, someone could contend that the speech pretest was more likely to stimulate improvement even in the absence of the treatment than was the math pretest. This is what we mean when we say that variable B must be one that would show an improvement if a threat to internal validity is having an impact but one that would not be expected to improve if the treatment were having its impact on the targeted outcome (variable A).

The weakness of this design is that it relies heavily on finding and measuring variables that logically meet the criteria for variables A and B. Not every treatment lends itself to easy identification of variables that would register gains if the threats to internal validity were the critical factor but if the treatment were not having an impact. In other cases, variable B can be identified, but it may be expensive (in terms of time or money) to measure, or the researcher may simply not have access to measurement of this second variable. In addition, sometimes there are indirect effects by which the treatment works but also causes improvements in the second variable. For example, a child might be the recipient of a new reading program that causes him to read better, which in turn causes him to have an improved self-concept, which in turn causes him to work harder in all his academic subjects, which causes him to score higher on his math tests. A researcher using the nonequivalent dependent variable design might wrongly conclude that the treatment had been effective because the child had improved on both the reading and math variables. Because the logical prerequisites for variable B are difficult to demonstrate, this design is often recommended as a supplement to other designs (see page 286) rather than as a design to be used alone.

The results of this design are straightforward and easy to interpret *if* the logical assumptions of the design are met. Diagram A in Figure 12.4 provides an example of an experiment where the treatment apparently caused an outcome. (In reading these diagrams, remember that the different sets of data refer to two separate outcome variables—not to two groups of subjects, as has been the case in previous diagrams.) Diagram B, on the other hand, indicates that the treatment did not produce an outcome.

It is possible, of course, to combine this quasi-experimental design with the untreated control group design discussed earlier in this chapter. By doing so, we can rule out some of the interactive threats that remained with that design. For example, when we discussed the untreated control group design, we used the example of the teacher who used her five-year-old nonverbal children as an experimental group and some three-year-old nonverbal children as a control group. Since it was possible that the three-year-olds would mature at a different rate

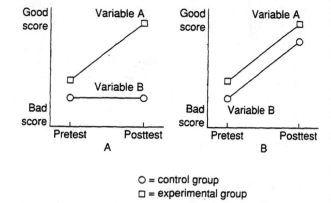

Figure 12.4 Sample Results from the Nonequivalent Dependent Variables Design

than the five-year-olds, this teacher had a problem with the interaction of selection bias and maturation. However, if she would select and measure *two* verbal outcomes (variable A and variable B), she could rule out this interactive threat. If her results were like those shown in Figure 12.5, then she could safely conclude that maturation was not a threat—even in interaction with selection bias. Using this design as a supplement to other designs *is a highly recommended strategy.*

REPEATED TREATMENT DESIGN

Repeated treatment design is another strategy useful when only one group (often a very small group, such as just a single subject) is available for the experimental treatment. This design is often employed in special-education research—especially when strategies such as behavior modification are applied to individual learners. Keep in mind that the "group" in the following discussion is often one person. This design is diagrammed as follows:

O_1 X O_2 X_0 O_3 X O_4 (Just one group)

If you wanted to use this design, you would measure the performance of the group (O_1). Then you would introduce the treatment (X) and afterwards measure the group's performance a second time (O_2). Next

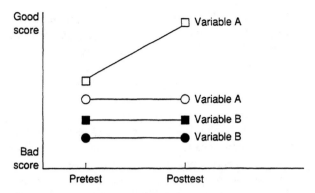

Figure 12.5 Sample Results of Nonequivalent Dependent Variables Design Combined with Untreated Control Group Design

you would *remove* the treatment (X_0). After this withdrawal, you would measure the group's performance a third time (O_3). Then you would reintroduce the experimental treatment (X) and finally measure the group's performance a fourth time (O_4). In many instances, each observation in this design consists of a series of measurements—for example, the researcher might observe and record behaviors for a week, then introduce the treatment, then observe and record for another week, and so on. The time between each of the measurement occasions should be approximately equal. If the treatment is successful in producing the desired outcome, the groups will score high on occasions O_2 and O_4 and low on occasions O_1 and O_3.

This design is useful only when the treatment produces a *transient* (nonpermanent) impact. It is useful in situations where a treatment must be continuously provided if it is to have its impact but not in situations where an outcome is permanently attained once a treatment has been successful. For example, a teacher might find that a child sits in his seat when he is given token reinforcement, engages in out-of-seat behavior during the period of time when tokens are not given, and again remains in his seat when the tokens are reinstated. This repeated treatment design is useful for ascertaining such transient impacts. However, this design would not be helpful to a teacher who wanted to teach her high school students to apply the formula for solving the quadratic

equation. If she would start out with her new approach, withdraw it, and then reinstate it, what would she find? It is unlikely that students who learned to solve such equations would forget how to do so as soon as the treatment was withdrawn, and therefore this design would lead to a false conclusion.

If the assumptions of this design are met (that is, if the treatment has a transient impact on the outcome variable), then the results are often easy to interpret. For example, diagram A in Figure 12.6 shows that the treatment appears to have been successful. Diagram B, on the other hand, suggests that some extraneous variable caused the initial improvement and the treatment probably did not produce the desired effect. Diagram C, however, is ambiguous. Would this pattern emerge because the treatment did not produce its effect, or could the pattern arise because the treatment did produce this effect but on a permanent rather than a transient basis?

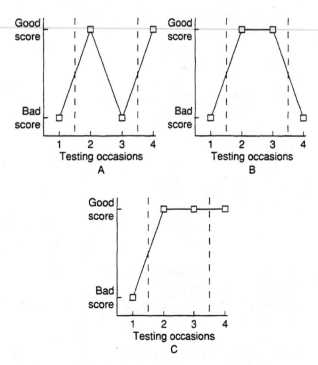

Figure 12.6 Sample Results from the Repeated Treatment Design

INTERRUPTED TIME SERIES DESIGN

The interrupted time series design requires several repeated measurements on the same group of subjects both before and after the administration of a treatment. Like the preceding design, this one is often employed with a single subject. It can be diagrammed as follows:

$$O_1 \; O_2 \; O_3 \; O_4 \; X \; O_5 \; O_6 \; O_7 \; O_8 \quad \text{(One group)}$$

The number of observations before and after the treatment in the diagram is arbitrary. We have selected a total of eight observations; we could just as easily have selected six or some other number. The principle is that there should be enough observations to detect any pattern that may occur. If you wanted to use this design, you would measure the group's performance on four equally spaced occasions, then administer the treatment, then measure the group's performance four more times. The length of time between testing occasions (including that between O_4 and O_5) should be equal.

The purpose of the multiple measurements is to use trends in the data as a basis for evaluating and eliminating threats to internal validity. For example, if maturation were causing improvements in the outcome variable, we would expect to see such gains all along the line, not just between O_4 and O_5. Likewise, statistical regression can easily be evaluated by examining the data pattern.

One threat that is not automatically controlled by this design is that of *history*. It is possible that some unique event might have occurred between O_4 and O_5. The way to deal with this threat is to look for historical events and see whether there are any ways in which the time interval between O_4 and O_5 differed from the other intervals. This design has the advantage over the nondesign on page 270 of having several sets of observations and permitting this comparison to be made over several time intervals. By examining the data and comparing the historical events that occurred during each of the intervals, it might be possible to conclude that it is extremely unlikely that a historical event just happened to occur at the precise time that the treatment was introduced.

The same thing can be said of *instrumentation*. It is possible that the instrument changed in some way between O_4 and O_5. This would be the case, for example, if a probation officer concluded that her new method of working with juvenile offenders worked, when in fact it only appeared to be successful because the court had redefined how to classify a person as a juvenile offender. However, this experimental design has the advantage over the nondesign of having several sets of observations and permitting comparison of several intervals. The possibility of changes in instrumentation can be evaluated in the same way as the threat of history described in the preceding paragraph.

The interpretation of the results of the interrupted time series design is easy—if your results provide a simple pattern of data. For example, in Figure 12.7, diagram A clearly suggests that the treatment caused the desired outcome—provided, of course, that the problems of history and instrumentation mentioned in the preceding paragraphs are taken care of. Likewise, diagram B suggests a causal impact, since the continuous upward pattern took a dramatically more upward shift after the treatment was introduced and continued to progress from this higher level. Diagram C is also easy to interpret as *no* causal impact, since it suggests that the original pretest pattern simply continued in the posttests. Diagram D is more ambiguous. This diagram *could* reflect a slight initial but transient increase after the treatment, but since there was no stable pattern before the treatment, it is more likely that this merely represents a chance fluctuation and no treatment effect. Diagrams E and F are also ambiguous. Diagram E could indicate a transient improvement after the treatment, or it could be evidence of some temporary anomaly followed by a return to normal on testing occasions 6 through 8. To interpret diagram E we would need further information—such as an explanation of whether the treatment is theoretically supposed to produce a transient or a permanent impact. Likewise, diagram F *could* be evidence of a causal impact, but it could also be an indication of some other factor, since the previous pattern of growth did not continue after the treatment. Incidentally, you might have noticed that both diagrams E and F could be influenced by ceiling (instrumentation) effects during the later testing sessions.

It is possible (and often useful) to combine the interrupted time series design with some of the other quasi-experimental designs. The results of some of these combinations are presented in Figure 12.8. Diagrams A1 and A2 in Figure 12.8 are modifications of diagram A of Figure 12.7, with a control group added. The result is a hybrid quasi-experimental design that could be diagrammed as follows:

$$O_1 \quad O_2 \quad O_3 \quad O_4 \quad X \quad O_5 \quad O_6 \quad O_7 \quad O_8 \quad \text{(Exp.)}$$
$$\overline{O_1 \quad O_2 \quad O_3 \quad O_4 \qquad O_5 \quad O_6 \quad O_7 \quad O_8} \quad \text{(Control)}$$

The results of this hybrid quasi-experimental design presented in diagram A1 suggest that the treatment probably did not cause the desired effect. These results support the alternative explanation that some extraneous event (such as a historical event or a sudden change in instrumentation) could best explain the abrupt improvement in performance. On the other hand, diagram A2 provides stronger evidence that the treatment did produce its desired impact, since the experimental group showed an improvement while the control group stayed at the same level of performance after the introduction of the treatment. As you can see, the combined use of these two quasi-experimental designs provides clearer information than would be provided by either design alone.

Similarly, diagram E1 in Figure 12.8 (a modification of diagram E in Figure 12.7) suggests no causal impact, whereas the results shown in diagram E2 suggest that the treatment (which was at best ambiguous in diagram E of Figure 12.7) probably did produce the desired impact. Diagram F1 is ambiguous. Do we have a temporary fluctuation in the data of the experimental group between O_4 and O_5, or do we have an actual improvement that is clouded by some kind of instrumentation effect? On the other hand, diagram F2 suggests a clear causal impact—suggesting that both groups were receiving some sort of temporary stimulation that stopped just as the treatment began.

There are many possibilities for combining the interrupted time series with other quasi-experimental designs. Hybrids from other basic designs are also possible, and many of these are discussed in Cook and Campbell (1979). Your task should not be to memorize the labels and diagrams attached to each of these hybrid designs but rather to understand the fundamental idea that it is possible (and often desirable) to combine the various quasi-experimental

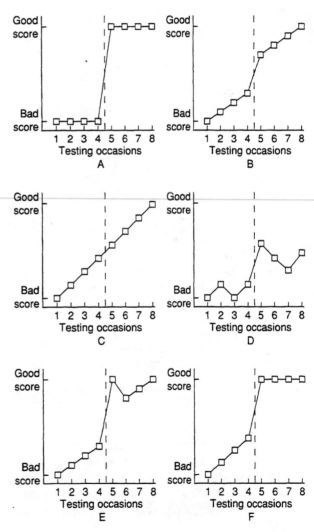

Figure 12.7 Sample Results from the Interrupted Time Series Design

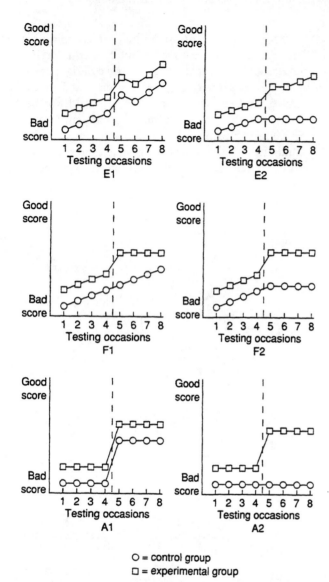

O = control group
□ = experimental group

Figure 12.8 Sample Results of Hybrid Designs Combining the Interrupted Time Series Design with a Control Group

designs. Do not combine designs just to see how complex and esoteric you can make your design. Combine designs for a purpose. Find a basic design and modify or adapt it in such a way as to clarify some of the ambiguities that existed in the original design.

COHORT DESIGNS

The term *cohort* refers to successive groups of same-age subjects or other groups of subjects who follow each other through some institution. The term *institution* can refer to any organized group, including schools, classes, basketball teams, and so on. The simplest cohort design is diagrammed as follows:

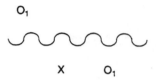

To use this design, you would test one group of subjects before the treatment has been administered within the institution. Then you would administer the treatment to another group, and finally you would test the group to which the treatment was administered. (The wavy line in the diagram indicates that the comparison is with a cohort group.) This basic design can be improved by combining it with other quasi-experimental designs, as by adding observations or control groups.

Cohort designs are often useful for three reasons: (1) it often happens that a cohort receives a treatment that its predecessors did not receive; (2) although they are not randomly assigned, cohorts often differ only in minor ways from their predecessors and successors; and (3) it is often possible to use existing data to compare cohorts receiving a treatment with other cohorts in the same institution who have not received the treatment.

An example of the use of a cohort design could occur in a high school that has implemented a new English curriculum. Did the curriculum have a favorable impact? One way to find out would be to compare the performance of the freshmen at the end of the first year after the start of the new program with the performance of their freshmen cohorts in the same school who last experienced the old curriculum. Assuming that some sort of standardized test is administered at the end of the freshman year, the simplest cohort design could easily be expanded to become a hybrid of the interrupted time series and the cohort designs, which could be diagrammed as follows:

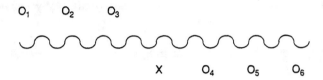

$$O_1 \qquad O_2 \qquad O_3$$

$$X \qquad O_4 \qquad O_5 \qquad O_6$$

The critical comparison, of course, focuses on comparing the performance of the cohorts after the treatment with the performance of the groups preceding the treatment.

It is possible, of course, that the nature of the groups changed just as the treatment was introduced. This possibility can be evaluated by examining the performance of both cohorts with regard to additional characteristics, such as IQ or math ability. If the cohorts are the same with regard to these characteristics, this similarity increases the validity of the conclusions drawn from a cohort design. Likewise, it is possible that some extraneous historical event could account for the improvement, and this threat has to be evaluated the same way as in the other quasi-experimental designs.

The results of the cohort designs are interpreted in the same way as the results of the other quasi-experimental designs. Sample results are presented in Figure 12.9. Diagram A suggests that an improvement occurred as a result of the treatment. The evidence presented in diagram B is more persuasive in this regard, since it rules out the likelihood of a chance instability at the time of the treatment. Diagram C presents results that show a temporary improvement at O_4, followed by a return to the previous pattern. This is probably not evidence of a causal impact.

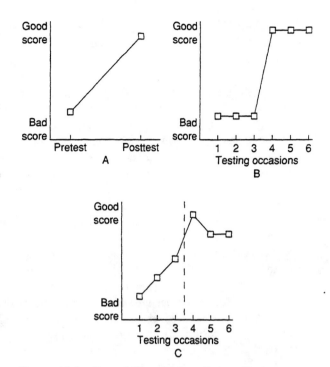

Figure 12.9   Sample Results from Cohort Designs

SUMMARY OF QUASI-EXPERIMENTAL DESIGNS

Many more quasi-experimental designs than we have presented can be devised. The designs we have discussed have been selected because they are representative of what is possible through quasi-experimentation. By understanding the logic behind these designs, you should be able to devise your own designs as needed and thereby strengthen the validity of your cause-and-effect inferences.

Although quasi-experimental designs are sometimes not quite as good as true experiments for supporting causal inferences, they are generally very effective, if they are carefully implemented. True experimental designs are often easier to interpret because the assumptions underlying them are stronger than the assumptions underlying nondesigns. A true experiment employing a large number of subjects and careful experimental procedures controls the major threats to internal validity through simple statistical probability. A quasi-experiment, on the other hand, lacks some of these controls and attempts to compensate with reasoning like this: "If this threat were a problem, it would show up at this point in my observations. My results contradict this, and so I am going to assume that this threat is not a serious factor." Quasi-experiments, in other words, may rely on a lengthy series of inferences, whereas true experiments are based on simple, straightforward statistical probability. If you have a choice, the true experiment is usually the design you should choose.

Another difficulty with quasi-experimental designs is that the results of such experiments are not always as straightforward and easy to interpret as the results we have used for demonstration in this chapter. These results were provided to show you how to interpret the designs, and for such purposes nonambiguous results were usually chosen. In actual practice, the results are often more ambiguous, and in such cases it becomes more difficult to draw inferences. The results of true experiments, on the other hand, are less likely to be clouded by ambiguity, which is why true experiments are preferable to quasi-experiments.

The major advantage of quasi-experiments over true experiments is that they can often be carried out with less disruption to ongoing educational activities. In many cases, a teacher or researcher would be prohibited from conducting a cause-and-effect study if she insisted on interrupting things so that she could obtain random assignment to treatments. On the other hand, a quasi-experimental design can be carried out in almost any situation where the researcher is able to arrange for the collection of data. Quasi-experiments are often nondisruptive and nonartificial. There are instances where the artificiality of the true experiment reduces the degree to which the results can be generalized, whereas the less artificial quasi-experimental results can be generalized much further, since the experimental situation is much more similar to real-life settings. The topic of generalizing results will be explored further in chapter 15.

The quality of inferences that can be drawn from quasi-experimental designs can often be improved by combining several designs for use in the evaluation of a single treatment. Your goal as a researcher should be to select a design (or combination of designs) to help you satisfy yourself (and others who are interested) that you have controlled as many threats to internal validity as possible and that will enable you to draw inferences that are as valid as possible.

It has been suggested that all teachers do Level I research often. At this point it should be obvious that all teachers should at least occasionally engage in Level II research. Quasi-experimental designs are effective tools for Level II research because they enable you to make judgments about the causes of the various desirable and undesirable outcomes you observe in your classroom. You should be concerned about such cause-and-effect relationships in your classroom. You will find that by understanding the principles discussed in this and the preceding two chapters, you will be able to make more intelligent inferences about cause-and-effect relationships in your classroom, even when you are not able to undertake a true experiment. At least occasionally you will find it helpful to examine causal relationships using one or more of these designs.

PUTTING IT ALL TOGETHER

There was a neatly wrapped package under the Christmas tree. In it Mr. Anderson found the most wonderful present he had ever received in his life. It was not a piece of jewelry. It was not a necktie. Nor was it a gift certificate to a fast-food restaurant. Rather, his niece had given him a copy of the very textbook you are now reading. As others continued to open their presents, Mr. Anderson's heart leapt within him as he eagerly curled up by his fireplace and began reading the chapter he had dreamed about for the past 41 days: "Experimental Design: What to Do When True Experiments Are Impossible."

There it was! He had been offered many classrooms for his research, but in each case he had rejected the opportunity to test his Animal Life Program (ALP) because random assignment had been impossible. But this chapter suggested that he could use intact groups in an untreated control group design with pretest and posttest. In addition, he could buttress the evidence from this design by combining it with aspects of the other designs discussed in this chapter.

Shortly after school resumed, Mr. Anderson obtained permission to evaluate the ALP in a local school system. He chose a school with two fourth grades, two fifth grades, and two sixth grades. Although the students in the classes had not been randomly assigned, they were comparably grouped, and standardized test scores showed that the classes performed about the same within each grade level. Mr. Anderson planned to use his Fireman Tests as pretests and posttests. All students would be tested on both occasions, and between testing occasions Mr. Anderson would administer the ALP to one of the classes at each grade level.

As an additional control for the threats to internal validity, Mr. Anderson cooperated with the local humane society, the police department, and the principal of the school to obtain a listing of animal-related bad deeds and good deeds. Such a listing would not be available for all the schools, but in this case it was possible to compile a list of children who had been reported to one or the other of these agencies as having performed either a good deed or a bad deed toward animals. This information was available for the past three years. He recognized that this sort of data would be somewhat unreliable and invalid, but he decided to use it in a supplementary analysis. These data would fit into a hybrid combination of a cohort and an interrupted time series design, which would be used to supplement the main untreated control group design.

If the ALP was successful, Mr. Anderson expected to see the following results. The experimental and control groups would score about the same on the pretest of the Fireman Test, but the experimental students would do much better on the posttest. Likewise, although he already knew that over the past three years the number of reported good deeds and bad deeds had been about the same for the experimental and control groups, he expected the experimentals to do even better after receiving the ALP. Finally, he could not retroactively give the Fireman Test to previous cohorts within the school,

but he could use the good deed versus bad deed data to compare this year's experimental students with their cohorts from previous years. He expected his experimental subjects to show more good deeds and fewer bad deeds than their cohorts from the past three years.

With these carefully laid plans and predictions, Mr. Anderson approached his experimental study with confidence and enthusiasm.

SUMMARY

Chapter 11 showed how all the major threats to internal validity can be controlled through a combination of careful experimental procedures and an experimental design based on random assignment. The present chapter has recommended procedures for use in situations where such ideal experimental designs are impossible. Although it is sometimes possible to draw conclusions based on the nondesigns, these strategies are extremely weak and should be upgraded to a more useful design whenever possible. The quasi-experimental designs do not use random assignment, but they compensate for this shortcoming through careful scheduling of observations and treatments in such a way as to overcome many of the threats to internal validity.

This chapter has described several of the basic strategies of quasi-experimentation to help you understand how such strategies can overcome specific threats to internal validity. Table 12.2 describes the quasi-experimental designs discussed in this chapter and summarizes their major strengths and weaknesses. By combining several of these designs into a single hybrid design, it is possible to control most of the threats to internal validity almost as thoroughly as they could be controlled in a true experiment.

What Comes Next

Chapters 13 and 14 will discuss statistical tools that help report relationships and estimate the likelihood that the results of experiments are not merely the outcome of chance fluctuations in data.

Table 12.2 Summary of Important Features of Quasi-Experimental Research Designs

Design	Diagram	Number of Groups	Advantages	Disadvantages
Untreated control group with pretest and posttest	O_1 X O_2 ------- O_3 O_4	Two or more	This design is often necessary when random assignment is impossible. Selection bias is controlled by the pretest. To the extent that the groups are similar, this design is similar to the true experimental designs.	The pretest is essential. If groups are not initially equal, then problems of interpretation occur. Interaction of selection with other factors may occur.
Nonequivalent dependent variables	O_{A1} X O_{A2} O_{B1} O_{B2}	One group	Only one group is necessary.	It is often difficult to find a non-equivalent dependent variable that fits the logic of this design.
Repeated treatment	O_1 X O_2 X O_3 X O_4	One group	Only one group is necessary.	If the treatment has a permanent impact, this design becomes difficult to interpret.
Interrupted time series	O_1 O_2 O_3 O_4 X O_5 O_6 O_7 O_8	One group	Only one group is necessary.	If the data do not follow a simple pattern, the results become difficult to interpret.
Cohort	O_1 ~~~~~ X O_2	One group (actually, several consecutive groups in one institution)	Cohorts are often easy to find.	Cohorts may not actually resemble one another.

DOING YOUR OWN RESEARCH

The untreated control group design is by far the most common of the quasi-experimental designs. The pretest is an essential feature of this design. Even with the pretest, however, it leaves uncontrolled some of the threats to internal validity (selection and the interaction of selection with other threats). Therefore, if you use this design you should seriously consider supplementing it with another design. For example, by giving two pretests a month apart, you can easily have a combination of untreated control group and interrupted time series designs. This will make the data arising from your study much more useful.

Quasi-experimental designs can often be conducted with almost no interruption of the normal flow of events. This ease of implementation can serve you in two ways: (1) you can easily gain the cooperation of others to enable you to do your research, and (2) the research can be conducted in a realistic situation that will permit generalization to nonexperimental settings.

FOR FURTHER THOUGHT

1. The textbook says that to establish cause-and-effect relationships it is necessary to assign subjects to experimental conditions. But with the cohort design, the experimenter examines naturally occurring cohorts coming through an institution. How can this design examine cause-and-effect relationships?

2. Can quasi-experimental designs ever be preferable to true experiments for minimizing the threats to internal validity?

3. Complete this sentence by answering the designated questions: "Quasi-experimental designs ...(do what?) (To what or whom?) (When?) (Where?) (How?) (Why?)"

ANNOTATED BIBLIOGRAPHY

Alberto, P., & Troutman, A. (1990). *Applied behavior analysis for teachers* (3rd ed.). Columbus, OH: Merrill.

Chapter 5 of this book describes several single-subject research designs that are particularly useful for evaluating the effectiveness of behavior modification strategies in special-education programs.

Campbell, D. T., & Stanley, J. C. (1966). *Experimental and quasi-experimental designs for research.* Chicago: Rand McNally. This book is also included as a chapter in N. L. Gage (Ed.), *Handbook of research on teaching* (Chicago: Rand McNally, 1963). Everything in this resource is contained and improved upon in the Cook and Campbell reference cited next. However, when you read older research studies, this source will be cited as the main authority for quasi-experimentation.

Cook, T. D., & Campbell, D. T. (1979). *Quasi-Experimentation: Design and analysis issues for field settings.* Chicago: Rand McNally. This book has become the bible of quasi-experimentation. It describes how to conduct quasi-experiments and how to analyze the results. The chapters on analysis are perhaps more complex than novice readers would care to handle. On the other hand, the chapters on how to devise quasi-experimental situations are easily understandable and useful to readers at any level of expertise. The terminology employed in the present text has been made compatible with that used in this more extensive resource, and thus readers who wish to look to Cook and Campbell for further information will find the transition easy.

Fitz-Gibbon, C. T., & Morris, L. L. (1987). *How to design a program evaluation* (2nd ed.). Newbury Park, CA: Sage. This is a book in the Program Evaluation Kit cited under Herman, Morris, and Fitz-Gibbon in chapter 1. This volume presents practical guidelines to assist practitioners in setting up quasi-experimental designs to evaluate programs.

CHAPTER 12

Research Report Analysis

The study described in the report in Appendix C attempts to show that the guided use of computer simulations caused the students to develop problem-solving abilities to a greater extent than would have been possible with the traditional approach to teaching the same topics or with the unguided use of the same programs.

1. Which research design described in the present chapter does this study employ?

2. In what ways does this research design contribute to controlling the threats to internal validity?

ANSWERS:

1. This study uses the untreated control group design with pretest and posttest (a quasi-experimental design).

2. This design helps us control several of the threats to internal validity. Most important, it controls the threat of selection bias. That is, we know that the superior performance of the guided students at the end of the experiment did not already exist at the beginning of the experiment. In addition, having two groups helped control maturation, instrumentation, and pretesting. In each of these cases, if the threat influenced one of the groups, it should have been equally likely to influence the others. (A threat that is not directly controlled by this design is the interaction of selection bias and the other threats. That threat is mentioned but not emphasized in detail in the present textbook.)

CRITERION GROUP AND CORRELATIONAL RESEARCH: NONEXPERIMENTAL METHODS FOR EXAMINING RELATIONSHIPS

■ WHERE WE'VE BEEN

We have examined the major threats to internal validity and have seen how experimental and quasi-experimental research designs help control the major threats to it.

■ WHERE WE'RE GOING NOW

In this chapter we'll discuss strategies for determining that relationships exist—even though these may be noncausal relationships. The strategies described in this chapter often serve as a useful preliminary to conducting the types of research described in chapters 11 and 12. As part of the discussion, we will describe various types of correlation coefficients, which are useful statistical tools in many areas of educational research.

■ CHAPTER PREVIEW

The previous two chapters focused on designs (both strong and weak) for scheduling treatments and observations to develop a basis for causal inference. All the designs discussed there required the manipulation of subjects—the introduction of a treatment and the evaluation of the subjects' response to this treatment. In some cases such manipulation is impossible, but it may still be useful to determine whether a relationship exists, even if we cannot be sure that this is a causal relationship. The present chapter will describe some useful strategies for examining such relationships.

After reading this chapter, you should be able to

1. Describe and give examples of the use of criterion group designs.
2. Describe and give examples of the use of each of the following correlation coefficients:

Pearson correlation coefficient

Partial correlation coefficient

Eta coefficient

Multiple correlation coefficient

3. Given an example of each of the preceding correlation coefficients, interpret it accurately.

4. Given a relationship that could be examined using a correlation coefficient, select the correct coefficient for that situation.

5. Evaluate the strengths and weaknesses of criterion group and correlational research strategies.

■

NONEXPERIMENTAL RESEARCH

Occasionally, you will speculate about a cause-and-effect relationship and discover that the experimental strategies described in the last two chapters simply cannot be applied to the problem at hand. This will be the case because in a given situation it may be impossible, inconvenient, or inappropriate to manipulate the subjects—to assign some to a treatment and to withhold that treatment from others. We have already discussed some nonexperimental, descriptive research in chapters 4 through 9. The present chapter will focus on some descriptive methods that examine relationships—and may even imply causality—without directly addressing the causal nature of the relationships.

For example, examine the following cause-and-effect question: Do unfavorable preschool models lead children to develop attitudes of antagonism toward school? To settle this question through either true experimental or quasi-experimental designs, it would be necessary to have an experimental group of children who would receive unfavorable preschool models and a control group from whom unfavorable preschool models would be withheld. Such a research experiment is impossible for ethical reasons: no sensible researcher would expose young children to unfavorable models just to see whether

these models would have an adverse impact on the children.

Likewise, we might want to investigate this question: Does the gender of a child lead to (i.e., cause) stereotyped attitudes toward scientific professions? To employ a true experimental design, we would have to find a large group of children and randomly assign some of them to the male treatment and some to the female treatment. This is not easy to do.

There are numerous cause-and-effect questions to which the experimental methodologies discussed in the previous two chapters cannot reasonably or easily be applied. Does a child's birth order cause him to have a certain type of self-concept? Does the environment in which a child is raised influence her attitude toward poetry? Does going to college actually cause a person to attain a higher income after graduation? Does an excessive reliance on a certain counseling strategy lead to an increase in suicides among clients? Do pilot trainees who crash their planes do so because they were subjected to unusual anxiety during training? These are all interesting questions, and there are people who want to know the answers, but none of them can be answered by assigning some participants to an experimental group and others to a control group. In each case, such assignment to treatments (either randomly or otherwise) is either impossible or unethical.

Some of these questions can be addressed through the qualitative and quantitative descriptive strategies discussed in chapters 4 through 9. In addition, researchers employ criterion group or correlational methodologies. Since these methodologies do not manipulate subjects (i.e., either assign them to treatments or withhold treatments from them), they do not lead to causal inferences as directly as would a true experimental or quasi-experimental methodology. Instead, they demonstrate that there is a consistent relationship between something that could be called a treatment and a designated outcome.

For example, such a correlational study might show that there is indeed a relationship between going to college and earning a high income later in life. A careful examination of the data indicates that college graduates do, in fact, earn more money than do nongraduates. However, such a relationship is not proof (or even strong evidence) that going to college causes an increase in income. It is possible (since there was no random assignment to the college treatment) that most of the people who go to college are those who would have made more money anyway. The researcher who wants to establish a causal connection between college attendance and financial success would have to think of all the plausible explanations for earning the higher income and then rule out the likelihood that any of these alternatives (rather than college attendance) could be responsible for the higher wages. Without experimental research, it is impossible to predict how much the non-attenders would have earned if they had gone to college. Ruling out these alternative explanations without the benefit of an experimental research design is a taxing (and sometimes impossible) occupation. On the other hand, if only the researcher could randomly assign 100 subjects to the college condition and another 100 to the noncollege condition, then it would be quite a bit easier to rule out these threats to the internal validity of the conclusion that attending college causes an increased income. For practical and ethical reasons, however, random assignment is impossible in this case, and researchers have to do the best they can with weaker methodologies.

A similar problem arises in birth order research. A consistent finding is that lastborns perform more poorly (on the average) on most tests than do firstborns. The most widely held inference based on this relationship is that being born last in a family of siblings causes one to be weaker with regard to certain traits than someone born first. This sounds like a plausible explanation, but is it not also possible that being weak with regard to certain characteristics is what causes a person to be born last? A child who is bright, friendly, and cooperative will be likely to score high on various tests; and because of these favorable characteristics his parents may feel inclined to have another child, and therefore he will not be a lastborn. However, if this was a difficult child to raise, his parents might have been less inclined to have more children, and therefore he would have become a lastborn. This chain of events would lead to lastborns performing more poorly (on the average) than firstborns on various tests. In the absence of random assignment to the conditions of firstborns and lastborns (which is biologically impossible), it is difficult to establish the causality behind this relationship.

On the other hand, if a researcher is able (even in the absence of an experimental design) to demonstrate that there is no relationship between a selected treatment and an outcome, then this is strong evidence that the treatment did not cause the outcome. For example, if a researcher would demonstrate that among people coming from the same social background, college graduates earn no more than nongraduates, then this would be compelling evidence that college attendance does not cause an increase in income. Likewise, if a researcher could demonstrate that among families of the same size, lastborns score about the same as firstborns on most tests of academic achievement or of personality variables, this would lead to a reasonable inference that birth order does not cause differences in the characteristics measured by these tests.

The present chapter will describe useful methodologies for ascertaining whether such relationships exist. They are introduced because they are the most common methodologies and because they provide a good understanding of what is possible in this regard. If you are interested in additional methodologies, refer to the source cited in the Annotated Bibliography at the end of this chapter.

CRITERION GROUP DESIGNS

A criterion group design is one in which groups of subjects are gathered into treatment groups and control groups on the basis of naturally occurring circumstances (after these events have already occurred) rather than on the basis of random or nonrandom assignment to treatment and control conditions. For example, we might want to know how English teachers differ from math teachers in their use of a motivational strategy, how boys compare with girls in verbal ability, or how baseball players

---

BOX 13.1

Post Hoc Ergo Propter Hoc (Or, After This Therefore Because of This)

The post hoc error refers to the tendency to assume that because there is a relationship between two events or characteristics, the first event or characteristic causes the latter. The following examples demonstrate that this conclusion does not always follow. In each case, there is a relationship, but the conclusion that this is a causal relationship is obviously absurd. See if you can identify the real cause in each case.

As the temperature of the water off the coast of California increases, the number of drownings also increases. A recent study has found the same relationship off the coast of North Carolina. The researchers recommend keeping your water at a low temperature in your swimming pool, since warmer water obviously leads to more drownings. (In fact, a research study has shown that if the temperature of swimming pools is kept below 50 degrees, almost nobody drowns—of course, almost nobody swims.)

Good news for people with big feet! A recent study shows beyond any doubt that people with big feet read better than those with smaller feet. A study of 1,000 randomly selected citizens between the ages of 5 and 50 from a Midwestern state showed that people with larger shoe sizes read much better than people with smaller shoe sizes. (Oddly enough, when this study was replicated among citizens between 25 and 50, the relationship disappeared. Likewise, when only fifth graders were included in the study, there was no noticeable relationship.)

Research shows that there are more storks in England during March than during any other month. Likewise, more babies are born in England during March than during any other month. The implications of this finding for sex education programs are still being discussed.

---

differ from tennis players in muscle coordination. Although data tabulated to answer such questions may often look exactly like the results of an experimental or quasi-experimental design, the absence of a manipulation of the treatment makes a crucial difference in interpretation.

There are many possible formats that criterion group designs can employ. The following is the simplest:

$$C \qquad O_1$$
$$O_2$$

In this design, the C (for *criterion*) replaces the X for representing the treatment. To use this design, you would find one group of subjects who are already receiving (or have previously received) a treatment (or possess a certain characteristic) and measure that group's performance with regard to a specified outcome variable. Then you would find another group similar in all respects to the first group, but whose subjects are not receiving the treatment, and then measure this second group's performance regarding the same outcome variable. Finally, you would compare the performance of the two groups to see whether their scores differed on the outcome variable.

This is obviously a very weak design. The most glaring difficulty is that there is no control whatsoever over the selection of subjects into the criterion group. Therefore, both simple selection and its interaction with other factors are extremely serious threats to the internal validity of cause-and-effect conclusions you might try to draw from this design. Nearly all the other threats to internal validity can also pose problems when this design is employed. The only way to control these threats is to collect additional data to try to demonstrate that the groups really are quite similar and to try to rule out other likely explanations of the observed outcomes.

Let us examine the question of whether unfavorable preschool models lead to attitudes of antagonism toward school. The criterion group design would dictate that we operationally define unfavorable preschool models and on the basis of this definition assemble the records of a criterion group of children who have been exposed to such models. We would then operationally define antagonism toward school and find a way to measure it. We would also find another group of children who appear to be similar in all respects to the children who have received the unfavorable models but who have not themselves been exposed to unfavorable modeling. Finally, we would measure the second group's antagonism toward school. If the criterion group (the children who received unfavorable modeling) displays more antagonism, then this would indicate that the expected relationship exists. However, because of the severe limitations of the design, we would still be far from having a sound basis for a causal inference that unfavorable preschool models cause antagonism toward school.

It is possible (and, intuitively, even likely) that unfavorable preschool models do often cause such hostile attitudes. But a skeptic might point out that it is also possible that some other factor (or set of factors) could both cause people to become unfavorable preschool models and cause children to develop attitudes of antagonism. If this were the case, then attempts to improve attitudes toward school by reducing the unfavorable modeling would be ineffective. For example, our skeptic might argue that maybe some environments (such as inferior schools or administrators who do not understand the culture of their students) make people cynical toward schools, and the same environments might cause children to develop attitudes of antagonism toward schools. There are several ways that we could deal with our skeptic's objection. First, we could look

into published literature or examine the environment closely to determine whether there are factors having a dual impact of this kind. (The application of principles of qualitative research, discussed in chapter 9, would be helpful in making this analysis.) Second, we could try another criterion group design, this time comparing unfavorable preschool models from a favorable environment with unfavorable preschool models from an unfavorable environment. This process, as you can see, would eventually become very complex—perhaps even futile. Note, however, that if the above study would have shown that unfavorable preschool models did *not* have different attitudes than other children, this would have been convincing evidence that unfavorable preschool models do *not* cause such attitudes.

In addition to using the criterion group design when other designs are impossible, some researchers select this design because it is easier (and faster) to employ than one of the stronger designs. Sometimes this reasoning exhibits laziness or incompetence, but in certain cases there is validity to this use. Criterion group design being relatively easy to employ suggests that we might want to use it as a preliminary step before employing a better design. For example, we might want to know whether open classrooms cause improved self-concepts without a loss of academic skills. We are able to operationally define both *open classrooms* and *self-concept*. The best way to collect evidence for such a causal inference would be to use an experimental or quasi-experimental design. Such designs would be expensive in terms of time and money; however, and we might feel better about undertaking such an expense if we at least knew beforehand that a relationship existed. Therefore, we might find two colleagues—one who uses a traditional approach and the other who uses an open classroom approach—and conduct a criterion group design in their classrooms. We might discover that the two teachers appear to be about equally competent and that the students seem to be similar in most respects, but that the self-concepts are superior in the open classroom. Because of this observation we might be inclined to go ahead with a quasi-experimental design. (While we are conducting this criterion group design, we could also save some time and improve efficiency by collecting baseline and qualitative data that could later be incorporated into our quasi-experiment.) On the other hand, if the criterion group design shows no such relationship, then we might decide not to pursue the research any further.

CORRELATIONAL STUDIES

All the methodologies for establishing relationships that have been discussed so far in this and previous chapters have relied on the administration of a treatment and a comparison of the average performance of groups of subjects. A group is exposed to a treatment, and the impact of this treatment is in some way evaluated. Correlational studies are different. They are performed by calculating correlation coefficients, which are discussed later in this chapter. These studies do *not* give a treatment to one or more groups of subjects while withholding it from a control group, analyzing performance before and after the treatment. Rather, they take a single group of subjects and compare the performance of the people within this group with regard to two different characteristics. For example, a researcher doing a correlational study might have all the sophomores in her school take both a creativity test and an IQ test and analyze the data to see whether there is a pattern in the way the scores relate to each other. Correlational studies can be diagrammed as follows:

$$O_1 \qquad O_2$$

To perform a correlational study, we would identify a group of subjects and measure all the people in that group with regard to the two or more characteristics of interest. Then we would examine the data to see whether there is a relationship between the two sets of scores.

Note how correlational studies differ from experimental and criterion group studies. Until now we have focused on comparing means—usually of two or more groups. Now we are focusing on one group and two or more variables.

These are the results of some sample *experimental* studies:

1. The experimental group averaged 85% correct answers on the test, while the control group averaged 75% correct answers (two groups, one outcome variable).

2. The students in the cooperative learning group were on task 45.8 minutes out of the hour; those in the competitive group were on task only 33.2 minutes out of the hour (two groups, one outcome variable).

These are the results of some sample *criterion group* studies:

3. The boys averaged 84% correct answers on the test, as did the girls (two groups, one outcome variable).

4. The dropouts had been referred for disciplinary problems 6.3 times per year; the nondropouts had been referred only 2.1 times per year (two groups, one outcome variable).

These are the results of some sample *correlational* studies:

5. The more homework the students were assigned, the better they did on the test (one group, two variables).

6. The more the students watched television, the worse they did in school (one group, two variables).

Sometimes, a slight rewording can turn an experimental study into a correlational study. For instance, assuming the students were assigned to either a peer-tutoring experimental group or a nontutoring control group, this is an example of an experimental study:

7. Students who attended the peer-tutoring sessions averaged 85% correct answers on the final exam, whereas those who did not attend the sessions averaged only 75% correct (two groups, one outcome variable).

Assume, on the other hand, that the tutoring sessions were available to everyone. The researcher waited until after the final exam and then found out how many tutoring sessions each student attended and how each student did on the final exam. The following would be the result of a sample correlational study:

8. The more tutoring sessions students attended, the better they did on the final exam (one group, two variables).

or

9. Students who attended more sessions did better than those who attended fewer sessions (one group, two variables).

Statements 1, 2, and 7 express the results of experimental or quasi-experimental research. There is a stronger possibility of a causal relationship in these statements than in the others, which express the results of either correlational or criterion group research.

As a result of a correlational study, we might be able to conclude that two characteristics are correlated in the group of subjects in the study. This means that these two characteristics occur together according to some predictable pattern. For example, we might conduct a correlational study with a group of high school students to see whether there is a relationship between sense of humor and performance in English class. We could administer to all the students a test that measures sense of humor and then compute a correlation coefficient between these scores and the students' first-semester grades. If there was a high correlation coefficient, this would mean that persons who were assessed as having a good sense of humor are also assessed as doing well in English class. Conversely, if we knew that a person did well in English class, we could predict that she had received a high score on the sense of humor test; on the other hand, students with a weak sense of humor would tend to perform poorly in English class. Students with a mediocre sense of humor would perform at an average level in English class.

Note that in the preceding example, we have not demonstrated a causal relationship. We have not shown that a good sense of humor causes a person to do well in English class. It is possible that such causality explains the relationship, but it is also possible that the causality is reversed: a person's success in English class may cause that person to be evaluated as having a good sense of humor. In addition, it is possible that some third variable (such as intelligence or creativity) causes a person to receive high scores both in English class and on the instrument measuring sense of humor.

There are many other questions about relationships that could be investigated through correlational studies. The following are some examples:

Are teachers who spend a great deal of time reading professional journals actually perceived as more effective by their students than those who do very little professional reading?

Do children from large families show more respect for teachers than do children from smaller families?

Do students who borrow more library books spend less time than do others playing intramural sports?

Do counselors who listen more often to contemporary rock music have better rapport with the students they counsel than do those who spend less time listening to such music?

Is there a relationship between academic rank in class and popularity?

Is it possible that students who finish exams either very quickly or very slowly do better than those who take intermediate amounts of time?

In each of the preceding cases we could conduct a correlational study. We would find a valid way to measure each pair of characteristics, record these measurements in a given group, and then see whether there is a pattern. An important caution is in order at this point. Even though we may be interested in speculating about whether one characteristic causes the other, correlational studies tell us little about such causality. If we wanted to show that listening more frequently to rock music to the point of liking it actually caused counselors to develop better rapport with students, we would have to use an experimental methodology rather than a correlational study. Simple correlational studies help us establish the existence of relationships, but they seldom enable us to determine the causes of these relationships.

The results of correlational studies are often expressed in terms of correlation coefficients. There are several different types of correlation coefficients, and each serves a specific purpose. The following sections of this chapter will describe the major types of correlation coefficients. This discussion will be nontechnical; no attempt will be made to teach you how to compute these coefficients. Your goals should be to understand the purpose of each coefficient, know when to use each of them to help you solve a specific problem, and know how to interpret each coefficient when you see a reference to it in the professional literature.

PEARSON CORRELATION COEFFICIENT

The Pearson correlation coefficient is the most common of the correlation coefficients. (It is often abbreviated as *r*, for *relationship*.) Many of the other types of correlation coefficients are adaptations or modifications of the Pearson coefficient. By understanding this coefficient, you will have a basis for understanding any other correlation coefficient. The Pearson correlation coefficient expresses the strength of a relationship in numbers falling between the limits of +1.00 and -1.00. A high absolute value indicates a strong relationship, whereas a near-zero value indicates a weak or no relationship between the two variables. (The term *absolute value* indicates that you should ignore the plus sign or the minus sign.) Table 13.1 gives some examples of correlation coefficients and their meanings. (Note that perfect relationships of +1.00 and -1.00 are only theoretical limits. In education, it is never possible to have a perfect correlation for any meaningful pair of variables.)

It is useful to think of the strength of the relationship between two variables in terms of how accurately we can use our knowledge of a person's score on one characteristic to predict that person's score on a second characteristic. If there is a strong relationship, we can make a very accurate estimate of the second characteristic. If the relationship is weak (near zero), it is difficult or impossible to make an accurate prediction about the second characteristic. Putting this into terms of correlation coefficients, if there were a correlation of 1.00 between two characteristics, then we could make an absolutely perfect prediction of the person's performance on the second variable if we know the person's score on the first. On the other hand, if the correlation were .00, then knowing the person's score on the first characteristic tells us nothing about performance on the second. A correlation of .90 indicates a stronger relationship than one of .80. This means that if we made an estimate of a second characteristic based on what we knew about that person's performance on a first characteristic, we would be more likely to be accurate in a situation where the correlation was .90 than if the correlation were .80.

A coefficient of either 1.00 or -1.00 would indicate a perfect correlation between two variables. In either case, if we knew a person's score on one of the variables, we could make a perfect prediction regarding the person's score on the other. The difference between positive and negative correlations is that with a positive correlation, as a person's score on one variable increases, the score on the other variable also increases. On the other hand, a negative correlation means that as a person's score on one variable increases, the score on the other decreases.

To take an example, there is a high positive correlation (say, r = .80) between a person's score on an IQ test and her score on a standardized reading test. This relationship is diagrammed in Figure 13.1. Students with high scores on the IQ test are also likely to have high scores on the reading test. Students with low scores on the IQ test are likely to have low scores on the reading test. People in the middle range on the IQ test are likely to be in the middle range on the reading test. (We could also make predictions in the opposite direction. Persons with high scores on the reading test are likely to have high IQ scores; and so forth.)

Table 13.1 Some Sample Correlation Coefficients Between Performance on Test A and Test B and Their Meanings

Correlation Coefficient	Interpretation
1.00	There is a perfect (positive) relationship between scores on the two tests. If you know a person's score on one test, you can predict with perfect accuracy that person's score on the other. As scores on test A increase, scores by the same people on test B also increase to the same degree.
.80	There is a strong (positive) relationship between scores on the two tests. If you know a person's score on one test, you can predict with very good (but not perfect) accuracy that person's score on the other. As scores on test A increase, there is a strong tendency for scores by the same people to increase on test B also.
.75	There is a strong (positive) relationship between scores on the two tests. If you know a person's score on one test, you can predict with very good accuracy that person's score on the other test—but the accuracy would be slightly worse than if the correlation were .80. As scores on test A increase, there is a strong tendency for scores by the same people to increase on test B also.
.15	There is very little relationship between scores on the two tests. If you know a person's score on one test, you can make no reasonable prediction about that person's score on the other test. There is a very slight (probably chance) tendency for scores on test A to be accompanied by similar scores on test B.
.00	There is no relationship whatsoever between scores on the two tests. If you know a person's score on one test, you can make no reasonable prediction about that person's score on the other test.
−.12	There is very little relationship between scores on the two tests. If you know a person's score on one test, you can make no reasonable prediction about that person's score on the other test. There is a very slight (probably chance) tendency for high scores on test A to be accompanied by low scores on test B.
−.90	There is a strong (negative) relationship between scores on the two tests. (This relationship is stronger than the .80 correlation stated above.) If you know a person's score on one test, you can predict with very good (but not perfect) accuracy that person's score on the other. As scores on test A increase, there is a strong tendency for scores by the same people to decrease proportionately on test B.
−1.00	There is a perfect (negative) relationship between scores on the two tests. If you know a person's score on one test, you can predict with perfect accuracy that person's score on the other. As scores on test A increase, scores by the same people decrease on test B to a precisely similar degree.

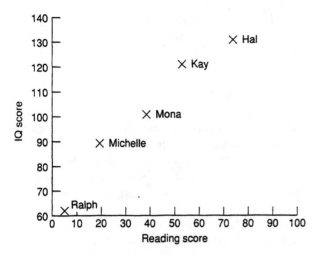

Figure 13.1 An Example of a Positive Correlation between IQ Scores and Reading Scores

On the other hand, there is a *negative* correlation (say, r = -.80) between a person's score on an IQ test and the number of days he is likely to be absent from school. This relationship is diagrammed in Figure 13.2. A person with a high IQ score is likely to be absent a very low number of days. A person with a low IQ is likely to be absent quite often. A person in the middle range of IQ is likely to be present an average number of days.

Finally, there might be a very weak relationship (say, r = -.13) between IQ scores and the amount of time children can hold their breath under water. This relationship is diagrammed in Figure 13.3. Some persons with high IQ scores can hold their breath for a long time, others only briefly. The same is true of low and average IQ scorers. There is no predictable pattern. The absence of a pattern is signified by the low correlation coefficient.

You may have realized by now that whether a relationship will be described as positive or negative is often an arbitrary decision, based on how the researcher chooses to define the variables. For example, the negative relationship in Figure 13.2 can become the positive relationship shown in Figure 13.4 if we simply measure days present instead of days absent and change the correlation coefficient from -.80 to +.80.

When applied to the reliability and validity of measurement processes, the Pearson r represents the reliability and validity coefficients described in chapter 5. For example, in terms of the present chapter, a high test-retest reliability coefficient would mean that if you know a person's score derived from a measurement process on one occasion, you can make a good estimate of that person's score on that same measurement process on a different occasion. Low test-retest reliability, on the other hand, would mean that knowledge of the results of one administration

Figure 13.2 An Example of a Negative Correlation between IQ Scores and the Number of Days Absent During a Quarter

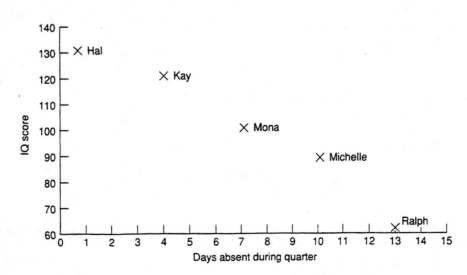

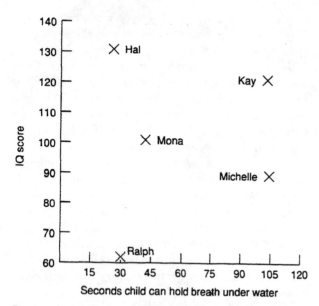

Figure 13.3 An Example of a Near-Zero Correlation between IQ Scores and the Length of Time a Child Can Hold His or Her Breath Under Water

of the measurement process would give us little ability to estimate a person's performance on a different occasion.

HOW TO READ A SCATTERGRAM

Figures 13.1 through 13.4 presented scores in scattergrams. In Figure 13.1, for example, the range of IQ scores is written along the left side of the diagram, and the range of reading scores is written across the bottom. Low and zero scores are at the bottom and left, respectively; high scores are at the top and right. Since each student has two scores (an IQ score and a reading score), it is possible to describe each student's performance by placing a mark at the point in the diagram that corresponds to his or her performance on the two tests. Thus, Ralph had an IQ of about 62 and a reading score of 5; and therefore in Figure 13.1 we can indicate Ralph's performance to the right of 62 on the IQ scale and above 5 on the reading scale. (Note that neither 62 nor 5 is actually written on the scales, but these points can easily be estimated from other numbers that are there.) Likewise, Kay had an IQ score of 123 and a reading score of 55, and therefore her performance is recorded by putting a mark to the right of 123 on the IQ scale and above 55 on the reading scale.

Figure 13.4 The Data from Figure 13.2 Reversed to Show a Positive Rather than Negative Correlation between IQ and Attendance in Class

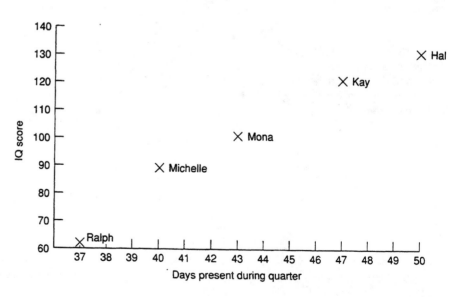

Let us apply the same logic to Figure 13.2. Ralph has an IQ of 62 and was absent 13 days. Therefore, his performance is indicated with a mark to the right of 62 on the IQ scale and above 13 on the days-absent scale. And so on.

After this brief introduction, test your knowledge by answering the following questions:

1. In Figure 13.1, what are Hal's scores?
2. In Figure 13.1, what are Michelle's scores?
3. In Figure 13.2, what are Mona's scores?
4. In Figure 13.3, what are Ralph's scores?
5. In Figure 13.3, what are Hal's scores?

Answers:

1. IQ about 130, reading about 80
2. IQ about 90, reading about 20
3. IQ about 100, days absent about 7
4. IQ about 60, breath held for about 30 seconds
5. IQ about 130, breath held for about 30 seconds

If you got any of these wrong, and if you cannot understand the basis of your errors, you should ask someone for help. Reading these diagrams is actually not difficult, and this skill will be helpful to you in reading the text and in your professional reading. Figures 13.1 to 13.4 show relatively simple diagrams, since each contains data on only five persons. Scattergrams containing many more data points are interpreted in exactly the same way as these simplified examples.

THE STRENGTH OF RELATIONSHIPS

How high does a correlation coefficient have to be to indicate a strong relationship? There is no single answer to this question. A good way to answer it is by asking another. Earlier we talked about correlations as indicating how accurate a prediction about a second characteristic would be, based on our knowledge of a first characteristic. How accurate would such an estimate have to be for you to consider it a good estimate? A relationship of 1.00 or -1.00 would indicate a perfect relationship, but such relationships do not appear in educational studies. The closer you get to a value of 1.00 (or -1.00), the stronger the relationship is. A relationship of r = .70 is stronger than one of r = .50, and so on. A useful interpretation of such correlation coefficients is shown in the following:

There is a Pearson correlation of .50 between IQ and the number of books a child reads during the school year, and there is a correlation of .75 between self-concept and the number of books read. This means that we can make a much better estimate of how much reading children will do by measuring their self-concepts than by assessing their IQ.

To summarize, Pearson correlation coefficients range between theoretical limits of +1.00 and -1.00. The strength of the relationship is indicated by the absolute value of the coefficient, disregarding the sign. A strong positive relationship indicates that a person with a high score on one of the variables is likely to have a high score on the other as well. A moderate positive correlation has the same meaning, but predictions of the second characteristic based on knowledge of the first are not as likely to be precise. A negative correlation indicates that a person who has a high score on one variable is likely to have a low score on the other variable. If this negative relationship is strong, then estimates of the second variable based on knowledge of the first are likely to be accurate. However, as the correlation coefficient approaches zero, the relationship grows weaker. When correlations are weak (near zero), there is little or no relationship between the two variables; it is impossible to make consistently good predications about one characteristic based on knowledge of the other.

And now here is an important technical note. The Pearson correlation coefficient is calculated with the mathematical assumption that the scores represent interval or ratio data (discussed in chapter 7). When the coefficient is computed with ordinal or simple nominal data, it still indicates the strength of a relationship; but it must be kept in mind that ordinal and nominal scores convey different information than interval or ratio scores. For example, a correlation of r = .57 between gender and reading achievement would mean that there was a moderately strong relationship between gender and scores on a reading test. To calculate this coefficient, the researcher could have arbitrarily classified males as "0" and females as "1" (or vice versa). As you can see, these numbers are merely labels (nominal data); it is not logical to assume that the numbers indicate a degree of "maleness" or "femaleness" that can be quantified. The coefficient merely indicates that there is a tendency for persons labeled as female to score higher on the reading test than those labeled as males; and this tendency is stronger than would be the case if the coefficient were, say, r = .26.

The preceding discussion has merely indicated that there are further statistical considerations in calculating and using correlation coefficients. More detailed information can be found in Appendix E of this book and in the reference cited at the end of this chapter.

REVIEW QUIZ 13.1

1. Which of the following coefficients indicates the strongest observed relationship?

    .35
    .79
    .01
    -.85
    -.14

2. Which of the following coefficients indicates the weakest relationship?

    .27
    .04
    -.17
    -.86
    .80

3. Let's say that there is a moderate positive relationship between creativity and scores on the Art Proficiency Test. This relationship would best be described by which of the following coefficients?

    .60
    .95
    .17
    -.25
    -.60

4. Let's say that there is a strong negative relationship between creativity and the amount of time a student can stay in Mr. McDonald's class. This relationship would best be described by which of the following coefficients?

    .57
    .96
    .01
    -.63
    -.86

5. Let's say that there is almost no relationship between creativity and the number of boxes of cookies a girl scout can sell. This relationship would best be described by which of the following coefficients?

    .18
    .88
    -.79
    -.16
    .51

6. Let's say that there is a Pearson correlation of -.80 between ability in Mrs. Schmidt's French class and performance in Mr. Tut's geometry class. What does this statement mean?

7. Let's say that the correlation between the amount of time spent watching television and scores on the current events exam is .17. What does this statement mean?

COMPUTING THE STATISTICS

This is not a statistics book. Statistics are introduced in this text as tools to accomplish research goals. Chapter 14 will introduce a few more statistics, and Appendix E offers a brief summary of a larger number of statistical procedures. Neither the underlying mathematical theory behind procedures nor the method of computing these statistics is discussed in detail in this book.

However, since some statistics are extremely important to compute, a cookbook approach to computing some elementary statistics is included in Appendix D. In cases where you have a large number of subjects for whom you wish to analyze data, or if the statistic you wish to compute is more complex, you should do your analysis by computer. The use of the computer for such purposes is discussed in Chapter 18.

If you wish to obtain additional skills in statistical analysis, you should read further textbooks, consult the references in the Annotated Bibliographies at the end of this and the next chapter, take appropriate courses, or consult with someone who can help you with your analysis. A major goal of the present text is to enable you to develop a basic understanding to help you use computers appropriately for computation, to read further references and professional literature intelligently, and to ask the right questions when looking for help regarding statistical matters.

PARTIAL CORRELATION

Sometimes it is useful to know what the relationship would be between two variables if the influence of a third variable were reduced or eliminated. For example, in Box 13.1, it was suggested that there is a high positive correlation between the temperature of water and the number of drownings in the ocean. You might rightly have noted that this occurs because more people go swimming when it is warm; and if there are more people in the water, there is a greater likelihood that someone will drown—warm water doesn't cause people to drown.

Let us assume that the correlation between maximum daily water temperature and number of drownings is .80. The question you might want answered is this: What would the correlation have been if the number of people in the water was the same every day? A partial correlation coefficient mathematically adjusts for the influence of some third factor (such as number of people in the water) and estimates what the relationship between the other two variables would have been if the influence of this third factor were reduced or eliminated. For example, even though the Pearson correlation coefficient between water temperature and number of drownings might be .80, the partial correlation (with the number of people in the water taken into consideration) would probably be closer to .00.

Partial correlations have the same theoretical range (1.00 to -1.00) as the other coefficients discussed in this chapter; partial correlation coefficients are interpreted in the same way as these others. However, the reference to the third variable makes it a bit more complicated to state this relationship in simple English. Here are a few hypothetical examples of partial correlations accompanied by brief paraphrases:

1. When IQ is controlled through partial correlation, the correlation of .60 between scores on creativity tests and grades in art class drops to .20.

   If all the students had similar IQs, then there would have been little or no relationship between creativity and art performance.

   (The apparent moderate relationship between creativity and art performance probably occurred because students with higher IQs did well both on the creativity tests and in the art class.)

2. The Pearson correlation between mechanical aptitude and performance on the electronics exam was .75. With IQ held constant, the partial correlation was .70.

   Even when the influence of IQ is eliminated, there is still about the same moderate relationship between mechanical aptitude and performance on the electronics exam.

(The relationship between mechanical aptitude and electronics performance is probably not caused by IQ.)

3. The correlation between number of hours of therapy and currently rated personality adjustment after one year of therapy was -.60. However, when severity of initial prognosis was controlled, the partial correlation was .40.

There was a strong tendency of those who received more therapy to have a lower current personality adjustment index. If everyone had an equally severe prognosis, however, then there would have been a moderate tendency for those who had more treatment to have better personality scores after therapy.

(The reason for the original relationship was probably that people who had more severe troubles took more treatment. Even if people who had more troubles improved substantially, their scores would still be lower than those who had fewer troubles at the start and therefore required less treatment. This difference in initial prognosis clouded the relationship between the amount of treatment and the status of clients after the treatment.)

Partial correlations are often identified by the notation $r_{12,3}$. The correlation is between two variables (1 and 2), with the third variable (3) partialed out.

As we have noted elsewhere in this chapter, although the existence of a correlation does not demonstrate causality, the finding of no correlation is a strong step toward demonstrating that there is no causal relationship. If there is no relationship between two variables, then certainly one of them cannot be the cause of the other.

Partial correlations can have an even more important bearing on causal inferences than can Pearson correlations. By using partial correlations, a researcher may be able to either verify or rule out many of the alternative explanations for an observed correlation, and eliminating alternative hypotheses is a major part of the scientific research process. If there is a high Pearson correlation between two vari-

ables, a researcher might compute a partial correlation, controlling (i.e., partialing out) the influence of some third variable. If the correlation drops dramatically when this is done, this is strong evidence that there is not a causal relationship between the original two variables. On the other hand, if the partial correlation is about as strong as the original Pearson correlation, the assumption that there is a causal relationship between the original two variables is strengthened, because the likelihood that the relationship was caused by one specific alternative variable has been ruled out as a result of the partial correlation analysis. By measuring enough variables and running enough partial correlations, the researcher can rule out many of the alternative explanations for the observed relationship. Although this procedure does not *prove* causality, it can be a significant step toward strengthening the acceptance of a causal inference, since it helps eliminate rival explanations. This is a useful strategy in situations where experimental research is difficult or impossible. This method of partialing out the influence of many variables to determine the resulting interrelationships is the basis of *path analysis,* a strategy for determining probable causality (path analysis is reported in many educational research journals).

REVIEW QUIZ 13.2

1. Which of the following is a Pearson correlation coefficient, and which is a partial correlation coefficient?

    -.14

    .86

    .35

2. Which of the following would require a Pearson correlation coefficient, and which would require a partial correlation coefficient?

    a. If we rule out the common influence of socioeconomic status on both IQ performance and appreciation of poetry, can it still be said that more intelligent students have a greater appreciation for poetry?

b. Did those who finished closer to first place in the tennis tournament spend more time jogging than those who finished near last place?

c. Is the amount of time a student spends in the assistant principal's office when called in for an infraction related to the severity of the punishment the child will receive?

CURVILINEAR CORRELATIONS

Is the overall level of excitability of the human organism related to a person's ability to learn? In other words, do we become more capable of learning as our level of arousal increases? The answer seems to be that humans do show an increasing ability to learn as level of arousal increases up to a certain point of arousal. After that point is reached, however, the pattern reverses itself: the more aroused the person becomes, the less the person learns. This relationship is diagrammed in Figure 13.5. The diagram shows that a person who is either nearly asleep or near panic will learn little, whereas a person at a medium level of arousal will learn a great deal.

Is there a strong relationship between level of arousal and ability to learn? Obviously, Figure 13.5 shows a very strong relationship—a very predictable pattern. However, the Pearson coefficients would indicate a near-zero correlation. This low correlation would be found because those coefficients are designed to measure only linear (straight line) relationships, like those previously diagrammed in Figures 13.1 through 13.4. If ability to learn kept increasing as level of arousal increased (so that the most aroused person would also be the most able to learn), this pattern would have resulted in a strong linear (straight line) relationship, and the Pearson correlation coefficient would have been high. However, since the pattern reversed itself at midpoint, this would drastically reduce the magnitude of the Pearson correlation coefficient.

To measure curvilinear relationships, we need a more advanced type of correlation coefficient—one that is sensitive to nonlinear patterns. One such coefficient is the eta coefficient. Eta coefficients have a theoretical range from 1.00 to .00. (There are no

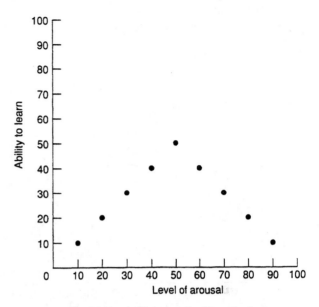

Figure 13.5 Diagram Showing the Hypothetical Relationship between Level of Arousal and Ability to Learn. (This is a curvilinear relationship. The numbers on the side and bottom of the diagram refer to scores that could be obtained on hypothetical tests measuring level of arousal and ability to learn.)

negative curvilinear relationships.) Other than that, the interpretation of the eta coefficient is basically the same as that of other correlation coefficients. A high value indicates a strong tendency to adhere to the curvilinear pattern, and a low value indicates a weak relationship. However, to interpret the eta coefficient, you need a scattergram or graph of the formula representing the relationship. The scattergram indicates the pattern of the relationship, and the eta coefficient indicates how strongly the scores adhere to this pattern. For example, Figure 13.6 shows an eta coefficient of .83 between level of arousal and ability to learn.

The diagram in Figure 13.6 is essential to interpreting eta coefficients. If all we knew was that there was an eta correlation of .83 between two variables, this relationship could take a number of forms, such as those shown in Figure 13.7. The diagram provides the pattern, and the eta coefficient indicates how strongly the data adhere to this pattern.

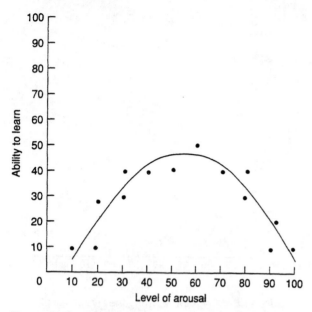

Figure 13.6 Diagram Showing a Hypothetical Less than Perfect Relationship (eta = .83) between Level of Arousal and Ability to Learn

Those readers who are mathematically oriented might have noticed that the eta coefficient could be used even for linear relationships. This is because a straight (linear) line can be viewed as a specific type of curved line. Therefore, it would be possible to replace the Pearson correlation coefficient with the eta coefficient. For several reasons, this has not happened. Mainly, the Pearson correlation coefficient is more readily interpreted (no need for a diagram) than the eta coefficient and more easily integrated with other statistical procedures. In addition, most relationships in the educational and psychological worlds are reasonably linear. When they are not linear, the Pearson correlation coefficient underestimates the degree of the relationship. Thus, if a reported Pearson correlation coefficient is strong, it can be assumed that the eta coefficient is even stronger. The eta coefficient can be a useful tool for discovering curvilinear relationships, when such relationships are thought to be important.

REVIEW QUIZ 13.3

Which of the following relationships would be described by an eta coefficient?

a. The hungrier children get, the less they learn. This is true both right after children have eaten and several hours later.

b. As time passes after a meal, children learn well. This is true up to a certain point. After that point, as time passes, they learn less well.

MULTIPLE CORRELATION COEFFICIENTS

It is possible for a certain ability to be caused or predicted not by a single factor but by a combination of two or more factors. Likewise, a more accurate prediction could be made about a certain event not by using a single variable for making this prediction but rather by combining our knowledge about several different variables. This is what multiple correlation does. It enables us to state the relationship between a combination of several variables and some outcome variable. Multiple correlation coefficients are differentiated from simple Pearson correlation coefficients by using a capital R instead of a lowercase r to indicate the relationship. Like the other correlation coefficients, multiple correlation does not necessarily show causality; it merely indicates that a relationship exists.

Let us examine one instance of a multiple correlation coefficient. Assume that there is a multiple correlation of $R = .65$ among a combination of manual dexterity, rating during an initial interview, and rating from a previous employer and later success as a computer operator. This means that a weighted combination of these three predictor factors is as strongly related to the criterion variable (success as a computer operator) as would be a single variable (if one could be found) with a correlation of .65. Taken separately, manual dexterity might correlate .50 with success as a computer operator; initial interview, .35 with success as a computer operator; and previous employer's rating, .45 with success as a computer

Figure 13.7 Four Possible Diagrams of the Relationship Described by an Eta Coefficient of .80 between Two Variables

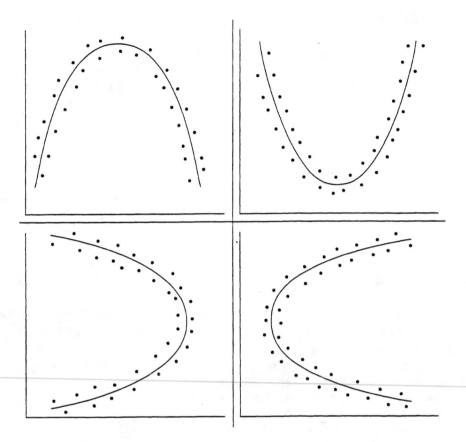

operator. But when they are combined and used simultaneously for prediction, they show a much stronger relationship. If a prospective employer could use either IQ (which we'll speculate correlates .60 with success as a computer operator) or any of these other variables to select her new computer operators, she should use IQ, because it is more strongly related to future performance than any of the others. On the other hand, if she can combine the three into a single, weighted package and make a prediction, then this combination will yield a more accurate selection process than would the single variable of IQ.

The topic of multiple correlation is usually introduced in an intermediate- or advanced-level statistics course rather than in a general educational research methods course. This is because performing multiple correlations requires relatively complex computational procedures and because it is possible to do some relatively complicated things with this technique. It is introduced here to indicate an additional direction that correlation coefficients can take and to enable you to recognize and interpret them in your professional reading. You are likely to come across "multiple R's" in your professional reading, and this brief introduction can help you understand them. Likewise, in your own research it will be useful to know that there is a technique for combining several variables to ascertain their relationship to another variable, and the information given here will enable you to seek help in developing multiple correlation coefficients.

REVIEW QUIZ 13.4

Which of the following statements would be based on a multiple correlation coefficient?
   a. There is a correlation of .75 between a combination of IQ and creativity and performance in art class.
   b. There is a correlation of .80 between creativity scores and performance in art class, and there is a correlation of .69 between creativity scores and performance in English class.

PUTTING IT ALL TOGETHER

Part of the research Mr. Anderson performed fits into the categories of criterion group and correlational studies described in this chapter. For example, he wanted to find out whether being the owner of a pet caused children to have a more favorable attitude toward animal life. The only way he could examine this question was through a criterion group design. He obtained access to several classes of children, identified the pet owners and non-pet owners, and then compared the performance of these two groups on the Fireman Test. He had to use a criterion group research design rather than an experimental design because pet ownership was not a variable over which he had any control. (True, it was theoretically possible that he could have found a group of 50 non-pet owners and assigned pets to 25 and withheld pets from the others. But aside from being of dubious ethical and practical merit, this experiment would not have addressed the same question as that addressed by examining the naturally occurring pattern of ownership.) Mr. Anderson administered Johnny and the Fireman Test to about 200 pet owners and 100 non-pet owners and he found that the mean number of animals chosen was 1.20 by the non-pet owners and 1.15 by the pet owners. This difference was not substantial. (The idea of assessing the statistical significance of the results will be discussed in the next chapter.) Mr. Anderson concluded that there was no relationship between pet ownership and attitudes toward animal life.

Mr. Anderson was at first surprised to find no difference in attitudes between pet owners and nonowners, but soon he realized that this was actually quite logical. There were a lot of children who would have liked to own a pet and would be kind to a pet but simply did not own one for reasons beyond their control. Likewise, many children who owned pets viewed them as objects rather than as living things. He decided to pursue a new line of reasoning. He wondered whether among pet owners there was a relationship between the amount of time children spent caring for their pet and their attitudes toward animal life. He subdivided the 200 pet owners from his previous study into three groups, based on how much time per week they spent actively caring for their pets. When he examined the scores, he found these results:

Pet owners who spent at least 30 minutes per day caring for their pets: 1.5 animals chosen

Pet owners who spent between 15 and 30 minutes per day caring for their pets: 1.2 animals chosen

Pet owners who spent less than 15 minutes per day caring for their pets   0.8 animals chosen

He saw a clear pattern in these results. Pet owners who spent more time caring for their pets did, in fact, display more favorable attitudes toward animal life. (Again, the concept of statistical significance, treated in the next chapter, would be relevant here.)

Note that Mr. Anderson has examined two different questions. In one case he found no relationship, and in the other he found a relationship. In the first case, when he found no relationship between pet ownership and attitudes toward animal life, this could be taken as evidence about a causal relationship. If there was no relationship between pet ownership and attitudes toward animal life, then a fortiori (as the logicians say) pet ownership cannot cause these attitudes. (If pet ownership did cause the attitudes, then there would be a relationship.) On the other hand, the finding that the amount of time spent taking care of one's pet is related to attitudes toward animal life cannot be taken as evidence that there may be a causal relationship. It may be possible, for example, that friendly attitudes cause the children to spend more time taking care of their pets. On the other hand, it may also be possible that spending more time with one's pet causes friendlier attitudes. Without further information, all we can say is that there is a relationship, and this may be a causal relationship.

SUMMARY

Criterion group designs and correlational research are useful for demonstrating the existence of relationships. They do not, however, provide direct, compelling evidence with regard to cause-and-effect relationships. The only strong cause-and-effect conclusion that can be based on these designs is that if no relationship is found using a criterion group or correlational design, then there is probably not a causal relationship. When such designs do uncover a

relationship, however, further information is needed to determine the causal direction, if any, of this relationship. Such further information can be obtained from nonexperimental research design and reasoning, including the elimination of rival hypotheses and the examination of further criterion groups and correlations. However, the strongest evidence regarding cause-and-effect relationships has to be acquired from the experimental research designs discussed in the previous two chapters.

This chapter has also examined specific correlation coefficients for estimating the strength of a relationship. Table 13.2 summarizes the major characteristics of the correlation coefficients discussed in this chapter. Table 13.3 shows examples of each coefficient. The absolute (nonsigned) value of a correlation coefficient determines the strength of a relationship, and the sign indicates whether the relation-

Table 13.2 Summary of Important Features of Statistics That Measure the Strength of a Relationship

Statistical Procedure	Description	Interpretation
Pearson correlation coefficient	Measures the strength of the linear relationship between two interval or ordinal scale variables	• The *absolute* value indicates the *strength* of the relationship • Either 1.00 or –1.00 would indicate a perfect relationship • Zero indicates no relationship whatsoever • The sign indicates direct or inverse relationship
Eta coefficient	Measures the strength of the curvilinear relationship between two interval or ordinal scale variables	• The coefficient must be accompanied by a diagram or verbal description of the relationship. The coefficient indicates how strongly the scores adhere to this pattern • Zero is no relationship; 1.00 would be a perfect relationship • Eta coefficients are always positive
Partial correlation coefficient	Estimates what the strength of the linear relationship between two variables would be if the influence of a third variable were controlled	• Same as for Pearson coefficient — with the further condition that the influence of an additional factor(s) is removed
Multiple correlation coefficient	Measures the strength of the relationship between a combination of two or more predictor variables and a criterion variable	• Same as Pearson coefficient, except that the variable is actually a combination of several variables • Zero indicates no relationship; 1.00 would indicate a perfect correlation

Table 13.3 Examples of Correlation Coefficients and Their Meanings

Correlation Coefficient	Example	Interpretations
Pearson correlation coefficient	There is a correlation of .75 between students' verbal SAT scores and success in the English class.	• There was a fairly strong tendency for persons who did well on the verbal portion of the SAT to do well in the English class (and for those who did poorly on the SAT to do poorly in English). • If we knew a student's SAT score, we could make a good guess about how well that student would do in the English class.
Eta coefficient	The researcher found an eta coefficient of .75 between the amount of time the students spent preparing for the test and how well they did on the test. (This statement would be accompanied by a diagram to show the nature of the relationship.)	• There was a fairly strong tendency for students who spent either very little time or a great deal of time preparing for the test to do well on it, whereas those who spent a medium amount of time tended to do more poorly. (Other interpretations would be possible with different diagrams.) • If we know how much time a student spent preparing for the test, we can make a pretty good guess about that student's performance - but this relationship may not be as simple as with the Pearson coefficient).
Partial correlation coefficient	There was a Pearson correlation of .75 between performance in the algebra class and performance in the geometry class. However, when the role of IQ was taken into consideration, the partial correlation dropped to .25.	• If all the students would have been of comparable intelligence, there would have been little relationship between performance in the two classes. • The relatively strong relationship between performance in the two classes probably occurred because IQ is an important factor in both classes.
Multiple correlation coefficient	There was a Multiple R of .75 between the combination of school rating, rank in class, and GPA and subsequent performance as a freshman in college.	• We can predict performance in college fairly accurately from information about the students' GPA and class rank and the rating of their school. • By combining these three factors we can predict students' performance in college as well as we could with a single factor (if we could find one) that had a Pearson correlation of .75 with performance as a college freshman.

ship is positive or negative. The Pearson correlation coefficient is by far the most widely used coefficient. The partial correlation coefficient estimates what the strength of a relationship would be if the influence of a specified extraneous factor were removed. The eta coefficient is an example of a statistical method for estimating the strength of curvilinear relationships. Finally, the multiple correlation coefficient combines several predictable variables and estimates the strength of the relationship between this combination of predictor variables and a criterion variable.

The research designs discussed in this chapter have two major uses. First, we can use them as a patchwork method when time is a factor or when a better design is impossible. Such designs enable us to examine on a minimally controlled basis relationships that would otherwise go unexplored if we had to wait for actual experimental evidence. It is important to note at this point that a large amount of our daily thinking about relationships necessarily goes on without experimentation. We must constantly make decisions based on what we perceive in our world. In making these decisions, we necessarily develop our own criterion groups and estimate our own correlations, even if we are not specifically aware of doing so. A knowledge of the uses and limitations of non-experimental research design, therefore, can help us in this routine, nonexperimental decision making.

Second, these designs are generally useful preliminary designs to use before undertaking data collection in experimental or quasi-experimental designs. If we know that a relationship exists, then we can undertake further, more scientifically controlled efforts to determine whether this is a causal relationship.

What Comes Next

Chapter 14 will conclude the discussion of statistical tools by describing tests of significance, which help estimate the likelihood that the results of experiments and other research designs are not merely the result of chance fluctuations in data. Chapter 15 will begin the treatment of Level III research, which builds upon Level II research.

DOING YOUR OWN RESEARCH

Correlational and criterion group research are often more convenient to conduct than experimental research. This is because all you have to do is collect data about existing situations rather than assigning subjects to treatments and timing the collection of data to rule out threats to internal validity. Because these forms of research are relatively easy to conduct, beginning researchers often choose them for research projects.

While correlational and criterion group research are often useful in their own right, a major purpose of conducting such research is to lay the basis for future research to examine the cause-and-effect nature of these relationships. Therefore, it is important at this stage to learn as much as possible about the nature of these relationships. The usefulness of correlational and criterion group research can be enhanced by collecting valid data for all variables involved in the study and supplementing the quantitative data with qualitative data that will lead to more complete interpretation and testable hypotheses.

FOR FURTHER THOUGHT

1. In what ways are correlational and criterion group research similar? In what ways are they different?

2. In what ways are criterion group and experimental research similar? In what ways are they different?

3. Complete this sentence by answering the designated questions: "Correlational research . . .(does what?) (To what or whom?) (When?) (Where?) (How?) (Why?)"

4. Complete this sentence by answering the designated questions: "Criterion group research . . .(does what?) (To what or whom?) (When?) (Where?) (How?) (Why?)"

ANNOTATED BIBLIOGRAPHY

Guilford, J. P., & Fruchter, B. (1978). *Fundamental statistics in psychology and education* (6th ed.). New York: McGraw-Hill. This book provides a good discussion of correlation coefficients.

In addition to the Guilford and Fruchter text, many of the sources cited in the bibliography at the end of the next chapter are closely related to the topic of this chapter as well.

ANSWERS TO QUIZZES

Review Quiz 13.1

1. -.85 indicates the strongest relationship. If you answered .79, you forgot that it is the absolute value (disregarding the sign) that indicates the strength of the relationship.

314 ■ CHAPTER 13

2. .04 indicates the weakest relationship. If you answered -.86, then you are letting the negative sign distract you. The coefficient -.86 actually indicates the strongest relationship in this set of coefficients.

3. .60 indicates a moderate positive relationship. .95 indicates a strong positive relationship; .17 indicates a weak positive relationship. The others indicate a negative relationship.

4. -.86 indicates the strongest negative relationship.

5. Either .18 or -.16 would show almost no relationship. Remember: -.79 shows a strong (but negative) correlation.

6. There is a fairly strong relationship. People who do well in the French class tend to do poorly in the geometry class. Likewise, the weaker students in the French class are likely to be among the stronger students in the geometry class.

7. There is practically no relationship between the two variables. If we know how much time a child spends watching television, we could not reasonably use this as a basis for estimating that child's performance on the current events exam.

Review Quiz 13.2

1. It is impossible to tell. Both correlation coefficients are reported in the same way.

2. a. partial
   b. Pearson
   c. Pearson

Review Quiz 13.3

The second relationship would be described by an eta coefficient.

Review Quiz 13.4

The first statement would be based on a multiple correlation coefficient. Note that b is actually two separate Pearson correlation coefficients.

CHAPTER 13

Research Report Analysis

Experimental studies often contain partial examples of other research strategies as well. There is one respect in which the research report in Appendix C incorporates criterion group or correlations research. Can you find it?

1. In what way does this research report incorporate the results of a criterion group study? (Hint: The answer can be found in a one-sentence reference to a moderator variable.)

ANSWER:

1. The researchers report, at the end of the Results section, that the boys and girls responded similarly in the study. Boys and girls were not assigned by the researchers to their respective genders. This minor aspect of the study represents criterion group research.

TESTS OF STATISTICAL SIGNIFICANCE

■ WHERE WE'VE BEEN

We have examined the major threats to internal validity and seen how experimental and quasi-experimental research designs help control them. We have also examined correlational and criterion group research and seen how these nonexperimental procedures help establish the existence of relationships, without providing direct information about causality.

■ WHERE WE'RE GOING NOW

In this chapter we'll discuss tests of statistical significance, which help rule out the likelihood that the results of experiments are merely an outcome of chance fluctuations in data. These statistical procedures will be treated in a conceptual rather than a mathematical manner.

■ CHAPTER PREVIEW

Two serious problems in establishing cause-and-effect relationships were mentioned near the beginning of chapter 11. The first of these was that it is impossible to find groups that are actually equal in every respect with regard to all variables except the treatment. Solutions to this problem were discussed in chapters 11 and 12. The second problem was that it is often difficult to tell whether groups are still the same with regard to the outcome variables after a treatment. This is the problem referred to as instability, and it is one of the major threats to internal validity.

The results of collecting data before and after a treatment are clouded because the unreliability of the measurement processes and natural fluctuations found in small samples will introduce chance variations in scores. This threat to internal validity cannot be controlled by eliminating it, but it can be mathematically assessed to determine whether differences in the scores obtained from the data collection processes exceed the natural amount of fluctuation that would occur because of instability. The researcher and the users of the research can then judge whether such instability is an important factor influencing conclusions drawn from the experiment. The basic strategies for estimating the likelihood of such chance fluctuations in scores are the topic of this chapter.

After reading this chapter, you should be able to

1. Describe the underlying principles behind statistical tests of significance.

2. Describe what is meant by level of statistical significance and interpret statements regarding such levels.

3. Describe the purposes of each of the following statistical procedures:

    t test

    F tests in the analysis of variance

    Chi square

4. Identify situations in which each of the preceding statistical procedures would correctly be used.

5. Given a situation in which each of the preceding statistical procedures is used, interpret the situation correctly.

6. Use an appropriate statistical table to identify the level of significance of a *t* statistic.

7. Define statistical power and give examples of its application.

■

THE BASIS OF STATISTICAL REASONING

If you flipped a quarter 10 times and came up with 6 heads and 4 tails, would you be astonished at this outcome? If you then flipped a half dollar 10 times and came up with 5 heads and 5 tails, would this result surprise you? Comparing the two results, would you conclude that quarters were more likely than half dollars to come up heads? In the preceding series of events, you would probably be unimpressed by the evidence. You would rightly point out that simply because the flip of a quarter comes out 6

heads and 4 tails one time, this does not mean that the result will always be that way. You know that the odds are that coin tosses will come out about half heads and half tails, and slight deviations from this norm are to be expected. The 6 heads represent a chance fluctuation; they are a concrete embodiment of the research threat of instability—nothing to get excited about.

Similar problems of instability arise in educational research. If the experimental class scores 80% on a test and the control class 70%, is this enough of a disparity to convince us that the treatment caused the difference, or could this be the result of imprecision of measurement and the natural fluctuations of groups of students? As we discussed in chapter 5, neither educational tests nor the people who administer them are perfectly reliable; and the absence of reliability introduces an element of chance into educational research comparisons. Likewise, there is a certain amount of chance variation arising from random assignment of subjects to groups as part of the experimental design. Because of this unreliability, we know that the scores of 80% and 70% are not precise measurements. These scores would probably have been different if we had measured the same students at a different time, under slightly different circumstances, or with a different form of the test, or if we used two different groups of students. Therefore, it is possible that the difference between the experimental and control groups' scores is no more real than was the difference between the tosses of the quarter and the half dollar in the situation we presented in the preceding paragraph. The difference between the two coins was *probably due to chance*. The difference between the scores of the experimental and control groups was also *probably due to chance*.

This is the problem dealt with by statistical tests of significance. *Such tests provide an estimate of how likely it is that two or more observed outcomes are merely chance fluctuations arising from attempts to measure an identical outcome*. Note that instability is the *only* threat to internal validity that statistical tests of significance help control. These statistical analyses do nothing to control any of the other threats; the other threats must be dealt with by experimental design or the other strategies discussed in chapters 11 and 12. Tests of significance are derived from underlying mathematical theories and are accomplished through computational procedures, which will not be discussed in this book. By applying one of these tests to the coin tossing example, we can specify that odds are about 75 in 100 that the quarter results (6 heads) and the half dollar results (5 heads) are really just chance variations of patterns that are thought to be identical in their long-range results. On the basis of this information, if you and a friend were flipping a coin to see who got a date with a bright, attractive person, you probably would not care whether the coin used for this purpose was a quarter or a half dollar. On the other hand, if the results of this statistical test would have shown that there was only 1 chance in 1,000 that the results were chance variations from coins likely to be identical, then you *would* be concerned about which coin would be used.

The same logic can be applied to educational research. *By applying statistical procedures, we can make an estimate of how likely it is that two observed outcomes are really just chance variations (instability) arising from identical capabilities.* Such information can be used to help us make judgments about educational experiments. In the educational example cited previously, we had an experimental group that scored 80% correct after a treatment, while the control group scored 70%. If we applied a statistical test of significance to these results, we might discover that the chances are about 75 in 100 that the scores of 80% (experimentals) and 70% (controls) on a grammar test could well be chance variations of actually identical grammar abilities influenced by instability. If we knew this, then we would conclude that the groups were probably not really different after the treatment. Furthermore, we would also conclude that the treatment had not produced an observed outcome greater than would be expected by mere chance. On the other hand, if our statistical test had shown that there was only one chance in 100 that the scores of the two groups were likely to represent chance variations of an identical capability, then we would conclude that the groups probably were different after the treatment. More-

over, if we had previously ascertained that the groups were equal before the treatment, we would be justified in concluding that the treatment had produced an outcome greater than would have been expected by chance alone. This logic of statistical reasoning in experiments is schematically summarized in Figure 14.1.

Let us incorporate this statistical reasoning into the basic research strategy discussed in chapter 11. If we found that the difference was so small that it was likely to have occurred by mere chance, then our reasoning would go like this:

The two groups were identical to begin with, except for minor, chance variations.

The two groups were treated essentially identically, except that one of them received the treatment.

Afterwards, the groups still did not differ, except as would be expected by mere chance variations.

Therefore, since the groups are still the same, the treatment must not have made a difference.

All this reasoning, of course, relies on the basic assumptions that the groups really were equal to begin with, that we really did treat them identically with regard to everything except the treatment, and that we are validly measuring the outcome we think we are measuring. If we have failed to meet any one of these assumptions (for example, if we have used an invalid or totally unreliable test measuring something other than what we intended to measure), then our research conclusion would be wrong. *Statistical procedures cannot rectify faulty logic or faulty research procedures!*

If we found that the difference between the two groups was *not* likely to have occurred by mere chance, then our reasoning would go like this:

The two groups were essentially identical to begin with, except for chance differences.

The two groups were treated essentially identically, except that one of them received the treatment.

Figure 14.1 Summary Diagram of the Logic Behind the Statistical Tests of Significance

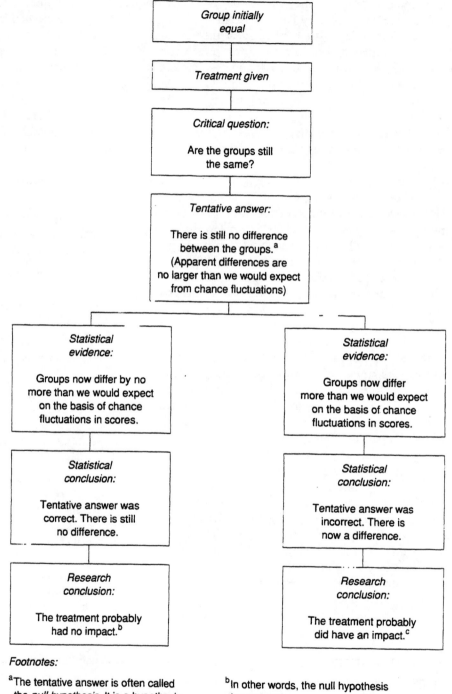

Footnotes:

[a]The tentative answer is often called the *null hypothesis*. It is a hypothesis that there is *no* difference between the two groups.

[b]In other words, the null hypothesis is accepted.

[c]In other words, the null hypothesis is rejected.

Afterwards, the groups differed by a greater amount than would be expected by mere chance variations.

Therefore, since the groups are no longer identical, the treatment must have caused this difference.[1]

Note that the statistical reasoning discussed in the previous paragraphs is based on the assumption that the groups were *initially identical;* this assumption, in turn, requires random assignment. Strictly speaking, therefore, many statistical tests of significance relying on this type of reasoning should be applied only to true experiments, where random assignment has been employed. Statisticians who have pursued the matter, however, have ascertained that within certain guidelines these same procedures can be applied—with much the same meaning—to situations in which random assignment was not used. The precise nature of these guidelines is beyond the scope of this book. The same or similar reasoning and statistical tests can be applied to quasi-experiments.

Also note that it is not possible to make a sound judgment about the probability that the performance of the experimental and control groups differed by more than chance variation merely by examining their scores of 80% and 70%. To make such a judgment, additional information would be needed. At the least, we would need the means and standard deviations of the two groups, but the easiest way would be to have the exact scores of all the students and plug these into a computer program, as chapter 18 will describe. Some simple computational procedures are described in Appendix D, but for other procedures you should take courses in statistics and refer to more detailed statistics texts.

The following sections of this chapter are intended to introduce you to some basic statistical tests of significance. This introduction will help you understand their use when you read about these statistics in professional journals and will enable you to know which procedures can help you solve a given problem in your own work. Before actually trying to use some of these statistical procedures, you should seek information beyond that contained in this book regarding their computation and the basic assumptions underlying them.

STATISTICAL SIGNIFICANCE

A dictionary definition of the word *significant* would indicate that it means *important*. Using the logic described in the previous section of this chapter, we could say that the difference between the two groups is significant (important) if the difference is unlikely to be a chance occurrence. Likewise, we could say that a difference is insignificant if the results are likely to have occurred by chance. This is the meaning the word *significant* has in statistical usage. Saying that something is statistically significant is a way of saying how likely it is that observed outcomes are merely chance variations from the measurement of an identical capacity or from fluctuations from sample to sample in small samples (any number fewer than 7,000 is a small sample).

Statistical significance should not be confused with such ideas as social significance, relevance for society, practical applicability, and educational importance. For example, one of our children has a dice baseball game. By applying methods similar to our earlier coin tossing analysis, we might discover that he gets more 2s (home runs) than could reasonably be expected by chance alone when he plays this game. We might do a statistical analysis and conclude that there is only about 1 chance in 100 that he could get 2s as often as he does. This would be statistically significant evidence of cheating. However, in terms of what it reveals about his personality, what impact this finding will have on society, or what it means regarding what he will be when he grows up, the social and personal significance of this

---

[1]Technically, the reasoning process discussed in the previous two paragraphs is referred to as *testing the null hypothesis.* References to the null hypothesis are included in the footnote to Figure 14.1. Although the logic behind the null hypothesis is essential to educational research, the term itself is often confusing to students, and therefore it has been avoided in this text.

finding appears to be trivial. This would be an example of a statistically significant but practically inconsequential finding. Thus, when applied to statistical tests, the term *significant* entails a narrow, specific usage and has little to do with research design or with personal or social importance.

When we make statements about statistical significance, we do so in terms of a specific number. This number states the mathematical probability that the observed outcomes are merely chance variations arising from small samples and the unreliable measurement of identical capabilities. For example, an experimental group may be said to differ from a control group at the .01 level of significance. (This is often referred to as a *p* [for *probability*] *value*.) This means that there is less than 1 chance in 100 that the two groups are really equal with regard to the specified outcome and that the observed scores are merely chance variations arising out of some sort of instability. On the other hand, if the two groups differed at only the .50 level of significance, this would mean that there are about even odds that the obtained, apparent difference would occur if the groups were really equal and the observed outcomes were influenced only by chance variations arising from small samples and imprecise measurement processes. Thus, the *lower* the number included in the statement of significance, the *stronger* the degree of confidence we can have that the observed differences are not the result of chance fluctuations. In other words, the lower the level of significance, the stronger the differences.

This is an important idea to understand. Some students confuse level of significance with correlation coefficients. Since a high number indicates a strong correlation, they assume that a high number likewise reflects a strong difference between groups. This is not the case. It is easy to make the distinction, if you keep in mind the meaning of a statement of significance. A difference at the .01 level indicates a rarer probability than a difference at the .05 level of significance. That is, if there is only 1 chance in 100 that the results have occurred by chance, then the observed differences are more likely to be "real" than if there were 5 chances in 100 that the differences arose from random variations. Our confidence

in an outcome would be greater if there were only one chance in a thousand that an outcome occurred by chance than if there were 5 chances in 100 that it was a chance result.

There are several ways of stating the level of significance. All of the following statements mean exactly the same thing:

The two groups differed at the .01 level of significance.

The two groups differed significantly ($p < .01$).

The two groups differed significantly (alpha level = .01).

The first two statements employ terminology we have already discussed. In the second statement, "$p < .01$" means that the *probability* of the results arising from chance fluctuations is fewer than 1 in 100. In the third statement, "alpha level = .01" means that when the person interpreted this result, he or she entered the statistical table under the .01 column. The use of such a table will be described in the next section of this chapter.

Prior to the widespread availability of computers for calculating statistics, certain specific decision points were used to express levels of significance. A researcher would select a decision point (such as .01) and check to see whether the observed difference between means was more significant or less significant than would be indicated by that decision point. Thus, if a researcher selected a decision point at the .05 level of significance and there were 6 chances in 100 that the results were chance fluctuations, this outcome would be considered not significant. On the other hand, if there were only 4 chances in 100 that the difference represented a chance fluctuation, then this result would be significant at the .05 level.

Using this method, it is possible to develop a highly structured system of significance levels. Traditionally, a result with fewer than 5 chances in 100 was considered significant; a result at the .01 level of significance could be considered very significant; and one at the .001 level, extremely significant. Going in the other direction, a result significant near the .10 level was sometimes called nearly significant.

Perhaps a result above the .50 level of significance could be considered not even remotely close to approaching significance. With the exception of the last, all of these interpretations have actually been in vogue at one time or another.

Currently, however, the trend seems to be toward reporting exact levels of significance whenever possible. If your computer tells you that a difference was significant at the .02 level, why convert this to "significant beyond the .05 level"? Just report the exact level, and let your readers have full access to this more precise information. The strategy of labeling levels of significance at preconceived decision points arose out of an arbitrary consensus among researchers in the social sciences that if an outcome had a probability of greater than 1 in 20 of occurring by chance, it was beyond a reasonable doubt that the groups differed by instability alone. Such reasoning has some validity behind it, and you can use this logic if you like, even if you have access to precise levels of significance from computers. If you have access to a computer that gives exact levels of probability (as described in chapter 18), then it is better to use the more explicit information. On the other hand, if you have access only to a table (as we describe in this chapter), use the decision points—but use them intelligently, not as part of a blind ritual.

t TESTS

If you want to determine how likely it is that the means of interval data for two groups differ by more than would be expected by chance, you can do this with a t test. If you have more than two means to compare, you should not use a t test for your statistical analysis. Likewise, if you have nominal or ordinal data, you cannot use a t test. Note that t tests are actually a bit more complex than this brief discussion may seem to indicate. For example, there are different procedures for computing t tests when the same group is compared on two occasions than when one group is compared with another group. In this discussion, both procedures are covered jointly. A t test could be used to test the significance of the following differences between means of groups:

The mean of a group of students prior to a treatment compared with the mean of that same group after the treatment

The mean of the experimental group on a posttest compared with the mean of the control group on the same posttest

The gains of the experimental group compared with the gains of the control group (this one is tricky; in this case, four scores would become two *gain scores*, because each pretest score would be subtracted from a posttest score)

A t test could *not* be used to test the significance of the following differences between means of groups:

Scores on a pretest compared with performance on a posttest and performance on a delayed posttest (in this example, if you wanted to do two separate pretest-posttest comparisons, it would be possible with two separate t tests)

A comparison of the scores of fourth graders with those of fifth graders on an attention span test

A comparison of the performances of freshmen versus sophomores, where the classes are subdivided into groups of boys and girls (in this case, there are actually four groups)

If you wish to compare the means of more than two groups, you should use analysis of variance, which is described in the next section of this chapter.

A t test is performed by following an appropriate mathematical formula or accessing an appropriate computer program based on that formula. There are minor variations in t test formulas, depending on the precise nature of the comparisons being made. (The computational procedure for one of the most common t tests is included in Appendix D.) The output from the application of this formula is called a t statistic. To interpret a t statistic computed by hand, it is necessary to refer to a table, like the one in Appendix B.

To use such a table, you have to calculate a t statistic and determine your degrees of freedom and alpha level. (No discussion will be provided here of why these apparently obscure labels exist.) The degrees of freedom is usually the number of subjects minus two. The alpha level is the level of significance that you select—traditionally, the .05 or .01 level.

With this in mind, let's pursue an example and use the statistical table. Suppose we ran a *t* test with 32 subjects (16 in each group) and derived a result of $t = 2.30$. Is this result significant at the .05 level? To answer this question, we would look down the left-hand column of the table of significance in Appendix B (which is labeled *d.f.* for *degrees of freedom*) until we came to 30 (because 32 - 2 = 30). We would then look under the alpha level of .05 (alpha levels are written across the top of the table). Then we would go down the .05 column to the place where the .05 alpha level intersects with the row for 30 degrees of freedom. The number appearing at this intersection is 2.042. We would then ask ourselves: Is 2.30 greater than 2.042? The answer is yes, and therefore our result is statistically significant at the .05 level.

To pursue this example further, let us see whether this result is also significant at the .01 level. To answer this question, we would move over to the .01 alpha level column. Then we would look for the number at the intersection of the .01 alpha level and 30 degrees of freedom. We would then ask ourselves: Is 2.30 greater than 2.750? Since the answer is no, we could state that our result is *not* significant at the .01 level. The way statistical logic works, we can imagine the following conversation with ourselves:

What are the chances that the two groups have the same ability but that instability helped generate these two seemingly different mean scores from the measurement process? The answer is that there are somewhere between 1 and 5 chances in 100 that the two groups have the same ability but that instability helped generate these two seemingly different mean scores from the measurement process.

If the chances of the observed difference occurring because of instability are so remote, then it seems probable that the groups actually do differ from each other.

If we have effectively controlled the other threats to internal validity, then it seems likely that the treatment really did cause the observed differences.

In general, almost all tables of significance are interpreted in this manner. Some tables are more complex, but the strategy of interpretation is always the same. No further examples (e.g., for F tests from analysis of variance) will be provided in this text. Once the level of significance is obtained from such a table, it is interpreted in the way we described in this paragraph and in more detail earlier in this chapter.

REVIEW QUIZ 14.1

1. Which of the following questions would be answered using a *t* test?

   a. The boys averaged 4.5 correct answers; the girls averaged 5.1 correct. Is this difference likely to be the result of chance instabilities?

   b. Our students averaged 60.3% correct answers before the lecture and 75.1% after the lecture. Is this likely to be a real difference or a chance fluctuation?

   c. What is the relationship between test anxiety and scores on the final examination? Do those with higher anxiety do worse than those with lower anxiety? As anxiety decreases, does performance improve?

   d. We taught some students using computers and others with traditional methods. Did the computer work differently at each of three distinct levels of aptitude? Within both the experimental and control groups we had some high-ability, some medium-ability, and some low-ability students. We have mean scores on an achievement test for each of these groups of students.

2. Is each of the following comparisons significant at the .05 level? at the .01 level? at the .001 level?

a. Pretest mean = 51.5; Posttest mean = 53.2; $t = 2.70$ (number of subjects = 60)

b. Experimental group mean = 15.6; Control group mean = 23.7; $t = 1.13$ (number of subjects = 20)

c. Boys' average score = 34.9; Girls' average score = 27.3; $t = 2.99$ (number of subjects = 100)

d. $t = 5.45$; Number of subjects = 50

ANALYSIS OF VARIANCE

Analysis of variance examines the significance of the differences among *two or more* groups. Thus, it can be employed in any situation in which a *t* test would be appropriate; in addition, it can be used when there are more than two groups. The output of an analysis of variance (called an F statistic) is evaluated in a way similar to that of evaluating the *t* statistic.

In dealing with two groups, therefore, we have the option of using either analysis of variance or a *t* test. The *t* test has the advantage of being somewhat easier to compute by hand. If both statistics were used to evaluate the same set of data for two groups, the test of significance for the analysis of variance would be identical to the statistical significance of the *t* test.

When we use analysis of variance with more than two groups, the output tells us the level of significance of the differences *among the several groups*. For example, if we compared the average performance of the Cardinals, Crows, and Robins in music class and found a difference significant at the .01 level, all we would really know is that *at the very least* the highest-scoring group differed from the lowest-scoring group to a degree that would be unlikely to occur because of chance instability. To determine whether specific groups (e.g., the middle-scoring and the lowest-scoring groups) differed from one another, we would need further tests. These additional tests (which are similar to *t* tests and not described further in this book) are interpreted in exactly the same way as *t* tests and analysis of variance.

REVIEW QUIZ 14.2

For each of the following, state whether the question could be examined by a *t* test, by analysis of variance, or by either *t* test or analysis of variance.

1. The football players were able to bench press only about 100 pounds at the beginning of the season. By the end of the season, they had advanced to an average of about 150 pounds.

2. The experimental group gained more than the control group. Within the experimental group, those with the highest self-concepts did better than those with either medium or low self-concepts. The differences based on self-concept did not appear in the control group.

3. The television sets repaired by Mr. Kern's trainees lasted an average of 34.8 days before they needed further repairs. The sets repaired by Mrs. Foster's trainees lasted 63.2 days. Those repaired by members of the control group lasted an average of 28.3 days.

CHI SQUARE

Another useful statistical tool is chi square (abbreviated X^2), which provides an estimate of how likely it is that an obtained distribution of scores is merely a chance variation from a theoretical or expected distribution of those scores. For example, at the beginning of this chapter we discussed coin tossing—how surprised should you be if your friend flips a quarter 10 times and gets 6 heads and 4 tails? The expected outcome (based on a 50% probability) would be 5 heads and 5 tails. How likely is it that the deviation occurred as a chance fluctuation? If your friend obtained 8 heads and 2 tails, how likely is it that *this* deviation occurred as a chance fluctuation? If he flipped the coin 100 times and got 80 heads, how likely is it that *this* deviation occurred as a chance fluctuation? This sort of question can be answered by using a simple chi square test.

(Note: In keeping with the spirit of this book, we are not going to present any mathematical computations in this chapter. The formula for chi square is easy to compute and is given in Appendix D, along with a cookbook approach for making the actual computations. At this point, we shall simply present the results of some chi square analyses.)

A. The examples of chi square that we shall deal with involve data that can be fit into a contingency table, like the one shown here. In this case, the columns show heads and tails, and the rows show what was expected and what was observed. In this example, we would have expected 5 heads and 5 tails, but our friend obtained 6 heads and 4 tails. Running this through the chi square formula, we get a result of $X^2 = .20$. To be significant at the .05 level, X^2 has to be greater than 3.84; thus, there are more than 5 chances in 100 that our friend's coin flips could have occurred that way by chance.

	Heads	Tails
Expected	5	5
Observed	6	4

$$X^2 = .20$$

B. Let's suppose our friend obtained 8 heads and 2 tails. How likely is it that this outcome occurred by chance? Again, we can put the information into a contingency table and run it through the chi square formula. The result is $X^2 = 1.98$. This still is not above 3.84, and so we would conclude that there are more than 5 chances in 100 that this outcome occurred by chance fluctuations.

	H	T
E	5	5
O	8	2

$$X^2 = 1.98$$

C. Let's suppose our friend got 9 heads and 1 tail. Again, we can put the results in a contingency table and run the formula. This time the result is

$X^2 = 3.81$. This is just barely below 3.84, and so we would say that there are slightly more than 5 chances in 100 that this outcome occurred by chance fluctuations. It's not that unusual to get a 9–1 split when flipping a coin 10 times; it's likely to happen about 1 time out of 20.

	H	T
E	5	5
O	9	2

$$X^2 = 3.81$$

D. Let's say our friend flipped his coin 100 times instead of just 10, and obtained 80 heads and 20 tails. The results here show that this outcome gives a result of $X^2 = 19.78$. This is greater than 3.84. In fact, it's greater than 10.83, which makes it significant at the .001 level. In other words, it's extremely unlikely that this result occurred because of chance fluctuations.

	H	T
E	50	50
O	80	20

$$X^2 = 19.78$$

How do we explain these findings? Do we assume that in the first three examples our friend played fairly but that he cheated in example D? This would be a rash assumption. Our friend *could* have cheated in example A—the fact that the results were fairly likely to occur that way by chance does not mean that they *did* occur by chance alone. Likewise, our friend *could* have been honest in example D—the fact that it's unlikely for an outcome to occur by chance does not mean that it's *impossible* for that outcome to occur by chance. Let's look at some examples from education:

E. Assume that a professor gives a history test. Thirty liberal arts majors and 5 engineering majors pass; 20 liberal arts majors and 10 engineering majors fail. The engineers cry foul! They say the test was biased because two-thirds of the engineering majors but only two-fifths of the liberal arts majors failed. How likely is it that the difference between liberal arts majors and engineering majors was just a chance fluctuation? In this case, we are not comparing an observed distribution with a theoretical distribution (as in the previous examples) but rather one distribution (liberal arts majors) to another (engineering majors). We can put the results into a contingency table and compute chi square. The result is $X^2 = 3.30$. This chi square value is below 3.84, so we would say that there are more than 5 chances in 100 that the differences in failure rate between liberal arts majors and engineering majors occurred by chance.

	P	F
LA	30	20
ENG	5	10

$$X^2 = 3.30$$

F. Assume that in the previous example there were 3 engineering majors passing and 12 failing. Would this be stronger evidence of bias? Running the chi square analysis, we would obtain a result of $X^2 = 7.39$. This is significant at the .05 level. In fact, it's significant at the .01 level. There is fewer than 1 chance in 100 that this difference in failure rates occurred by chance fluctuations.

	P	F
LA	30	20
ENG	3	12

$$X^2 = 7.39$$

What do we conclude about test bias in examples E and F? Does the chi square value in example F prove that the test was biased against engineering majors? No, it does not *prove* anything. It is one piece of evidence, which suggests that differences of this magnitude in failure rate are not likely to occur

by chance. Assuming that the results did not occur by chance, does it mean that bias is what *caused* the difference? Again, the answer is no. These are not the results of an experimental study, and there are many factors that could have caused the difference in distributions. To suggest just two possible explanations, perhaps the liberal art majors had greater aptitude for the subject matter on the test or they studied harder. The professor would be well advised to consult chapter 5 of this book to make sure the test is valid and chapter 9 to develop qualitative research strategies to determine why there is this difference in failure rates in example F.

Chi square analysis of this kind can be used in situations like those cited in the previous examples, when you have two categories in which to classify subjects (like *boys* and *girls, expected* and *observed, engineers* and *liberal arts majors*) and a distribution consisting of a dichotomous (yes/no) frequency count for the subjects classified within those two categories. This sounds more complicated than it really is—if the information will fit into a contingency table like those shown in the preceding examples, then it can be analyzed through a chi square analysis to determine statistical significance. (Note that we have presented as an example only a specific type of chi square analysis. Chi square analysis for more complex distributions follow the same logic, but they are not discussed in this book.)

OTHER STATISTICS

This discussion of tests of significance has focused on *t* tests, analysis of variance, and chi square. Similar procedures can be applied to determining the significance of correlation coefficients. In this case, the level of significance refers to the probability that a correlation coefficient of the observed magnitude would be likely to arise because of chance fluctuations in the sets of scores. Therefore, if we have a Pearson correlation coefficient of .35 and are told that p = .01, this would mean that there was fewer than 1 chance in 100 that with that sample size a correlation of r = .35 would arise as a result of chance fluctuations.

Many statistical procedures have not been covered in this book. The discussion here has been brief and incomplete; only a few of the most basic techniques have been introduced. Consulting the resources listed in this chapter's Annotated Bibliography and taking statistics courses will enable you to better understand the procedures described here and learn about those that have not been discussed in this text. In addition, Appendix E provides a brief description of most of the major statistical techniques you are likely to encounter in your research or professional reading. As you examine Appendix E, you will discover that even the most complex statistical procedures are interpreted in ways similar to those described in this and the preceding chapter.

SELECTING A STATISTICAL PROCEDURE

Table 14.1 summarizes the major characteristics of the tests of significance discussed in this chapter. A comparable summary of correlation coefficients was provided in Table 13.2. The statistical procedures described in this and the previous chapter will help you solve many of the statistical problems you will encounter in your research. In addition (and frequently), knowledge of these techniques will enable you to understand the use of statistical procedures in many articles and reports you will read.

A problem that you may encounter when you first start using statistical procedures is how to decide which statistic to employ. You might understand the basic logic behind these statistics, and you might be able to describe what is meant by a statistical statement when you see one written down, but how do you decide which statistic to use to solve a problem you wish to explore? How do you choose from the apparent maze of statistical procedures available to you? Figure 14.2 perhaps can help you with this problem.

Figure 14.2 presents an algorithm related to the statistical procedures discussed in this book; the figure can help you narrow the field as rapidly as possible, so that you can select the one that will help you investigate a given problem. The first question that you should ask yourself, according to this decision rule, is whether your data will fit into a chi square

Table 14.1 Summary of Major Tests of Statistical Significance

Statistical Procedure	Description	Example
t test	Estimates the probability that the difference between two groups is likely to be the result of chance variations in scores	• Compare the means of the experimental and control groups in a study • Compare the performance of boys to that of girls on a test • With just one group, compare its pretest mean to its posttest mean on an achievement test
Analysis of variance	Estimates the probability that differences among two *or more* groups is likely to be the result of chance variations in scores	• Compare the means of the experimental, control, and placebo control groups • Compare the performance of low-, middle-, and high-SES students on a test • Use in any situation when a *t* test would also be possible
Chi square	Estimates the probability that an obtained pattern of scores is merely a chance variation of a theoretical or expected pattern	• In one class 15 students passed and 12 failed. In the other, 12 passed and 13 failed. Is this difference greater than would be expected by chance? • The membership of the senior class is 35% white, 50% Black, and 15% Hispanic. Yet 7 out 13 of the students who were offered scholarships were whites. How likely is it that this would occur by chance?

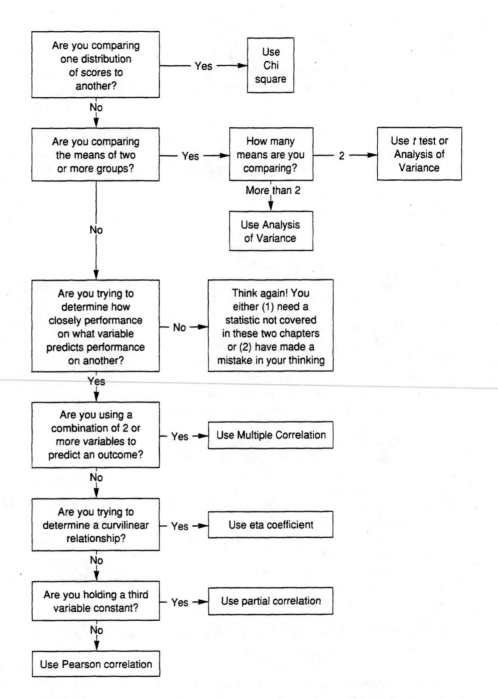

Figure 14.2 An Algorithm for Selecting a Statistical Procedure

contingency table. In other words, do you have two categories with frequency counts for another variable broken down by these two categories? If this is the case, you need a chi square analysis. The second question is whether you plan to compare the means of interval data for two or more groups of subjects. If the answer is yes, then your menu of choices is immediately restricted to the statistics that test for the differences between means. It is merely a matter of asking one more question to find the appropriate statistic.

If your answer to the first two questions was no, then you should proceed to the next question in the left column of the figure: "Are you relating the performance of the same group on two or more variables?" This is another way to ask, "Can your question be diagrammed with a scattergram?" or "Do you need a correlation coefficient?" If your answer to this second question is yes, then the rest of the questions in the left column will direct you to one of the correlational procedures described in the preceding chapter. By answering a few more questions, you can select the exact statistic you need. Note that the algorithm arranges questions in such a way as to eliminate inappropriate statistical procedures as quickly as possible.

If you answered no to all three of the preceding questions, then you either need a statistic not covered in the present text or you made a mistake in your answer to the first three questions. Unless you have already become fairly sophisticated in your research needs, you should probably think things over before you conclude that you have come up with a problem that goes beyond the present textbook. On the other hand, if you were to reexamine your problem and discover that the answer to the first two questions is still no, then you might want to look for statistical help (several relatively common techniques—such as factor analysis and nonparametric statistics—are not covered in this book).

Figure 14.2 presents an oversimplified view of selecting a statistical procedure. Were we to add even a few more procedures, it would become much more difficult to select a procedure merely by answering a few simple questions. The algorithm would expand quickly. Nevertheless, all users of sta-

tistics, no matter how sophisticated, should use an algorithm something like that shown in Figure 14.2 when selecting a statistical procedure. This is true even though some users may do this without realizing that they have such an algorithm in mind and even though the algorithms used by more sophisticated users are considerably more complex than this one. Therefore, practice in using this algorithm will help you in two ways: (1) it will make you more familiar with the application of the statistics covered in this book, and (2) it will help you to think along appropriate lines so that if you care to learn more about statistical procedures, you could fit new ones into an expanded algorithm of your own.

REVIEW QUIZ 14.3

This quiz assumes that you will use the algorithm described in Figure 14.2. Choose the correct statistical procedure to help you answer each question. Then compare your answer with the answer provided in the text. The text answer is accompanied by the reasoning (based on the algorithm) that led to the selection of that statistic.

In selecting your answers, choose from the following list:

Pearson correlation coefficient

Partial correlation coefficient

Eta coefficient

Multiple correlation coefficient

t test

Analysis of variance

Chi square

1. Fifteen out of 20 students in a class that used computers passed the state proficiency test; only 10 out of 20 in the class that did not use computers passed the same test. Is this difference greater than would be expected by chance?

2. Do children with permissive parents become more open-minded thinkers as adults than children with nonpermissive parents?

3. Is it likely that the more familiar a word is the easier it will be to recognize it when its letters are scrambled, as in an anagram?

STATISTICAL POWER

If an experimental treatment or condition has an impact, will statistical tests of significance *always* verify whether there is a significant difference between the experimental and control groups? The answer is no. It often happens in educational research that statistical tools lead to inaccurate inferences.

There are two types of error that can arise when we use statistical analysis to make inferences (see Figure 14.3). Type I errors occur when our statistical procedure leads us to conclude that there is a relationship when in fact there is none. For example, a mathematics program may be ineffective, but because of the unreliability in testing procedures and in the characteristics of the subjects, the *t* test may generate a *t* statistic indicating that the results of the measurement process were unlikely to have occurred by chance. This is relatively rare, but it happens. Researchers generally avoid Type I errors by setting the level of significance at a low level of probability. That is, Type I errors are less likely to occur when the results are significant at the .001 level than at the .01 level.

Type II errors occur when our statistical procedures lead us to conclude that there is no relationship when in fact there is a difference. For example, a reading program may be truly effective, but because of unreliable measurement processes and a small number of students who took part in the study, the *t* test produced a *t* statistic that was lower than necessary to indicate statistical significance at an appropriate level. It should be obvious that the most common procedure for minimizing Type I errors (using low levels of significance) actually increases the likelihood of Type II errors.

Educational researchers have traditionally taken the attitude that a conservative approach is best (i.e., it's best to be cautious before concluding that a relationship does exist). In other words, they have put a priority on minimizing Type I error—avoiding the mistake of a chance statistically significant result. It is considered safer to conclude that a study has not provided satisfactory evidence that the treatment produced an impact than to run the risk of falsely believing that the treatment did produce an impact.

This conservative attitude has merit, but the result is that by reducing Type I errors researchers have markedly increased Type II errors. In other words, there are many research studies in education in which relationships did exist but the statistical tools for making inferences were unable to verify their existence.

Figure 14.3 Types of Errors That Arise with Statistical Analysis

		Reality	
		The relationship actually exists	The relationship actually does not exist
Conclusion	There is a relationship	No error	Type I error
	There is no relationship	Type II error	No error

The term *power* refers to the ability of a statistical analysis to reduce Type II errors. Higher-power tests are more likely to find a statistical relationship when there is one. The three most important ways to increase the power of tests are to (1) increase the number of subjects in an experiment, (2) increase the reliability of the measurement processes employed in a study, and (3) increase the level of significance at which statistical results will be considered to warrant an inference that the treatment has had an impact. The reason most educational experiments have low power is because they tend to have a relatively small number of subjects (fewer than 70) and tend to employ measurement processes that are not fully reliable.

There are four main ways to deal with the problems of weak power in educational studies:

1. In general, keep in mind that a finding of not statistically significant is not the same as proof that the treatment did not work.

2. Remember that statistical power is likely to be low when the number of subjects in a study is small. When conducting studies of your own, try to obtain as large a number of subjects as possible. Cohen (1992) gives specific recommendations for group size. When reading published reports, be cautious in drawing a conclusion of "no real difference" when the number of subjects in an experiment is small.

3. Use data collection processes that are as reliable as possible. When reading research reports, examine the reliability data carefully before drawing a conclusion of "no real difference." To the extent that the data collected from both experimental and control groups are unreliable, they are likely to obscure real differences among groups.

4. Use the results of meta-analyses when they are available. Meta-analysis is a strategy described in chapter 16 that combines the results of several studies; by combining results, it increases the number of subjects and thus the statistical power of the studies. In addition, meta-analysis offers an additional index, called the effect size, which is easier than level of significance to interpret for practical applications.

This discussion of statistical power and types of error has been brief and nontechnical. While our examples have focused on *t* tests, the same principles can be applied to F ratios from an analysis of variance, correlation coefficients, and the statistical procedures described in Appendix E. More detailed information regarding power can be found in Runyon and Haber (1988) and Freedman, Pisani, Purves, and Adhikari (1988). Cohen (1992) is a resource designed for nonstatisticians.

PUTTING IT ALL TOGETHER

After Mr. Anderson carried out the experiment outlined at the end of chapter 12, it was necessary to analyze the results of the children's performance on the various tests. The results on the Fireman Tests are shown in Figure 14.4. The experimental group chose an average of 0.96 animals on the pretest and 2.01 on the posttest. The control group chose an average of 0.78 animals on the pretest and 0.48 animals on the posttest.

A *t* test for the pretest scores produced a *t* statistic of 1.12. With 48 degrees of freedom, this was not even close to being significant at the .05 level. However, on the posttest, the *t* statistic was 3.80. This difference was significant beyond the .001 level. Mr. Anderson concluded that the groups had been initially about equal but that they differed on the posttest by more than could be expected by chance.

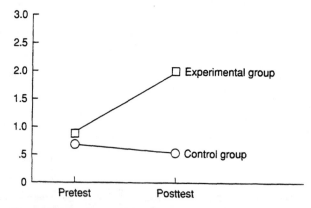

Figure 14.4 Average Number of Animals Chosen on Fireman Tests

Plugging this information into the basic strategy of research design, Mr. Anderson concluded that the Animal Life Program had caused an improvement in attitudes toward animal life.

Mr. Anderson also had supplementary data based on the number of good deeds and bad deeds reported to various agencies. These results, which are summarized in Figure 14.5, show that there was a low incidence of good deeds during the three years before the program and that the number of good deeds increased dramatically among the experimental students (but not among the control students) after the treatment was given. In addition, bad deeds had occurred at a high rate in both groups prior to the treatment; after the program, these bad deeds continued at a high rate among the control students, while they dropped substantially among the ALP students.

To analyze these results, Mr. Anderson reported the average number of good deeds and bad deeds for the students in each class prior to the experiment. He then compared the average number of good or bad deeds after the treatment for each group with this baseline information. The results showed that the ALP students had averaged 5.33 good deeds per class per year during the baseline period, and this average jumped to 14.33 after the ALP was introduced. The control group averaged 6.67 good deeds per class per year during the first three years, and this average edged up to just 7.00 good deeds during the fourth year. This posttest difference between the ALP and non-ALP classes was statistically significant at the .01 level. The two groups had also been similar with regard to reported bad deeds before the ALP

program. After the experimental program, the number of bad deeds reported among the experimental classes dropped, whereas the number reported for the control classes remained higher. This difference between the two groups on the posttest was again significant at the .01 level.

Mr. Anderson knew that although the groups had not been randomly assigned, the pretest scores had shown that the experimental and control groups were about equal on all observed variables before the ALP was administered. After the treatment, however, the ALP students surpassed the control students in increases on the Fireman Test, in increases in the number of good deeds, and in the reduction in the number of bad deeds. Although he would have been happier with a true experimental design, Mr. Anderson was nevertheless satisfied that his quasi-experimental design had demonstrated a causal relationship. The ALP, he felt, had *caused* improved attitudes toward animal life, and he had statistical evidence to support this belief.

SUMMARY

Statistical tests of significance are tools for assessing how likely it is that an observed difference between groups might have arisen as a result of mere chance fluctuations in group scores rather than as a result of the treatment under consideration. If there is a low degree of probability that the observed difference is one that could have arisen by chance, then this difference is referred to as significant.

Figure 14.5 Average Number of Good Deeds and Bad Deeds Reported per Class During Three Years Before Treatment and One Year After Treatment

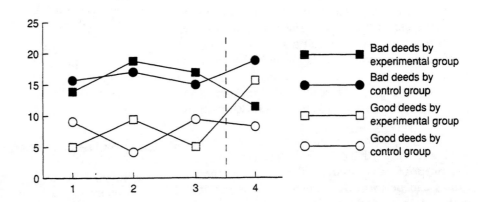

The simplest method for estimating the significance of the difference between the means of two groups is the *t* test. Analysis of variance is a slightly more complex but more versatile method, which can be applied to the means of two or more groups.

In selecting an appropriate statistical procedure, it is essential to keep in mind the question you want answered by the statistic and the contribution that each statistical procedure can make. The algorithm in Figure 14.2 combines these two factors in such a way as to allow you to quickly and easily determine which statistic will help you solve a specific problem.

What Comes Next

This chapter almost—but not quite—concludes our treatment of Level II research; we shall return again to Level II in chapter 16, which introduces meta-analysis, a powerful research tool that helps the researcher establish cause-and-effect relationships derived from a whole series of experiments and determine how far the results of those studies can be generalized. In the meantime, chapter 15 will begin the treatment of Level III research.

DOING YOUR OWN RESEARCH

Don't be afraid of inferential statistics like those described in this chapter. Computing them by hand may be difficult, but understanding them is not, nor is it difficult to calculate them by computer. After reading this chapter, you should be capable of interpreting many statistics. If you have access to a statistical consultant, you should also now be capable of enlisting that person's help to use a computer to perform the statistical analyses necessary to do fairly sophisticated research. If you plan to work independently, you should take an appropriate series of statistics courses or carefully read texts like Fitz-Gibbon and Morris (1987); Freedman, Pisani, Purves, and Adhikari (1988); Moses (1986); and Runyon and Haber (1988).

Most good computerized statistical packages (e.g., SPSS and Systat) have manuals that clearly explain the purpose of the statistical procedures the programs can perform. All you need do is put in the right numbers and interpret the results correctly.

However, it is essential that you understand what you are doing clearly enough to enter the appropriate numbers into the computer.

To use inferential statistics correctly, it is important to plan ahead. The time to plan your statistical analysis is before you collect any data. If you sit down at the computer and discover that you failed to collect the proper data, it is not likely that you will be able to perform as useful a statistical analysis as would have been possible had you collected the data more appropriately.

FOR FURTHER THOUGHT

1. When the results of the analysis of variance indicate that the differences between two groups are not significant, what does this mean? Does it mean that the treatment did not work? What other explanations could there be for a lack of statistical significance?

2. When the results of the analysis of variance indicate that the differences between two groups *are* significant, what does this mean? Does it mean that the treatment caused the difference? What other explanations could there be for the presence of statistical significance?

3. Complete this sentence by answering the designated questions: "A *t* test . . .(does what?) (To what or whom?) (When?) (Where?) (How?) (Why?)"

4. Complete this sentence by answering the designated questions: "Analysis of variance . . .(does what?) (To what or whom?) (When?) (Where?) (How?) (Why?)"

5. Complete this sentence by answering the designated questions: "Chi square . . .(does what?) (To what or whom?) (When?) (Where?) (How?) (Why?)"

ANNOTATED BIBLIOGRAPHY

Bruning, J. L., & Kintz, B. L. (1988). *Computational handbook of statistics* (3rd ed.). Glenview, IL: Scott, Foresman and Company. This book provides a cookbook format for computing most of the important statistics that are used in educational research. If you know what statistic you need, know how to put numbers in columns, and have access to a calculator, it is easy to compute statistics with this book.

Cohen, J. (1992). A power primer. *Psychological Bulletin*, *112*, 155–159. This is a moderately technical but readable discussion of the concept of power in statistical analysis.

Fitz-Gibbon, C. T., & Morris, L. L. (1987). *How to analyze data* (2nd ed.). Newbury Park, CA: Sage. This book is in the Program Evaluation Kit, cited under Herman, Morris, and Fitz-Gibbon in chapter 1. This volume presents practical guidelines for analyzing the data collected during the evaluation process.

Freedman, D., Pisani, R., Purves, R., & Adhikari, A. (1988). *Statistics* (2nd ed.). New York: W.W. Norton. This text covers the important, basic statistics in a detailed and comprehensive fashion. This is a medium-level book that should be comprehensible to the serious reader of the present textbook who wants to come to a better understanding of the important concepts of statistics.

Huff, D. (1954). *How to lie with statistics*. New York: W.W. Norton. Huff teaches us to respect descriptive statistics by showing how easy it is to falsify data by misusing them. Reading this book will help you develop a healthy skepticism.

Moses, L. E. (1986). *Think and explain with statistics*. Reading, MA: Addison-Wesley. This book approaches introductory descriptive and inferential statistics from a practical perspective. It includes numerous examples from many fields, including education.

Popham, W. J., & Sirotnik, J. A. (1973). *Educational statistics: Use and interpretation* (2nd ed.). New York: Harper and Row. The choice of statistics texts depends largely upon the taste of the reader. This book may appeal to novices because it deals in simple terms and uses good, concrete examples. The computational chapters are presented separately from the conceptual chapters, and so a person who is not currently interested in computation can skip those chapters until the need arises. This is a useful book for a person who wants to learn more about statistics without taking a course on the subject. It does not go into the level of detail covered by Freedman et al. (1988).

Runyon, R. P. (1977). *Winning with statistics*. Reading, MA: Addison-Wesley. This book covers basic descriptive statistics and provides a minimal introduction to tests of significance. It is a short and enjoyable book. It may be hard for many readers to imagine a statistics book that is difficult to put down, but this book fits that description.

Runyon, R. P., & Haber, A. (1988). *Fundamentals of behavioral statistics* (6th ed.). New York: Random House. This is a good introductory text. It differs from the Popham and Sirotnik (1973) text in that it is more informal in its presentation and goes well beyond the limits of education for its examples. This book could easily be read by a person who wants to learn more about statistics without taking a stat course.

Spatz, C. (1993). *Basic statistics: Tales of distributions* (5th ed.). Pacific Grove, CA: Brooks/Cole. This creatively written book is designed to be comprehensible for persons who take only a single course in statistics as well as those who will take additional statistics courses. It may be ideal for those who took a statistics course, then read the present book as part of the educational research course, and next plan to move on to more advanced study.

ANSWERS TO QUIZZES

Review Quiz 14.1

1. a and b would be tested with a *t* test because each uses interval data and includes two (and only two) means for comparison; c would not be tested with a *t* test because this is a comparison of the performance of a single group of students with regard to two variables; it calls for a correlation coefficient (a *t* test is used only when two *means* are being compared); d would not be tested with a *t* test because this comparison involves more than two groups. There are three different levels of ability for students using the computers and three levels for those not using computers. This is six groups altogether and would require an analysis of variance, discussed later in this chapter.

2. a. Significant at the .05 level; significant at the .01 level; not significant at the .001 level

    b. Not significant at any of these levels

    c. Significant at the .05 level; significant at the .01 level; not significant at the .001 level

    d. Significant at the .05 level; significant at the .01 level; significant at the .001 level

Review Quiz 14.2

1. Could use either (two groups)
2. Analysis of variance (two groups subdivided into three self-concept groups, making six groups)
3. Analysis of variance (three groups)

Review Quiz 14.3

1. Chi square. Reasoning: Will the data fit into a chi square contingency table? Yes. Then use chi square analysis. There's no need to pursue the algorithm any further.
2. A *t* test or analysis of variance. Reasoning: Will the data fit into a chi square contingency table? No. Am I comparing the means of two groups? Yes; the two groups are *children with permissive parents* and *children with nonpermissive parents*. Are there two groups or more than two? Two

groups. Therefore, I can use either a *t* test or analysis of variance.

3. Pearson correlation coefficient. Reasoning: Will the data fit into a chi square contingency table? No. Am I comparing the means of two groups? No. Am I relating the performance of subjects in a group on one variable to the performance of the subjects in that same group on another variable? Yes. (This is tricky because you have things, rather than persons, as your subjects. You have a group of words. Each word will have one score describing its degree of familiarity and a second score describing ease of recognition in scrambled format.) Am I using a combination of two or more variables to predict a single outcome? No. Am I trying to measure a curvilinear relationship? No. Am I trying to reduce the influence of a third variable? No. Therefore, I need a Pearson correlation coefficient.

CHAPTER 14

Research Report Analysis

The statistical analyses described in Appendix C are a major part of the research. The report described the results of an analysis of covariance. This statistical procedure is interpreted in the same way as an analysis of variance.

1. What do the results of the analysis of variance of the pretest scores tell us?
2. What do the results of the analysis of variance of the Watson-Glaser test tell us?

ANSWERS:

1. The results of the analysis of variance tell us that there are fewer than 4 chances in 100 that the differences in gains between the guided students and the other two groups occurred as the result of chance variations in the scores. (Actually, the results say that the difference *among* the three groups is significant. We would need additional tests—called planned comparisons—to pinpoint

the differences more specifically. The planned comparisons are not presented in this report. However, an inspection of the gain scores shows that the guided students gained vastly more than the other two groups, and so the interpretation that they gained significantly more is probably valid.)

The results of the analysis of variance also tell us that there are fewer than 2 chances in 1,000 that the differences in gains between the guided students and the other two groups occurred as the result of chance variations in the scores. (Actually, the results say that the difference *among* the three groups is significant. We would need planned comparisons to pinpoint the differences more specifically. However, an inspection of the gain scores shows that the guided students gained vastly more than the other two groups and that the unguided students gained an intermediate amount, so the interpretation that they gained significantly more is probably valid.)

An additional analysis of variance on the cumulative gains on pretests is presented in the text but not in the tables. This shows that the students using the simulations (either with or without guidance) outgained the control students. There was fewer than 1 chance in 1,000 that this difference would have occurred by chance. (These data were complex and have been omitted from the abridgement presented in Appendix C.)

2. On the Watson-Glaser test, the guided students gained more than either of the other groups. There are fewer than 5 chances in 100 that a difference of this magnitude would be likely to occur as a result of chance fluctuation in scores. (Again, this statement actually related to a difference *among* the three groups; visual inspection of the data shows a large discrepancy between the guided students and the other two groups. Planned comparisons could pinpoint this difference more accurately.)

EXTERNAL VALIDITY: GENERALIZING RESULTS OF RESEARCH STUDIES

■ **WHERE WE'VE BEEN**

We have examined the major threats to internal validity and seen how experimental and quasi-experimental research designs help control them. We have also discussed methods for examining relationships that may be noncausal. Finally, we have seen how tests of significance can help us evaluate the level of confidence we can place in the results of experimental studies.

■ **WHERE WE'RE GOING NOW**

In this chapter we'll discuss Level III research, which deals with external validity, or how far the results of a research study can be generalized. This chapter will show how we can minimize the probability that unique persons, settings, or historical events will interfere with the generalizations that can be made from a research study.

■ **CHAPTER PREVIEW**

External validity deals with the problem of whether the cause-and-effect results of a research study can be applied to other persons, in other settings, and at other times than those involved in the original research study. In other words, it deals with how far we can generalize the results of a study. Educators will often have less time to spend worrying about external validity than about internal validity; after all, their job is usually to solve their own problems, not to suggest to other educators how to solve theirs. Those interested in evaluation or action research (discussed in chapter 1) are likely to be particularly uninterested in external validity because their concern is with practical issues that are likely to be restricted to local settings. Nevertheless, the question of external validity is still important to educators as consumers of educational research. Only if we can understand the limitations and restrictions that must be placed on generalizations can we make efficient use of the research of others in seeking solutions to our own problems.

After reading this chapter, you should be able to

1. Define *external validity*.
2. Define and give examples of each of the threats to external validity.
3. Describe how each of these threats operates to weaken the external validity of a research study.
4. Describe strategies for overcoming these threats to external validity.
5. Describe and identify examples of correctly written operational definitions.
6. Given a research variable, write an operational definition of it.

■

THE PROBLEM OF EXTERNAL VALIDITY

External validity deals with the problem of whether a result obtained in one setting would be likely to occur in another setting. Internal validity deals with cause-and-effect results and is *internal* in the sense that it involves problems that occurred *within* the time span, *within* the research design, and *within* the context of a particular experiment. In a similar way, external validity is *external* in the sense that it deals with considerations *outside* the time span, *outside* the research design, and *outside* the context of a particular experiment. (The logic of generalizability discussed in this chapter applies to nonexperimental as well as experimental research.) External validity deals with the problem of how far we can generalize the results of a research study beyond the original research setting. It deals with the question of whether the same result would occur with other persons, in other settings, and at other times.

To a major extent, when we are dealing with experimental research, internal validity is a necessary prerequisite for external validity—much as reliability is a prerequisite for validity in test construction. In other words, it would be pointless to ask whether a treatment would cause an effect in a setting beyond the experimental context unless it has previously been shown that it had caused an effect in the experimental setting.

As the previous chapters have indicated, teachers and educators should be doing research on a regular basis. The kind they will most frequently find helpful is Level I research—employing the strategies that enable them to discover what outcomes are actually occurring in their educational settings. Although teachers are legitimately concerned about cause-and-effect relationships, they may find that they have less time to devote to the experimental and quasi-experimental research of Level II. This trend continues as we progress toward the higher levels of research: higher levels depend on lower levels, but active professionals often find they have less time and less inclination to engage in these higher levels. Teachers are constantly concerned about what is happening in their classrooms and schools. Even though they are interested in what is causing outcomes to occur, they are often unable to devote time and attention to determining whether the same thing would happen somewhere else.

Although this relative lack of interest holds true for educators doing their own research, it does not hold true for educators reading the professional literature. When teachers pick up an article about a seemingly successful experimental innovation or insight, one of the paramount questions in their minds is "Will it work in my classroom?" This question lies at the heart of external validity. A closely related question is "Are there specific types of learners in my classroom who would benefit from this program even though others may not?" What we need to determine as we examine professional research articles is the likelihood that we can generalize the results of the research to the learners in our own classrooms. Even if an innovative treatment worked as the article says it did, we need evidence that it will work *for us*.

THE THREATS TO EXTERNAL VALIDITY

Since external validity deals with the generalization of results to other persons, settings, and times, then anything that prevents or limits such generalizations is a threat to external validity. Therefore, it is easy to see that there are three basic threats to external validity:

1. Interactions of the treatment with *persons*
2. Interactions of the treatment with the *setting*
3. Interactions of the treatment with the historical context (*time*)

The term *interaction* means that it could be a *combination* of the treatment plus unique persons, settings, or times, rather than the treatment by itself, that caused the observed outcome. We can strengthen the external validity of a study by demonstrating through qualitative observations and interviews that there are no unique persons, settings, or historical events that were essential features of the study and that would therefore limit the generalizability of the findings.

You have perhaps noticed that some of these same features can also limit the *internal* validity of an experimental study. It will be useful to demonstrate how these threats can have an impact on external validity that is different from their impact on internal validity. The difference can be seen in Figure 15.1. Diagram A presents an example of an uncontrolled experiment in which the unique features of the subjects, of the setting, or of the time interact with the treatment in such a way as to threaten the internal validity of a research study. In this diagram it is impossible to determine whether the enhanced performance of the experimental group is a result of the treatment or the result of one or more of the extraneous threats.

Diagram B shows the application of experimental design (discussed in chapter 11) to control the threats to internal validity. From diagram B one can conclude that the treatment caused the improved performance because the extraneous threats are the same for both the experimental group and the control group. The treatment is the only variable that is different, and therefore the treatment must be responsible for the difference in observed outcomes. However, in diagram B we still do not know whether the same outcome would have occurred if

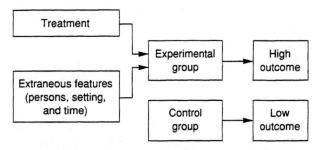

A. An experiment with weak internal validity (unique features influence only the experimental group)

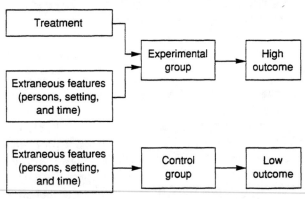

B. An experiment with strong internal validity (unique features influence *both* experimental group and control group)

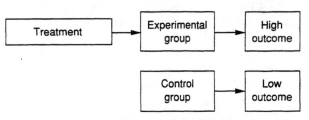

C. An experiment with strong external validity (unique features influence *neither* group)

Figure 15.1 Three Diagrams Showing the Impact of Unique Features of Persons, Setting, and Time on Internal and External Validity

the extraneous factors were not present to *either* of the groups. This is the problem with regard to external validity: how do we know that it was not a *combination* of the treatment plus one or more of these extraneous factors that caused the observed difference in outcomes?

Diagram C of Figure 15.1 presents a perfectly clear conclusion. The treatment, and only the treatment, can be said to be responsible for the outcome in this situation. The problem with diagram C, however, is that it is virtually impossible to attain this degree of clarity. To attain this degree of external validity, we would have to either remove each of the extraneous factors completely or show that each extraneous factor is actually much like the situation to which we wish to generalize and is therefore not a threat to generalization. Since the first course of action is a practical impossibility, the latter is the course of action most often to be followed.

The Interaction of the Treatment with Persons

The *interaction of the treatment with persons* is a threat to external validity to the extent that the subjects involved in the research situation are different or function in different ways from those to whom we wish to generalize the results. This is a problem of external validity if the subjects in the whole research study (not just in the experimental group) are atypical in this way. (If the problem is that the subjects in the experimental group are different from those in the control group, this is a problem of *internal* validity. Refer to diagrams A and B of Figure 15.1 for a clarification of this distinction.)

A frequent problem of research studies reported in educational journals is that the studies are based on volunteers (such as sophomores in college courses or graduate students needing course credit). When we try to generalize such results to our own settings, we are making the assumption that the people in our own settings are similar to these subjects. In many cases, this is an accurate assumption, but we should be aware that such groups sometimes have unique features—or perhaps *our* group has unique features—that prevent accurate generalizations.

Likewise, it is not safe to make the assumption, for example, that an AIDS prevention program that worked with the students in a large city 2,000 miles away will work with the students in our small town, that a program that teaches reading to highly motivated readers will work just as well with children of lower motivation, or that a method for cultivating

new teaching strategies among first-year teachers will be equally successful with teachers who have 10 years or more of experience. In each case, it is possible that the subjects who have derived demonstrable benefits from the treatment have unique features that make it improper to generalize the results to a second group of subjects with unique features of their own.

The Interaction of the Treatment with the Setting

The *interaction of the treatment with the setting* can occur in several ways. The obvious existence of a pretest can sometimes provide an artificial setting that makes the results difficult to generalize. The pretest may sensitize subjects in such a way that it makes them profit from the treatment. If this sensitization occurs, then it is by no means obvious that the treatment would have the same impact in the absence of a pretest. (Of course, if the treatment sensitizes the experimental group alone and not the control group, this would be a threat to internal rather than external validity.) If our intention is to generalize the treatment to a situation in which there will be no pretest, or if there was no control goup, then the existence of a sensitizing pretest in the experimental situation would present a serious threat to external validity. An example of such pretest sensitization is presented in Box 15.1.

A similar problem occurs to the extent that an experimental situation is artificial. If the participants in both the experimental group and the control group know that they are part of a research study, this knowledge may sometimes affect their performance. Sometimes this artificial atmosphere leads to expectations of certain outcomes, such as success. (If this knowledge causes them to expect the treatment to work and the control condition to fail, then this is a threat to internal validity. If it provides a positive expectancy for both groups, then this would be a threat to external validity.) When such artificial expectations exist, it is possible that the treatment will work *only* when such positive anticipations are aroused; if such expectations of success are not present in the situation to which the results are to be generalized, then there will be serious problems with

BOX 15.1 | How Far Can We Generalize Results?

Mr. Weller wanted to find out whether a new antismoking program would actually lead to a reduction in smoking among the persons to whom it was administered. He located 50 volunteers to take part in the experimental program. (The fact that these subjects volunteered for the program did not bother him, because he intended the program to be administered only to people who wanted to voluntarily quit smoking.) He randomly divided the 50 subjects into two groups and told 25 that they could start right away and the other 25 that they would have to wait for two weeks before they could receive the program. During the first interview, Mr. Weller also had all 50 subjects fill out a questionnaire regarding their attitudes toward smoking and indicating how many cigarettes they smoked each day. He then administered the program for two weeks to the first 25 subjects (the experimental group) and retested all 50 with the same measuring instrument at the end of the two-week period. He discovered that the experimental subjects smoked significantly fewer cigarettes and displayed attitudes more strongly opposed to smoking than the control subjects. He did a follow-up study six months later, and found that the experimental subjects maintained their antipathy toward tobacco. Mr. Weller was pleased with these results.

Did Mr. Weller demonstrate that his program worked? It sounds as though he did a good job. His treatment seems to have caused a reduction in smoking. Is it possible that the pretest rather than the treatment caused the reduction in smoking and the changed attitudes? Not really, because if the pretest had been responsible for the changes, then the same effect would have occurred in both groups, because both received the pretest. However, it is possible that the pretest sensitized both groups to profit from the treatment, but because only the experimental group received the treatment, only this group showed the improvement. A person taking the pretest might have said to herself, "I didn't realize that I smoked 34 cigarettes a day!" This and similar self-reflections might have influenced the participants to develop a proclivity to benefit from the program. Without such predispositions, the treatment might not have been so successful. Mr. Weller could eliminate this possibility by replicating his study without the pretest. (In fact, because he had relatively large, randomly assigned groups, the pretest was superfluous in this study. Mr. Weller should have omitted it to improve the external validity of the experiment.)

external validity. Even if there is no widespread expectancy of success, it is still possible that the artificiality of an experimental situation will evoke features that will not appear in the setting to which the treatment is to be generalized. Such features could include greater attention than usual to record keeping, accidental additional consideration for classroom details, the presence of additional teaching or supervisory personnel, and the availability of research consultants to help the teachers. If such features are present in the experimental setting but not in the setting to which the results are to be generalized, then such factors pose a threat to external validity.

Even if there is no artificiality in the research setting, there can be numerous unique features in the contexts or settings that could influence the degree of generalization that will be appropriate. Such obvious features as the size and atmosphere of the school, the size and ambience of the class, and special techniques (such as learning centers, computerized instruction, and team teaching) would obviously influence the validity of generalizing to other settings. In addition, the exact way an instructional method is actually implemented in the specific research setting is a crucial factor and should be documented by qualitative strategies such as observations and interviews. For example, if a researcher reports that a whole-language approach to reading and writing was effective, then it is important to other language arts teachers to know whether this researcher's definition of whole-language instruction matches their own. Mismatches in operational definitions are a recurrent threat to external validity, and because of the importance of this matter, considerable emphasis will be devoted later in this chapter to methods for clarifying such definitions.

The Interaction of the Treatment with Historical Context

The *interaction of the treatment with historical context* is an important factor when there is anything unusual about either a research situation or the setting to which we plan to generalize the results of the research. If historical events occur to an experimental group but not to the control group, or if there is no control group, this is a threat to internal validity. If the historical events occur to both the experimental group and the control group, such events may pose a threat to external validity, even if the threat to internal validity is controlled. The following examples show the difference between history as a threat to internal validity and as a threat to external validity:

Miss Smith is evaluating the effectiveness of a social studies program. She has an experimental group and a control group. During the course of the experiment, a popular television program coincidentally discusses topics similar to those covered in the social studies program. Her experimental group does better than her control group on the posttest. This is a threat to *external* validity. If the study has been otherwise well done, Miss Smith can assume that the social studies program helped cause the improvement. (If the television program were the causal factor, then both the experimental group and the control group would have improved.) However, she cannot be certain whether the social studies program would

have worked without the television program. It might have been the *combination* of the television program and the social studies program that produced the desired outcome.

Mr. Brown is evaluating the effectiveness of a social studies program. He has an experimental group and a control group. During the course of the experiment, the fifth-period students (including the experimental students) see a popular movie that discusses topics similar to those covered in the social studies program. Because of scheduling problems, the third-period students (including the control students) do not see this movie. Mr. Brown's experimental group does better than his control group on the posttest. In this case, history is a threat to *internal* validity. Even if the study has been otherwise well done, Mr. Brown cannot assume that the social studies program caused the improvement. (The social studies program might have been ineffective, but the movie might have caused the improved performance of the experimental students. Because of the threat to internal validity, Mr. Brown simply does not know what caused the improvement.)

Note that even in the case of Mr. Brown, it is also possible that the *combination* of the movie and the social studies program produced the desired outcome, but this is a moot question for Mr. Brown. Since he has no proof of a cause-and-effect relationship, it would be pointless to ask whether this unproven relationship could be generalized.

It seems obvious that some educational techniques that were demonstrated to be effective in 1910 may not be equally effective right now. On the other hand, historical events and historical contexts often do not have a major impact on educational techniques. The point is that we have to be aware of such threats and determine whether they pose a problem for a particular generalization. The threat of history is particularly cogent when an experimental treatment is demonstrated to be successful on only one occasion, at a time when additional unusual events related to the treatment or outcome variable were simultaneously occurring.

CONTROLLING THE THREATS TO EXTERNAL VALIDITY

The threats to *internal* validity can be controlled largely through the use of appropriate experimental research designs and procedures. The same high degree of control is usually impossible to attain with regard to *external* validity. Research design plays a comparatively insignificant role in the control of external validity of individual studies, but meta-analysis (a method discussed in chapter 16 for combining the results of a group of experiments on the same problem) markedly enhances external validity. With external validity, a much heavier emphasis falls on the careful, logical analysis of similarities and differences among the circumstances surrounding the research study and target situations with regard to the persons, settings, and historical contexts involved. This qualitative analysis of similarities and differences is by logical necessity always less than perfect, and for this reason there is almost always some doubt about the external validity of an experimental study.

The threat of an interaction between the treatment and the persons involved in the study can theoretically be brought under control by randomly selecting the subjects for the research study from the target population. In ideal experimental studies, this would mean first randomly selecting the subjects from the target population and then randomly assigning them to the experimental and control groups. In reality, this process for generalization is almost never actually followed in experimental research. Almost always there is an attempt to generalize to a population from which subjects were not randomly selected. It is generally not feasible to identify the entire population to which the researcher will want to generalize and then randomly select subjects from this population. Try to imagine how you would derive a list from which you could randomly draw a sample for any of the following populations: the children you will teach in the next five years; readers with learning disabilities; U.S. teachers; or students interested in learning drama. If you could define such a population, and if you drew a random sample from that population, and if you could bring them

together and randomly assign some to an experimental group and others to a control group—*then* you would be able to generalize your results to that population! However, you would find that you could accomplish this in only the most trivial cases. In real life, meaningful populations are either very large or change very often, and thus an authentic random sample would be difficult to capture.

Qualitatitve analysis of similarities and differences is always less than perfect, and so there is almost always some doubt about the external validity of an experimental study.

Instead of random sampling, therefore, experts recommend a strategy called *purposive sampling for heterogeneity*. With this procedure, an experimental researcher does not try to get a random sample but rather tries to make sure that the pool of subjects from which the experimental and control groups are drawn will include representative numbers of the whole variety of subjects to whom the results will be generalized. For example, if you intend to generalize your results to whites, blacks, Hispanics, persons with learning disabilities, those without learning disabilities, motivated learners, and unmotivated learners, then you should be sure that the subjects in your study include representatives of all these categories. If you plan to generalize your results to Oriental students or to students with low self-concepts but have included no subjects representing these classifications in your study, then your generalizations will be weakened to the extent that there is any logical reason to expect that such learners would be likely to respond differently than others to the treatment.

Even more useful than merely including representatives of each relevant category within your study is the strategy of *isolating relevant characteristics of subjects and analyzing their impact by treating them as moderator variables* (described in chapter 2). For example, if you included a sufficient number of white, black, and Hispanic subjects in your study, you could compute the average performance of each of these groups separately and determine whether the treatment affected the groups similarly or differently. With such information, you might find that the treatment worked the same for all three groups, and this would lead you to believe that race or ethnic background is not a barrier to generalizations. On the other hand, you might find that the treatment worked for one group but not for the other two. Such information would not only limit your generalization, it would also tell you how to state these limits. Likewise, if you included a substantial number of both motivated and unmotivated learners, you could state whether the treatment worked equally well for both groups or whether one group benefitted more than the other. Such information can be extremely useful either to a researcher or to a reader of research in determining the specific groups and subgroups to whom the results of a study can be generalized. (The process described in this paragraph consists of identifying interactions by analyzing moderator variables, which will be described in detail in chapter 17.)

A similar aid for determining the limits for generalizations from a study can be found in *the careful statement of control variables* (which were described in chapter 2). If a researcher states clearly the exact nature of the subjects included in the study, this provides users of the research with helpful information regarding populations and settings to which the results can and cannot be generalized.

Finally, *replication* is an important way to increase the validity of generalizing results to varying populations and settings. Replication refers to the repetition of a research study in a new setting (and often by a different researcher) to see whether similar results will be obtained. To the extent that results are replicated with varying populations and different settings with variations in the operational definitions of the research variables, it becomes increasingly likely that a generalization to other populations will be valid. For example, by carefully specifying the nature of the population in each replication of an experimental study, it becomes possible to identify specific groups of subjects with whom a treatment is likely to work and other groups with whom it is unlikely to work.

The threat of an interaction between the treatment and the setting can be brought under partial control by making sure that the setting of the research study resembles as closely as possible the setting to which generalizations will be made. Basic research is often criticized on the basis of external validity, because human learning does not closely resemble either a rat maze or the memorization of nonsense syllables. The fact that a treatment has worked in an unrealistic, isolated context does not immediately lead us to believe that it will work the same way in the real-life situation to which we want to apply the results. For this reason, studies done in real-life situations are preferable to those done in laboratories. A study that allows us to retain the original setting undisturbed will be more easily generalized to other settings that resemble this original setting.

In addition, generalizability can be increased by attention to any other steps that reduce the artificiality of the experimental setting. For example, if an experimental treatment is accepted as a routine part of the educational setting or if a participant observer is truly accepted as part of the ordinary environment, then artificial behaviors and artificial expectations will be kept to a minimum. Since testing is often one of the most artificial aspects of a research study, the use of unobtrusive measurement (discussed in chapter 6) can be helpful in this respect.

For experimental research, there are two design strategies that can help reduce threats to external validity arising from the experimental setting. First, it is possible to control expectancy effects by employing a placebo control group. This is an additional control group that receives a treatment that is not really likely to have an impact on the outcome variables—but if expectancy were a factor, subjects receiving this pseudotreatment would be expected to change their performance with regard to these outcome variables. This placebo group can be added to the experiment in such a way that the artificial pressures of the experimental setting will influence both the experimental group and the placebo control group. If the experimental group thereafter outperforms both the control group and the placebo control group, then it is unlikely that the artificial expectations were a significant factor.

An important strategy for controlling threats to external validity arising from the experimental setting is to develop and report accurate operational definitions of the treatment and all the other variables in the study. This strategy will be the detailed topic of the next section of this chapter. In addition, it is important to use qualitative descriptions of contexts, participants, and treatments to "inform" the results of the study and to keep the researcher (or readers) from drawing naive conclusions.

Finally, replication is an important strategy for increasing the validity of generalizations to new settings. As a study is replicated with similar findings in different settings and with different methodologies, there is a corresponding increase in the range of settings to which generalizations would be appropriate. Likewise, if the results are replicated in certain settings but not in others, it becomes possible to systematically differentiate between appropriate and inappropriate settings in which to apply the results of the experiment.

The threat of an interaction between the treatment and the historical context can best be controlled by carefully looking for and identifying extraneous events that might be the source of such interactions and replicating the study in different historical contexts. Remember that *historical context* does not refer merely to the older, significant events that appear in newspapers and history books but also to the qualitative aspects and contextual variables that surround a current research study. If the results of a study performed on one occasion are to be applied on another occasion, then it is important to determine whether additional events are a prerequisite for the duplication of the outcome. Such events as a successful football season, the airing of a popular novel on television, the assassination of a political leader, the death of a classmate, and the rewarding of scholarships during the school year are all part of the current historical context. By identifying such qualitative events and contexts and by replicating the study in a variety of historical contexts in which these events change, we can reduce the likelihood that generalizations will be limited by interactions with the historical context.

OPERATIONAL DEFINITIONS

As we discussed in chapter 4, operational definitions of a variable state the observable behaviors, events,

or characteristics that we are willing to accept as evidence that the variable exists. All the major types of variables introduced in this text can be operationally defined. The nature and functions of each of these types of variables were introduced in chapter 4 and will be summarized in the following chapter.

Operational definitions are important sources of control for external validity. Although they do not eliminate extraneous sources of bias, they assist us in the generalization process by specifying more precisely the nature of the persons, materials, and events involved in a study. Such specifications make it possible for us to identify more clearly the specific populations and settings to which we can generalize the results of a study.

Operational definitions assist us in the generalization process by specifying more precisely the nature of the persons, materials, and events involved in a study.

If you read that someone has demonstrated that an open classroom has caused improved performance on science tests, would you be able to generalize this finding to the open classroom that you might set up in your own school? The answer is no—not unless you knew what the researcher did that enabled the students to learn according to their own needs and how the researcher operationally defined *open classroom*. On the other hand, if the researcher defined the open classroom in terms of the exact activities the teacher and students performed during class sessions, then you could examine this definition to see whether it matched what you had in mind as your own idea of an open classroom. This examination would enable you to estimate the likelihood that similar results would occur in your own open classroom.

Let us look at another example of the value of such operational definitions. Suppose you read an article indicating that frustration leads to aggression among elementary school students. You might consider conceptual definitions of these variables that go something like this: Frustration is the feeling that occurs when people are deprived of what they feel legitimately belongs to them, and aggression is a deliberate attempt to inflict pain on another person. These are two widely accepted definitions of the terms, and you might discover that they are fully shared by the author of the article. However, as you read the article, you might come across this sentence: "Frustration was induced by telling the children that they would not be able to see a movie that had previously been promised to them." This is, in fact, the author's specific operational definition of *frustration*. Later, you might find this sentence: "Aggression was assessed by having the students rate the teacher and counting the number of negative evaluations given to the teacher." This is the author's specific operational definition of *aggression*. Armed with these two operational definitions, you can now see whether you can generalize these results to your own situation. (At this point, you may rightly express exasperation that the definitions are so narrow and based on a single method of data collection. It would be easier to derive insights from richer, more fully developed operational definitions—and many good studies assist readers with multiple, fully developed operational definitions that lead to data collection through strategies that supplement and complement one another.)

Perhaps you are interested in rearranging the seats in your classroom so that friends will no longer sit together. Does the researcher's finding that "frustration leads to aggression among elementary school students" lead you to conclude that the pupils will probably fight with each other if you frustrate them by carrying out your plan of action? Based on the operational definitions given and looking at no other information, this conclusion would hardly seem warranted. The researcher's operational definition of *frustration* hardly seems to match the frustration you plan to impose upon your pupils, and likewise the researcher's definition of *aggression* doesn't match your operational definition of this feeling among your students. Only with this knowledge of the operational definitions can you determine the generalizability of such results.

Just as the outcomes and the treatment can be operationally defined, the other variables in the study must also be defined in terms of the observable behaviors, events, and characteristics that provide evidence of their existence. For instance, in the example cited in the previous paragraph, it would be useful if the researcher would operationally define *elementary school students*. Such a definition would consist of a simple, exact description, in observable terms, of the elementary students in the study. If they were predominantly white, middle-class third graders, this may give you reason to pause before you generalize the results to your predominantly Hispanic, inner-city fifth graders. Likewise, the setting can be operationally defined in terms of such variables as the size of the class, the physical construction of the school, the context and setting of the city or neighborhood in which the school is located, and many other qualitative characteristics. To the extent that any such factors can limit or extend the ability to generalize the results, the operational definitions provide useful information for the external validity of a study.

Examine the following detailed example. It provides an illustration of the use of operational definitions in drawing generalizations from a research report.

The following is a conclusion from a research study: Positive reinforcement of incompatible behaviors was found to be more effective than punishment in reducing aggressive behaviors among elementary school children.

Mrs. Cox wanted to know whether the results of this study were applicable to her own classroom. She first examined the study and found that it was flawless with regard to internal validity. There was absolutely no question in her mind that *within the study* the results really did lead to the conclusion stated in the research report. As she examined the study more closely, she discovered that the operational definitions of the important variables were these:

Positive reinforcement consisted of awarding a point that could be turned in for material rewards or privileges at a designated time once a week. (Mrs. Cox recognized this as a form of token reinforcement, which she had read about in professional publications.)

Punishment was defined as spanking the child with a paddle. The spanking was administered by the teacher in accordance with the guidelines of the school in the study. (She examined these guidelines and found that they were about the same as those employed by her own school system.)

An **aggressive behavior** was defined as an overt attempt to inflict pain or injury on another pupil. The pain could be either physical or psychological; thus, insults would count as aggressive behavior. (The research report included a list of examples of aggressive behaviors, and Mrs. Cox agreed that each of the examples fit within her own personal definition of *aggression*. In addition, she could think of nothing that she considered aggressive classroom behavior that was not close to one of the behaviors listed in the report.)

An **incompatible behavior** was defined as any nonaggressive and socially acceptable behavior that the child could perform instead of an aggressive behavior. A further qualification was that the behavior had to be one that could not be performed while the child was simultaneously performing an aggressive behavior. (Mrs. Cox examined the list of examples and determined that all of these were examples of behaviors that she would consider socially acceptable, nonaggressive, and incompatible with aggressive activities.)

Elementary school children were operationally defined as third through sixth graders in a traditional middle-class neighborhood. The children were 75% white, 20% black, and 5% Hispanic. There were about equal numbers of boys and girls in the study. (After examining the brief paragraph that clarified what was meant by a traditional school, Mrs. Cox quickly recognized that these pupils were much like her own.)

Mrs. Cox summarized the entire experiment for herself in operational terms: In this study, consisting of children much like my own, children who received token points for engaging in socially acceptable, nonaggressive behaviors that were incompatible with aggressive behaviors showed a greater reduction in the infliction of deliberate pain or injury upon other pupils than children who were spanked for engaging in these same aggressive behaviors. (In this summary, the word *aggressive* could have been replaced with an operational definition each time it occurred, but that would make the sentence exceedingly cumbersome. Mrs. Cox felt uncomfortable with cumbersome sentences. As long as the word *aggressive* was operationally defined in her own mind, she was satisfied with the summary.)

Now Mrs. Cox turned to the problem of applying the results to her own classroom. Almost all the operational definitions matched her own setting. (Note: Mrs. Cox should demand multiple operational definitions

and supplementary qualitative data. We have omitted these to keep the example from becoming too lengthy.) The one serious difficulty, however, was the operational definition of *punishment*. In her classroom, she punished her children, but she did this primarily by taking away privileges. Keeping this difference in mind, Mrs. Cox realized that the researcher had not provided evidence that rewarding an incompatible behavior *instead of punishing by removing a privilege* would result in a greater reduction of aggressive behavior. Therefore, since there was a substantial difference in the operational definitions of punishment employed by Mrs. Cox and by the researcher, there was serious question regarding the external validity of the study for Mrs. Cox. In other words, it was not immediately obvious that the results could be generalized to Mrs. Cox's setting.

What should Mrs. Cox do? Should she ignore the results of this study? Or should she decide that the operational definitions were close enough and go ahead and apply the researcher's results in her own setting? The answer is that Mrs. Cox should examine the situation based on what she knows. What she knows is this: If the dominant method for controlling aggressive behavior in her classroom were spanking children whenever they performed such behaviors, then replacing this method with the reinforcement of incompatible behaviors would lead to better results. However, Mrs. Cox does not use spanking in her classroom; she uses removal of privileges instead. Her immediate task is to determine how alike are her form of punishment and the form used in the study. If she concludes that her removal of privileges is really quite similar to spanking, then she will conclude that the results are applicable to her own classroom. On the other hand, if she concludes that her form of punishment is not even remotely similar to that employed in the study, then she will conclude that the study has told her little useful for her own classroom. Note that Mrs. Cox would not have to rely exclusively on her own speculation or intuition in making these judgments. She could consult the professional literature for other research on various types of punishment and reinforcement. (If the article that she originally read was well written, it is possible that the author of that article might include references that would help her find these other sources of information.) By consulting such sources, she might, for example, find that the effects of her type of punishment were not at all similar to the effects of spanking, and this might lead her to give less credence to the results under consideration.

After a close examination of the study and other related literature, Mrs. Cox might decide that the results of the original study cannot be directly generalized to her own classroom. Nevertheless, she might decide that the idea is worth trying anyway. She would therefore implement the researcher's ideas in her own classroom, using an appropriate experimental or quasi-experimental design to evaluate the outcomes. If she would do this while using much the same operational definitions as the previous researcher (with the exception that she would redefine *punishment* to fit her technique), then she would actually expand the state of knowledge on this topic. For example, if she discovered that the reinforcement of incompatible behaviors worked better than her own form of punishment, this would lead to an increase in the range of generalization that could be based on the conclusion stated at the beginning of this example. On the other hand, if she would discover that the same results did *not* occur with her redefinition of *punishment,* this would lead to a statement of specific limitations of the degree to which the results could be generalized. In either case, Mrs. Cox's replication of the study would lead to an improvement of the quality of generalizations that could be based on this research. The range of generalization could be further extended or refined in additional replications by systematically altering other operational definitions—for example, by altering the operational definition of *elementary school children.*

When you read research studies or listen to research reports, the operational definitions are not always clearly stated. It is safe to say that one of the most serious weaknesses in educational research is the *absence* of adequate multiple operational definitions and the reliance on single methods of data collection. Without operational definitions it is difficult to know what to make of the results. It is important that you learn to look for the operational definitions. In some cases these will be clearly stated and all you will have to do is figure out where to look for them. In other cases the operational definitions are not at all clearly stated, and no matter how hard you look you will not be able to find them. You should develop a willingness to look for operational definitions and ask about them when they are not obviously stated. You should likewise develop the ability to recognize weak, inadequate, single operational definitions and realize the threats to external validity

posed by such inadequacies. When you are presenting your own results, you should be willing to state clear operational definitions to help others determine how fully your results can be generalized to their settings.

The importance of operational definitions is not unique to educational research. They are just as necessary in most areas of social science—research in these other fields is often weakened by inadequate operational definitions. Politicians have been known to run for office with promises of wonderful benefits from their programs, but they give no operational definitions of these programs. A colleague of ours once listened to a foreign diplomat speak of peace and freedom in his country. At the end of the speech, our friend mumbled, "I would like to know his operational definition of *peace and freedom.*" It would be equally interesting to hear certain pop philosophers give their operational definitions of *happiness* and *the good life.* While such concepts are usefully discussed on a purely conceptual level, even an occasional operational definition can add insights to the discussions. The use of multiple operational definitions can provide a valuable service to any thoughtful undertaking.

SUMMARY OF STRATEGIES FOR OVERCOMING THE THREATS TO EXTERNAL VALIDITY

Table 15.1 provides a summary of the principal strategies for overcoming the major threats to external validity. These strategies cannot provide the same high degree of control for external validity that we can provide for internal validity. Nevertheless, by following these guidelines we can extend the range of situations to which generalizations can be made and identify specific restrictions that must be placed on generalizations.

Table 15.1 shows that one strategy common to the control of all three major threats to external validity is the careful examination of the context of the research setting and of the setting to which generalization is to be made. This examination is undertaken in order to look for unique features of the subjects, setting, or historical context that might restrict

Table 15.1 Summary of the Major Strategies for Overcoming Threats to External Validity

I. Threats arising from interactions of the treatment with *persons*.

    A. Examine the persons in the experimental context and in the setting to which generalization will be made, and look for unique features.

    B. Use random sampling from an overall population.

    C. Use purposive sampling for heterogeneity.

    D. Isolate and identify important interactions within the study (moderator variables), and use these as a basis for stating precise generalizations.

    E. State any control variables focusing on persons.

    F. Operationally define all variables related to persons.

    G. Replicate the study with varying subjects.

II. Threats arising from interactions of the treatment with the *setting*.

    A. Examine the experimental setting and the setting to which generalization will be made, and look for unique features.

    B. Use a placebo design.

    C. Use designs without pretests.

    D. Use unobtrusive measurements on pretests.

    E. Make the experimental setting as nonartificial as possible.

    F. State any control variables focusing on the setting.

    G. Operationally define all variables related to the setting.

    H. Replicate the study in varying settings.

III. Threats arising from interactions of the treatment with the *historical context*.

    A. Examine the historical context of the experimental setting and the setting to which generalization is to be made, and look for unique features.

    B. Replicate the study in varying historical contexts.

generalizations. In our previous discussions of internal validity, this strategy of looking over the setting qualitatively to see whether anything unusual was happening was viewed as one of the weakest ways to control the threats to internal validity. And yet, this is one of the strongest ways to control the threats to external validity. Reliance on strategies other than design strategies is the main reason why external validity is so much harder to establish than internal validity. We are forced to rely much more heavily on our observations and insight than on any systematic procedure to control the extraneous variables. The resulting inferences are necessarily weakened.

Another strategy that is common to the control of all three major threats to external validity is that of replicating the study in a different setting. If a study can be replicated in a variety of settings, then the variety of persons, settings, and contexts to which generalizations can be made will increase. Likewise, by being systematic in the way we vary subjects, settings, and contexts for these replications, we can derive specific statements of the limits that must be imposed on generalizing results arising from a study.

In addition, the adequacy of operational definitions is a crucial factor in establishing the external validity of a study. An operational definition states the observable events, behaviors, actions, characteristics, or data that we are willing to accept as evidence that a treatment, outcome, or other factor exists. By stating clear and precise operational definitions, we provide guidelines regarding the limits that must be imposed on the results of a research study.

The other strategies listed in Table 15.1 are uniquely useful for specific threats to external validity. A specific strategy will not always be feasible or useful, but used in accordance with the guidelines described earlier in this chapter, these strategies can greatly enhance the validity of research studies. Random sampling in experiments, for example, is almost never possible, but in situations where it *is* appropriate, it greatly improves the external validity of the study in which it is used. Purposive sampling is more often employed and is also valuable. It is necessary to examine a specific situation to determine what guidelines are appropriate.

This chapter has focused largely on generalizing the results of experimental research studies. The same logic of generalization can be applied to nonexperimental research—such as correlational and qualitative studies. The basic point is that results can be generalized only to persons, places, and contexts similar to the original, and this chapter has offered guidelines for making such generalizations.

PUTTING IT ALL TOGETHER

As we left him at the end of the last chapter, Mr. Anderson was satisfied that he had demonstrated that his Animal Life Program (ALP) had actually caused the development of improved attitudes among the children to whom he administered it. He realized his proof was not perfect (and could never be), but he was at least temporarily satisfied. Now he wanted to know how far he could generalize his results. This was the question of external validity. Among what other persons, settings, and historical contexts could he expect similar results?

It was immediately obvious to him that such generalizations had to be restricted to children like those in his study, until evidence could be supplied that the conclusions could be extended to children with varying characteristics. Therefore, since the children in his study came from mostly middle-class backgrounds, he was reluctant to offer any assurance to a colleague who taught in a poor neighborhood that the ALP would work equally well in her school.

Likewise, generalizations were restricted because the school in which Mr. Anderson had conducted his experiment had unique characteristics. An obvious problem was that the school had volunteered itself for the program. Would a program that worked in a school where the humane educator had been warmly welcomed with open arms be equally effective in a school where the reception would be apathetic or even hostile? It was obvious that further information would be needed before this generalization would be warranted.

In addition, it was possible that other subtle, qualitative characteristics of the setting could influence the external validity of generalizations, even though Mr. Anderson was not yet aware of what these other factors might be. To minimize this possibility, Mr. Anderson replicated the study on similar populations in two additional, geographically separated schools. The results were almost identical, and so these replications minimized the probability of accidental threats. Nevertheless, all three schools had volunteered and were located in middle-class neighborhoods, and therefore the generalizations were still restricted.

Mr. Anderson saw little threat from the interaction of the treatment with the historical context. He had carefully watched for unusual events both in the newspapers and at the schools involved in the studies, and he had found no unusual events that might enhance attitudes toward animal life. In addition, the replications had occurred over a period of seven months, which helped minimize the likelihood that some unique historical event was essential for the ALP to be successful.

The generalizations would be limited by the narrow operational definitions of the variables (these were discussed at the end of chapter 4). After reading the next chapter, it should be obvious to you that the operational definition of the ALP will influence how far Mr. Anderson can generalize his results to additional similar programs. It would be useful to estimate how closely his operational definition of *a favorable attitude toward animal life* matched the operational definition possessed by others who might wish to implement similar programs.

SUMMARY

This chapter has discussed the factors that influence the generalizability of the findings from an experimental research study. The question of whether cause-and-effect experimental results can be generalized to other persons, settings, and historical contexts is the focus of external validity. Threats to external validity arise when unique or unusual characteristics of the persons, settings, or historical contexts restrict the generalizations that can be drawn from a research study. This chapter has described each of these threats and has outlined strategies for overcoming or minimizing such threats. In addition to helping identify overall populations to which generalizations can and cannot be made, the principles discussed in this chapter can help us identify specific subgroups within a larger group about whom it is or is not appropriate to generalize. In this way, results can be applied in a prescriptive manner.

This chapter has also described the importance of devising appropriate, multiple operational definitions of concepts and variables in a study and using these to clarify how the results of a research study can be generalized. Operational definitions are helpful in communicating the results of research and clarifying the limits that must be applied to generalizations arising from a research study.

What Comes Next

Chapter 16 will introduce meta-analysis, a powerful research tool that integrates the results of a whole series of experiments—generally conducted by completely unrelated researchers. This procedure combines principles from the present chapter with those of preceding chapters to help researchers establish cause-and-effect relationships and determine how far the results of their studies can be generalized. In chapter 17, we will provide an integration of nearly everything covered in the preceding chapters: we will review information regarding each of the types of educational research; discuss the ways that various research variables interact in such research; and then discuss the concept of interactions. We will also present a brief discussion of theoretical (Level IV) research, which examines the underlying principles that explain the relationships observed in educational research.

ANNOTATED BIBLIOGRAPHY

Agnew, N. M., & Pyke, S. W. (1987). *The science game: An introduction to research in the behavioral sciences* (4th ed.). Englewood Cliffs, NJ: Prentice-Hall. Chapter 13 presents a brief but good discussion of the problems of external validity.

Cook, T. D., & Campbell, D. T. (1979). *Quasi-Experimentation: Design and analysis issues for field settings.* Chicago: Rand McNally. The index of this book lists only about 15 pages on external validity, but this brief discussion is very good.

CHAPTER 15
Research Report Analysis

One of the main reasons for publishing the results of the study reported in Appendix C is to enable readers to decide whether their own science students could benefit from the use of similar programs.

1. How well did the study described in this report control the interaction of the treatment with history?

2. How well did the study described in this report control the interaction of the treatment with persons?

3. How well did the study described in this report control the interaction of the treatment with setting?

4. In what ways do the authors of the report use operational definitions to enhance the external validity of the report?

5. In what ways do the authors of the report use experimental design to enhance the external validity of the report?

6. In what ways do the authors of the report use replication to enhance the external validity of the report?

ANSWERS

1. It is not obvious that the threat of interaction with historical context is well controlled. The report simply doesn't say much about the historical context. Without further qualitative information, we don't know much about what else was happening to all three groups, and these additional events could limit how far we can generalize these results. Note that this answer differs from the parallel answer to history as a threat to internal validity in chapter 10. There we were concerned that something might happen to one of the groups but not the others; here we are concerned with what happened to all three groups that might differ from what's happening where we want to generalize the results.

2. The authors have described the subjects in reasonable detail. Readers can assess the degree to which these subjects are similar to those to whom they wish to generalize the results. If readers want to generalize the results to students who are radically different—for example, gifted students in suburban schools—they should probably hesitate. However, to the extent that learners are similar to the inner-city high school students described in this study, generalizations are probably reasonable.

3. The interaction with setting presents considerable problems. The problems of expectancy were discussed in the answer to question 1 of chapter 10, and that discussion applies also to external validity. In addition, computer simulations were a novelty in the school where this study was conducted. It is possible that it was a combination of the novelty effect and the treatment that made the guided students perform so well. It is not clear that computer simulations employed in a more routine environment would have had an equally strong impact.

4. The authors use operational definitions of the research variables as a primary way to deal with external validity. In other words, although they themselves do not control many threats to external validity, they provide information that will enable readers to appropriately restrict their generalizations. These operational definitions are a strength of the report.

5. The authors do not use experimental design to support external validity. Experimental design is of primary importance for supporting internal, not external, validity.

6. The authors themselves did use replication, but the replications have been abridged out of the current report. In fact, the original report included three separate studies, all of which came to the same conclusions. These replications enhance the external validity of the research. In addition, it would be useful for other researchers to replicate the study with different subjects, new operational definitions, new experimental designs, and new data collection strategies and in new settings.

META-ANALYSIS: COMBINING THE RESULTS OF SEVERAL STUDIES

■ WHERE WE'VE BEEN

We have examined the major threats to internal and external validity. We have seen how experimental and quasi-experimental research designs help control the major threats to internal validity and how the threats to external validity are most often controlled by such processes as replication and careful operational definitions of all the variables in the study. We have also seen how tests of significance can to an extent help us evaluate the level of confidence we can place in the results of experimental studies. In addition, we have found that statistical tests as done in education and psychology lead to wrong inferences as a result of low power that occurs when the numbers of subjects or effect sizes are small.

■ WHERE WE'RE GOING NOW

In this chapter we'll discuss meta-analysis—a powerful research tool that integrates the results of whole sets of experiments. Meta-analysis is generally conducted by completely unrelated researchers to enhance both the internal and the external validity of the conclusions that can be drawn from those studies, giving us far more definitive statistical conclusions as a result of the much larger combined samples in all of the studies.

■ CHAPTER PREVIEW

The weight of cause-and-effect evidence from a single experimental study is weak, compared with the evidence that could be derived from a large number of studies on a single topic. Likewise, the ability to generalize from a single experimental study is much weaker than would be possible from numerous replications of the same type of study. This chapter discusses meta-analysis, a research tool that integrates the results of whole sets of experiments to strengthen the internal validity of cause-and-effect conclusions and enhance the external validity of the conclusions that can be drawn from those studies. Meta-analysis uses tests of statistical significance to evaluate the overall confidence we can place in these combined results. Because of their improved power to detect real differences among groups, these statistical tests are more likely than similar tests applied to isolated studies to reflect accurately the real world.

After reading this chapter, you should be able to

1. Describe the major problems in reviewing and integrating the results of experimental studies and the ways meta-analysis helps solve these problems.

2. Define the concept of effect size and describe how to compute and interpret it.

3. Describe the role of moderator variables and interactions in meta-analysis.

4. Describe the major steps in conducting and reporting a meta-analysis.

5. Describe guidelines for reading and interpreting a meta-analysis in such a way as to avoid errors and misinterpretations.

■

GOING BEYOND INITIAL STUDIES

Meta-analysis is a relatively new methodology, developed by Glass (1976) and further refined by Hedges (Hedges & Olkin, 1985; Hedges, 1986). *Meta* is a Greek prefix that means "beyond"—in effect, *meta-analysis* refers to a method that goes beyond an initial set of analyses or studies. It is a method for reviewing and synthesizing previously completed or published experimental studies. With meta-analysis, one synthesizes the prior data in a research area into a more organized and meaningful body of knowledge. In fact, many consider it to be the best way of reviewing the quantitative literature in a research field.

Many consider meta-analysis to be the best way of reviewing the quantitative literature in a research field.

Before we continue, let's restate some of the principles discussed in this book that are related to meta-analysis:

1. In chapter 5 we showed that there can be no perfect reliability of a test or observations, or really anything even close to the precision of measurement that technicians and workers in the physical or biological world make in their everyday work. Imprecision of measurement processes is a fact of life in educational research and the social sciences.

2. In chapter 4 we discussed the problems that arise when measurement processes employ only a single operational definition or a small number of operational definitions for the major variables in a research study or a similarly small number of methods for measuring outcomes. The validity of research conclusions is jeopardized when researchers do not employ multiple operational definitions and varied methods of data collection.

3. We presented in chapter 10 the threats to cause-and-effect relationships in experimental research (i.e., the threats to internal validity).

4. One of the threats to internal validity is instability—the substantial variations in the results of experiments due simply to the combination of the imprecision of measurement and the scatter of results from study to study because of sampling variations.

5. In chapter 14 we discussed tests of statistical significance, which help solve the problem of instability by using mathematical principles to make estimates of how likely it is that instability has introduced artificial differences into the results of an experiment. However, conclusions based on statistical inference can be wrong. In chapter 14 we also briefly introduced the concept of

power, which refers to the likelihood that we can avoid the error of concluding that a treatment has made no difference when in fact it has really produced an impact. The results of many educational experiments are especially prone to errors arising from low power, which are particularly likely to occur when the number of subjects in an experiment is small—say, fewer than 70.

6. In chapter 15 we discussed ways to strengthen external validity to support generalizations about cause-and-effect experimental results by considering whether the subjects, treatments, and criterion variables were much like the students, instruction, and objectives in your classes and whether schools were rather like those in the experiment you were reading. Our attempts to generalize the results of experiments are hindered because the isolated circumstances of an experiment may not resemble those to which generalization must be made. We suggested that you consider possible interactions of variables that might change the results of the particular experiment with respect to your own situation. However, the judgments we asked you to make were essentially qualitative, in part a matter of opinion.

7. In chapter 2 we discussed moderator variables, which we described as factors that can influence the way a treatment affects the outcome variables under consideration. These will be discussed further when we discuss interactions in chapter 17.

As the preceding list shows, many of the major problems in interpreting and applying the results of experimental research in education arise because we usually have relatively small numbers of subjects in educational research experiments, measurement processes employed in research experiments are limited and imprecise, and the contexts in which these experiments occur are usually restricted (perhaps unique).

The effect of studies with relatively small numbers of subjects has been to accumulate Type II errors (incorrectly concluding statistically that a treatment made no difference) when we combine the results of several studies. For example, we may examine 20 studies on a particular topic, find that there were significant differences in 10 of them and no significant

---

BOX 16.1	Unanswered Questions

One of the major advantages to making the exhaustive literature search that occurs at the beginning of meta-analysis is that the researcher is able to determine exactly what questions have and have not been tested experimentally. This search for experimental studies may show gaps in the research literature. For instance, when one of the authors of this book started a meta-analysis of the effects of teaching English literature, as far as he could determine there had not been a single experimental study ever done in that important field.

About $1.5 billion a year is spent on drug education in the United States—not for enforcement or medical or psychological treatment but strictly for drug education, certainly an enormously important problem of our youth. The federal government's General Accounting Office's review of the evaluation of the results stated that there were fewer than a dozen good evaluations. In our own start of a meta-analysis in this area, we have been able to find no more than a dozen experimental studies with which to work. In the absence of cause-and-effect evidence, one can only speculate about how the drug education program decisions are made and how effective they are.

Some critics are concerned that experimental studies are overemphasized. In some instances, this is certainly not the case.

differences in the other 10, and then conclude that the results are ambivalent. This vote-counting method of summarizing the results of educational research has often been done in the past and is very likely to be seriously misleading.

Drawing firm conclusions on the basis of isolated studies is analogous to deriving similar conclusions from case studies of isolated students.

Based on the information in the preceding paragraphs, teachers and researchers should be cautioned against drawing anything close to definitive conclusions from a single study. Drawing firm conclusions on the basis of isolated studies is analogous to deriving similar conclusions from case studies of isolated students. As chapter 9 has shown, there is much that can be learned from careful, qualitative observations of individual learners and groups of learners; likewise, single, well-done experimental studies can generate useful information. However, the quality of information from experimental studies can increase astronomically when the results of several studies are integrated into a meta-analysis.

WHAT META-ANALYSIS DOES

The best way to draw conclusions from the experimental literature is to assemble all of the results of several similar studies into one overall analysis—the meta-analysis. The arithmetic of doing this statistical analysis is not all that difficult or esoteric, but it is still outside the scope of this book, which is a research methods text and not a statistics text. For readers who have had a beginning statistics course, we recommend Hedges and Olkin (1985, pp. 110–114, 163–165) and Hedges (1986). Also, certain computer programs will do a great part of the arithmetic for you, since meta-analysis is essentially a spreadsheet methodology.

Meta-analysis helps solve problems of both internal and external validity:

1. Errors of measurement arising from reliability are minimized because such errors are likely to balance out in the long run. (This addresses a problem of *internal* validity.)

2. Different studies often use different operational definitions of the variables in the studies; therefore, the highly desirable strategy of using multiple operational definitions and multiple methods of measurement will almost automatically be incorporated into the meta-analysis. (This helps solve a problem of *internal* validity as well as *external* validity.)

3. The likelihood of specific threats to internal validity diminishes because these, too, are more likely to be a problem in a single experiment than to occur repetitively over a series of experiments. If there is a concern that a threat is likely to be an issue in a specific meta-analysis, then that threat can be coded as a moderator variable, and its impact can be empirically investigated. (This helps solve a problem of *internal* validity.)

4. The problem of instability is radically reduced as the overall number of subjects in the meta-analysis increases. With the much larger number of participants in the combined experimental studies, the likelihood of Type II errors (concluding that there is no difference when there actually is a difference) is reduced substantially. (This markedly helps solve the *internal* validity problem of instability.)

5. The ability to generalize results increases because with the wider range of subjects and contexts it becomes less likely that specific factors unique to a single experiment will restrict generalizability. (This helps solve a problem of *external* validity.)

6. By treating possible contaminating factors as moderator variables, the actual likelihood that these factors threaten the conclusions of research on a designated topic can be systematically examined. (This helps solve problems of *internal* or *external* validity, depending on the nature of the interaction.)

Several problems that can be at least partially solved by meta-analysis are summarized in Table 16.1. In addition, because the meta-analysis generates effect sizes, a cost-benefit relationship can be calculated. This cost-benefit analysis will be relatively unimpaired by the "muddiness" of our inability to interpret the data arising from random sampling variability and the inherent lack of perfect reliability of measurement. The cost of implementing an experimental treatment or condition compared with the cost of implementing a standard method or other alternatives can be determined.

THE CONCEPT OF EFFECT SIZE

The basic unit of data for meta-analysis is the effect size from an experiment. The effect size is defined as the standard score difference between the experimental group average minus the control group average. (A standard score is a derived score with a range of about +3.00 to -3.00, with a standard deviation of 1.00. For example, an effect size of .35 means that the experimental group scored .35 standard deviations above the control group in the study under consideration. Standard scores were discussed in chapter 7. The computation of effect sizes is described in greater detail later in the chapter.)

By examining the effect sizes from several experiments, meta-analysts try to determine whether, with all of these effect sizes combined, the size of this overall, average, cause-and-effect difference is enough to recommend changes in educational practices. Typically, although statistical tests of significance are made, they are reduced in importance compared with the usefulness of the size, or strength, of the overall difference.

With a reasonable number of studies (even 5 to 10), the combined number of subjects or participants in the set of studies will usually be several hundred or more. Thus, the power of the statistical tests to detect differences among groups is markedly enhanced. With meta-analysis, it is unlikely that researchers will fail to find differences because of low reliability or because of a small number of subjects.

An effect size of .35 means that the experimental group scored .35 standard deviations above the control group in the study under consideration.

The effect size is based on the difference between the mean (the average) of the experimental group minus the mean of the control group. To get a standardized effect size, that difference is divided by the combined standard deviation of the scores of these groups. This can easily be seen in the following examples:

	n	Mean	S.D.
Experimental Group	10	40.0	2.0
Control Group	10	39.0	2.0
Difference		1.0	
Effect size	.50		

The numbers in this example have been kept simple. We gave both groups the same standard deviation, and so the computation was straightforward. In real situations, the computation becomes slightly more complex.

Effect sizes are standard scores based on the standard deviation (discussed in chapter 7). They have a possible range of about -3.00 to +3.00. An effect size of .20 is considered small; .50, medium; and .80, large (Hedges & Olkin, 1985, p. 5). The discussion of the normal curve in chapter 7 showed that about six standard deviations encompass the whole range of scores on a criterion variable; thus, it is clear that an effect size of 1.00 would be a gain of about one-sixth of the range of scores of a group. Another way to say this is that a gain of 1.0 would take a group from a mean at the 50th percentile to a mean at the 84th percentile in the normal distribution. This would be a major cause-and-effect accomplishment or benefit.

A meta-analysis uses the effect sizes from several studies that focus on a common topic and combines these to determine the overall impact of a treatment. For example, from the results of the meta-analyses that he reviewed, Wahlberg (1986) found that teaching strategies that emphasized cooperative learning tended to have an effect size of about .80. This is tantamount to moving average students from the 50th percentile to the 79th percentile. This information strongly suggests to practitioners that the results of cooperative learning are worth the effort it takes to develop the cooperative learning environment. Wahlberg also found that while studies that focused

Table 16.1 Problems Solved by Meta-Analysis

	Problem	Explanation	Solution offered by Meta-analysis
1.	Unreliability	Imprecision of measurement processes obscures search for real differences.	Such errors are likely to even out in the long run when multiple studies are combined in meta-analysis.
2.	Limited operational definitions and data collection methods	Employing only a single definition or a small number of operational definitions and data collection methods in a measurement processes reduces its validity.	If different studies used different operational definitions of the variables in the studies, the strategy of using multiple operational definitions and multiple methods of measurement will almost automatically be incorporated into the meta-analysis.
3.	Threats to internal validity	Threats to internal validity reduce validity of conclusions from research studies.	These threats are more likely to be a problem in a single experiment than to occur repetitively over a series of experiments (see also Excessive subjectivity).
4.	Instability	Results of experiments will vary markedly due to the combination of the imprecision of measurement and the scatter of results from study to study because of sampling variations.	The problem of instability is radically reduced as the number of subjects increases.
5.	Inaccurate statistical conclusions	Conclusions based on statistical inference can be wrong. The results of many educational studies are especially prone to errors arising from low power, which are particularly likely to occur when the number of subjects in an experiment is small.	With the much larger number of subjects or participants in the combined experimental studies, the overwhelming error of statistical inference of "no difference" is reduced nearly to unimportance.
6.	Excessive subjectivity regarding external validity	Judgments about external validity (and some aspects of internal validity) are often essentially qualitative, in part a matter of opinion.	The ability to generalize results increases, because with the wider range of subjects and contexts it becomes less likely that specific factors unique to a single experiment will reduce generalizability. In addition, specific threats to both internal validity (chapter 10) and external validity (chapter 15) can be coded and their impact can be examined empirically. Qualitative judgments, of course, will still play an important role in interpretations; but these can be backed up by more solid quantitative data.
7.	Interactions often are unexamined	The nature of interactions from moderator variables often cannot be adequately examined in a single study.	By treating possible contaminating factors as moderator variables, the actual likelihood that these factors threaten the conclusions of research on a designated topic can be systematically examined.
8.	Results not directly practical	Tests of significance almost never give useful information about the practical usefulness of a treatment.	An effect size and ultimately a cost-benefit relationship can be established.

on *assigning* homework tended to have an effect size of about .30, the effect size for *graded* homework tended to be about .80. This kind of pragmatic information makes the effect size a powerful and practical tool for educational decision making. (Bloom's two-sigma problem, which is discussed in Box 16.2, is based on research similar to that analyzed by Wahlberg.)

Using the effect size, a cost-benefit ratio can be computed to compare the costs of implementing various educational treatment methods with their effect size benefits. Indeed, Glass, McGaw, and Smith (1981) essentially did this in a meta-analysis of the effectiveness in instruction of various class sizes. They found all the experimental studies of instructional achievements of various group sizes and then calculated the effect sizes of each. They then drew a graph with a line comparing the relative effect size strengths with the size of the instructional group. (See Figure 16.1.) As might be expected from the qualitative observations of teachers in their daily classes, the smaller the class, the greater the effect size. However, the researchers' result was clearly based on cause and effect and combined the results of several experiments, done in a variety of conditions and schools; thus, the external validity and generalizability of the results were good. Indeed, the state of Indiana used Glass as a consultant and implemented, as educational policy, a program called Prime Time, with strict limits on class size in the primary grades in order to enhance the educational achievement of the children in these important years. Clearly, the costs are major. If class size is reduced by half, then costs approximately double. Are the gains worth the costs? This is an important question, and with the cost-benefit review from meta-analysis we have a basis for answering this question.

The next question could be this: Are there other ways to maintain the achievements reflected in the effect sizes at a lower cost? It is believed that the numerous uses of teachers' aides, clerks, and cooperative learning groups might do this, while at the same time the productivity and status of the teachers as instructional team leaders could be enhanced. Again, the cost-benefit analysis gives us a basis for answering these questions.

Figure 16.1 Effect sizes that resulted from various class sizes in well-controlled versus poorly controlled studies in Glass, McGaw, and Smith (1981)

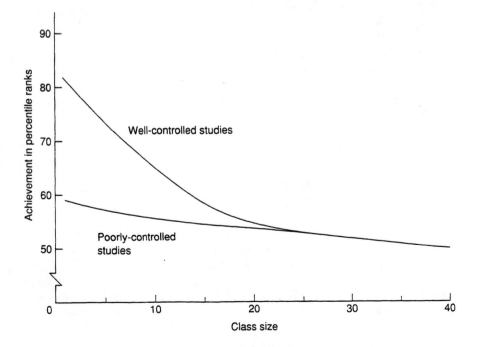

BOX 16.2 | **The Two-Sigma Problem**

One of the most stimulating recent developments in the field of educational psychology has been Bloom's (1984) statement of the two-sigma problem. Bloom theorized that students who received individualized tutoring would do better in any subject area than those taught under normal classroom instruction. Of course, this theory assumes that other factors, such as the quality of the instructor, would somehow be held constant. Bloom verified his theory by reviewing the results of published meta-analyses, which showed that students who received individualized tutoring displayed an effect size of 2.0 compared with those who received normal instruction. In other words, students who received individualized tutoring scored an average of two standard deviations above others on achievement tests. To put this yet another way, individualized instruction would take a person from the 50th to the 98th percentile on a standardized test.

Bloom decided to arbitrarily consider this gain of two standard deviations the ideal toward which normal, group-oriented instruction should strive. Since the Greek letter *sigma* is the abbreviation for *standard deviation*, he began referring to the two-sigma problem as the quest for ways that the quality of group instruction can approximate that of individualized tutoring. Many other researchers have taken up this search. Table 16.2 gives a list of several variables and their effect sizes with regard to academic achievement. Notice that each of the variables listed in this table is modifiable; that is, the teacher or school system can make changes that are likely to lead to gains in achievement among students. Bloom's eventual goal is to find some combination of these procedures that can approach individualized tutoring as a means of delivering instruction. Even if this goal cannot be reached, the effect size offers a basis for comparing different approaches to delivering instruction.

Research like this is based on effect sizes, which are at the heart of meta-analysis. This focus on effect sizes has led to much livelier discussion and practical implementation than would be possible with the more ambiguous concept of statistical significance.

LOOKING FOR INTERACTIONS

Meta-analysis also permits the systematic analysis of interactions over a series of experimental studies. This means that the factors that vary from study to study can be coded as moderator variables, which were discussed in chapter 2, and the researcher can look for and interpret interactions, which will be discussed in chapter 17. In this way, one can examine more thoroughly the moderator variables and interactions that are typically examined in individual experimental research studies. However, an even greater advantage is that by looking for interactions

through meta-analysis, we can dramatically enhance our ability to deal with the threats to internal and external validity. That is, we can code these as moderator variables during meta-analysis, and this will enable us to analyze statistically the likelihood that these threats have reduced the ability to make inferences from a series of studies.

By looking for interactions through meta-analysis, we can dramatically enhance our ability to deal with the threats to internal and external validity.

For example, imagine that there are 50 studies on the impact of Factor A on reading ability. Since some of the studies involved volunteer subjects, it is possible that selection bias would have affected both the internal and external validity of those studies. If the studies employing volunteers were adversely affected by selection bias, this would weaken their usefulness.

Table 16.2 Selected Alterable Variables that Influence Student Achievement

Effect Size	Percentile*	Strategy
2.00		Tutorial instruction
1.20		Reinforcement
1.00		Corrective feedback
1.00		Cues and explanations
1.00		Student classroom participation
1.00		Student time-on-task
1.00		Improved reading/study skills
.80		Cooperative learning
.80		Homework (graded)
.60		Classroom morale
.60		Verifying initial cognitive prerequisites
.50		Home environment intervention
.40		Peer and cross-age remedial tutoring
.30		Homework (assigned)
.30		Higher order questions
.30		New science and math curricula
.30		Teacher expectancy
.20		Peer group influence
.20		Advance organizers
.25		Socioeconomic status (included for contrast—SES is not easily alterable by teachers)

By simply coding each study's participants as volunteers or nonvolunteers, one could ascertain not only whether this factor makes a difference but also what the magnitude of the difference (if there is one) is. If there is no interaction, it would be appropriate to generalize across volunteer and nonvolunteer studies and to draw a single conclusion. On the other hand, if an interaction is found, the researcher would have to decide whether to exclude these studies from further analysis, to analyze their results separately, or to make more refined conclusions. The point is that with meta-analysis, we are not forced to speculate that there might be an interaction; we can empirically check to see whether an interaction occurs.

In the preceding example there are many other interactions related to internal or external validity that could be examined as part of the meta-analysis. The following are a few examples:

The various researchers used a number of different operational definitions of reading achievement, which can reasonably be classified into five categories. Do the results differ based on these variations?

In some cases the teachers themselves administered the posttests, whereas in other cases an outsider administered the posttests. Does it make any difference who administers the tests?

Five of the studies were conducted outside the United States. Were there any differences related to nations?

About two-thirds of the experiments used a quasi-experimental design, while the others used a true experimental design. Did the results of the true experiments differ from those of the quasi-experiments?

Some of the children received Factor A in their own classrooms, others received it in resource rooms, and still others received it in artificial situations that hardly resembled schools. Did these settings make a difference?

BOX 16.3	Actually Doing It

To actually do a meta-analysis requires the calculation of effect sizes. When a meta-analysis includes moderator variables to test for interactions, there will be effect sizes for each level of each moderator variable. On page 359, we have presented the basic strategy for calculating effect sizes. For the extraction of effect sizes from the data of more difficult reports (e.g., when the standard deviations of the groups differ greatly or when the research uses more complex analyses but does not report means and standard deviations), we recommend that you refer to Glass, McGaw, and Smith (1981).

The basic arithmetic of a meta-analysis is best done by the spreadsheet type of computer programs. Templates for meta-analysis are available via the "invisible college" networks of computer users and meta-analysts. Announcements of published meta-analysis programs have been made, but the actual programs have not appeared yet. We recommend that you test these computer programs by inserting the open education data analyzed by Hedges and Gage and used as an example on pages 163–165 of Hedges and Olkin (1985). If your meta-analysis program produces the same results as their analysis, you are ready to use the program for your own analysis.

Hedges and Olkin also have five pages (110–114) of formulas and development. These pages discuss material that is the key to understanding the arithmetic of meta-analysis. To understand what is influencing the results of meta-analysis, it is helpful to go through the arithmetic of some simple examples and illustrations of the equations used.

Asher (1990, pp. 146–156) presents the basic rationale of meta-analysis, illustrations of effect size results, the basic data sheets and coding of several variables for hypothesis testing, and eight basic formulas needed for meta-analysis. The enormous range of effect sizes from a set of sentence-combining studies is also illustrated in Asher. The effect sizes of the sentence-combining studies ranged from -.46 to +1.14. Think how a researcher might try to interpret the results of any one of these studies! No wonder a traditional reviewer generally concludes that there are conflicts in the literature.

Vaughn, Feldhusen, and Asher (1991) also offer an illustrative example of an actual meta-analysis from the field of the gifted and talented.

In about three-fourths of the studies, everyone knew that there was an experiment going on, but in the other one-fourth, Factor A was introduced unobtrusively. Did the degree of obtrusiveness make a difference?

Factor A has actually been studied for 10 years. Do the results of the earlier research show a different impact than those of later research?

These are examples of the alternative explanations, or hypotheses, that could be examined through meta-analysis. There are many more examples that could be listed; the possibilities are limited only by the data that can be described and collected from the combined studies. As these examples show, meta-analysis allows the researcher to systematically test various hypotheses about possible differences in methodology or research conditions that might restrict external validity and generalizability. This can be done with formal statistical analyses rather than the more subjective qualitative judgments that we presented in chapter 15, where we speculated that *maybe* the students in the reported study performed in a rather different way than one's own students would perform. With a large number of studies it is quite possible to code the students in the several studies as inner-city, urban, suburban, rural, East Coast, Southern, gifted, average, below average, and so on, and then statistically test whether indeed the original differences between the experimental and control groups differed among themselves as the result of these coded classifications.

Interactions found in a meta-analysis often generate new ideas for subsequent research hypotheses and even entirely new theories in a given area.

In addition to improving the internal or external validity of generalizations from a set of studies, the analysis of interactions during meta-analysis offers another advantage. These interactions often generate new ideas for subsequent research hypotheses and even entirely new theories in a given area. As chapter 2 showed, the statement, elimination, and refinement of rival hypotheses is at the very basis of the development of scientific theory.

In general, the specific threats to internal and external validity in the studies included in a meta-analysis can be coded as described on page 360. These threats to internal and external validity can then be related to the effect sizes of the studies. If the studies with major threats have effect sizes that differ from the studies judged to be without them, then they can be set aside and the meta-analysis conclusions can be based on the higher-quality research data. If there are no differences, then we know that the specified threat is of minimal importance in the particular area of research and broad generalizations are appropriate.

STEPS IN META-ANALYSIS

Like all research projects, meta-analysis starts by defining a problem and its relevant variables. Next it is necessary to search the literature and retrieve all the experimental studies pertaining to the problem stated. Chapter 3 described procedures for conducting such a search as effectively as possible. The object of this search is to obtain all of the existing experimental evidence relative to the problem. To exclude any of it on the basis of the meta-analyst's judgment is to allow possible biases to enter. It is more appropriate to include all the studies, flag and code the studies perceived as possibly weak or differ-

ent, and systematically evaluate them on the basis of shown differences in the statistical analyses in the meta-analysis. If the apparently weak studies do, in fact, lead to different outcomes, then they should be excluded from subsequent stages of meta-analysis because of this confirmed interaction. These methods of meta-analysis are public and replicable, and alternative, more explicit hypotheses about the influence of possible poor methodology or biasing factors can be statistically tested by others as well.

Perhaps the major contribution of meta-analysis is that it has produced the best method of reviewing and synthesizing the experimental research literature in education.

This emphasis on exhaustive retrieval of the literature and use of statistical tests (with good statistical power) produces findings of a quality that was simply not available before Glass and others developed the basic methods. Perhaps the major contribution of meta-analysis is that it has produced the best method of reviewing and synthesizing the experimental research literature in education. There is scholarly and research literature developing continually from philosophical, curricular, and naturalistic and experiential work, but certainly the method of using meta-analysis to synthesize the crucially important results is absolutely necessary for establishing a factual, cause-and-effect base for educational practice.

After the questions have been formulated and the experimental studies assembled, the effect sizes are calculated, as suggested earlier. On the surface, these calculations are simple. You expect that reported in the literature (whether a journal article, book, dissertation, ERIC report, or other form of media) will be the experimental and control group means, standard deviations, and number of subjects in each study, and that the effect size can be quickly calculated from these basic elementary descriptive statistics (which all the research methods texts say should be reported in any research report). However, in reality, these data are frequently not reported, and thus the effect sizes need to be developed or inferred, or the basic data must be obtained directly from the researcher.

The challenge in meta-analysis is not in actually doing the calculations. The real challenge lies in extracting and developing the effect sizes from the reports of the research. The results of experimental studies are often reported in ways that make it difficult to locate the effect sizes for use in a meta-analysis. A knowledge of basic inferential statistics or advice from a statistician can help overcome this problem. In addition, as meta-analysis continues to become more common as a statistical tool, more researchers are likely to report their results in formats that are easily compatible with meta-analysis. It is also useful to avoid being compulsive about getting every effect size for every experimental study found; even Gene Glass himself (who largely invented the procedure) reported that he could seldom obtain more than 90% of the effect sizes from the studies he found in an area (Smith, Glass, & Miller, 1980).

Once you have assembled all the studies and calculated all the effect sizes possible (and attached all the footnotes explaining how you estimated several of them), you should code each study for analysis of moderator variables to see whether there are important interactions, as described earlier in this chapter. The next step is to actually compute the meta-analysis, probably using a computer program. If interactions are discovered and studies are eliminated from subsequent analyses, the meta-analysis will have to be calculated in several repetitive, successive stages. Finally, it is necessary to compile a report of the meta-analysis, focusing not only on overall significance and effect sizes but also on interactions, qualitative data, and the relationship of the results to related theory. It is also necessary to summarize descriptions of operational definitions, data collection processes, threats to internal validity, and any other information that was involved in coding the individual studies for analysis with regard to the independent, dependent, moderator, or control variables in the meta-analysis.

In our discussion of external validity in chapter 15, we pointed out that results were easier to generalize if the researcher included qualitative information that would give rich, interpretive insights to the results of individual experiments. An analogous situation arises with meta-analytic reports. Just as a pure mathematical presentation of data from an individual study is enriched by the inclusion of objective, anecdotal, qualitative information, so also a meta-analysis can be enriched if specific details of at least some of the representative studies are summarized in the report. Hedges (1986, p. 393) strongly advises that "the most persuasive meta-analysis is likely to be one that combines the strengths of qualitative reviews and those of serious quantitative methodology."

GUIDELINES FOR INTERPRETING META-ANALYSIS

Well-done meta-analyses are powerful contributors to educational theory and practice. Most Level I and II researchers will be readers and users of the results of meta-analyses. It is important for readers of meta-analyses to realize the strength of their cause-and-effect results and the breadth and power of the theory involved. This merit arises from the integration and statistical analysis of a broad range of students, school contexts, educational treatments and conditions, and operational definitions of criterion variables. A good meta-analysis increases the power of statistical tests, employs the principle of triangulation by using multiple operational definitions and multiple methods of data collection, tests for possible interactions, and generates effect sizes that can be easily interpreted.

However, all good things come to an end. As could be expected, weak meta-analyses have begun to appear in the literature. One of our colleagues recently approached us with an article in hand and said, "This is a *meta*-analysis. It *must* be true." The simple fact is that readers must be alert that meta-analyses, too, can and are being badly done and badly interpreted. Meta-analysis has become the latest fashion, yet many such studies are ill-conceived, poorly done, and just plain bad scholarship. One of the authors of this textbook once did a government report that was published in ERIC with himself as the second author. When the same research was incorporated into a journal article, he was the first author. In a subsequent meta-analysis, the study was cited twice—once with an effect size of -.06 and once with an effect size of +.34! Transcribing (or calculating) errors of this sort can certainly reduce

---

BOX 16.4	Calculating the Meta-Analysis

The mathematical equations and methods for calculating effect sizes and study weights and for doing the statistical analyses generally will be of interest to those doing research for publication (usually, Level III and IV research). However, teachers who are not afraid of arithmetic can certainly do meta-analyses—especially if they are able to work with Level III and IV researchers.

For instance, Mrs. Vicki Vaughn (now Dr. Vaughn), an elementary teacher of gifted and talented children, became intrigued with meta-analysis in an introductory educational research methods course as "the only way to review the literature." (She was working on her doctorate part-time while teaching full-time.) When she read the results of several meta-analyses in the field of the gifted and talented, with respect to full-time classes and early entrance to school, she noticed there were no meta-analyses of the results of pull-out programs for such students, an educational accommodation for them that is far more common than the other two methods. Dr. Vaughn decided to do a meta-analysis herself. She worked with her major professor (an expert in the field of gifted and talented students) and with another professor who was an expert in meta-analysis. The results of her work were deemed so important to the field that they were published even before she could formally finish her doctoral work (Vaughn, Feldhusen, & Asher, 1991).

---

the validity of a meta-analysis. Armed with the brief introduction from this chapter, you should be able to avoid being victimized by faulty meta-analytic reports.

The following are some guidelines for reading and interpreting research:

1. A good meta-analysis should report reliability data regarding the coding of studies. Since coding usually involves a qualitative classification of the study into various categories, the most common type of reliability reported is interobserver agreement. It is reasonable to expect this percentage (normally, above 95%) to be reported.

2. The report should indicate how studies were gathered for inclusion in the meta-analysis. Using strategies described in chapter 3, you can easily do a spot-check to verify that the sources and descriptors employed by the researchers would have obtained the appropriate set of studies to include in the meta-analysis.

3. You should examine the list of moderator variables (which should be described in the methods section of the report) to verify that

the researchers have looked for appropriate interactions. You can also examine the operational definitions by which studies were categorized into these moderator variables and evaluate the suitability of these classification systems. Be very skeptical of studies that examine no interactions.

4. You can compare the effect sizes with those you have found in other meta-analyses and determine whether the researchers' conclusions are warranted by these effect sizes. In general, you can also apply the information in this chapter to verify that the researchers have interpreted their meta-analysis sensibly.

5. It seems appropriate to expect (perhaps demand) that editors of journals and textbooks take steps to ascertain that published reports contain the information necessary to determine effect sizes of experimental studies and to incorporate the results into meta-analyses.

If you read a large number of meta-analyses or perform them, it would be useful to pursue the references cited in the Annotated Bibliography at the end of this chapter.

CRITICISMS AND ALTERNATIVES TO META-ANALYSIS

Along with very many educational research theorists, we believe everyone should be aware of the advantages of meta-analysis and that everyone should know how to read the results of a meta-analysis research report. However, not everyone looks quite so favorably on the method. The distinguished English psychologist Hans Eysenck is one critic. He declared meta-analysis to be "an exercise in mega-silliness" (1978, p. 517).

Some theorists have suggested modifications or alternatives to meta-analysis for reviewing and integrating the literature on an educational topic. Slavin (1986) prefers to summarize the literature using a procedure followed in the legal profession called *best evidence*. Slavin declines to accept evidence that does not meet the minimum conditions of quality that he has developed. Thus, he usually bases his summarized conclusions on only a few studies. However, there are several problems with the best-evidence analysis:

1. The biases (even the unconscious ones) of selection by the reviewer-summarizer could easily influence the nature of the conclusions drawn from the review and integration. (How can professors gain national recognition if they say what everyone else says? Isn't it likely that a person who sees a trend or pattern will look extra hard for reasons to include studies that fit the pattern and to exclude those that don't?) This is analogous to the expectancy threat to the internal validity of individual experimental studies.

2. Instability from small samples and imprecise reliability is likely to lead to false conclusions when only a few studies are included in the analysis.

3. Finally, the external validity and generalizability of results based on a few operational definitions of contexts, treatments, conditions, teachers, and criterion variables are likely to be far weaker than that attained with the rich variety of situations, contexts, students, teachers, and operational definitions of criterion variables found in a meta-analysis of, say, even a dozen studies.

Thus, while there seem to be intuitive advantages to a best-evidence analysis, such an approach appears to have some obvious weaknesses—all of which are dealt with effectively by meta-analysis.

BOX 16.5

Expanding Theories with Meta-Analysis

Meta-analysis can help answer theoretical as well as practical questions. For example, it might be useful to examine the effectiveness of theoretically different approaches to solving an educational problem. The differing theoretical approaches of the various researchers can be coded into groups (and these codings can be replicated by an independent coder as a reliability check via a percentage agreement figure) and the effect sizes can be statistically tested.

Do the two extensively discussed theories of sentence combining in composition instruction (open and closed) really differ in their effectiveness? In the 27 experimental studies of sentence combining, the type of theory used in the instruction was coded by examining the descriptions of the instructional materials used and reported in the articles and dissertations. The meta-analysis showed that there were, in fact, no differences. This would lead one to suspect that after the first several articles preparatory to experimental data collection, the extensive discussion of philosophies of instruction and theoretical reasons for using open versus closed sentence combining were of dubious value (Asher, 1990).

Table 16.3 Major Variables Coded for Each Study in the Ryan (1991) Meta-analysis (see Box 16.6)

Substantive variables

Demographics
    Grade level
    Socioeconomic status
    School type
    School area
Ability level
Hardware features
    Presentation
    Computer make
    Color
    Music and sound
    Synthesized speech
Instructional features
    Subject area
    Software written by teacher
    Mode of application (drill, tutorial, etc.)
    Size of instructional units
    Supplemental or replacement unit
    Type of outcome (level of thinking)
Physical setting features
    Local area network
    External telecommunications
    Location (classroom, laboratory, library)
Time features
    Duration of treatment
    Length of sessions
    Frequency of sessions
Instructor features
    Professional level
    Hours of pretraining
    Coordination with project teachers

Methodological features

Instrumentation
Sample size
Subject assignment
Controls for internal validity
    Instructor effect
    History
    Time-on-task
    Test-author bias
    Bias in scoring

PUTTING IT ALL TOGETHER

While attending a World Series game between the Cubs and White Sox one day in October, Mr. Anderson slipped into a time warp. He journeyed forward 30 years and found himself in an air-conditioned meeting room in a convention center in a western part of the United States, where he saw his own granddaughter, Marie Anderson-Witherspoon, presenting the results of her master's thesis: "A Meta-Analysis of Research on Ways to Improve Humane Attitudes."

Marie's interest had been piqued when she discovered that her parents had met at a humane education conference years ago, where her paternal grandfather and maternal grandmother had both been presenting results of their own experimental studies on "Developing Humane Attitudes." As Marie examined the original papers on microfiche, she discovered that the two papers differed markedly. Her grandfather had employed a role-playing strategy and had found significant differences on the Fireman Tests between experimental and control groups on the posttest. Marie's grandmother had reported on two studies: one that had employed role-playing but led to no significant differences on the Fireman Tests and one that had employed trips to zoos integrated with group discussions that did lead to significant improvements by the experimental group on those same Fireman Tests. (Both the grandmother and the grandfather had employed additional measurement processes as well, and these led to essentially the same conclusions.)

As she read a summary of the convention proceedings, Marie had noticed that the discussant for the symposium had commented on the ambivalence of humane education research: some studies showed positive results, while others using the same methods showed no significant differences. As she continued to read studies from subsequent years, Marie discovered that this ambivalence persisted down to her own time: sometimes results were significant, and sometimes they were not. She thought she saw a pattern: role-playing seemed to work better when the children lived in suburban rather than rural or urban neighborhoods, but even this pattern was murky.

| BOX 16.6 | A Detailed Example of Meta-Analysis |

(This example is summarized from Ryan [1991].)

Researchers collected 40 studies dealing with the impact of the computer on various areas of achievement of elementary school students. The criteria for inclusion of studies were as follows:

1. Experimental or quasi-experimental design
2. Quantitative results of academic achievement
3. Use of microcomputers as an instructional tool in the experimental treatment
4. Kindergarten through sixth-grade classroom sites
5. Sample size of at least 40 students (minimum of 20 students in experimental and control groups)
6. Duration of eight weeks or longer
7. Release date of 1984 or later
8. Report available through university or college libraries or from ERIC or *Dissertation Abstracts International*

Each study was coded, whenever possible, for each of the variables listed in Table 16.3 on page 367. It was hypothesized that each of these variables might influence the impact of computers on achievement. Therefore, they were coded as moderator variables. Note that it would be impossible to have so many variables in a single, experimental study.

Some of the studies reported more than one set of results, and so the number of effect sizes available from the 40 studies was 58. The mean effect size was .31, indicating that students using computers scored about three-tenths of a standard deviation above those not

---

Marie knew exactly what to do. She went straight home and pulled from the table by her bedside her copy of the second edition of this book, which her grandfather had bequeathed to her in his will. (She kept her grandmother's copy of the third edition in a safe deposit box at the bank. The copies of the fourth through twelfth editions, of course, were on CD-ROM, but her computers had mysteriously developed a virus recently.) She opened the book to the chapter on meta-analysis. There it was: the basis of her master's thesis!

Over the next four months, Marie tracked down 47 reports that had focused on developing humane attitudes among children. Seven of these were unpublished manuscripts by her own grandfather, and two were rebuttals by her grandmother. Several additional studies that had claimed to be experimental were merely anecdotal descriptions by well-meaning people who had collected no data at all. She discovered that most of her grandmother's research had been of a qualitative nature—carefully collected and reported descriptions but without any quantitative information that could be incorporated into a meta-analysis. She eventually found 12 experimental studies in the published literature, 18 others on ERIC microfiche, and 17 more that she had tracked down by writing to authors, contacting universities, and interviewing presenters at conventions. She found 7 other reports that she had to exclude from her analysis because she found it impossible to determine the effect sizes for the experiments (those reports did not include means and standard deviations—only statements that results were significant or not significant).

The 47 reports actually contained information on 63 experiments. Many of these included multiple

using computers. The authors correctly interpreted this to mean that, projected over the span of a year, the students who used computers gained approximately three months in grade-equivalent units.

Many of the coded variables were likely to produce small cells. For example, since only a few of the studies mentioned color as a variable, it was impossible to make a reasonable comparison of students using color monitors with those using monochrome monitors. In almost every case where reasonable comparisons were possible (i.e., when there were at least four effect sizes in each cell for comparison), the differences were not significant. The only exception was pretraining of teachers, and the results of that comparison are summarized in Figure 16.2. These results indicate that students performed much better when their teachers received 10 hours or more of training in the use of computers for instruction.

Note that when someone conducts a similar meta-analysis in five years, many of these cells will contain additional effect sizes, and it will be possible to make additional comparisons. In addition, a future analyst may further subdivide the pretraining category and discover that teachers receiving training of type A display an average effect size much greater than those receiving training of type B. The authors of the study suggest that administrative coordination may be an important factor, but since only three studies mentioned that variable, they were unable to explore it as a factor in this meta-analysis. The authors reported an additional interesting result: when the software was written by the teacher, the effect size was .82; when commercial software was used, the effect size was only .29. However, they considered this result to be tenuous (since only 3 studies were based on software written by teachers, while 52 used commercial software), and they recommended further research in this area. The authors also suggest that future researchers examine such variables as type of reinforcement, pace, amount of student control, and the amount of computer/student interaction to determine their influence as moderator variables on the impact of computerized instruction.

treatments, several groups, or multiple outcome variables. Marie sorted the information carefully. She coded each study according to the type of treatment used; the type of outcome variables; the way these variables were operationally defined and measured; the age, gender, and ethnicity of the children; the type of neighborhoods from which the children came; and many other variables. In many cases, effect sizes for a particular variable (such as ethnicity) could not be determined for some of the studies, and so Marie had to add an additional level called "unavailable" for these moderator variables. She asked a colleague to make the same categorizations for all these variables, and she discovered that they agreed about 95% of the time. For those judgments about which she and her colleague disagreed, the two raters reexamined them and came to an agreement regarding classification.

The results of Marie's research are too complex to report here. We'll focus on just a few issues. Her first discovery was that there was an interaction between quality of research and outcomes: the 8 studies in which expectancy was uncontrolled showed much larger effect sizes than those in which expectancy was controlled. Therefore, she excluded these 8 studies from further analysis. When she analyzed the remaining studies, Marie discovered that the overall effect size for experimental programs designed to improve humane attitudes among children was .54. Focusing on the area where her grandparents had originally disagreed, she found an effect size of .59 for role-playing studies and .27 for those involving field trips. She further found that the effect size of .59 stayed roughly the same for role-playing studies, no matter what moderator variables she examined for interactions. When she examined the

Figure 16.2 Mean Effect Sizes by Hours of Pretraining in Ryan (1991) Study (see Box 16.6)

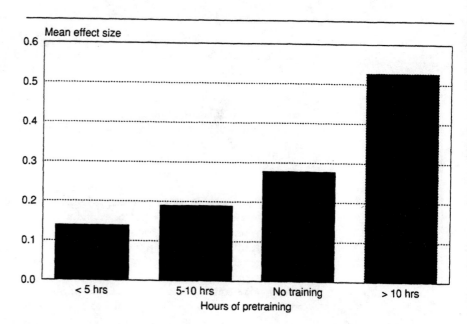

field trip studies, however, she found interactions with neighborhood that ranged from effect sizes of .87 to .04. This led her to the conclusion that role-playing worked equally well for all groups of children but that field trips were especially likely to be helpful for children who came from lower-income neighborhoods.

A questioner at the convention asked Marie how she explained the initial ambiguity in the results of humane education research. Marie's reply was that the original fuzziness had probably occurred because sample sizes were small in the individual studies and because the measurement processes were imprecise. Results that appeared to be contradictory would be likely to occur by chance, and just counting the votes to see whether a method worked would be likely to give a false impression. Marie added that, in addition to other benefits, her meta-analysis had combined the subjects from several studies, thereby enabling her to see the big picture rather than apparent ambiguities. After Marie's presentation, a principal from the audience mentioned to her that role-playing was considerably less expensive than field trips and that it was more easily integrated with other subjects (specifically, language arts) than field trips, which tended to be, in his experience, enjoyable but dis-

tracting. Marie was able to refer to her grandmother's qualitative research to point out that the principal's insights were corroborated by empirical data. However, she suggested that since her meta-analysis had shown an interaction, it might be useful to continue to use field trips in schools where children came from lower-income neighborhoods.

Mr. Anderson enjoyed his evening spent in the time warp. However, he had to get back to find out whether the Cubs could beat the Sox.

SUMMARY

This chapter has discussed meta-analysis, a research tool that integrates the results of a whole set of experiments to strengthen the internal validity of cause-and-effect conclusions and enhance the external validity of the conclusions that can be drawn from those studies. Meta-analysis uses tests of statistical significance to evaluate the overall confidence we can place in these combined results. These statistical tests are more likely than similar tests applied to isolated studies to reflect accurately the real world because of their improved power to detect real differences among groups. In addition, meta-analysis focuses on the examination of effect sizes, which are easier to interpret and often of more practical importance than tests of significance for computing cost-benefit ratios and for making decisions regarding the adoption of appropriate educational strategies.

In addition, this chapter has focused on several of the specific problems solved by meta-analysis, including the increased power to identify real differences among groups, the easy incorporation of multiple operational definitions and multiple methods of data collection into the data analysis, and the qualitative concerns of contexts and anecdotal descriptions. This chapter has also described the role of moderator variables and interactions in meta-analysis. By examining interactions, the researcher can often rule out threats to internal and external validity, as well as be more precise in describing the conclusions that can be drawn from a study. Finally, the chapter has described guidelines for reading and interpreting meta-analysis in such a way as to avoid errors and misinterpretations.

What Comes Next

We have now completed our treatment of Levels I, II, and III research. Chapter 17 will further integrate this information and present a discussion of theoretical (Level IV) research. Chapter 18 will discuss how to use the computer in your research endeavors. Finally, Chapter 19 will describe effective strategies for carrying out research studies and writing research reports.

DOING YOUR OWN RESEARCH

One of the most important points to be made in this chapter is that many readers of this book should consider performing a meta-analysis of the literature related to the topic they have chosen to research. The hardest part of a meta-analysis is often finding the research reports, reading them carefully, and extracting the effect sizes. If you are planning to conduct a thorough review of the literature, you may

want to consider doing a meta-analysis of the research on your chosen subject.

When performing a meta-analysis, it is important to code the data correctly. You can do the best possible job if you plan the meta-analysis carefully and code all the important variables during a single run through the reports. If you fail to plan properly, you will waste time. For example, if your meta-analysis will cover 50 research reports and you discover while reading the 35th that you really should have categorized the studies on the basis of the operational definition of the outcome variable, then you'll have to go back through the first 34 studies to code all of them on this new variable. It would have been more efficient to code this variable during the initial reading of each report.

If you are interested in doing a meta-analysis, don't be deterred if someone else has already published a meta-analysis in the area in which you are interested. In addition to updating the previous study with more recently published effect sizes, you can add additional moderator variables to make your own meta-analysis more useful.

Finally, when writing your research report, consider qualitative as well as quantitative information.

FOR FURTHER THOUGHT

1. Some researchers would argue that only good research should be included in a synthesis of research information on a given topic. Some meta-analysts respond that weak studies do not really invalidate the results of a meta-analysis, as long as the meta-analysis is conducted properly. How can this be true?

2. What kind of information would be provided to you in the ideal synthesis of research on a given topic? How close does meta-analysis come to meeting this ideal?

3. Complete this sentence by answering the designated questions: "Meta-analysis . . .(does what?) (To what or whom?) (When?) (Where?) (How?) (Why?)"

REFERENCES

Bloom, B. S. (1984). The search for methods of group instruction as effective as one-to-one tutoring. *Educational Leadership, 41,* 4–17.

Eysenck, H. (1978). An exercise in mega-silliness. *American Psychologist, 33,* 517.

Ryan, A. W. (1991). Meta-analysis of achievement effects of microcomputer applications in elementary schools. *Educational Administration Quarterly, 27,* 161–184.

Smith, M. L., Glass, G. V., and Miller, T. L. (1980). *The benefits of psychotherapy.* Baltimore, MD: Johns Hopkins Press.

Wahlberg, H. J. (1986). Synthesis of research on teaching. In M. C. Wittrock (Ed.), *Handbook of research on teaching* (3rd ed.). New York: Macmillan.

ANNOTATED BIBLIOGRAPHY

Asher, J. W. (1990). Educational psychology, research methodology, and meta-analysis. *Educational Psychologist, 25,* 143–158. This article presents an overview of the value of meta-analysis in building theory in educational research. It includes a more detailed description of the sentence-combining example presented on page 366.

Glass, G. V. (1976). Primary, secondary, and meta-analysis of research. *Educational Researcher, 5,* 3–8. This is widely regarded as the first and classic description of what meta-analysis is and does.

Glass, G. V., McGaw, B., & Smith, M. L. (1981). *Meta-analysis in social research.* Beverly Hills, CA: SAGE. Chapter 5 describes the methods for the extraction of effect sizes from the data of more difficult reports.

Hedges, I. V. (1986). Issues in meta-analysis. In E. Z. Rothkopf, *Review of research in education,* vol. 13 (pp. 353–398). Washington, DC: American Educational Research Association. This chapter provides a good discussion of problems likely to be encountered during a meta-analysis and how to deal with them.

Hedges, I. V., & Olkin, I. (1985). *Statistical methods for meta-analysis.* Orlando, FL: Academic Press. This book presents an authoritative treatment of how to perform and interpret meta-analyses.

Lauer, J. M., & Asher, J. W. (1988). *Composition research: Empirical designs.* New York: Oxford University Press. Chapter 10 gives a simple but complete description of meta-analysis with examples related to English composition.

Slavin, R. E. (1986). Best evidence synthesis: An alternative to meta-analysis and traditional reviews. *Educational Researcher, 15,* 5–11. This modification of traditional strategies for meta-analysis provides an alternative way to combine the results of several studies.

Vaughn, V. L., Feldhusen, J. F., & Asher, J. W. (1991). Meta-analyses and review of research in pull-out programs in gifted education. *Gifted Child Quarterly,* 92–98. The researchers combine the results of all known studies of pull-out programs in gifted education to ascertain the degree to which that strategy is likely to be effective.

CHAPTER 16

Research Report Analysis

The results of the study reported in Appendix C could be incorporated into a meta-analysis. A researcher conducting a meta-analysis would have to code this study with regard to important variables and extract the effect size(s).

1. What are some of the important variables for which this study could be coded in a meta-analysis?

2. What effect size(s) would the researcher obtain from this study?

ANSWERS

1. Depending on the goal of the person conducting the meta-analysis, this study could easily be coded with regard to its subjects (inner-city students), subject matter (science education), the way the computers were used (guided versus unguided), and outcomes (thinking skills). (Coding on other variables would also be possible.) By coding the study in this way and entering the effect size from this study into a meta-analysis with effect sizes from many other studies, the

authors would be able to address questions such as the following:

a. Does using computer simulations result in different effect sizes for inner-city students than for suburban or rural students?

b. Does using computer simulations result in different effect sizes for science education than for social studies, mathematics, or foreign languages?

c. Does using computer simulations with guidance result in different effect sizes than using the same or similar programs without guidance?

d. Does using computer simulations result in different effect sizes when the goal is to teach generalized thinking skills than when the goal is to teach specific content information?

The preceding list is only a sample of the variables that could be coded when this study is included in a meta-analysis. By coding with regard to these and similar variables, the research could look for interactions (discussed in chapter 17), and the results could become much more useful than if the researcher simply reported an overall effect size for computer simulations in science education.

2. Actually, this is a difficult question. The problem is that the person conducting the meta-analysis would want to select a single effect size that represents the results of the entire study or perhaps select several effect sizes to examine several hypotheses. There are several strategies that could be employed:

a. Take the average of all the effect sizes in Table C.1 in Appendix C. This procedure would require computing the effect sizes for the six separate tests listed in that table,

adding them together, and dividing by six. This strategy would have the advantage of including all of the variables discussed in the study, but it would have the disadvantage of giving disproportionate weight to the five unit tests compared with the more comprehensive Watson-Glaser test. (Using this approach, we would get an effect size of .40 for the guided group compared with the control group.)

b. Use the Watson-Glaser test alone. This strategy would be based on the theory that the Watson-Glaser test is the most valid measure of thinking skills of all those employed in this study. (Using this approach, we would get an effect size of .61 for the guided group compared with the control group.)

c. Get an average of the unit pretest effect sizes (by computing them separately, adding them up, and dividing by five). Then average this with the Watson-Glaser effect size. (Using this approach, we would get an effect size of .35 for the guided group compared with the control group.)

Other strategies would also be possible. Whatever strategy the researcher decided to use should be specified in the methods section of the meta-analysis report.

Note that these examples focused on the effect size for guided use of simulations compared with a traditional approach. Other effect sizes would be possible for *unguided use compared with traditional approaches* or for *guided use compared with unguided use of simulations*. It would also be possible to obtain a combined effect size for *guided or unguided use of computer simulations compared with traditional approaches*. All this would be specified in the methods section of the report.

EXAMINING INTERACTIONS AND INTERPRETING THEORETICAL RESEARCH

■ WHERE WE'VE BEEN

We have examined research problems, research hypotheses, and the variables that they involve. We have also discussed strategies for collecting and interpreting reliable and valid data. In addition, we have discussed strategies for conducting qualitative and quantitative research studies and for controlling the major threats to internal and external validity. Finally, we have discussed meta-analysis as a strategy for integrating the results of several studies.

■ WHERE WE'RE GOING NOW

In this chapter we'll provide an integration of nearly everything covered up to this point. First we will review and integrate information regarding each of the types of educational research. Second, we will discuss the ways that various research variables interact in such research. And third, we will discuss the concept of interactions. We will also present a brief discussion of theoretical (Level IV) research, which examines the underlying principles that explain the relationships observed in educational research.

■ CHAPTER PREVIEW

This chapter will in several ways integrate many of the ideas discussed in previous chapters. First we will discuss the concept of interactions, which play an especially important role in experimental, criterion group, and meta-analytic research. Then we will discuss the role of theoretical research in education. Both of these topics have been at least briefly described in earlier chapters.

After reading this chapter, you should be able to

1. Read and interpret published reports of research.
2. Conduct effective research of your own.

3. Define interactions and describe how they influence educational research.

4. Given a description or diagram of an interaction, interpret it correctly.

5. Describe the similarities and differences between theoretical and applied research.

6. Describe strategies for identifying the intervening variables that are responsible for the relationships observed in education.

7. Describe how the methodologies of applied research can be integrated into the process of theoretical research.

■

INTERACTIONS

An *interaction* is said to occur when two variables act together to produce an effect that is different than would occur with the variables acting separately. Sometimes interactions confuse issues, and in such cases the researcher tries to minimize them. For example, chapter 10 discussed threats to internal validity as interactions that were to be avoided if possible. Chapter 15 provided a similar discussion of interactive threats to external validity. These threats were called interactions because they act together with the treatment to produce an effect. It is desirable to eliminate these interactions because they cloud the issue regarding the precise effect produced by the treatment.

The main reason for identifying moderator variables is to look for interactions.

Moderator variables also lead to interactions. They act together with the treatment to produce an outcome. However, instead of trying to eliminate the interactions caused by moderator variables, the researcher tries to isolate these variables and to measure the size and direction of the interaction. Instead of getting rid of the interaction, the researcher describes the interaction as precisely as possible and

makes this description available for use in interpreting the results of the study. The main reason for identifying moderator variables is to look for interactions.

Let us examine some diagrams showing the results of studies containing moderator variables.[1] The following is one of the hypotheses used as an example in chapter 2:

Behavior modification will reduce creative behavior among elementary school children in middle-class schools but will increase creative behavior in lower-middle-class schools.

Figure 17.1 shows the results of a study undertaken to test this sample hypothesis. These results show that the middle-class children who received no behavior modification averaged about 50 on the creativity test, whereas the middle-class children who did receive the behavior modification program averaged about 30. This is what a prediction based on the hypothesis would expect. On the other hand, the lower-middle-class children without the behavior modification averaged about 30, whereas the lower-middle-class children who received behavior modification averaged about 50. Again, this is what the hypothesis would predict. The results summarized in the diagram, therefore, support the belief expressed in the hypothesis. The hypothesized interaction of the moderator variable with the independent variable has been found to exist. The effect that behavior modification would produce was influenced (moderated) by the child's social class. The combination of middle-class status and behavior modification led to low average performance on the creativity test, whereas the combination of lower-middle-class status and behavior modification led to higher average performance on the creativity test.

One reason why this interaction might occur is shown in Figure 17.2, which suggests that behavior modification introduces structure (an intervening variable) that causes some children (who need more structure) to become more creative, while it

---

[1]These studies and results are fictional. They have been invented to provide clear examples.

BOX 17.1

Dear Researcher: My nephew was ferreting through a garret in an ancient parsonage in Stratford near Avon, when he came upon a tattered manuscript. Much of it was illegible. However, it seems that the scrawlings were the rough draft of a poem or play in iambic pentameter, dedicated to the theme of educational research. It is my belief that this is the original version of Hamlet's third soliloquy. Is it possible that the enclosed lines were written by Shakespeare himself?

> To be, or not to be? that is the question:
> Whether 'tis nobler in the mind to suffer
> The slings and arrows of external invalidity,
> Or to take arms against a sea of threats,
> And with a moderator variable isolate and control them.
> (Here some lines are lost, eaten by moths.)
> Thus conscience does make researchers of us all,
> And thus the native hue of true experimentation
> Is sickled o'er with the page cast of factorial design,
> And experiments of great pith and moment
> With this regard their generalizations expand
> And lose the name of irrelevance.—Soft you now:
> The fair Ophelia:
> (The rest of the text is lost, eaten by moths.)

(signed) *Scholarly Inquirer from Phoenix*

Dear Scholar: No, this was not written by Shakespeare. It was written by Sir Francis Bacon. So were the rest of Shakespeare's plays.

(signed) *The Lonely Researcher*

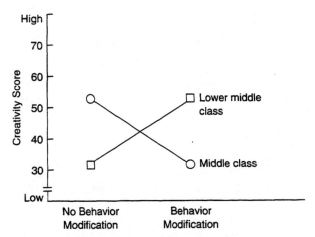

Figure 17.1 Results of a Hypothetical Study Confirming Hypothesis 2 (stated on page 376). The added structure of behavior modification has moved the middle-class scores *down*. The added structure has moved the lower-middle-class scores *up*.

causes other children (who already have plenty of structure) to become less creative. The diagram in Figure 17.2 suggests a way that interactions are related to theoretical research, which is discussed later in this chapter.

Here is another hypothesis, which was also operationally stated in chapter 2:

Delaying reading instruction until the sixth grade will have no adverse impact on reading ability by the time the child reaches adolescence. This absence of impact will be equally true among low-IQ, medium-IQ, and high-IQ students.

This hypothesis states that a moderator variable (IQ) will be examined, but it predicts that there will not be an interaction. The results shown in Figure 17.3

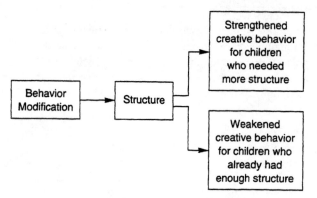

Figure 17.2 Diagram of the Effects Shown in Figure 17.1

support this hypothesis. Low-IQ subjects averaged about 25 in both the delay and the no-delay conditions. Likewise, the medium-IQ subjects averaged higher than the low-IQ subjects, but they scored about the same in both conditions. The high-IQ subjects also averaged the same score in both conditions. These results show that there was no interaction between the treatment and the IQ level of the subjects. IQ *by itself* made a difference in reading achievement, but it did not *combine* with the treatment to produce outcomes.

There is an easy rule that will enable you to estimate whether there is an interaction through visual inspection of such diagrams. If the lines are parallel or nearly parallel, there is no interaction. If the lines cross or come toward each other so sharply that they would cross if they were allowed to continue a little farther, then there is an interaction. This rule covers obvious cases, like those represented in Figures 17.1 and 17.3. In more subtle cases, it is hard to ascertain by visual inspection alone whether the lines are nearly parallel; in such cases it is necessary to rely on statistical procedures (e.g., analysis of variance) rather than visual inspection to interpret the results. Nevertheless, this is a useful rule that will help you interpret research reports containing moderator variables and interactions.

If the lines are parallel or nearly parallel, there is no interaction.

Figure 17.4 shows the results of a study undertaken to examine the following hypothesis:

Programming in Logo will cause substantial improvements in higher-order thinking skills among slow readers who are not classified as having learning disabilities. However, no such improvements will occur among slow readers who are classified as having learning disabilities.

In the study under consideration, the pupils with learning disabilities performed about the same in both experimental conditions, whereas the pupils with no learning disabilities performed much better when they programmed in Logo.

The results in Figure 17.4 show that the experimental results supported the belief that the predicted interaction would occur. Of course, it would be possible that the hypothesized results might not be found in the experiment. For example, Figure 17.5 shows a different set of results from an experiment examining

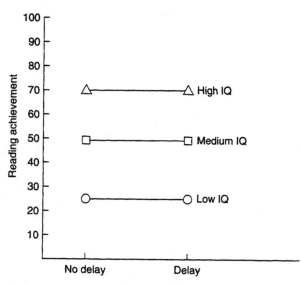

Figure 17.3 Results of a Hypothetical Study Undertaken to Test the Hypothesis That Delaying Reading Instruction Until the Sixth Grade Will Have No Adverse Effect on Reading Ability by the Time the Student Reaches Adolescence. (The results show 10th-grade reading achievement tests, reported for low-, medium-, and high-IQ students.)

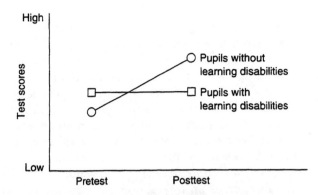

Figure 17.4 Results of a Hypothetical Study on the Effects of Logo Programming on Test Scores with *Learning Disabilities* as a Moderator Variable

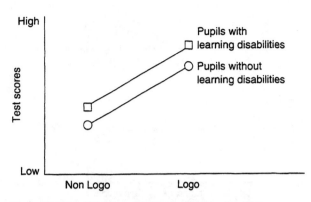

Figure 17.5 Results of a Study Testing the Same Hypothesis Shown in Figure 17.4. (This time, there is no interaction.)

the same sample hypothesis. These results indicate that both sets of pupils performed better when they programmed in Logo. The lines in the diagram are nearly parallel; this means that there is no interaction. Researchers interpreting results such as those shown in Figure 17.5 often state that there was an overall effect of both the treatment and the moderator variable but that there was no interaction between the two variables. In other words, the average score of the students who programmed in Logo was higher than that of those who did not, and the average of the pupils with learning disabilities was superior to that of the pupils without learning disabilities. However, being in one or the other experimental condition did not have a different effect on either of the sets of pupils, as had been the case in Figure 17.4. The results in Figure 17.5, therefore, do not support the belief that the hypothesized interaction exists.

The value of looking for such interactions can be seen from an examination of Figure 17.6. This diagram shows no moderator variables. A researcher undertaking a study to ascertain the effects of Logo programming might examine the results shown in this figure and conclude that Logo programming makes no difference. By selecting the appropriate moderator variables, however, the same researcher might find the rather dramatic interaction displayed in Figure 17.4. Identifying the correct moderator variables and integrating them into our research design can enable us to gain useful insights from experimental studies. Students and professional researchers can find interesting topics for research by

adding moderator variables to studies they read about and then replicating the earlier research with a design that incorporates these moderator variables.

The discovery of interactions as well as the verification of their absence provide useful information to the researcher and the consumer of research.

Which is better: to hypothesize and discover interactions, or to look for and verify the absence of interactions? The answer is that the discovery of interactions as well as the verification of their absence provide useful information to the researcher and the consumer of research. Figures 17.7 and 17.8 show the results of a sample study undertaken to

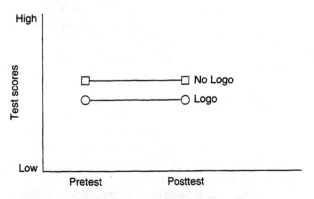

Figure 17.6 Results of a Hypothetical Study on the Effects of Logo Programming on Test Scores *with No Moderator Variable*

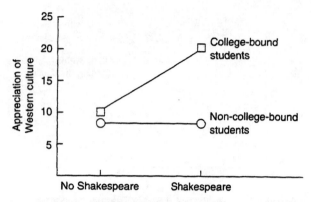

Figure 17.7 Results of a Study Testing the Hypothesis That Studying Shakespeare Leads to Greater Appreciation of Western Culture Among College-Bound Students but Not Among Non-College-Bound Students. (These results show an interaction. Those in Figure 17.8 show no interaction.)

examine related hypotheses that differ only because they predict a different interaction. Figure 17.7 shows an interaction, whereas Figure 17.8 shows no interaction. They both provide useful results. A researcher or other reader examining the results in Figure 17.7 would conclude the following: spending time teaching Shakespeare achieves the desired effect among college-bound students but not among non-college-bound students; we should continue using Shakespeare for this purpose among the college-

bound students, but maybe we should seek a different approach for our non-college-bound students. On the other hand, the same researcher or reader examining Figure 17.8 might conclude this: spending time teaching Shakespeare achieves equally desirable benefits among both college-bound and non-college-bound students; unless we find an approach that is even more successful, we should continue using Shakespeare for this purpose among both groups. Thus, either finding an interaction or finding the absence of an interaction can provide useful information for making decisions based upon the results of a research study.

REVIEW QUIZ 17.1

1. Here is a research hypothesis: Students in grades 9 to 12 who complete two elective years of the Latin curriculum will score higher on a standardized vocabulary test than those who do not enroll in an elective Latin class at all. This difference will occur both among those students enrolled in advanced-placement English at any time in their high school career and among those never enrolled in advanced-placement English.

The following are the results of a fictional study to test this hypothesis. Do these results support the hypothesis?

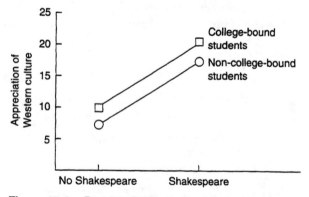

Figure 17.8 Results of a Study Testing the Hypothesis That Studying Shakespeare Leads to Greater Appreciation of Western Culture Among College-Bound Students as well as Among Non-College-Bound Students. (These results show no interaction. Those in Figure 17.7 do show an interaction.)

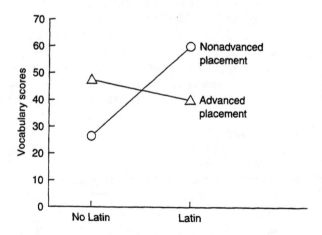

Diagram of the Results of a Study to Test Whether Taking an Elective Latin Curriculum Will Improve Vocabulary Scores

2. Here is a research hypothesis: Clients who enroll for counseling at the Roberts Psychiatric Clinic and are initially diagnosed as passive-aggressive will later show more assertiveness by resisting a mock telephone solicitor with cogent reasoning after treatment employing Transductive Role Modeling (TRM) than similar clients receiving the traditional treatment. However, clients at the same clinic diagnosed as passive-withdrawn will show more assertiveness after receiving the traditional treatment than passive-withdrawn clients receiving the TRM treatment.

The following are the results of a fictional study to test this hypothesis. Do these results support the hypothesis?

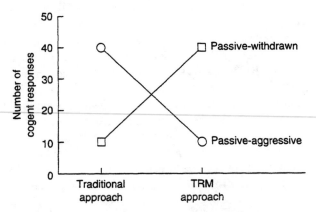

Diagram of the Results of a Study to Determine the Effect of Transductive Role Modeling

THEORETICAL RESEARCH: THE UNDERLYING PRINCIPLES BEHIND THE OUTCOMES OF RESEARCH

Often it is important to know not only whether a particular treatment works but also what underlying principle is at work to produce the observed outcome. In other words, we may be interested in knowing not only what outcomes are occurring (Level I research), what is causing those outcomes to occur (Level II), and whether the same events would cause the same outcomes in a different situation (Level III), but also whether there are underlying principles that can be generalized to other treatments

and to other outcomes. The search for such underlying principles is the essence of Level IV research.

The discussion of this type of research has been reserved to last not because it is unimportant but for two main reasons. First, the lower levels of research receive a priority in terms of how much time inservice educators can actually devote to research. Second, the other types of research are necessary prerequisites to successful higher-level research. Higher-level research is built upon sound foundations of lower-level research.

An emphasis on practicality should not prohibit attention to the theoretical aspects of our work.

It is important to stress that just because inservice educators often have little time for Level IV research does not mean that they should be unconcerned about such research. That suggestion would be an insult to professional educators. Just as we assume that physicians and surgeons are interested in the theoretical aspects of medical science and that engineers are interested in current physical science developments, it is safe to assume that educators are interested in the theoretical aspects and current developments in the behavioral and social scientific fields related to education. While we do not assume that every physician is capable of performing a detailed chemical analysis that will lead to a new discovery or that every engineer can function as a theoretical physicist, we do anticipate that most doctors and engineers spend some time thinking about such theoretical issues. We also presume that they are capable of reading and understanding the information provided to them by the theoretical researchers who are examining problems related to their fields of professional interest. It seems equally appropriate to expect that professional educators will spend some time with theoretical speculations regarding the principles involved in their daily work. An emphasis on practicality should not prohibit attention to the theoretical aspects of our work.

How is theoretical research conducted? What does it mean to say that high-level research builds upon lower-level research? How does a person who is actively engaged in solving practical, concrete, daily problems find time to develop a simultaneous interest in abstract questions? Let us answer some of these questions by giving you an example from our own professional experience.

Recently in a course he was teaching, one of our colleagues tried a different way of teaching a very difficult concept. He usually asked three questions on the final exam dealing with this particular topic. By looking at his previous tests (he keeps many of the tests that his students return to him, so he was able to use a cohort design to evaluate his new method), he knew that in the past the students had consistently averaged 70–75% correct on these questions. This had disturbed him because on most concepts the students (who were dedicated people taking the course on a mastery basis) averaged 85–95% correct.

After he tried his new way of teaching this concept, our colleague continued to insert three previously used items on that concept on the final exam. He found that the scores on these items jumped the next three semesters to 90%, 80%, and 90%, respectively. He found a similar high level of performance when he used his new method again the next semester. He was impressed. He had evaluated his new instructional method with a fairly sound research design and had pretty well proved to himself that this new method worked. In his elation, he even contacted a colleague who taught a similar course; she tried the same approach and found it successful in her course too. Our colleague was impressed again, since he was now moving toward external as well as internal validity.

In a certain sense, it did not matter why this new method worked; all that really mattered was that it did work. Even if he could never figure out why the results came out the way they did, both his colleague and he intended to keep using this new method, because they had good evidence that it caused their students to master an important concept more effectively. But in another sense, it did matter why this new method worked the way it did. If he could find out what underlying principle was at work in making this new method produce its desirable outcome, he (and others) could apply that same principle to other appropriate instructional situations.

In identifying this underlying principle, our colleague did not have to start from scratch or guess blindly. After all, when he had chosen his new method, he had made this choice for a reason. He had chosen the new method because he felt that the traditional way of teaching the concept had involved terminology that the students were likely to find confusing because they had used similar terminology in defining similar but distinct concepts. Therefore, he had decided to avoid the traditional terminology and had invented some new terms, which were not confusing because the students associated these terms with nothing at all. In using the new terms the students were able to examine the concept without confusion, and this enabled them to understand and apply it more easily.

In developing the new method, our colleague had derived ideas from the concept that educational psychologists refer to as *proactive inhibition*. This concept refers to the fact that concepts we learn earlier are likely to interfere with our future attempt to learn concepts that are in any way similar to the earlier learning. Our colleague's belief was that he could minimize proactive inhibition by using terms that did not remind students of earlier, incorrect concepts. When the new approach worked, therefore, he naturally took this as a verification of his belief that using terms that did not remind students of previously learned concepts reduced proactive inhibition and thereby enhanced learning of the new concept.

Had our colleague really, at this point, proven that his theory was correct? Had he proven that this underlying principle had actually been at work in causing the beneficial outcomes that followed his new method? No, at this point, his proof regarding the underlying principle was actually quite weak—even though his evidence regarding the success of the new method itself was strong. His evidence was weak because there were several other factors that could have caused the beneficial outcome. For example, maybe his new terms were more precise and descriptive than the traditional terms, and therefore the principle at work would be that more precise and descriptive terms lead more effectively to learning than terms that are not as precise and descriptive. Or perhaps when the traditional terms are taken away from teachers, these teachers are forced to become more creative, and perhaps it was this increase in creativity on the part of his colleague and himself (rather than a decrease in proactive inhibition) that led to the improved performance of the students. These and similar alternative explanations could not be ruled out on the basis of a small number of experiments.

At this point our colleague's curiosity was temporarily satisfied. He knew his new method worked, and he had a suspicion that he knew what caused it to work. At the same time, he was aware that he had not really provided solid evidence that it was this underlying principle that had been responsible for his improved outcomes. He was actually very interested in knowing whether he had successfully circumvented proactive inhibition, but he had important, practical things on his mind, such as teaching the next unit in that class and performing the rest of his teaching responsibilities. Therefore, he was able to devote no more time to the theoretical aspects of this problem. However, even though he had to put it out of his mind, he knew that a good way to pursue the issue further would be to replicate the study with expanded operational definitions of proactive inhibition and of the outcome variables and to conduct studies applying the same principle to new concepts. He kept this in mind, and he looked for other situations in which he could apply the principle. Eventually, he did find other situations, and he discovered that the principle worked again. Such replications strengthened his belief that his principle was based on accurate generalizations. He continued to pursue this issue, always on an informal basis while carrying out his professional responsibilities.

If our colleague wanted to devote a greater portion of his life to examining the theory that proactive inhibition can be reduced by using terminology that does not remind students of unrelated concepts, what else could he do? There are two important steps that he could follow: (1) he could identify additional settings in which the principle should operate and then set up experiments to see whether this hypothesis would be confirmed in these additional settings, and (2) he could draw up an exhaustive list of other plausible explanations of the outcomes and set up additional experiments to test these alternate explanations. He should set up these additional experiments in such a way that if his theory is correct, one result will occur, whereas if the alternative explanation is correct, then a different result will occur. For example, we suggested earlier that perhaps his new terms were more precise and descriptive than the traditional terms and that it may have been this difference rather than the reduction of proactive inhibition that caused the improved learning. The researcher could check this possibility by setting up a situation in which the experimental group received the terms that reduced proactive inhibition but the control group received terms that were more precise and descriptive. If the experimental group still surpassed the control group under these circumstances, this would indicate that the alternative explanation was less plausible than the proactive inhibition theory. Such results would strengthen the theory.

Likewise, we suggested that the removal of the traditional terms might have forced the teachers to be more creative and that it might have been this increased creativity rather than the reduction of proactive inhibition that caused the improved learning. The researcher could check this possibility by giving an experimental teacher the new terms and a control teacher some placebo terms. If both sets of terms would arouse equal amounts of creativity (and he could check this through some system of observation) and if the experimental group still surpassed the control group in performance, then this would indicate that this alternative explanation was not as plausible as the proactive inhibition theory. This would further strengthen the hypothesis.

If the researcher could come up with a comprehensive list of alternative explanations and rule each of these out, and if he could apply the principle in a wide variety of situations with the expected outcomes, the theory would gain strength. Quite likely, he would not meet with unmitigated success in each test of the hypothesis. Occasionally he would find discrepant results. If he found enough discrepant results, he would abandon the theory. However, another very strong possibility is that when he encountered results that contradicted the theory, he would modify the theory rather than abandon it. For example, he might find that the principle works well when applied to abstract concepts but fails miserably when applied to concrete concepts. He would then change the theory to state that the use of terms that do not remind learners of unrelated concepts will minimize proactive inhibition and enhance the learning of abstract concepts. A lengthy series of tests of this theory would undoubtedly lead to a large number of revisions, and such revisions would make the theory more precise and resistant to subsequent refutation.

In this process of theory verification, our colleague would not have to work alone. The theory is likely to be of interest to other professionals. Somebody else has undoubtedly done research at least indirectly related to the topic, and he can find the results of such research by consulting appropriate library references. He could also publish the results of his own research. This would subject the theory to the professional scrutiny of his peers. Such publication might arouse considerable interest, and perhaps other researchers would test some of the alternative hypotheses or replicate his study in various settings. The exchange of information resulting from such publication could spread valuable information to interested professionals and speed up the process of theory refinement by enlisting the aid of more researchers. As the next section will show, whenever we pursue theoretical questions in the systematic manner described in this example, we are engaging in what can be called the science of educational research.

BOX 17.2

Does Frustration Lead to Aggression?

Professor Froid had a theory that frustration leads to aggression. He devised multiple operational definitions of the concepts of frustration and aggression, and his graduate students conducted the following experiments (the operational definitions of the concept of frustration are *italicized*; the operational definitions of the concept of aggression are in **boldface**):

1. One of them watched little children in a naturalistic setting. She noticed that *when children had their toys taken away from them,* they were more likely **to hit other children.**
2. Another set up an experiment among college sophomores. He discovered that *when students received a lower grade than they felt they deserved,* they often responded by **giving the teacher much lower ratings on the teacher evaluations.**
3. Another discovered that when fourth graders *were forbidden to watch their favorite television show and were required to play with dolls instead,* they were more likely to **engage in hostile activities toward the dolls, such as hitting them, poking them, and pulling their hair.**
4. Another student gave extra free time to a large number of elementary school students. She discovered that if she *took back this extra free time,* the students were more likely to **make critical comments about their classmates' oral presentations** than other students who were allowed to retain the extra free time.

Since Professor Froid agreed that all of these operational definitions were valid, we can arrive at a reasonable understanding of his concepts of frustration and aggression. In addition, Professor Froid has reason to believe that frustration (rather than a more narrowly defined experience such as having a toy taken away) is at the basis of the observed hostile activities.

To make this into good theoretical research, Professor Froid would continue to replicate his experiments with additional operational definitions and multiple methods for measuring these operational definitions. By doing so, he would continue to refine his theory.

THE RELATIONSHIP BETWEEN THEORETICAL AND APPLIED RESEARCH

The main difference between theoretical research and the more practical or applied research described throughout the earlier chapters is that theoretical research focuses primarily on the intervening variable. It is important to note that except for this focus, the methodologies employed in theoretical and applied research are similar. In fact, theoretical research is correctly viewed as an extension of the nontheoretical levels of research. Theoretical research must build upon the successful implementation of these applied levels in order to produce useful theoretical results. The kinship between theoretical research and the more applied levels can be seen in Figures 17.9 and 17.10.

Figure 17.9 diagrams the statement of the theoretical hypothesis. This relationship is stated at Step 2 as the scientist pursues Dewey's scientific method. Figure 17.10 shows what happens to this abstract hypothesis when the scientist proceeds to Step 3 of the scientific method. At this step, the scientist asserts that if the hypothesis is correct, then a certain observable event will lead to a certain observable outcome—assuming that one or more abstract concepts intervened between the two observable events. (The scientist has to resort to observable events and outcomes in this prediction; otherwise, the prediction would merely be another unverifiable hypothesis.)

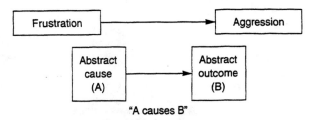

Figure 17.9 The Abstract Hypothesis Is Describing the Theoretical Relationship at Step 2 of the Scientific Method

What the prediction at Step 3 really states, therefore, is that a certain observable cause will produce the hypothesized interaction between the abstract cause and the abstract effect, and this interaction will in turn produce a specified observable outcome. The series of events diagrammed in Figure 17.10 is really just another way of saying that the observable cause in the prediction is an independent variable that leads to an intervening variable (the interaction between the abstract cause and the abstract effect), and this intervening variable in turn leads to a dependent variable (which is really an operational definition of the abstract dependent variable).

Thus, one of the major ways that theoretical research differs from applied research is that the theoretical researcher must spend a large amount of time setting up the operationally defined hypothesis in Figure 17.9 in such a way as to make sure that it

Figure 17.10 The Deduced Prediction from Step 3 of the Scientific Method. The components of Figure 17.9 have been compressed into the middle box of this diagram.

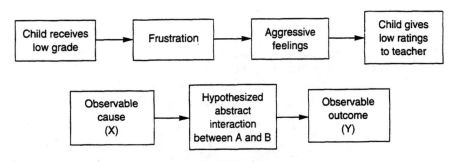

really is a prediction based on the conceptual hypothesis of interest. Once the operationally stated hypothesis has been formulated, the methodologies employed by the theoretical researcher to verify or reject this hypothesis are exactly the same as those employed by nontheoretical researchers.

A second difference between theoretical and applied research arises from the setting in which the hypothesis must be tested. To provide the most efficient and useful information relevant to the theoretical hypothesis, the prediction that emerges from Step 3 of the scientific method should be stated in such a way that insofar as possible the theoretical hypothesis and only the theoretical hypothesis will be able to explain the results obtained from the experiment. To accomplish this, the experimental setting has to be carefully structured to focus on this one intervening variable. The difficulty or artificiality involved in careful structuring often makes practical researchers shy away from theoretical endeavors. Once such settings are established, however, the procedures used to carry out the experiment and evaluate its outcomes are the same as those described in the earlier chapters of this book.

Applied research is not inherently incompatible with theoretical research.

Applied research is undertaken to solve specific problems. It enables us to find out what is happening in our educational settings, determine what is causing these outcomes, and determine how far such findings can be generalized. Applied research is not inherently incompatible with theoretical research. In many cases, applied researchers can help solve theoretical questions, and in many cases theoretical researchers can help solve practical problems. Such mutual helpfulness depends on planning and communication. A knowledge of the scientific processes involved in theoretical research will enable us to contribute more effectively to this process of planning and communication.

This textbook is written primarily for educators who are actively engaged in such processes as teaching, counseling, and administering educational programs. Because of this orientation, the text has focused on the practical and applied types of research that are most likely to be helpful to the readers in this audience. The present chapter has provided a brief introduction to how theoretical, nonapplied research is conducted. To a certain extent, you may be able to do some of this theoreti-cal research while you pursue more practical concerns. Readers who will need to do a great deal of theoretical research will almost certainly wish to acquire more information about the processes of theoretical research than is contained in this text. For example, most doctoral students take courses that deal with the philosophy of science and the logic, statistical analysis, and measurement of psychological constructs, and such courses would enable them to develop skills in those areas of theoretical research that have minimal overlap with the methodologies used in the more applied research discussed in this textbook.

Figure 17.11 summarizes how the various research variables work together to produce a result. The independent, moderator, and control variables are under the researcher's control. They cause an impact within the subject. This impact is referred to as the intervening variable. In addition, the extraneous variables have an impact on this intervening variable. Because these extraneous variables are not under the researcher's control, their presence weakens a study. One of the goals of a researcher is to eliminate as many factors as possible from the extraneous category by employing an effective research design and bringing these factors into the categories of moderator and control variables. This process of removing extraneous threats strengthens a study.

Figure 17.11 Summary of the Variables in the Research Process

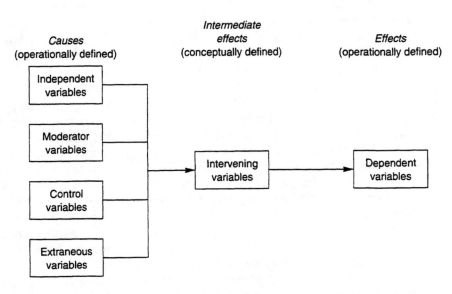

The intervening variable is merely hypothesized; it cannot be physically observed. It is defined in conceptual terms. The intervening variable is produced by some combination of the causal variables in the left-hand column of Figure 17.11. It produces the dependent variable. Thus, the dependent variable is an indirect result of the variables in the left-hand column.

Figure 17.11 is a highly simplified diagram. In addition to the interactions shown here, the independent, moderator, control, and extraneous variables could be pictured as interacting with one another, as well as having an impact on the intervening variable. Arrows portraying such interactions have been omitted for the sake of simplicity. In addition, the role of the intervening variable has been oversimplified; in many cases, there could be a whole string of boxes rather than a single box. For example, a certain set of causal variables might lead to a combination of increased psychological arousal, a sense of self-efficacy, and altruistic feelings, and these might lead to increased motivation (as well as to other intervening outcomes), which might lead to improved personal awareness, which might lead to more efficient selective attention, which might lead to new insights, which might (finally) lead to higher scores on the science test. This whole complex chain has been compressed into a single box in Figure 17.11.

Although theoretical research has been treated only briefly and incompletely, the topic will be pursued no further in the present text. This brief introduction will enable you to do theoretical research on a minimal basis. In addition (and probably more important), this introduction will enable you to understand and formulate evaluations of the theoretical research that you will read as a professional educator. It should be obvious that much of the thinking you do requires focusing on abstract theories. This is often true even when you are neither reading research nor explicitly devoting your time to a research project. An understanding of how theoretical research works and an ability to focus the principles discussed in this text on theoretical problems will enable you to think more carefully and clearly about theoretical issues. Many thinkers and philosophers have defined *science* as organized common sense—but common sense is sometimes uncommon. To the extent that this is an accurate definition, an improved ability as a scientific thinker will make you a better thinker.

THE RECURSIVE NATURE OF THEORETICAL RESEARCH

Figure 17.13 summarizes the recursive and integrated pattern that theoretical research typically follows in education. Researchers interested in theoretical issues often begin with qualitative, exploratory studies that focus on a broad range of variables in their natural context. At this stage, they collect field data and engage in a combination of developing new theories and integrating their field data with previous theories. The dominant factors at this stage are the careful collection of data and the insight of the researchers.

The results of the initial qualitative observations often lead to additional qualitative studies and to either quantitative descriptive or experimental studies. As these studies expand and become refined, they take on an increasingly sharp focus to integrate and develop the theoretical concepts under consideration. However, the conclusions at this stage—while more formal—are still tentative.

The results of the studies at the second stage often lead to the formulation of hypotheses that can be tested in more formal experimental studies with careful controls designed to examine cause-and-effect relationships. While many of these studies are designed to support practical decisions, they can be integrated with other quantitative research and with qualitative research to strengthen generalizations about underlying principles. In addition, the results of these more formal experiments feed back into the qualitative and quantitative studies of the second stage.

Finally, meta-analyses combine the results of previously conducted experimental studies. In addition to providing direct and useful information to further theoretical knowledge, the results of these meta-analyses help interpret and generate new hypotheses for research at the second and third stages. The activities at all four stages are summarized in Table 17.1 on page 392.

BOX 17.3	## An Example of Theoretical Research

Figure 17.12 shows an example of a theoretical model of school-related behavior. It shows a filter model of social knowledge acquisition and social performance. This imposing diagram is not all that complicated to interpret.

Reading from left to right, the figure suggests that there is social information available to the child. This information (listed in the leftmost box) is the input that feeds into the filters.

The first set of filters consists of environmental factors. These factors filter social information in the sense that cultures and sanctions influence the information the child is likely to get from the environment.

Social information that comes through the first filter is then filtered by physiological factors. For example, a child with a short attention span would get different information from the environmental filter than a child from the same culture with a longer attention span.

After social information is filtered by the physiological factors, it is passed along to the information processing filter. For example, children are likely to encode social information with different degrees of efficiency.

This information processing filter interacts with the social knowledge filter. This means that what a child already knows will both influence and be influenced by what he or she already knows about social activities.

After a child knows what social behaviors are appropriate, the decision to actually engage in social behavior will be influenced by the motivation filter.

(The additional lines in the diagram indicate further complexity in the learning and performance of social behaviors.)

This diagram was derived from a careful analysis of the research of many researchers in education and the other social sciences.

A model like this is more than a tool for ivory tower researchers. It also has practical value for classroom teachers. For example, if a child is having problems getting along with peers, the teacher can use this diagram to pinpoint the problem and to generate ideas to help the child overcome these problems. Without this model, a teacher may perhaps assume that a child who disrupts other students should be punished. By using this model to guide remediation, however, the teacher would realize that punishment would have a chance of being effective only if the problem were that the child knew what to do but was refusing to do it. This model may suggest that for a given child, the problem may be in the second (physiological) filter, and this would lead to a different course of action than would be appropriate for a child for whom the breakdown was in the operation of the motivation filter.

A model like this suggests both theoretical and applied research. At the theoretical level, it can be integrated with the social learning theory of Bandura (1986) and the social cognition theory of Fiske and Taylor (1991). At the practical level, it would be useful to develop data collection strategies to diagnose where breakdowns occur and to evaluate specific programs designed to remediate various social information shortcomings, such as the Think Aloud program advocated by Camp and Bash (1981).

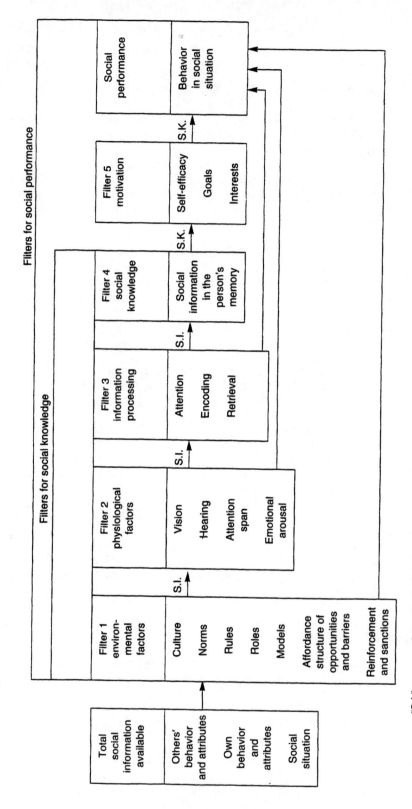

"S.I." appears above the 2nd, 3rd, and 4th arrows to indicate that social information is being passed through to the next filter.
"S.K." appears above the last two arrows to indicate that social knowledge is being passed through to the next filter.

Figure 17.12   A Filter Model of Social Knowledge Acquisition and Social Performance (Based on Bye & Jussim, 1993.)

Figure 17.13 The Recursive and Integrated Pattern of Theoretical Research in Education

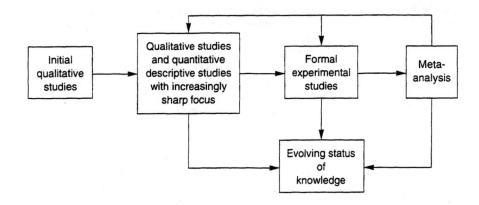

PUTTING IT ALL TOGETHER

In addition to being a practical man, Eugene Anderson prided himself on being a philosopher of sorts. He did not drink hemlock juice nor suffer from existential angst, but he did like to speculate about such issues as why people act they way they do, what is meant by morality, and what it really means to be a humane person. Combining his educational vocation with his philosophical avocation, he wondered why some people are humane toward animals and others are hostile. He wondered why his Animal Life Program (ALP) worked with some children and not with others. He wondered what it was that in general made some programs work while others failed.

Mr. Anderson worked with organizations that wanted to imbue an appreciation of animal life in the American population. These organizations worked by promoting a love of animals in their programs. From his early work with his Fireman Tests, Mr. Anderson wondered whether his colleagues might be barking up the wrong tree. He had noticed that about 25% of the children who took his tests chose to save no animals whatsoever. In their explanations for their choices, these children indicated no animosity toward animals. Rather, they simply ignored animals and chose material objects because the objects had monetary value. Moreover, he had noticed that he could predict with considerable accuracy that if a child chose a wallet, a credit card, or color television as his or her first choice, that child would not choose an animal for the second or third choice. Based on this information, Mr. Anderson had a hunch that it

might make more sense to focus on fighting materialism than on trying to make children love animals.

Note that Mr. Anderson's hunch was based on weak evidence. He had merely noticed an apparent relationship between choosing things with monetary value and rejecting animals. Such a correlation does not necessarily indicate a causal relationship. In addition, he has a rather poorly defined concept—materialism—which would have to be more fully operationally defined before he could strengthen his conclusions. Mr. Anderson was aware of these shortcomings, but he still enjoyed his speculations.

The primary focus of Mr. Anderson's theoretical speculations was the question "What was it that caused some programs to work while others failed?" The first programs he had evaluated had not succeeded in changing attitudes toward animal life. In discouragement, he had gone through the psychological literature on attitude change research and had discovered that an important principle was that attitudes were more likely to change if the participants in a program felt some sort of dissonance within their value systems. Applied to elementary school children, this meant that if children felt that they were basically decent and kind people, and could be convinced that some behaviors they engaged in were incompatible with this perception of themselves, then they would change these behaviors to bring them in accord with the image they wanted to have of themselves. When he developed the ALP, therefore, he designed it in such a way that the early part of the program focused on creating this dissonance and the latter part of the program showed the children how to overcome the

Table 17.1 Summary of the Activities Involved in Theoretical Research

Stage	Role of Qualitative Research	Role of Quantitative Research	Who Conducts It?	Input	Output
1. Initial qualitative studies	• Dominant	• Sometimes no role—may be deliberately avoided • Often supports and refines qualitative	• Field researchers (often experts at qualitative research cooperating with practitioners)	• Field data • Previous theories • Insights and reasoning of researchers	• Practical overview • Broad, integrated view of many developing and emerging variables • Emphasis on insights and interpretation • Exceptionally useful for developing new variables
2. Qualitative studies and quantitative studies with increasingly sharp focus	• Generates insights for quantitative research • Interprets and refines the conclusions of quantitative research	• Tests insights from qualitative research • Generates conclusions to be refined and expanded by qualitative research	• Practitioners supported by research specialists • Research specialists and their students	• Variables and hypotheses from qualitative research • Experimental data to test hypotheses.	• Generally tentative conclusions, but more formal than Stage 1
3. Formal experimental studies	• Interprets and refines conclusions of quantitative research	• Dominant	• Some practitioners and research specialists, often supported by practitioners and students	• Variables and hypotheses from previous stages • Experimental data to test hypotheses • Some qualitative experimentation	• Cause-and-effect decision oriented information • Focuses on fewer variables developed from earlier qualitative and quantitative research
4. Meta-analysis	• Interprets and refines conclusions of quantitative research	• Dominant	• Research specialists with experience in meta-analysis supported by others	• Results (effect sizes) of previous experimental studies	• More definite conclusions based on overall analysis of the previous experimental studies interpreted by all other research

dissonance. When the ALP worked on repeated occasions, Mr. Anderson took this as evidence that this theory of induced dissonance was accurate. (Mr. Anderson's colleagues felt that he took delight in uttering the words *induced dissonance*. Perhaps one of the rewards of seeing a theory work is being allowed to attach a name to it.)

The practical nature of Mr. Anderson's job prohibited him from exploring this theoretical question through additional research of his own. However, he took the liberty of sending a copy of his results to one of the leading experts on attitude change research, and that author had responded by sending Mr. Anderson some additional information, which he found to be very helpful. Mr. Anderson made it a point to read each issue of the *Journal of Personality and Social Psychology,* for he found that this journal published high-quality research that occasionally touched upon ideas of particular interest that could be incorporated into his humane education programs. In addition, he frequently consulted *Psychological Abstracts* to see what new ideas were published on topics of interest to him. Mr. Anderson discovered that whenever he integrated these new ideas into his ALP, the results seemed to improve.

Although Mr. Anderson was not doing a great deal of theoretical research of his own, he had become an intelligent consumer of such basic research. He had become successful at understanding theoretical research and adept at taking ideas from it as a basis for shaping his applied research. Although he rarely isolated and manipulated the intervening variable, he let his awareness of it generate new hypotheses and new operational definitions that led him to more successful results in his applied endeavors.

SUMMARY

This chapter has reviewed, summarized, and integrated information regarding the different types of educational research. In doing so, this chapter has also identified likely errors and ways to avoid them, and it has described guidelines for conducting each type of research.

This chapter has also discussed interactions, which are said to occur when two variables act together to produce an effect. The main reason for identifying moderator variables is to look for interactions. By identifying moderator variables and looking for interactions, we can understand relationships more thoroughly and can describe more precisely how results of research can be generalized. This chapter has also described how to draw and interpret diagrams of interactions.

Finally, this chapter has discussed theoretical research, which focuses on the underlying causes behind the observed outcomes of research studies. Although many educators do not have a great deal of time to spend performing research of a purely theoretical nature, it is important that educators become intelligent consumers of basic research. An educator who can understand theoretical research can use its findings as an important source of ideas to attack the many practical problems that occur at the more applied levels of research.

Theoretical research focuses on the intervening variable. In addition, such research must often take place in a more artificial setting than applied research. Aside from these differences in focus and setting, however, theoretical research depends on the same methodologies as applied research. In fact, theoretical research can come to accurate conclusions only to the extent that it incorporates the strategies discussed in the earlier chapters to provide valid data collection and good internal and external validity.

What Comes Next

Chapter 18 will present a discussion of how to use the computer as a tool to carry out educational research activities. Chapter 19 will discuss strategies for planning a study, carrying out the practical steps in that study, and reporting the results of the research.

DOING YOUR OWN RESEARCH

Looking for untested interactions can be a productive source of research ideas for persons interested in both applied and theoretical research. The following are some good ways to generate research ideas:

1. When you read the results of an interesting study, consider the possibility that apparently simple relationships may not really be all that simple. For example, if a report says that "X causes Y," ask yourself, "How likely is it that X always causes Y?" Think about some possible exceptions, and then conduct a study to see whether these really are exceptions—that is, whether these moderator variables interact with the treatment.

2. Simply replicate the results of other research that claims to have found an interaction. In general, the results of studies that report interactions are not as well replicated as those that report simple, overall effects of the treatments. In fact, when there is no interaction, some researchers tend to simplify their reports by not even mentioning that they included the moderator variables in their studies.

3. Replicate an earlier study with a new operational definition of the moderator variable or of the other variables in the study that found the interaction.

4. Find moderator variables that interacted in a published meta-analysis, and conduct a study to test a revised hypothesis.

5. Conduct a meta-analysis in an area of interest, and code as moderator variables factors that have not previously been checked for interactions.

The strategies in the preceding list can lead to fruitful insights that may not only satisfy your own curiosity but also advance the state of knowledge within an area of interest to you.

FOR FURTHER THOUGHT

1. In many experimental studies that demonstrate interactions, the moderator variables are really examples of criterion group research. What does this mean with regard to the cause-and-effect nature of the findings of such studies?

2. Learning styles are an example of interactions. Learning style theorists maintain that people with different learning styles should be taught in ways that accommodate these styles. When critics point out that the published research often fails to demonstrate an interaction, the proponents reply that this is because there are no good tests to measure many of these learning styles. How would you respond to these arguments?

3. Proponents of cooperative learning claim that such a method is likely to be ineffective unless it is conducted in an atmosphere of positive interdependence and individual accountability. Positive interdependence refers to the idea that learners feel that the members of the group all must work together in order for the group to succeed. Individual accountability refers to the idea that each student's performance is frequently assessed and the results of that assessment make a difference to the individual. How would theorists prove that these two factors really are critical to the success of cooperative learning?

REFERENCES

Bandura, A. (1986). *Social foundations of thought and action*. Englewood Cliffs, NJ: Prentice-Hall.

Bye, L., & Jussim, L. (1993). A proposed model for the acquisition of social knowledge and social competence. *Psychology in the Schools*, 30, 143–161.

Camp, B., & Bash, M. (1981). *Think aloud*. Champaign, IL: Research Press.

Fiske, S., & Taylor, S. (1991). *Social cognition* (2nd ed.). New York: McGraw Hill.

ANSWERS TO REVIEW QUIZ 17.1

1. No. These results show an interaction. They indicate that the Latin curriculum helped the non-advanced-placement students but not the advanced-placement students. This is not what the hypothesis predicted.

2. No. These results show exactly the opposite of the stated prediction. Here, the passive-aggressive clients did better with the traditional approach, and the passive-withdrawn clients did better with the TRM approach. These results do not support the hypothesis at all.

CHAPTER 17
Research Report Analysis

In addition to its practical implications, the study reported in Appendix C examines some theoretical issues.

1. What interaction is examined in this report? Did the interaction actually occur?
2. What is the intervening variable discussed in this report?
3. To what extent have the researchers demonstrated that this intervening variable really has had the effect they claim it has had?

ANSWERS:

1. The only interaction examined in this study was that between gender of students and the computer simulations with regard to performance on the outcome variables. Since the interaction did not actually occur, it is described in passing (just before the conclusions section) and is discussed no further. Confirming the absence of an interaction is a useful research activity.

2. The intervening variable is *focused reinforced practice*. In the review of the literature (following the abstract), the authors develop the theory that guided reinforced practice is a critical factor in developing problem-solving skills. In the discussion and conclusions section they argue that their results have supported this theory.

3. The results of this isolated study actually provide relatively weak evidence to support this claim. The authors are obviously aware of this. A series of additional studies with more explicit control of alternative explanations (that is, of alternative intervening variables) would be necessary to thoroughly support the belief that the simulations had the observed impact because of focused reinforced practice rather than because of some other reason.

COMPUTERIZED DATA COLLECTION AND ANALYSIS

■ WHERE WE'VE BEEN

We have completed our study of the major strategies for conducting research.

■ WHERE WE'RE GOING NOW

In this chapter we'll discuss effective ways to use the computer as a tool to organize information and analyze data while conducting research at all levels.

■ CHAPTER PREVIEW

In addition to helping researchers obtain information, the computer can be a valuable tool to help researchers collect and analyze data. With the computer it is possible to perform statistical and mathematical calculations and summarize masses of data in a short time. In addition, the computer enables a researcher to have a high degree of confidence that the calculations are accurate, as long as the numbers given to the computer for analysis were accurate. All of the statistics that have been described in this text, as well as those covered in statistics courses, can easily be performed by the computer. This chapter will show you how to put data into an appropriate format for analysis by computer and how to use the computer to perform statistical analyses.

After reading this chapter, you should be able to

1. Describe how to put data into an appropriate format for subsequent computer analysis.
2. Interpret statements from a computer program designed to perform a statistical analysis.
3. Perform a computer analysis of data, using a commercial statistical package.
4. Interpret the output provided by a computerized statistical analysis.

5. Use programs commonly available for personal computers to organize, analyze, interpret, and present data and results from a research study.

■

THE ADVANTAGES OF THE COMPUTER

Computers are becoming increasingly accessible to educators, and they can make an important contribution to research tasks at any level of sophistication. All the statistical procedures described earlier in this book (plus many more) can be performed by computer. Once the data have been correctly prepared and entered into the computer, a large number of analyses and subanalyses can be performed on the same set of data with a minimum of additional effort.

Besides saving a great deal of time, the computer offers another advantage. Computer analysis enables researchers to be confident of the results of calculations. Many statistical procedures require complex mathematical computations, in which errors can be made; even minor errors can render the whole computational process inaccurate. With the computer, once the data and commands are correctly entered according to prescribed instructions, the possibility of errors is vastly reduced.

Even if you use the computer for analysis, however, there is still a possibility that you will get inaccurate results. This will usually occur not because of any error the computer will make but rather because of errors you make as you are feeding the data into the computer. Computer programmers have a saying: "Garbage in, garbage out." This means that the computer just does what it is told to do. No matter how smart we view computers to be, they still are not smart enough to know when the programmer has made an error. Therefore, if you give the computer an order that it is capable of carrying out, it will carry out that command, no matter how absurd it may be. This means that if you reverse the order of data, instruct the computer to read the wrong entries, or simply enter incorrect information, you will get erroneous results. Likewise, if you use the computer to perform a statistical analysis that should not appropriately be performed on a set of data (for example, if you instruct it to compute a correlation coefficient for sets of unordered, nominal scale data), it will have no way of knowing about your theoretical error and will go ahead and perform the calculations. The result will be misleading.

Even if you use the computer for analysis, there is still a possibility that you will get inaccurate results.

Computers do, in fact, occasionally make mistakes. However, the vast majority of errors that novices attribute to computers occur because the person entering the data or program commands made a mistake. This chapter is written to help you use the computer to obtain helpful and accurate results. It provides only a brief introduction, but by understanding this chapter and following a few more instructions that will be unique to your own computer system, it will be possible for you to use the computer to calculate all the statistics discussed in this book and in basic statistics books. In addition to the information provided here, you will find that most colleges and universities employ computer consultants who are familiar with statistical programs and will help you analyze your data if you organize them correctly.

There are several sets of statistical programs available to researchers in education. Only a few of these packages will be discussed in this chapter. However, they are typical of many other programs, and a reader who can understand how to use these programs will easily be able to shift to other statistical packages, if the need should arise. If you decide to use these programs, you will certainly want more information about them; you can obtain this information by consulting manuals such as the one listed in the Annotated Bibliography at the end of this chapter.

The main examples of statistical programs used in this chapter are taken from the *Statistical Package for* the Social Sciences (SPSS). The SPSS programs were chosen as examples because they are well designed and widely available even for personal computers, and because their usage is easily understood by persons with little background in computer programming. Additional examples are taken from Systat, a program that was selected because it also exemplifies the work one can do with personal computers in the home or office, without access to the major computing facilities often found on university campuses.

The purpose of this introduction to computerized data analysis is to let you know what is possible and to show you some general guidelines for using statistical packages on computers. The concepts and strategies discussed in this chapter are applicable to all statistical programs. We will not attempt to teach you how to use any specific program. If you decide to use a particular program to analyze data, you should assume that it is necessary to read parts of the program's manual or to seek the help of specialists in your computing facility. Only the principles of computer usage that are essential to understanding the use of the statistical programs will be discussed in this chapter.

PUTTING THE DATA INTO A PROPER FORMAT

To analyze data, it is necessary that they be arranged in a systematic format. This requirement is typical of all computer programs, but some statistical packages allow more leeway than others. When the computer is instructed to calculate a statistic (for example, the mean of a set of scores), it can accomplish this only by reading the information in specifically designated formats and acting upon this information in a prescribed way. The computer does not know whether the contents of the designated columns consist of mathematics scores, bowling averages, or locker numbers; all it does is accept the numbers and do what you tell it to do with them. Therefore, it is obviously important that you enter the data appropriately, so that the computer can find the correct numbers and do the work you want it to do.

It is important to enter the data appropriately, so that the computer can find the correct numbers and do the work you want it to do.

Figure 18.1 contains all the information needed about a hypothetical student to include him in a statistical analysis for a research project. However, this information is not arranged in a systematic manner that would make it ready for the computer to analyze.

In Figure 18.2, the data available for analysis on eight similar students have been more systematically arranged. The haphazard, chain-of-thought approach has vanished, and now the data are arranged in columns, with the same information placed in the same order for every student. The family income has been changed from a phrase ("over $50,000") to a number ("4") according to the following scale:

1 = under $10,000
2 = between $10,000 and $20,000
3 = between $20,000 and $50,000
4 = over $50,000

Note that the arrangement of data for computer analysis is much like that for test scores in a teacher's

Jeff Jones is a 12-year-old boy. He attained a score on the I.Q. test of 104. He should be classified as coming from a high socioeconomic class, since his parents have an income over $50,000 a year. He scored 14 correct on the pretest. At about the same time he scored 60 on the self-concept test. Later, he scored 34 on the posttest.

Figure 18.1 An Example of Data That Must Be Put into a More Systematic Format Before It Can Be Analyzed by the Computer

---

BOX 18.1

Dear Researcher: I've got you this time! Look how impersonal and degrading computers can be. In Figure 18.1, we had a nice, personal note about Jeff Jones. By the time he's ready to go into the computer, he's become not Jeff Jones but "01." How impersonal can you get? I protest this dehumanizing process. What do you have to say about that?
(signed) *Anonymous*

Dear Anonymous: Mathematics, by its very nature, is a bit impersonal. I don't see how putting a person's score on a card along with a code number is any more impersonal than writing the score in a column before you add the column, divide the result, or do whatever you want with it. Actually, the anonymity of the computer card can provide a valuable service by protecting the confidentiality of the person whose response is recorded.
(signed) *The Lonely Researcher*

---

gradebook. Students (or subjects) are listed in the left column, and the other columns contain scores for each student.

With some computer programs, the data shown in Figure 18.2 would already be arranged in a format satisfactory for statistical analysis. Some programs, however, require a few additional steps. One of the remaining problems is that many computer programs can deal with numbers more easily than with words; therefore, "Jeff Jones" and "male" would be inappropriate. This problem is easily solved by coding Jeff Jones as "01" and categorizing all males as "1" and all females as "2" (this decision was arbitrary; we could just as easily have made "Jeff Jones" "7149" and males "7"). The important consideration is to be systematic and to remember what you did. In Figure 18.3, the process of arranging the data for

analysis has been completed. The only information that will be entered into the computer about Jeff Jones will be this:

011124104143460

As you can see, this is the first data line (row) of Figure 18.3, with all the spaces omitted.

A further change that has been made is that additional zeros have been added in front of such numbers as the IQ of Mary Smith (ID number 02) and the pretest score of Albert Brown (ID number 03). These additional zeros have been inserted to make it more likely that the correct scores will always appear in the correct columns for every student. Without the additional zero, for example, we might accidentally put Mary Smith's IQ of 94 right next to her income of 1. This would cause everything from that point onward

Figure 18.2 An Example of Data for Eight Students That Have Been Partially Systematized for Computer Analysis

	Sex	Age	Income	IQ	Pre.	Post	Sc.
Jeff Jones	Male	12	4	104	14	34	60
Mary Smith	Female	12	1	94	24	35	59
Albert Brown	Male	13	2	100	4	14	42
Tom Williams	Male	12	4	130	30	40	64
Bob Jamison	Male	13	3	101	20	24	65
Alice Wilson	Female	13	2	85	5	7	40
Teresa Smith	Female	12	3	80	15	15	65
Brenda Johnson	Female	13	4	120	30	40	65

Figure 18.3 The Data from Figure 18.2 Put Completely into a Format Ready for Computer Analysis

ID	Sex	Age	Inc.	IQ	Pre.	Post	So.
01	1	12	4	104	14	34	60
02	2	12	1	094	24	35	59
03	1	13	2	100	04	14	42
04	1	12	4	130	30	40	64
05	1	13	3	101	20	24	65
06	2	13	2	085	05	07	40
07	2	12	3	080	15	15	65
08	2	13	4	120	30	40	65

to be read erroneously, and such an error (an IQ of 942!) would seriously distort the results. The impact of such an error is shown in Figure 18.4. (Note that not all statistical packages require this addition of leading zeroes. For example, most programs that accept input from spreadsheets would accept 94 as well as 094 for Mary Smith's IQ.)

Once the data have been systematically arranged, the numbers are ready to be entered and analyzed by the computer. The computer can read this information and compute means, standard deviations, correlation coefficients, analysis of variance, chi square, and many other statistics. The advantage of having access to a computer for computations regarding eight students is slight, but the same procedures that we shall apply to these eight subjects could be applied to hundreds or even thousands of subjects with no loss in accuracy and no increase in the complexity of the instructions we would give to the computer.

Remember, any error made up to this point is likely to go uncorrected by the computer. This applies not only to transcribing and data entry errors but also to errors of logic. For example, in Figure 18.2, the financial income data were converted to categories labeled 1 through 4. The researcher would probably consider the lowest category to be poor and the highest to be wealthy. If this is an incorrect or unsound classification, the computer will never correct the mistake; it will merrily go on comparing 1s with 4s, with no regard for what the researcher thinks the numbers stand for.

PERFORMING A STATISTICAL ANALYSIS

Let us suppose we want to take the data from Figure 18.3 and compute a Pearson correlation coefficient between IQ and self-concept. This could be accomplished by entering the following SPSS commands:

```
TITLE          'PRACTICE DATA'
DATA LIST      SEX 3, AGE 4-5, INCOME
               6, IQ 7-9, PRE 10-11,
               POST 12-13, SC 14-15
CORRELATIONS   IQ, SC
 /STATISTICS   1
BEGIN DATA
```

[Here we would insert the eight lines with each student's information on a line.]

```
END DATA
FINISH
```

This is a partial listing of a set of SPSS commands. One command is written per line. The following paragraphs will provide a brief description of each command.

The TITLE command gives a label that will be written at the top of each page of the printed output. If you run a similar program, you will probably want to insert a TITLE command to include a description that will help you distinguish your computer output from other similar printouts. For example, your command might read

TITLE 'MY FOURTH TRY TO GET IT RIGHT'

If the original TITLE line were removed and this one inserted in its place, the program would run the same way the original ran. The only exception is that "My Fourth Try to Get It Right" would appear at the top of each page in the computer output instead of the original heading.

The DATA LIST command attaches labels to each variable for the computer's use. In addition, it tells the computer in which column to find each variable. In this example we have indicated that our analysis will focus on a maximum of seven variables. (We have chosen to ignore the "ID" in the first two columns because we intend to perform no calculations on that variable.) The computer will refer to the first variable (in column 3) as "sex," the second (in columns 4 and 5) as "age," and so on, until it finds all seven variables. There are some simple rules that must be followed in composing labels, and you can find these rules in the SPSS manual. Notice that the computer does not know what "sex" or "age" means; it will simply assume that there are variables with those names located at specified locations on the data lines and will perform the calculations we instruct it to perform.

The CORRELATIONS command tells the computer that we want to calculate a Pearson correlation coefficient. The terms "IQ" and "SC" with this com-

	Line A	022121094243559
	Line B	02212194243559
	Line C	022121 94243559

Line A is the correct data for Mary Smith.

Line B contains the error of omitting a zero and moving Mary's IQ and all following data one space to the left.

Line C is exactly the same as Line A, except that a blank space has been inserted before the IQ rather than a zero. This is a correct line; but keypunchers are very likely to omit spaces, whereas they are less likely to omit zeros.

If Line B were punched instead of Line A or C, the following errors would be fed into the computer:

		Mary's Real Data	What the Computer Would Read as Mary's Data
Col 1–2	ID	02	02
Col 3	Sex	2	2
Col 4–5	Age	12	12
Col 6	Income	1	1
Col 7–9	IQ	94	942 (The 9 and 4 have moved over) (The 2 from the pretest has moved over)
Col 10–11	Pretest	24	43
Col 12–13	Posttest	35	55
Col 14–15	Self-concept	59	90 (The computer would add the zero automatically)

Figure 18.4 An Example of What Happens When Data Are Arranged and Entered into the Computer in the Wrong Columns

mand tell the computer which two variables we want to include in this calculation. The computer recognizes IQ and SC as terms from the DATA LIST. IQ is the fourth variable, located in columns 7 through 9; SC is the seventh variable, located in columns 14 and 15.

The STATISTICS command lets us identify certain other statistics (in addition to the correlation coefficient) that we can have the computer calculate for us while it is computing the Pearson coefficient we have requested. The SPSS manual provides a list of the additional statistics that are available with each statistical procedure. By consulting this manual, we would know that "1" means that we will get the mean and standard deviation for each of the variables in our DATA LIST. This command is optional; if we omitted it, the only effect would be that the mean and standard deviation would not be included as output.

Requesting a calculation of the mean from the computer is often a good way to check your work. It is possible that you had incorrectly entered some of the data—for example, by putting some numbers in the wrong columns. Since the mean is an extremely easy statistic to calculate by hand, you can check your work by comparing your own mean with that generated by the computer. If they match, you have reason to believe that the computer is reading the correct data. In addition, if the mean is correct, then it is likely that any other statistics the computer calculated based on the same set of numbers are also correct.

The BEGIN DATA command informs the computer that the next lines will be data lines—that is, lines on which the student information will be entered in the previously designated format.

The END DATA command informs the computer that it has reached the end of the data to be analyzed. Any additional lines will include additional commands, not data to be analyzed.

The FINISH command comes last. It means that the run is over—that there are no more statistics to compute. It would be possible (and a later example will demonstrate this) to perform additional statistical procedures prior to the insertion of the FINISH command.

Figures 18.5 and 18.6 show three pages of the output we would get from this input. (Note that it would also be possible to have the output appear on the computer monitor rather than to have it printed on paper.) Figure 18.5 shows the second and third pages. Page 2 is self-explanatory. Page 3 presents the Pearson correlation coefficient. Actually, it presents four correlations: IQ correlated with IQ, IQ with SC, SC with IQ, and SC with SC. Most of this information is either redundant or useless, and the only thing we care about is the correlation of .38 between SC and IQ. (The statement p = 0.176 indicates level of significance. That is, there are about 18 chances in 100 that a correlation of this magnitude would occur when two sets of chance scores of 8 subjects are correlated.)

If we wished to do so, we could do further statistical analyses simply by inserting a few additional lines before the FINISH command. For example, we may wish to obtain a breakdown of mean IQ scores by gender to see whether the boys had higher IQ scores than the girls (Figure 18.6). We might also wish to perform an analysis of variance, estimating the probability that the difference between IQs of boys and girls is merely a chance variation. These and other calculations can easily be performed by giving the computer appropriate commands.

An advantage of programs like the SPSS package is that they are designed in such a way as to help you correct many of the errors you make. Everything has to be entered into the computer according to a carefully selected format. If you wander from this format, it is likely that the computer will recognize your error and tell you what you did wrong. For example, if we would have mislabeled SC as SG by mistake, the computer would be unable to proceed, because it would not know what SG means. In this case, the computer output would look like this:

```
CORRELATIONS IQ, SG
THE FOLLOWING SYMBOL HAS CAUSED AN
ERROR.."SG"
ERROR NUMBER 850. PROCESSING
CEASES, ERROR SCAN CONTINUES.
```

```
SPSS HYPOTHETICAL PRACTICE DATA                          10/30/94        PAGE 2
FILE    NONAME    (CREATION DATE = 10/03/94)
            VARIABLE        CASES           MEAN        STD DEV
            IQ                8          101.7500       16.7054
            SC                8           57.5000       10.4608




SPSS HYPOTHETICAL PRACTICE DATA                          10/30/94        PAGE 3
FILE    NONAME    (CREATION DATE = 10/03/94)

------------------------------PEARSON CORRELATION COEFFICIENTS-----------------------

            IQ              SC
IQ          1.000           0.3809
            (       8)      (       8)
            p = *****       p = 0.176
SC          0.3809          1.0000
            (       8)      (       8)
            p = 0.176       p = *****

(COEFFICIENT / (CASES) / SIGNIFICANCE)       A VALUE OF 99.0000 IS PRINTED IF A
COEFFICIENT CANNOT BE COMPUTED)
```

Figure 18.5   The Second and Third Pages of the Output from the SPSS Program Described in "Performing a Statistical Analysis"

This message means that the computer cannot do what you told it to do (because it does not know what SG means), but it will examine the rest of the program to see whether there are any more errors to call to your attention. At the end of the printout, there would be the following explanation:

```
ERRNO = 850
THE CORRELATIONS LINE CONTAINS AN
INVALID DATA LIST
```

The error messages are specific, and it is possible to use such messages to locate and remove errors quickly.

There are many statistical procedures that are possible through the SPSS package, and there are similar systems that have not been discussed here. All the statistical procedures mentioned in this text and all those encountered in elementary statistics courses can be computed through the SPSS system. In addition, many more advanced statistics programs are available. Besides the statistical procedures, there are other functions that can be performed by the computer. It is possible, for instance, to have the computer do mathematical computations for us. For example, in the data we have been using for illustration, we might want to compute the amount of gain each student showed between pretest and posttest;

```
SPSS HYPOTHETICAL PRACTICE DATA                    10/03/94        PAGE    6
CRITERION VARIABLE IQ

-------------------------------ANALYSIS OF VARIANCE------------------------------

VARIABLE    CODE    VALUE LABEL        SUM        MEAN     STD DEV    SUM OF SQ        N
SEX          1.                     435.0000   108.7500   14.2683    610.7500   (    4)
SEX          2.                     379.0000    94.7500   17.8022    950.7500   (    4)
                                   ----------------------------------------------------
            WITHIN GROUPS TOTAL    814.0000   101.7500   16.1323   1561.5000   (    8)

*********************************************************************************
*                             ANALYSIS OF VARIANCE                              *
*********************************************************************************
*  SOURCE              SUM OF SQUARES    D.F.     MEAN SQUARE         F      SIG.   *
*  BETWEEN GROUPS          392.000        1         392.000        1.506   0.2657  *
*  WITHIN GROUPS          1561.500        6         260.250                        *
*                    ETA = 0.4480    ETA SQUARED = 0.2007                          *
*********************************************************************************
```

Figure 18.6   The Breakdown of Mean Scores by Sex and the Accompanying Analysis of Variance from the Program Described in "Performing a Statistical Analysis"

this could be done by inserting the following line before the PEARSON CORR command:

COMPUTE   GAIN = POST - PRE

By doing this, we could get a printout that would include the analysis we wanted. The many possibilities of what can be accomplished through the use of the computer can be explored by examining the manual for either the SPSS programs or whatever system is available at your computer facility.

The use of the computer is by no means reserved to the more sophisticated levels of research. Even at Level I research the computer can provide considerable advantages. Tests can be scored and item-analyzed by computer. Reliability coefficients, which are annoying or time-consuming to compute by hand, are easy to calculate on the computer. Whatever your research needs may be, it is important to plan ahead so that you can take full advantage of what the computer has to offer. With proper planning, you can save steps when the time comes for analysis.

Look ahead, determine how you should format the information to make it most easily accessible to the computer, and then collect the data as much as possible in that format. Think ahead and eliminate, insofar as you can, the need for painstaking recopying and recoding of data before it can be entered into the computer. In some cases, it may even be possible to record the initial data on optical scanning sheets that can be read by some computers, thus eliminating the need for you to do that portion of the data entry.

The computer can save you time, and the amount of time you save will become greater as the number of subjects or the complexity of the analysis increases. Computers are available to almost every researcher. It is just a matter of knowing where to find them and how to access them. By becoming familiar with the computer, you can greatly expand your capabilities as a researcher.

Note that programs vary in their degree of user friendliness. Users of the SPSS programs must essentially write simple computer commands every time they perform a data analysis. This is a relatively simple, straightforward task, but some researchers may find the mini program on page 401 to be an imposing task. It would be possible to use a program that would prompt you with specific questions, such as the following, as you ran the program:

What statistical procedure do you want?

What is the first variable you want to include in the computation of the correlation coefficient?

What is the second variable you want to include in the computation of the correlation coefficient?

What is your first subject's name?

What is John's math score?

Most users would discover that this degree of user friendliness is unnecessary. After running a few statistical analyses, most researchers discover that writing instructions like those shown on page 401 is a logical and understandable way to obtain essential information.

OTHER TOOLS FOR DATA ANALYSIS

In addition to formal statistical packages, there are other computerized tools for analyzing data. For example, researchers should consider taking advantage of computerized data input by having subjects put their responses to tests and questionnaires onto answer sheets that can be read by Scantron or similar machines. These answer sheets come in standard formats, but they can also be tailored to meet individual needs. When letting subjects respond through computerized input, however, it is important to consider the possibility that this may lower the reliability of the data. For example, young children may inadvertently give responses they did not intend to give because they are unfamiliar with the data entry format. Even when subjects cannot themselves respond in a computerized format, it may be desirable to transfer the data to answer sheets to facilitate entry into the computer.

Electronic data base management systems provide useful formats for organizing data.

Electronic data base management systems provide useful formats for organizing data. Especially in cases where no sophisticated statistical analysis is necessary (see Figure 18.7), a data base may enable a researcher to collect and organize information effectively. With just a few keystrokes, the user can go from the list format (screen a) to the individual record format (screen b). In addition, it is easily possible to rearrange the data (e.g., by alphabetizing names or arranging scores in order), to select specific records, or to print out any portion of the data in a specified format. A major advantage is that data base management systems can often be easily integrated with word processors, and this facilitates report writing. Data base management programs are often preferable to spreadsheet programs (discussed next) for analyzing qualitative information.

Electronic spreadsheet programs not only enable users to organize information, they also perform mathematical calculations easily and efficiently. Figure 18.8 shows an example of the data contained in a spreadsheet. Entries are made in *cells* (e.g., cell D2 contains Karen Bench's midterm score of 98, cell D3 contains Judith Brown's midterm score of 85, etc.). Cells off the screen and not shown in this figure contain formulas for computing totals and averages (e.g., cell D28 computes the class average on the midterm and cell N2 computes Karen Bench's average on the three LIT tests).

A major advantage is that these programs almost instantly recalculate results when input is changed. For example, in Figure 18.8, if Karen Bench's final score were incorrectly recorded, the researcher could correct that score, and instantly, Karen's own average and the class average (as well as any other scores that depended on these) would be recalculated. The advantages of recalculation become greater when the computations become more complex. Using a spreadsheet, a researcher could calculate many of the statistics described in this book.

Last Name	Activities													Total Activity	Total
Bench	30	10	10	10	20	10	20	10	5	10	10			145	544
Brown	40	80	10	10	20	20	10	20	20	10	10	10	10	270	520
Brown	20	10	20	10	10	10	10	10	5	10	10	10	10	145	553
Busch	30	10	10	10	10	10	10	10	10	10	5	10	10	10	185	560
Collins	20	20	10	10	10	10	10	10	10	10	10	10	10	150	556
Dunstan	10	20	30	10	10	10	10	10	10	10				130	537
Hall	20	40	10	10	10	10								100	508
Jefferson	20	10	20	10	10	10	20	10	10	10	10	10		150	525
Kemp	30	10	20	10	20	20	10							120	506
Lennon	10	25	60	10	10	10	10							135	495
Letterman	30	10	10	20	10	10	20	10						160	538
Lincoln	30	10	10	10	20	20	30	20						150	545
Marx	90	10	10	10	10									130	503
Nixon	100	50	10											160	525
Rose	100	50	20	20	10	10	10	10	10					240	525

Type entry or use @ commands   @-? for Help

Screen A

Record 2 of 21   (21 selected)

===

Last Name: Bench
First Name : Karen
Group: 2
Midterm Exam: 98
Final Exam: 97
Literacy I: 50
Litercy II: 44
Literacy III: 50
Group Bonus Points: 60
Activities: 30 10 10 10 20 10 20 10 5 10 10
Total Activity Pts.: 145
Total Exam Points: –
Total Points: 544
Grade: –

Type entry or use @ commands   @-? for Help

Screen B

Figure 18.7 Examples of Screens from the AppleWorks Database Management Program. (This example presents information from a teacher's gradebook, which could be used to evaluate the effectiveness of instruction.)

```
File: Demo SS                        01/30/94   4:49 pm                    Escape: Main Menu
===========A=========B=========C=========D=========E=========F=========G=========H====
    1) LAST NAME    FIRST      GROUP      MIDTERM    FINAL      LIT 1      LIT 2      LIT 3
    2) Bench        Karen      Control        98        97         50         44         50
    3) Brown        Judith     Exp            85                   25         50         50
    4) Brown        Diana      Control        98       100         50         50         50
    5) Busch        Mary       Control        75        90         50         50         50
    6) Collins      Keith      Control       100        98         50         48         50
    7) Dunstan      Carolyn    Control       100        97         50         50         50
    8) Hall         Patricia   Exp           100        98         50         50         50
    9) Jefferson    Linda      Exp           100       100         20         50         45
   10) Kemp         Candace    Control        88        98         40         50         50
   11) Lennon       Thomas     Exp            75        95         35         50         45
   12) Letterman    Oran       Exp            80        90         50         48         50
   13) Lincoln      Susanne    Exp           100       100         50         50         35
   14) Marx         Mariana    Exp            83        90         45         50         45
   15) Nixon        Stacey     Exp            92        98         25         50         40
   16) Rose         Sue        Control       100                   45         50         50
   17) Smith        Annamari   Exp            95        97         15         50         50
   18) Thomas       Deborah    Exp           100       100         40         48         50
--------------------------------------------------------------------------------------------
A2: (Label) Bench

Type entry or use @ commands                                                 @-? for Help
```

Figure 18.8 An Example of a Screen from the AppleWorks Spreadsheet Program. (These are the same data that were included in Figure 18.7. In addition, the graphs in Figure 19.6 are based on these data.)

Teachers often have access to electronic gradebooks. When doing research on classroom performance, it is often possible to transfer data from these gradebooks into data base management programs, electronic spreadsheets, and statistical programs to perform statistical analyses without reentering the data. After analysis, the results can often be transferred electronically to word processing and graphing programs for inclusion in reports. Such electronic strategies not only save time, they also minimize the possibility of errors that occur when data or results are recopied.

Systat is a statistical package that combines data base and spreadsheet features with a powerful set of statistical tools. The user enters information as if the program were a computerized gradebook (or perhaps electronically copies it from an electronic gradebook, if this is possible)—no knowledge of programming or of any system of commands is necessary. To perform a statistical analysis, the user identifies variables and selects options from a menu. This kind of user-friendly interface makes it extremely easy to perform statistical analyses.

PUTTING IT ALL TOGETHER

Early in his career in humane education, Eugene Anderson learned the advantages of using the computer. He discovered that he could use it to score tests and compare means of various groups to whom he administered humane education programs. He could also compute correlation coefficients between scores on his tests and other characteristics that he expected to be either related or unrelated to performance on the tests.

Figure 18.9 The Data Tabulation Sheet from Which Mr. Anderson Entered His Humane Education Data

								Johnny			Janet						
School	Year	I	D	Sex	Gr	Pct	1	2	3	1	2	3	vv	I	Q	Read
1	4	7	9	0	0	1	1	4	2	2	4	8	2	4	8	3	1	0	6	6	0
1	4	7	9	0	0	2	2	4	1	9	2	5	0	3	1	1	1	1	0	4	9
1	4	7	9	0	0	3	2	4	1	2	9	1	2	3	5	1	0	9	5	4	0
1	4	7	9	0	0	4															
1	4	7	9	0	0	4															
1	4	7	9	0	0	5															
1	4	7	9	0	0	6															
1	4	7	9	0	0	7															
1	4	7	9	0	0	8															

One important use of the computer occurred in the process of validating his tests. As you may recall, such a process of validation would involve demonstrating that the tests correlate substantially with other measures of humane attitudes and that they correlate negligibly with characteristics theoretically unrelated to positive attitudes toward animal life. On one occasion, Mr. Anderson was able to administer his tests to 31 fourth graders, and he was able to obtain additional information regarding sex, reading ability, and IQ from this same group. To this group he gave not only two forms of the Fireman Test ("Johnny and the Fireman" and "Janet and the Fireman"), but also a TV test, which gave children a chance to hypothetically choose to watch current TV shows that either did or did not feature animals.

Mr. Anderson had previously decided to use a standardized format for data tabulation. By using the same format every time he administered his tests, he could eventually combine the data from several different administrations and make more complete comparisons. The form on which he tabulated his data is shown in Figure 18.9.

The commands that Mr. Anderson used to analyze his data are listed in Figure 18.10. Let us briefly examine the listing for this program. The DATA LIST command tells the computer that there will be 12 variables; it also tells where to find these variables. Notice that the computer has been instructed to ignore the first seven columns. These columns contain information that Mr. Anderson may be interested in on some other occasion (for example, if he would combine the data from several administrations of the tests), but at the present time he is not interested in an analysis using this information.

By using a series of COMPUTE and IF commands (the 7th through 16th lines), Mr. Anderson arranged to have the computer score the Fireman Tests. On the data tabulation sheet (Figure 18.9) he entered not scores but rather the first, second, and third choices for each student on the Johnny test and on the Janet test. He then instructed the computer to examine each choice and give the student one point for any number (2, 4, or 8) that corresponds to the choice of an animal. The computer obtains a separate score for Johnny, a separate score for Janet, and a Fireman score that combines the Johnny and Janet scores. If you examine lines 7 through 16 closely, you can probably determine the logic of this computerized scoring process.

With the SELECT IF commands, Mr. Anderson instructed the computer to include in the analysis only the students who completed both a Johnny test and a Janet test. The other students may be used for another analysis some other time, but at present Mr. Anderson wished to exclude them from the computations.

Mr. Anderson requested his first statistical analysis on the CORRELATIONS line. This is a command

```
                                                                      PAGE 0001

      TITLE              HUMANE EDUCATION TEST VALIDATION
      ATA LIST           SEX 11, GRADE 12, PET 13, JOHN1 14, JOHN2 15, JOHN3 16, JANET1 17,
                         JANET2 18, JANET3 19, TV 20, IQ 21-23, READ 24-25
      RECODE             SEX TO READ (BLANK=-9)
      COMPUTE            JOHNNY=0
      COMPUTE            JANET=0
      COMPUTE            FIREMAN=0
      IF                 (JOHN1 EQ 2 OR JOHN1 EQ 4 OR JOHN1 EQ 8)JOHNNY=JOHNNY+1
      IF                 (JOHN2 EQ 2 OR JOHN2 EQ 4 OR JOHN2 EQ 8)JOHNNY=JOHNNY+1
      IF                 (JOHN3 EQ 2 OR JOHN3 EQ 4 OR JOHN3 EQ 8)JOHNNY=JOHNNY+1
      IF                 (JANET1 EQ 2 OR JANET1 EQ 4 OR JANET1 EQ 8)JANET=JANET+1
      IF                 (JANET2 EQ 2 OR JANET2 EQ 4 OR JANET2 EQ 8)JANET=JANET+1
      IF                 (JANET3 EQ 2 OR JANET3 EQ 4 OR JANET3 EQ 8)JANET=JANET+1
      COMPUTE            FIREMAN=JOHNNY+JANET
      MISSING VALUES     SEX TO READ(-9)
      SELECT IF          (JOHN1 GE 0)
      SELECT IF          (JANET1 GE 0)
      CORRELATIONS       JOHNNY,JANET,FIREMAN,TV,IQ,READ
      STATISTICS         1
      BEGIN DATA
      END DATA
      BREAKDOWN          TABLES=JOHNNY,JANET,FIREMAN BY SEX, PET
      STATISTICS         1
      FREQUENCIES        INTEGER=JOHNNY,JANET,FIREMAN(0,6)
      OPTIONS            8
      ANOVA              JOHNNY,JANET,FIREMAN BY SEX (1,2) WITH IQ/
      CROSSTABS          TABLES=JOHNNY,JANET BY SEX
      OPTIONS            3 , 5
      FINISH
```

Figure 18.10 Mr. Anderson's Computer Program. (Note that several commands that put labels on the printouts have been omitted from this list.)

that you have seen previously. The output from this analysis is shown in Figure 18.11. Notice that although there were 31 subjects for whom data were entered, the number of subjects in each actual calculation ranged from 23 to 26. This reduction in numbers occurred because of selections the computer made based on the SELECT IF and MISSING VALUES commands.

Next he requested a breakdown comparing the means of boys with those of girls and the means of pet owners with those who didn't own pets. This breakdown was accompanied by an analysis of variance (signified by a "1" on the STATISTICS line that follows the BREAKDOWN command). This BREAKDOWN command actually yielded six analyses of variance, and one of them is shown in Figure 18.12. You have already seen a printout like this, and you can tell from examining it that the difference between pet owners and those who don't own pets is quite small and is likely to have arisen by chance.

```
HUMANE EDUCATION TEST VALIDATION                    10/02/94       PAGE   4
FILE:      NONAME    (CREATION DATE = 10/02/94)
```

---PEARSON CORRELATION COEFFICIENTS---

	JOHNNY	JANET	FIREMAN	TV1	TV2	IQ	READ
JOHNNY	1.0000	0.7584	0.9377	0.2660	0.1060	0.2531	0.2565
	(26)	(26)	(26)	(25)	(25)	(24)	(24)
	P=*****	P=0.000	P=0.000	P=0.099	P=0.307	P=0.116	P=0.113
JANET	0.7584	1.0000	0.9377	0.1715	0.0846	0.3180	0.2077
	(26)	(26)	(26)	(25)	(25)	(24)	(24)
	P=0.000	P=*****	P=0.000	P=0.206	P=0.344	P=0.065	P=0.165
FIREMAN	0.9377	0.9377	1.0000	0.2322	0.1012	0.3020	0.2464
	(26)	(26)	(26)	(25)	(25)	(24)	(24)
	P=0.000	P=0.000	P=*****	P=0.132	P=0.315	P=0.076	P=0.123
TV1	0.2660	0.1715	0.2322	1.0000	0.9269	0.1677	0.2956
	(25)	(25)	(25)	(25)	(25)	(23)	(23)
	P=0.099	P=0.206	P=0.132	P=*****	P=0.000	P=0.222	P=0.085
TV2	0.1060	0.0846	0.1012	0.9269	1.0000	0.1871	0.2278
	(25)	(25)	(25)	(25)	(25)	(23)	(23)
	P=0.307	P=0.344	P=0.315	P=0.000	P=*****	P=0.196	P=0.148
IQ	0.2531	0.3180	0.3020	0.1677	0.1871	1.0000	0.7435
	(24)	(24)	(24)	(23)	(23)	(24)	(24)
	P=0.116	P=0.065	P=0.076	P=0.222	P=0.196	P=*****	P=0.000
READ	0.2565	0.2077	0.2464	0.2956	0.2278	0.7435	1.0000
	(24)	(24)	(24)	(23)	(23)	(24)	(24)
	P=0.113	P=0.165	P=0.123	P=0.085	P=0.148	P=0.000	P=*****

(COEFFICIENT / (CASES) / SIGNIFICANCE)   (A VALUE OF 99.0000 IS PRINTED IF A COEFFICIENT CANNOT BE COMPUTED)

Figure 18.11   The Correlation Matrix Resulting from Mr. Anderson's CORRELATIONS command. (The number of cases in parentheses varies because some students were excluded from specific analyses by the MISSING VALUES command.)

Next, with a FREQUENCIES command, Mr. Anderson requested a simple frequency count. The selection of "8" on the OPTIONS line accompanying this FREQUENCIES command enables him to obtain the frequency histogram shown in Figure 18.13. (Mr. Anderson learned this from the SPSS manual.)

Mr. Anderson found these results to be useful. He also found it impressive that the computation of all these statistics (including the many shown in the list but not in the figures) took only 12.16 seconds of computer time.

SUMMARY

The computer can be a great help to researchers at any level of sophistication. If you put accurate information and correct instructions into the computer, it will provide you with accurate statistical analyses in a remarkably short time. On the other hand, if you enter faulty data or provide incorrect instructions, it will provide you with inaccurate and possibly misleading information. This chapter has provided guidelines on how to put data into an appropriate format for submission to the computer. It has also

```
HUMANE EDUCATION TEST VALIDATION                  10/02/94       PAGE 9
CRITERION VARIABLE FIREMAN

-------------------------------ANALYSIS OF VARIANCE-------------------------------

VARIABLE   CODE   VALUE LABEL        SUM      MEAN    STD DEV   SUM OF SQ        N
PET        0.                    37.0000    2.8462    2.5445    77.6923   (   13)
PET        1.                    29.0000    2.2308    1.7394    36.3077   (   13)
                                 -------------------------------------------------
        WITHIN GROUPS TOTAL      66.0000    2.5385    2.1794   114.0000   (   26)


* * * * * * * * * * * * * * * * * * * * * * * * * * * * * * * * * * * * * * * * * *
*                                                                                *
*                          ANALYSIS OF VARIANCE                                  *
* * * * * * * * * * * * * * * * * * * * * * * * * * * * * * * * * * * * * * * * * *
*                                                                                *
*  SOURCE             SUM OF SQUARES    D.F.    MEAN SQUARE        F       SIG.   *
*  BETWEEN GROUPS           2.462        1         2.462       0.518    0.4786    *
*  WITHIN GROUPS          114.000       24         4.750                          *
*                    ETA = 0.1454    ETA SQUARED = 0.0211                         *
* * * * * * * * * * * * * * * * * * * * * * * * * * * * * * * * * * * * * * * * * *
```

Figure 18.12   The Breakdown of Mean Scores by Pet Ownership and the Accompanying Analysis of Variance Resulting from Mr. Anderson's Breakdown and Statistics commands

provided basic guidelines for performing some statistical analyses. Additional information can be obtained by consulting manuals and more detailed resources dealing with computers.

What Comes Next

Chapter 19 will discuss ways to integrate everything covered in this book to carry out a research project and write a research report.

DOING YOUR OWN RESEARCH

It is important to start planning your computer analysis when you first begin planning your research project. While it is possible (and often necessary) to make adjustments during the early runs of a computerized analysis, it is generally not safe to simply collect data and to assume that the computer can "handle anything." The important point is that your analysis will go much more smoothly if you plan carefully and collect data in a format that can easily be analyzed by computer.

Even if you are inexperienced with both statistics and computers, it is still a reasonable task to use the computer for statistical analyses. Both of the statistical packages described in this chapter (as well as many others) have technical manuals that cover complex procedures that will be of no interest to you, but each also has simplified, step-by-step guidelines that enable even beginners to select and calculate the statistics they need.

Also note that these statistical packages are becoming increasingly capable of accepting input from almost any systematic source. For example, the first author of this book has already taken files with student data composed on an *AppleWorks* data base and transferred that to a Macintosh for analysis with Systat. The person who originally composed the student data base had no idea how to use a Macintosh computer or how to run the Systat program, but she received the complete analysis she had requested. It is likely that within your own university or school system there is someone who can perform a similar service for you.

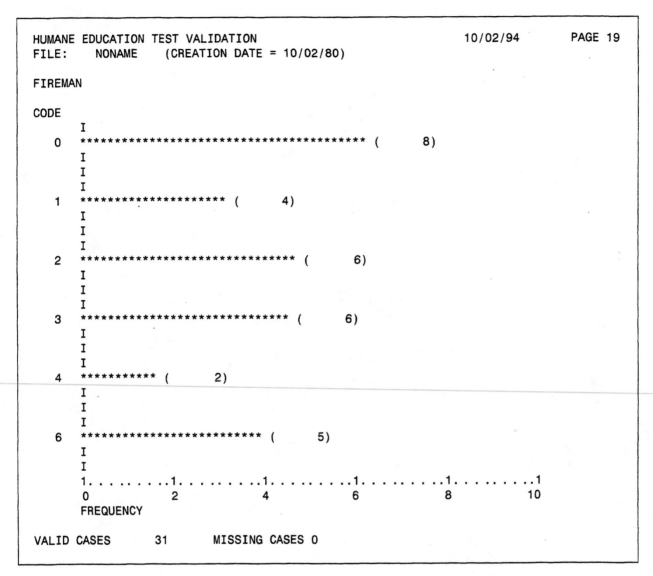

```
HUMANE EDUCATION TEST VALIDATION                    10/02/94        PAGE 19
FILE:    NONAME     (CREATION DATE = 10/02/80)

FIREMAN

CODE
         I
    0    ****************************************** (        8)
         I
         I
         I
    1    ******************* (        4)
         I
         I
         I
    2    ***************************** (        6)
         I
         I
         I
    3    ***************************** (        6)
         I
         I
         I
    4    ********** (        2)
         I
         I
         I
    6    ************************ (        5)
         I
         I
         I........1.........1.........1.........1.........1
         0        2         4         6         8         10
         FREQUENCY

VALID CASES      31      MISSING CASES 0
```

Figure 18.13 The Frequency Histogram Resulting from Mr. Anderson's FREQUENCIES and OPTIONS command. (The numbers 0 through 6 under the word "Code" indicate scores on the combined Fireman Tests.)

ANNOTATED BIBLIOGRAPHY

Norusis, M. J. (1989). *SPSS-X introductory statistics guide.* New York: SPSS. This is the manual for the SPSS programs. It provides comprehensive and detailed instructions on how to write the commands and to format the data to perform statistical analyses using these programs. This manual should enable you to do most of your own programming, but if you need additional help, there is probably a consultant available at your computing center.

CARRYING OUT A RESEARCH PROJECT AND WRITING THE REPORT

■ **WHERE WE'VE BEEN**

We have completed our study of the major strategies for conducting research. We have also discussed how to use the library and the computer as tools in the research process.

■ **WHERE WE'RE GOING NOW**

In this chapter we'll integrate everything covered in this book to suggest ways to carry out a research project and to write a research report.

■ **CHAPTER PREVIEW**

This chapter reviews, summarizes, and integrates the basic guidelines for carrying out a formal research project and writing a report on such a project. Aspects of these guidelines will also be useful for writing grant proposals and other types of educational reports and activities. It is assumed that the reader is already familiar with the principles discussed in previous chapters. The information here will be useful to readers who are required to do a research project as part of their course work or thesis requirements or who need to write other kinds of reports. It will also be useful to professionals who wish to perform research for their own satisfaction or because of the requirements of their jobs. It will likewise help those readers who want to write research proposals to submit to funding agencies to obtain grants.

After reading this chapter, you should be able to

1. Identify and describe the major steps in conducting a research study.

2. Describe the purpose of each of the following types of research, ways to conduct each type, problems that are likely to occur with each, and ways to overcome these problems:

a. Quantitative descriptive research (status research)

b. Qualitative research

c. Experimental and quasi-experimental research

d. Correlational research

e. Criterion group research

f. Meta-analytic research

3. Identify and describe the major components of a research report.

4. Conduct a formal research study.

5. Write a research report.

■

FORMAL RESEARCH REPORTING

This chapter will discuss conducting and reporting the results of *formal research projects*. This term is used to distinguish formal undertakings from the more informal strategies used as a regular part of evaluating and improving educational efforts without disrupting ordinary routines.

In much of this chapter we shall focus on the steps involved in an empirical, quantitative research project or report. In many cases (for example, in reviewing the literature and conclusions), qualitative researchers would follow the same guidelines. Whenever appropriate, we shall give brief but specific treatment to parallel steps in a qualitative study. In addition, we shall provide synopses of each of the major types of research that have been discussed in this book. Each synopsis will include a statement of the purpose of each type of research, ways to conduct them, problems that are likely to occur with each, and ways to overcome these problems.

SELECTING AND CLARIFYING A PROBLEM

In chapter 2 we discussed strategies for selecting and clarifying a problem. Practical suggestions for select-ing a research problem were given in the "Doing Your Own Research" section at the end of that chapter. This book espouses the practical emphasis that all educators have problems that they can attack through educational research methodology. A useful strategy for finding a research problem is to identify outcomes that you want to either encourage or discourage. These are your dependent variables. Then, identify ways to increase or prevent these outcomes. These methods are your independent variables. State a research problem and use the strategies described in chapter 2 to refine it. The problems you face on your job are important, and if you are asked to do a research project to demonstrate your research capability, then certainly you should channel your energies into an area of direct relevance to your professional career.

An important step involved in choosing a research project is narrowing the field of prospects to one problem at a time. You have to use your own judgment in choosing which problem to work on. Certainly, the means to attack some problems in an effective manner may be beyond your control, and you would hardly want to tackle them as a course assignment, but all educators are beset with problems that can be successfully attacked and better understood through the research strategies discussed in this book.

Usually, the nature of the problem changes as it is clarified.

Usually, the nature of the problem changes as it is clarified. For example, a teacher may start by trying to solve the problem of how to make children be better behaved. As she clarifies her problem, she may realize that the children are misbehaving because her teaching methods are not suitable for dealing with their learning disabilities; so she may eventually shift to researching new methods for teaching math to pupils with learning disabilities. An assigned research project can be beneficial not only because you will learn how to do such assignments, but, more important, because it will encourage you to attack your problems in a more effective manner.

BOX 19.1

Dear Researcher: I am taking a course in which I have been given an assignment to do an educational research report. I have to select a problem by Wednesday evening. I am a very busy person, and I don't have time to look for research problems. I find this very irritating, because I have three children with learning disabilities who have been mainstreamed and I don't know what to do with them. In addition, I'm trying to develop a new method for teaching math that I think will help my pupils apply mathematics principles to their daily lives. Besides that, I'm trying to find out what causes so much anxiety when we watch the films in our new science series. How am I supposed to have time to find a research problem? Please help me. Tell me: what is the Great Unanswered Question of Educational Research? I need your help.
(signed) *Overwhelmed with Problems*

Dear Overwhelmed: The Great Unanswered Question of Educational Research is this: Why do teachers who spend all day dealing with problems have trouble finding a problem to do research on? In your letter you stated three different educational problems that have kept you from thinking of a problem. Do your research on one of them.
(signed) *The Lonely Researcher*

REVIEW OF THE LITERATURE

Once you have decided on a problem to attack, find out what is already known about it. Strategies for doing this were the topic of chapter 3. It is important to find out what others have said about defining the real nature of the problem and about solutions to it. You may decide to stay on a purely practical level and simply verify that a specific treatment can produce a specific effect in your own educational setting. This is itself a valuable outcome. On the other hand, you may decide to become a bit theoretical and develop a hypothesis that will expand upon someone else's theory. You may even become bold and add to a theory or develop one of your own.

When reviewing the literature, it is a good idea to look for moderator variables that are applicable to your problem. Even if you choose to operate at a very applied and nontheoretical level, the knowledge that a certain treatment will work differently with some subjects than with others can be a valuable discovery for your own professional use. In addition, if you choose to go a more theoretical route, identifying and testing new moderator variables while replicating another researcher's experiment can expand existing theoretical knowledge.

During your review of the literature, be particularly alert for meta-analyses (discussed in chapter 16) of studies related to your topic. Do not succumb to the belief that because someone else has performed a meta-analysis there is no need for further research in an area. Rather, use the meta-analysis as a basis to direct your energies into the most useful areas of unresolved problems. You should also consider the possibility of adding to existing meta-analyses or performing a meta-analysis of your own to help integrate and interpret the studies in your review of the literature. In doing so, be sure to look for pertinent interactions that may have been neglected by other researchers and get assistance from an experienced meta-analyst.

The review of the literature should be conducted in accordance with the guidelines described in chapter 3. Even while you are conducting this literature search, you can start organizing it into the portion of your paper that will be called "Review of the Literature." A useful approach is to write down on index cards specific ideas from various sources as you accumulate them and to modify and merge these cards in an appropriate order as the review of the literature leads to a clarified statement of the problem. An even more effective approach may be to enter the information in a systematic manner into a personal computer. The initial reaction of most readers of this book may be to enter research notes and information into a word processor. However, it may be a better idea to use a data base management program (Figure 19.1).

Figure 19.1 shows how one of the authors used the *AppleWorks* data base program to generate the "Annotated Bibliography" examples at the end of most of the chapters of this book. Whenever he read a book or journal article that exemplified concepts discussed in this book, he entered pertinent information about it into the format shown in Figure 19.1. This enabled him to keep track of these resources. When it came time to transfer this information to the book manuscript, he used the mail merge option of *AppleWorks* to transfer the information into a word processing program so that the books and articles could be cited at the end of the appropriate chapters. By doing different sortings of the same data base, he was easily able to insert into the instructor's manual a list of all the resources cited (so that instructors could easily give assignments involving books or journals in their schools' libraries) and a cross-referenced list of books and articles whose secondary topics would make them useful in various chapters.

In addition to generic data base programs, there are computer programs specifically designed to facilitate note taking and the generation of bibliographies. For example, *EndNote* from Niles & Associates enables computer users to enter information into a flexible format and generate output that is likely to be helpful at various stages of the research process. Personal Bibliographic Software's *ProCite* likewise enables researchers to store notes and automatically generate reference lists in a designated format [for example, American Psychological Association (APA) style].

Let your literature search be guided by the question "What do I need to know before I can take some reasonable action?" or "What are the right themes?" Then look for answers to these questions. Do not let the review of the literature be a mere formality.

Record 260 of 395 (1 selected)
==
Author: Patton, M.Q.
Title: How to Use Qualitative Methods in Evaluation
Subtitle: –
Place of Pub: Beverly Hills, CA
Publisher: Sage Publications
Date of Pub: 1987
Library: PUC
Catalog Number: H 62 P3216 1987
Book Chapter: 9
Summary: This book covers issues to consider when deciding whether to use
  S2: qualitative research methods as well as strategies for conducting
  S3: qualitative studies.
  S4: –
  S5: –

Type entry or use @ commands   @-? for Help

Figure 19.1 A Database Entry for Keeping and Organizing Notes. (The authors used the mail merge capability of AppleWorks to generate an annotated bibliography entry directly from this database, selecting only the appropriate information in the proper order, with no need to retype it.)

STATEMENT OF THE HYPOTHESES

When you think you have solutions to the problem (no matter how tentative), write these down as your hypotheses. Then go about refining them until you feel a degree of satisfaction with them. Include appropriate control and moderator variables, as well as the dependent and independent variables. After you have devised clearly stated hypotheses, write out some research predictions in which all the terms of the hypotheses are operationally defined. Most researchers find that this process helps them to clarify the problem into a much better formulation. It is perfectly legitimate (and often desirable) to go back to earlier steps by modifying the statement of the problem, looking for more information in the professional literature, and restating the hypotheses as often as necessary. Avoid making changes in your statement of the problem and hypotheses just to make the problem easier to solve. Your changes should be directed toward helping you solve as thoroughly as possible the problem you want to solve. In stating your research hypotheses and research predictions, follow the guidelines given in chapters 2 and 4.

Changes in the statement of the problem and hypotheses should be directed toward helping you solve as thoroughly as possible the problem you want to solve.

It is quite legitimate to change the hypotheses as often as you wish, up until you begin the actual collection of data. After that, it is scientifically unsound to change the hypotheses. Science (and educational research) would not make noteworthy progress if the researcher were allowed to look at the results first and then decide what the hypotheses should be. This would allow chance factors to play an important part and render the research less valuable. The scientific method depends on first stating a prediction and then conducting research to verify or refute the prediction. It is important that you adhere to this convention.

The discussion in this section has focused on situations in which it is appropriate to state the research hypothesis in the early stages of the research process. As the summaries in this chapter indicate, the hypothesis is usually stated early in quantitative research studies. However, in qualitative research projects, an early statement of the hypothesis might bias the data collection process. Note that in situations where the statement of hypothesis is delayed, research predictions will also be delayed; or, the predictions may be replaced completely by greater emphasis on interpretation in the final stages of the research project.

PLANNING THE RESEARCH PROCEDURES

Once you have satisfactorily stated your hypotheses and research predictions (if these are appropriate), it is time to plan and carry out the data collection process to verify or refute these predictions. By looking at the research predictions that you derived from your hypotheses, you should be able to determine exactly what information you will need to test these predictions. For example, here is one of the sample quantitative, experimental research predictions from chapter 4, which was derived from a hypothesis stated in chapter 2:

> Reading *Julius Caesar* in accordance with our school's curriculum guidelines will cause sophomore students to make more references to a wider variety of aspects of Western civilization in an essay on Western culture written at the end of the semester than students who do not read *Julius Caesar.*

A teacher/researcher looking at this research prediction could easily tell that a study to test this prediction would consist of assembling an experimental and a control group of sophomores, having the experimental group read *Julius Caesar* in accordance with the school's curriculum guidelines while the control group did not, and then having both groups write an essay on Western culture at the end of the semester. If the experimental students made more references to a wider range of aspects of Western civilization, then the hypothesis from which this prediction was derived would be supported. (There are also many other possible ways to test this research prediction.) The knowledge you have gained from previous chapters will help you decide what research design or other procedures will help you acquire this information. In fact, one of the criteria for recognizing good research is that it often generates more good questions than it answers.

Since most research in education involves humans as subjects, it is possible for researchers to inadvertently do something during a research project that would be harmful to the participants. Researchers should take careful precautions to see to it that no such harmful effects occur. Almost all school systems, universities, government agencies, and professional organizations have specific guidelines for research involving human subjects. If you adhere to the guidelines, you can be fairly certain that harmful effects will be ruled out. These guidelines are designed to prevent participants from being hurt, embarrassed, frightened, or in any other way imposed upon or negatively affected by research procedures.

Researchers should take careful precautions to see to it that no harmful effects happen to human subjects in their studies.

In many cases, such guidelines indicate that participants have a right to be "informed" before consenting to be subjects in a study, to refuse to participate in a research study, to remain anonymous if they wish, and to have responses kept confidential. Participants also have the right to expect that researchers behave in a responsible manner in all respects during the experiment. Ethical guidelines obligate us to behave responsibly when we collect data. The guidelines do not by any means prohibit useful educational research. In most cases, these guidelines simply ensure that one will behave in the same way that ethical persons would wish to behave in performing responsible research even if there were no guidelines. They ensure that common sense is observed in research on human subjects. The guidelines are most likely to restrict the activity of researchers who use measuring instruments that are

not normally part of the school's testing program or who require the students to do something that is not part of the school curriculum. The researcher should always obtain the approval of appropriate administrative officials, curriculum committees, or teachers before introducing the data collection process or altering the curriculum.

Extraordinary measures may be essential in research of a major theoretical nature, but most of the research projects conducted by the readers of this text will typically involve no more than measuring or observing student performance to assess the effectiveness of instructional techniques. In such cases, the educators will often do what they normally do but more systematically and effectively, and they will analyze the results. There is usually no reason for concern about the welfare of the participants, provided the research fits into the routine educational procedures of the school and the data are handled confidentially. Specific, formal permission from administrative officials or a curriculum committee may not even be necessary, although they should be kept informed. If the treatment is not an actual part of the curriculum or employs a type of data collection that would not routinely be used as part of student evaluation, then evidence must be supplied to demonstrate that no harm will occur. Even if only routine permission is required, of course, it is expected and required that the researcher act responsibly and ethically. Similar guidelines probably apply in your educational setting. If you are in doubt, err on the side of safety, and ask permission.

In addition to being concerned about ethics, it is important to be concerned about what is possible and practical. For example, it might seem obvious that the clearest and best way to test your research predictions would be by having randomly assigned experimental and control groups whose performance would be measured by interviews and a carefully validated battery of tests. However, you might quickly discover that randomly assigned groups are not going to be available to you or that the interviews and the desired battery of tests would be both too costly and too time-consuming to warrant their use. Therefore, you might have to settle for a quasi-experimental design using a less than perfect measuring device. However, although it is important to be aware of what is practical, it is equally important not to be too quick to abandon the search for the near ideal. In many cases it is possible to have the administration cooperate with you in advance to achieve random assignment, and it is likewise possible to obtain or develop data collection strategies that provide a high degree of validity.

It is important to obtain or develop and field test all the instruments, materials, and methods that will be needed for the study. An appropriate research design must be selected that will provide the control necessary to maximize internal and external validity. Appropriate scheduling must be arranged so that unusual events will not ruin the timing of the treatments or observations. Insofar as possible, problems should be anticipated so that few emergency adjustments have to be made as the study is being carried out.

It is important to plan any statistical analysis before the data are collected.

In types of research where it is possible to do so, you should plan the statistical analysis at this point, before any data are collected. By doing this, you can make sure that you will obtain all the data you need to test your hypotheses. You will be able to ascertain that you will know what to do with the data after you have obtained your results. Once you have conducted the study, it will be too late to go back and collect data that you really should have collected in the first place. In quantitative studies, it is also important to plan to collect qualitative data to supplement and help interpret the quantitative conclusions of your study.

If you plan to use the computer for data analysis, make plans to do this before you collect the data. It may be possible to devise measuring instruments so that data can be initially recorded in a fashion that is easily compatible with data entry and analysis. If you fail to plan ahead, analyzing the data by computer will be time-consuming; at worst, you may even discover that your data are simply not compatible with the types of computer analysis that would be most appropriate.

Note that some studies do not permit the precise kind of planning described in the preceding paragraphs. This is because many of the researcher's activities during the study may depend on what had happened at a previous point, which cannot be determined before the start of the research project. This does not mean that planning is unnecessary. It merely means that flexible but careful thinking for naturalistic research (described in chapter 9) must be undertaken.

CARRYING OUT THE STUDY

After appropriate planning, you should implement the strategy according to the prescribed plan. Stick to the proposed plans as closely as possible. Even the most careful plans, however, sometimes go awry; when something surprising comes up or something just plain goes wrong, adjustments have to be made. When it is necessary to make changes in plans, do so as much as possible within the guidelines of sound educational research procedures. *Modify* your original plan, but do not abandon it. Come as close as you possibly can to getting a full test of your research predictions. In some cases, of course, the changes will be positive rather than negative. For example, you may discover an additional group for comparison or an extra opportunity for data collection that would strengthen the findings. By all means, take advantage of such opportunities if they strengthen your research design. Keep a close record of whatever changes you make, so that you can analyze the impact of these changes on your study.

ANALYZING THE DATA

If you have planned appropriately, analyzing the data is not difficult. You simply do what you said you would do. (Qualitative data analysis is often very time-consuming; guidelines are given in chapter 9.) The real problems occur if you fail to plan your analysis ahead of time. Researchers who wait until after they have collected their data to decide how to analyze their results may discover that there is no acceptable way to do a sensible analysis for their inappropriately collected data.

While doing your analysis, you may discover that additional analyses would be helpful. Perhaps you had forgotten or did not know about a certain analysis. Or perhaps a certain result might be surprising and a further analysis (perhaps taking into consideration new moderator variables) would be helpful to clarify this confusion. In such cases, it is appropriate to do the additional analyses and to report their results.

DRAWING CONCLUSIONS

After you have conducted your study and analyzed the results, it is necessary to look back and see how the results relate to your research predictions and hypotheses. Point out and clarify what you think the results have shown and how these results relate to what was previously known and discussed in your review of the research.

You may be forced to conclude that your results are ambiguous, perhaps because of some problem in your research procedures. Although this outcome may not be pleasant, it may sometimes be necessary. In such a case, admit the problem and recommend ways to clarify the results in the future. Even the best researchers arrive at ambiguous results. Any embarrassment lies not in attaining such results but in failing to recognize them as ambiguous.

WRITING THE REPORT

Once you have completed the study and drawn your own conclusions, you write the research report to convey the results to others. Writing the report need not be an onerous task. Even though this step is listed here after drawing the conclusions, much of the writing can be accomplished before the study is completed. As you read the sections beginning on p. 433 about the contents of the research report, it should be noted that almost everything in the main body of the report up to the results section can actually be written before the study is conducted (for example, you can write the methods section while

planning that part of your study). The rest is a matter of modifying the initial manuscript, writing down what happened, discussing these data and events, and drawing conclusions.

Almost everything in the main body of the report up to the results section can actually be written before the study is conducted.

At this point, it may be useful to summarize the major steps involved in carrying out a research project. Table 19.1 provides such a summary. In examining this table, recall that although these steps are listed sequentially, there may be alterations in the order. For example, although writing the report is listed as the last step, a major portion of the report can (and should) be written before the study is carried out. The second column provides a brief list of chapters in which each of the guidelines is discussed. Such a list is necessarily an oversimplification, since many topics are covered in more than one chapter. Nevertheless, even a tentative list may be helpful to a researcher who needs to know where to look for more information.

The following section contains guidelines for conducting specific types of educational research. Each set of guidelines includes a description of the designated type of research, cautions regarding possible errors, and important steps for conducting that type of research.

QUANTITATIVE DESCRIPTIVE RESEARCH (STATUS STUDIES)

Quantitative descriptive research studies describe the status of subjects or programs with regard to context or outcome variables. A quantitative descriptive study is an example of good research to the extent that it collects accurate information and reports this information accurately. Chapters 4 through 8 of this book have described the strategies for conducting effective quantitative descriptive studies. In addition to being important sources of information in themselves, these methods provide the

Table 19.1 The Major
Steps in Carrying Out a
Research Study

Step	Chapter in This Book Where You Can Seek Guidelines
Select a problem	Chapters 2 and 17
Determine which of many to focus on	
Clarify the problem so that you know what your real problem is	
Review the literature to seek solutions	Chapter 3
Perform meta-analysis	Chapter 16
State your hypothesis	Chapter 2
Identify all variables (dependent, independent, moderator, control)	
State research prediction	Chapter 4
Plan research procedures	
Check ethical considerations	Chapter 19
Select a design or strategy	Chapters 9, 11, 12, 14
Develop, obtain, and field test all instruments	Chapters 4 to 8
Anticipate any problems that may arise	Chapters 9, 11, 12, 14
Plan for statistical analysis	Chapters 7–13, 14
Plan for computer usage	Chapter 18
Carry out the study	Chapters 9, 11, 12, 14
Stick to your plan	
Note modifications	
Analyze the data	Chapters 13–14
Do all analyses that were planned	
Do supplementary analyses, if any	
Draw conclusions	Chapters 9, 17
Write report	Chapter 19

foundation upon which other research builds to establish cause-and-effect and theoretical relationships.

The following are hypothetical examples of quantitative descriptive studies:

1. Fifty-five percent of the students interviewed said that they would oppose the extension of the school year by an additional week.

2. The students responded with a mean rating of 3.52 on a Likert scale (with 5 being "strongly agree") to the statement "The instructor seems to be well prepared for the class."

3. The third-grade students averaged at the 76th percentile on the state competency test.

4. Eighty-one percent of the students passed the GED test at the end of the course.

5. The student received a combined score of 890 on the SAT, which was well below the median of the college to which she was applying.

Certain things can go wrong with quantitative descriptive studies. The collection or reporting of data can be inaccurate for one or more of the following reasons:

1. The outcome variables may be improperly operationally defined. (chapters 4 and 5)

2. The data collection methods may not match the operational definitions. (chapters 5 and 7)

3. The data collection may not be conducted reliably and accurately. (chapter 5)

4. The sample of respondents may be inappropriate to permit generalization to the intended population. (chapter 8)

5. The information may be analyzed, summarized, or presented in a manner that does not convey the information accurately. (chapter 6)

6. The reader or researcher may try to generalize the findings to populations and situations to which generalizations are inappropriate. (chapter 15)

The chapters cited in the preceding list contain guidelines that can help you avoid these errors. In addition, since this type of research often serves as the basis of other research, these same guidelines will be helpful in performing correlational and experimental research.

The following are important steps involved in quantitative descriptive studies:

1. State the problem clearly before you begin to collect data. Continue to modify, revise, and clarify this statement of the problem as you move through subsequent steps in the research process. (chapter 2)

2. Examine information in the library and reference sources to find out how the work done by others can help you solve your own research problem. (chapter 3)

3. State operational definitions of the outcomes regarding which you want to collect data. In general, it is best to state multiple operational definitions of each outcome variable. (chapter 4)

4. Select appropriate formats that will enable you to collect accurate data related to the outcome variables you have identified. (chapter 7)

5. Follow appropriate procedures to make your data collection process reliable and valid. (chapter 5)

6. If you are not able to collect data from the entire population of respondents, make the research

feasible by selecting a sample of respondents that will permit generalizations to that population. (chapter 8)

7. Use appropriate reporting processes to record, analyze, and summarize the data you have collected. (chapter 6)

8. Supplement the findings of quantitative research with qualitative data whenever possible. The integration of qualitative and quantitative insights is more likely to lead to a complete picture than is the isolated use of either approach. (chapter 9)

QUALITATIVE OR NATURALISTIC RESEARCH

Qualitative researchers use observations, interviews, content analysis, participant observers, and other data collection tools to report the contexts, feelings, personal interpretations, and behavior of participants. Qualitative research is generally conducted in naturally occurring social situations. A qualitative study is well done when the comprehensive data are collected accurately in natural contexts, the relationships among all the variables in the natural setting are identified, and the events and relationships are interpreted in the way they would be interpreted by the people in that environment.

Chapter 9 described the strategies for conducting effective qualitative studies. In addition to being important sources of information in themselves, qualitative methods often provide the foundation upon which other research builds to establish cause-and-effect and theoretical relationships and adds to the depth and breadth of understanding in predominantly quantitative research.

The following are hypothetical examples of qualitative descriptive studies:

1. In their private conversations around the school, the faculty members expressed themselves in ways that could best be described as hostile and defensive toward the principal.

2. Observation of students in the English writing lab indicated that although these students did not spend as much time on the revision process as those in the regular classrooms, they tended to focus on more significant issues and to share this information more often with their peers.

3. Careful observation of children during their activities in the computer lab suggested that many of them tended to focus on superficial aspects of the software rather than on the key elements of the instructional unit.

4. After working with the third-grade students and their new science materials for an entire year, the teacher concluded that the new materials worked better this year because the students using them showed a higher degree of ownership and a stronger urge to internalize the information than had been the case in previous years.

5. Mrs. Simmon's program for at-risk students had a much higher success rate at keeping students motivated and in school than similar programs in the district. Observations and interviews with Mrs. Simmon and her students suggested that this was because she had found several ways to establish rapport with the students and to build upon this rapport to integrate academic needs with intrinsic motivation for individual students.

Certain things can go wrong with qualitative studies. The collection, interpretation, or reporting of data can be inaccurate for one or more of the following reasons:

1. The data collection process may be inaccurate. (chapter 9)

2. The data collection process may be incomplete. (chapter 9)

3. The analysis of the data may be inaccurate. (chapter 9)

4. The reader or researcher may try to generalize the findings to populations to which generalizations are inappropriate. (chapter 15)

5. The data might be interpreted in an unwarranted cause-and-effect manner. (chapter 9)

Chapter 9 contains guidelines to help you avoid errors in qualitative research. The following are important steps involved in qualitative research studies:

1. Avoid biases that may improperly filter information or invalidate the way it will be recorded or interpreted. These biases may occur during the preparation, discovery, interpretation, or explanation stages of the research process (pages 207–209 of chapter 9).

2. Avoid disrupting the natural setting while collecting data. One good way to accomplish this is to assume the role of the participant observer (page 196 of chapter 9).

3. Find a way to record data accurately without distracting yourself from attending to what is happening and without disrupting the natural settings. Using field jottings and field notes (described on pages 201 and 202 of chapter 9) is an example of an effective strategy.

4. Support the findings of qualitative research with quantitative data whenever possible. The integration of qualitative and quantitative insights is more likely to lead to a complete picture than is the isolated use of either approach.

CORRELATIONAL RESEARCH

Correlational research studies use statistical techniques such as correlation coefficients to examine the relationships among two or more variables, without necessarily making generalizations about the causal nature of these relationships. A correlational study is an example of good research to the extent that it collects accurate data on the selected variables, accurately calculates and interprets interrelationships among them, and incorporates appropriate contextual data. Chapter 13 has described the strategies for conducting effective correlational studies. In addition to being important sources of information in themselves, correlational studies provide information about relationships, which sometimes can be further explored through experimental and quasi-experimental methods to establish cause-and-effect and theoretical relationships.

The following are hypothetical examples of correlational studies (for each statement, the information in parentheses gives the correlation coefficient and sometimes the reasoning that would lead to the stated conclusion):

1. Students who were weak readers also tended to be weak in arithmetic. (The correlation between reading and math scores was .75.)

2. Students who rated the teacher high in "preparation for class" also tended to rate her high with regard to "taking another class from this teacher." (The correlation between the two ratings was .68.)

3. Success in college is more strongly related to a combination of high school performance and student support systems than to SAT scores. [The correlation between SAT scores and the criterion of college grade point average was .53. On the other hand, the multiple correlation between the combination of (a) high school grade point average and (b) the rating of the students' support systems and the criterion of college grade point average was .65.]

4. The more formal education a person has, the higher the person's income will be. (The correlation between years of education and income is .67. This suggests that formal education causes an increase in income. If this conclusion were true, this would be a good reason to invest money in a college education.)

5. When intrinsic motivation to succeed is held constant, there is no relationship between years of formal education and income. (The partial correlation between years of education and income is .15, when intrinsic motivation is held constant. This statement assumes that intrinsic motivation was measured and entered into the equation to compute the partial correlation. It is

plausible that intrinsic motivation contributes both to the number of years a person goes to school and to a person's income. If this conclusion is true, then one should consider factors in addition to personal income when deciding whether to invest in college.)

Certain things can go wrong with correlational studies. The collection or reporting of data can be inaccurate for one or more of the following reasons (chapter 13 contains guidelines that can help you avoid errors in correlational research):

1. One or more of the variables may have been measured incorrectly. (chapters 4 through 8)

2. The researcher may have chosen the wrong statistic to measure the relationship or may have calculated it incorrectly. (chapter 13)

3. The reader or researcher may assume a causal relationship when none has been demonstrated. (chapter 13)

4. The reader or researcher may try to generalize the findings to populations to which generalizations are inappropriate. (chapter 15)

The following are important steps involved in correlational studies:

1. State the problem clearly before you begin to collect data. Continue to revise and clarify this statement of the problem as you move through subsequent steps in the research process. (chapter 2)

2. State operational definitions of the predictors and outcomes regarding which you want to collect data. In general, unless you are dealing with very specific predictions (e.g., predicting college grade point average on the basis of high school grade point average), it is best to state multiple operational definitions of each variable. (chapter 4)

3. State the research predictions. (Revise this as necessary as you move through Step 4 and repeat Steps 1 and 2.) (chapter 2)

4. Examine information in the library and reference sources to find out how the work done by others can help you solve your own research problem. (chapter 3)

5. Determine what kind of data analysis will enable you to test your research prediction. If a correlational strategy is appropriate, proceed to Step 6; otherwise, use a different strategy. (chapter 13)

6. Select appropriate formats that will enable you to collect accurate data related to the variables you have identified. (chapter 7)

7. Follow appropriate procedures to make your data collection process reliable and valid. (chapter 5)

8. If you are not able to collect data from the entire population of respondents, select a sample of respondents that will permit generalizations to that population. (chapter 8)

9. Use appropriate reporting processes to record, analyze, and summarize the data you have collected. (chapter 13)

EXPERIMENTAL AND QUASI-EXPERIMENTAL RESEARCH

Experimental researchers use the systematic scheduling of the times at which treatments are administered to participants and at which data are collected about the performance of the subjects to examine the nature of cause-and-effect relationships among variables. This kind of research builds upon a foundation of good descriptive research. It often tests hypotheses derived from qualitative or correlational research. An experimental study is well done to the extent that it controls the threats to internal and external validity. Experimental research addresses the need for cause-and-effect information necessary for decision making in the applied field of education.

The following are hypothetical examples of experimental or quasi-experimental studies:

1. The students who participated in the Higher Order Thinking Skills (HOTS) program averaged at the 76th percentile on the state competency test, whereas the students from the same grade level who did not take part in the HOTS program averaged at only the 34th percentile.

2. More students who took part in the evening program passed the GED test than did those who took part in the Saturday program.

3. The faculty members expressed themselves less often in ways that could best be described as hostile and defensive toward the principal after the sensitivity training sessions than had been the case before the sessions.

4. Students assigned to the English writing lab did not spend as much time on the revision process as those in the regular classrooms, but they shared information more often with their peers.

5. Mrs. Simmon's program for at-risk students had a much higher success rate at keeping students motivated and in school than similar programs in the district.

Certain things can go wrong with experimental and quasi-experimental studies. The results of these kinds of research studies can be inaccurate for one or more of the following reasons:

1. The data collection process may be inaccurate. (chapters 4 through 8)

2. One or more threats to internal validity may be uncontrolled. (chapters 10 through 12)

3. The analysis of the data may be inaccurate. (chapter 14)

4. The reader or researcher may try to generalize the findings to populations to which generalizations are inappropriate. (chapter 15)

The following are important steps involved in experimental and quasi-experimental research studies:

1. State the problem and hypothesis clearly before you begin to collect data. Continue to revise and clarify these statements as you move through subsequent steps in the research process. (chapter 2)

2. State operational definitions of the variables in your proposed study. In general, unless you are dealing with evaluating a very specific treatment with regard to a very specific outcome (for example, whether the use of a specific computer program enables counselors to record absences more accurately), it is best to state multiple operational definitions of each variable. (chapter 4)

3. State the research prediction. (Revise this as necessary as you move through Step 4 and repeat Steps 1 and 2.) (chapter 2)

4. Examine information in the library and reference sources to find out how the work done by others can help you test your own research hypothesis. (chapter 3)

5. Determine what kind of data analysis will enable you to test your research prediction. If an experimental or quasi-experimental strategy is appropriate, proceed to Step 6; otherwise, use a different strategy. (chapters 11 and 12)

6. Select an experimental design that will test your research prediction while minimizing the threats to internal and external validity. (chapters 10 through 13)

7. Use appropriate strategies of quantitative and qualitative descriptive research to collect data. (See chapters 5 through 9.)

8. Use appropriate statistical procedures to estimate the likelihood that observed differences exceed chance expectations. (chapter 14)

9. When appropriate, look for interactions—that is, situations where moderator variables make a significant difference in the way the independent variable (treatment) influences the dependent (outcome) variables. (chapter 17)

10. Support the findings of quantitative research with qualitative data whenever possible. The integration of qualitative and quantitative insights is more likely to lead to a complete picture than is the isolated use of either approach. (chapter 9)

CRITERION GROUP RESEARCH

Criterion group research studies gather groups of subjects into treatment and control groups on the basis of naturally occurring circumstances (after these events have already occurred) rather than on the basis of random or nonrandom assignment to treatment and control conditions. They use statistical techniques such as t tests, analysis of variance, and chi square to determine whether membership in a group is related to performance regarding one or more outcome variables, without making generalizations about the causal nature of these relationships. A criterion group study is an example of good research to the extent that the researcher collects accurate data to classify the participants and to measure the outcome variables and accurately calculates and reports the degree of relationship among them. Chapter 13 has described the strategies for conducting effective criterion group studies. In addition to being important sources of information in themselves, criterion group studies provide preliminary information about relationships, which can be further explored through experimental and quasi-experimental methods.

Criterion group studies closely resemble correlational studies in that it is not possible to make direct inferences from them regarding the cause-and-effect nature of relationships. They resemble experimental and quasi-experimental studies in that they compare the performances of groups.

The following are hypothetical examples of criterion group studies. They are accompanied by extensive explanations to clarify the distinctions among three types of research that are often confused: criterion group, correlational, and experimental research. The distinctions are summarized in Table 19.2 on page 431.

1. Students who drop out of school before completing the 12th grade earn significantly less money than those who complete the 12th grade.

It would be unethical to require some students to drop out of school in order to conduct an experiment, so an experimental study in this case would be impossible. Instead, the researcher would find a sample of persons in the designated age range and ask them for at least two pieces of information: (1) whether they completed the 12th grade and (2) their current income. The respondents would be divided into two groups (graduates and nongraduates), and the mean for each group would be calculated. The researcher could use a t test or analysis of variance to ascertain whether the difference between these means was statistically significant.

Since participants were not assigned to the dropout and nondropout conditions by the experimenter, there is little evidence that dropping out directly causes a reduction in income or that staying in school causes an increase in earning power.

2. Students who drop out of school before completing the 12th grade are more likely to be involved in automobile accidents between the ages of 21 and 30 than those who complete the 12th grade.

This study is basically the same as the first study. It would be unethical to require some students to drop out of school in order to conduct such an experiment, and so an experimental study would be impossible. Instead, the researcher would find a sample of persons who were at least 30 years old and ask them for at least two pieces of information: (1) whether they completed the 12th grade and (2) the number of automobile accidents they had been involved in during the designated time period. The respondents would be divided into two groups (graduates and nongraduates), and the mean number of automobile accidents per person for each group would be calculated. The researcher could use a t test, analysis of variance, or chi square to ascertain whether the difference between these means was statistically significant.

Since participants were not assigned to the dropout and nondropout conditions by the experimenter, there is little direct evidence that dropping out causes persons to become involved in accidents.

3. Teachers who allow students to retake tests on a mastery basis are viewed more favorably by their students than those who do not do so.

There are two basic ways that this study could be conducted. First, it would be possible to collect information from all the teachers in a school with regard to two variables: (1) whether they permitted their students to retake tests on a mastery basis and (2) the ratings of these teachers by their students. The teachers could then be divided into two groups—permitters and nonpermitters—and the mean rating for favorableness could be calculated for each group. The researcher could use a t test or analysis of variance to ascertain whether the difference between these means was statistically significant. This procedure is an example of criterion group research.

On the other hand, the researcher could solicit the participation of all the teachers in a school. She could select half of these teachers at random and persuade them to permit their students to retake tests on a mastery basis, while the other half would continue with their ordinary procedure of not permitting such retests. At the end of a designated period of time, she could obtain ratings of all the teachers. She could then compare the mean ratings of the permitters with those of the nonpermitters. She could use a t test or analysis of variance to ascertain whether the difference between these means was statistically significant. This procedure is an example of experimental research.

The first procedure did not involve assignment of the teachers to the treatments. It is possible that the teachers who were inclined to permit the retests were also the ones who would be inclined to do other things that would result in high ratings. Therefore, this first procedure presents little evidence that permitting retests directly causes higher ratings. On the other hand, the second procedure did involve assignment of teachers to a treatment and control condition. Teachers who were initially inclined to do things that would result in high ratings were equally likely to be included in either group. Therefore, this procedure presents considerably more and better evidence that permitting retests actually causes the higher ratings.

4. Boys have more favorable attitudes than girls toward adventure-style arcade games.

Without some formidable genetic engineering, once they have been born, boys and girls cannot be assigned to one gender or the other. A study like this would be conducted by measuring the attitudes of boys and girls toward adventure-style arcade games. The researcher would use a *t* test or analysis of variance to compare the mean attitude of the boys with that of the girls.

5. Children who are permitted to watch violent television shows at home are likely to engage in more antisocial behavior in school than children who are not permitted to do so.

The way this conclusion is stated seems to indicate that the researcher examined a large group of students (perhaps a sample from several schools) and obtained two pieces of information about each student: (1) whether the child was permitted to watch violent television shows and (2) the number of times the child engaged in antisocial behavior. The researcher would use a *t* test or analysis of variance to compare the mean number of antisocial behaviors of the watchers with that of the nonwatchers. This would be a criterion group study and would not provide direct evidence that watching violent television caused antisocial behavior.

Almost the same hypothesis could be tested in a second way. The researcher could obtain a large group of students (perhaps a sample from several schools) and obtain two pieces of information about each student: (1) the number of violent television shows the child watched each week and (2) the number of times the child engaged in antisocial behavior. The researcher would use a correlation coefficient to determine the degree to which these two variables were related. This study would be an example of correlational research. However, the hypothesis tested by this study would be slightly different from the original. It could be stated as "The more violent television shows a child watches, the more antisocial behavior that child is likely to engage in" or "There is a positive relationship between the amount of violent television a child watches and the amount of violent behavior engaged in by that child."

There is a third way to test almost the same hypothesis. The researcher could obtain a large group of students (perhaps a sample from several schools). Half the students could then be exposed to violent television shows and the other half could watch nonviolent shows. The researcher could use a *t* test or analysis of variance to compare the mean number of antisocial behaviors of the watchers of violence with that of the watchers of nonviolence. This would be an experimental study, and it would suggest more direct evidence that watching violent television caused antisocial behavior. However, this hypothesis would be slightly different from the original. It could be stated as "Students who are experimentally exposed to violent television shows are likely to engage in more antisocial behavior than those who are exposed to nonviolent television shows."

Certain things can go wrong with criterion group studies. The collection or reporting of data can be inaccurate for one or more of the following reasons (chapter 13 contains guidelines that can help you avoid errors in criterion group research):

1. Participants may be classified into the criterion group on the basis of an inappropriate operational definition. (chapter 4)

2. The outcome variables may have been measured incorrectly. (chapters 4 through 8)

3. The researcher may have chosen the wrong statistic to measure the relationship or may have calculated it incorrectly. (chapter 13)

4. The reader or researcher may assume a causal relationship when none has been demonstrated. (chapter 13)

Table 19.2 Comparison of Major Features of Correlational, Criterion Group, and Experimental Research Studies

	Correlational Study	Criterion Group Study	Experimental Study
Number of groups	One at a time	Two or more	Two or more
How are subjects assigned to groups?	Not applicable	Self-selection (identified after the treatment)	Usually assigned by experimenter (identified prior to the treatment)
What is usually compared?	Performance of individuals on two or more variables	Means of groups	Means of groups
Typical statistics	Correlation coefficients	t test Analysis of variance Chi square	t test Analysis of variance Chi square
Conclusion	Descriptive	Descriptive	Causal
Example of typical diagrams			

The reader or researcher may try to generalize the findings to populations to which generalizations are inappropriate. (chapter 15)

The following are important steps involved in criterion group studies:

1. State the problem clearly before you begin to collect data. Continue to revise and clarify this statement of the problem as you move through subsequent steps in the research process. (chapter 2)

2. State operational definitions of the criterion group and of the outcome variables regarding which you want to collect data. In general, unless you are dealing with very specific predictions (for example, whether boys or girls weigh more at a certain age), it is best to state multiple operational definitions of each variable. (chapter 4)

3. State the research prediction. (Revise this as necessary as you move through Step 4 and repeat Steps 1 and 2.) (chapter 2)

4. Examine information in the library and reference sources to find out how the work done by others can help you solve your own research problem. (chapter 3)

5. Determine what kind of data analysis will enable you to test your research prediction. If a criterion group strategy is appropriate, proceed to Step 6; otherwise, use a different strategy. (chapter 13)

6. Select appropriate formats that will enable you to collect accurate data related to the variables you have identified. (chapter 7)

7. Follow appropriate procedures to make your data collection process reliable and valid. (chapter 5)

8. If you are not able to collect data from the entire population of respondents, select a sample of respondents that will permit generalizations to that population. (chapter 8)

9. Use appropriate reporting processes to record, analyze, and summarize the data you have collected. (chapters 13 and 14)

META-ANALYSIS

When conducting a meta-analysis, researchers use the results of other experimental studies as the raw data for a study that combines the results of the other studies. The meta-analysis estimates the average effect sizes from the other studies and permits the researcher to look for interactions that influence the way the effect sizes are interpreted. Meta-analytic research builds upon a foundation of experimental and quasi-experimental research; these in turn build upon a foundation of criterion group, correlational, descriptive, and qualitative research. A meta-analysis is an example of good research to the extent that it objectively analyzes the data from other studies and interprets it validly.

The following are hypothetical examples of meta-analyses:

1. Students who participate in thinking skills programs gained an average effect size of .43 on tests of higher-order thinking compared with students who participate in traditional educational programs.

2. Students who participate in cooperative learning gained an average effect size in academic achievement of .56 compared with those in competitive environments and an average effect size of .12 compared with those in individualistic environments.

3. Students who participate in cooperative learning gained an average effect size of .56 in social skills compared with those in competitive environments and an average effect size of .12 compared with those in individualistic environments. (Conclusions 2 and 3 would be likely to appear in the same meta-analysis.)

4. Students who participate in cooperative learning gained an average effect size in academic achievement in language arts skills of .56 compared with those in competitive environments and an average effect size of .12 compared with those in individualistic environments. In mathematics, students who participated in cooperative learning gained an average effect size of .49 compared with those in competitive environments and an average effect size of .23 compared with those in individualistic environments. (Conclusions 2 through 4 would be likely to appear in the same meta-analysis.)

5. An analysis of several studies showed that there is an average correlation of .45 between SAT performance and college grade point average. (While it is possible to perform a meta-analysis of correlational studies, methods for doing so are not covered in this book.)

Certain things can go wrong with meta-analytic studies. The results of a meta-analysis can be inaccurate for one or more of the following reasons:

1. The studies that supplied the raw data for the study may themselves be inaccurate. (This is not

a serious problem. One way to control it is to look for systematic sources of bias in the studies and include these as moderator variables in the data analysis. This makes it possible to ascertain the degree to which "good" studies would lead to different conclusions than would "weak" studies. In addition, when the results of a large number of studies are combined, random errors tend to balance out.)

2. The rules for including studies in the meta-analysis may be illogical. These rules are essentially operational definitions, and the meta-analysis can be improved by making the inclusion rules more logical and well defined.

3. Important moderator variables may be omitted. As a result, effect sizes will be inappropriately lumped together and important interactions will be ignored.

4. The effect sizes or other statistics involved in the meta-analysis may be calculated incorrectly.

The following are important steps involved in conducting a meta-analysis:

1. State the problem and hypotheses for which you want to perform the meta-analysis.

2. State the rules for including studies in the meta-analysis.

3. Identify moderator variables that will be coded to look for interactions.

4. Examine information in the library and reference sources to find out how the work done by others can help you conduct your own meta-analysis. Use this information to revise Steps 1 through 3, as necessary.

5. Conduct an appropriate search of published and/or unpublished resources to find all the studies that meet the criteria for inclusion.

6. Find the studies identified at Step 5. If studies cannot be located, specify these omissions as part of your revised inclusion rules.

7. Examine the studies identified at Steps 5 and 6, and code this information for analysis.

Occasionally you may discover a need for an additional moderator variable. It is legitimate to make adjustments in the coding, but such alterations should be made early in the analytic process to avoid confusion.

8. Calculate the effect sizes and other statistics [described in Hedges and Olkin (1985), which is described in chapter 16's Annotated Bibliography. These calculations are not discussed in detail in this book].

9. Summarize the results of the meta-analysis.

10. Support the findings of the meta-analysis with anecdotal information from specific studies and with qualitative data whenever this will make the conclusions clearer. The synthesis of qualitative and quantitative insights is more likely to lead to a complete picture than is the isolated use of either approach.

THE PARTS OF A RESEARCH REPORT

The parts of a research report will now be described in the order in which they normally appear. Grant proposals and other reports often follow a similar format. In many cases, the actual order in which the parts are written will vary from the order described here. For example, although the title and abstract are described first and come at the beginning of the report, they should be written last, after the rest of the report has been compiled. Otherwise it may be difficult for the title and the abstract to catch the full sense of what has been reported. In addition, even though each part is labeled separately here, sometimes labels are omitted and parts are combined. For example, "Statement of the Problem" is often directly attached to the end of the review of the literature rather than constituting a separate section. Many reports merge related sections into such combinations as "Results and Discussion" or "Discussion and Conclusions." The important thing is to use a writing style that will convey the information clearly to the reader; if departing from these guidelines will enable you to do a better job, then you should certainly let your own wisdom guide you.

The Title of the Report

Make your title succinct and meaningful. Avoid lengthy titles. When the first author of this book wrote his doctoral dissertation, the original title was "The Relationship Between the Perceived Quality of Educational Research Reports as Viewed by Educational Researchers and by Educational Decision Makers." After refinement, the title had become "Information Quality and Educational Decision Making." Reducing the title from 20 to 6 words had lost little information, forced the author to communicate more precisely, and made it more likely that people would read the research.

The word *relationship* can almost always be deleted from a title. Words describing the nature of the participants or the type of instrument used to collect data can usually be omitted unless this information is likely to be of use to the reader. Your title should communicate as briefly and directly as possible the precise nature of your report.

Your title should contain key words that will be recognized by others who might be interested in your research.

Your title should contain key words that will be recognized by others who might be interested in your research. This is important because your report may be picked up by an abstracting service like ERIC, and such services index reports by key words in the titles and abstracts. With this in mind, you may want to be sure that your title and abstract contain the relevant key words from the *ERIC Thesaurus,* for example, if you expect your report to be indexed in any of the ERIC dissemination services. The title should be written *after* the report is written. Of course, the title may occur to you during the project, while you are writing the report, or even before you have begun the research. In such cases, do not throw the title away. Examine it and revise it carefully *after* the report is written to make sure it conveys what it is expected to convey.

The Authors and Affiliation

The statement of authorship tells readers who is responsible for the research. If there is only one author, there are no problems. When there are multiple authors, it becomes a problem to determine the order in which the authors are to be listed. Being first author is somewhat more prestigious. When people refer to a research article, they often refer to it as "so-and-so's work"; in doing so, they often use the name of only the first author. The decision regarding the order of authors has to be made among the persons involved in the project, of course, but the basic guideline is that the person who bore the major share of the responsibility in performing the research should be listed as first author.

It is worth noting that many journals currently permit the authors to add a footnote indicating that the article was written under conditions of equal coauthorship. If there are more than two authors, the same guidelines apply; whoever assumes a greater amount of responsibility should receive greater recognition.

A statement of institutional affiliation should accompany the article to show the reader what institution supported the research and to tell readers where the author can be reached and where there is likely to be some interest in this area of research. In addition, many journals request additional information about the author and include this information in a footnote or a separate section of the journal where all the authors for a given issue are described. Make this information brief and accurate. If you make it too lengthy, someone may edit it, and editing may result in a different impression than you would want to give of yourself.

Some journals, conventions, and funding organizations follow a process of blind review. This means that the paper will be read by reviewers who will not know who wrote the report and therefore cannot let information about the author influence their judgments regarding its quality. If you are submitting a report to blind review, follow the guidelines indicated by the journal or other organization.

The Abstract

The abstract should include a brief summary of the key points of the report. It is usually limited to 50—150 words, so you have to be concise. The abstracts give a reader a good idea of what the report is about. The most important component of the abstract is a brief summary of the results, but it also can include a brief statement of the hypotheses or research predictions. In addition, a brief statement of why the research is worth doing is sometimes important. It is not necessary (or even advisable) to write these ingredients as separate parts. Rather, they should be integrated in a meaningful fashion. One good strategy is to have the abstract consist of a statement of the results inserted into the format of the operationally defined research predictions. The reader can then tell by reading this abstract why the research should be of interest, what the specific problem is, and what the results are. As stated earlier, it is usually a good idea to write the abstract *after* the rest of the report has been written. It is an easy task to go through a well-written report and pull out the material needed for a concise abstract.

We recommend always including an abstract, even if the person or organization to whom you are submitting the report does not ask for one.

A well-written abstract is a great service to everyone concerned. We recommend always including an abstract, even if the person or organization to whom you are submitting the report does not ask for one. Abstracts are the main tool you have to put your ideas quickly in front of the people whom you want to read your research. The importance of abstracts can be seen in writing grant proposals. When reviewers are reading many grant proposals to decide which ones they will fund, the decision may be influenced by what you said (or failed to say) in your abstract. Likewise, decisions regarding whether to read an article or to accept it for publication are often influenced by an assessment of the abstract.

Your abstract may be picked up by an indexing and abstracting service. If an article is not accompanied by an abstract, someone who works for the indexing and abstracting service will have to write one for you, or the report will merely be indexed without an abstract. Both of these alternatives are undesirable. In addition, such services index the report under key words, and they often allow you to suggest them yourself. You can often identify key words beyond your title by underlining up to 10 important words throughout the abstract. In choosing such words, you should use terms that are taken insofar as possible from the thesaurus of the organization or service that you expect to index your report. The idea is to make your report as readily available as possible to persons who will want to find it.

The Review of the Literature

The main purpose of the review of the literature is to put the hypotheses to be examined in the research report into proper perspective by supplying a theoretical foundation for the research—not to overwhelm readers with a large number of impressive citations. A secondary purpose of this part of the report is to provide readers with guidelines regarding where they can look to find more information about the topics.

The length and contents of the review of the literature will vary depending on whom the researcher expects to read the report. If the target audience consists of readers who have no knowledge whatsoever about a topic and who will want background information, then time will have to be spent developing and explaining the variables and contexts cited in the sources. At the other extreme, if the intended audience consists of persons who will already be familiar with the background research, then a simple reference (in a few sentences) to four or five researchers and their findings may provide a satisfactory perspective on how their research relates to the problem at hand. Decide what your audience needs, and then provide that information. Confine yourself to the relevant aspects of the sources you cite. If a source has an elaborate theory that relates to many aspects of education, focus only on how that theory relates to the problem at hand. If readers want more information, they can always read the sources you have cited.

One of the best reporting styles and easiest methods of citation is that shown in the publication manual of the American Psychological Association. This style is also widely used in educational journals. A sample citation to an article in a review of literature might look like this:

Kosmoski and Vockell (1978) found that learning centers stimulated both cognitive and affective growth among elementary school students.

This citation format immediately tells the reader who wrote the article and how recent it is. This is accomplished without any footnoting. If readers want to know more about the cited article, they can look in the list of references at the end of the article and find the article written by Kosmoski and Vockell in 1978. At that point, there will be an indication of the exact title of the article, the name of the journal, and the issue and pages upon which the article appeared. This method conveys useful information without needlessly disrupting the reader's attention.

The Statement of the Problem

The review of the literature should clearly and naturally develop a basis for the statement of the research problem. In most cases the statement need not even be in a separate section of the report. It can simply be part of the concluding paragraph of the review of the literature. The train of thought should go something like this: "These various sources have shown that. . . . All this leads us to wonder about the relationship between X and Y." Such a statement of the problem leads to a natural transition to the statement of the hypotheses.

The Statement of the Hypotheses and Research Predictions

The hypotheses or research questions should be clearly stated immediately before the methods section of the report. These statements or questions can be couched in purely conceptual terms at this point; or, if it seems natural to do so, this section can employ operationally defined terms. In general, more specific and thorough operationally stated predictions should be reserved for a later point in the methods section.

If the hypotheses are complex, do not be afraid to state them in several sentences instead of trying to compress too many ideas into a single, complicated sentence. In applied areas, it might seem more natural to state questions at this point and then follow these with research predictions that answer these questions in the methods section. This is an acceptable practice, so long as the questions clearly and unambiguously ask about the relationships that would be contained in the hypotheses if they were stated in that form.

In dissertations and formal research papers, the statements of the hypotheses are often contained in a separate section of the report. In most journal articles and for situations that are less academic, the hypotheses fit easily and naturally at the end of the review of the literature. The last paragraph could summarize the review by stating a concise set of problems, and then the hypotheses could provide a tentative answer to these problems.

The Methods Section

Within the methods section, all the important variables in the study should be stated and operationally defined. In experimental studies, this will include control and moderator variables as well as the dependent and independent variables. This operational definition process should be so complete that another knowledgeable researcher could duplicate the research methods by simply doing what you said you did in the methods section. In fact, few readers will actually wish to duplicate the process, but only such a precise description will enable others to make judgments regarding the validity of the research.

The operational definition process should be so complete that another knowledgeable researcher could duplicate the process by simply doing what you said you did in the methods section.

A detailed description of the participants and contextual setting should be provided. In quantitative studies it should be clear to the reader which variables were treated as moderator variables and which were treated as control variables. All variables should be operationally defined and described in detail so that a reader could duplicate the research if time and resources were available. A description should be given of any instruments used to measure the research variables. In qualitative reports, the description of participants and variables must sometimes be delayed until the results section. In such cases, the methods section describes the plan of action as clearly as possible, so that the readers can determine that an appropriate level of objectivity and scientific methodology has been incorporated into the study.

In providing operational definitions, you can use a certain amount of brevity. For example, if you employ a commercially developed product with which your readers are likely to be familiar, you can merely mention the label attached to this product and indicate where readers can get further information. If you use the Stanford-Binet IQ test or some other standardized test about which the readers are probably already well informed or can easily obtain additional information, then a detailed operational description of such variables is unnecessary. On the other hand, whenever there is any ambiguity, provide additional specific information. Sometimes it will be necessary to state that you used an instrument you developed yourself and describe it as fully as possible. Then tell the readers to contact you if they want more details.

The methods section should also include a statement of the research design and of any statistical procedures used in the analysis of the data. Again, this should be stated in such a way that the readers could replicate your analysis if they had access to your data. (In fact, if some other competent researcher should ask to see your data, you should permit this, if this can be done without infringing on the confidentiality of your subjects.) At this point you should be aware of the wide variety in levels of expertise that may exist among your readers. For example, some may be qualified statisticians, whereas others may not even know what a t test is. You yourself may not be highly proficient in research design or statistics. You may have used a certain statistical procedure, for instance, simply because a textbook specified that you should do so. In such cases, it is a good idea to provide a brief description of the research design or the statistical procedure and then insert a bibliographic citation indicating where the reader can find more information about the topic. If you used a computer to perform your analysis, it is often helpful to specify the names of your computer programs and cite the source in which the reader can learn more about these programs.

It is often useful to conclude the methods section with one or more operationally stated research predictions. Such predictions should follow a format similar to that shown in the examples in chapter 4. A statement of this prediction in operational terms at this point will enable the reader to have clearly in mind what the results would look like if they supported the hypotheses, and this will make more meaningful the examination of the results that follow immediately thereafter.

The Results Section

The Results section makes available to the reader an analysis of the data that were collected as described in the methods section. All the results that the previous sections led the readers to believe they would see should be presented in this section. In many cases, researchers combine this and the following section into a "Results and Discussion" section. This is an especially good idea if the discussion is brief and is most appropriately presented when the results are fresh in the mind of the reader. At the least, you should point out to the reader what hypotheses or aspect of the hypotheses a given result refers to and whether this result verifies or rejects that aspect of the hypotheses.

Of course, if you are writing a proposal rather than a report, you will not yet have any results to report. In such a case, you should speculate about what the results are likely to be and how these results will serve the world of education.

Table 19.3 Mean Performance and Gains of Experimental and Control Groups on Critical Thinking Test and Analysis of Variance of Posttest Scores with Pretest Scores as the Covariate

Experimental group pretest	(n = 25)	Mean = 18.0	S.D. = 3.0
Control group pretest	(n = 13)	Mean = 18.5	S.D. = 3.4
Experimental group posttest	(n = 25)	Mean = 20.0	S.D. = 2.5
Control group posttest	(n = 13)	Mean = 18.4	S.D. = 4.4
Gain by experimental group	(n = 25)	Mean = 2.0	S.D. = 3.4
Gain by control group	(n = 13)	Mean = 0.1	S.D. = 2.5

F ratio for analysis of covariance of posttest using pretest as covariate: $F = 3.97$ (d.f. = 2.35). Level of significance = .05.

It is advisable to make use of tables and figures in presenting your results. In doing so, refer to these as tables and figures, not as charts, graphs, and diagrams. This terminology is the more standardized. A *table* is an organized summary of quantitative information, usually in labeled rows and columns. A *figure* is any other type of illustration—often a diagram or graphic representation of information that could also be presented in a table. Number your tables and figures consecutively, sequencing your tables and figures separately (for example, the first figure is Figure 1, even if it comes after Table 3). When you write your report, it is a good idea to put all the figures and tables on separate pages rather than in the running text and then to make a notation like the following in the actual text:

Insert Figure 5 about here.

One advantage of this approach is that it is considerably easier for the typist. Reviewers and editors can set the tables and figures in a separate pile and refer to them whenever necessary, even moving them along as they proceed to new pages in the text that continue to refer to the same figure. Journal editors prefer this style because it is much easier to make arrangements for printing if they do not have to adjust to the idiosyncrasies of your typing format. In some cases, journals merely photocopy what is given to them and insert the results into the journal. If this is the case, there may be specific guidelines to follow to provide photo-ready copy.

Organize your information in such a way as to give a clear and accurate impression of what your results show. Badly organized tables create confusion and encourage readers to ignore them. For example, Tables 19.3 and 19.4 both present the same results of an experiment in which an attempt was made to teach critical thinking skills to an experimental group of college students. Both tables show the number of subjects in the experimental and control groups, and both show the means and standard deviations of both groups on both testing occasions. Both tables show the gains made by each group, the F ratio obtained from an analysis of variance, the degrees of freedom, and the exact level of significance. This information is obscured in Table 19.3, but the same information is much clearer in Table 19.4. The difference is that the data in Table 19.4 are arranged in such a way as to allow easy comparisons among the numbers.

As an additional visual aid, it would be useful to accompany your table with a graph. Figures 19.2 and 19.3 present the results shown in Table 19.3. A

Table 19.4 Mean Performance and Gains of Experimental and Control Groups on Critical Thinking Test

	Pretest	Posttest	Gain
Experimental (n = 25)	18.0 (3.0)	20.0 (2.5)	2.0 (3.4)
Control (n = 13)	18.5 (3.4)	18.4 (4.4)	−0.1 (2.5)
F ratio (d.f.)		3.97 (2.35)	
Level of significance		.05	

Standard deviations in parentheses. The F ratio is a result of an analysis of covariance in the posttest scores with pretest scores as the covariate.

reader looking at Figure 19.2 is given no clear impression about the data. What is there to conclude? This figure shows four columns of about equal height with one edging slightly above the others. This would not show a reader that the treatment had produced an impact. On the other hand, Figure 19.3 presents the same data in such a way as to show that the treatment did produce an impact. The sharply crossing lines indicate that the treatment made a difference.

It is impossible in this brief and general text to explain in detail how to draw good figures and tables. The important point is to organize the information in a logical fashion and to present it so that it conveys the information you want to convey. Make it easy for readers to focus their attention where you want it and to make the comparisons you want them to make. In addition to presenting the data in tables and figures, of course, it is necessary to provide a brief narrative description in the text interpreting each of the tables and figures.

Tables and figures are most effectively designed when it is possible for the reader to understand them without referring constantly to the text. You should consider a table or figure well done when you can

show it to someone who has not seen the narrative accompanying it, and that person can make a correct interpretation of the results.

Recent developments in software for personal computers have made it easier to incorporate clear and attractive tables and figures into reports. For example, many spreadsheet programs enable users to generate graphs by following simple instructions. These programs usually permit users to change from one form of a graph to another, to change the dimensions or scale of a graph, or to replace old data with new data and immediately redraw the graphs (Figure 19.4). In addition, desktop publishing programs and presentation graphics packages enable researchers to integrate graphs and tables with efficient word processors and attractive artwork.

The number of tables and figures and the amount of results presented will vary, depending on the nature of the report and the audience for which it is intended. In general, a doctoral dissertation or master's thesis will contain a much lengthier results section than a journal article based on the same research. The dissertation or thesis contains an abundance of details, whereas the article reports only those results that are necessary to demonstrate to readers what they need to know. Interested readers can always consult the original report for more details if they want more specific information. Include all the results that your readers will need in order to formulate a decision of their own concerning whether the results support the research hypotheses.

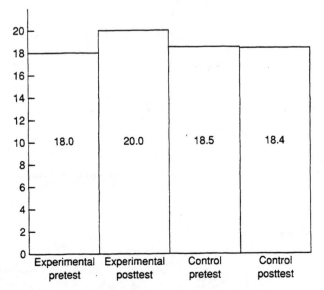

Figure 19.2 Mean Critical Thinking Performance of Experimental and Control Groups on Pretest and Posttest

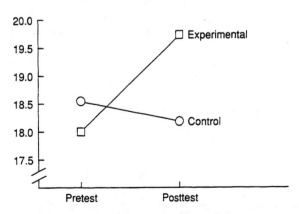

Figure 19.3 Mean Critical Thinking Performance of Experimental and Control Groups on Pretest and Posttest

Figure 19.4 A Bar Graph (Screen A) and a Line Graph (Screen B) Based on the Same Set of Data. (The researcher was able to change graphs with just a few keystrokes.) These graphs are based on data previously shown in Figures 18.7 and 18.8.

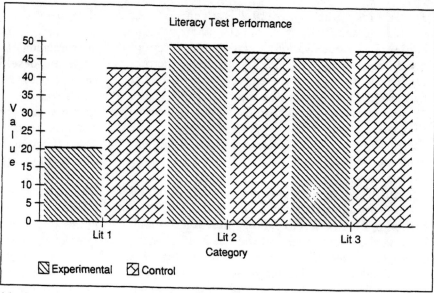

(a)

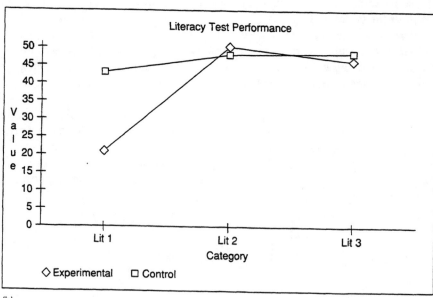

(b)

The Discussion Section

The methods section described how the data were collected, and the results section presented the results of the analysis of the data collected through these methods. The discussion section relates your results to the results of other studies and discusses problems that may have arisen during your study. It focuses on how the results have confirmed or rejected the research predictions and thereby confirmed or rejected the research hypotheses. It is appropriate at this time to show how expectations from the review of the literature have been verified, rendered suspect, or put into a new context by the research from the current study and to show how the current results relate to prior research and theory. It is likewise appropriate at this time to point out how results may have failed to support the research predictions and to suggest reasons for any failures. Results from the current study are not introduced here. Rather, this section explains how the results already presented can be interpreted and explained.

This section is the place where limitations should be clearly recognized. Do not artificially deride your research, but honestly indicate its limitations. For example, in an experimental study, state what shortcomings there were with regard to internal validity, and specify how these weaknesses affect the inferences about the cause-and-effect relationships emerging from your study. If the research of others cited in your review of the literature has some bearing (for example, by providing evidence that a certain threat was probably not a significant factor), then cite such evidence at this point. This is the place to state as accurately as possible the limitations regarding the generalizability of your study. No study has perfect generalizability; by stating the specific limitations of your study and bringing to bear whatever other researchers have had to say about factors related to generalizability, you will help your readers draw useful generalizations from your research.

This section is often combined with either the results section or the conclusions section of the report.

The Conclusions Section

This section returns to the conceptual level. Previously, the results have been discussed in terms of operational definitions. Now this section devotes its attention to what the results really mean—what do they have to say about the concepts involved in the research? This section is where the intervening variables are discussed. At this time you should help your readers determine what conclusions they can actually draw based on the research you have presented. The conclusions are often combined with either the discussion section or summary section of the report. This section may also contain recommendations for implementation or further research.

The Summary

The summary restates the hypotheses and major findings of the study, pointing out how the findings have confirmed or rejected the hypotheses. This is usually not a section by itself, but rather the summary is given in the final paragraph or two of the previous section. In many respects, the summary looks a lot like the abstract. The major difference is that when writing the summary you can assume that the reader has read the rest of the report. This is often a short section, but it can be lengthened considerably by being combined with the conclusions section of the report.

The References Section

Any source that you cited in the report should be listed in the references at the end of the report. We believe that the APA style of listing references (compatible with the citation style mentioned in the review of the literature section) provides the best format. Avoid the temptation to cite impressive references without good reason. List in the references section only those sources to which you actually made a reference in the text of the report. (Some research reports have a bibliography section for additional sources not specifically cited in the report.) The list of references can be a valuable resource to others who might want to pursue your line of research beyond where you have led them. Proofread the references as carefully as you do the text of the report. This is more difficult than proofreading the text, because volume and page numbers are not very exciting. However, errors at this point can be a serious disservice to the avid reader whom you would most like to serve by providing leads to further information.

SOME GENERAL COMMENTS ON THE WRITTEN REPORT

The main point of writing a report is to convey meaningful information to other persons. This should be done in an objective manner, but objectivity does not necessitate boredom or lack of creativity. By following the guidelines provided here you can write a good report, provided you have good information to convey. On the other hand, it may be wise under certain circumstances to modify some of the guidelines to fit your specific needs.

Since most writers have a tendency toward verbosity, we hesitate to give the following advice. When you are submitting a report, it is often better to provide more information than necessary, with the assumption that readers can ignore what they do not want. If you include too much information in an article submitted to a journal, the editor can always tell you that the article will be acceptable if you revise and shorten it. On the other hand, if you err on the side of brevity, the editor and other readers have no way of knowing whether you could add further information if given a chance to do so. Under such circumstances, editors tend to reject manuscripts instead of asking authors to add more information. This advice means that when in doubt you may prefer to add additional, relevant, cogent ideas. It does not mean that you should pad the report with irrelevancy or use circumlocutions in order to consume enough space to appear impressive. In general, the more concisely you can state your point, the more your readers will appreciate you.

If you create a good piece of research, you should consider submitting it to a professional journal. Publishing your research will enable you to benefit from the comments of your peers, advance the state of knowledge on a given topic in education, and provide readers with concrete information that can lead to better solutions for some of their own problems. If you follow the guidelines described in this chapter, you should be able to write a presentable report. To submit an article, first find a journal that is likely to be interested in your work. *The Educator's Desk Reference* (Freed, Hess, & Ryan, 1990) includes a chapter that describes the major features of many education journals and pertinent information for submitting manuscripts to them. A good way to identify a journal is to select one that you cited in your own review of the literature. Your research will be viewed as a follow-up to the research already in that journal. Then look for the section "Guidelines for Manuscript Submission" in that journal. These guidelines are often inside the front or back cover or somewhere near the table of contents. Follow the guidelines carefully. Submit the required number of copies together with a letter briefly stating that you want to submit the manuscript for possible publication and that you have not already published the same article or submitted it to another journal.

Normally, you will receive an acknowledgment that the article has been received within a week or two, but then there follows a period of two to three months (or more) during which the article is reviewed. Sometimes your article will be accepted. Often, however, it will be rejected on the first submission, but the reviewers or editors may suggest some modifications and recommend possible resubmission with revision. If you receive a request for modifications, take the editor's suggestions seriously. Resubmitting often leads to acceptance of the article for publication.

Even after the article has been accepted, there will be a publication lag of four months to a year, since the journal is likely to have a backlog of articles already accepted for future issues. Once the article appears, you will be pleasantly surprised to see how many comments you will receive from colleagues you do not know, asking for further information or offering you ideas of their own on the same topic. This exchange of professional information is a fruitful and enjoyable enterprise.

SUMMARY

This chapter has provided a summary of the major steps involved in carrying out a formal research project. In addition to restating and integrating the important points from previous chapters, these guidelines have focused on ethical and practical considerations involved in carrying out such a project. This chapter has also presented a series of synopses of guidelines for conducting each of the major types of research discussed in this book. Finally, the chapter has discussed the major components of a research paper and provided practical suggestions on how to submit a report to a journal for publication. By following these guidelines, you will find that the pursuit of formal educational research projects can be a fruitful enterprise.

ANNOTATED BIBLIOGRAPHY

American Psychological Association. (1982). *Ethical principles in the conduct of research with human participants*. Washington, DC: Author. These guidelines are widely accepted as appropriate for protecting the rights of participants involved in experimental studies.

American Psychological Association. (1983). *Publication manual of the American Psychological Association* (3rd ed.). Washington, DC: Author. These guidelines for writing research reports are acceptable to an ever increasing number of schools, conventions, journals, and funding organizations. Your library should have a copy.

Freed, M. N., Hess, R. K., & Ryan, J. M. (1990). *The educator's desk reference*. New York: Macmillan. In addition to providing summaries of much other information, this book lists journals that publish research within specific areas of education. It also provides such detailed information as how to submit articles to these journals.

Martin, D. W. (1991). *Doing psychology experiments* (3rd ed.). Monterey, CA: Brooks/Cole. Chapter 10 provides good guidelines on how to write a report based on psychological research.

Strunk, W., & White, E. B. (1979). *The elements of style* (3rd ed.). New York: Macmillan. This brief book provides valuable information on how to express yourself briefly and cogently. It provides guidelines that will help you write your report without sounding like the stereotypical social scientist.

GLOSSARY OF IMPORTANT TERMS

achievement test   An instrument designed to measure the degree of mastery of academic skills.

action research   The practical application of the scientific method or other forms of disciplined inquiry to the process of dealing with everyday problems.

affective outcomes   Events or behaviors that arise out of changes in such things as emotions, attitudes, and personality traits within a subject.

alpha level   The statistical probability that an observed result (such as a difference between two means) is likely to be a chance occurrence.

analysis of covariance   A statistical procedure that is similar to analysis of variance, except that it also attempts to control the influence of one or more independent variables on the dependent variable. (Attempts to use this strategy to equate initially unequal groups are often misleading.)

analysis of variance   A statistical procedure for determining the likelihood that the observed difference on a criterion variable among means occurred by chance. This procedure can be used with two or more groups.

analytic notes   The written results of the qualitative researcher's conceptualizations of how culture and social groupings are structured and organized.

applied research   The use of research strategies to determine the nature of relationships and to make generalizations about such relationships in order to help solve specific, practical problems. The term overlaps with what some textbooks refer to as action research or evaluative research. (Often contrasted with *theoretical research*.)

attitude test   A measurement instrument designed to assess the feelings and emotions a respondent possesses toward people, places, events, and so on.

behavioral objective   The observable behavior that the teacher is willing to accept as evidence that learning has occurred. A behavioral objective is a specific type of operational definition.

C   A symbol used in diagrams of research designs to indicate that the members of a group were selected on the basis of possessing a certain characteristic (criterion group design) rather than through assignment to experimental and control groups.

central tendency   An estimate of the typical or average score in a set of scores. Measures of central tendency include the mean, the median, and the mode.

chi square   A statistical procedure (abbreviated X^2) used with counted or frequency data that provides an estimate of how likely it is that an obtained distribution of scores is merely a chance variation from a theoretical or expected distribution of those counts or frequencies.

coding   The transfer of unstructured data into a format that can be numerically tabulated in quantitative research or summarized in some other way in qualitative research.

coefficient alpha   The most general statistical procedure for estimating the internal consistency reliability of a data collection process.

cognitive outcome   A change in behavior that arises out of new learning in such areas as knowledge, concept formation, understanding of principles, and problem solving.

cohort design   A quasi-experimental design in which a group of subjects is compared with another group that has preceded or will follow the first group through an institution. The institution can be either narrowly defined (such as a school) or broadly defined (such as American society or childhood). For example, sociologists might compare current adolescents with their pre-Vietnam-era cohorts.

comparison group   A group of subjects that does not receive a treatment or a condition, or receives a standard treatment, and whose performance is compared with that of the experimental group. Sometimes the comparison group experiences an alternate treatment or condition.

compensatory demoralization   The social-psychological threat to internal validity that arises when subjects in one group or another reduce their efforts for emotional or social reasons.

compensatory equalization of treatments   The social-psychological threat to internal validity that arises when there is a demand that the apparent benefits of the experimental treatment be extended to the control group as well.

compensatory rivalry   The social-psychological threat to internal validity that arises when subjects in one group have emotional responses to the other group and work harder to compete with that group.

concurrent validity   A type of measurement validity that deals with the question of whether a given data collection technique correlates highly with another data collection technique that is supposed to measure the same thing.

confidence interval   The boundaries within which a population's score on a measurement or statistical process most likely falls. The term is used when the score or statistic is estimated from sampling procedures. Confidence intervals are placed around the statistic obtained from the sample to indicate the range within which the population score probably lies.

construct validity   A type of measurement validity that deals with the question of whether a data collection technique is actually providing an assessment of an abstract, theoretical psychological characteristic.

content validity   A type of measurement validity that deals with the question of whether a given data collection technique adequately measures the whole range of topics it is supposed to measure (rather than a restricted, nonrepresentative range of such topics).

continuous behavior   A behavior that cannot be meaningfully counted by merely enumerating specific instances of the behavior but rather occurs over a prolonged period of time. (Contrasted with *discrete behavior*.)

control group   The group of subjects from which the treatment or condition is withheld in an experiment or which receives a standard treatment. The performance of this group is compared with that of the experimental group.

control variable   A factor whose impact upon an experiment is reduced or eliminated through either random assignment, statistical control, or isolation and removal.

convenience sample   A sample of subjects who are selected simply because they are available.

correlation   The degree to which two or more variables are related. A high correlation means that two events are strongly related—the occurrence of one event is associated with a predictable pattern in the other. A low correlation means that two variables have little relationship.

correlation coefficient   A statistical index for estimating the strength of a relationship. Such coefficients range from near +1.00 to near -1.00. A high absolute value (either positive or negative) indicates a strong relationship. A low absolute value indicates a weak relationship.

criterion group research A descriptive, nonexperimental approach to ascertaining the nature of relationships among variables in a group. Usually, numerous variables are measured in one group at a time and then interrelated. It is difficult to draw causal inferences directly from such results.

criterion-referenced test A measurement process with which a respondent's performance is judged by comparison with a preestablished standard (the criterion) rather than by comparison with the performance of other respondents who experienced the same measurement process.

criterion-related validity This term refers to how closely performance on a data collection process is related to some other measure of performance. Methods of establishing the criterion-related validity of a data collection process rely primarily on computing correlation coefficients between the results of the data collection process being validated and the results of another data collection process; this other data collection process is referred to as the criterion. Specifically, concurrent and predictive validity are examples of criterion-related validity.

curvilinear relationship A relationship that is not represented by a straight line. That is, the relationship is predictable, but it must be diagrammed by a curved line rather than a straight line.

data A term that refers to the results (including tests, questionnaires, observations, and interviews) obtained from a data collection process.

data base management program A computer program that enables users to store information in an organized manner and to retrieve the information in a logical manner. Personal computer users can use these programs for purposes such as entering and organizing their notes during the review of the literature and recording data during the data collection stage of a research project.

data line In computerized statistical programs, one of the lines in the program on which the information (data) about the subjects is listed.

degrees of freedom A term derived from theoretical statistics and closely related to the number of subjects or the number of observational categories in an analysis. The term is important because it refers to the point at

which a researcher enters a statistical table to determine the level of significance of a statistical analysis (as in the use of the *t* statistic). (In this book, instructions accompanying the computation of statistics in Appendix D indicate how to determine the degrees of freedom.)

dependent variable The outcome that is measured after an experimental treatment has been administered to determine whether the treatment had the expected effect. The dependent variable has been referred to throughout this text as the outcome variable. It is dependent in the sense that it depends on the treatment for its value.

descriptive research See *quantitative descriptive research*.

descriptive validity The overall accuracy of the descriptions that make up a qualitative research study.

design See *research design*.

desktop publishing program A program that integrates a word processing program with a graphics program on a personal computer.

diachronic reliability A term used by qualitative research theorists to describe the stability of an observation over time.

diffusion The social-psychological threat to internal validity that arises when participants in one group communicate information about the experiment to members of another group.

discrete behavior A behavior that can be counted by enumerating specific instances of it. (Contrasted with *continuous behavior*.)

effect size The difference between the experimental group average minus the control group average divided by the pooled standard deviation of the groups. Effect sizes are thus standard scores. They are the basic data for meta-analysis and have the advantage of being easy to interpret.

emerging theories The theoretical formulations or explanations of behavior that arise from the analysis of exploratory, qualitative research.

equivalent-forms reliability The form of reliability that estimates the degree of similarity between two forms of the same data collection process. Statistically, equivalent-forms reliability is estimated by computing the correlation coefficient between scores by the same persons on both forms of the data collection process.

ERIC (Educational Resources Information Center) A national information system comprising clearinghouses throughout the country. It publishes two main indexing and abstracting services: *Current Index to Journals in Education* (CIJE) and *Resources in Education* (RIE).

eta coefficient A statistical procedure for estimating the strength of curvilinear relationships. Eta coefficients are always positive and must be accompanied by a diagram to show the nature of the relationship.

ethnography (a) A field within cultural anthropology. Ethnographers view and describe human actions in broad social contexts and look for multiple meanings that the participants have for their actions. Qualitative researchers typically use ethnographic methods in educational research. (b) The results of research using the methods of ethnography.

evaluation research The application of the scientific method or other forms of disciplined inquiry to the process of making decisions about the quality of educational products or outcomes.

evaluative validity The degree to which judgments based on a research study are legitimate.

expectancy effects The threat to internal or external validity that arises when the attitudes the subject or experimenter has toward the experimental situation, rather than the treatment itself, cause an observed outcome.

experiment A strategy for examining cause-and-effect relationships by administering treatments to one or more groups of subjects, withholding the treatments from another group of subjects, and making assessments of the groups.

experimental design The use of systematic methods for assigning participants to treatment groups in an experiment, applying various treatment conditions, and collecting data about the performance of the subjects in the various groups.

experimental group A group of subjects to whom the experimental treatment is administered in an experiment.

experimental mortality The threat to internal validity in an experiment that arises when observed differences in the outcome variable occur because of subjects dropping out rather than because of an effect of the treatment.

experimental research The use of experimental or quasi-experimental designs to examine the nature of cause-and-effect relationships among variables.

external validity The degree to which the cause-and-effect conclusions from an experiment can be generalized to other subjects, other situations, other similar variables, and other times.

extraneous variables Factors whose influence upon a data collection process or upon an experimental design is uncontrolled and therefore unknown. Extraneous variables introduce error and uncertainty into data collection and into the interpretation of research.

factorial design A research design that takes into account moderator variables and other treatment variables and examines their impact upon the relationships among the independent and dependent variables.

field data The generic name given to the data collected in the real world (applied or nonlaboratory settings) from such processes as observations, interviews, and documentary analysis in educational research.

field diary A personal chronicle of how the participant observer in qualitative research feels about the social situation that he or she is in, as well as of the relationship of the observer to those in the social situation.

field jottings Brief notes that are taken whenever the qualitative researcher observes or hears something important. They are written on the spot to avoid the problems of forgetfulness and selective memories.

field log A chronicle of daily events: how the qualitative researcher planned to spend time, how time was actually spent, who was seen, what their names were, what they talked about, who else needed to be seen, and what needed to be asked.

field notes Summaries of field data collected by a qualitative researcher during the day or over a designated period of time.

formative evaluation The type of evaluation of a product or program that occurs during its planning and operation. Its purpose is to provide information that may result in the improvement of the product or program.

F ratio The statistic resulting from analysis of variance. To interpret an F ratio, it is necessary to refer to an F table. However, computer printouts typically give the exact level of statistical significance associated with an F ratio.

generalizability The degree to which an account can be extended to situations or populations not directly studied. External validity deals with the degree to which generalizability exists for a given study.

grounded theory Theory that is generated from the data, rather than developed first and then tested through the collection of data.

history Extraneous events occurring in the experimental research environment at the same time the experimental variable (the treatment) is being tested. Such events can pose a threat to either internal of external validity of an experiment.

human ecology   The study of the total system of influences in the social and biological world, as a unit, surrounding people and their relationships. Qualitative researchers often use the methods of human ecology in educational research.

hypothesis   A statement of the possible relationships among the variables in a research study. The research hypothesis is a proposed, tentative answer to the research question or research problem. The purpose of research is to support or reject this hypothesis. Because of the nature of the inferential logic that forms the basis of the scientific method and because of the imperfections inherent in educational data collection processes, the hypothesis can never really be fully confirmed or rejected, since there is always the possibility of a subsequent rejection or confirmation.

Independent variable   A treatment or condition variable in an experiment; also, the treatment that is administered to the experimental group and withheld from the control group in an experimental study. In a more general sense, it is the treatment that leads to the outcome—the cause that produces the effect. It is independent in the sense that it does not depend upon the dependent variable for its value.

instability   The threat to internal validity that arises when chance fluctuations in measurement processes, variables, and people, rather than the actual treatment itself, cause the observed differences in an outcome variable. This is the only threat to internal validity that is controlled by statistical analysis.

instrument   See *measurement instrument.*

instrumentation   The threat to internal validity in an experiment that arises when observed differences in an outcome variable are the result of changes in the data collection process (including the observers) rather than the result of the treatment itself.

intact group   A group of subjects in an experiment that was already formed prior to the experiment or that was assembled on a basis other than random assignment. This prior formation and absence of random assignment are the essential characteristics of an intact group.

interaction   Something that occurs in an experiment when two or more variables together have an effect different than either would have had alone. If a mod-

erator variable or treatment has an impact on the way another treatment influences the dependent variable, this is referred to as an interaction. Researchers often deliberately look for interactions and make them the focus of their studies. Other interactions introduce ambiguity into a study that is focusing on something else. For example, when extraneous variables (such as selection bias) have an effect on the relationship between the independent and dependent variables, this is an interaction that leads to threats to either internal or external validity.

internal consistency   The degree to which all or most of the parts of a data collection process, such as the items on a test or observers, tend to agree. The term is generally used in association with discussions of reliability.

internal validity   The degree to which conclusions about cause-and-effect relationships arising from an experiment are accurate.

interobserver agreement   The degree to which two or more observers tend to agree that an event does or does not occur during a series of observations.

interpretive validity   The degree to which the researcher correctly interprets the activities and feelings of the people in a qualitative research study—that is, as the participants themselves would interpret them.

interscorer reliability   The degree to which two or more scorers tend to give the same scores to the same set of responses during a data collection process.

interval data   The results of a data collection process that do more than merely rank the respondents; these results actually assign scores with equal intervals between adjacent numbers.

intervening variable   The hypothetical factor that is considered responsible for the interaction observed in an experiment. This variable intervenes in the sense that the independent variable produces the intervening variable, and the intervening variable in turn produces the impact upon the dependent variable.

interview   A data collection format in which a person (the interviewer) questions the respondents and records their answers.

item   A question, statement, or other element presented to a participant to respond to and provide information on during a data collection process. A series of items makes up a test.

item analysis   A set of statistical procedures that can be used to estimate the quality of test items. Item analysis tends to select items that, in general, measure the same thing as the other items on the same test.

Kuder-Richardson reliability coefficient A statistical procedure for estimating the internal consistency of a data collection process; answers can only be coded as right or wrong or can be interpreted as percentages or proportions.

learning An internal change in the organization of knowledge that results from insight or reinforced practice. Learning cannot be directly observed; its existence has to be inferred from observed behaviors.

level of significance See *statistical significance*.

Likert scale A technique of equal-interval measurement whereby a respondent is given a statement and is asked to place his or her response into one of these five specific categories: strongly agree, agree, uncertain, disagree, and strongly disagree.

linear relationship A relationship between two variables that follows a pattern that can be diagrammed as a straight line.

manipulation A method that provides an experimental treatment to one group of subjects while withholding it from another.

matching A system of pairing subjects for an experiment on the basis of measured characteristics and subsequently assigning one member of each pair to the experimental group and the other to a control group at random. All other uses of matching on the basis of measured characteristics (not followed by random assignment to treatments) generally present problems of regression toward the mean. Matching on nominal characteristics such as gender, race, and neighborhood is acceptable.

maturation The threat to internal validity in an experiment that arises from changes in an outcome variable that may occur routinely as a result of the passage of time rather than as a result of the treatment that occurred while time was passing.

mean The arithmetic average of a set of scores. The mean is obtained by adding the scores and dividing by the total number of scores. The mean can be computed with interval ratio data, but other measures of central tendency are more appropriate for nominal or ordinal data.

measurement An attempt to assign numerical values to characteristics possessed by the persons being studied. This is done through the process of choosing operational definitions and then observing the subjects' performances with regard to these definitions.

measurement instrument A device for carrying out the measurement process. The instrument is usually software (e.g., a test or questionnaire), rather than hardware, as the name may imply. In the present textbook, the terms *measurement instrument* and *test* are used interchangeably.

measurement process The process of collecting data to estimate the occurrence or status of a variable, usually by administering and tabulating the results of some kind of data collection instrument or observation strategy.

median The middle score in a set of scores that are arranged in ascending or descending order. When data are ordinal, the median is used to indicate the average or typical score.

member check The strategy in qualitative research of asking participants if they think the participant observer's interpretation is valid.

meta-analysis A powerful research analysis method that integrates the results of a set of experiments to enhance both the internal and external validity of the conclusions that can be drawn from those studies.

mode The most frequently occurring score in a set of scores. The mode must be used to indicate the average or typical outcome when the scores are nominal data.

moderator variable A variable that influences (moderates) the impact of the independent variable upon the dependent variable in an experiment.

mortality See *experimental mortality*.

multiple correlation coefficient A statistical procedure for estimating the strength of the relationship between a criterion or dependent variable and a combination of two of more predictor or independent variables.

naturalistic research See *qualitative research*.

negative correlation A relationship between two variables in which the scores on one increase as the scores on the other decrease. (Also referred to as an *inverse relationship*.)

nominal data The use of numbers or names to merely categorize or label subjects or responses. There is no meaning (such as an implication that "2" is higher than "1") beyond merely being a classification. Nominal data convey less information than ordinal or interval data.

normal distribution A distribution of scores that fall in a pattern represented by the bell-shaped curve. The mode, the median, and the mean all fall at the midpoint of this distribution.

norm-referenced test   A measurement process with which a respondent's performance is judged by comparison with the performance of other respondents (the norms) rather than with regard to a preestablished standard.

norms   A set of scores that provides a basis for comparing the performance of a respondent or group of respondents with the performance of other respondents during the same measurement process.

O   A symbol used in diagrams of research designs to indicate the occurrence of an observation or testing occasion.

observable behavior   A behavior of a person that is external to the extent that two or more observers can reliably agree that the behavior is or is not occurring.

observation   The act of collecting data about the performance of subjects by watching them or listening to them, recording their behaviors, and inferring their feelings, attitudes, knowledge, and so on.

observational technique   A data collection technique whereby an observer watches someone else's behavior, judges that behavior in some way, and then records this judgment.

open-ended question   An item on a questionnaire or in an interview on which the respondent is given considerable freedom to compose his or her own responses. (Contrasted with *structured question*.)

operational definition   The definition of observable behaviors or events that a researcher accepts as evidence that a variable exists.

ordinal data   Results of a data collection process that do more than classify but do not give precise meaning to the size of intervals between scores (as would interval data). Such results merely rank the respondents but do not assign exact scores. The normal usage of the word *ordinal* as opposed to *cardinal* should enable you to remember this, since all ordinal data contain a ranking of first, second, and so on.

outcome variable   The outcome that occurs as a result of a treatment or activity. In formally defined hypotheses, the outcome variable is referred to as the dependent variable.

outliner   A computer program that assists users in the efficient generation of outlines of ideas. These programs are usually integrated with word processing programs.

partial correlation   A statistical method for estimating what the relationship between two variables would have been if the correlated influence of a third variable is removed.

participant   A person from whom data are collected in a research study. The words *participant* and *subject* are often used interchangeably.

participant observer   A person who participates in the research setting or process being studied and also observes and reports what is happening. The participant observer is a key data collector in qualitative research.

Pearson correlation coefficient   The most frequent procedure for computing the index of relationship between two variables.

percentile rank   A score indicating the percentage of scores equal to or below a respondent's score derived from a data collection process. (These are ordinal data. *Percentages,* on the other hand, are interval data.)

population   In sampling theory, the larger group from which the sample is drawn.

positive correlation   A relationship between two characteristics of the subjects in a group such that as the score on one increases, the score on the other also increases. (Also referred to as a *direct relationship*.)

posttest   An observation or measurement of the subjects in an experiment that is conducted after the treatment has been administered to the experimental group.

predictive validity   A type of measurement validity that deals with the question of whether a measurement process forecasts a person's performance on a future task.

pretest   An observation or measurement of the subjects in an experiment that is conducted before the treatment is administered to any of the subjects.

pretesting   The threat to internal validity that arises when the changes observed in an experiment are a consequence of the participants' having taken the pretest rather than of the treatment itself.

purposive sampling   A nonrandom sampling technique, often used in qualitative research, whereby subjects are selected to meet particular goals of the researcher, such as ensuring heterogeneity or involving key persons in the research sample.

qualitative research   Research in which researchers use observations, interviews, content analysis, and other data collection methods to report the responses and behavior of subjects. This kind of research is often conducted in naturally occurring social situations and gives considerable attention to describing the context of the social environment. A key feature is its concern with the relationships among all the variables in the natural setting and the interpretation of events in the environment by the people in it.

quantitative descriptive research Empirical data collection that numerically describes the status of subjects or programs with regard to specified context or outcome variables.

quantitative research Research in which researchers count or measure behaviors or in some other way assign scores, as a result of a data collection process, and use these scores as a basis for making comparisons and drawing conclusions.

quasi-experiment An experiment that is not based on random assignment of subjects to groups. It uses another strategy, such as pretesting or relatively continuous testing between experimental conditions, to determine the relative effect of the treatment.

questionnaire Any data collecting instrument, other than an achievement or ability test, on which the respondents directly report their own answers to a set of questions.

quota sampling A sampling procedure whereby the researcher identifies a set of important characteristics of the population and then selects the sample to match the population with regard to this set of characteristics.

r A symbol for a correlation coefficient.

R (a) A symbol for a multiple correlation coefficient. (b) A symbol used in diagrams of experimental research designs to symbolize that the subjects have been assigned to groups at random.

random assignment The process of placing subjects into groups in such a way that chance is the only factor that determines which subjects go into which groups. The result is groups that can be considered equal except as they happen to differ by chance with regard to all variables at the time of random assignment and (if not *treated* unequally) into the future. (Also referred to as randomization.)

random sampling A sampling procedure whereby the decision regarding who will be taken from the population and included in the sample depends on chance alone. The result is a subgroup (the sample) that represents the population with regard to all characteristics except as it happens to differ by chance. The degree to which this group is likely to differ from the population by chance is based on the size of the sample and can be estimated by confidence intervals.

range The difference between the highest and lowest scores in a group.

ratio data Results of a data collection process that are expressed not only in terms of meaningful, equal intervals but also in relation to an absolute zero. (There is no meaningful difference between interval data and ratio data presented in this book, since no psychological variables have a true zero.)

regression toward the mean See *statistical regression.*

reliability The degree of stability or consistency with which a data collection process will produce similar results on occasions when it theoretically should produce the same result. The term also refers to the degree of consistency among items or observations in a data collection process.

reliability coefficient An index, ranging from .00 to near 1.00, that indicates the degree of internal consistency or stability displayed by a data collection process. In most cases, the reliability coefficient is a correlation coefficient and is interpreted in much the same way as a correlation coefficient.

research design The systematic scheduling of the observations, tests, measurements, treatments, interviews, and so on that are to be administered to the participants in the research process.

research prediction A logical consequence derived from the research hypothesis and stated in operationally defined terms. The research prediction is the statement of the research hypothesis with all the variables stated in terms of operational definitions.

respondent A person whose behavior is measured (by giving responses in some way) during a data collection process.

sample A subgroup taken from a larger group (called a population) in such a way as to make it similar to the larger group with regard to important characteristics.

sampling The inductive reasoning process by which a smaller group (a sample) is selected from among the members of a larger group (a population) so that the characteristics of the smaller group can be used to estimate or make inferences about the characteristics of the larger group.

scattergram A type of picture or diagram used to display the relationship between two variables for a group of subjects.

scientific method The process of advancing theoretical knowledge by drawing inferences based on the careful observation of facts. A popular formulation of the scientific method was stated by John Dewey. This formulation focuses on the following: perceiving a problem, stating a hypothesis as a tentative solution of the problem, deducing predicted consequences based on that hypothesis, collecting data to verify or reject that prediction, and drawing conclusions about the hypothesis based on an analysis of the results of the data collection.

selection bias   The threat to internal validity that arises when a group's performance on an outcome variable is the result of initial differences among the groups themselves rather than of the treatment that is supposed to have produced the outcome.

significance   See *statistical significance*.

social-psychological threats   Threats that arise from the psychological dynamics of the social situation surrounding the introduction of the treatment in an experiment. These threats include diffusion, compensatory equalization of treatments, compensatory rivalry, and compensatory demoralization. These factors have the impact of setting up so-called rival treatments that compete with the experimental hypothesis to explain the research results.

split-half reliability   The type of reliability that can be computed by correlating one-half of the test with the other half of the test. This measure of internal consistency is now rendered obsolete by coefficient alpha.

spreadsheet   A computer program that permits users easily to perform calculations and recalculations on a personal computer.

SPSS (Statistical Package for the Social Sciences)   A popular set of programs that permit the computerized calculation of most of the statistics employed in the social sciences, including education.

stability   The tendency for the same result to occur on different occasions when the data collection process *should* produce similar results. The stability of a data collection process is estimated by a test-retest (over time) reliability coefficient.

standard   A level of performance that has been designated as a goal.

standard deviation   A statistic that describes the individual differences of scores within a group. The larger the standard deviation, the greater the spread among the scores. In a normal distribution, one standard deviation represents about one-sixth of the entire range of scores.

standard error of measurement   A statistic that indicates the range within which the true score of an individual

is likely to fall, taking into consideration the unreliability of the test.

standardized instrument   A data collection instrument with highly structured guidelines for administration and scoring and with norms available to provide comparisons with other persons who have responded to the same data collection process.

statistical procedures   Mathematical methods for summarizing and making judgments and inferences about the results obtained from data collection processes and research methods.

statistical regression   The threat to internal validity that arises from the tendency of subgroups that have been selected on the basis of extreme scores to have a mean score closer to the mean on subsequent retests.

statistical significance   The statistical probability that an observed result (such as the difference between two means) is likely to be a chance occurrence.

status research   See *quantitative descriptive research*.

stratified sampling   A strategy for selecting samples in such a way that specific subgroups (strata) will have a sufficient number of representatives within the sample to provide ample numbers for subanalysis of the members of those subgroups.

structured question   A question on a questionnaire or in an interview to which the respondent merely selects one of several possible answers rather than creating his or her own answer. (Contrasted with *open-ended question*.)

subject   A person who takes part in an experiment by either receiving the treatment or having it withheld from him or her, or a participant whose characteristics are studied as part of a research process.

summative evaluation   The type of evaluation that occurs after a product has been developed or a program has been completed. Its purpose is to provide evidence regarding the effectiveness of the product or program.

synchronic reliability   A term used by qualitative research theorists to describe the similarity of observations within the same time period (agreement among observers or interviews).

systematic sampling   A strategy for selecting the members of a sample that allows only chance and a "system" to determine membership in the sample. The system is a planned strategy for selecting members after a starting point is selected at random, such as every 10th subject, every 11th subject, and so on.

table of random numbers   A list of numbers whose sequence is determined purely by chance. Such a table can be used to select subjects at random from a population or to assign subjects at random to treatment groups.

test A set of items for measuring a characteristic of a respondent. In this book, the term refers to any measurement procedure or instrument, not merely to academic tests.

test-retest reliability A type of measurement reliability that is estimated by computing the correlation between the same people's performance on two administrations over time of the same measurement process.

theoretical research Research that focuses primarily at the conceptual level, as distinguished from applied research, which focuses on the use of research methods to solve practical problems. The methodologies of the two types of research are quite similar, but theoretical research gives primary attention to intervening variables, whereas applied research gives only minimal attention to these variables.

theoretical sampling A sampling procedure, often employed in qualitative research, in which informants and events are selected for their unique ability to explain, understand, and yield information about the meaning of expressive behavior or the way the social system works.

theoretical validity The degree to which the qualitative researcher's explanations represent a legitimate application of the concepts or theories that the researcher thinks they represent.

treatment An event or activity that is imposed on subjects and is expected to produce an outcome. Determining whether this outcome indeed occurs is the purpose of an experiment.

triangulation The process of using multiple operational definitions and/or multiple data collection strategies to measure an outcome variable. By zeroing in on the variable with different measures or procedures (in a process similar to triangulation in surveying or navigation), the researcher is able to more validly measure that outcome.

true experiment An experiment based on random assignment of subjects to groups and the administration of possibly different treatments, followed by observa-tions or measurements to assess the effects of the treatments.

t statistic The statistical result of a test of the significance of the difference between the means of two groups on a measurement process. The t statistic is compared with numbers on an appropriate table to determine the probability that the result would be likely to occur by chance.

t test A statistical procedure for determining the likelihood that an observed difference between the means of two groups on a measurement process occurred by chance.

unobtrusive measurement Data collection techniques that enable the researcher to collect data in such a way that respondents are unlikely or less likely to be aware that data are being collected. Respondents are therefore unlikely to "react" to this data collection process.

validity The strength of a conclusion or the degree to which the conclusion arising from a data collection process or an experiment is likely to be true. For example, the various types of measurement validity (content, criterion related, construct, concurrent, and predictive) all deal with whether a data collection process measures what someone claims the data collection process measures. Likewise, the forms of experimental validity (internal and external) deal with the question of whether an experimental treatment has caused an effect or can be generalized beyond the original experiment.

variable A conceptual entity. Any construct or characteristic to which different numerical values can be assigned for purposes of analysis or comparison. The term is usually synonymous with the terms *factor* and *characteristic*. The specific types of variables that can be identified in an experimental research project are the independent, dependent, moderator, control, and intervening variables.

X A symbol used in diagramming research designs to signify the administration of an independent variable (treatment or experimental condition).

STATISTICAL TABLES

Table B.1
Critical Values of *t*

	Level of Significance					
d.f.	.20	.10	.05	.02	.01	.001
1	3.078	6.314	12.706	31.821	63.657	636.619
2	1.886	2.920	4.303	6.965	9.925	31.598
3	1.638	2.353	3.182	4.541	5.841	12.941
4	1.533	2.132	2.776	3.747	4.604	8.610
5	1.476	2.015	2.571	3.365	4.032	6.859
6	1.440	1.943	2.447	3.143	3.707	5.959
7	1.415	1.895	2.365	2.998	3.499	5.405
8	1.397	1.860	2.306	2.896	3.355	5.041
9	1.383	1.833	2.262	2.821	3.250	4.781
10	1.372	1.812	2.228	2.764	3.169	4.587
11	1.363	1.796	2.201	2.718	3.106	4.437
12	1.356	1.782	2.179	2.681	3.055	4.318
13	1.350	1.771	2.160	2.650	3.012	4.221
14	1.345	1.761	2.145	2.624	2.977	4.140
15	1.341	1.753	2.131	2.602	2.947	4.073
16	1.337	1.746	2.120	2.583	2.921	4.015
17	1.333	1.740	2.110	2.567	2.898	3.965
18	1.330	1.734	2.101	2.552	2.878	3.922
19	1.328	1.729	2.093	2.539	2.861	3.883
20	1.325	1.725	2.086	2.528	2.845	3.850
21	1.323	1.721	2.080	2.518	2.831	3.819
22	1.321	1.717	2.074	2.508	2.819	3.792
23	1.319	1.714	2.069	2.500	2.807	3.767
24	1.318	1.711	2.064	2.492	2.797	3.745
25	1.316	1.708	2.060	2.485	2.787	3.725
26	1.315	1.706	2.056	2.479	2.779	3.707
27	1.314	1.703	2.052	2.473	2.771	3.690
28	1.313	1.701	2.048	2.467	2.763	3.674
29	1.311	1.699	2.045	2.462	2.756	3.659
30	1.310	1.697	2.042	2.457	2.750	3.646
40	1.303	1.684	2.021	2.423	2.704	3.551
60	1.296	1.671	2.000	2.390	2.660	3.460
120	1.289	1.658	1.980	2.358	2.617	3.373
*	1.282	1.645	1.960	2.326	2.576	3.291

Table B.2
A Table of Random Numbers

33	60	43	33	62	85	62	50	12	32
48	34	14	98	42	73	94	95	32	14
44	59	72	63	99	70	63	81	20	70
94	70	33	25	95	10	41	42	23	54
89	17	95	88	29	34	87	20	48	10
63	62	06	34	41	67	17	36	50	51
65	37	37	29	84	30	17	13	77	41
58	12	47	01	33	18	93	60	21	38
14	16	02	95	59	24	45	77	78	97
29	12	64	11	16	93	87	53	23	76
16	13	72	58	23	28	62	99	45	25
16	18	73	57	30	16	96	38	31	78
91	50	65	27	37	11	37	46	30	63
79	92	23	09	50	42	46	03	86	38
20	78	92	34	91	04	97	32	72	01
05	82	48	68	46	99	25	46	76	32
61	26	45	86	42	59	24	10	89	12
21	04	62	69	87	28	21	97	37	34
35	79	55	62	06	04	14	21	62	68
22	47	87	38	87	32	09	44	88	25
36	09	55	06	91	13	20	41	36	90
45	14	15	34	54	55	83	15	29	42
58	84	34	52	00	21	11	46	26	38
08	84	19	78	78	00	99	52	10	44
07	39	32	41	68	48	80	43	66	96
39	73	72	75	37	14	58	40	44	90
70	20	39	40	94	87	26	13	00	56
59	37	20	90	75	71	13	76	90	45
68	84	30	36	46	32	08	57	45	74
65	57	41	63	80	80	59	23	81	76
16	39	72	85	22	38	56	01	94	30
03	74	09	42	16	21	21	55	44	91
82	21	60	43	97	03	79	85	18	08
38	29	40	02	99	37	46	46	25	20
65	25	96	25	80	94	24	60	42	38
43	06	85	00	76	21	36	16	48	16
27	21	42	26	02	98	34	60	72	53
39	86	64	69	17	17	97	76	88	77
15	38	71	28	56	66	22	73	83	58
58	05	25	01	31	71	29	33	39	84

Lengthier tables of random numbers can be found in most books of statistical tables.

Example of a Research Report[1]

COMPUTER SIMULATIONS TO STIMULATE SCIENTIFIC PROBLEM SOLVING

(Abstract)

Computer simulations were employed by high school biology students in an attempt to enhance their problem solving skills. The simulations were administered under two conditions: (a) Unguided discovery and (b) Guided discovery. In addition, a control group received no simulations. To ascertain the effectiveness of the simulations in enhancing problem solving abilities, performance was compared on (a) subsequent unit pretests, (b) standardized tests measuring scientific thought processes, and (c) a standardized test of critical thinking.

The results indicate that (a) the students using the simulations met the unit objectives at least as well as the control students, and (b) the students using the guided version of the simulations surpassed the other students on the subsequent simulation pretests, on the tests of scientific thinking, and on the test of critical thinking. The authors discuss the apparent usefulness of the programs in terms of the opportunities they provide students (a) to be actively involved in the learning process and (b) to repeatedly practice applying principles that would otherwise be practiced much less often.

An important goal of science education is to help students develop an understanding of principles and to generalize these principles through experiential problem solving to new situations (Linn, 1986). "In addition to traditional competencies, students increasingly should learn the thinking skills to manage information, formulate effective probing questions, test hypotheses, make judgments, express themselves logically and lucidly, and solve problems" (Committee on Science, Engineering and Public Policy, 1984).

The logic of the introduction and review of the literature goes like this:

I. Science education should teach students to develop thinking skills like problem solving.
II. Here are some ways that students learn to solve problems (including reinforced practice). . . .
III. Computer simulations should be able to help students solve problems. Here are some reasons to support this belief. . . .
IV. Here is a general description of the kinds of simulations we used in our study. . . .
V. Here are the results of some comparable studies. . . .
VI. Here's what we plan to do. . . .
VII. By the way, guidance should help students develop problem solving skills, and so we tested for its effect on our simulations.

---

[1]This is an abridgement of an article that was published in the *Journal of Research in Science Teaching*, vol. 24, no. 5, (May 1987), pp. 403–415.

The process of acquiring specific problem solving skills is facilitated by active, reinforced practice (e.g., DeCecco, 1974; Beyer, 1984b). However, many researchers and theorists have found that attempts to teach generalized problem solving skills have proven to be ineffective (DeCecco, 1974; Hudgins, 1977; Gagne, 1977; DeBono, 1983; Beyer, 1984a). In contrast, Bruner (1973) suggests that a person solves new problems by placing the current problem into a more generic coding system. The problem solver then "essentially reads off from the coding system additional information either on the basis of learned contingent probabilities or learned principles of relating material" (p. 224). More recently, Papert (1980) has advocated the generalizable benefits arising from such activities as learning to program the computer, using Logo.

(Additional paragraphs that have been omitted to conserve space continued to discuss how students develop thinking skills.)

Here is the statement of the hypothesis.

We hypothesized that computerized science simulations could provide students in science classrooms with enough productive practice in novel problem solving to help develop a generalized skill in scientific problem solving.

Compared to traditional laboratory settings, computerized science simulations allow students to solve more problems. By performing peripheral tasks (such as data tabulation) that could consume time without developing problem solving skills, the computer may enable the student to work much more efficiently. As a result, students go through a plan-execute-evaluate cycle several times when solving a problem. In the plan phase, the student designs an experiment to help solve the problem. In the execute phase the student carries out the experiment and collects the data. In the evaluate phase, the student analyses the data and develops an inference or hypothesis on the basis of the data. In our simulations, students were allowed to conduct as many of these plan-execute-evaluate cycles as they wished, up to a reasonable limit (between 5 and 10 times), thus giving them considerable flexibility to restate and retest hypotheses.

(Additional paragraphs that have been omitted to conserve space continued to discuss potential advantages of the computer in teaching thinking skills.)

The computerized simulations used in this study were carefully designed to help teachers develop scientific problem solving in their students: (a) The simulations could easily fit into the existing curriculum. (b) Each simulation was based on an accurate model for the scientific problem it presented. (c) A carefully designed laboratory guide that emphasized all three elements of problem solving (planning, executing and analyzing) accompanied each program. (d) A thorough teacher's guide that provided background on the simulation model and its assumptions and appropriate teaching aids and strategies accompanied each program.

Studies examining the effect of the use of computer simulations in science on either scientific or general problem solving ability have provided divergent results. Hughes (1974) found no significant differences in science problem solving ability between students in laboratory, combined computer laboratory, and computer simulation groups. Alternatively, Donaldson (1972) found students in computer-supplemented science classes seemed to use the problem solving strategies generated in those classes in non-computer science classes. This inference was based on informal observation of some students in the experimental group.

The present study employed computer simulations designed to enhance scientific problem solving skills. They presented a variety of problem situations for participants to solve. While the participants solved these problems, they were expected to acquire a wide variety of specific problem solving skills. In addition, because the simulations required essential research and idea-generating strategies, the participants were expected to integrate these specific strategies into an enhanced overall problem solving strategy. The success of the computer simulations in developing problem solving abilities was ascertained by analysis of posttest scores on problem solving tasks varying in degree of remoteness from the type of problems in the simulations.

Finally, guidance to the learner may facilitate the acquisition of problem solving skills. Generic guidelines may assist students in formulating a useful model of the scientific phenomena under investigation. It is possible to analyze the knowledge structures required for the performance of problem tasks and to offer advice to learners regarding how to use knowledge acquired in one domain to solve problems in another (Greeno, 1983). A guided, experiential approach to solving concrete problems should help students develop generalized problem solving skills. Therefore, the effects of guidance while the problem solvers were interacting with the simulations was examined to ascertain whether a pure discovery-oriented use of computer simulations was more or less effective than a guided discovery use of the simulations.

Methodology

This report summarizes the results of a study conducted in a school system in a midwestern metropolitan area. Because of space restrictions, numerous details have been summarized or omitted for this report. (For complete details, see Vockell and Rivers, 1984a, 1984b.) The students in this study were mostly minority students of middle-class and lower-middle-class socioeconomic status. All the students in six beginning biological science classes during the 1981–82 school year participated in the study. The students in the other six beginning biological science classes in the same school served as controls.

This section includes the operational definitions of the research variables.

This description of the school and the type of students is an operational definition of the control variable.

This description of the computer simulations and the way in which they were used is an operational definition of the independent variable. If the reader wants a more specific description, it would be possible to look in the manuals accompanying the software.

Treatment

The treatment classes ran computer simulation programs on Apple II computers. Teachers attended a workshop during which they were briefly instructed in the use of the computers and programs. Learning guidelines for integrating the computer simulations with their regular classroom and laboratory instruction were routinely available within the teacher's guide that accompanied the simulations. The students in the experimental classes then interacted with the computers as an integrated part of the laboratory experience in their science courses. This interaction usually consisted of small groups of three to five students preparing for the simulations by studying the laboratory guides and determining what variables to manipulate in the simulation. Then they conducted the planned experiments using the simulations on the computers. Finally, they analyzed the data and drew their conclusions, again in small groups away from the computers.

The following programs were included in the study:

BALANCE: A Predator–Prey Simulation. BALANCE is a student-interactive simulation which explores the interrelated variables affecting predator–prey relationships. Manipulation of variables of food supply, carrying capacity, environmental conditions, and external pressures is possible. Tabular and graphic output is provided to illustrate the effects of the variables on the related population. The student develops scientific problem solving skills as well as skills of tabulation, graphing and interpretation. The students record data in a student laboratory guide which provides realistic scenarios for exploration.

PLANT: A Plant Growth Simulation. PLANT is a student-interactive simulation which explores the relationship of light intensity and light duration to the growth and development of a green plant.

OSMO: Osmosis in Red Blood Cells. OSMO is a student-interactive simulation which explores various osmotic conditions in red blood cells.

MOTHS: Peppered Moth Evolution. MOTHS is a student-interactive simulation based upon the historical occurrence of peppered moth evolution in industrial England.

MONOCROSS: Monohybrid Crosses. MONOCROSS is a student-interactive program which simulates various monohybrid genetic crosses.

DICROSS: Dihybrid Crosses. DICROSS is a student-interactive program which simulates various dihybrid genetic crosses.

POLLUTE: Impact of Water Pollutants. POLLUTE is a student-interactive simulation which examines the impact of various pollutants on typical bodies of water.

Each of the programs described more briefly included characteristics similar to the more detailed description of BALANCE. Each computer simulation is integrated with a teacher's guide and a student laboratory guide which provides additional laboratory and real life experiences. All of these programs are published by Diversified Educational Enterprises (West Lafayette, Indiana).

Programs were selected to correspond to topics normally covered in the biology curriculum in the study schools. Treatment classes used the simulations to assist in dealing with those topics while control classes were taught the equivalent topics in a non-computerized fashion (using textbook, lecture and traditional laboratory). Approximately the same amount of time was spent on each topic in control and treatment classes.

Treatment classes were further divided into two groups, guided and unguided. Students in unguided classes received only a short introduction to the simulation given to them as they began the program. Students in guided classes received, in addition to the introduction, two to ten brief paragraphs of strategies to use as they solved the problems presented in the simulation. For example, each of the following paragraphs appears as part of the directions for the guided version of BALANCE:

IT IS A GOOD IDEA TO CHANGE ONLY ONE VARIABLE AT A TIME.

THE POPULATION OF THE PREDATOR AND PREY ARE INTERRELATED. A CHANGE IN ONE GENERALLY HAS AN EFFECT ON THE OTHER.

IF THE DEER POPULATION BECOMES TOO LARGE, IT WILL EXCEED THE CARRYING CAPACITY OF THE ENVIRONMENT. EVENTUALLY THEIR FOOD WILL RUN OUT AND THEY WILL DIE OFF. (CARRYING CAPACITY IS THE NUMBER OF DEER THE ENVIRONMENT CAN SUPPORT WITHOUT HAVING THE FOOD RUN OUT.)

THE DENSER THE VEGETATION OF THE ENVIRONMENT, THE EASIER IT IS FOR THE WOLVES TO CAPTURE THE DEER.

EACH WOLF HAS TO FIND AND EAT ABOUT 26 DEER PER YEAR TO SURVIVE.

USE THIS PROGRAM TO TEST YOUR HYPOTHESES. LOOK FOR PATTERNS OR RELATIONSHIPS BETWEEN POPULATIONS AS YOU SYSTEMATICALLY CHANGE THE VARIABLES.

This is the operational definition of guidance. The operational definition of unguided is "running the same programs without this kind of guidance."

The guidance was supplied at a controlled pace as part of the computer program, and students could not by-pass its presentation. Each paragraph of guidance appeared on a separate screen, and the instructions permitted the learner to re-examine previous screens upon request. An accompanying student manual provided study questions and problems to solve. Therefore, structuring the guidance and providing it to designated students was easily accomplished.

These are the operational definitions of the dependent variable.
Problem solving is operationally defined in two ways: (1) improved performance on successive pretests, and (2) performance on the Watson-Glaser test.

Information about the reliability of the unit tests is not specifically stated. The reader can only assume from the fact that the items were based on the same set of objectives that the pretest and posttest were equivalent. This would also increase the content validity of the test. In addition, standardizing the administration contributed to the reliability—and hence to the validity—of the data collection process.
Information regarding the reliability and validity of the Watson-Glaser test is not specifically given. However, readers can obtain this information by checking either (1) the reference cited in the text, (2) a source like the *Mental Measurements Yearbook,* or (3) the test manual. Any of these sources would provide good evidence about this test's reliability and validity.

The analysis of variance shows differences among the three groups. Further analyses—called planned comparisons—would help pinpoint these differences more specifically.

Analysis of covariance is a procedure similar to analysis of variance for determining whether the differences among means is statistically significant. This procedure is briefly described in Appendix E. It is interpreted in the same way as analysis of variance.

The reference to percentiles makes possible a comparison of performance on the two forms of the test. A simple comparison of mean raw scores would be confusing.

Evaluation

To assess the effect on subject matter and problem solving, the performance of the students was monitored on the pretest and posttest for each simulation. These tests were included as a part of each simulation's teacher's guide. The individual unit tests measured specific problem solving skills directly related to each unit. In addition, improved performance on successive pretests would indicate a generalized ability to solve problems.

The tests were based on the stated instructional objectives for each unit. These objectives were communicated to students in all groups, and the tests were administered according to standardized instructions to all groups.

To assess general problem solving, we used the Watson-Glaser Critical Thinking Appraisal (1964, 1980) as a measure of the ability to make inferences, to recognize assumptions, to deduce conclusions, to decide whether conclusions are warranted, and to evaluate the strength of arguments. This test was administered according to the instructions in the manual.

Results

Table C.1 summarizes the results of the pretests and posttests on the individual unit mastery tests and uses an analysis of covariance to compare the various groups for each of these units. For three simulations, there was no significant difference in the rate of gain. On PLANT and BALANCE, however, the Guided students gained more than the others, and the Unguided students gained more than the Control students.

We hypothesized gains on subsequent pretests due to generalized problem solving skills. Table 1 shows this pattern of improved performance on each subsequent pretest. An analysis of covariance of later scores with the initial (PLANT) pretest scores as the covariate shows that the two computer groups significantly outgained the control students on subsequent pretests (F = 11.47, d.f. = 2, 191, sig. = .001). This cumulative gain on consecutive pretests would tend to make it harder for the experimental students (who had already improved on subsequent pretests) to improve even further on each posttest.

On the more generalized Watson-Glaser test, the Guided students gained significantly more than either of the other two groups. Note that the apparent "losses" of two of the groups are actually a result of transfer to Form A from Form ZM of the Watson-Glaser, and not an indication of an actual reduction in critical thinking ability.

In actual fact, as Table 1 shows, the Guided students progressed from the 14th to the 72nd percentile, while the Control students went from the 19th to the 60th percentile. . . .

Table C.1 Results for Study 1

Simulations	Control		Unguided		Guided		F-Ratio*	d.f.	Significance
	M.	S.D.	M.	S.D.	M.	S.D.			
PLANT									
Pretest	7.95	(3.30)	7.52	(3.53)	7.02	(3.46)			
Posttest	11.88	(4.16)	12.28	(4.44)	13.40	(4.14)	3.27	2,222	0.04
Gain	4.05	(4.81)	4.98	(4.71)	6.38	(4.28)			
OSMO									
Pretest	6.46	(2.68)	6.57	(2.95)	6.64	(3.03)			
Posttest	6.97	(3.06)	7.38	(2.63)	7.43	(3.17)	0.49	2,215	0.62
Gain	0.51	(3.32)	0.81	(3.14)	0.79	(3.56)			
MONOCROSS									
Pretest	6.07	(2.95)	7.67	(2.57)	6.81	(3.03)			
Posttest	7.46	(3.09)	9.09	(3.10)	8.56	(3.41)	1.64	2,217	0.20
Gain	1.39	(3.03)	1.42	(2.92)	1.74	(2.73)			
BALANCE									
Pretest	16.02	(3.85)	15.74	(3.56)	17.70	(4.40)			
Posttest	16.52	(4.10)	17.23	(4.31)	20.65	(2.31)	6.84	2,101	0.002
Gain	0.50	(3.81)	1.48	(3.32)	2.95	(3.49)			
MOTHS									
Pretest	13.98	(3.52)	15.41	(4.26)	15.31	(3.91)			
Posttest	14.55	(4.80)	17.53	(3.73)	16.26	(5.03)	1.62	2,99	0.21
Gain	0.57	(4.27)	2.12	(2.64)	1.24	(3.74)			
WATSON-GLASER									
Pretest	47.26	(7.78)	45.40	(6.53)	45.00	(10.61)			
%-ile	26		21		20				
Posttest	43.44	(6.60)	40.33	(7.10)	46.18	(7.64)	3.13	2,90	0.05
%-ile	60		45		72				
Gain	−3.82	(7.42)	−4.93	(8.82)	+1.18	(9.52)			
%-ile	+34		+24		+52				

* F-Ratios and levels of significance are derived from an analysis of covariance of posttest scores with each appropriate pretest used as the covariate.

A separate analysis of covariance revealed that there were no differences in the ways boys and girls responded to the treatment conditions.

This statement describes the moderator variable. The researcher checked, and there was no interaction of gender with the treatment. Boys and girls performed similarly.

Discussion and Conclusions

In general, the results support the hypothesis that the computerized simulations used in this study enabled students to master the objectives of a biology course as effectively as did more traditional methods. Students using the simulations mastered the instructional objectives for each unit "at least as well" as students taught through conventional methods.

This part of the report interprets the results that appeared in the previous section and relates these results to the hypotheses and to the reasoning in the introduction.

The authors are discussing the intervening variable. They are trying to convince their readers that reinforced practice is the critical factor that accounts for the improved performance. More specifically, they are arguing that focused reinforced practice—when the guidance provides the focus—leads to improved problem solving skills.

This is a good example of using qualitative information to support a predominantly quantitative set of inferences.

The reasoning in this section goes like this:

I. We told you what we thought would happen, and it happened:
   A. Students in the Guided group showed a slightly greater tendency to improve on successive pretests.
   B. Students in the Guided group surpassed the others on the Watson-Glaser test.
II. We believe that these differences occurred because the Guided students had more effective reinforced practice.
III. The results differed with regard to various specific outcomes. If we wanted to do a really good job, we should focus the practice on each of these specific outcomes. (Maybe someone else will do this.)
IV. The informal perceptions of the teachers support our own conclusions about the simulations.

The teachers' comments are another example of qualitative data that supports the planned, quantitative research.

In addition, students experienced more generalized benefits. One evidence of this was the significant difference in cumulative pretest gains. This suggests that problem solving strategies learned from one unit were being transferred (generalized) to subsequent units.

Additional evidence for a generalized impact from the use of the simulations can be found in an examination of the Watson-Glaser results. These results suggest that the students using the computerized simulations were developing generalizable skills which transferred to novel settings.

(The study also examined performance on Watson-Glaser subscales. These results showed that the simulations had different effects on the various components of critical thinking. This discussion has been omitted to save space.)

The previous paragraphs indicate that in order to do a thorough job of teaching problem solving or thinking skills, the programs described in this report are helpful. However, the programs do not cover the entire spectrum of appropriate thinking skills. To teach generalized problem solving skills effectively, it would be necessary to either (a) restructure the simulations (or ancillary materials) to focus more specifically on the specific skills (such as deductive reasoning) to be covered in the curriculum; or (b) combine the programs with other experiences which address these additional skills.

Finally, it is useful to consider the informal perceptions of the teachers. In all of the schools the teachers intended to continue using the programs after the university's support was withdrawn. The reasons the teachers most frequently gave were (a) the students seemed to learn from them, (b) the programs were cost effective, (c) the computerized experiments were easier to set up and run than conventional experiments, (d) the support materials made it easy to integrate the simulations into the curriculum and to evaluate student performance, and (e) while the students used the computers, the teachers themselves would be able to individualize in other ways.

The teachers made these judgments before they had access to the formal data contained in this report. It seems proper to say that simulations of this type would be useful instructional tools, even if they did nothing more than help students meet the objectives of isolated instructional units. However, the results of this report indicate that such simulations can promote additional generalized outcomes as well.

SUMMARY

Students using computerized science simulations in beginning biological science classes met the unit objectives at least as well as the control students. In addition, the students using the simulations often surpassed the control students on the pretests for subsequent units and on a test of critical thinking. In most cases, the students using the Guided version of the simulations developed these generalized skills more effectively than those using an Unguided version.

These results suggest that computerized simulations can help high school students substantially increase their problem solving abilities. This may occur because students using computers have more opportunities for active, reinforced practice. To be most effective, it appears that these simulations should be integrated with curriculum objectives and should provide guidance to direct students to use the simulations efficiently.

REFERENCES

Beyer, B.K. (1984). Improving thinking skills—Defining the problem. *Phi Delta Kappan*, 65, 486–490.

Bruner, J.S. (1973). *Beyond the Information Given.* New York: W.W. Norton.

DeBono, E. (1983). The direct teaching of thinking as a skill. *Phi Delta Kappan*, 64, 703–708.

DeCecco, J.P. and Crawford, W.P. (1974). *The Psychology of Learning and Instruction.* Englewood Cliffs, N.J.: Prentice-Hall. (2nd Ed.).

Donaldson, W.S. (1972). Computer supplemented instruction in secondary school science: Implementation proceedings and survey findings from a one-year program. Paper presented at National Association for Research in Science Teaching Annual Meeting, Chicago, Illinois, April.

Gagne, R.M. (1977). *The Conditions of Learning.* New York: Holt, Rinehart and Winston. (3rd Ed.).

Greeno, J.G. (1983). Research on cognition and behavior relevant to education in mathematics, science, and technology. In *Educating Americans for the 21st Century. Volume 2.* Washington: The National Science Board Commission on Precollege Education in Mathematics, Science, and Technology.

Hudgins, B.B. (1977). *Learning and Thinking.* Itasca, Illinois: F.E. Peacock.

Hughes, W.R. (1974). A study of the use of computer simulated experiments in the physics classroom. Dissertation Abstracts International, 34, 4710A.

Linn, M. (1986). *Establishing a Research Base for Science Education: Challenges, Trends, and Recommendations.* Washington: National Science Foundation.

Papert, S. (1980). Teaching children thinking. In *The Computer in the School: Tutor, Tool, Tutee.* R. Taylor (Ed.). New York: Teachers College Press.

Vockell, E.L. and Rivers, R. (1984a). Computerized science simulations: Stimulus to generalized problem-solving capabilities. Paper presented at the annual meeting of the American Educational Research Association, New Orleans, LA.

Vockell, E.L. and Rivers, R. (1984b). *Computer Simulations to Stimulate Problem Solving Skills.* Final Report to the National Science Foundation.

Watson, G. and Glaser, E.M. (1964). *Critical Thinking Appraisal.* New York: The Psychological Corporation. (Revised, 1980).

COMPUTATIONAL PROCEDURES FOR STATISTICS

This appendix contains a cookbook approach to computing the Pearson correlation coefficient, the t test, and X_2.

Note that to compute some of these statistics, you have to compute a square root (for Step 23 of the t test computation and Step 21 of the Pearson computation). Be sure you can accomplish this before you start. It is very disheartening to get that far along and discover that you cannot go any further. If the square root is the only thing preventing you from performing these calculations, do not overlook the possibility of dialing up a friend on the telephone and having your friend calculate the square root for you from a more sophisticated electronic calculator than you have access to.

Even with this cookbook approach, using a computer is usually an easier way to obtain your results.

The following pages contain a list of steps for each procedure, plus an example of how to perform each computation. If you follow the steps carefully, you will get the right answer.

t-TEST

Step 1. Arrange the scores according to the two groups. The order of the scores within each group is irrelevant.

Step 2. Add together all the scores in the first group.

Step 3. Square each of the scores in the first group.

Step 4. Add together all the squared scores from Step 3.

Step 5. Square the number obtained in Step 2.

Step 6. Count the number of scores in the first group.

Step 7. Divide the result of Step 5 by the result of Step 6.

Step 8. Subtract the result of Step 7 from the result of Step 4.

Step 9. Add together all the scores in second group.

Step 10. Square each of the scores in the second group.

Step 11. Add together all the squared scores from Step 10.

Step 12. Square the number obtained in Step 9.

Step 13. Count the number of scores in the second group.

Step 14. Divide the result of Step 12 by the result of Step 13.

Step 15. Subtract the result of Step 14 from the result of Step 10.

Step 16. Add together the results of Step 8 and Step 15.

Step 17. Add together the results of Step 6 and Step 13 and subtract 2.

Step 18. Divide the result of Step 16 by the result of Step 17.

Step 19. Divide the result of Step 6 *into* 1.

Step 20. Divide the result of Step 13 *into* 1.

Step 21. Add together the results of Step 19 and Step 20.

Step 22. Multiply the result of Step 18 by the result of Step 21.

Step 23. Take the square root of the result of Step 22.

Step 24. Divide the result of Step 2 by the result of Step 6.

Step 25. Divide the result of Step 9 by the result of Step 13.

Step 26. Subtract the result of Step 24 from the result of Step 25. If the result is negative, drop the minus sign.

Step 27. Divide the result of Step 26 by the result of Step 23. The result is your *t* value.

Step 28. Make the result of Step 17 your degrees of freedom.

Step 29. Read the table for *t* values. If your *t* value is higher than the *t* value in the table for the correct degrees of freedom, your result is significant at the designated level.

SAMPLE COMPUTATION

Step 1.

Males	*Females*
34	35
14	7
40	15
24	40

Step 2. $34 + 14 + 40 + 24 = 112$

Step 3.
$34 \times 34 = 1156$
$14 \times 14 = 196$
$40 \times 40 = 1600$
$24 \times 24 = \underline{576}$

Step 4. 3528

Step 5. $112 \times 112 = 12{,}544$

Step 6. Number of scores = 4

Step 7. $12{,}544 \div 4 = 3136$

Step 8. $3528 - 3136 = 392$

Step 9. $35 + 7 + 15 + 40 = 97$

Step 10.
$35 \times 35 = 1225$
$7 \times 7 = 49$
$15 \times 15 = 225$
$40 \times 40 = \underline{1600}$

Step 11. 3099

Step 12. $97 \times 97 = 9409$

Step 13. Number of scores = 4

Step 14. $9409 \div 4 = 2352.25$

Step 15. $3099 - 2352.25 = 746.75$

Step 16. $392 + 746.75 = 1138.75$

Step 17. $4 + 4 = 8\ 8 - 2 = \underline{6}$

Step 18. $1138.75 \div 6 = 189.79$

Step 19. $1 \div 4 = .25$

Step 20. 1 ÷ 4 = .25

Step 21. .25 + .25 = .50

Step 22. 189.79 × .50 = 94.895

Step 23. √94.895 = 9.74

Step 24. 112 ÷ 4 = 28

Step 25. 97 ÷ 4 = 24.25

Step 26. 24.25 − 28 = −3.75 = 3.75

Step 27. 3.75 ÷ 9.74 = 0.38

Step 28. df = 6

Step 29. 0.38 is not even close to 2.571, and therefore the difference is not significant at the .05 level.

PEARSON CORRELATION COEFFICIENT

Step 1. Arrange the scores in matching columns. Pair each of the scores that belong together in adjacent columns.

Step 2. Count the number of pairs.

Step 3. Multiply the two numbers in each pair times each other.

Step 4. Add the products obtained in Step 3.

Step 5. Multiply the number obtained in Step 4 by the number obtained in Step 2.

Step 6. Square each number in the first column.

Step 7. Add the squared values found in Step 6.

Step 8. Multiply the number from Step 7 by the number from Step 2.

Step 9. Add together all the scores in the first column.

Step 10. Square the number obtained in Step 9.

Step 11. Square each number in the second column.

Step 12. Add the squared values found in Step 11.

Step 13. Multiply the number from Step 12 by the number in Step 2.

Step 14. Add together all the scores in the second column.

Step 15. Square the number obtain in Step 14.

Step 16. Multiply the number obtained in Step 9 by the number obtained in Step 14.

Step 17. Subtract the result of Step 16 from the result of Step 5. Note that the result of Step 17 can be either positive or negative.

Step 18. Subtract the number obtained in Step 10 from the number obtained in Step 8.

Step 19. Subtract the result of Step 15 from the result of Step 13.

Step 20. Multiply the result of Step 18 by the result of step 19.

Step 21. Take the square root of the number obtained in Step 20.

Step 22. Divide the result of Step 17 by the result of Step 21. Unless you are computing a split-half reliability coefficient, you are finished. The result of Step 22 is the Pearson Correlation Coefficient.

SAMPLE COMPUTATION

Step 1.

Column A	Column B
104	60
94	59
100	42
130	64
101	65
85	40
80	65
120	65

Step 2. Number of pairs = 8

Step 3.
104 × 60 = 6240
94 × 59 = 5546
100 × 42 = 4200
130 × 64 = 8320
101 × 65 = 6565
85 × 40 = 3400
80 × 65 = 5200
120 × 65 = 7800

Step 4. 47,271

Step 5. 47,271 × 8 = 378,168

Step 6.
104 × 104 = 10,816
94 × 94 = 8,836
100 × 100 = 10,000
130 × 130 = 16,900
101 × 101 = 10,201
85 × 85 = 7,225
80 × 80 = 6,400
120 × 120 = 14,400

Step 7. 84,778

Step 8. 84,778 × 8 = 678,224

Step 9. 104 + 94 + 100 + 130 + 101 + 85 + 80 + 120 = 814

Step 10. 814 × 814 = 662,596

Step 11.

60	×	60 =	3600
59	×	59 =	3481
42	×	42 =	1764
64	×	64 =	4096
65	×	65 =	4225
40	×	40 =	1600
65	×	65 =	4225
65	×	65 =	4225

Step 12.   27,216

Step 13. $2 \bar{\,} ,216 \times 8 = 217,728$

Step 14. $60 + 59 + 42 + 64 + 65 + 40 + 65 + 65 + = 460$

Step 15. $460 \times 460 = 211,600$

Step 16. $814 \times 460 = 374,440$

Step 17. $378,168 - 374,440 = 3728$

Step 18. $678,224 - 662,596 = 15,628$

Step 19. $217,728 - 211,600 = 6128$

Step 20. $15,628 \times 6128 = 95,768,384$

Step 21. $\sqrt{95,768,384} = 9786.13$

Step 22. $3728 \div 9786 = .38$. This is the Pearson corelation coefficient.

SAMPLE COMPUTATION

Step 1.

	Pass	Fail
Lib Arts	30	20
Eng.	5	10

Step 2. 30 + 20 + 5 + 10 = 65

Step 3. Lib Arts Row = 50
Eng Row = 15

Step 4. Pass column = 35
Fail column = 30

Step 5. 50 × 15 × 35 × 30 = 787,500

Step 6. 30 × 10 = 300

Step 7. 20 × 5 = 100

Step 8. 300 − 100 = 200

Step 9. 200 × 200 = 400

Step 10. 40000 × 65 = 260,000

Step 11. 2,600,000 ÷ 787,500 = 3.30. Since 3.30 is less than 3.8, this difference in patterns between liberal arts and English majors has greater than .05 probability of occuring by chance

CHI SQUARE

Step 1. Arrange the scores in a contingency table, like that shown in Chapter 14 or in Step 1 of the sample computation.

Step 2. Add together all the numbers in the table.

Step 3. Add together the numbers in the rows to get the *row sums*.

Step 4. Add together the numbers in the columns to get the *column sums*.

Step 5. Multiply together the four numbers obtained in Steps 3 and 4.

Step 6. Multiple the upper left number by the lower right number in the contingency table.

Step 7. Multiply the upper right number by the lower left number in the contingency table.

Step 8. Take the results of Steps 6 and 7, and subtract the smaller from the larger.

Step 9. Square the result of Step 8.

Step 10. Multiply the result of Step 9 by the result of Step 2.

Step 11. Divide the result of Step 10 by the result of Step 5. The answer is Chi square.

A Chi square value of greater than 3.8 is significant at the .05 level. A chi square greater than 6.6 is significant at the .01 level. A Chi square greater than 10.8 is significant at the .001 level.

STATISTICAL PROCEDURES: BRIEF DESCRIPTIONS

This appendix includes brief, nontechnical descriptions of many statistical procedures and terms. These descriptions should help you read research reports that employ these statistics. To obtain a more complete understanding of these procedures, you should take appropriate statistics courses or refer to the references at the end of chapters 13 and 14 of this book.

alpha level   A statement of the level of statistical significance.

analysis of covariance (ANCOVA)   A statistical procedure that attempts to estimate whether two or more groups would have differed on a criterion variable if the effects of related variables associated with the criterion variable were removed. (Attempts to use this strategy to equate initially unequal groups are very often misleading. See also chapter 14.)

analysis of variance (ANOVA)   A procedure for estimating the probability that the apparent differences among the means of two or more sets of scores are the result of mere chance fluctuations in those scores. (See chapter 14.)

ANCOVA   See *analysis of covariance*.

ANOVA   See *analysis of variance*.

beta weights   The weights used in regression equations when the raw scores of the predictor variables have been replaced by standard scores. They have theoretical value in determining the relative importance of each of the predictor variables. (See also *B weights*.)

biserial correlation   An *estimate* of the correlation Pearson coefficient between two variables when one is artificially dichotomized and the other is an interval variable. With the availability of computers, it is unnecessary to calculate this statistic; the point biserial coefficient (a form of the Pearson correlation coefficient) should be used instead.

Bonferroni significant difference test   A statistical procedure for making individual comparisons among the means of group scores in an analysis of variance.

B weights   The weights used in regression equations when the raw scores of the predictor variables are being used in making the prediction. They are of practical use in making predictions from the test scores or observations.

canonical correlation   A procedure for determining the relationships among sets of two or more predictor variables and two or more criterion variables.

central tendency   A score that indicates the most typical or average score within a set of scores. The mean, the median, and the mode are measures of central tendency. (See chapter 7.)

chi square   A statistic using frequency counts that estimates the degree to which one distribution corresponds to another. (See chapter 14.)

coefficient of concordance   A nonparametric correlation coefficient, interpreted in much the same way as other correlation coefficients.

coefficient of determination   A statement of how much of the variance in a criterion variable is determined by a predictor variable. It is obtained by squaring a correlation coefficient and multiplying by 100 to get a percentage.

Cohen's kappa   A nonparametric procedure that estimates the percentage of agreement among observers and applies a correction factor for chance agreement. It is a type of reliability coefficient.

correction for attenuation   A method for stating the correlation between two variables if both variables were measured with perfect reliability.

correlation   An index of the strength of the relationship between two variables. Most correlation coefficients theoretically range from -1.00 to +1.00. A high absolute value (ignoring the sign) represents a strong relationship. (See chapter 13.)

Cronbach's alpha   The most general procedure for determining the internal consistency reliability of a measurement process.

degrees of freedom (df)   A term that defines the point at which a table will be entered to interpret an inferential statistic. With parametric statistics (such as t tests and analysis of variance), degrees of freedom are related to the number of subjects involved. With nonparametric statistics, the degrees of freedom generally are related to the number of categories employed in an analysis. Degrees of freedom are often given in parentheses after a statistic. For example, $F(2, 88)$ means to read the F table at the juncture of 2 and 88 degrees of freedom.

descriptive statistic   A statistic (such as a mean, standard deviation, or correlation coefficient) that merely describes a set of scores rather than attempting to draw inferences about that set of scores. The statistics discussed in chapters 7 and 13 are descriptive statistics.

df   See *degrees of freedom*.

dichotomous variable   A variable that is scored with just two possible numbers, such as "1" and "0." A true dichotomy occurs when these scores represent reality—as "male/female" or "right/wrong." A forced dichotomy occurs when these scores represent an invented or artificial status.

discriminant analysis   A procedure for using a set of predictor variables to estimate the likelihood that a subject will belong to a group or category. The procedure essentially uses a clustering of the predictor variables and multiple regression methods to predict membership in one of several groups.

Duncan's multiple-range test   A statistical procedure for computing individual comparisons in analysis of variance.

Dunnett's test   A statistical procedure for computing individual comparisons in analysis of variance.

effect size   A standard score that represents the strength of a treatment in an experiment. It is calculated by dividing the difference between the means of the experimental and the control group by the pooled standard deviation. The effect size is the major piece of data entered into a meta-analysis. (See chapter 16.)

factor analysis   A procedure for sorting a large number of variables into smaller clusters of related variables (factors) and for determining the interrelatedness of the variables within these clusters. It attempts to maximize the correlation of the variables within a cluster of variables while minimizing the correlations among the separate clusters of variables.

factorial analysis of variance   See *two-way analysis of variance*.

Fisher's significant difference test   A statistical procedure for computing individual comparisons in analysis of variance.

F ratio   The statistic that results from an analysis of variance. It is interpreted by reference to a statistical table, stating the probability that the several means are likely to differ by chance. (See chapter 14.)

homogeneity of variance   The degree to which two or more distributions of scores are comparable. This is an important factor in data analysis, since it is improper to use certain inferential statistics when the distribution of one set of scores is substantially different from that of another.

honest significant difference test   A statistical procedure for computing individual comparisons in analysis of variance.

Hotelling's T   The multivariate equivalent of the t test, employed when there are just two treatment groups and multiple outcome variables.

individual comparisons   Follow-up statistics performed after an initial analysis of variance when there are more than two groups involved in the analysis. The individual comparisons test for significant differences between individual pairs of means and among sets of means.

inferential statistics   Statistics (such as *t* test or F ratio in analysis of variance) that help the researcher or reader make a judgment about the apparent differences among means of sets of scores or about correlations between variables. They estimate the likelihood that a difference between means or the relationship among variables arose only because of chance fluctuations in scores. The statistics discussed in chapter 14 are inferential statistics.

Kendall's tau   A nonparametric correlation coefficient, interpreted in much the same way as other correlation coefficients.

Kruskal-Wallis H test   A nonparametric equivalent of a one-way analysis of variance, employed with ordinal data.

kurtosis   The degree to which a distribution is "flat" or "peaked" compared with a normal, bell-shaped distribution. *Leptokurtic* refers to a "high and skinny" distribution, and *platykurtic* refers to a "low and fat" distribution.

least significant difference test   A statistical procedure for computing individual comparisons in analysis of variance.

level of significance   The probability that a statistical result could have occurred as a result of mere chance fluctuations among scores. (See chapter 14.)

log-linear analysis   A recently developed strategy for analyzing frequency data into a form more suitable for analysis. A form of analysis of variance for frequency data.

Mann-Whitney U test   A nonparametric equivalent of a *t* test, employed with ordinal data.

MANOVA   See *multivariate analysis of variance*.

McNemar's chi square   A statistic employed with frequency (nominal) data that are repeated observations. A type of chi square.

mean   The sum of all the scores in a distribution divided by the number of scores. Symbolized by $\bar{X}$ or *M*. (See chapter 7.)

median   The middle score in a set of scores that are arranged in order from lowest to highest. (See chapter 7.)

median test   A nonparametric statistic that performs much the same function as a *t* test.

mode   The most frequently occurring score in a set of scores. (See chapter 7.)

multiple comparisons   See *individual comparisons*.

multiple correlation   A statement of the relationship between one criterion (or dependent) variable and a combination of two or more predictor (or independent) variables. (See chapter 13.)

multiple regression   The use of a regression equation to state the mathematical relationships between the set of predictor variables and the criterion variable in a multiple correlation.

multivariate analysis of variance (MANOVA)   An analysis of variance procedure employed when two or more outcome (dependent) variables are being analyzed simultaneously.

Neuman-Keuls test   A statistical procedure for computing individual comparisons in analysis of variance.

nonparametric statistics   Inferential statistics (such as chi square) that are *not* based on the assumption that the scores upon which they are calculated fall into a normal distribution.

normal distribution   The distribution of a set of scores that approximates the bell-shaped curve. (See chapter 7.)

one-tailed test   See *two-tailed test of significance*.

one-way analysis of variance   An analysis of variance used when there is just one mean for each of the several groups involved in the analysis and when there are no moderator variables involved in the analysis.

p   A symbol for *probability* or *level of significance*.

parametric statistics   Inferential statistics (such as a *t* test or analysis of variance) that are based on the assumption that the scores on which they are used are distributed into a normal, bell-shaped distribution.

partial correlation   A statement of what the relationship would probably have been if the correlated influence of some other variable(s) had been removed. The resulting partial correlation coefficient is interpreted in much the same way as the Pearson correlation coefficient. (See chapter 13.)

path analysis   A nonexperimental procedure that builds upon correlation coefficients and partial correlation coefficients to develop inferences about causal relationships among variables.

Pearson correlation coefficient   The most commonly calculated and reported index of relationship between two variables. Its theoretical range is from -1.00 to +1.00. A high absolute value (ignoring the sign) represents a strong relationship. The complete name is the Pearson product moment correlation coefficient. (See chapter 13.)

percentile score   A score that indicates the percentage of individuals within a distribution that fall below a designated score. (See chapter 7.)

phi coefficient   The name given to a Pearson correlation between two dichotomous variables.

planned comparisons   See *individual comparisons*.

planned orthogonal comparisons   A statistical procedure for computing individual comparisons in analysis of variance.

point biserial correlation   A statement of the relationship between a dichotomous variable and an interval variable. It is interpreted in much the same way as the Pearson correlation coefficient.

post hoc test   See *individual comparisons*.

power   The ability of a statistical test to detect real differences when they exist (as opposed to concluding that a treatment has made no difference when in fact it has). In general, setting the significance level low or reducing the number of subjects will *reduce* the power of a statistical test. Increased power reduces Type II errors. (See chapter 14.)

protected rank sum test   A nonparametric individual comparisons test employed as a follow-up to the Kruskal-Wallis H test.

protected *t* test   A statistical procedure for computing individual comparisons in analysis of variance.

r   The traditional symbol for a correlation coefficient. It specifically refers to the Pearson correlation coefficient. (See chapter 13.)

R   The traditional symbol for a multiple correlation coefficient. (See chapter 13.)

r²   The symbol for the coefficient of determination.

R²   A symbol for the coefficient of determination, used when the coefficient is derived from a multiple correlation coefficient.

range   The highest score minus the lowest score in a distribution (for purists, the highest score minus the lowest score, plus 1). (See chapter 7.)

rank-sum test   A nonparametric equivalent of a *t* test, employed with ordinal data.

regression equation   A mathematical equation that uses one or more variables to predict a criterion variable. These equations have terms in them that are closely related to correlation coefficients. A regression equation is really a formula for the line that can be drawn to show a relationship between variables in a scattergram.

repeated-measures analysis of variance   An analysis of variance computed when there are two or more mean scores or sets of observations for each of the individuals and groups involved in the analysis.

restriction of range   The phenomenon that occurs when the magnitude of a correlation coefficient is likely to be smaller when the scores are narrowly distributed (restricted) than when they are broadly distributed.

robustness   The ability of any statistical test to yield valid inferences even when the assumptions underlying the test are violated. For example, when statisticians say that an analysis of variance procedure is robust, this means that it is legitimate to use it even when data are not normally distributed (even though normal distribution was an assumption when the procedures for analysis of variance evolved).

scattergram   A diagram of the scores involved in a correlation. (See chapter 13.)

Scheffe test   A statistical procedure for computing individual comparisons in analysis of variance.

significance   See *level of significance*.

skewness   The degree to which there is a "tail" to a distribution of scores (scores are "right tailed" or "left tailed," depending on which way the tail is extended).

Spearman-Brown formula   An equation for estimating what the internal consistency reliability of a measurement instrument would be if the test were lengthened or shortened.

Spearman rho   A statement of the relationship between two variables that are (or can be treated as) ordinal data. It is interpreted in much the same way as a Pearson correlation coefficient.

standard deviation   A measure of the average spread among the individual scores in a set of scores. It is a measure of individual differences. In a normal distribution, six standard deviations cover the range of all the scores—three standard deviations above and three below the mean. (See chapter 7.)

standard error of measurement   An estimate of the accuracy of scores, based on the standard deviation of the scores in the norm group, the number of observations, and the reliability of the test. (See chapter 5) There are about two chances in three that a person's true score on a test is within one standard error either above or below the obtained score. A standard error is interpreted in the same way as a confidence interval (discussed in chapter 8).

standard scores   Derived scores that have a mean of zero and both a standard deviation and variance of 1.00. (See chapter 7.)

tetrachoric correlation coefficient   An estimate of the Pearson correlation coefficient between two interval variables when both have been artificially dichotomized. (With the availability of computers, it is generally unnecessary to calculate this statistic.) It is interpreted in much the same way as a Pearson correlation coefficient.

t test   A procedure for estimating the probability that the difference between the mean of two sets of scores is the result of mere chance fluctuations in those scores. (See chapter 14.)

Tukey's significant difference test   A statistical procedure for computing individual comparisons in analysis of variance.

two-tailed test of significance   The most commonly accepted strategy for interpreting levels of significance. We won't describe the theory in detail here. If a researcher instead uses a one-tailed test of significance, this doubles the chances of finding significance at any level—if the difference is in the hypothesized direction (if not, considerable embarrassment ensues).

two-way analysis of variance   An analysis of variance in which it is possible to look for interactions of moderator variables with independent variables and with each other, as well as differences among the independent variables. A sentence describing the variables that are hypothesized to interact usually contains the variables separated by an *x* (which is read as "by"). For example, a researcher may refer to a 2-x-2 analysis of variance or to a treatment by IQ analysis. (See chapter 14.)

type I error   The error in statistical interpretation that occurs when a researcher concludes that an observed outcome is statistically significant (a real difference) when it really could be the result of chance. Setting the level of significance high (.10 instead of .05) will increase the likelihood of Type I errors. (See chapter 14.)

type II error   The error in statistical interpretation of failing to detect true differences or relationships. Setting the level of significance low (.01 instead of .05) will increase the likelihood of Type II errors. (See chapter 14.)

variance   The square of the standard deviation. The variance is another way to describe the spread or individual differences among individual scores in a distribution. Researchers try to identify factors that explain variance, and some studies will report the amount of explained variance—indicating that they have identified variables that explain a relationship.

Wilcoxon test   A nonparametric test for ordinal data that is analogous to a matched-pairs two-group *t* test.

Wilks's lambda   The statistic resulting from a multivariate analysis of variance (MANOVA). The equivalent of the F ratio in a univariate analysis of variance.

X   The traditional abbreviation for an individual score within a set of scores.

X̄   The traditional abbreviation for the mean.

z score   A standard score with a mean of 0 and a standard deviation of 1. Z scores range from about -3.00 to +3.00. (See chapter 7.)

Σ   The traditional abbreviation for the sum of a set of scores.

Author Index

SUBJECT INDEX